Adult Life

Developmental Processes

FOURTH EDITION

Judith Stevens-Long
University of Washington, Tacoma
The Fielding Institute, Santa Barbara

Michael L. Commons
Harvard Medical School

Mayfield Publishing Company
Mountain View, California
London • Toronto

Copyright © 1992 by Mayfield Publishing Company

Library of Congress Cataloging-in-Publication Data
Stevens-Long, Judith.
    Adult life ; developmental processes. — 4th ed. / Judith Stevens
-Long. Michael Commons.
      p.   cm.
    Includes bibliographical references and indexes.
    ISBN 1-55934-082-7
    1. Adulthood.   2. Life cycle, Human.   3. Maturation (Psychology)
I. Commons, Michael L.   II. Title.
HQ799,95.S74   1992
305.24—dc20   91-33062
                                                    CIP

Manufactured in the United States of America
10 9 8 7 6 5 4 3

Mayfield Publishing Company
1240 Villa Street
Mountain View, California 94041

Sponsoring editor, Franklin C. Graham; managing editor, Linda Toy; production editors, Sondra Glider and Lynn Rabin Bauer; manuscript editor, Lauren Root; text and cover designer, Andrew Ogus; photo researcher, Stephen Forsling; illustrator, Judith Ogus. The text was set in 10/12 Bembo by G&S Typesetters and printed on 50# Finch Opaque by R. R. Donnelley & Sons.

Cover photo: Paul Klee, *Pyramide,* 1930.138. Paul Klee-Stiftung/Kunstmuseum Bern.
Text and photo credits appear on a continuation of the copyright page, p. 622.

For my final husband, Larry
JS-L

For the staff of the Dare Institute
MLC

Contents

Preface

Since its inception fifteen years ago, when I was thirty-two, this textbook has changed with me as well as with the field. The field has grown so quickly and in such complex ways that it is in fact no longer possible for one person to possess the expertise (or the time and energy) to cover all the new research with any confidence. In this regard, I am pleased and honored to welcome Michael L. Commons on board with this edition. Michael is a groundbreaking researcher who has contributed broadly to the study of adult cognition, moral development, and creativity. Having done an extraordinary amount of cross-cultural research on the constructs they have described, he and his associates are now working their way across the spectrum of developing systems outlined in Chapter 2 of this textbook.

Themes of *Adult Life*

Still my intellectual pet, Chapter 2 has received a good deal of attention in this revision. In particular, it has been enhanced by the growing articulation of the contextual view. Writers like Dannefer and Perlmutter, Featherman and Lerner, Baltes and Riley have made us all so much more aware of the degree to which it is necessary to talk about the social context of development, the part we all play in creating and maintaining our social environment. They have also continued to highlight the problem of continuity and discontinuity in adulthood and the issue of how to optimize development across the life span. These ideas have influenced the treatment of theory in Chapter 2 as well as much of the discussion of cognitive and social development elsewhere.

Organizing Our Thinking about *Adult Life*

The distribution of topics throughout this book highlights another important change in this edition. The organization of *Adult Life* has always seemed like a "clothesline" approach to me. Although the topics are organized chronologically, there is no underlying notion that marriage and divorce are best accomplished in young adulthood or that personality change and sameness is a topic only relevant in middle age. The topics are simply strung out across the adult years in a way that reflects the focus of researchers in various areas. Most researchers looking at love and marriage study young adults, whereas those most interested in personality change are likely to include and often emphasize the middle years of adulthood. As there is nothing sacred about this particular distribution, we have added a table of contents in the instructor's manual, showing how the textbook might be used with equal success in a topical approach.

Not only can the book be easily used by those who prefer a topical approach, but its chronological framework makes it especially well suited to this particular version of a course on adult development. The text can be followed by topic, but within each topic a chronological approach helps to organize the vast amount of material. Thus, the section on cognition in the alternative table of contents is internally organized into cognition in young adulthood, middle age, and later life. This approach gives students the best of both worlds—a sense of the life course as well as the time to focus on topics in a more intense way than is often possible with a strictly chronological format.

The Content of *Adult Life*

As I look over the manuscript pages, still in the print form of my "near letter quality" printer, I realize how much time and intensity I have devoted to the issues of love and marriage, divorce and family. Between this edition and the last, I have remarried, experiencing all the joys and frustrations of trying to build a functional blended family. My stepfather died, leaving my mother on her own; as a result, the issues of the caregiving middle-aged woman became clearer to me. I also found myself more interested in personality change and adjustment at midlife. I even began to feel the topics in Chapters 10 and 11 on aging were not only interesting in the abstract, but becoming more and more relevant.

Other major changes in this edition include much more emphasis on everyday problem-solving and creativity in the chapters on intelligence and cognition (thanks to Michael and his associates), as well as a very much updated discussion of the literature on memory, where recent work has suggested whole new processes, like the idea of working memory or memory for discourse discussed in Chapter 9. I have also been able to include, for the first time, a fairly respectable amount of research on ethnicity and aging. Since the last edition, this literature is represented by a section on demography of aging in Chapter 10, as well as more information throughout the book on the particularities of development among African Americans, Hispanic Americans, Asian Americans, and Native Americans. This is only the barest beginning, however. I hope that by the next edition much more information will be available.

The latest research on work in adult life is covered, including current discussions of the "fast track," and the "mommy track," in Chapters 5 and 8 and the problem of empowerment in the workplace. There is also a much more informed discussion of women's career development from adolescence through middle and later adulthood.

Besides the expanded coverage of love, marriage, divorce, and remarriage, *Adult Life* gives due attention to the burgeoning literature on caregiving families in middle age. There appears to be much concern for the health and well-being of those who assume charge of their parents, particularly when many are still caring for adolescent or college-aged children.

Work on personality development continues apace. Much controversy has arisen over change and sameness, but at least the basis for the conflict is becoming clearer. Recent attempts have been made to take a more qualitative approach to this literature, asking people how they experience aging and whether they feel they have changed. I was struck by the fact that few people ever feel old as long as they are healthy and mobile. Nevertheless, the elderly are always "other" people.

Finally, I was intrigued by the practical turn of the literature in this area of death and dying. There was much more information about how to make life-threatening decisions, how to create and give force to a living will, what to expect in bereavement, and how to cope with it. I think Chapter 12 may well contain the most useful information available in the area at this time.

As before I have not ignored ideas or topics because they were difficult or complicated. Having used this book myself at California State University, Los Angeles, as well as the University of Washington, Tacoma, I have found that a wide variety of students can appreciate even the most complex ideas and feel good about themselves for the attempt to understand them. In response to reviewers, I have been careful about vocabulary and the unnecessarily abstract quotation. I have tried hard to make issues even more accessible than they were in earlier editions.

Aids to Learning about *Adult Life*

Pedagogically useful are the vignettes that open many of the chapters. They are designed to illustrate the problems and adaptations of real people over the life span. Many of these stories are about people I have known whose lives and circumstances were brought to mind by the research literature. I have also tried to include a greater number of examples drawn from everyday life. Within each chapter, great care was given to the inclusion of line drawings, charts, and tables that reinforce content in the clearest and most effective manner possible. Finally, this edition includes four color sections that serve to focus the reader's attention on the core interest of this textbook, adults in development. These sections are intended to add appeal to the content without increasing the cost to the reader.

In the new instructor's manual, a wealth of experiential learning exercises and discussion topics make the literature in adulthood come alive. The test files for this edition, available both in print form and on computer disk, contain nearly 1,000 questions. For each chapter there are at least thirty multiple choice questions, as well as true/false, short answer, and essay questions. Additional test files are included, based on each of the four parts of the text and on an overview of the entire text (a good resource for final examination questions), containing 216 questions. The computerized testbank, Brownstone's Diploma II, is available upon request from Mayfield Publishing Company.

Acknowledgments

Many thanks to the people who have reviewed this edition for me. I found their comments most helpful and have tried to incorporate most of their ideas. In fact, I believe that either I am getting much more mature about criticism or this is the best group of reviewers I have had since I began writing the book. They include Marvin W. Berkowitz, Marquette University; Elaine Blakemore, Indiana University–Purdue University at Fort Wayne; James Buchanan, University of Scranton; Bernard S. Gorman, Nassau Community College; Rosellen M. Rosich, University of Alaska at Anchorage. Special thanks to L. E. Thomas for his helpful advice.

Thanks also to the staff at Mayfield, especially Linda Toy and Frank Graham, who, as usual, put so much thought and energy into each new edition, Lynn Rabin Bauer, Sondra Glider, Jeanne Schreiber, and to my copy editor, Lauren Root.

Finally, I want to thank my friends and family: to Susan Macdonald, who took on the writing of the instructor's manual again; to my husband, Larry, and my daughter, Alexis, who both put up with all the stress of my starting a new job, writing a book, and trying to adjust to being married again after ten years of the single life. It's been a challenging couple of years and makes me wonder how things will be the next time I check in with all of you, in the preface to the fifth edition.

JS-L

Special thanks to the people who were so helpful in the reworking of chapters 3, 6, and 9. They included Catherine Kaczowka, Joseph Morissey, Timothy Saburn, Hadley Anna Solomon, and Tanya Wong.

MLC

Foundations of Adult
Development and Aging

The Graying of America
The Baby Boom
The Study of Adult Development

Introduction

At thirty, Barry has decided he'd like to settle down finally. He'd like to get married and start a family. The problem is, almost every woman he's met lately is older than he is. He doesn't know how he feels about that. He'd really like to marry someone close to his own age or younger.

Besides that, Barry doesn't know if he can get the money together to make a down payment on a house. He had a really hard time finding a decent job, even had to live with his parents for a while after college to make ends meet. He also knows his parents won't be able to help him out much. They're talking about early retirement now and at the same time they're still putting his younger sister through college and trying to help take care of their own parents. Sometimes, Barry wonders if he's ever going to feel like a full-fledged adult. It seems as though he's been "starting out" forever.

WHAT IS ADULTHOOD? When does it start? Is it divided into stages? Do you have to be "on your own" to be an adult? What kind of physical, social, and psychological changes can a person expect over the span of adult life? These are some of the questions this book addresses. In particular, this book is about the issue of change and stability in adulthood. What sort of changes can Barry look forward to in the next forty years of his life? What features of his life are likely to remain the same? If he does get married, will that make a difference in his personality? How will having children affect his experience of himself and his life?

It is only fairly recently that psychologists, sociologists, and biologists have begun looking for the answers to questions about the course of adult life between adolescence and old age. During the first half of this century, researchers tended to look at the adult years as a relatively stable period in which **development,** if it could be said to occur at all, slowed to a standstill, picking up momentum only on the downhill stretch. In most textbooks about human development, few chapters cover the adult years. Books on the history of psychology seldom mention the study of adult development (Birren & Birren, 1990). For the most part, the study of human development has been the study of child psychology.

Consider Barry's case, for example. Certainly he is a young adult. But he doesn't feel like an adult yet because he doesn't have many of the trappings of adulthood. What if Barry finally marries at forty and has a first child at the age of forty-five? In a sense, he will be chronologically middle-aged but will have the career and family patterns of a typical thirty-year-old. At the same time, Barry may have a forty-year-old co-worker who has two grown children, ages twenty and twenty-two. Let's say she's been working full-time for twenty years and is Barry's boss. Which of these people best represents what it means to be middle-aged?

Only in the last two decades have researchers begun to appreciate the complexity of even the simplest questions about adulthood. In 1945, only 500 items were published in the field of psychology on the subjects of adulthood and aging. The literature in the field has doubled every year since (Birren & Birren, 1990). The tremendous economic and social changes of this century, especially since the end of the Second World War, have forced us to address adulthood and aging.

The Graying of America

Demography is the scientific study of human population statistics. Demographers are interested in how the makeup of a population changes. Demographers ask questions such as how many people will turn sixty-five over the next ten years; what proportion of the population will they represent; how many of them will be male or female, black, white, or hispanic; how does the data for the next ten years compare with what is known about the last ten years; and what can one surmise about the future (Myers, 1985)? Demographers are also interested in why population changes takes place. For example, are there more elderly people because some people live to be very, very old, or because very few people die early in adulthood?

George Myers, the Director of the Center for Demographic Studies at Duke University, points out that aging is a worldwide phenomenon. It is not unique to the United States. In international terms, the United States is a "Type II" country. Populations have been typed by the rate and length of increases in the elderly. Since the turn of the century, there has been a sharp increase in the proportion of the population that is elderly, as in the United States. In some countries, the increase in the proportion of elderly has been steadier (Type I); in some, most of the increase has taken place since the end of the Second World War (Type III); and in developing countries, the increase is less prominent but still apparent (Type IV). Figure I.1 presents data on the growth of the elderly population in selected countries.

This circumstance can be understood better in historical perspective, as the social sciences, like all sciences, are shaped by historical forces. Sometime around the turn of the century, social and economic forces like the spread of compulsory education and the exclusion of children from the labor market established the perception of childhood as different from the rest of the life span. People began to consider the uniqueness of childhood; childhood became a complex and interesting phenomenon in the eyes of the social scientist.

At about the same time, adolescence was acknowledged as a separate developmental period. The study of adolescence did not begin in earnest, however, until after World War II, when the American family moved off the farm and into the cities and adolescents remained at home through high school and even college. Today, the study of adolescence is subdivided into three distinct phases (as is the study of childhood): early, middle, and late adolescence. Each phase is no longer than two or three years (Stevens-Long & Cobb, 1983).

The study of adulthood is also divided into three fairly distinct phases: early, middle, and late. Each phase, however, spans twenty to twenty-five years, which creates great ambiguity about how people in each age range might be characterized. People often ask for a definition of middle age or old age. These questions sound simple, but in fact, terms like *middle-aged* or *elderly* are very crude and can be difficult to define.

The number of aged throughout the world in the year 2025 will have tripled since 1985. And, although the proportion will be higher in the developed countries, two-thirds of all the elderly will live in developing countries. Large gains in life expectancy may occur over the next few decades in the countries of Asia and Africa (Myers, 1990).

What does it mean to be living in a Type II country? Since the turn of the

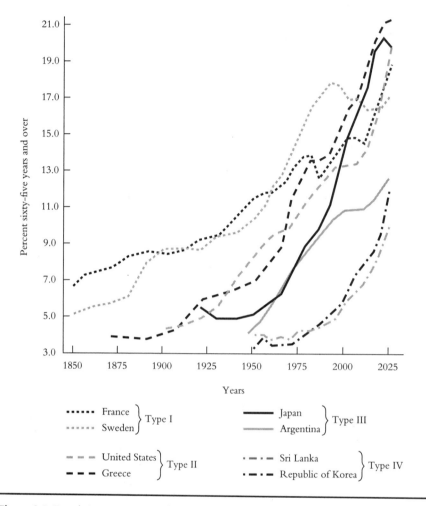

Figure I.1 Trends in percentage of population sixty-five years and over, selected countries, 1850–2025.

SOURCE: Myers, 1985, p. 180.

century in the United States, the number of people over the age of sixty-five has increased seventeenfold, three times the rate of the general population. In 1900, people over sixty-five represented just 4 percent of the population. To-day, this group represents over 10 percent, a figure that is expected to rise to 16 or 17 percent by the year 2030. Expressed another way, in 1900, 3.1 million Americans were over sixty-five. By 1970, this number had increased to 20 mil-lion, and by the year 2025, there will be an estimated 58.6 million people over

In 1900 the average span of life in the United States was forty-five years. By the year 2000, the average American male will live about seventy-five years. How well one lives out one's life span is of growing concern to developmental psychologists.

the age of sixty-five (Decker, 1980; Myers, 1990; U.S. Department of Commerce, 1981).

These astounding changes have been created by two very different trends. First, there has been a decline in *mortality,* and second, there has also been a decline in *fertility.* In other words, more and more people are living long enough to become elderly, and people are also choosing to have fewer children, both of which factors are reducing the proportion of young people in the population.

At the turn of the century, the average person in this country lived to be forty-five, a gain over the average life span during the previous century (twenty-eight years), but just the beginning of a trend. By the year 2025, perhaps 25 percent of the aged will be over eighty-five years old. Today, the average life expectancy for adults who are now middle-aged or older is about sixty-seven for males and seventy-five for females. In 1983, the Department of Agriculture estimated that the average life span for American males will reach

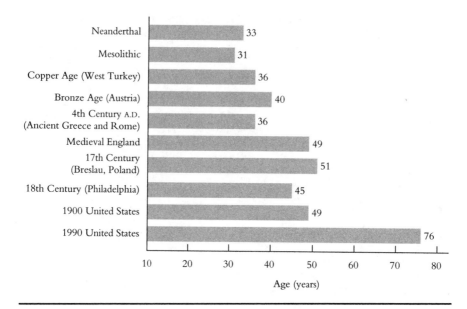

Figure I.2 Expectation of life in past societies.

SOURCE: Laslett, 1985, p. 210.

seventy-five by the year 2000, by which time the average female will live to be eighty-five or more (*Los Angeles Times,* 1983). It is also possible that unpredicted medical advances over the next ten years will have spectacular effects. The control of cardiovascular and renal diseases or major breakthroughs in the prevention and treatment of cancer might easily extend the life span an additional ten years (Decker, 1980). Figure I.2 presents some historical data on the average life span in past societies.

Today the study of human development must address the impact of increased life span and aging on social, political, and economic institutions. Can people stay married for sixty or seventy or eighty years? Will people stop working at sixty-five or seventy and be retired for the next thirty or even forty years? What if the life span is dramatically extended? Can a 90-year-old son be expected to take care of his 110-year-old mother? Because a very rapid reduction of mortality rates occurred for people over age seventy-four between 1960 and 1980 (Myers, 1990), we may have to face these questions much sooner than expected.

Not only are people living to be older, they are also choosing to have fewer children. In the United States, a larger and larger portion of the population is adult. In fact, the median age in the United States has been increasing for at least 150 years. The median age represents the age below which exactly one-

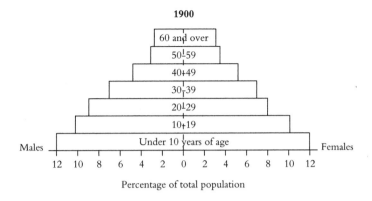

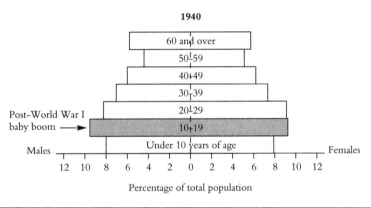

Figure I.3 Population pyramid for the United States for the years 1900 and 1940.

SOURCE: Both Figures I.3 and I.4 are based on Decker (1980) and Bowmer (1980).

half of the population falls. In 1820, for instance, one-half of the population was less than seventeen years old. In 1980, the median age rose to thirty. Declines in fertility of up to 50 percent are expected in developing countries over the next few decades (Myers, 1990).

Figure I.3 shows how the shape of the population of the United States changed between 1900 and 1940. Figure I.4 shows its shape in 1970 and the projection for the year 2030. The changes in these figures have occurred partly because the life span has been extended, but also because of changes in the birthrate that have produced a very special demographic phenomenon: the post–World War II baby boom. Barry is a younger member of that group. In 1991, the first "baby-boomers" will turn forty-five while the youngest of them will turn twenty-seven. As this huge group enters each new phase of the life span, the number of people representing that phase sky-rockets, usually alter-

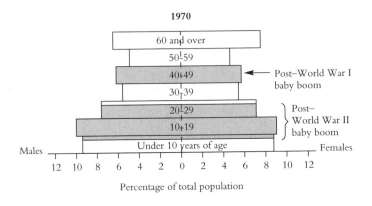

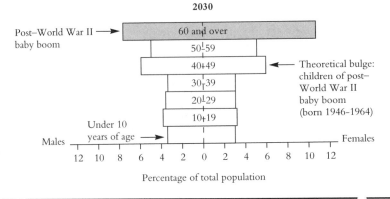

Figure I.4 Population pyramids for the United States for the years 1970 and 2030.

ing basic notions about that age group and posing new sorts of problems—like those Barry has experienced, for example, in just becoming an adult.

The Baby Boom

In "America's Baby Boom Generation: The Fateful Bulge," Leon Bower (1980) wrote: "The sudden 'dumping' of an extraordinarily large number of people of a specific age on society necessarily results in certain upheavals in that society's institutions" (p. 29). Seventy-six million Americans were born in the years between 1946 and 1964. Demographers have called the baby boom a "pig in the python." Figure I.5 gives some idea why.

The baby-boomers have changed the shape of American society, partly because of their numbers and partly because they have been a vocal group. Al-

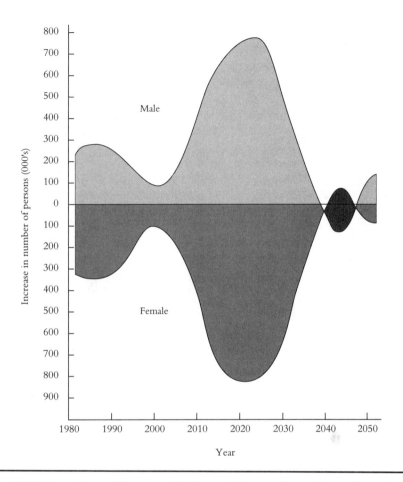

Figure I.5 Projected annual increase of U.S. population aged sixty-five and over, by sex, 1980–2050.

SOURCE: Middle Series, Projections. From U.S. Bureau of the Census, 1989.

though they are better educated than any previous generation, they have not done as well economically as their parents and may never do so. Between 1973 and 1983, "the median real income of a typical young family headed by a person ages 25 to 34 fell by 11.5 percent. In the 1970s, for the first time in history, the economic value of a college degree declined. An awful lot of physics majors found themselves driving cabs" (*Time,* May 19, 1986, p. 25).

Partly because of economic circumstances, the baby-boomers will contribute to the eventual graying of America. They have had fewer children and had them later than the previous generation. They are much more likely to be divorced than their parents were. They are much more likely to be engaged in a

Rapid decline in the birthrate over the last decade is changing the meaning of family life, our most important social institution.

two-paycheck marriage, often of necessity. Sixty-five percent of all first-time home buyers needed two incomes to make payments on their mortgages in 1983.

Barry is a member of the "second wave" of the baby-boomers, and at least some of his complaints may be the result of demographic realities. The second wave is simply the second half of the boom, those born between 1954 or so and 1964. These are the people who have had the most difficult time in some ways. By the time they got to college, most of the best jobs had already gone to their older brothers and sisters, so they had to wait for desirable positions to open up again. Barry is meeting more "older women" because there just are an awful lot more women who are five to ten years older than he is rather than his age or younger. The price of housing increased at a very rapid rate during the years that the first wave bought their first house, so it was harder for the second wave to find the down payment. Barry's grandparents have both lived longer than any previous generation, so his parents are in the unique position of trying to cope with both college-aged or young adult children and the needs of their aging parents.

On a more positive note, Barry and his generation have had and will continue to have a strong impact on every institution it enters. As *Time* Magazine (1986) put it: "Through high times and hard times, no other group of Americans has ever been quite so noisily self-conscious. . . . the Baby Boomers have indeed turned old values upside down, revolutionizing the role of women and transforming American taste, music and sexual mores" (p. 23). The influence of this outspoken generation is one of the major reasons why the study of adulthood and aging is not only exciting to developmental researchers and theoreticians but critical to an understanding of society's future.

The Study of Adult Development

Everything happens to everybody sooner or later if there is enough time.

— George Bernard Shaw

In this book biological and social events and a variety of psychological events, including motivational, cognitive, emotional, and behavioral phenomena, are considered. Faced with a growing wealth of material, researchers and writers are continually redefining the study of adult development, hoping to achieve a more comprehensive, meaningful statement. The first edition of this text relied on the work of James Birren, one of the seminal researchers in the area. Birren referred to aging as a series of changes that individuals characteristically experience as they progress toward maturity and through adulthood into old age (Birren, 1964). In 1977, Birren elaborated on this basic definition, pointing out that researchers should be concerned not only with the description of these changes but should also engage in the attempt to understand the evolution and genetic limits of age-related behavior and explain how such limits might be modified.

In the latest edition of the *Handbook of the Psychology of Aging*, Birren and Birren (1990) suggest that the term *development* implies a change in the organization of behavior "from simple to complex forms, from small to large repertoires of behaviors, from fixed ways of responding to demands and needs to large repertoires of behaviors that can be strategically chosen" (p. 9). This new definition suggests that human development need not end at any special point in the life span. In fact, Birren and Birren even argue that aging and development are, to some extent, independent processes and that people age and develop concurrently.

Elsewhere in the *Handbook*, Schroots and Birren (1990) contend that aging is a progressive **desynchronization** between different developing systems in the individual and between the individual and the environment. So, in some places in this book, we will be looking at the ways in which people age, that is, how their functioning loses a certain kind of smooth organization. The colloquial use of the phrase "out of synch" actually captures much of what is meant here. In other places, we will focus on how people continue to develop, that is, continue to learn new behaviors and to make good strategic choices about which behaviors are appropriate to specific situations.

However, Birren's definition may overemphasize what is universal and irreversible about aging. Another important researcher, Paul Baltes (Baltes, 1979; Baltes, Dittmann-Kohli, & Dixon, 1984; Baltes & Willis, 1977) believes that Birren has neglected both the historical influences on human development and the unique events that make each person's life different from any other. Baltes refers to the effects of the biological and environmental events strongly associated with age as **normative age-graded influences.** Biological maturation and the acquisition of age-appropriate behavior are examples of these. Baltes also talks, as does Birren, about the importance of studying the modification or optimization of developmental change. Unlike Birren, however, Baltes discusses two classes of events he believes must be addressed if one is to account for the complexity of life span development:

1. **Normative history-graded influences:** The general social and historical background of particular groups of people that are born into a culture at the same time. For instance, how will the turmoil in Kuwait affect the lives of people living in this particular historical period?

2. **Nonnormative influences:** Environmental and biological events that do not occur universally or in regular patterns. Such events include marriage, parenthood, and career junctures. To what extent will Barry's late start on marriage, family, and career affect his development over the life span?

Baltes's definition reflects a shift over the past decade or so from the idea that aging is a unitary, universal process to an emphasis on the tremendous variation in development from one adult to another, from one culture to another, and from one generation to another. Current research indicates that the cross-cultural generalizability of numerous developmental functions is limited. In fact, at least one important researcher, Jochen Brandtstädter (1984a, 1990), maintains that adult development is most strongly shaped by historical influences like education, nutrition, health care, and general social values. He contends that development can be described only in terms of a particular social context. In other words, one can only say that certain developments occur with age so long as the relevant social context remains unchanged. Brandtstädter believes the social context is so influential because it shapes a person's beliefs about aging and his or her evaluations of the events that occur with age. In other words, what people believe about aging may be as important as any more concrete force.

Certainly, one of the most important changes in the developmental literature in the last ten years has been a shift toward the study of more subjective phenomena. Researchers and theorists have become increasingly intrigued by how cognition, emotion, and values influence behavior—the role people play in their own development. There is also growing respect for complexity of the interactions between the person and the culture in the shaping of beliefs, feelings, and thoughts. In fact, Birren (1980) has argued that development over the life span is strongly characterized by an increased interdependence of person and environment. The exchange of influence between people and the social and historical context is more important in adolescence than in childhood, and more important in adulthood than in any earlier period.

This book is organized to take advantage of the idea of context. There are three major chronological sections: one deals with early adulthood, one with middle age, and one with later life. In each section, the chapters move from research on the internal context, including biological events, cognition, and emotional development; to the personal context, covering such topics as personality, family, and friends; to the expanded context of work, leisure, and one's relationship to the larger social and political environment. Before the chronological sections begin, however, there are two overview chapters, one devoted to research methodology and the other to theory. The book concludes with a chapter on death and dying framed as a final context for human development.

1

Design and Methods

ELAINE IS STARTING TO FEEL like herself again, at least part of the time. It has been pretty rough this time around even though she didn't have to go through the agony of a long illness, as she did with her first husband, six years ago. After Ed died, Elaine married her childhood sweetheart, Wayne. She was seventy at the time. Wayne was seventy-one. Six months ago, Wayne died of cancer. Elaine still feels disoriented half of her waking hours. It happened so fast. She can't seem to quite take in all the changes. It's affected her memory too. She'll go upstairs to get something and forget what it was by the time she's at the top of the stairwell. She can't remember where she puts her knitting bag.

It doesn't seem as though she was so forgetful before Wayne died. But maybe it was just because he was so good at remembering things for her—before he got sick, of course. Anyway, she still has awfully difficult moments, but she is living on her own again, paying the bills, keeping up a great big house and, recently, she's even started painting a little. As a girl, she thought she had some talent. Now she wonders if seventy-five isn't too late to develop it.

IN THIS CHAPTER, WE'RE GOING TO LOOK at some of the ways researchers might try to sort out all of the influences that are at play in the complicated lives of people like Elaine. To what extent is her forgetfulness normal? Is it a product of aging itself or due to the shock of bereavement? Is she actually more forgetful now, or does she simply notice her absent-mindedness more because she is elderly and people expect to forget things more often when they grow old? And what about that talent? Can an elderly person develop an entirely new skill very late in life? What might be the best ways to go about answering each of these questions? That is the basic issue of research design.

The Basic Questions

What can I know? What ought I to do? What may I hope?
                                        —Immanuel Kant

Jum Nunnally (1982), a researcher who has focused on basic questions and research methods in human development, once wrote: "It is not difficult to make the case that most scientific theories and related research activities are concerned with some natural or experimentally induced change" (p. 133). In other words, scientists of all kinds, whether they are interested in human, animal, plant, or physical nature, are basically trying to identify and explain change. Yet, in the study of human development, some have raised the question of whether the changes that occur during most of adulthood are of a sufficient magnitude to be considered truly developmental (Flavell, 1970).

Certainly, there are aspects of adult experience that do not change very dramatically over fairly long periods. For example, general levels of adjustment, integration, and competence are relatively stable over the years from ages twenty to seventy (Newman, 1982; Thomae, 1979). Studies of various personality traits including egocentrism, dependency, decision making, the need for achievement, creativity, and hope have generally reported essential stability over the adult years (Plomin & Thompson, 1988; Neugarten, 1977). Studies of cognitive style, that is, of insightfulness and interest in intellectual matters, also show little change over the adult years (Costa & McCrae, 1981; Haan, 1976). Researchers are, in fact, very likely to turn up evidence for the stability of adult personality and behavior when they measure general characteristics, like dependency or the need to achieve, especially if they use only one set of responses to define that characteristic (Neugarten, 1977).

On the other hand, autobiographical material and long-term interview studies of the same individuals over a number of years regularly report change. In one study, the autobiographies of 180 men and women born around the turn of the century were analyzed (Thomae, 1979); the average participant reported about seventeen major changes or turning points over the course of adult life. Most frequently people report changes in their own attitudes, in self-esteem, and in how aware they are of their own ideas, beliefs, and attitudes.

Some researchers have suggested that whether people see themselves as stable or not simply depends on the stability of their commitments, relationships, and the degree to which stability or change is rewarded (Wells & Stryker, 1988). These researchers have argued that all adults have a set of identities that are organized into a hierarchy reflecting their commitments. Some of the identities may change and some may not, depending on whether the activities associated with them are stable. The longer one remains a worker, for example, the harder it may be to retire and the greater changes one might expect in retirement.

Most research does suggest that the most dramatic changes take place in the subjective aspects of experience: in how we see ourselves and in how we feel about ourselves, others, and life. Often, it is not clear how such changes affect behavior. Jochen Brandtstädter (1984a, 1990) has attempted to address this issue with a model suggesting how beliefs and values might affect personal development. He shows how one's appraisal of the prospects for and outcomes of development might produce attempts at personal change, emotional effects, and further evaluations. From this point of view, the possibility of Elaine's learning to paint well depends to a large extent on her own personal appraisal of whether she is any good at it. If she thinks she is, she will make efforts to improve her work. If not, her early attempts may simply add to her feelings of depression and despair. So she is taking a very risky step in trying a completely new activity at this point in her life. If she is successful, especially at something others consider difficult, she may be rewarded with strong feelings of joy and relief, pride and competence.

Of course, no one has ever argued that there were no changes in adulthood to be studied at all. Decline has always been assumed in the study of later life, and much of the traditional research data has supported the stereotype of decline with age. Elaine's memory problem is a typical phenomenon that researchers have found of interest. This makes sense for two reasons. First, researchers too are affected by social stereotypes, and the American stereotype of age emphasizes loss. They have spent little time considering functions that might improve. Second, American scientists usually assume that behavior can only deteriorate, improve, or remain stable. They have rarely examined the possibility that complex phenomena, like memory, constitute an array of functions, some of which might deteriorate with age, some remain stable or improve, and some even undergo transformation (Horn, 1982; Schaie & Hertzog, 1982, 1985; Schaie, 1988).

Throughout this book, an effort is made to remain open to various ways of conceptualizing changes that take place over the life span. As John Nesselroade (1977) put it: "Behavioral change over the life span is a complex, multifaceted phenomenon whose proper study requires the researcher to utilize methodological tools which are sufficiently complex to match it" (p. 59). Of course, the idea that anything can happen—that developmental changes can be expansive or represent decline or even be transformational, that they may be gradual or fairly rapid—demands the use of sophisticated research designs and measures. Of equal value are a flexible conception of the life course and a means of dividing it into periods or phases for study.

Defining the Life Span

A variety of terms have been used to refer to the sequence of events that make up a person's life experience. **Life span** is often used by developmental psychologists, whereas **life course** has been more popular among sociologists. Psychologists generally tend to be more interested in internal, subjective events (although this is certainly not true of all psychologists), whereas sociologists focus on "socially created, socially recognized, and shared" events (Hagestad & Neugarten, 1985). Specifically, the life course reflects "how society gives social and personal meanings to the passage of biographical time" (Hagestad, 1990, p. 151). Technologically, the life span may be longer than the life course. That is, people may live longer than the number of years assigned important social or personal meanings by the society (Hagestad, 1990).

Life cycle is also a term in current usage, although it has been suggested that it be reserved for talking about development that takes place not only over the life span of an individual but also over generations (O'Rand & Krecker, 1990). Life cycle has been used to refer to the normal, predictable sequence of events within a culture (Hagestad & Neugarten, 1985) or to the underlying order in the life course (Levinson, 1986), made up of a sequence of eras, each with its own psychological, biological, and social character.

Table 1.1 presents some of the ways the life course has been divided into phases, or eras. Among these possibilities, Daniel Levinson's has probably been the most thoroughly researched.

Levinson postulates the existence of definite age-linked periods. His research has shown regularity of pattern over much of adulthood for both males and females (Levinson, in press). It has also underlined the developmental importance of the transitional periods between eras. Levinson maintains that each of us builds a sequence of *life structures,* a concept he defines as a pattern of

Table 1.1 Dividing up the life course

Bromley (1974)	Levinson et al. (1974)	Gould (1972)	Havighurst (1972) and Neugarten (1974)
Juvenile Phase			
0–11 Childhood			0–6 Early childhood
			7–12 Middle childhood
12–16 Adolescence	16–20 Leaving home	16–18 Ambivalence	13–18 Adolescence
17–20 Transition	21–29 Getting into the world	19–22 Leaving home	19–35 Early adulthood
		23–28 Establishment	
Adult Phase			
21–25 Transition		29–32 Thirties transition	
26–40 Middle adulthood	30–34 Settling down	33–40 Adulthood	36–60 Middle adulthood
	35–39 BOOP*a*	41–43 Midlife transition	
41–60 Late adulthood	40–42 Midlife transition	44–50 Midlife	
	43–50 Restabilization	51–60 Flowering	
61–65 Preretirement			61+ Later maturity
66–70 Retirement			55–75 Young-old
71+ Old age			75+ Old-old
Terminal stage			

a Becoming one's own person

relationships with people, groups, objects, and institutions over the life cycle. Each one of these structures lasts five to seven years, ten at the most, ending in a transitional phase during which the current life structure is reappraised, alternatives explored, and new choices made.

Levinson's eras are not really stages in the sense that developmental theoreticians ordinarily use the term *stage*. A stage is traditionally defined as a new organization, whether psychological, biological, or social, that is "higher" or more mature than the last. Usually, stage theorists posit that people have to resolve the issues or develop the abilities characteristic of one stage before they can enter the next (McHale & Lerner, 1900). Levinson doesn't make this kind of claim for his concept of stages. He doesn't think the structure one builds at midlife is necessarily any more mature than the one constructed in early adulthood, but he does feel that structures vary in "*satisfactoriness.*" A satisfactory structure is one which is both *suitable* and *viable*. When important aspects of the self are expressed rather than neglected or repressed, a structure is suitable. If the structure allows one to operate well in the outside world, it is viable. As Levinson points out, however, a structure can be viable without being suitable, or vice versa.

Another way to discuss the life span is to use the concept of **developmental tasks.** For instance, one early researcher, R. J. Havighurst (1972), approached the study of adulthood through the description of the obligations and responsibilities he felt produced healthy, satisfactory growth in society. Havighurst described developmental tasks as "bio-socio-psychological" in origin; he also believed they could be accomplished only at one particular, critical period in the life course.

A more recent treatment of the same idea (Oerter, 1988) has emphasized the need to analyze what kinds of skills underlie coping with developmental tasks as well as what environmental objects are involved and what competencies develop. Developmental tasks may vary, from this point of view, from something as simple as a person's "first date" to a lifelong goal such as "becoming mature." Oerter believes that the tasks a society sets out for a particular period reflect the wisdom and historical experience of a culture. In his view, although some skills may depend on the acquisition of certain earlier skills, the tasks themselves need not be considered hierarchical. That means, a person does not necessarily have to complete one to be able to complete the next. A person might become a mature adult, for instance, having never had a date at all.

It has also been argued, however (Keating & MacLean, 1988), that we have to be very careful about accepting the idea that developmental tasks reflect what has "worked" historically or represent some kind of wisdom because certain voices have been systematically excluded from the shaping of social norms and expectations. For example, historically women have had little impact on defining either what was normal or what was optimal in human development.

Whether or not stages or eras can be said to characterize the life span, re-

"Life with Father" as pictured here was once considered an ideal image of the American family. The recent rapid decline in the birthrate may have forever changed the way American family life is defined.

searchers have to find a reasonable way to divide up the adult years in order to make the comparisons that would tell us whether development occurs and how it proceeds. Unfortunately, there is little agreement about where important transitions are to be found. Nonetheless, research goes on, and researchers make educated guesses about what kinds of comparisons make the most sense for different areas of study. For example, in studying memory, it makes some sense to compare twenty-, forty-, and sixty-year-olds because the processes change rather slowly. On the other hand, attitudes toward sex-role behavior might change dramatically between groups separated by as little as five or ten years.

All of which leads to one of the thorniest problems in developmental research. Although there are many differences between people of different ages, only some of these differences are related to the passage of time, or to maturation, or to increased experience—some of the forces we might think of as developmental. Many important differences between people of various ages are social and historical. A sixty-year-old person grew up in a very different society than a person who is twenty, and the differences between their societies may be responsible for much of what is ordinarily attributed to aging. The recognition of historical context as an important determinant of age differences has served as a wellspring for work in research design and analysis.

Research Designs

Research activities are concerned with change. In the case of research in adult development, then, researchers focus on the change that occurs in the lives of adults, change that takes place over time. That is, researchers look for **time-** or **age-related change.** It turns out that time- and age-related changes are difficult to distinguish from each other. For instance, executive burnout at forty-five may seem to be an age-related change but may actually occur because a person has spent twenty years on the job. It crops up at age forty-five only because most executives begin their jobs at age twenty-five (Schaie, 1988; Schaie & Hertzog, 1985). In the first stages of research, changes related to age and those related to the passage of time are often not sorted out.

Researchers tend to be interested in identifying any kind of regular changes that take place over the life span. Only later do they try to determine what processes might be responsible for the changes and whether the changes can be influenced by the person or the environment. For example, let's return to the problem of explaining why Elaine can't remember where she put her knitting bag. This is a particularly important example because so much of the research on adult development has been devoted to the study of mental abilities. It could be that if Elaine's memory is getting worse, it is related to her age. That is, maybe people do lose the ability to remember certain kinds of information as well as they used to. It is also possible, however, that it's been a long time since Elaine *had* to remember anything. Remember, she says that Wayne used to remind her. Perhaps her memory lapses are worse than they used to be because she is unused to keeping track of things herself.

Deterioration of memory is not typical of all aging people. Elaine may be having a difficult time remembering because of the psychological and physical changes associated with recent bereavement. Or it could be that some of her memory loss is due to the way she and her peers were taught to memorize things as children. In the last case, we might guess that twenty years from now, people Elaine's age would not show the same kinds of change.

In recent years, researchers have spent a great deal of energy trying to sort out the influences that might be responsible for the differences people exhibit with age. In particular, they have been concerned with trying to determine which differences are most strongly related to aging, which ones are most likely to be the product of a person's social history (for instance, how Elaine was taught to use her memory as a child), and which ones might be due to circumstances in the current environment (Elaine's bereavement). The differences one observes among people of various ages might be a product of any or all of these forces. In casual observation, then, age differences are evident that may have been produced by age changes; historical, or **cohort,** changes; or a variety of factors peculiar to the environment at the time of measurement (Schaie, 1967, 1973, 1979, 1988; Schaie & Hertzog, 1982, 1983, 1985).

Probably the key term for understanding this problem is cohort. A cohort is a group of people who were all born at or about the same time. For a researcher the delineation of a cohort depends on the problem to be studied. Thus, all people born in 1945 might constitute a cohort in one inquiry, whereas everyone born between 1940 and 1950 might be a significant cohort in another.

Let's consider Elaine's situation one more time. How might memory deficits be explained by cohort differences? Let's say that the average forty-year-old person performs far better on a researcher's test of memory than the average person Elaine's age. Today, people who are forty are likely to have finished high school and to have attended at least a year or two of college. Most people over seventy do not have a high school education. If scores on a memory test are affected by education, cohort differences may explain the observed differences in performance. People who are forty are also more familiar with memory tests, often having been tested during their school careers. So that is another way that cohort influences might be at work. Furthermore, people who are forty have only been out of school for fifteen to twenty years, whereas people who are over seventy have been out of school for longer than the entire life span of the forty-year-olds. Dozens of other cohort differences may affect performance, and cohort differences are usually greater than the differences due to age. Determining what is age-related and what is cohort-related change has been a central challenge of research on adult life.

It is also true that the current environment may affect performance in a variety of ways, producing what is generally referred to as **time-of-measurement** effects. Returning to our example, consider how social stereotyping might affect Elaine's behavior. Most people, including Elaine herself, tend to believe that memory fails with age. Such attitudes may shape the behavior of people who belong to different age groups and also influence the ways in which researchers interpret that behavior. Thus, age differences can reflect the bias of the subjects, the researchers, and the general culture at a particular time of measurement.

Finally, Elaine's bereavement and her general health status may be influencing her performance. Because health and **bereavement** are related to age, it is especially difficult to distinguish their effects. Therefore, it is critical researchers describe the general health of their subjects and that they try to gather information about events that could affect subjects' responses to a study. It may also make sense for researchers to screen for deficits in vision or hearing among older subjects (Schaie, 1988).

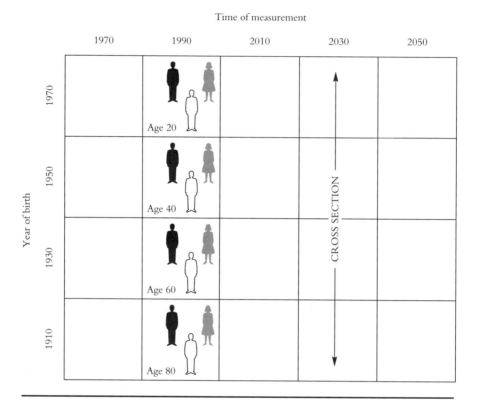

Figure 1.1 Cross-sectional design.

What method of observation might allow the researcher to determine which explanation best accounts for observed age differences? Part of the answer lies in choosing the right method of observation, or *research design*. Part involves the careful construction of measures and proper subject selection, and, ultimately, part lies in how one interprets the results of the observation. Consider first the problem of choosing a research design.

Cross-sectional Designs

The most common research design, and, unfortunately, the least informative, is called a **cross-sectional design.** In a cross section, people from two or more cohorts (people born at the same time) are observed at one time of measurement. Time of measurement is simply the date of the experiment. In the cross section shown in Figure 1.1, for instance, an investigator doing research in 1990 selected a group of people born in 1970 as representative of all twenty-

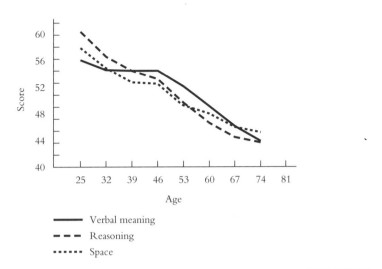

Figure 1.2 Cross-sectional results on subtests of Primary Abilities Test given in 1963.
SOURCE: After Schaie & Labouvie-Vief (1974).

year-olds, a group born in 1950 as representative of all forty-year-olds, a group born in 1930 as representative of all sixty-year-olds, and a group born in 1910 to represent all eighty-year-olds. In a cross section, age groups are necessarily represented by people who differ not only in age but also in cohort.

If one collects data on mental abilities using a cross section, it will be impossible to say whether any age differences that emerge are the result of age changes, cohort differences, or time of measurement effects. All three of these major forces are *confounded,* that is, they cannot be sorted out. For years, however, researchers did not realize the implications of using a cross-sectional design, assuming that the age differences they found in a cross section represented the effects of age. Much of the early research on mental abilities relied on cross-sectional designs, consistently reporting steep declines in performance over the adult years. Figure 1.1 presents a model of the simple cross-sectional design, whereas Figure 1.2 presents typical cross-sectional data on mental abilities as reported by Schaie in a 1974 study comparing different kinds of research designs.

Cross-sectional research has consistently supported what has been called the **irreversible decrement** model of aging. In other words, cross-sectional research on a wide variety of functions, including intelligence, learning, memory, and biological functions, has usually produced data suggesting decline over the life cycle. Much, if not most, of this decline probably reflects cohort differences rather than age changes, however. For that reason, researchers in-

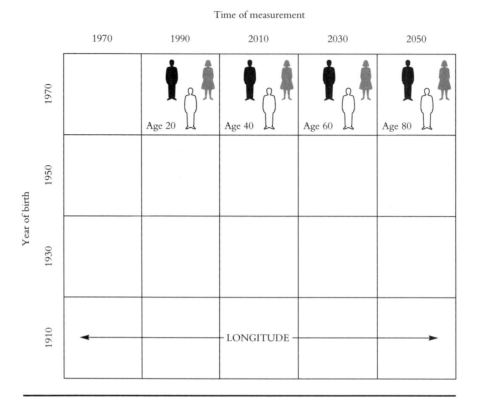

Figure 1.3 Longitudinal design.

terested in identifying developmental changes over long periods of the life span have turned to different kinds of designs.

Longitudinal Designs

Because it is so difficult to interpret evidence collected in a cross-sectional design, many developmental researchers consider a **longitudinal design** superior. In longitudinal research, the investigator observes the same people over and over again; thus, there are several times of measurement and several ages observed as the same people get older. Figure 1.3 represents a typical longitudinal approach to the same age groups represented in Figure 1.1. Age differences found in a longitudinal study may reflect age changes or they could be produced by changes in cultural conditions from one time of measurement to the next, but they cannot be a product of cohort differences, because there is only one cohort.

Unfortunately, longitudinal research is plagued by special curses that are the side effects of observing the same people again and again, over time. Participants may become more proficient at some tests over the years (the **practice effect**); they may become bored; they may even become hostile or annoyed. Repetition alters the behavior of participants, the meaning of measures, and the perceptions of the experimenters as well. The potential **test-retest effects** in a longitudinal study are many, varied, and difficult to foresee (Baltes, Reese, & Nesselroade, 1977; Schaie & Hertzog, 1982, 1983, 1985; Schaie, 1988).

Special problems also arise when experimenters have to keep in touch with the same people often over twenty years or more. Some people move and leave no forwarding address; some lose interest; some decide they don't like the experiment; some may even die. When subjects don't return to a longitudinal study, for whatever reason, **experimental mortality** is said to occur. Experimental mortality wouldn't be so bothersome if it occurred randomly, that is, if the people who didn't come back were identical to the ones who did. Usually, however, the less intelligent, more rigid, less healthy subjects disappear. Subjects who are lost over the years also seem to be of lower socioeconomic status, to show lower self-esteem, and to engage in less frequent social interaction than those who return (Riegel, Riegel, & Meyer, 1967; Rusin & Siegler, 1975; Siegler, 1975).

Imagine how longitudinal studies of mental abilities over the adult life span might be influenced by experimental mortality. For instance, longitudinal studies typically show less decline than cross-sectional studies. Is that because only the most intelligent, high-status, high self-esteem subjects consistently return?

Finally, if a longitudinal study follows the performance of only one cohort, researchers may learn much about age changes among members of that cohort but be unable to say whether anything they have learned applies to people born at any other point in history. Performance on some tests of mental abilities declined during adulthood for the cohort born in 1920, but will the same thing happen to the cohort born in 1960? The cohort of 1960 will have more education, on average, and probably hold more skilled jobs than those held by the cohort of 1920. Data from one cohort are very hard to generalize to another, untested cohort especially during periods of great social change.

In the last few years, researchers have made progress toward solving some of the problems of simple cross-sectional and longitudinal designs, combining and extending them to reap the advantages of both. These combinations have been called **sequential designs,** since they call for sequences of cross-sectional or longitudinal studies.

Sequential Designs

A sequential study includes the observation of at least two simple cross sections or two longitudinal analyses (see Figure 1.4). The researcher must observe people from at least two different cohorts, at two or more times of measurement. The increased information produced by this simple extension of the designs already considered here allows the researcher to estimate the effects of

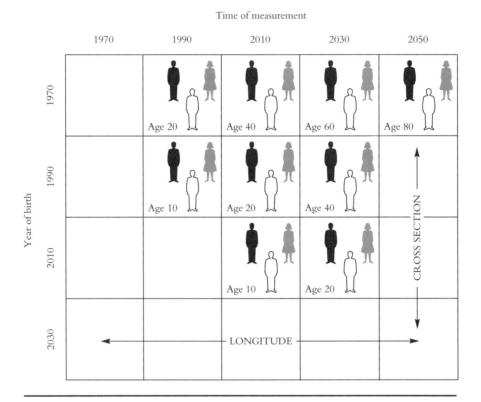

Figure 1.4 Sequential design.

age, cohort, and time of measurement separately. Remember, a cross section includes only one time of measurement, and a simple longitudinal study relies on data from only one cohort. To apply the sophisticated statistical analysis required to estimate the effects of age, cohort, and time of measurement, a design must include two groups representing each effect; that is, two age groups, two cohorts, and two times of measurement. The sequential design accomplishes this goal.

The most sophisticated sequential design, which Schaie has dubbed the "most efficient design," calls for both cross-sectional and longitudinal sequences (1982). At each time of measurement, new subjects are added to each age group, and subjects from the last time of measurement are retested. By comparing the behavior of new subjects with subjects tested before, researchers can begin to estimate the influence of practice or test-retest effects, as well as age, cohort, and time-of-measurement effects. They can also decide whether experimental mortality is affecting the data in an important way (Baltes & Schaie, 1976).

Schaie's data, seen in Figure 1.5, show how people of different cohorts per-

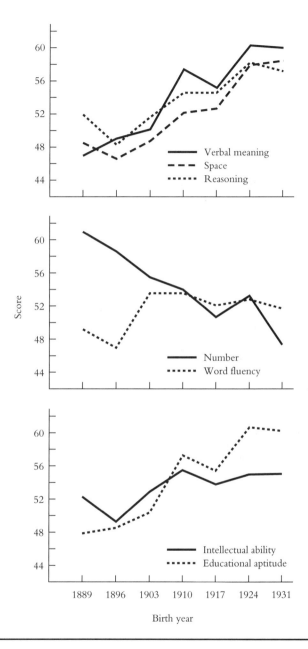

Figure 1.5 Results from a sequential research design for the primary mental abilities.

SOURCE: From Schaie, Labouvie, & Buech (1973).

formed on tests of mental abilities. Note that data for the oldest subjects appear first on the gradients presented.

In an overview of work using longitudinal and sequential designs, Paul Baltes and his associates (Baltes, Dittmann-Kohli, & Dixon, 1984) conclude: "General decline (across persons and abilities) of intellectual performance does not seem to occur until the seventh or eighth decade of life in most individuals of presently aging cohorts in the United States" (p. 40).

Even with its high level of sophistication, however, sequential design cannot answer all the questions researchers pose about aging. For example, both longitudinal and sequential research designs produce data that are presented in the form of curves based on averaging over a number of people. It has been argued that such average growth curves don't really tell us anything about individual growth. They can't answer questions like "Why do some people remain stable even into their seventies and eighties?" or "Under what conditions do people appear to deteriorate early?" (Rogosa, 1988). More in-depth exploration of the people who lie at the extremes of these average growth curves would add immeasurably to what we already know.

Interpretive Science   There are a variety of ways that such information might be gathered. One could, for instance, observe a small number of people over and over again, trying to discover the conditions under which change occurs. John Nesselroade (1988) has used this kind of design to study fatigue and anxiety, demonstrating that scores on tests of anxiety are dependent on fatigue. Interview data, the analysis of literary texts, and participant observation are other ways that rich data may be collected (Thomas, 1989). These methods are sometimes called **interpretive science** because they are directed more at understanding and less at predicting human behavior than the more traditional scientific methods. Whether one is analyzing texts or interpreting interviews or working as a participant observer, the basic idea is to try to understand the data through the eyes of the informants and in light of the political, social, cultural, economic, and historical context.

At the other extreme, some researchers choose to continue the analysis in the laboratory. Given good descriptive data about what changes are clearly associated with aging, researchers formulate hypotheses about why such changes occur and try to recreate those conditions in the controlled setting of the lab.

Laboratory Research Designs

The most extensive literature using laboratory methods has appeared in work on cognition and memory. Often, the goal of the researchers is to see whether elderly performance can be improved or optimized. In one very interesting example, the investigators hypothesized that directions given to subjects of different ages might influence performance. The experimenters were studying memory of a 500-word narrative under different conditions. Under two of the

The potential for physical labor and strenuous athletic endeavor is greatest in the mid-twenties, enabling the young adult to perform a multitude of physically demanding tasks, including giving birth.

When they reach the stage of formal operations, young adults can think logically about the possible as well as the real. This ability to generate and test alternatives enables them to manipulate systems of abstract symbols, to negotiate complex social interactions, and to develop independent moral and ethical beliefs.

In childhood, creativity usually means technical expertise in one particular endeavor. In adulthood, however, creativity means original approaches to problem solving in all aspects of life.

Self-disclosure is a necessary ingre-
dient of any intimate relationship,
whether between close friends
or between lovers. Because self-
disclosure depends on self-
knowledge, a strong sense of
identity is a prerequisite for close
adult relationships.

Achieving an equitable, loving relationship doesn't guarantee that it will last. Maintaining a relationship past the initial passion as both partners develop and as their family grows requires the ability to tolerate and even appreciate change and conflict.

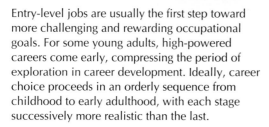

Entry-level jobs are usually the first step toward more challenging and rewarding occupational goals. For some young adults, high-powered careers come early, compressing the period of exploration in career development. Ideally, career choice proceeds in an orderly sequence from childhood to early adulthood, with each stage successively more realistic than the last.

According to Kohlberg's theory of moral development, people who reason at the higher stages tend to make moral judgments based on universal principles. Young adults who have reached this stage are more likely than their more conventional peers to work actively for the good of their community.

The sudden death of a young adult, for whatever reason, is an unexpected tragedy, especially for the surviving spouse and children. In spite of the disruption of their entire life, young survivors are expected to grieve only briefly and then to rebound quickly.

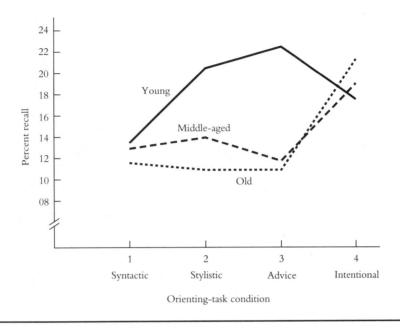

Figure 1.6 Mean percentage of propositions recalled as a function of orienting task and condition.

SOURCE: Simon et al., 1982.

orienting conditions, subjects were asked to correct errors (syntactic and stylistic) in the narrative; in another to write a letter of advice to the family described in the story; in the last to read and remember the story. The results of the study demonstrated that elderly and middle-aged subjects performed best when they were simply told to remember the story. Figure 1.6 presents the complete data from this study.

In studies like this one, researchers test hypotheses about what causes age-related changes. In this case, the researchers concluded that older subjects do not use the same processes younger subjects do to transfer material to memory. It is possible that cohort differences in how people were taught to use their memories produced these differences. That is one of the explanations we looked at for Elaine's apparent memory loss. Attempts have been made to teach older people how to process information in new ways. This research is discussed in a later chapter; the important point here concerns the advantages and disadvantages of work done in the laboratory.

If one knew whether laboratory research recreated events similar or at least analogous to the events of ordinary development, one could generalize experimental findings to the outside world with confidence. But often laboratory interventions are very different from what are probably the normal developmental processes. When a particular procedure, like teaching a new way to

A general decline of intellectual performance does not seem to occur until age seventy or even eighty. Grandparents can be important sources of advice and knowledge about family in the lives of their children and grandchildren.

transfer information to memory, improves performance among elderly subjects, it may mean little about the process that caused the differences in performance between young and old in the first place. It is possible, for instance, that biological decline produces poor memory performance among the elderly, and learning new ways to process memory materials in the laboratory simply permits elderly subjects to overcome an inevitable biological decrement (Baltes, Reese, & Nesselroade, 1977; Birren & Renner, 1977). As Birren and Cunningham (1985) put it: "The demonstrated improvement of an ability with practice does not contradict decrement models but does clearly show that declines are neither inevitable nor immutable. The distinction between what is natural and what is inevitable is an important one for aging" (p. 25).

Discovering what is natural about aging in the laboratory is very complicated. There are both ethical and practical problems. Usually, the researcher assumes that the processes causing age-related changes occur over several years of the life cycle or gradually over the entire life span. In the laboratory, however, investigators must recreate such processes in a few minutes or a few hours. As is the case for research that employs computer models or other species, we can't be sure how much of what is learned in the lab applies to life in the real world. Some authors have even argued that the real world is so complex and changes so rapidly that human development will never be completely understood or explained. Kenneth Gergen (1980) maintains, for example, that the forces behind development are in a constant state of flux, and the true role of the researcher is not verification, but vivification. By this he means that observation and experimentation can sensitize us and motivate us to question our assumptions, but we cannot expect predictive value from laboratory research and statistical analysis.

Concern about the significance and validity of developmental research does not end with criticisms of design or questions about the generalizability of laboratory results. There are also problems of subject selection, the construction of measures, and the interpretation of results. All of these will lead to questioning much of the research literature in chapters to come. In any science, however, one must be able to question the accepted ways of doing and interpreting things, to push for better, more exact methods.

Subject Selection

In truly experimental studies of psychology, sociology, or biology, the experimenter is able to assign each subject to a condition of interest. If, for instance, the researcher is interested in the effects of television violence on aggression, some subjects are assigned to view violent television programs and some are assigned to view nonviolent programs. After the subjects have been exposed to these conditions, the experimenter tries to determine whether there are significant differences in the attitudes, beliefs, or behaviors of subjects who have viewed violent versus nonviolent programs.

In the study of adult development, the conditions of interest are actually various lengths of the life span. We are interested in whether significant differences in the attitudes, beliefs, and behaviors of people occur as a function of age. Obviously there is no way to assign ages to subjects, so it is necessary to study naturally existing groups. When the assignment of subjects to conditions cannot be controlled, the research is considered **quasi-experimental** (Campbell & Stanley, 1963; Ray & Ravizza, 1985). Subjects in quasi-experimental studies are influenced by forces over which the experimenter exercises no control.

When an experimenter chooses subjects of different cohorts to represent age groups, those subjects differ not only in ways related to aging but in ways related to cohort as well. When subjects are chosen at random, cohort differences are likely to be maximized. For that reason, investigators often try to match subjects from different age groups on certain characteristics they feel might influence the phenomenon of interest. For example, in a 1982 study of problem solving, Nancy Denney (1982) matched her elderly and young subjects for years of education. This study suggested that even when subjects are matched for educational background, decrements in problem-solving ability can be observed among elderly persons. In this case, the matching of subjects for education worked. However, educated elderly people are actually an elite

What really happens inside a single-parent family after the first year of a divorce? All the subtle interactions that profoundly influence people's behavior in the real world cannot be replicated and examined in any controlled environment.

group of older people, whereas educated young subjects are more representative of the average young person. Most younger people have at least high school educations and are healthy. But among the elderly, only the most advantaged are well educated and in good health, especially among the oldest groups. If Denney had not found differences in performance, it might have been because her elderly subjects were a rather privileged group.

There may be no optimal way to select subjects for developmental research. However, it is important that the researcher understand and describe the critical characteristics of the people who participate in it. This is seldom the case. Even basic information about health and education are often missing from investigator's descriptions (Schaie, 1988). For instance, the majority of studies published in the *Journal of Gerontology* do not adequately specify the health of elderly subjects (LaRue & Jarvik, 1982). An accurate, complete description of the subjects in a study allows one to generalize the results to the appropriate group in the larger population.

Subjects are not the only thing that experimenters select, of course. They also select setting, treatment conditions, measures, observers, and a time of measurement. A truly complete picture of how people develop will only come over time through repeated research with variations in selection criteria (Nesselroade, 1990).

Instrumentation and Measurement

Probably the most important issue in selecting a test or measure for use in developmental research is **age equivalence.** Age equivalence means the researcher can be confident the measure reflects the same set of abilities or attributes for all of the ages included in a particular study. It also means that this set of abilities is equally important for each age group (Eckensburger, 1973; Schaie & Hertzog, 1985).

In a test comparing the mental abilities of eighty-year-olds and twenty-year-olds, it would be crucial to know that it meant the same thing to both sets of participants. If the sample of older people contained a large number of immigrants, the test might reflect ability to speak English among the eighty-year-olds but not among the subjects in their twenties. Schaie and Hertzog (1985) remind us that there are "substantial differences in language behavior and educational exposure between successive cohorts that may readily affect test comprehension and verbal performance" (p. 66). They argue that it makes some sense to use older forms of certain tests when working with older cohorts. For example, Gribben and Schaie (1976) found that the more recent versions of the test for Primary Mental Abilities did not reflect competence as well for older subjects as did earlier versions of the test.

Even if the test meant exactly the same thing to both groups, it is still not clear that the kinds of abilities tested for are as important to intelligent behavior in eighty-year-olds as in twenty-year-olds. The problems of people who are twenty (e.g., how to read an entire textbook in one night) are very different from those of eighty-year-olds (e.g., how to go up a flight of stairs with limited physical mobility). The factors that predict intelligent behavior in the real world may differ greatly over the life span and may not be predicted equally well by the measures ordinarily available in developmental research.

One approach to the age-equivalence problem is to develop measures specifically designed for each age group. Denney's (1982) work provides an example. Box 1.1 illustrates some of the items she formulated for her study of problem solving. Age equivalence might also be assured by using a set of measures rather than a single measure. When several measures are used, sophisticated statistical analyses can be applied to discover whether there is a profile of pattern of abilities that might be said to represent changes over the life span (Nesselroade, 1977).

Clearly, measurement issues are as complex as any problem discussed so far. Nunnally (1982) has even declared that the worst problems in the area of developmental research are problems of measurement construction, especially if an investigator plans to use the same test over and over again in a longitudinal design. Over successive administrations, performance may be distorted by practice and by the fact that some of the test items become dated over the years.

Research design, sample selection, and text construction all influence the results of a study. Furthermore, each of these is influenced by any preconceived

---

Box 1.1 Real-life problems constructed for three different age groups

1. Let's say that a twenty-five-year-old woman comes home to her apartment, where she lives alone, at 1:00 A.M. When she gets to the door she notices that the front door is unlocked and standing open. It is dark inside. The woman is surprised because she usually locks her door when she leaves her apartment. What should she do?

2. If a middle-aged man is on vacation in a foreign country and he loses his wallet, which contains all his money and all his credit cards, what should he do?

3. Let's say that a sixty-year-old man who lives alone in a large city needs to get across town to a doctor's appointment. He cannot drive because he doesn't have a car, and he doesn't have relatives nearby. What should he do?

---

notions the experimenter has about the subject of study. At every turn, the researcher's beliefs, expectations, attitudes, and decisions are influential in determining the outcome of the study. The next few pages contain a summary of the design issues discussed so far and detail some effects that both experimenters and subjects can have on the outcome of research.

Interpretation of Research Results

As you read through this book, you will be introduced to a wide variety of research results. What should you look for in evaluating these studies? To summarize much of what has already been said, most of the basic criticisms of research design and application can be divided into two general categories. Research may have problems of **internal validity,** or it may have poor **external validity** (Campbell & Stanley, 1963).

Internal validity refers to the extent to which a research design allows the investigator to rule out alternative explanations of the results. John Nesselroade and Eric Labouvie (1985) assert that "internal validity is the *sine qua non* without which the outcomes of research investigations are uninterpretable" (p. 41). The examples of research designs presented in this chapter can be used to illustrate the concept. For instance, in a cross-sectional research study, it is impossible for the investigator to know whether any age differences observed are actually age-related changes because it may be equally easy to show how the differences may be related to cohort change or time of measurement influences. In a longitudinal design, one cannot say whether changes are most strongly related to age or to time of measurement. It may also be that some of the changes observed in a longitudinal design are due to experimental mortality or test-retest effects. All of these problems threaten the internal validity of the research design.

Members of different generations differ not only in age and experience and health but in thousands of ways defined by the history unique to each cohort and by the attitudes all of us have toward that history.

Poorly chosen instruments or inadequate procedures for the selection of subjects also reduce internal validity. Problems of internal validity exist whenever it is possible to explain differences between age groups in a way that is unrelated to aging. If an instrument measures different characteristics in one group than another, internal validity is challenged. The practice of using average growth curves to talk about individual development (Rogosa, 1988) is also a problem of internal validity because it is possible to explain the results of the study as a product of a particular way of averaging the data rather than a reflection of true age changes.

External validity refers to the degree to which the relationships an investigator reports can be generalized to other subjects or settings or times of measurement (Nesselroade & Labouvie, 1985). Results based on the longitudinal study of one cohort cannot necessarily be applied to people born at a different time. Results of a cross-sectional research design may not be generalized to a different time of measurement. The conclusions formulated in a laboratory experiment may not generalize to real-life situations. Nesselroade and Labouvie (1985) maintain that "relationships that are not generalizable beyond the particular samples and situations in which they are observed cannot contribute directly to the body of scientific knowledge" (p. 44).

Finally, the behavior and beliefs of both subjects and experimenters can affect the validity of research results. William Ray and Richard Ravizza (1985) have advanced the idea that research must have **ecological validity,** in addition to internal and external validity. They use the term **ecology** to emphasize the fact that the scientist, the subject, and the experimental, or observational, situation are continuously influencing one another, and this interplay must be considered before research conclusions can be considered valid.

A variety of forces need to be considered in evaluating the ecological validity of a piece of research. These can be divided into four major categories: experimenter effects, subject effects, situational effects, and the more general effects of the social and cultural context.

A researcher influences the outcome of a study at every step along the way, from the formulation of hypotheses, to the selection of subjects and design, to the statement of conclusions. Experimenter effects are both powerful and subtle. Every researcher begins with some idea of how the data will look before the first piece of data is collected, and it is clear that a researcher's expectations can influence the outcome of behavioral studies involving adult subjects, school children, and even white rats (Rosenthal, 1966, 1979).

In a set of classic experiments in psychology, Robert Rosenthal produced a spectacular demonstration of experimenter effects. Rosenthal (1969) recruited a number of college students to act as experimenters in these studies. In one demonstration, student experimenters were instructed to ask subjects to rate photographs of people they had never seen. Subjects were asked to indicate whether the photos depicted people who were successful in life or unsuccessful, using a rating form that ranged from −10 (extremely unsuccessful) to +10 (extremely successful).

One group of student experimenters were told to expect an average rating of −5 from the subjects in their study. A second group was led to expect an average rating of +5 from their subjects. Subjects were then randomly assigned to student experimenters; all the experimenters read exactly the same instructions to their subjects.

Rosenthal found that the experimenters saw just what they were told to see. The lowest average rating of any experimenter expecting high ratings was higher than the highest rating obtained by any of those who expected low ratings. Similar effects have been found using animals as subjects, when one group of experimenters is led to expect a particular kind of performance (like fast learning) and another is led to expect the opposite (Rosenthal, 1979).

How might such effects be produced? Two possibilities exist. The first is that the experimenter is more likely to record data that support the hypothesis of a study than data that do not. When any ambiguity exists (is that a 5 or a 3?), the experimenter may unconsciously push the data in the direction of the expected outcome. Furthermore, unintended variations from the original experimental plan (should data be used from a subject who was ill?) tend to favor the expected outcome (Rosenthal, 1979).

Experimenters can also bias the behavior of their subjects in unintentional ways. In Rosenthal's photo study, student experimenters might have frowned when subjects gave ratings that the experimenters considered incorrect. To use a more germane example, researchers might react with surprise and displeasure when a young subject does poorly on a test of memory but with sympathy and understanding to the mistakes of an elderly person.

The second category of ecological concerns—subject effects—refers to the interpretation of subjects' behaviors that do not fit the experimenters' expectations. One classic example of this problem has been dubbed the **Hawthorne effect,** because it was first observed at the Hawthorne plant of Western Electric during a study of working conditions. The researchers found that workers were equally productive under very poor and very good working conditions. Apparently, workers included in the experiment considered themselves special just by virtue of being observed, so they continued to work hard no matter what the experimental conditions. In the case of the **placebo effect,** subjects can even show improved health when they are included in medical or therapeutic studies but not given any real treatment (Hass, Fink, & Hartfelder, 1963).

A third category of ecological factors includes ways in which the research setting may influence subjects' behavior. Situational effects include the assumptions subjects make about what the experimental setup demands. Subjects may believe they are supposed to behave in a particular way because of the nature of the research problem. For example, subjects who believed they were being exposed to sensory deprivation reported unusual visual imagery and fantasies even under conditions that did not really produce true deprivation (Orne, 1962). In the study of adult development, consider the influence of widespread publicity about the experience of midlife crisis. Middle-aged subjects interviewed about their current emotional life by psychologists might well feel obligated to describe some form of discomfort or distress. The subject's notion of what the experimenter is trying to find can influence the outcome as strongly as can the experimenter's notions about what is likely to occur.

There are also very general shared social and cultural assumptions held by both experimenters and subjects that affect research outcome and interpretation. Worldview not only affects the interpretation of data but also limits the range and nature of hypotheses themselves. As long as the culture encourages the notion that aging consists largely of a series of irreversible declines, it may not be easy to spot how this proposition fails. As John Meacham (1980) has pointed out, research is usually thought of as a monologue or one-way interrogation of subjects, whereas the reality is much closer to a dialogue in which subjects both sense and respond to a variety of unstated and unexamined beliefs and expectations in the experimenter.

The experimenter may interpret small differences as signs of universal changes. In a recent review titled "Ageism in Psychological Research," K. Warner Schaie (1988) concludes that small declines with age should not be interpreted as universal. The researcher needs to estimate the number of subjects who have remained stable or even improved with age. Schaie believes at least 50 percent of the subjects in an experiment must be affected adversely before the researcher is justified in suggesting adverse social consequences. Schaie also points out that even substantial declines may have very little social meaning. For instance, the average decline in reaction time (the time it takes to respond to a signal) declines by 100 to 150 percent between thirty and seventy, but the absolute difference is very small (less than one second).

Finally, researchers seldom look for compensating changes when they explore the problems of aging. Personality characteristics, such as evenness of temperament, or social skills, such as the ability to resolve conflicts, may compensate for small decrements in competency. Even in jobs where technical skill is important, people are apparently able to find ways to compensate. For instance, in a study of typists (Salthouse, 1987), decline in speed with age turned out to be of no consequence in overall performance. Apparently older typists learn to compensate: experience may allow them to read farther ahead, turn the head less often, even anticipate what word sequences are most likely.

Birren and Cunningham (1985) offer a valuable outline of issues in the evaluation of research. Here are some of the questions they pose in evaluating research results.

1. Does the author draw conclusions about the major problem posed in the study?

2. Are the conclusions clearly supported by the data?

3. Are the problems and limitations of the study stated clearly?

4. Are the results generalized appropriately?

5. Has the researcher rejected unexpected results because they do not match the hypothesis or because they really conflict with common sense?

6. Are statistically nonsignificant tests evaluated or are they interpreted as meaningful?

7. Are important reservations or qualifications pointed out?

8. Can additional questions be generated from the study and are they stated?

9. Is sufficient information present to replicate the study?

10. What are the implications of the results for knowledge in the field?

11. Does the researcher critically evaluate the method chosen in light of the results obtained?

12. What is the potential importance of the study and what scientific or practical benefits may follow?

13. What contributions have been made to theory?

At this point, when confronted with a piece of research, a newcomer to the field of research evaluation should be able to deal with many of the issues that Birren has raised in the first twelve questions. Chapter 2 begins to address question 13: What contributions have been made to theory?

Summary

I. Basic Questions
   A. Is there developmental change in adulthood?
      1. Personality traits, insightfulness, intellectual interests, adjustment, and competence change little.
      2. Subjective phenomena like attitudes toward the world, impulse control, and self-esteem seem to change the most.
      3. Aging needs to be considered a complex, multifaceted phenomenon that will include a variety of functions over time.
   B. How should the life span be defined and divided up?
      1. A number of schemes for dividing up the life span have been presented, including Levinson's stage theory of life structures and the idea of developmental tasks.
      2. The recognition of the part social history plays in human development has made it more difficult for researchers to agree on definitions and divisions for the life span.

II. Research Design
   A. Research designs should distinguish between age-related change, cohort changes, and time of measurement effects.
      1. The cross-sectional design has been used quite frequently, but does not provide a basis for distinguishing age-related changes and cohort changes. Furthermore, time-of-measurement effects may also influence research results in this design.
      2. Longitudinal designs fail to distinguish between age-related and time-of-measurement effects. Furthermore, one cannot generalize from longitudinal data on one cohort to the development of another cohort. Longitudinal designs also suffer from test-retest effects and experimental mortality.
      3. Sequential designs constitute an attempt to overcome the prob-

lems created by cross-sectional and longitudinal research by combining and extending these two simple types of designs.
  B. The biological and experiential aspects of aging cannot be manipulated in the laboratory, therefore, researchers have relied on the use of sophisticated statistical analyses, computer simulation, research with other species, and the simulation of age-related processes.
    1. Experimental research has most often focused on trying to modify age differences in cognition and memory.
    2. There are both ethical and practical problems in designing laboratory research that may make it difficult to predict age-related change.

III. Subject Selection
  A. Because subjects cannot be assigned to ages, researchers must study naturally occurring groups that differ in ways other than age alone.
  B. Some researchers have tried to overcome the problem of using natural groups by matching old and young subjects for factors assumed to differ between these groups, like education and health.
  C. Matched groups may not overcome the problems of subject selection because healthy, well-educated older subjects constitute an elite group, whereas healthy, well-educated younger subjects are in the majority.
  D. Careful, complete description of subject samples is required if generalization of research results is to be valid. The setting, observers, and times of measurement may also be considered problems of sampling.

IV. Instrumentation and Measurement
  A. Age-equivalence ensures that a measure or test reflects the same set of abilities or attributes for all ages observed.
  B. Measures may not tap the same abilities in the old as the young and may not predict performance outside the test setting equally well for both groups.
  C. Measures designed specifically for each age group may be useful if we can be sure that the same abilities are tested in all groups.
  D. Longitudinal designs present very difficult measurement problems, as the same measures are used over and over again.

V. Interpretation of Research Results
  A. Internal validity is the extent to which a research design allows the investigator to rule out alternative explanations of results and includes consideration of cohort effects, design of measures, and subject selection procedures.
  B. External validity refers to the degree to which the relationships an investigator reports can be generalized to other observations and includes the problems of one-cohort longitudinal designs and the generalization of cross-sectional research results to another time of measurement.

C. Ecological validity includes four categories of experimenter, subject, and setting effects.
   1. The beliefs of the experimenter can influence research results at every step, including design, collection of data, and interpretation of results.
   2. Subjects' beliefs about the purpose and effect of the experiment can influence results.
   3. The demand characteristics of the research problem can influence subjects to behave in ways they believe congruent with the research problem.
   4. The worldviews of both the experimenter and the subject affect research outcome and interpretation.

2

Theories of Adult Development

TONIGHT IS SARAH'S BIRTHDAY. She's forty-two years old and in the middle of what people have been calling her "midlife crisis." She's been working as a substitute teacher off and on since the kids were little, but her baby is a sophomore in high school this year and the older one is a sophomore in college. Substitute teaching, in fact, any kind of teaching, just doesn't appeal to her much. She and Jack still need the money. Sending a kid to college is an expensive proposition. So she knows she can't quit working entirely, but she just has to find something else. After all, she could end up working for another twenty or twenty-five years and some days it seems as though one more week of substitute teaching will kill her.

She got her credential twenty years ago, just before she got pregnant. If she wants to get anywhere as a teacher, she'd have to go back for the Master's Degree and it seems like a lot of work to put into a career she's not crazy about. On the other hand . . . Well, she just doesn't have any idea what to do. She's been depressed and irritable about the whole thing and taking it out on Jack, who's having problems of his own. Tonight she's going to put it all aside and try to just have a good time. Jack's gone to a lot of trouble to plan this party. All their best friends are coming. Maybe she'll get a chance to talk to Marcia. Marcia's in the same boat as Sarah. Her kids are leaving and she doesn't know exactly where she's headed either. Maybe Marcia will have come up with some good ideas by now. Sarah applies the last stroke of mascara and straightens out her collar. She doesn't look too bad for forty-two and confused.

WHAT'S GOING ON WITH SARAH? Why is she having such a difficult time at this stage of her life? Isn't midlife supposed to be a time when people finally settle down and act stable? Can she really expect to make a successful change at the age of forty-two? What is causing her to be so depressed and irritable? Does everybody have to go through a midlife crisis? These are some of the kinds of questions that theories of adult development address. Theories can show how a variety of forces may be converging to create the situation Sarah is experiencing. Theory can create understanding, suggest ways that Sarah might want to approach problems, give one an idea of how common those Sarah is facing might be, and guide future researchers and theory builders toward new areas to explore in the study of adulthood.

In this chapter, we will look at some of the basic beliefs that have shaped the growth of theories about human development in general and adulthood in particular. We'll also examine how those beliefs are expressed in specific theories and look at some of the current attempts to integrate existing theories into a more general framework. We begin with the problem of defining what a theory is and what theories are supposed to do for those of us interested in the study of human development.

Defining Theory

Fully to understand a grand and beautiful thought requires,
perhaps, as much time as to conceive it.

—Joubert

A **theory** is a set of abstract principles that can be used to predict facts and to organize them within a particular body of knowledge. For example, a theory of adult development would suggest how cognition, personality, behavior, and so on, might change over the adult life course. Ideally, however, a theory allows one to go beyond prediction and to explain development (Salthouse, 1985a). That is, theory should offer new ideas about how events not currently understood (like memory deficits in old age) are related to things already understood (like the principles of learning or arteriosclerotic brain disease).

In some sense, theories are just like ordinary explanations. Let's return to the story of Sarah at forty-two. You might try to explain her situation by saying that certain kinds of external events, like the absence of her oldest child and the growing independence of her youngest one, are making her feel irritable and depressed because she is losing an important role that has organized her life for the last twenty years or so. Until she finds some meaningful way to fill that vacuum, she will continue to experience a problem. This kind of theorizing refers to things that are going on outside of Sarah and suggests that the solution lies in her acquiring some new behaviors. Such an explanation is in keeping with a long tradition in the study of human development, and it makes certain assumptions about what causes people to make changes and have internal events like "feeling irritable" or "depression."

You might ask, on the other hand, whether Sarah is experiencing any of the signs of menopause. You could wonder whether Sarah's mother was able to handle this transition in her own life very well. You might even refer to a childhood experience in which Sarah lost someone very close to her in order to explain the strong feelings she is experiencing. These ways of explaining Sarah's situation suggest a rather different set of assumptions than we made when we were most concerned with Sarah's loss of the role of mother.

Of course, the formal theories we will review in this chapter are somewhat more elaborate than the simple explanations just suggested. Still, the goal of these more formal theories is the same. As David Magnusson has written, the goal of any theory of psychology is "to understand and explain why individuals think, feel, act and react as they do in life situations" (1988, pp. 16–17). Magnusson believes that the unique contribution of developmental theory is to show how a person's developmental history affects his or her feelings and actions. As we shall see, however, not everyone would agree with this position. Like our simple explanations, not all theories of human development emphasize a person's history. Some tend to focus on what is happening in the immediate environment; some focus on biological events; some even refer to goals and intentions or how a people's ideas about the future affect their development in the present.

The study of adulthood has not produced rigorous theories yet; current theories offer interesting but untested predictions about the course of adult life. Convincing explanations of age changes are limited to quite specific phenomena, such as declines in certain problem-solving performances, rather than the broader problem of general cognitive development. Still, even a theory that turns out to be wrong can prompt scientists to dig deeper, to observe more rigorously, and to generate a more satisfactory idea (Achenbach, 1978; Baldwin, 1980).

Despite, or perhaps because of, the lack of a grand, established theory, now is an exciting time to be studying developmental theory. A strong movement is afoot toward increased sophistication and even integration by some of the most influential thinkers in the field. This chapter builds toward an understanding of that movement, beginning with two seminal articles written in the early 1970s (Overton & Reese, 1973; Reese & Overton, 1970). In these works, Hayne Reese and William Overton tried to articulate the reasons that integration of the existing theories of human development had not been, and perhaps could not be, undertaken.

Theoretical Paradigms

There are trivial truths and great truths.
The opposite of a trivial truth is plainly false.
The opposite of a great truth is also true.

—Niels Bohr

Reese and Overton argued that certain basic questions about human development may just be unanswerable. To what degree is human behavior determined by external, environmental forces? What is the role of internal, biological events? Is the human organism basically passive, or does it play some part in its own development? What is the nature of behavioral change? Do humans develop bit by bit, response by response—or does change occur in larger, more predictable leaps? Reese and Overton noted that all developmental researchers and theoreticians are guided by a set of beliefs about such questions, beliefs they may not even be aware they hold. Furthermore, Reese and Overton wrote that these beliefs could be divided into two coherent **models** or **paradigms** of development: the **mechanical model** and the **organismic model.**

A model or a paradigm can be formally defined as a set of untestable assumptions a person makes about the nature of human development, human beings, and human behavior. Although the word *model* has been used extensively to refer to such assumptions, *paradigm* may be a better term because model is also used to talk about more specific kinds of explanations (Salthouse, 1985b).

The Mechanical Paradigm

Life is like playing a violin solo in public, and learning the instrument as one goes on.

—Samuel Butler

From the mechanist perspective, the computer serves as a very satisfactory analogy for human development. The mechanist model suggests that the best way to understand human behavior is to assume that people behave like very sophisticated machines. Human beings are viewed as receptive organisms, not active players in the construction of their own lives. All behavior, from the skillful performance of a master chess player, to the first tentative words of an infant, is ultimately explained as a set of responses to objective environmental forces.

The mechanist holds that change in behavior is cumulative and predictable. Change emerges as new responses are acquired or as old ones are chained together in more elaborate sequences. First, one learns to play one note on the piano, then another, then to chain the two—until at last one learns a whole tune. From this point of view, human behavior is quite **plastic;** it can be molded in an infinite variety of ways at any point in the life span. If children learn slowly, it is the fault of the teacher. If the elderly cannot remember, it is because they never learned the most effective way to store information (Lerner, 1983). Both human failures and accomplishments are often attributed to forces wholly outside the self (Skinner, 1971).

B. F. Skinner's work on operant conditioning and Ivan Petrovich Pavlov's principles of respondent conditioning are classical illustrations of the mechanist position. Even though Skinner insisted that a scientist should put aside all abstract ideas in the search for principles of human behavior, many writers have pointed out that Skinner believed very wholeheartedly in the mechanical paradigm of human development.

In terms of the example that we have been developing, Sarah's feelings, actions, and reactions could be explained by the fact that she is losing the reward structure that has defined her life for the last twenty years. She is no longer reinforced for helping her children, for advising them or looking after them. In fact, whatever attempts she makes to supervise them or express her love the way she did when they were infants or children are probably most unwelcome, even punished. She is feeling depressed and irritable because she hasn't found a new role that offers comparable rewards yet, but her distress will probably result in trying out new roles or behaviors and eventually, she may find new patterns that are as successful as those she is leaving behind. If she does not find new ways to gain rewards, she may be unhappy for a considerable time.

The Organismic Paradigm

Evolution is a change from a nohowish untalkaboutable all-likeness
to a somehowish and in general talkabout-able no-all-likeness by
continuous sticktogetherations and somethingelseifications.

—William James

The organismic paradigm is strongly related to concepts used in the study of evolution, biology, and philosophy. The organismic thinker believes psychological and behavioral development, like biological growth, depend on maturation rather than external environmental forces. The developing embryo

Perhaps we are attracted to people who look and act as we do because they are unlikely to demand big changes in the way we live our lives.

serves as a metaphor. Inner, biological events are far more influential in embryonic development than external events, as long as environmental effects stay within normal limits. This focus on the role of maturation leads to an emphasis on universal, maturationally determined changes and is often expressed as a description of developmental stages (Dixon, 1990).

From the organismic standpoint, psychological changes, like biological ones, may occur in stages characterized by rapid transitions during which internal, unobservable structures undergo qualitative transformation. To illustrate the idea, consider how, shortly after conception, the embryo consists of a mass of rapidly dividing cells, all essentially alike. In time, however, cells begin to *differentiate;* some form a primitive nervous system; some become part of developing organ systems. Soon there are many functioning groups of cells that are qualitatively different from the original amorphous mass and from one another as well. The organism has been transformed, a leap, or *discontinuity,* in development has occurred (Diamond, 1982).

Behavior, according to the organismic thinker, also develops by qualitative leaps. New stages emerge because the organism is active, always structuring and interpreting its own experience. Like a filing system that is rendered obsolete by new information, thinking, emotion, and behavior are periodically reorganized as new strategies for coping with experience become available. External stimulation may be essential to normal development, but such experiences are not thought to be critical, as the proponents of Skinner or Pavlov would maintain (Crain, 1980). The work of Jean Piaget on the development of cognition in childhood and adolescence is a classic example of organismic thinking.

In terms of our discussion of Sarah, an organismic thinker might suggest that there is a stage of adult life that ought to be called "midlife crisis," and most people will pass through this stage sometime in their late thirties or early forties—perhaps even as late as forty-five or forty-six. While the exact age at which people pass through this stage may not be the same, if people reach later life not having renegotiated the decisions and commitments they made in early adulthood, they are not likely to experience later life in a very satisfactory way. Sarah is going through a perfectly normal and predictable stage of adult life. If she is able to develop a new structure for her life, or if she is able to find new ways to make the old structure continue to work, she will feel better and more satisfied now and also have a better chance of creating a satisfactory life structure as an older person.

The key to identifying organismic assumptions is to listen for statements about the universality of certain kinds of developments and the notion that one must deal with certain developmental issues or tasks in a particular order if the life course is to proceed in a satisfactory way.

Another form of the organismic model stresses the role of genetics in shaping the course of human development. Although this view has been more prominent in theories of child development, some recent work suggests that heredity may be a more important force in adult life than previous work has suggested. For example, research on identical twins as well as pairs of people who were adopted and reared in the same family have been used to argue that the impact of inherited differences becomes more apparent with age (Plomin & Thompson, 1988). Such personality characteristics as emotionality and activity level show greater genetic influence in later life than they do in youth. Furthermore, sharing an environment, as pairs of adopted children do, contributes in fact very little to understanding how those individuals will develop. Far more revealing are the kinds of nonshared events, like accidents or illnesses, or differences in parental attention that have occurred.

Plomin and Thompson conclude that "the influence of heredity on individual differences in development is nearly ubiquitous. So far, only a handful of traits appear not to be influenced by heredity" (p. 23). However, the effects of heritability rarely exceed 50 percent. The rest may be attributable to environment, mostly to the nonshared aspects of environment. Figure 2.1 presents the estimated effects of genetic heritability over the life span as presented by Plomin and Thompson.

Having described these two competing worldviews in terms of basic assumptions, Reese and Overton declared it unlikely, if not impossible, that any integration could be achieved between two such different paradigms. Six years later, Reese (1976) changed his mind, partly due to the articulation of a third

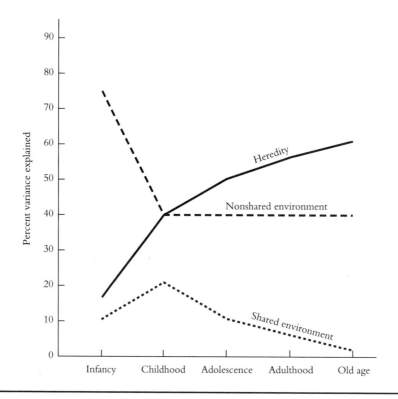

Figure 2.1 A life-span profile of genetic and environmental influences on individual differences in mental development.

SOURCE: Reproduced, with permission, from R. Plomin (1986), *Development, genetics and psychology,* Lawrence Erlbaum.

and perhaps integrative worldview called the **dialectical paradigm** (Riegel, 1975a, 1975b, 1977).

The Dialectical Paradigm

Throughout the 1970s an increasing emphasis on the role of large social and historical forces in the human life course emerged. As we saw in Chapter 1, the recognition of birth cohort as a developmental influence revolutionized research design. The dialectical view grew, to some extent, from this social-historical thinking and from the idea that both internal, maturational forces and more external, environmental effects must be simultaneously considered in the explanation of individual development.

The term *dialectics* comes from the concept of dialogue, or to paraphrase

Charles Tolman (1983), dialectic implies movement from one state (e.g., ignorance) to another (e.g., knowledge) by means of a process (dialogue) characterized by opposition (contradiction) and governed by internal necessity (logic). The dialectical paradigm emphasizes the role of contradiction or conflict in human development. Conflict is said to produce change; and change, in turn, to produce further conflict (Dixon, 1990).

The relationship between internal and external forces is conceptualized as a dialogue. In a dialogue, the speaker is also a listener and the listener is also a speaker. As a speaker, one is changed by the responses of others as well as by the things one says oneself. Likewise, the individual is changed by external conditions and, at the same time, participates in the construction of those conditions (Buss, 1979; Reese, 1983; Riegel, 1975a, 1975b, 1977). Dialectics has been considered an integrative paradigm because it includes important ideas found in both the mechanist and organismic models (Labouvie, 1982).

Klaus Riegel (1975, 1977) was one of the first theorists to describe a dialectical paradigm for development. He did not consider any contemporary theory truly dialectical; however, he thought that psychodynamic theories, especially the work of Erik Erikson might be a good place to begin. Riegel was impressed by Erikson's emphasis on the role of conflict in development and by Erikson's idea that interactions between the individual and society were both inevitable and critical. Erikson's ideas will be discussed in more detail shortly.

Dialectical thinkers have renewed the interest of many developmental psychologists in psychodynamic ideas. More than anything, however, the dialectical paradigm has stressed the possibility that development is multidimensional and multidirectional. Dialectical thinkers emphasize the need to consider a wide variety of forces in the study of human development and to think about the many ways such forces may interact. Dialectics has also focused attention on the role of conflict and long-term historical changes (Lerner, 1983).

Development as a Multidimensional Process

Very recently, an important paper on the idea of development as a multidimensional process appeared in the journal *Human Development*. Dale Dannefer and Marion Perlmutter (1990) point out that a variety of terms, including *dialectical, contextual, life-span, ecological,* and *interactive* are currently used to refer to the notion that development is driven by a variety of forces that may interact in quite complex ways. Perhaps different processes are best understood in terms of different models, or paradigms. These authors have proposed that the central problem is to understand how "much explanatory power ought to be expected of 'the environment' in accounting for individual change" (p. 109). They go on to suggest there are at least three processes underlying human development and each may develop differently over the life span, reflecting a particular kind of interaction between the environment and forces within the person.

Physical ontogeny represents development that is largely dependent on biological regulation, like learning to walk or sensory acuity, whereas **habitu-**

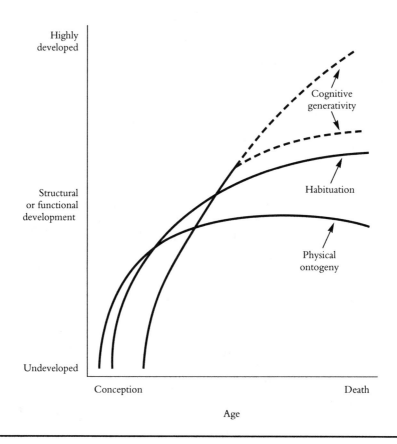

Figure 2.2 Age trajectories of development for three developmental processes.

ation represents types of development that are largely dependent on environmental experience. Habituation refers to most of what is called learning in laboratory research with animals. It probably includes behaviors that are acquired through classical and operant conditioning, and perhaps modeling or observation. A third type of development, **cognitive generativity** refers to the kind of development that occurs when the individual is actively recombining experience with logic, memory, and imagination. "It allows the individual to interpret the past and present, as well as to envision alternative lives and alternative futures" (p. 110).

Figures 2.2 and 2.3 show how these three capacities may develop over the life span and suggest how effective each might be at different points. "Functional effectiveness" refers to the relative effectiveness of each process, and as you might note from the figure, these authors propose that habituation becomes less effective in later life. They believe that older people often exhibit "overlearned" or "hyperhabituation" behaviors that actually interfere with

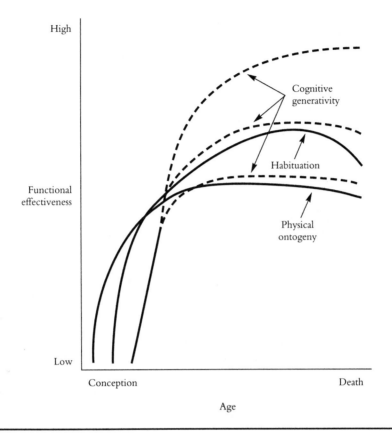

Figure 2.3 Age trajectories of functional effectiveness for three developmental processes.

SOURCE: Figures 2.2 and 2.3 from Dannefer & Perlmutter, 1990, p. 111.

their effectiveness. The different dashed lines for cognitive generativity show how it might develop and how effective it might be under favorable and unfavorable conditions. We have recently reported, for instance (Stevens-Long & Macdonald, 1991) that empathic conflict appears to promote cognitive generativity. That is, when people are able to identify with people on both sides of an issue, they are likely to produce more creative social solutions. In terms of how we have been conceptualizing theories of human development so far, you might think of the work that has been done using an organismic approach as reflective of cognitive generativity while the mechanistic model would be useful in understanding habituation.

In expanding on the idea of cognitive generativity, Dannefer and Perlmutter talk about the experience of reflection and imagination and the ability to take oneself as an object of thought; that is, to think about the self. They also

Box 2.1 Focus on Application: Labeling theory

Although the concepts and ideas of the dialectical or contextual paradigms seem very abstract and complicated at first glance, there are some quite practical, down-to-earth examples of how they might apply to everyday human affairs. One of the most important of these is "labeling theory" (Dannefer & Perlmutter, 1990). The basic argument is that labeling people in particular ways can actually produce behavior and beliefs that have no real basis in the labeled person's personality or development.

Most people occasionally engage in some kind of behavior that might be considered negative or "deviant." If those instances are noticed by significant others and labeled, it may well direct the attention of others to any further evidence of "deviance." At the same time, the "normal" behavior that belies the labeling goes unnoticed. If people create their social reality in concert with others and their development is strongly influenced by that reality, then labeling can become a "self-fulfilling prophecy."

Let's return to the example we started with: Sarah at midlife crisis. That's a label itself: midlife crisis. But it is one that is usually considered within the normal range of human development—even predictable and typical. If Sarah is labeled as a victim of midlife crisis (and she accepts that label), she is likely to think about lifestyle changes that include education, changing jobs, maybe even divorce or separation, as those are the kinds of events that the society seems to associate with midlife crisis.

What if, on the other hand, Sarah's doctor decides she has *involutional melancholia*, a rather old-fashioned term meaning depression associated with menopause? Sarah might consider taking hormones or mood elevators and never think about going back to school. In fact, she might be discouraged from trying something new because she has a "medical" problem.

What if Jack decides Sarah is hysterical or neurotic and encourages her to seek psychotherapy? What if Sarah's best friend tells her that there's nothing really wrong with her at all? She is just being "dramatic" and living her life like a soap opera. Each one of those possibilities suggests a whole range of implications. If Sarah accepts one of them, she will feel differently about herself, make different plans, and consider different options than if she accepts another. Once she is seen in a certain way, people are likely to treat her differently and have a different sense of what is possible for her.

As Dannefer and Perlmutter point out, however, labeling is not a complete explanation for human behavior. But it describes an important piece of the process, one of the many forces that must be considered if we are to build a complete understanding of human development in all its variety.

refer to such "irreducibly generative dimensions as imagination, resourcefulness, empathy, and reflection," (p. 115) and they point out that cognitive generativity actually gives human beings some control over habituation. In other words, these authors believe that through intentionally compensating for or changing the ways in which the environment affects behavior, people overcome certain debilitating effects that might be predicted by their environmental circumstances.

The degree to which we are able to understand which aspects of development might best be considered a result of physical ontogeny, which are linked to habituation and which are the product of cognitive generativity, will depend on the degree to which we understand social reality. What kinds of resources do people have that allow them to engage in cognitive generativity? What ideas or beliefs are typical of people who seem unable to produce creative thinking and behavior?

The idea of cognitive generativity also points to the importance of studying what is optimal in human development, rather than what is average. Much of the research you will encounter in this book concerns itself almost exclusively with averages. Very little attention has been devoted to what is *optimal*. In the next few pages, we will review a variety of specific theories about human development and adult development in particular with an eye to what they have to say about the problem of optimal development.

Theories: A Multiplicity of Views

We owe almost all our knowledge not to those who have agreed,
but to those who have differed.

—Charles Caleb Colton

Scientific theories of human development first appeared around the turn of the century with the work of G. Stanley Hall, who believed that the development of the individual repeated, or recapitulated, the evolutionary history of the species. His theoretical framework was clearly organismic, ascribing little significance to external forces (Lerner, 1983).

By the middle of this century, theories that emphasized the role of nature in human development had been discarded in favor of mechanistic theories advanced by behaviorists and learning theorists working in controlled laboratory settings. Then, during the 1960s, the work of European thinkers once again challenged the hold of mechanism in America. Psychodynamic theories, especially those proposed by Carl Jung and Erik Erikson, grew in popularity. At the same time, interest in the development of cognition, especially the work of Jean Piaget, began to attract the attention of young American researchers.

Through the early seventies, work on cognition in adulthood, along with the more abstract study of paradigms or models, combined to broaden the variety and range of useful, workable theory. Writers began to argue that different types of development might demand different theoretical approaches (Baltes, 1979; Birren & Cunningham, 1985; Lerner, 1983), and that it might be necessary to define and track a multitude of developmental dimensions in pursuit of a coherent, comprehensive theoretical framework. Developmental patterns may be *multicausal,* shaped by a variety of forces, both internal and external, acting in isolation or in concert. In fact, most contemporary theorists, whether they begin with mechanist, organismic, or dialectical assumptions, have addressed the notion that development entails a strong interaction between an active organism and a changing environment. Behaviorists talk more about cognition these days, and organismic thinkers are paying more attention to social and cultural forces. Psychodynamic theorists speak more often about thought and language as well as emotion (Skolnick, 1986b).

As we move into the nineties, the most productive course seems to be, as Daniel Keating and Darla MacLean (1988) have written, to "entertain many possibilities" and to pursue each of them thoroughly in the attempt to isolate all the pieces of the puzzle as we begin to put the larger integrated picture together. The objectives of developmental theory are summarized by Richard Lerner and Patricia Mulkeen (1990) as an emphasis on differences in individual development, on how much people change over the life course, on the potential optimal levels of development, and on the investigation of *change processes.*

It may be best to think of existing developmental theories as a set of lenses, each one most sharply focused on a different dimension or system of development. Somewhat arbitrarily, the theories reviewed in this chapter are assigned to one of four such systems: motivation, emotion, cognition, and behavior. Beginning with a discussion of motivational theories seems appropriate since motivation seems to have inspired some of the grander, more general conceptions of current thinkers.

Theories Focusing on Motivation

The works of Erik Erikson and Abraham Maslow come from two very different worldviews. Erikson was a student of Anna Freud, and his ideas have been called a starting point for a dialectical theory of the life span (Riegel, 1977). Maslow was much more of an organismic thinker, although he was strongly influenced by psychoanalytic thought and believed that certain environmental preconditions had to be fulfilled before the mature personality could emerge (Maddi, 1980).

Erikson believed that development occurs in a series of universal stages governed by a genetic ground plan. The ground plan, he contended, determines the time at which certain developmental issues become ascendent in the individual life course (Erikson, 1963, 1968a, 1982). Erikson also assumed, however, that biological factors in development interacted with personal, cultural, and even historical forces and that such interactions produced the central issues or conflicts. Because he viewed development as a product of interaction and conflict, his view is more dialectical than most (Riegel, 1975a, 1975b, 1977), Table 2.1 outlines each of Erikson's eight stages.

Erikson had a complex notion about how interaction develops between the society and the individual. He argued that this interaction produced age grading (Erikson, 1963; Lerner, 1976; Riegel, 1977). All societies are age-graded;

Table 2.1 Erikson's eight stages of life

Conflict at each stage	Emerging value	Period of life
Basic trust versus mistrust Consistency, continuity, and comfort produce a feeling of security and predictability.	Hope	Infancy
Autonomy versus shame and doubt Parental firmness allows for the experience of demand fulfillment with limits that produce self-control.	Will	Early childhood
Initiative versus guilt The development of the superego and cooperation with others support the growth of planning and a sense of responsibility.	Purpose	Play age
Industry versus inferiority Working and learning with others produces skill and the ability in using tools, and weapons, and method, as well as feelings of self-esteem.	Competence	School age
Identity versus role confusion The physical changes of adolescence arouse a new search for sameness and continuity and the need for a coherent sense of self.	Fidelity	Adolescence
Intimacy versus isolation A new ability to tolerate the threat of ego loss permits the establishment of mature relationships involving the fusion and counterpointing of identity.	Love	Young adulthood
Generativity versus stagnation The adult need to care for children and to guide the next generation produces the desire to leave something of substance as a legacy.	Care	Maturity
Integrity versus despair An accrued sense of order and meaning allows one to defend one's own life cycle as a contribution to the maintenance of the human world.	Wisdom	Old age

that is, they make new demands and present new challenges as people age. Cross-cultural evidence also convinced Erikson that every society sets up institutions that help people cope with the changes that occur during development (Miller, 1983). For instance, Erikson saw religion as the social institution that both reflected and supported the development of basic trust. Likewise, he argued that the institutions of law and order reflect and support the development of autonomy. He believed that positive development would become difficult if social institutions began to deteriorate. He felt that human development changed the structure of social institutions, just as social institutions influenced development. For instance, he believed that marriage and divorce could promote (or prevent) the emergence of intimacy in young adulthood, and intimacy, when it developed, would support certain institutions (like monogamy) and not others.

Ideas like his hypothesis about monogamous heterosexual marriage led some critics to accuse Erikson of overvaluing institutions and concepts, like personal identity, that tend to be rather Western in flavor, if not exclusively American. Erikson has acknowledged that his theory is shaped by its own historical context. Perhaps because much of his basic work was done in the context of America in the fifties, he seems to admire conformity rather more than rebellion and doubt. For instance, Allan Buss (1979) has written that Erikson's definition of integrity as the acceptance of one's life underemphasizes the possibility of growth in the final stages of the life span. Buss does not think that acceptance should be heralded as the capstone of personal growth.

Furthermore, Erikson's work grew, like Freud's, from an interest in case study and psychoanalysis, and some of his concepts are left essentially undefined. We don't know, for instance, how intellectual development might be influenced by each stage, or how learning and modeling might shape the resolution of crisis. As Patricia Miller (1983) observed, "Erikson presents his theory as would a novelist or an artist rather than a scientist. At most, the theory is a loosely connected set of ideas and observations that could not, strictly speaking, be called a . . . theory" (p. 173).

In his own defense, Erikson has maintained that he prefers to use the everyday words of the "living languages," words like *love* and *wisdom,* because they "express both what is universally human and what is culturally specific" (1982, p. 58). Terms like *hope, faith,* and *will* must harbor some fundamental relationship to human development, Erikson has said, and simple, objective definitions may miss the most important aspects of their meanings.

In one recent critique, Paul van Geert (1987) states: "Perhaps Erikson's theory is not a theory in the classical sense, but a heuristic framework, continuously changing, lacking a sufficient amount of logical-conceptual rigor. . . . Let us hope that the theory is more than a loose amount of assumptions, a therapeutic I Ching, useful to get understanding started, but to be abandoned as soon as the feet touch firmer ground" (p. 254). In this paper, van Geert presents a formal analysis of the properties and assumptions of Erikson's theory and makes some predictions and extensions specific to the theory. If such pre-

The AIDS epidemic has affected future generations because of the drastic way it is changing our lifestyles.

dictions or extensions could be demonstrated by van Geert or other researchers, this would validate Erikson's theory.

Other researchers have tried to determine whether or not Erikson's stages can be seen in the responses people make to interviews or to paper-and-pencil tests developed to measure concepts like psychosocial maturity. One such effort (Viney, 1987) produced evidence that many people tend to describe their lives in ways that conform to Erikson's ideas about the life span. However, some interesting differences were also found, especially in interview data gathered from adolescents and young adults. In particular, researchers reported that good interpersonal relationships could serve as a basis for identity. In other words, participants in the study often exhibited the capacity to forge a sense of identity as a function of their interpersonal relationships rather than depending on a strong sense of identity to form good interpersonal relationships.

Like Erikson, Abraham Maslow tends to rely on everyday words to express the content of development. He too postulated that development took place through a series of stages, but he did not believe that the stages represented particular age-related periods of the life cycle nor that they represented an inevitable sequence. It seems likely, however, that the later stages he described are more often achieved in adolescence or adulthood, although the precursors of adult achievements may be seen in childhood. Figure 2.4 presents Maslow's stages in the form of a pyramid.

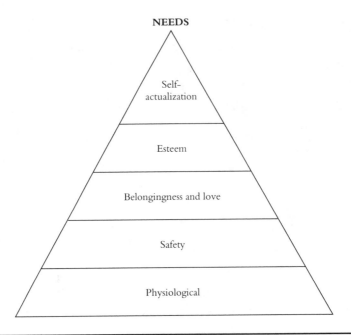

Figure 2.4 Maslow's needs hierarchy.

Maslow's ideas are a little different from those proposed by most developmental psychologists, as he was more interested in clinical than developmental psychology. Rather than talking about developmental tasks or issues, Maslow defined two basic kinds of human needs: deficiency needs and higher, or **meta-, needs.** Deficiency needs include biological requirements like food, water, and air, as well as the need for safety, the need to belong and to be loved, and the needs for esteem (including self-esteem and the esteem of others). The more basic the need, the lower on the pyramid in Figure 2.4.

The meta-needs (which are referred to collectively as the need for **self-actualization**) appear at the top of the pyramid because they cannot, Maslow argued, be fulfilled until all the basic needs are met. Self-actualization is the realization of the self through the fulfillment of individual creative potential. Maslow believed that self-actualization is an innate motive composed of a variety of needs like the need for truth, beauty, and self-sufficiency. People are compelled to fulfill the meta-needs once deficiency needs are met, according to Maslow, and self-actualization is thereby produced.

In his attempt to delineate self-actualization, Maslow studied the lives of such historical figures as Abraham Lincoln, Thomas Jefferson, Albert Einstein, Albert Schweitzer, Eleanor Roosevelt, and Baruch Spinoza. These were people he considered self-actualized and without any obvious signs of pathology. He found them more likely to perceive the truth than other people, more able to detect dishonesty and fakery, and less influenced by social stereotypes. Their lives, he wrote, showed an acceptance of self, nature, and others. He saw them as problem-centered rather than self-centered, and capable of intense, profound relationships. Yet they were not all seriousness and intensity. He noted that they were also hearty in their appetites and able to enjoy the pleasures of the world without shame or doubt (Maslow, 1970).

Maslow believed that every human being has the potential for being and feeling in a way that is organized, peaceful, intact, and harmonious (Mahrer & Gervaize, 1990). Whereas self-actualized people live in greater peace and harmony than most of us, "Maslow is quick to point out that self-actualizing people have the usual short-comings of all human beings. Thus, they also exhibit silly, wasteful, thoughtless and irritating behavior" (Bammer, 1990, p. 316).

Like Erikson, or any theorist operating on such a grand scale, Maslow has been criticized for his failure to specify the mechanisms of self-actualization. Some of the meta-needs (like truth and beauty) are very abstract indeed. Despite the scale of the theory, Maslow never expressed much interest in the more intellectual aspects of maturity, simply noting that more self-actualized people were more problem-centered. Until the midseventies, most psychologists who focused on the development of intelligence and cognition were students of childhood and adolescence. In recent years, however, interest in the unique aspects of adult cognitive and intellectual development has grown, and some very sophisticated new ideas have emerged.

Theories Focusing on Cognition

Because it posits an active organism that constructs and interprets its own experience, the organismic paradigm tends to emphasize the role of intellectual, or cognitive, development. So it is not surprising to learn that the most elaborate theories of adult cognition have grown from the work of Jean Piaget, whose theory is also a stunning example of organismic thinking. Piaget's stages of intellectual development reflect strict adherence to the assumptions of the organismic view: Human beings construct reality through action on the environment, and change occurs in a series of qualitatively different stages. Table 2.2 presents an overview of the course of intellectual development according to Piaget.

Piaget believed that the last true stage of intellectual development, formal operations, emerged in adolescence. Over the past fifteen or twenty years, a number of writers have taken exception to this notion, describing a fifth, adult stage of thinking (Basseches, 1984; Commons, 1982; Edelstein & Noam, 1982; Labouvie-Vief, 1982a, 1982b; Riegel, 1975b). Of these several attempts, two of the most elaborate are the **structural analytic stage** described by Michael Commons and Francis Richards (1978, 1982), and **dialectical thinking** as outlined by Basseches (1984).

To understand these ideas, however, it helps to know a little about Piaget's

Table 2.2 Piaget's stages of cognitive development		
Stage	Age (approximate)	Description
Sensorimotor	Birth to two years	Behavior suggests child lacks language and does not use symbols or mental representations of objects in the environment. Intentional behavior begins, such as learning to seek objects and to make interesting sights last.
Preoperational	Two to seven years	Child begins to represent world mentally, but is unaware that others do not see the world in the same way. Child is unable to focus on two aspects of a situation at the same time.
Concrete operational Operational	Seven to twelve years	Child can adopt viewpoint of others, can classify objects in a series (longer, shorter) or as subordinate and superordinate (a dog is an animal) but cannot systematically formulate and test alternative solutions to a problem.
Formal-operational	Twelve years and above	Mature, adult thought emerges, characterized by deductive logic and the consideration of various possibilities prior to solving a problem. The ability to abstract and to form and test hypotheses systematically appears.

SOURCE: Based on Rathus, 1981, p. 386.

idea of formal operations. Piaget believed that formal operations allowed one to consider all the variables in a problem and to make hypotheses about how changes in one variable might be related to changes in another. For instance, formal operators understand that varying the length of a string will change the speed at which a pendulum swings. Formal operators can test an idea in a controlled way, holding some elements in a problem constant while systematically changing other elements. In other words, formal operations allow for the scientific method of the laboratory.

As an example, consider the problem of matching a sample of turquoise paint by combining white, blue, and green. The best strategy requires holding the amount of two of the colors, blue and white, constant while progressively adding more green. If this approach does not produce the right shade of turquoise, then hold green and white constant and vary the amount of blue. Finally, hold blue and green constant and vary the amount of white.

It should be noted, however, that among the criticisms leveled at Piaget's work, perhaps the most serious is research suggesting that basic ideas or operations, like those described in formal operations, may develop long before adolescence. Some investigators believe that some of the developments Piaget describes in children may even be present at birth. In one clever research study, the investigators were able to show that even infants have pretty sophisticated ideas of how the world works before they have a chance to develop. For instance, where confronted with a display in which one solid object seemed to move through another, infants registered surprise (as measured by the amount of time they spent looking at the display). This means that infants might be said to "know" that solid objects can't pass through one another (Baillargeon, Spelke, & Wasserman, 1985). Research like this has led away from the description of particular cognitive feats and toward a more general emphasis on the kinds of thinking people are able to do at various stages of the life span. Piaget too was interested in such general, underlying principles.

At each stage of his scheme, Piaget described new abilities that are essentially *content-free;* that is, abilities that might be applied to a variety of intellectual problems. At the formal level, the ability to formulate and test hypotheses in a systematic way is as useful in sustaining an intimate relationship as it is in running a physics lab. At the structural analytic stage, Commons and Richards propose that people move beyond the analysis of single elements in a problem and begin to look at the relationships between sets of relationships. For instance, instead of focusing on how to match a sample of turquoise paint, the structural analytic thinker becomes interested in how matching paint samples is similar to or different from other problems in logic.

Basseches' (1984) description of dialectical thinking also assumes that people who have mastered formal operations are able to move from the analysis of relationships within a problem or a **system** to the analysis of competing systems. A system is any coherent set of relationships. For instance, the mechanical paradigm is a system for thinking about human development. So is the organismic paradigm. In talking about how these two systems are alike or different, structural analytic or dialectical thinking (if the discussion is sophisticated enough) takes place. Basseches argues that the ability to think at the dialectical level requires one to understand how people and information interact to produce the ideas that dominate different historical periods. What passes for truth today differs from what people believed 500 or 1,000 years ago. Either thinking has changed or the truth has changed. Certainly, for example, the truth about human development may change with human history (Gergen, 1977, 1985; Skolnick, 1986b).

Basseches has argued that dialectical thinking depends on an appreciation of change and on a sensitivity to contradiction. For example, a real appreciation of the contradictions between the mechanistic and organismic models has led to movement in developmental theory toward greater integration. Basseches contends that dialectical thinkers see contradictions not as unfortunate problems but as positive sources of change. Every system of thinking leaves something out, Basseches writes, and that something eventually creates a contradiction in the system. The dialectical thinker sees the contradiction as an opportunity for a new and better idea. Because dialectical thinkers assume that current systems of thought are only partly true, or only true for a particular period of history, they are able to value many different perspectives on reality and to enjoy the generation of rich, even paradoxical ideas.

The work of Commons and Richards as well as Basseches suggests that adult thinking becomes ever more abstract and complex. These authors generally ignore the evidence of decline in some aspects of intelligence (Rybash, Hoyer, & Roodin, 1986; Salthouse, 1985b). They do not deny the validity of such evidence; they are just not particularly interested in the development of the average thinker. They are intrigued by the possibility of optimal development. Chapter 3 covers the data on average performance more thoroughly (Horn, 1982; Schaie & Hertzog, 1985). For now, suffice it to say that most research shows decline in intellectual performance after middle age, including performances on problems that require formal operations (Denney, 1986; Labouvie-Vief, 1982a, 1982b). At least one author, Gisela Labouvie-Vief, has tried to include this data in her version of adult thinking and concludes that a new, more pragmatic type of cognition arises sometime in adulthood.

Labouvie-Vief has noted that formal operations are most useful in problems of formal logic, when a single, correct answer can be deduced from the premises of a problem. Life, however, is not always logical, and most problems do not have one single, best solution. Reality is full of uncertainty and paradox. Labouvie-Vief believes that the clash between logic and reality requires at least three stages of thought beyond formal operations: **intrasystemic thought, intersystemic thought,** and **autonomous thought.**

Intrasystemic thought is rather like a last phase of formal operations. The relationships within a single system are well understood, and the truth is considered universal and unchanging by the intrasystemic thinker. In the next stage, intersystemic thought, people begin to understand that truth can be a product of a particular system, and that multiple intellectual perspectives are possible in a changing reality. In the final stage, autonomous thinkers are able to see their own role in the creation of personal truth, and to see how social and personal motivations have influenced their own construction of reality. Any decline in performance on problems that require formal operations in old age, according to Labouvie-Vief, may arise from an "increasingly complex understanding of real-life system(s)," which finally subordinate the "buoyant and naive if brilliant thought derived from 'pure logic'" (1982b, p. 76).

To exemplify her point, Labouvie-Vief uses a study (Cohen, 1979) in which college students were asked to draw inferences about the following problem:

"Downstairs, there are three rooms: the kitchen, the dining-room, and the sitting-room. The sitting-room is in the front of the house, and the kitchen and the dining-room face onto the vegetable garden at the back of the house.

The noise of the traffic is very disturbing in the front rooms. Mother is in the kitchen cooking and Grandfather is reading the paper in the sitting-room. The children are at school and won't be home 'til tea-time."

When asked who is being disturbed by the traffic noise, college students almost invariably answer "the grandfather," thus giving evidence of having processed the logical relationships embedded in the test. . . . Older adults, on the other hand, do not appear to engage in this mode of analysis and thus fail to infer that it is only the grandfather who might be disturbed . . . many adults might point out that the grandfather may have been deaf or that the noise may not have been disturbing at the moment in question. Indeed, some might convert the causal direction readily adopted by Cohen's college students by arguing that the grandfather could not possibly have been disturbed since, had that been the case, he would not have chosen to read in the sitting room or would have chosen to leave it . . . the grandfather's behavior can be seen as motivated, free, and responsible. (Labouvie-Vief, 1985, pp. 524–525)

From Labouvie-Vief's perspective, the failure of the older adult to infer the "logical" relationships may not suggest a decline in the ability to interrelate information logically. It may reflect a profoundly different interpretation of the situation described by the experimenter, and may even suggest a more mature, realistic kind of thinking.

Other writers taking a similar stand have suggested that "the formal thinker is infatuated with ideas, abstractions, and absolutes" (Rybash, Hoyer, & Roodin, 1986, p. 31), and that mature adult thinking reconnects reason with emotional and social reality. Adults must be able to cope with contradictions, especially in social situations, and to create compromises between the demands of logic and emotion. They must find an adequate or effective solution to a problem rather than defending the most "logical" solution (Edelstein & Noam, 1982).

This most recent work on adult cognition seems to acknowledge the interaction between thinking and feeling in everyday life. Several writers have considered the notion that mature thinking allows one to separate thought and emotion, while others have emphasized the role of cognitive conflict in producing emotion. In either case, emotion is not the central focus but something to be eliminated or discriminated from thought. In the next section, we look at theoretical work more specifically devoted to the place of emotion in development.

Theories Focusing on Emotional Development

Perhaps because the American hero has, for so long, been the strong, silent type, the study of emotions has been relatively neglected over the years by American psychologists. In particular, the positive emotions, like love and happiness, have seldom been considered a proper arena for scientific psychology. Most students come to the study of psychology because they are interested in motives and feelings, but in most courses that deal with such matters, more time is devoted to hunger and thirst in animals than to love, hate, sorrow, and anger in human beings.

No research on emotional development appears in the first edition of the *Handbook of the Psychology of Aging* (1977) or the *Handbook of Developmental Psychology* (1982). In the second edition of the *Handbook of the Psychology of Aging* (1985), Richard Schulz sums up the work on emotional development as follows: "Emotions are . . . rarely addressed from a developmental perspective. Major textbooks on adult development and aging devote little space to it; moreover, major theories regarding the determinants of human emotions . . . have little to say about emotionality through middle and old age. It is unclear whether this neglect is due to oversight, to the unavailability of the necessary data, or to the assumption that age, beyond early adulthood, is an irrelevant dimension for the understanding of emotionality" (p. 531).

At this stage of the game, no one is even sure how to define different emotional states. For instance, how should one distinguish between strong emotions, moods, and long-duration affective states like depression (Schulz, 1985)? Schulz suggests that strong emotions are accompanied by high levels of arousal over brief periods, while moods are of moderate duration and involve moderate levels of emotions. Emotion, he argues, has its primary effect on the environment, whereas moods and affective states primarily affect the individual. He believes the only difference between moods and long-term affective states is duration. Table 2.3 presents Schulz's model of emotion, mood, and affect.

Beginning with the distinctions outlined in Table 2.3, Schulz contends that emotional development over the life span may be experienced in at least six different dimensions:

1. Intensity: Does the intensity of emotional experience decline over the life span (a hypothesis suggested by the common stereotype of elderly people)?

2. Duration: Does emotional experience last longer with age because the physiological events that accompany emotions return to normal more slowly?

3. Variability: Does emotional experience become more or less variable with age?

4. Frequency: Is negative affect more frequent with age (again, a hypothesis based on common social stereotypes)?

5. Quality: Are there any qualitative differences in emotions, like love or sorrow, over the life span?

6. Elicitors: Do different stimuli elicit emotional experiences at different stages of the life span?

Based on his review of the literature, Schulz concludes that there is decreasing emotional stability with age, but the ratio of negative to positive emotions

Table 2.3 Dimensions used to differentiate emotions, moods, and personality types

	Dimensions		
Affective category	*Intensity of arousal*	*Primary locus of effects*	*Duration*
Strong emotions	High	Emotions	Short (e.g., minutes)
Moderate emotions, moods	Moderate	Individual	Moderate (e.g., hours, days)
Affective disorders	Moderate	Individual	Long (e.g., years)

SOURCE: Schulz, 1985, p. 532.

is fairly stable. Survey research (Cameron, 1975) has shown no increase with age in the frequency of negative emotions like anger, fear, and unhappiness. On the other hand, the data do show an increase in the frequency of depression among the elderly. Schulz speculates that a new class of emotional events—the loss of significant others and important objects or roles—may cause new, intense, and long-lasting negative affective states. Schulz also points out that one of the most persistent themes in the study of age and emotion has been the control of emotional experience.

The issue of control has been addressed in several important sets of research articles on emotion (Leventhal, 1982; Linville, 1982; Mandler, 1982; Berkowitz, 1990). How a researcher approaches the issues has partly to do with how he or she conceptualizes the relationship between emotion and cognition. For example, George Mandler (1982) believes that emotional experience is determined by the cognitive evaluation of emotional arousal. In other words, when emotion occurs, the label we give it (e.g., fear vs. excitement) depends on what we know about the world. In a familiar situation, where we know how to respond, our emotional experience is likely to be positive and relatively mild. When knowledge is insufficient, the outcome may be positive or negative depending on whether we are able to cope with the situation. From Mandler's point of view, experience over the life span should produce increasing emotional control.

Like Schulz, Mandler would predict that new emotional events, such as bereavement and the interruption of normal response patterns caused by illness or loss, would produce new emotional experiences (Berscheid, 1982). However, whether these experiences are negative or positive will depend on whether the person is able to adjust.

Evidence suggests that people who possess more complex self-concepts show fewer, less intense mood swings than those with relatively simple self-concepts (Linville, 1982). A complex self-concept means that the individual feels able to function in a variety of different, clearly distinguishable roles. Developmentally, the complexity of the self-concept probably increases in adulthood as people take on new roles and activities, and even as they cope with loss and change in old age.

Researchers have approached the issue of emotional control in a second major way. Those who believe that cognition and emotion should be considered partially independent systems, argue that people learn to use reasoning to control emotional experience over the life span (Leventhal, 1982). Howard Leventhal, a major proponent of this view, believes that people learn to control their emotional responses because they become increasingly able to predict those responses. Over the course of adulthood, he argues, emotional responses cease to have an impulsive quality and become more deliberate and controlled. The ability to predict your own behavior allows you to control it.

Leventhal's research has demonstrated that people who have emotional control can actually experience a wider range of emotions in a given situation. For instance, his studies show that once cancer patients learn to cope with terror, they can also experience joy and happiness in the context of dying. Leventhal views emotion as a kind of cognition itself, different from abstract reasoning or perception, but capable of integration with other cognitive processes over the course of development.

Leonard Berkowitz (1990) has demonstrated that angry feelings and thoughts are experienced as less intense when people are simply told to focus on them and use a rating scale to rate their intensity. Berkowitz asserts that negative feelings can be "countered by higher-level cognitive processes. . . . Here, as in so many other ways, it is thought and not suffering that makes us better" (p. 502).

Except for the notion that there may be some new, intense emotions associated with loss in old age, few psychologists have suggested that anything beyond control might develop in adult life. Erikson (1963) believed that love emerged in young adulthood as a product of intimacy, and he spoke of the development of compassion in middle age, but he did not suggest any emotional experience associated with integrity. Only recently have psychodynamic thinkers expanded on the notion that love emerges in young adult life, and no one has done much work yet on the development of compassion.

An exception exists in the work of Carl Jung (1933, 1960). Jung contended that the first real opportunity for maturity emerged as a person turned from biological and social interests and activities to a concern for the inner, spiritual world at midlife. Jung thought people became more religious, philosophical, and intuitive in the second half of life, that they were more capable of integrating unconscious experience into everyday life, and that wisdom and patience developed beginning in middle age.

Jung used the term **self-actualized** to talk about maturity. He believed that the mature person could tolerate and eventually transcend conflict and opposition even within the self. He thought that self-actualization produced integration and harmony among conflicting personality tendencies, a concept

Erikson believes that values like love, hope, faith, and charity are universal because they express the developmental rudiments of human strength.

somewhat reminiscent of Erikson's **integrity.** Finally, the self-actualized person, according to Jung, possessed the ability to identify with all living things in an uncritical, appreciative way.

In those cases where research has been done on emotional development in adulthood, such development has most often been tied to changes in cognition. For instance, one group of psychoanalytic thinkers interested in interpersonal

Major theories regarding the determinants of human emotions seem to ignore middle and old age. And yet it is a common assumption that aging adults enjoy a longer and better quality of life if they remain active and engaged in enjoyable activities.

relationships (Bergman, 1980; Coen, 1981; Kernberg, 1976) have offered some thoughts on the nature of mature love. These writers have been called the **object relations** school because their primary interest is in how people relate to the significant people, objects, and ideas they encounter over the life course. Specifically of interest here, Otto Kernberg (1980) has defined mature love as the ability to identify with a partner such that the interests, wishes, feelings, and shortcomings of the partner attain about the same importance as one's own. Kernberg also maintains that mature love does not develop unless certain cognitive abilities are present. One must be able to think abstractly enough to develop adult ethics and commitment in order to love.

In a book entitled *Complexity of the Self,* Vittorio Guidano (1987) has argued that development over the life span proceeds toward greater complexity and order of the self through the integration of experience. Part of this process involves becoming aware of and integrating "implicit" knowledge. Implicit knowledge includes the emotional patterns a person develops based on repeated experiences that start in infancy. To some extent, becoming mature means becoming aware of these patterns and how they motivate behavior; progressively more integrated self-awareness emerges through comparing one's ongoing emotional reactions to related reactions in the past.

One of the basic ideas Guidano develops is the notion that all thought is influenced by emotion. Our earliest thoughts appear in the context of the family, a context that is emotionally charged. Becoming aware of the emotional aspects of cognition is extremely important from this point of view. Guidano might argue that there is no such thing as "objective thinking." All thinking is influenced by emotion. A similar position is taken by Elsa Schmid-Kitsikis (1990), a psychoanalytic thinker concerned with the relationship between logical thought, as described by Piaget, and emotion. She believes that all thought is exposed to emotional processes and "for the individual to be truly creative, it is necessary for these processes to combine and not to be antagonistic" (p. 191). She also believes that mature functioning involves being able to take into account the emotionally conflicted aspects of our experience rather than denying or cutting it off.

Schmid-Kitsikis even goes so far as to say that the emotional aspects of thought are terribly important to creative mental activity—or cognitive generativity as Dannefer and Perlmutter (1990) might call it. She believes that the emotions provide energy, clarify meanings, and create connections for people as they develop intellectually. It may be that answering the question "Why do people develop?" or "What causes development?" lies in the closer study of the relationship between emotion and cognition. It has been suggested that a central problem in the study of cognitive generativity is the issue of how it arises (Featherman & Marks, 1990; Stevens-Long & Macdonald, 1991). The work of Guidano and Schmid-Kitsikis may offer a direction for addressing these questions.

Theories Focusing on Behavior

So far, several perspectives on each of the major developmental systems have been considered, and, while opinions differ, some agreement prevails about what cognition or emotion or motivation looks like. What is interesting about the study of behavioral development is that the description of behavior itself is seldom undertaken. Behavior is usually ascribed to external environmental circumstances or cognitive intention, rather than perceived as a separate developmental system. No one yet has suggested that behavior becomes more mature without changes in motivation or cognition, but it is easy to conceptualize changes in motivation or cognition that do not show up in a person's behavior. Even B. F. Skinner's radical behaviorism is usually considered a theory of motivation, since he contended that change in the nature or timing of reinforcement motivates all changes in behavior. Skinner has described behavior primarily in terms of accuracy and frequency but ignores the qualitative aspects of behavior. What about terms like *grace, dignity,* or *productivity?* Do these ideas have any objective properties?

Table 2.4 Social readjustment rating scale	
Life event	**Mean value**
1. Death of spouse	100
2. Divorce	73
3. Marital separation	65
4. Jail term	63
5. Death of close family member	63
6. Personal injury or illness	53
7. Marriage	50
8. Fired at work	47
9. Marital reconciliation	45
10. Retirement	45
11. Change in health of family member	44
12. Pregnancy	40
13. Sex difficulties	39
14. Gain of new family member	39
15. Business readjustment	39
16. Change in financial state	38
17. Death of close friend	37
18. Change to different line of work	36
19. Change in number of arguments with spouse	35
20. Mortgage over $10,000	31
21. Foreclosure of mortgage or loan	30
22. Change in responsibilities at work	29

Theories of adult behavior have taken two general forms: those that stress the role of external, environmental events, and those that are concerned with how internal, cognitive events influence behavior. Of the first sort, one interesting example is found in the work of David Chiriboga and Loraine Cutler (1980), who have studied how stressful events affect behavior. Chiriboga and Cutler do emphasize how people perceive events, an idea that shows how the organismic paradigm has influenced mechanistic explanations of behavior.

In keeping with the mechanical model, Chiriboga and Cutler set out to quantify the amount of stress people experience in response to a variety of life events. They began with the Holmes and Rahe Social Readjustment (1967) scale as presented in Table 2.4. To use the scale, one simply adds up the points

Table 2.4 *(continued)*

Life event	Mean value
23. Son or daughter leaving home	29
24. Trouble with in-laws	29
25. Outstanding personal achievement	28
26. Wife begin or stop work	26
27. Begin or end school	26
28. Change in living conditions	25
29. Revision of personal habits	24
30. Trouble with boss	23
31. Change in work hours or conditions	20
32. Change in residence	20
33. Change in schools	20
34. Change in recreation	19
35. Change in church activities	19
36. Change in social activities	18
37. Mortgage or loan less than $10,000	17
38. Change in sleeping habits	16
39. Change in number of family get-togethers	15
40. Change in eating habits	15
41. Vacation	13
42. Christmas	12
43. Minor violations of the law	11

SOURCE: Holmes & Rahe, 1967, p. 216.

assigned to each of the events one has experienced in the last six to twelve months. The total number of points is used to predict the probability of stress-related illness during the following year.

Like many critics of the Holmes and Rahe scale, however, Chiriboga and Cutler felt that the assignment of a standard number of points to each event, regardless of a person's particular experience, made the scale less useful than it might be. Divorce is more stressful at the end of a long marriage where there are children and community property, than at the end of a three-year union between two young adults who had neither property nor children. Therefore, Chiriboga and Cutler asked people to assign their own point values to each event and to say which were positive and which negative. They also added a number of events Holmes and Rahe had omitted, including some that are especially typical of old age, like losing a driver's license because of failing eyesight.

Chiriboga and Cutler identified four major behavior patterns among the people who used the new scale. One group managed to avoid stress altogether; one was characterized by increases in positive stress without any increase in negative stress (the "lucky" group); another group was "overwhelmed" by large amounts of negative stress; and a final group appeared to be stress-prone (subject to high levels of both negative and positive stress).

What makes an event more difficult for one person than another? One critical predictor of how much stress people experience is the distribution of an event (Brim & Ryff, 1980). **Distribution** refers to how many people are likely to experience that event, whether the event is age-related, and whether it is likely to occur in the life of a particular person. Table 2.5 illustrates the distribution of various types of events.

When people are asked to explain their own behavior, they usually refer to vivid or recent events. For example, Jon may attribute his erratic work record to the recent death of his father, or Elaine may explain that she can't sleep because she recently left her husband of thirty years. Brim and Ryff contend that the death of Jon's father is not as important as the fact that Jon's father was only fifty-six and that Jon wasn't ready for the loss. Elaine might sleep better if she had close friends who had been through a similar experience. If an event is a common occurrence, and if it takes place at the right time in the life span, **anticipatory socialization** occurs. Anticipatory socialization serves to prepare people for events that might occur through the delivery of information. Even if the event is very unusual (like succession to the throne of a Europen country), anticipatory socialization occurs if the person has always known it was going to happen. In a more common example, people who know they will inherit a great deal of money should be better prepared to handle wealth than someone who wins a lottery. People experience more anticipatory socialization for events of high probability. For instance, there is much common wisdom about marriage, starting work, or retirement. These are events that occur to most people. There is also much individualized anticipatory socialization for high-probability events that are experienced by only a few people. For instance, most people who will inherit a large estate or succeed a parent in a family business (or accede to a throne) know that event is likely to occur and are prepared by their family, their schooling and so on. These events are classified as high probability because one is likely to know for certain that the events will probably occur. Low-probability events may be infrequent (like spina bifida) or uncertain (like failure at school or unpopularity). One simply doesn't know before the event happens that it is about to occur and anticipatory socialization is, therefore, not available.

When a person is faced with a low-probability event, one that is unlikely to occur to many people, there are at least three properties that are important in predicting whether the event will be experienced as negative (Reese & Smyer, 1983). First, socially desirable events are experienced as positive (it is better to become King of England than to be imprisoned for espionage, both low-probability events). Second, if the event is age-related, people will be better prepared (certain diseases associated with age are low-probability events). Finally, cohort specificity will make a difference in how the event is experienced (the effects of Agent Orange on Vietnam vets are cohort-specific).

Theories that emphasize the role of external, environmental events emphasize the description, measurement, and objectification of those events. Another group of theorists, working from a more organismic perspective, has developed a framework called **action theory.** They are interested in how internal processes, like beliefs, plans, and expectations, influence subsequent behaviors (Baltes, 1984).

The study of action does not include the study of all behavior. Action theorists are only concerned with the explanation and prediction of **intentional behavior.** Action theory predicts what intentional behavior means to the actor, how feelings affect action, and how goals, evaluations, memories, and other cognitive events influence action (Eckensberger & Meacham, 1984). Action is self-planned behavior that is under personal control and can be explained in terms of expectations, beliefs, goals, and opportunities (Brandtstädter, 1984a).

Action theorists argue that the expectations people hold about aging are powerful predictors of behavior, and, therefore, development. If people believe they can change at any age, if they believe their own personal development is under their control, that they can create the conditions that enable change, their behavior will remain more flexible and adaptive over the life span (Brandtstädter, 1984a, 1984b). Beliefs about whether we determine our own development and can change our behavior are called **control beliefs** by action theorists. Action theorists have argued that people should learn how to analyze and evaluate their own potential in a positive way; people should believe they can shape their own development in order to optimize behavior over the life span (Brandtstädter, 1984b).

From an action-theory perspective, consideration of optimal development should begin with hypotheses about the needs and developmental motives of individuals and the conditions that might satisfy such needs. The problem then becomes how to meet these needs and fulfill these motives through certain types of active intervention. Optimal development would not, under this scheme, be the same for all individuals. In fact, Brandtstädter (1990) has argued that "under these premises, models of optimal development that claim to be valid for all individuals and all times seem suspect" (p. 163).

Action theory may eventually provide an opportunity for dialogue among environmental, organismic, and psychodynamic theorists. In a 1984 issue of *Human Development,* critics who held both more psychodynamic and more environmental points of view wrote about the pitfalls and potential of action theory. For instance, Adrienne Harris, a psychoanalytic thinker, points out the problem of divining people's intentions when they do things they don't want to do. "A woman of thirty-five who says she wants a relationship of communica-

Table 2.5 Life events typology

Corre-lation with age	Experienced by many		Experienced by few	
	High probability of occurrence	*Low probability of occurrence*	*High probability of occurrence*	*Low probability of occurrence*
Strong	Marriage	Military service draft	Heirs coming into a large estate	Spina bifida
	Starting to work	Polio epidemic	Accession to empty throne at 18	First class of women at Yale
	Retirement			Pro football injury
	Woman giving birth to first child			Child's failure at school
	Bar Mitzvah			Teenage unpopularity
	First walking			
	Heart attack			
	Birth of sibling			
Weak	Death of a father	War	Son succeeding father in family business	Loss of limb in auto accident
	Death of a husband	Great Depression		Death of daughter
	Male testosterone decline	Plague		Being raped
	"Topping out" in work career	Earthquake		Winning a lottery
	Children's marriages	Migration from South		Embezzlement
	Accidental pregnancy			First black woman lawyer in South
				Blacklisted in Hollywood in 1940s
				Work disability
				Being fired
				Cured of alcoholism
				Changing occupations

SOURCE: Brim & Ryff, 1980.

tion and trust lives in a series of masochistic and destructive relations with men who give her the silent treatment, who keep her in a state of hostile surveillance, but whom she cannot bear to leave. Wanting to live a good life, honorable and selfless, she compulsively shoplifts, always very beautiful things, sometimes items from people or settings she respects. Obviously, a full consideration of how and why these actions develop and persist . . . indicate(s) the need to flesh out and give complexity to the question of intention" (p. 201).

From a more mechanistic standpoint, "the use of action and intention may initially spell a return to a 'philosophical' rather than a 'natural-science' approach to human behavior" (Baltes, 1984, p. 137). The mechanist worries that action and intention are slippery concepts that need to be harnessed by careful and painstaking definition and analysis. Nonetheless, the ideas of action theory are related to some of the work of one major behaviorist, Albert Bandura (1981). Bandura has argued, after years of studying behavior therapy, that people's beliefs about whether they can change their own experiences are a major predictor of success in behavior therapy.

In general, most theorists have conceptualized behavior as a function of either environmental events or cognition, or, less frequently, emotion. It is hard to find descriptive qualitative studies of behavior itself. One of the few exceptions exists in the research of Robert White (1975) on the lives of young adults. Based on a number of intensive case studies, White concluded that behavior in young adulthood became more committed. Young adults, according to White, exhibit a deepening of interests that is accompanied by wholehearted activity and the progressive mastery of knowledge and skills. They learn to derive satisfaction from the activity itself, rather than the social gains that accompany activity. Social gains, approval, and attention from others may spark an initial interest, but, finally, it is the experience of competence that becomes the most important source of satisfaction.

Otto Kernberg's (1980) work on love indicates that love develops as behavior becomes more ethical and committed in young adulthood. Regarding moral development, Reid (1984) posits the emergence of committed, principled behavior in young adulthood. However, there is no current research on what constitutes committed, ethical behavior or how it differs from behavior at earlier points in the life span. Finally, other research has suggested that empathic behavior (Benack, 1984) and reciprocity (Edelstein & Noam, 1982) may develop over the adult life span. **Reciprocity** is an idea drawn from the work of Immanuel Kant. The Kantian principle, as it is called, defines optimal behavior as behavior that never involves the use of another person to gain one's own ends. In this sense, it is the opposite of Machiavellian or manipulative behavior, which involves using another person strictly as an instrument for meeting one's own needs.

Despite all the difficulties and oversights, this review of current theory does suggest some common ground among the different theorists. That development is multicausal and multidirectional lends legitimacy to the variety of theoretical voices speaking out on a wide range of issues in human development. In the final section of this chapter, these voices are arranged so that we can take a clear look at where new voices might be added to the growing chorus.

A Matrix of Theoretical Constructs

The knowledge we have acquired ought not to resemble
a great shop without order, and without an inventory;
we ought to know what we possess, and be able to make
it serve us in our need.

—Leibnitz

In the following few pages, the work we have discussed so far is summarized in the form of a chart, or **matrix**. A matrix is simply an array of elements arranged in rows and columns. In Figure 2.5, the columns are labeled with the names of the four developmental systems we have been studying: motivation, cognition, emotion, and behavior. The rows are labeled "young adulthood," "middle adulthood" (middle age), and "later adulthood" (old age). It is not that there is anything sacred about these basic age ranges but only that most of the theorists we have reviewed tend to use these categories. The matrix provides a visually effective summary of research and theory about development, and suggests sequences over the three principal stages of the life span.

It is unclear whether there is some kind of general change from one phase of the adult life span to another, and it is very unlikely that there are abrupt changes. In fact, Angela O'Rand and Margaret Krecker (1990) have written that neither historical studies, studies of populations, nor longitudinal studies of modern life have been able to establish the existence of true stages in the life cycle: "Life cycle stages can be reversible, repeatable, and only loosely coupled with biological and chronological age over the individual life-span" (p. 250). It is unlikely that the developments outlined in Figure 2.5 represent some kind of inevitable, universal ground plan for adult life. It is much more likely that motivational, cognitive, emotional, or behavioral developments that emerge at one period are gradually replaced by the developments typical of the next phase (Kagan, 1983; Labouvie-Vief, 1982a).

Furthermore, the developments in any one row, say, the row for young adulthood, probably do not emerge all at once. Development in one area, like cognition, may not be well related to development in behavior or emotional life (Campbell & Richie, 1983). It might be helpful to picture Figure 2.5 as a game board sitting on a table. Let's say that you can stack pieces on top of one another in any given square, making some of the piles higher than others. If we took the height of the piles in different squares to represent the degree to which a person had developed, you might start to think of development as having a certain texture that varied from one person to another. The board might begin

	Cognition	Emotion	Motivation	Behavior
I Young Adulthood	Structural Analytic Stage (Commons & Richards) Dialectical Stage (Basseches; Riegel) Intrasystemic Stage (Labouvie-Vief)	Love (Erikson) Mature Love (Kernberg)	Intimacy (Erikson) Self-actualization (Maslow)	Ethical behavior (Kernberg) Commitment (Kernberg; White; Erikson) Principled behavior (Kohlberg)
II Middle Adulthood	Wisdom (Jung; Edelstein & Noam) Intersystemic Stage (Labouvie-Vief)	Caring (Erikson) Control (Leventhal; Mandler) Patience (Jung) Responsibility (Edelstein & Noam)	Generativity (Erikson) Self-actualization (Jung)	
III Later Adulthood	Wisdom (Erikson)		Integrity (Erikson)	Reciprocity (Edelstein & Noam) (Kant)

Figure 2.5 A summary of theory and research in adult development. Blank cells indicate areas where no research or theoretical work exists.

to look like a child's flour-and-salt map of a mountain range. Now, for most people, the squares in the row labeled "young adulthood" would probably be higher if it is true that formal operations are necessary before dialectical thinking develops, or if love in close relationships develops before more general compassion. But it is quite possible that someone capable of mature love in close relationships would never demonstrate formal operations, or vice versa.

If we consider Figure 2.5 a chart of the ideas various theorists have had about what is optimal in human behavior, one overall theme might be an increase in self-awareness. As you move down the columns, there is a trend toward being able to see the broader context of one's own development. In young adulthood, for instance, the struggle to develop intimate personal relationships requires us to become more aware of how our own behavior affects the interaction between us and those we are close to. We begin to see that these relationships are things we participate in, not things that get done to us by someone else. We begin to analyze relationships to determine what our own contribution is and how our contribution is affecting the quality of our relationships. In other words, relationships become an object of thought rather than just an experience.

In middle age, or middle adulthood, the community, perhaps even the society, becomes the context in which people develop. Generativity, relative thought, and compassion contribute to and grow from our interactions with the broader social structure. Most people don't have much influence in the community or the society until middle age, so in that sense, there is a kind of age grading that makes certain sequences of development probable.

It is also unlikely, however, that the developments outlined in Figure 2.5 represent a universal path toward optimal development. It is much more likely that this is a description of what modern Western writers have seen as optimal at this point in historical time (Brandtstädter, 1990; Featherman and Marks, 1990). What may be most interesting about this scheme is that it says something central about the Western perception of maturity, even if it does not describe some universal truth. To some extent, then, we are limited by the values represented in Figure 2.5; that is, we cannot imagine a mature person who is incapable of love or commitment or logical thought.

In constructing Figure 2.5, one of the most interesting things that emerged was the blank cells. Contemporary theory suggests few ideals for middle-aged behavior, and offers no ideas about emotional development in old age. There were many more suggestions in some cells than others, often a reflection of how much research was available. For example, the cells representing work on young adulthood were much easier to fill than those for middle or later life. Since researchers have, in general, an easier time observing young adults than older people, there is more information about the young than the old. Furthermore, the column labeled "cognition" contains many more explicit suggestions, reflecting the emphasis Western culture places on the development of rational thought over emotion, motivation, or even behavior. Figure 2.6 presents some suggestions for filling the blanks. It also summarizes the concepts offered by various researchers working in the same area. Notice the addition of enabling/productive behavior in middle age and reciprocal behavior in later life. Patience has been suggested as a key emotional development in old age, or later adulthood. Some of the summary words require further discussion, particularly in terms of how they are related to each other, and how they meet the criteria for sequence (Campbell & Richie, 1983; Commons & Richards, 1982). One important question is about sequence: Does the development of an ability or characteristic listed at an early period seem necessary to the development of a trait or ability thought characteristic of a later period?

The developments of young adulthood seem logically related both to one another and to the developments of middle age. Erikson and other psychoanalytic thinkers tell us that development in young adulthood occurs in the context of intimate relationships. One learns to love, to care as much about another as about the self without losing one's sense of personal identity. Or, as

	Cognition	Emotion	Motivation	Behavior
I Young Adulthood	**Insight** The ability to analyze relationships within a system, to find logical solutions	**Mature Love** The ability to identify completely with another and maintain a strong sense of self	**Self-actualized Intimacy** The need to resolve the conflict between individuation and fusion in the context of close relationships; to be intimate and self-sufficient	**Ethical/ Committed** Behavior becomes ethical, driven by personal principles rather than conformity; interests deepen
II Middle Adulthood	**Perspective** The ability to compare relationships across systems and to find adequate solutions	**Responsibility** The ability to maintain a sense of self and exercise judgment in spite of personal and social disequilibrium: to exhibit both compassion and control	**Self-actualized Generativity** The need to develop and maintain the social system and continue to individuate in the context of pressure; to be stable and responsible	**Effective/ Enabling** One is able to meet one's own needs and to assist others without wasted effort; behavior becomes productive
III Later Adulthood	**Autonomy** The ability to see one's own role in the experience of reality; to mediate between emotions and cognition	**Patience** The ability to tolerate conflict, to identify with opposition	**Self-actualized Integrity** The need to accept one's past, one's life history as meaningful, and to continue to develop or individuate	**Reciprocity** One is able to meet one's own needs without using another person instrumentally

Figure 2.6 Development across the adult life span. Dark outlines indicate cells where the most research is available.

Maslow puts it, one learns how to have a profound relationship in the context of self-sufficiency. Learning how to discriminate one's own needs, abilities, and shortcomings from those of another person in a close relationship both requires and contributes to the fine-tuning of formal operations.

Remember that formal operations offer the ability to analyze relationships within a closed system. **Intimacy** provides a social context for this analysis. Within a close relationship one has to discover how to meet another person's needs and accept another person's identity without diminishing oneself or dominating the other. Another way to state the problem is to talk about the tension between individuation and fusion. In her presidential address to the American Psychological Association, Janet Spence (1985) argued that the conflict between individuation and fusion is one of the central issues of human development. Extreme individuation, the inability to see oneself as part of a broader context of relationship, produces the isolation Erikson describes. On the other hand, fusion, the inability to separate oneself from a significant other, makes self-sufficiency impossible.

The behavioral development (as seen in the column on the right in Figure 2.6) suggested by Kernberg, White, and others, echoes Erikson's concern for the role of commitment in the development of intimacy; work on the development of political thought and action also suggests that ethical behavior emerges at the end of adolescence (Conger & Peterson, 1984). Still, the hypothesis that principled, committed *behavior* is an achievement of late adolescence and early adulthood remains essentially unresearched. Because of the ethical problems posed for the researcher, very few studies of significant moral issues exist in the literature on adult development. It is difficult to construct a significant moral dilemma that does not affect the participant in a profound way.

Both Maslow's description of the self-actualized person as problem-centered and committed to the benefit of others and Erikson's notion that generativity and caring suggest a broadening of motivational development to a wider social context at midlife are illustrated in the second row of Figure 2.6. This period can be seen as the time when people begin to deal with a wider context than the intimate relationship provides. Middle-aged people are charged with the maintenance of society. At the same time, they must provide for change and continue to fulfill their own potential despite enormous pressures for personal stability. Emotionally, such a burden certainly requires the ability to empathize with and care for others. Furthermore, as researchers working on emotional development claim, emotional control seems essential. Middle-aged people are given the task of making long-term decisions affecting other people's lives, whether in the context of the family, the community, or the world.

In the cognitive domain, the ability to analyze the relationships between different systems, and to find adequate, effective solutions, contributes to and is supported by the emotional and motivational developments of middle age. The dialectical or intersystemic thinker realizes that solutions must be appropriate to the context. What works in one family or community may fail miserably in another. Middle-aged people are often in charge of finding solutions that work outside their own narrow social circles. Thought must be more realistic and consider context more often. In Figure 2.6 the term *perspective* appears. Perspective requires the thinker to consider his or her own system as only one in many that might be applied to a particular situation.

Although no one has spoken to the behavioral developments that might be associated with midlife, it seems probable that mature, middle-aged people be-

"Growing old is no more than a bad habit which a busy man has no time to form."
André Maurois

come increasingly productive and effective. That is, they learn to meet both their own needs and the needs of others with less trial and error. With perspective, with an ability to predict long-term consequences and to find socially adequate solutions, behavior can be said to be *effective*. In Figure 2.6, behavior at midlife is labeled "effective/enabling," reflecting a certain gap in language. It is hard to find a word that implies the right mix of productivity and concern for others. The assumption that adult ethics underlie effective behavior is critical. Without adult ethics and commitment, effective behavior is unrestrained by compassion and responsibility. Effective behavior requires commitment, but it also implies a certain kind of productive flexibility, the ability to try another strategy when one solution proves unworkable.

In the last row of Figure 2.6, the entries are the least well defined. Erikson's concept of integrity has been combined with Jung's thought on the mature personality to produce some of the ideas in this row. Jung believed that the first real opportunity for maturity occurred at middle age but continued through the second half of life. His notion that maturity was accompanied by increased introspection and concern for the integration of various elements in personality is supported by empirical data on declining concern for the external world among the elderly. As Leopold Rosenmayr wrote in the *Handbook of the Psy-*

chology of Aging (1985): "Late middle age is a phase of withdrawal and must perhaps be regarded as the key phase for gerontology in its classical sense" (p. 207). Rosenmayr has argued that the ability to question oneself gives a person control over defensiveness and regression in old age.

Labouvie-Vief's notion of autonomous thinking seems to fit nicely here. She spoke of how people begin to see that they have affected their own development. They begin to be aware of what has been unique to them and what is common to all human development. She has also argued that autonomous thought arises from a genuine awareness of the complexity of the social system, an awareness gained in middle age (Labouvie-Vief, 1985). In young adulthood insight develops about the differences between the self and other individuals. In middle age, one becomes aware of the differences between systems. In later life, **wisdom,** where it develops, may have something to do with seeing one's own role in the creation of these differences (Labouvie-Vief, 1985). Other suggestions about the nature of wisdom include the ability to mediate between thinking and feeling (Edelstein & Noam, 1982), and the ability to appreciate the self as part of the broader context of humanity (Chinen, 1984).

Jung's concept of patience seems a logical, emotional component of wisdom and integrity. No one has spent much time defining it, but patience seems to require attention and caring. Still, patience is more than caring, because it requires tolerance for opposition. In fact, it might be said to require the ability to identify with the very people or things that create opposition.

Finally, reciprocity stands as the only current suggestion about a final sort of behavioral development. Reciprocity, as defined by Kant, means never using another person as an instrument for meeting one's own needs. Reciprocity seems most likely to emerge in a person who is effective, compassionate, and patient. It might also require much insight into one's own development to be sure about what goals are one's own and what goals are someone else's and then to relate all of this to the larger social picture.

Filling in the blank cells and speculating about what concepts seem most apt in Figure 2.5 can be a revealing exercise. When I began thinking about the problem, I left a message on my answering machine asking callers to leave a single word they thought characterized mature people. I had an amazing number of thoughtful responses, including patience, responsibility, love, insight, and creativity. Two interesting ideas that don't appear in Figure 2.5 are facetiousness and courage. Facetiousness is wittiness, the ability to poke a kind of intelligent fun at oneself or the outside world. Certainly, humor develops over the life course, especially self-directed humor (Farrell & Rosenberg, 1981; Nahemow, McCluskey-Fawcett, & McGhee, 1986); and, although courage is difficult to define, it seems to imply the ability to deal with loss, even the loss of one's own life. Perhaps it could be placed at midlife when the ability to maintain one's sense of self in the face of personal and social pressure seems so important. Or, maybe it develops in the last stages of the life cycle, as one faces the loss of roles, significant others, and finally the self.

Summary

I. Theories and Models
    A. A theory is a set of abstract principles that can be used to predict facts in the context of a body of knowledge.
        1. Theories offer explanations for phenomena of interest in terms of what is already understood.
        2. Theories also help organize knowledge and generate new ideas.
        3. The study of adulthood has produced some limited explanations but not broad general theory.
    B. A model is an analogy or metaphor that guides research and theory.
        1. Models are based on assumptions about the nature of human beings and developmental change.
        2. There are three contemporary models of development: the mechanical model, the organismic model, and the dialectical model.
            a. The mechanical model uses the computer as an analogy for human development and assumes that change is produced by external events.
            b. The organismic model relies on the metaphor of biological development and assumes that change is produced by internal, qualitative changes.
            c. The dialectical model is based on the metaphor of dialogue and assumes that change is produced through the interaction of an active organism in a constantly changing environment.
            d. Recent work on development stresses how different kinds of development (physical ontogeny, habituation, and cognitive generativity) might reflect different models of the person-environment interaction.

II. Theories: A Multiplicity of Views
    A. A multicausal, multidirectional view of human development lends credence to a wide variety of theoretical positions focused on different developmental systems.
    B. Theories focused on motivation seldom have a developmental component, but the work of Erikson and Maslow are important exceptions.
        1. Erikson's stage theory has been labeled a starting point for a dialectical theory of development because it stresses the interaction between the individual and society.
            a. Erikson believed a biological ground plan was responsible for the emergence of different developmental stages.
            b. Erikson argued that social institutions develop from and, in turn, support individual development.
            c. Erikson's theory has been criticized for not presenting enough

specificity although it has generated a number of research hypotheses and guidance for evaluating interview data as well as paper-and-pencil tests.

2. Maslow also believed development occurred in a series of stages, but he defined two types of motivation: basic, or deficiency, needs and meta-needs, or the need for self-actualization.
   a. Self-actualization cannot occur until the deficiency needs are met.
   b. Self-actualized people are sensitive to deceit and fakery, are problem-centered rather than self-centered, exhibit a strong desire to benefit others, are capable of enjoyment without shame or doubt, and have intense, profound personal relationships.
   c. Self-actualized people are also human, however, and make many of the same silly, wasteful mistakes all humans make.

C. Theories that focus on cognition tend to be organismic in worldview, and are often derived from the work of Piaget.
   1. Piaget's definition of stage requires the emergence of general or content-free abilities that are derived from a logically necessary base in an earlier stage.
   2. The structural analytic stage meets Piaget's requirements and is defined by the ability to analyze the relationships between systems.
   3. Dialectical thinking is another version of postformal thought and is described in terms of the appreciation of change, sensitivity to contradiction, and the ability to discriminate general forms in the context of constant change.
   4. The decline of certain cognitive performances in later life has led to the proposal that a new stage in which pure logic is tempered by the experience of real-life complexity arises.

D. Theories that focus on affect rarely have a developmental component. It is unclear how emotional experience changes over the adult life course or whether qualitatively new emotions arise.
   1. The data suggest no changes in the frequency of negative emotions, but there may be new negative affective states as a result of significant loss.
   2. Both cognitive-emotional theorists, who think emotions involve the cognitive interpretation of arousal, and somatic theorists, who think emotions are a separate cognitive system from thought, believe emotional control should increase with age.
   3. It has also been argued that emotional complexity increases with age as people learn to deal with implicit emotional information in an explicit, integrated way.
   4. Jung argued that emotional developments like patience and feelings of integration and harmony developed during middle age.

     5. Erikson and other psychodynamic theorists argue that mature love emerges for the first time in young adulthood.

  E. Theories that focus on behavior rarely consider behavior an independent developmental system but treat it as a function of environmental events or cognition.

     1. Chiriboga and Cutler exemplify the environmental position in their attempt to quantify the personal perception of stress and use this to predict behavioral patterns.

     2. Brim and Ryff emphasize how the objective properties of events, like distribution, predict how well people will cope with them.

     3. Action theory is an attempt to explain intentional behavior in terms of cognitive events like beliefs, feelings, goals, evaluations, and memories.

        a. Control beliefs are thought to influence whether behavior remains flexible and adaptive throughout the life span.

        b. Action theory has provided a platform for the interaction of cognitive, psychodynamic, and environmentally oriented theorists. It suggests that optimal development is not the same for all individuals.

III. A Matrix of Theoretical Constructs

  A. If one divides the adult life span into early, middle, and late adulthood, and thinks in terms of four major developmental systems: cognition, emotion, motivation, and behavior, it is possible to develop a matrix that includes most of the concepts covered in this chapter.

  B. This summary matrix is probably best considered a series of probable sequences that represent a Western ideal of maturity.

     1. Data on the development of cognition through the life course are easiest to find, and there is more information on emotion, motivation, and behavior in young adulthood than other periods of adulthood.

     2. A summary of cognitive theory suggests development from the analysis of single systems, to the comparison of systems, to the discrimination between truth produced by a system and personal truth.

     3. The development of affect seems to proceed in the direction of greater control and from love to compassion to tolerance.

     4. Motivation may be cast in terms of the conflict between the self and others or the self and society. It may also derive from conflict within the self or between competing developmental or personality systems.

     5. Behavioral development is very poorly researched, but the evidence reviewed here suggests a progression from principled/committed behavior to effective/enabling behavior to reciprocity.

II

Young Adulthood

3

The Inner Context of Development: Physical and Intellectual Change

Well I hit the rowdy road,
and many kinds I met there,
many stories told me
of the way to get there, ooh
So on and on I go,
the seconds tick the time out,
There's so much left to know,
and I'm on the road to find out.

—Cat Stevens

THE FIRST YEAR OF COLLEGE was quite a change. I was on my own for the first time. My parents had always thought I should have a particular career. I started out studying for that. By the end of the year though, I knew it wasn't for me. That summer, what was so surprising was how my parents no longer seemed to understand me. They listened but kept saying the same old things. My father kept saying, "I do not understand what you have against making money." The next year, I experimented, trying out different subjects and a few majors. I got a good sense that I was people-oriented rather than thing-oriented. I did not know exactly where my interests would lead me. Around the time I was a senior, I was considering various jobs and possibly graduate school. My father just wanted me to get out and get a job. My mother wanted me to go to some professional school. I knew I wanted a break for a year or two, so after I graduated, I got a job. My first job was much harder to get than I thought. At first I found that the way they did a lot of things did not make a whole lot of sense. In school, I had hardly ever worked on a team. Here, I was just a junior member after having run my life for so many years. And the politics of it all. People were always gossiping about this and that and trying to impress this person or that person. I was frightened that I was not sophisticated enough to make a good impression. Work was much more demanding of me than I had remembered school being. I went home tired after each day. I did not know if this job was right for me even though I liked it OK. I thought a lot about going back to school but did not know exactly what to study.

EARLY ADULTHOOD: THE YEARS FROM TWENTY TO FORTY are a time of finding out and fitting in. During these years, the major themes of personal development are most often described by words like *insight, commitment,* and *intimacy.* By twenty, most people have some sense of who they are and what they want (or at least, do not want) but lack the experience and decision-making opportunities that produce maturity. The abilities and concerns expressed in adolescence—formal reasoning, the search for personal identity, and independence—continue to be refined and consolidated throughout the early years of adult life. In almost every way, one's twenties are a pinnacle of development. Mastery of the intellectual tools of formal thought and a deeper understanding of the self and others permit young adults to establish a niche in the world. Bones and skin are strong and supple, muscles are powerful, senses are keen, and almost everyone still has their own teeth. Old age seems as remote as Pluto.

Ironically, however, even by the age of thirty, physiological aging is measurable in a variety of ways. Some functions, for example, the performance of the heart and the circulatory system, pass the peak of optimal function at the end of adolescence. It has been estimated that general bodily functioning may decline at the rate of 1 percent per year throughout adulthood (Whitbourne, 1985b). The muscular development characteristic of adolescence continues, and many important signs of sexual maturity appear, from hair on the chest to the maturity of the uterus. At the same time, the data show subtle changes that occur with age in the organ systems of the body, processes that underline the importance of exercise, good nutrition, and beneficial health habits throughout adulthood (Fries & Crapo, 1981).

Development and aging are multidirectional processes. They are accompanied by the benefits of experience in increased power of reasoning, the comforts of a well-established life, as well as the problems of physical and emotional wear and tear. This chapter will examine the first boons and burdens of young adulthood, from sensory and perceptual functions to cognition and moral development. And it will look at the social and psychological tasks to which all of the systems and abilities of young adults respond.

Physical Functioning

Peak physical strength in the **striped muscles** is achieved between the ages of twenty-three and twenty-seven (Hershey, 1974). The striped muscles are commonly called the voluntary muscles; examples are the biceps and triceps. Thus, the capacity for physical labor and for strenuous athletic endeavor is generally the greatest during one's middle to late twenties. Injuries heal relatively quickly. Performance in the most vigorous sports, like tennis and boxing, seems to peak before the age of thirty, whereas top performance in such activities as billiards and golf tends to occur between twenty-nine and thirty-four (Lehman, 1953). The sports that require the greatest physical endurance and speed are generally the ones in which we pass our maximum capacity earliest.

The early effects of aging are also clear in measures of the maximum rate at which people work without fatigue, or the ability to climb stairs, run on a treadmill, or crank a wheel (Whitbourne, 1985b). The strength of the hand grip begins to decline after the age of twenty, although the decline from twenty to fifty is small. Peak leg strength is achieved between twenty and thirty (Buskirk, 1985).

Most people barely notice these changes, however, and adopt a variety of strategies that enable continued vigorous physical activity and peak work performance. People learn to use their strength wisely, expending maximum effort at the precise moment required (Timiras, 1972). Moreover, regular moderate physical recreation and exercise as well as a sensible diet can ensure many active years of adult living. Active people live much longer than people who do not exercise. On the other hand, people who place great value on feelings of physical strength and prowess—professional athletes, for example—may feel older and may experience more negative feelings about their age than people who do not assess themselves largely in terms of physical attributes (Buhler, 1972).

Vital Functions and Body Systems

The vital functions, which include the performance of the cardiovascular and pulmonary systems (see pages A-1 and A-2 in Appendix), undergo important changes during young adulthood. Evidence indicates a noticeable decrease in heart and lung function by the age of forty. Using Selective Service data from World War II, for example, Goldstein (1951) analyzed records of army physicals with particular attention to tests that measured recovery from strenuous physical activity. Between the ages of twenty and forty, the men being tested showed a substantial increase in the time required for recovery. Furthermore, recent comparisons of data for today's young adults with those of twenty or thirty years ago, indicate that current cohorts show a greater decline in measures of physical condition than young adults of the fifties. This trend has been attributed to the increasingly sedentary lifestyles of today's adults (Buskirk, 1985).

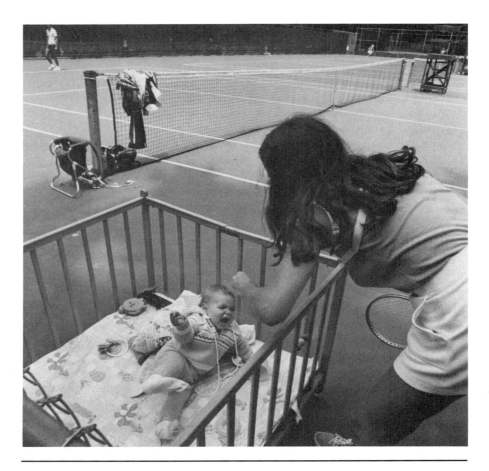

The capacity for strenuous athletic endeavor is greatest during one's middle to late twenties, a period when most married couples try to start families. Balancing leisure sports and parenting can produce stressful moments.

Both cross-sectional and longitudinal studies of cardiac function show a decline in output, defined as the quantity of blood ejected each minute by one of the ventricles of the heart. Maximum **cardiac output** is reached between twenty and thirty and slowly declines thereafter (Hershey, 1974). There is also a decline in the maximum heartbeat one can achieve. These changes occur for a variety of reasons, but the overriding event seems to be a decline in the power of the left ventricle of the heart. One of the central facts of aging is the stiffening of tissues throughout the body. In muscle tissue, like the heart, this means less power to pump blood through the body. Furthermore, there is increased resistance in the circulatory system, as the arteries become less flexible as well (Whitbourne, 1985b).

Similar changes characterize the respiratory system. **Vital capacity** is one

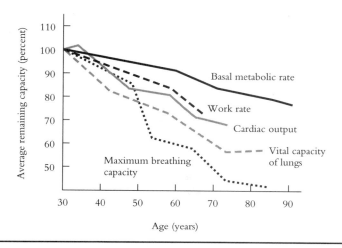

Figure 3.1 Decline of basic physiological capacities with age.

SOURCE: Insel & Roth, 1991, p. 521.

measure of pulmonary or lung function. The differences between the amount of air one takes in during a normal, relaxed breath and the amount one can take in during a maximum breath is called the **inspiratory reserve.** The amount of air one can still exhale after a normal breath is called the **expiratory reserve.** The sum of these two reserves is the vital capacity of the lungs, which decreases sharply between twenty and forty (Hershey, 1974). Decline in vital capacity approaches 40 percent over the course of adult life, and there is a decrease in maximum breathing frequency of up to 50 percent. All of this means that there is a decline in the amount of oxygen delivered from the outside air to the arterial system (Whitbourne, 1985a, 1985b). (See Figure 3.1.)

A variety of other measures, including the **basal metabolic rate** (a measure of oxygen consumption in the body), the functioning of the lymphatic system, and the output of the adrenal glands, show decline beginning around age twenty-five (Bromley, 1974; Timiras, 1972). Finally, some noticeable alterations take place in the structure and function of the nervous system during the early adult years. The number of cells in the central nervous system and the size of the brain actually decrease after puberty (Sinclair, 1969).

Whereas it is not clear whether regular exercise actually increases a person's life span, exercise does appear to delay or even reverse decline in cardiac function. If one begins exercising before age fifty, the result may also be an increase in vital capacity. The buildup of cholesterol in the arteries (**arteriosclerosis**) and high blood pressure can be reduced by a regular program of aerobic exercise. An increase in the maximum ventilatory rate and ventilatory flow of the lungs also results (Schneider & Reed, 1985; Whitbourne, 1985b).

Aside from the obvious physical advantages, exercise has also been associated with increased feelings of well-being and competence, and improved sleep, work performance, and sexual function. Part of the benefit of exercise derives from improved physical performance, but regular exercise also enhances a person's self-concept and body image. People who look and feel better, who are able to meet the demands of everyday life, and who work without undue strain or fatigue are likely to be generally more positive about themselves (Sonstroem, 1984).

Aside from exercise, the most important health choices one makes concern diet and smoking. Table 3.1 presents information about the risks associated with smoking cigarettes and the benefits one can expect to derive from quitting.

Overall, of course, the evidence does show that the years of young adult-

Table 3.1 Risks of smoking and benefits of quitting

Risks of Smoking	Benefits of Quitting
Shortened life expectancy. Twenty-five-year-old two-pack-a-day smokers have life expectancy 8.3 years shorter than nonsmoking contemporaries. Other smoking levels: proportional risk.	**Reduces risk of premature death** cumulatively. After 10–15 years, ex-smokers' risk approaches that of those who have never smoked.
Lung cancer. Smoking cigarettes is a major cause.	Gradual decrease in risk. **After 10–15 years, risk approaches that of those who have never smoked.**
Larynx cancer. 2.9 to 17.7 times that of nonsmokers. Risk is in all smokers (including pipe and cigar).	**Gradual reduction of risk** after smoking cessation. **Reaches normal after 10 years.**
Mouth cancer. Cigarette smokers have 3 to 10 times as many oral cancers as nonsmokers. Pipes, cigars, chewing tobacco also major risk factors. Alcohol seems synergistic carcinogen with smoking.	Reducing or eliminating smoking/drinking reduces risk in first few years; **risk drops to level of non-smokers in 10–15 years.**
Cancer of esophagus. Cigarettes, pipes, and cigars increase risk of dying of esophageal cancer about 2 to 9 times. Synergistic relationship between smoking and alcohol.	Since risks are dose related, reducing or eliminating smoking/drinking **should have risk-reducing effect.**
Cancer of bladder. Cigarette smokers have 7 to 10 times risk of bladder cancer as nonsmokers. Also synergistic with certain exposed occupations: dyestuffs, etc.	**Risk decreases gradually to that of nonsmokers over 7 years.**

Table 3.1 *(continued)*

Risks of Smoking	Benefits of Quitting
Cancer of pancreas. Cigarette smokers have 2 to 5 times risk of dying of pancreatic cancer as nonsmokers.	Since there is evidence of dose-related risk, reducing or eliminating smoking should have risk-reducing effect.
Coronary heart disease. Cigarette smoking is major factor; responsible for 120,000 excess U.S. deaths from coronary heart disease each year.	**Sharply decreases risk after one year.** After 10 years ex-smokers' risk is same as that of those who have never smoked.
Chronic bronchitis and pulmonary emphysema (COLD). Cigarette smokers have 4 to 25 times risk of death from these diseases as nonsmokers. Damage seen in lungs of even young smokers.	**Cough and sputum disappear** during first few weeks. **Lung function may improve** and rate of deterioration slow down.
Stillbirth and low birth weight. Smoking mothers have more stillbirths and babies of low birth weight—more vulnerable to disease and death.	Women who stop smoking before fourth month of pregnancy **eliminate risk of stillbirth and low birth weight** caused by smoking.
Children of smoking mothers are smaller, underdeveloped physically and socially, seven years after birth.	Since children of nonsmoking mothers are bigger and more advanced socially, inference is that **not smoking during pregnancy might avoid such underdeveloped children.**
Peptic ulcer. Cigarette smokers get more peptic ulcers and die more often of them; cure is more difficult in smokers.	Ex-smokers get ulcers but these are **more likely to heal rapidly and completely** than those of smokers.
Allergy and impairment of immune system.	Since these are direct, immediate effects of smoking, they are obviously **avoidable by not smoking.**
Alters pharmacologic effects of many medicines and diagnostic tests and greatly increases risk of thrombosis with oral contraceptives.	**Majority of blood components elevated by smoking return to normal after cessation.** Nonsmokers on oral contraceptives have much lower risks of thrombosis.

SOURCE: Adapted from American Cancer Society, *Dangers of Smoking, Benefits of Quitting and Relative Risks of Reduced Exposure* (rev. ed.): pp. 8–9.

hood are the peak physical years, despite the intimations of aging. During these years, one can stay out all night, dance until dawn, and still get to work the next day. This makes perfect biological sense from the standpoint of energy level, for these are also the reproductive years, when most people decide to settle into marriage and parenting.

Reproductive and Sexual Physiology

With the arrival of reproductive maturity in young adulthood, the demand increases for decision making and intimacy in heterosexual relationships. Luckily, most people have developed the intellectual ability to understand complex social interactions and can generate solutions for interpersonal problems. Of course, problem solving requires information, and, at the most basic level, sexual problem solving requires some understanding of the physiology of sexual arousal and its reproductive consequences. Knowledge alone doesn't guarantee a good sexual relationship, or more orgasms, or even a specific basis for making sexual decisions. It can, however, increase the probability of tolerant, reasonable attitudes toward sex, and the probability of responsible sexual behavior.

The Physiology of Sexual Intercourse   Basic sexual anatomy is presented on page A-6 in the Appendix. Of course, many other parts of the body also respond sexually, including the breasts of females (and of a surprising number of males), a good portion of the skin (especially the insides of the thighs, the small of the back, the mouth, and the back of the neck), as well as the anus, rectum, and buttocks.

Probably the most revolutionary findings about sexual responsiveness in this century are contained in the work of William Masters and Virginia Johnson (1966, 1970). One of their most significant conclusions was that male and female sexual arousal are alike, to a degree never before appreciated. According to these famous investigators, both sexes experience four stages of sexual arousal: excitation, plateau, orgasm, and resolution.

Excitation   **Excitation** occurs in both men and women in response to a variety of stimuli from sights and sounds to thoughts and dreams. Vasocongestion, the filling of the blood vessels near the surface of the body, is the most prominent sign of this stage. In men, erection results from **vasocongestion.** In women, vasocongestion causes sexual changes in the breasts as well as the genitals. About one quarter of all males experience vasocongestion of the breasts.

In neither sex does vasocongestion appear to be under much conscious control (Kaplan, 1980), although the fact is far more likely to be troublesome for a man than a woman. As Jack Litewka wrote of his adolescence, "You had to learn how to hide it or deal with the embarrassment of its discovery" (1977, p. 224). Secondly, and what is perhaps more relevant to adulthood, erection cannot be produced on demand even when all the right cues seem to be available. Men who have difficulty achieving an erection quite often have a medical problem such as diabetes or injury to the area. Also, men are often stuck with the stereotype of the male as a sexual expert or athlete. Masters and Johnson believe this stereotype is the leading cause of sexual dysfunction among American males. This form of impotence, which is the most anxiety-provoking male sexual dysfunction, occurs during excitation. The untimely failure of this involuntary vasocongestive response can be traumatic. The changes that ordinarily accompany age and may be apparent by age forty make it terribly important for a man to be able to deal with occasional erectile dysfunction. This enlightenment may be difficult to accomplish for anyone who believes his sex appeal depends on providing prompt, unflagging service.

For women, failure in the excitation phase may be unpleasant and upsetting, but it is less apparent. The inability to achieve orgasm despite normal arousal is the most common and distressing female complaint.

In addition to vasocongestion, excitation in both males and females is marked by increasing **myotonia.** Myotonia is the involuntary muscular contraction that builds throughout arousal to the point of orgasm. In fact, cramps of the hands and feet are not uncommon during intense sexual arousal. Facial grimaces or frowns may actually indicate high levels of involvement rather than pain or dismay (Masters, Johnson, & Kolodny, 1991).

Finally, lubrication is apparent in both sexes during the first stages of sexual arousal. Both males and females produce lubricatory fluids during excitation. Although the pre-ejaculatory fluid males secrete is produced by the Cowper's gland rather than the prostate (which contributes fluid to the semen), it may occasionally contain sperm. It is not clear exactly how vaginal lubrication is produced although the process has been labeled **transudation.** The walls of the vagina simply appear to sweat, but no one has identified the source of the fluid.

Plateau **Plateau** is a state of extremely high sexual arousal in both men and women. In females, the outer third of the vagina becomes engorged with blood, decreasing the size of the vaginal opening by as much as 30 percent and producing an orgasmic platform that "grips" the penis during intercourse. In males, an analogous response occurs with the elevation of the testes. Both of these responses make intercourse easier and, therefore, more productive—that is, reproductive.

Orgasm **Orgasm** is defined in both males and females as rhythmic contractions of the pelvic musculature that produce intense physical sensations. Lubrication and vasocongestion peak immediately prior to orgasm and males report feelings of "inevitability," as semen accumulates in the penis just prior to ejaculation. Furthermore, although there is evidence that orgasm can occur without ejaculation (reports of men with spinal injuries confirm this notion), and it is also clear that ejaculation can occur independently of orgasm, most men define orgasm in terms of ejaculation. The fact that men perceive orgasm in terms of ejaculation leads to the inevitable conclusion that men are capable of

A, B, and C are three different female sexual
response patterns, Female C — one orgasm,
Female A — two orgasms, Female B — no orgasms.

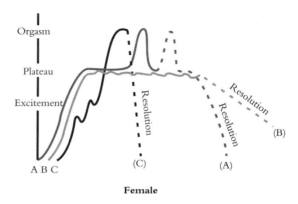

Female

The refractory period represents the last, irregular
contractions during which sexual tension rapidly
subsides.

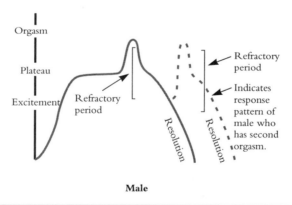

Male

Figure 3.2 Human sexual response cycles.

SOURCE: From Masters & Johnson (1966). Used by permission of Masters and Johnson Institute.

one orgasm at a time, whereas women have the "physical capability of being
multiorgasmic—that is, they can have one or more additional orgasms within
a short time without dropping below the plateau level of sexual arousal" (Masters, Johnson, & Kolodny, 1982, p. 68). The discovery of multiorgasmic
women may be one of the most widely publicized sexological events of the last
twenty-five years. Masters and Johnson even provide graphic illustration of
multiple orgasms, as presented in Figure 3.2. Despite the general acceptance

of the concept, however, multiple orgasm has not really been adequately defined.

If one accepts Masters and Johnson's (1966) definition of female orgasm as three to five contractions of the pelvic musculature, a number of interesting questions arise to challenge the concept of multiple orgasm. If a woman experiences fifteen contractions, is that tantamount to three orgasms or just one long one? Does a period of plateau always intervene between orgasms, and how long is this period? Might the man who experiences fifteen contractions during ejaculation be defined as multiorgasmic? In fact, some men report that if they think of orgasm as muscular contractions rather than ejaculation, they may be multiorgasmic too.

It ought to be noted, however, that even Masters and Johnson (1966) report it is "unusual for a woman to have multiple orgasms during most of her sexual activity" and they never considered the possibility that men could have more than one orgasm. Ejaculation can occur without erection. In fact, one popular author has suggested that it would make a big difference in male-female relationships if women understood how often this happens (Farrell, 1986). Erection often occurs without ejaculation. Ejaculation can occur in spinally injured men without orgasm and the reverse is also true, as noted earlier. And some who can achieve neither erection nor ejaculation still have dreams during which they report that orgasm occurs (McCary & McCary, 1982). Obviously, much work has yet to be done before the mechanisms behind male and female orgasm are understood.

Resolution   Most men move smoothly from orgasm into resolution, experiencing a **refractory period** after orgasm during which ejaculation cannot occur again. Women also move from orgasm into resolution, but there does not seem to be a female equivalent of the refractory period. For either sex, if orgasm is not experienced after a prolonged plateau, resolution may be lengthened and experienced as frustrating or irritating.

There is little doubt that there is an important subjective component to orgasm and resolution. For instance, writing about his experience in running personal growth groups for thousands of men and women, Warren Farrell (1986) notes that he finds that "approximately 90 percent of so-called 'impotence' is catalyzed by some combination of self-consciousness and fear of rejection or, on the other hand, simple distraction. When the catalyst occurs at a moment when we are expecting a body organ to change its shape, the body organ cannot concentrate" (p. 265). The comment probably applies equally well to women. In Shere Hite's famous report (1981), 70 percent of the women who responded reported that they could not achieve orgasm during sexual intercourse. Yet Freud believed that a shift from clitoral stimulation to orgasm induced by vaginal stimulation was a sign of maturity in women, and some modern researchers have argued that the inability to experience orgasm during intercourse is related to anxiety or low self-esteem. All of this discussion only indicates that the current understanding of sexuality in either its objective, physiological aspects or its subjective side is still rather limited.

Limited understanding does not, however, appear to be inhibiting behavior. Every available study of sexual behavior, including the premarital, marital, extramarital, and postmarital types, indicates that more and more North Americans and Europeans—men and women, from teens to seniors, of every religious, racial, or ethnic origin—are engaging in a wider variety of sexual activities with greater frequency and higher levels of reported satisfaction than researchers have ever found before. Furthermore, this trend is stronger among young adults, who appear more sexually uninhibited than middle-aged people. These findings hold true for females as well as males. The idea that females are at their sexual peak in middle age is not well supported by the literature. As Carlfred Broderick has written, "The current generation is getting off to a much faster start" (1982, p. 728). By 1988, 51.5 percent of women ages fifteen to nineteen had engaged in premarital sex. This is nearly double the 28.6 reported in 1970. Given the tremendous growth of heterosexual AIDS (Acquired Immune Deficiency Syndrome) cases, Sevgi Aral, chief of the behavioral studies section of the Centers for Disease Control (CDC) sees the 7.4 percent increase in sexual behavior between 1985 and 1988 as alarming. Also, as in the past, women still suffer unwanted pregnancies and people get sexually transmitted diseases other than AIDS.

Aside from AIDS, there are over twenty different organisms that have been identified as causing sexually transmissible diseases. Some of these are caused by viruses, some by bacteria, some by protozoa, and others by funguses and parasites. The most common of these is *chlamydia trachomatis,* which is estimated to infect three to four million Americans every year. Chlamydia is the leading cause of urinary tract infection in men and is responsible for approximately 50 percent of the estimated 500,000 cases of inflammation of the testicles seen each year in the United States. In women, chlamydia can cause inflammation of the cervix and fallopian tubes if left untreated. Sexually active women under twenty years old have chlamydia infection rates two to three times greater than women over the age of twenty. Chlamydia is easily treatable with antibiotics but far too often is left untreated, causing unnecessary suffering and biological damage (Insel & Roth, 1988).

Other common sexually transmitted diseases include *nongonococcal rethritis,* a urinary tract inflammation that is thought to be caused by several different organisms and that affects about 2.5 million Americans a year. *Gonorrhea,* affecting about one million people in this country every year, is caused by bacteria and can become a chronic, sterility-producing disease when it is treated late. *Syphilis* is much less common than it was only a few decades ago, when 5 to 10 percent of the population died of it, but it is extremely dangerous, particularly when carried by women, because it can infect infants after the tenth week of gestation. Finally, *herpes* is actually a group of viruses including *Herpes Simplex, Types I and II,* which are sexually transmitted and which infect at least 20 million people in this country, with 500,000 new cases appearing each year. Herpes can be successfully treated, but it cannot be cured (Insel & Roth, 1988).

It has been speculated that if a vaccine to prevent AIDS is not developed soon, sexual mores will change profoundly. Celibacy before marriage may become far more common than it has been in the last thirty years. There has also been a marked decrease in homosexual promiscuity in some regions such as San Francisco since the high rate of infection. A nationally representative 1989 survey by the National Opinion Research Center at the University of Chicago indicates high rates of monogamy—sex with one partner. They also report that most singles have rejected a lifestyle of numerous sex partners and casual encounters. Men and women are taking AIDS tests to assure their potential partners that they are free of AIDS. On the other hand, recent polls have suggested that adolescents ages fifteen to nineteen are still quite sexually active and are not practicing "safe sex." The University of Chicago may not have reached this group. More research is required to clarify whether there are important age differences and how age is related to attitudes about sexual monogamy and sexually transmitted diseases.

Despite the burgeoning literature on sexuality, the myths, the anxieties, and the general overemphasis on sexual attractiveness and performance in Western society, the job does get done. Men and women manage to overcome their fears, make commitments, and carry on the task of reproducing the species. It is interesting that with so much research on sex, there is so little information about the psychology of reproduction. Information about how people respond to pregnancy and childbirth is sketchy at best. Only three or four major studies have been done of the subject, based on interviews with limited numbers of women.

Pregnancy and Childbirth as Psychological Events

In 1977, Myra Leifer published an in-depth study of the reactions of twenty first-time mothers to pregnancy and childbirth. She conceptualized pregnancy as a series of developmental tasks, each representing a unique stress or conflict to which the pregnant mother must adapt for further maturation to occur.

Leifer found that those women who viewed motherhood as a chance for personal growth rather than a symbol of security or status were most likely to experience pregnancy as a positive state. She also found, however, that regardless of the degree of satisfaction a woman felt with pregnancy or with her own body image prior to pregnancy, the body changes associated with pregnancy evoked negative feelings. Those with the most positive attitudes toward pregnancy did not feel dissatisfied until the last trimester of childbearing, but eventually all of the women reported some negative feelings.

Many of the women Leifer interviewed were particularly embarrassed by the sexual implications of the changes in their bodies, especially during the first few months after childbirth, when the experience of fetal movements and the extra attention accorded a pregnant woman were no longer available. Leifer found very strong evidence for a general trend toward more negative mood

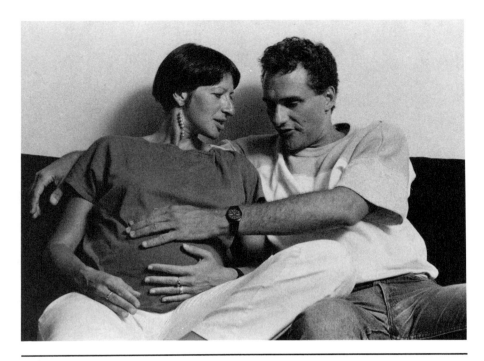

Despite the need to cope with radically changed body image, pregnancy can bring bursts of vitality and a heightened sense of well-being.

tone after the birth of the child, even in those women who made the best adjustments to pregnancy. She also reported these feelings persisted through at least the first seven months after the child's birth.

Leifer found that maternal anxiety during pregnancy, about the fetus, the self, or both, is a common experience. Contrary to much professional opinion, she argues that such anxiety about the fetus is not neurotic but is a normal part of the development of bonding between the unborn fetus and the mother. Leifer also believes that the bonding process is reflected by the pregnant woman's preoccupation with herself and her pregnancy, by her declining investment in the external world, and by a need to be alone, to withdraw, especially in stressful situations. According to Leifer, disengagement from social life accompanied by increased focus on the fetus is typical of the second trimester of pregnancy.

Leifer's sample also showed increased emotional vulnerability, marked mood swings, tension, and irritability during the last trimester of pregnancy. Yet there were also intensified feelings of well-being at times during the last few months. Immediately after birth, many of the mothers experienced great elation and satisfaction at the birth process itself. Within a few days, however, feelings of depression and anxiety were most common.

For more than two-thirds of the sample, the postpartum period was a very negative one, characterized by irritability and feelings of isolation and depression. In all, the immediate postpartum period seemed to be best characterized as a time of intense emotional stress. After about two months of motherhood, these feelings of depression and anxiety seemed to be replaced by boredom with the routine of child care. Seven months after childbirth, the mood of the women in Leifer's sample was still predominantly negative.

The transition to parenthood, Leifer contends, must be viewed as a period of emotional upheaval that is not necessarily related to emotional growth. Although some of the women in the sample did mature during this period, some did not. Whereas some experienced an increased sense of completeness as a person, some never became greatly attached to their children or enjoyed motherhood much. Leifer notes that a positive adaptation to pregnancy seems to predict good mothering behavior, and the degree of affective involvement a woman feels with the fetus by the third month of pregnancy is a relatively reliable predictor of maternal feelings. Even among those who made the best adjustments, however, feelings of depression, isolation, and increasing dissatisfaction and boredom with child care were common. Furthermore, the majority expressed moderate to high degrees of stress over general changes in their lifestyles. They were concerned about lack of household help, curtailment of their personal freedom, and changes in their marital relationships.

In a more recent treatment, Gabriele Gloger-Tippelt (1983) agrees that pregnancy should be considered a series of developmental tasks; however, she identifies four specific periods:

1. Disruption (zero to twelve weeks): A period during which the most radical changes occur and women worry about the termination of their educations and careers, decreased autonomy, deterioration of their appearance, and increased economic responsibilities. This developmental stage is difficult, because radical hormonal and physical changes occur as well as changes in how a woman views herself and her life.

2. Adaptation (twelve to twenty weeks): A time of greater stability, when there is a general reduction in negative physical symptoms. A strong positive force often emerges with the decision not to terminate even an unwanted pregnancy; emotional liability, anxiety, and depression usually decline.

3. Centering (twenty to thirty-two weeks): Now the mother's energies are focused on the child. Fetal movement or "quickening" occurs; the concrete evidence of new life often produces delight. On a social level, pregnant women begin wearing maternity clothes and take on the "pregnancy identity" (Wolkind & Zajicek, 1981), evoking all the social stereotypes. Other people often respond to women in this phase as pregnant first, and as women second.

4. Anticipation and Preparation (thirty-two weeks to birth): This time is one of rehearsal. Anticipatory socialization for birth occurs, and, as Brim and Ryff (1980) (see Chapter 2) suggest, anticipatory coping is associated with positive birth experiences. Women also may experience concern over the coming dissociation from the child.

Age, previous history of miscarriages or stillbirth, motivation for child-bearing, marital status, the father's attitude, and a huge number of social factors affect the individual experience of these stages.

Sensation, Perception, and Psychomotor Skills

The relationships between biological phenomena and psychological development in young adulthood are as yet poorly understood. Even in the study of types of development much more closely linked to biological change, **age-related** events have not been easily identified. Research on **sensation** and **perception** in young adulthood illustrates the point.

Sensation and Perception

Perception depends not only on sensation but on a number of other factors. These factors include the interpretation and analysis of stimulation. Sensations are interpreted and analyzed in terms of the perceiver's perceptual stage of development, prior experience, demands and expectations of the present, and a variety of individual or situational factors. These factors range from the health and personality makeup of the perceiver to weather conditions and the use of glasses. Perception can best be conceptualized as an active, constructive process (Neisser, 1976). Some of the most intriguing examples of the differences between sensation and perception come from studies that compare child to adult perception. For example, although both children and adults probably see certain things in similar ways, like the blue of the sky, they interpret this information very differently. Unlike adults, children often assume that the sky exists someplace far above their heads; it is impossible to convince them that the sky (or the atmosphere) comes all the way down to the ground (much less that it circles the globe).

Tests of visual perception are many and varied. They include examinations of spatial orientation, visual illusions, part-whole differentiation, perceptual closure, speed of recognition, causal illusions, and perspective taking. Studies of spatial orientation often require people to give responses such as the judgment of verticality for a luminiscent rod in a dark room when one's body has been tilted to one side. Visual illusions include geometric optical illusions, such as an apparent change in the length of a line when the ends of an arrow point away from a line, as shown in Figure 3.3. Part-whole differentiation involves the separation of an item from its background or context, as in a picture con-

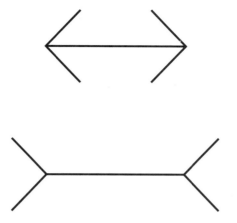

Figure 3.3 The Müller-Lyer illusion.

taining hidden figures. Perceptual closure tests focus on the recognition of incomplete forms. Speed of recognition is measured by presenting stimuli for extremely short periods (for example, for 0.01 second) and measuring the extent to which a subject can accurately describe the materials presented. Causal illusion tests show to what extent people see causes when no cause is present or when no presumed causal agent produces a cause. Causal insensitivity is tested by seeing when people fail to detect actual causes. Perspective-taking measures both apply to how objects would appear from a different viewing place and to how other people view each other's actions (Commons & Rodriguez, 1990).

Peak performance on experimental tests of perception of simple physical objects occurs during young adulthood (Kline & Schieber, 1985). Some evidence suggests that slight changes occur during early adulthood in performance on tasks involving part-whole differentiation (Comalli, 1962, 1965, 1970), the perception of tridimensionality (Plude, Millberg, et al., 1986) and spatial orientation (Comalli, Wapner, & Werner, 1959). Some evidence also shows that the complex causation (Armon, 1984; Commons & Richards, 1984) and social perspective taking do not fully develop until midlife (Rodriguez, 1991).

Some of the most extensive theorizing on the matter of perceptual change in adulthood is based on research concerning the propensity of people in different age groups to perceive certain of the visual illusions. For example, the effect of the Müller-Lyer illusion, as shown in Figure 3.3, declines throughout childhood and adolescence, plateauing between the ages of twenty and forty. On the other hand, if the Müller-Lyer illusion is presented sequentially (that is, if the line with the arrow pointing away is presented first and the line with the arrow pointing inward is presented alone later on), the illusion is perceived more strongly during adolescence and young adulthood. One group of researchers believes that the declining effect of certain illusions reflects subtle deterioration in sensitivity to patterned light, whereas the increased effect of sequentially presented illusions depends on one's ability to integrate perceptions over time and is a result of increasingly sophisticated intellectual functioning (Pollack & Atkeson, 1978).

Psychomotor Skills

Psychomotor skills require dexterity and agility and are generally believed to improve with practice. They vary from the mundane (running, skipping, dressing) to the sublime (gymnastics, ballet). These skills, which usually involve a pattern of movement, are influenced by the functioning of the central nervous system (Birren, 1964; Birren & Renner, 1977; Birren, Woods, & Williams, 1980). Psychomotor abilities, such as typing or tap dancing, can be automatic, but optimal performance depends on complex sequences of action in which timing is often a critical factor (Welford, 1977). These abilities eventually decline with age, and although the changes are almost imperceptible in young adulthood, some of the simple components of psychomotor abilities, such as speed, do begin to age.

Birren (1964) noted that among the "most reliable facts shown through research on human aging is the trend toward psychomotor slowness." Tests of reaction time in young adulthood foreshadow later psychomotor problems. **Reaction time,** the speed with which a person responds to a stimulus that initiates a response, increases noticeably between the ages of twenty and twenty-five (Salthouse, 1985b). Bromley (1974) estimated that a 17 percent increase in reaction time occurred between the ages of twenty and forty. Cerella's (1990) model suggests that the slowing is due to random cell deaths, lengthening the path a signal has to travel to produce the response.

Most of the psychomotor slowness observed in older people is probably a product of increased reaction time, because there are no apparent increases in the time it takes to complete a movement once a subject begins (Birren & Renner, 1977; Salthouse, 1985b). Furthermore, the time required by older subjects to perform psychomotor tasks can be reduced if the subject is warned that the stimulus marking the beginning of a trial is about to appear (Botwinick, 1959, 1981). Such warning signals are known to decrease reaction time. As with the other documented changes in physical capacities, the decline of the sensory systems and increase in reaction time are seldom important practical considerations until rather late in life. With increasing sophistication and experience, most adults learn to compensate for the gradual decline that accompanies age. "With a little extra effort or attention to particular features of the task, the performance may be maintained or even improved in the presence of physical limitation" (Birren, 1964).

Throughout young adult life, we learn to compensate for whatever physical changes occur. We are more careful about the level of illumination when reading. We squint at distant objects or get glasses, turn toward the source of a sound—all without seeming to notice. A tremendous amount of learning takes place during this stage of life, although little of it occurs in the classroom or

Finely tuned psychomotor skills enhance the quality of human life greatly by their contributions to the mundane necessities like dressing and driving and their role in great craftsmanship and art.

through any formal channels. Learning encompasses mastery of the major roles of adulthood, from spouse and lover to parent and citizen. We learn how to purchase a car and a house, the differences between term and whole life insurance, and, perhaps, how to balance a budget. Whereas there is no research on the kind of learning people do as young adults, a good deal of interest centers on the development of **cognition** and intelligence.

Intelligence and Cognition

The fundamental fact about the Greeks was that they had to use their minds. The ancient priests had said: "Thus far and no farther. We set the limits of thought." The Greeks said: "All things are to be examined and called into question. There are no limits."

—Edith Hamilton

In the sense that the Greeks may have been the first human beings to set no limits on thought, to call all things into question, they may have been the first modern adults. Actively questioning is certainly one of the hallmarks of the mature thinker. In fact, in perhaps the only cross-cultural studies of maturity Heath (1965, 1977) demonstrated that reflective, imaginative thinking that is clear and relatively free of repression is universally recognized as a sign of maturity.

Questions about how thinking differs from one person to another or from one period of life to another have captured the interest of many researchers. Such questions form the basis for the **qualitative approach** to the study of intellectual development. The work on postformal operations reviewed in Chapter 2 exemplifies the qualitative approach, which will be discussed later in this chapter. A very different point of view can be found in the study of specific skills like verbal fluency, memory, speed, and tests of mathematical or spatial abilities. Researchers who are interested in performance on standardized tests of intelligence like the Wechsler Adult Intelligence Scale or the Primary Mental Abilities Test are said to take a **quantitative approach** to the problem.

The Quantitative Approach

The quantitative approach usually assumes the existence of a variety of factors or abilities that account for the differences in people's performance on standardized intelligence tests.

Schaie and the Primary Mental Abilities Test   One standardized intelligence test, the Thurstone Primary Mental Abilities Test, reflects as many as sixty different factors or abilities grouped in five major categories: verbal meaning, reasoning, space, number, and word fluency. Verbal meaning is defined as the ability to understand ideas expressed in words and is tapped by items that require people to identify synonyms and antonyms. Items designed to test reasoning usually present a logical series of numbers or letters and require the person being tested to supply a missing member of a sequence. Items that require people to think about objects, for instance, to pick the mirror image of a sample figure, define the category called *space*. Number refers to items that test the ability to handle simple arithmetic problems. Word fluency is the ability to write and speak easily. Table 3.2 presents an outline of how the primary mental abilities have been defined.

Thurstone's test has formed the backbone of an exciting series of research projects conducted by Schaie and his associates. These projects have been designed using the sequential methodology discussed in Chapter 1, which involves presenting the same test or measure to the same group of cohorts at several different times of measurement. Data from these studies show clearly that early adulthood is the time of peak performance on all five of Thurstone's factors (Schaie, 1977, 1979; Schaie & Labouvie-Vief, 1974). Furthermore,

Table 3.2 The primary mental abilities

V.   **Verbal comprehension:** The principal factor in such tests as reading comprehension, verbal analogies, disarranged sentences, verbal reasoning, and proverb matching. It is most adequately measured by vocabulary tests.

W.   **Word fluency:** Found in such tests as anagrams, rhyming, or naming words in a given category (for example, boys' names or words beginning with the letter T).

N.   **Number:** Most closely identified with speed and accuracy of simple arithmetic computation.

S.   **Space (or spatial orientation):** May represent two distinct factors, one covering perception of fixed spatial or geometric relations, the other manipulatory visualizations in which changed positions or transformations must be visualized.

M.   **Associative memory:** Found principally in tests demanding rote memory for paired associates. There is some evidence to suggest that this factor may reflect the extent to which memory crutches are utilized. The evidence is against the presence of a broader factor through all memory tests. Other restricted memory factors, such as memory for temporal sequences and for spatial position, have been suggested by some investigations.

P.   **Perceptual speed:** Quick and accurate grasping of visual details, similarities, and differences.

I (or R).   **Induction (or general reasoning):** Early researchers proposed an inductive and a deductive factor. The latter was best measured by tests of syllogistic reasoning and the former by tests requiring the subject to find a rule, as in a number series completion test. Evidence for the deductive factor, however, was much weaker than for the inductive. Moreover, other investigators suggested a general reasoning factor, best measured by arithmetic reasoning tests.

SOURCE: Reprinted with permission of Macmillan Publishing Company from *Psychological Testing,* 6th ed., by Anne Anastasi. Copyright © 1988 by Anne Anastasi.

Schaie has argued these studies show that age decrement is not nearly as great or as uniform as the popular stereotype of old age suggests. The impact of cohort differences in early, cross-sectional research on intelligence in adulthood led many researchers to believe that there might be irreversible decrement in intelligence over time, according to Schaie. He has contested this point of view and labeled the entire period from thirty to sixty the *responsible stage.* Throughout early and middle adulthood, Schaie contends, people maintain high levels of intellectual performance, particularly when they lead complex lives. After age seventy, traditional measures of intelligence like the Primary Mental Abilities Test do show some decline, but Schaie does not believe that the Primary

Mental Abilities Test necessarily reflects the abilities that define intelligence during later life.

Working from studies like those by Schaie, researchers Willis and Baltes (1980) have applied the idea that age-graded influences, history-graded influences, and nonnormative critical life events each contribute to intellectual performance in adulthood. They do not believe that age-graded influences are of primary importance.

Age-graded influences are based on the changing biological and experiential foundations of thought and behavior and are highly correlated with chronological age. These events include biological aging as well as many familial, educational, and work-related events that almost always occur in certain periods of the life cycle. For example, the birth of a first child almost always occurs before the fortieth birthday of the mother, whereas learning to read and write nearly always occurs before age ten. All of the biological events associated with age, from the development of the spinal cord in the fetus to the deteriorating cell function in later life, are included in this category.

Willis and Baltes (1980) contend that social and historical events are much more powerful explanations of whatever declines occur in intellectual performance. History-graded influences include events like the Great Depression of the 1930s or the education push that followed the launching of Sputnik by the Soviets in the 1950s. Intellectual performance throughout life will depend on the amount and quality of education a person has, and the importance he or she has placed on continued, high-level performance. Social attitudes and historical events shape educational opportunities and individual values about intellectual performance. Nonnormative critical life events include opportunities that affect one person at a time, such as foreign travel, an automobile accident, or a death in the family. Nonnormative experiences present the opportunity for special learning, as is the case for the adolescent who must go to work because a parent dies.

Baltes's Dual-process Model of Intelligence   The Baltes research group (Baltes, Dittmann-Kohli, & Dixon, 1984; Smith, Dixon, & Baltes, 1987, 1989) has argued for a **dual-process model** of adult intelligence. Different classes of abilities show different courses of development over the life span, according to the dual-process model. Some abilities may in fact decline, many remain stable, and some may improve. Improvement is likely to occur, Baltes argues, in the **pragmatics of intelligence** as opposed to the **mechanics.** The mechanics of intelligence include basic tasks like perceiving relationships, classification, and logical reasoning. Pragmatics, on the other hand, involve the application of intelligence, or social wisdom. Baltes has defined wisdom as "good judgment about important but uncertain matters of life" (Baltes, Dittmann-Kohli, & Dixon, 1984, p. 66), a notion similar to the one encountered in Chapter 2. For example, Smith, Dixon, & Baltes (1987, 1989) have examined expertise in life planning, an aspect of wisdom.

Baltes's dual-process model of intelligence has been strongly influenced both by those who have studied cognition from the organismic view of thinkers like Piaget and by the very strongly empirical work of John Cattell and his student-colleague John Horn (Horn, 1978, 1982; Horn & Cattell, 1982; Horn, Donaldson, & Engstrom, 1981). Cattell and Horn believe that human intellectual functioning reflects a huge number of abilities, but they have been particularly concerned with two rather general types that they call fluid and crystallized intelligence.

Horn's Crystallized and Fluid Intelligence   Both fluid and crystallized intelligence are thought to be influenced by hereditary factors as well as environmental circumstances. **Crystallized intelligence,** however, is said to be most strongly shaped by the formal, institutionalized aspects of culture. In other words, education, social status, occupational requirements, and the like determine how people will perform on tests of crystallized intelligence. Crystallized intelligence includes many of the skills associated with verbal scales on standard intelligence tests. Examples include vocabulary, general information, the ability to generate new uses for familiar objects (How many ways can you use a brick?), and measures of verbal fluency, like the number of synonyms and connotations produced in response to a single word.

The tasks that Horn has used to measure **fluid intelligence** are very different from those that reflect crystallized intelligence. Some are like the tasks described for the space and reasoning scales of the Thurstone Test of Primary Mental Abilities, but some cannot be measured by way of paper and pencil. Horn (Horn, Donaldson, & Engstrom, 1981) defines fluid intelligence as those abilities that are dependent on the "memory involved in holding information in awareness while also manipulating it or doing other things . . . also, the processes at work in initially making sense of information, as when one intentionally classifies information" (pp. 73–74).

To illustrate, Horn might present a matrix of letters such as

```
YOUA
REAC
UTIE
```

The matrix is flashed on a screen for only a fraction of a second and the viewer is asked to recall as many letters as possible. If the viewer sees the words embedded in the matrix, he or she is likely to recall all twelve letters with ease. Meaningful material is stored more effectively than nonsense, but one has to produce meaning from the matrix. Examples of other tasks Horn has developed appear in Figure 3.4.

Horn's most controversial assertion has been the argument that fluid intelligence declines significantly throughout adult life, beginning in late adolescence. He bases this conclusion on at least a dozen studies from his laboratory

Fluid intelligence

Matrices. Indicate which figure comes next:

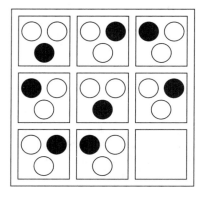 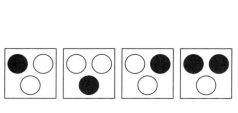

Letter series. Figure out which letter comes next in a series:

ADGJMP?

Topology. Find a figure on right where a dot can be placed in the same relation to triangle, squares, and circle as in example on left.

Crystallized intelligence

Esoteric analogies. Indicate which should go in the space.
Socrates is to Aristotle as Sophocles is to _____?

Remote associations. What one word is well associated with bathtub, prizefighting, and wedding?

Judgment. You notice that a fire has just started in a crowded cafe. What should one do to prevent death and injury?

Figure 3.4 Examples of test items that measure fluid and crystallized intelligence.

SOURCE: J. L. Horn, G. Donaldson, and B. Engstrom, "Apprehension, Memory, and Fluid Intelligence in Adulthood," *Research on Aging*, 3 (1981): 33–84.

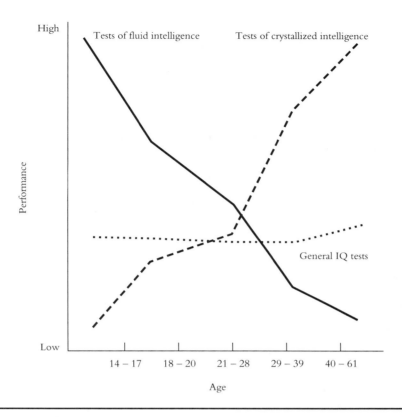

Figure 3.5 Performance of various age groups on tests used to define fluid, crystallized, and general intelligence.

SOURCE: Horn, 1970, p. 963.

representing eleven different samples of males observed between the years 1966 and 1982. Typical results from these reports appear in Figure 3.5.

According to Horn, crystallized intelligence may increase with age, at least in certain individuals. It does not undergo significant decline with age. As Figure 3.5 illustrates, the rise in crystallized intelligence often matches the decline in fluid intelligence. Furthermore, Horn believes that changes in fluid and crystallized intelligence over the life span are probably reflected in the nervous system.

Because fluid intelligence declines and crystallized intelligence does not, Horn has contended they must be associated with different parts of the brain. He has argued that the deterioration of the parts of the brain governing alertness and attention probably accounts for decline in fluid intelligence. Crystallized intelligence, he maintains, is probably associated with the storing and cross-referencing of information in the neocortex. With age, the neural nets that represent ideas, memories, and facts become more elaborated and more easily activated by remotely related ideas or facts. This process of elaboration accounts for the rise in crystallized intelligence in some individuals. In other words, one thought leads to another more and more often as people grow old (Horn, 1978).

At this point, some very general conclusions can be drawn from the quantitative study of human intelligence. For instance, as Schaie, Baltes, and Horn agree, intelligence is probably best conceptualized as a number, perhaps a rather large number, of different abilities. These abilities may overlap to some extent, yet they are probably shaped by different influences and may even be inherited separately, just as are height and weight. In other words, intelligence is *multidimensional*. Moreover, it seems that intellectual development is *multidirectional;* that is, different abilities may develop and age in different ways. The identification and description of different abilities and the patterns associated with each will, undoubtedly, keep researchers busy for some time to come.

Yet the quantitative approach is only one of several ways researchers have studied intellectual performance in adulthood. Other writers and researchers are equally busy observing, defining, and describing qualitative differences in intellectual performance, focusing on the process by which an individual solves a problem rather than on the accuracy or speed with which a solution is produced.

The Qualitative Approach

The qualitative approach proceeds from the assumption that there are stages in the growth of intelligence and that the way people approach problems at one stage is substantially different from the approach they use at another. The notion of stages implies that cognitive functions become more hierarchically complex as development takes place. That means the thoughts one is capable of at a higher stage allow one to "link up" or organize thoughts one was capable of at lower stages of development in ways that allow new perspectives to emerge.

Consider a concrete operational example in taking the perspective of another person. Almost all young adults successfully perform this task. The act of imagining how action will be viewed by another only requires you to imagine two causal sequences from the lower stage and to link them together at the higher stage. Let's say I want to know if the boss will give me a raise. I try to complete a causal chain from the perspective of my boss. There were two stimuli for my request: I was told that if I increase profits, I would get a raise. I have increased profits, thus my behavior is asking for a raise. The outcome event in the causal sequence is whether my boss will grant me the raise.

Likewise, I thought through the role of my boss. The stimulus is someone asking for something, and requests are granted if they follow company rules. The behavior is granting or not granting the request. The problem for me in taking my boss's perspective is to link the two perspectives. This requires thinking it through at the next higher stage. Thinking at the higher stage allows me to see my request as a stimulus for my boss's behavior. It also allows me to link my boss's behavior of granting the request to the outcome of my behavior of increased profits and making the request. At this higher stage, I am able to predict that the behavior of requesting the raise in the context of my having increased profits and the policy of giving raises for increasing profits should lead to the outcome of getting the raise.

Note that the rules or principles governing action change with stage. People exhibit different ranges of stages during different periods of the life span. Qualitative researchers are likely to study the responses people make in complex problem-solving situations and are usually interested in finding out why a person makes a particular response, that is, in the verbal explanations and justifications a person gives for the responses.

The qualitative approach to intellectual development is epitomized by the work of Piaget on the development of formal reasoning in childhood and adolescence. That approach is also represented by the post-Piagetians. See Chapter 2 for a discussion of the work of Riegel (1973) and his descendants (Basseches, 1984a, 1984b) as well as Commons and Richards. Others have extended Piaget's scheme to include a set of postformal operations (Arlin, 1983; Armon, 1984, 1989; Basseches, 1984; Commons & Richards, 1984a, 1984b; Kohlberg, 1990; Labouvie-Vief, 1984, 1990; Rybash, Hoyer, & Roodin, 1986; Pascual-Leone, 1990; Sinnott, 1989).

The three most common stages of adult reasoning are **abstract operations** (beginning formal), **formal operations,** and **systematic operations** (beginning postformal). An extension of the example of "asking for a raise" is used to illustrate these stages in social situations. In abstract-stage perspective taking, I would consider how the boss's behavior could effect additional outcomes for my behavior. I would think about what bosses in general would do. Formal-operational perspective taking would lead me to observe whether or not the particular boss in question usually keeps promises. With systematic-stage perspective taking (beginning postformal operations), I would look at what is going on in the company as a whole. This would include finding out what the boss's power was to grant raises and how the overall performance of my particular unit affects that power. I would consider my standing in the unit with respect to others and how a raise might affect them and the operation of the unit.

Formal operations represent the thinking most typical of young adulthood from Piaget's perspective, permitting people to apply fully mature logic to a huge number of problems and situations. Adults can think logically about the possible as well as the real and can use concepts like probability and chance to explain events. Adults can systematically generate small numbers of alternative solutions to problems and then test each of those solutions in turn, using any negative information they discover to eliminate more alternatives. This kind of thinking is what Piaget described, and he believed that the emergence of formal operations represented a universal pinnacle of adult thought.

As mentioned in Chapter 2, a number of researchers have challenged the notion that formal operations is the final, most mature stage of adult reasoning. And, on another front, adult developmental research has challenged the notion that formal operations are universal within Western culture.

The development of formal operations is facilitated by both cultural and individual factors, formal and informal education probably being the most important. Cross-cultural empirical studies have shown via standard Piagetian tasks (Dasen, 1981) that although formal operations are not found in everyday nonliterate cultures (Ure & Colinvaux, 1985), the sequence of stages prior to formal thought may be universal. Most recently, however, researchers have shown formal-operational reasoning in the moral domain in leaders in other countries (Galaz-Fontes, Ceron-Esquivel, Commons, Richard, Hauser, & Gutheil, 1988; Galaz-Fontes & Commons, 1989, 1990; Hernandez-Morelos, 1990).

Of course, one need not go to some isolated corner of the world to observe that many adults behave in intellectually naive ways. Anyone who has been to Las Vegas or Atlantic City can testify that many grownup people do not seem to understand or apply concepts like chance and probability very well. Some people really do believe that a particular pair of dice is lucky. Others become upset when another player at the blackjack table draws an extra card (thereby taking a card that might have been a loser for the dealer). Given behavior like this, many researchers have questioned whether formal operations appear regularly and to what extent they may appear in one arena (e.g., verbal reasoning), but not another (e.g., understanding probability).

Generally, education, westernization, and industrialization are important cultural predictors of the emergence of formal operations (Ashton, 1975; Price-Williams, 1981). From Sardinia to New Guinea, and from Australia to Zambia, most adults do not progress beyond concrete operations or abstract operations (beginning formal operations) unless they live in very complex, modern settings or have either formal or informal education. Informal education could consist of apprenticing at diagnosing and fixing machinery or being a political leader. Concrete operations rely on accurate perception of the external world, and include the ability to classify objects. They do not produce very abstract thinking. The concrete thinker does not use variables so does not consider hypothetical situations abstractly and systematically and cannot solve problems that assume counter-to-fact propositions. For instance, the concrete thinker cannot reason systematically about what people in general would think about having a shaved head.

The argument has been made, however, that formal operations may not be more adaptive than concrete operations in some settings despite the fact that they permit more complex, abstract thinking (Greenfield, 1976). For instance, Eskimos have a large number of words for different kinds of snow. The concrete operations associated with classification and categorization permit people to make very fine discriminations about their reality, such as the distinctions between wet and dry snow. If one were trapped in the snow, it would be quite useful to know such distinctions and the survival techniques best suited to different types of snow. On the other hand, in such an environment it would not be very useful to be able to explain the development of snow or derive the formula for the speed of a falling snowflake. Nor would it make any sense to think about how it might be if there were no snow (a counter-to-fact proposition). Vigilant, concrete observation and classification has some distinct advantages over more abstract, even scientific thought, when one is trying to survive in a snowstorm.

Not that formal operations are necessarily impractical, though they can be applied to everyday problems. For instance, formal operations might well generate some interesting uses for snow.

Even in industrialized societies, however, substantial numbers of adults do not exhibit formal operations, although most adolescents show at least some formal thinking (Kuhn, 1989; Kuhn, Amsel & O'Loughlin, 1988; Kuhn, Langer, Kohlberg, & Haan, 1977; Labouvie-Vief, 1985). The fact is, most people manage to live from one day to the next without worrying about the real versus the possible, or without working through hypothetical situations. For example, review Box 3.1 and then consider how rarely one has to deal with such problems.

When students in an undergraduate psychology class are presented with problems like the one in Box 3.1, they often report a sense of working very hard as they proceed through the verbal reasoning required to solve such problems. Certainly, they do not need to work that hard to get by in their daily lives, and it may be that people do not spontaneously develop or maintain formal operations unless they are required to by their occupations, their interests, or the complexities of their lifestyles.

To go beyond formal operations to systematic, metasystematic operations, or postformal dialectical thinking is somewhat uncommon. Although no random sample study has been done, it has been estimated that about 15–25 percent reach the systematic stage, and 1–2 percent the metasystematic stage (Demetriou & Efklides, 1985; Richards & Commons, 1984). Few people are strongly attracted to contradiction and paradox or are able to raise new and interesting problems. Conflict and contradiction are part of most important human affairs. There are always two sides to a story, two or more points of view, two realities in human interaction. It is much easier to ignore the complexities of any social problem. Nowhere is this more evident than in the study of moral thinking. The same act can be considered morally wrong one time and right another, depending on the motivation of the actor and the circumstances of the act. Hence, the study of moral reasoning has provided an inter-

---

Box 3.1 Some problems requiring formal operations

Read the statements about the two problems carefully. In each case, try to determine which of the conclusions are false and which are true. Circle the true statements.

Statements:

1. If the caretaker was an accomplice, then the door of the apartment was open, or the burglar entered through the basement.
2. If the burglar had an accomplice, the accomplice came in a car.
3. If the burglary took place at midnight, then the caretaker was an accomplice.

One has been able to prove that the door of the apartment was not open and that the burglar did not enter through the basement.

Conclusions:

a. The caretaker was not an accomplice.
b. The caretaker was an accomplice.
c. The burglary took place at midnight.
d. One cannot know if the burglary took place at midnight.

Statements:

1. You are going out with friends, or you are passing through the neighboring village.
2. If you are going out with friends, then you are going to the mountains or you are going fishing.
3. Finally, you are not going to the mountains and you are not going fishing.

Conclusions:

a. You are going out with friends.
b. You are not going out with friends.
c. You are passing through the neighboring village.
d. You are not passing through the neighboring village.
e. One cannot know whether you are passing through the neighboring village.

SOURCE: Anton Lawson, Arizona State University, Tempe, Arizona (personal communication, 1981).

esting example of how qualitative changes in cognitive development might make a difference in how people respond to social circumstances.

Moral Reasoning and Behavior

The study of moral judgment refers to the examination of the reasons people give, when faced with a moral dilemma, for the decisions about right and wrong. As approached by Lawrence Kohlberg and his associates, moral judgment is assessed by responses to a set of standard dilemmas. For instance, subjects are presented with a problem that requires a choice between the right to own property and the right to life. Kohlberg believes that the experiences of adult life play a critical role in the emergence of the most sophisticated forms of judgment. He has argued that maturation directs the growth of the intellect in childhood but that social and psychological forces are more important after adolescence (Kohlberg, 1973).

Box 3.2 presents an outline of the stages Kohlberg has proposed, beginning in early childhood with preconventional judgment and culminating in postconventional thought during middle age. Kohlberg based much of his thinking on an intensive longitudinal study of fifty subjects from the Chicago area (Kohlberg, 1984). The study began in 1958 and continues into the present. His belief in the importance of adult experience is partly based on his findings that not one of the subjects in his study appeared to achieve postconventional thought before the age of twenty-three, and that, even at age thirty, not one was predominantly functioning at the highest stages (either stage 5 or 6) (Kohlberg, 1973). In her longitudinal study of forty-three male and female subjects, Cheryl Armon (1991) found five subjects reasoning at stage 5 and above after age twenty-seven. The average age of the subjects reasoning at stage 5 and above was around forty-five. Figures 3.6 and 3.7 present her data. Her longitudinal research indicates that improvement continues between ages forty and fifty as suggested in Figure 3.6. Cross-sectional data has also indicated that moral judgment may continue to develop through age sixty-five. Figure 3.7 shows that this improvement was correlated with getting more education and not with age itself.

Kohlberg's work has evoked a great deal of related research and a fair share of criticism. At first it was thought that postconventional reasoning did not appear cross-culturally (Edwards, 1980). More recent work has reported the sequence of his stages in every culture studied (Colby & Kohlberg, 1987; Snarey, 1985). But postconventional performance is difficult to find in traditional rather than modern cultures. More recently, stage 5 reasoning has been reported in several other cultures, including Greece (Demetriou, 1990; Demetriou & Efklides, 1985), Mexico (Galaz-Fontes, Pacheco-Sanchez, Sierra-Morales, Commons, Gutheil, & Hauser, 1989), Taiwan (Li & Liu, 1991), and

Box 3.2 Kohlberg's proposed stages of moral reasoning

Preconventional Period

Few adults still reason at moral stages 1, 1/2, and 2. They consider such reasoning inadequate because it fails to fulfill conventional adult norms.

Conventional Period

This period begins at the onset of post-elementary school education and extends across the life span of all but a small portion of the population. This period generates the conventional norms of adulthood.

Moral Stage 3, *the Group stage.*   Actions are justified in terms of the reputation and characterization of the individuals or groups that are involved. People and groups can be good or bad, nice or nasty. Action is often judged on the basis of individuals' or groups' underlying sentiments or motives. Role and person may be confused.

Moral Stage 3/4, *the Bureaucratic stage.*   Actions are justified as fair and good if they are logical and abstract. Bureaucratic norms, laws, rules, and regulations guide behavior and are seen as "given;" they are not seen as responsive to individuals or particular situations. Role and person are no longer confused.

Moral Stage 4, *the Institutional stage.*   Actions are judged as to whether they preserve (or destroy) a system—or a society. Norms, laws, rules, and regulations form a logically coherent system. Actions are judged in terms of how they effect one's individual role and status within the system, as well as on the system's capability to function. Hence, there is a tension between societal and personal rights on one hand, and societal and personal duties on the other. For the individual, part of this tension is a conflict between independence from and dependence on both others and the system.

Postconventional Period

This period begins sometime after adolescence. Fully postconventional thinking and action appear only after early childhood (Colby & Kohlberg, 1987) and in a very small portion of society's members.

Moral Stage 5, *the Universal stage.*   Actions are justified on the basis of universal abstract principles. Many such principles can be found in the works of philosophic, political, and religious thinkers. The principles apply to all, irrespective of who is affected. Due process and social contracts are basic to changing the social system.

Moral Stage 6, *the Co-constructive stage.*   Actions are justified by co-constructing a moral framework with all the participants in an issue. The co-construction requires genuine real dialogue rather than the strategic jockeying for advantage quite often found earlier.

SOURCE: Based on Kohlberg (Colby & Kohlberg, 1987; Kohlberg, Levine & Hewer, 1983; Kohlberg, 1987) and his students (Commons & Grotzer, 1991; Sonnert & Commons, submitted).

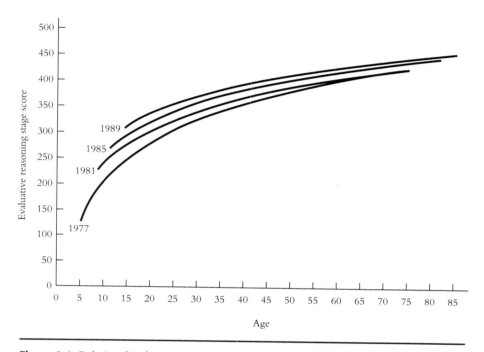

Figure 3.6 Relationship between age and evaluative reasoning stage scores at four test times (Ns=41,38,36,32).

SOURCE: Armon, 1991.

India (Vasasudev, 1987; Vasasudev & Hummell 1987). Even in this culture, most people do not show principled moral judgment. Stages 3, 3/4, and 4 represent the most usual forms of reasoning in America.

In the last work he undertook before his death, Kohlberg (Kohlberg, 1986, 1990; Kohlberg & Ryncarz, 1990) revised his postformal stages and realigned them with Piaget's. This work focused on how people make a transition from one stage to the next. It was related to Piaget's dialectical four-step transition model of changing stages (Flavell, 1963). The four steps that appear to be required are as follows:

Step A: Subjects attend to only one aspect of a problem (absolutism).

Step B: Subjects begin to alternate between attending to one aspect of the problem and another (relativism).

Step AB: A cognitive conjunction of the two aspects of the problem takes place (synthesis).

Step A with B: From the subjects' conjunction of the two aspects of the problem, they discover new relationships and interrelationships.

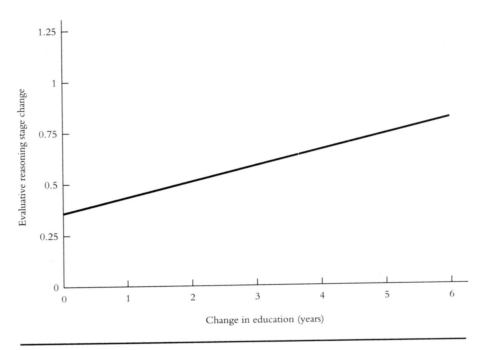

Figure 3.7 Relationship between change in education and changes in evaluative reasoning stage.

SOURCE: Armon, 1991.

During the transition from one stage to another, people take a *relativistic* position. For example, during the relativist transition from stage 4 to stage 5, the thinker sees that values vary from one social system to another, and is willing to take a perspective different from the one represented by his or her own society, but does not see any universal moral good or bad (Kohlberg & Candee, 1984).

The shift from stage 4 to stage 5 requires a change in perspective from law-abiding to law-giving. It requires that one develop a personal set of moral principles that is essentially free of cultural bias. Kohlberg believes that John Stuart Mill's **utilitarian principle** and Kant's **principle of justice** represent universal good. The utilitarian principle states that what is morally best is what maximizes human happiness. The principle of justice states that what is morally right is respect for individual rights and individual dignity and treating each person as an end in himself or herself, rather than a means. Although Kohlberg's original work placed the Kantian principle at stage 6 and Mill's utilitarianism at stage 5, he no longer claims to have succeeded in defining the

One of the hallmarks of middle age is the slowing of psychomotor responses. However, exercised abilities do not show signs of aging as
quickly unexercised ones do.

Intelligence does not decline with age, but it does change. A definition of intelligence in middle and later adulthood must take into account the qualities of responsibility, generativity, and integrity.

Although physical strength peaks during the young adult years, creativity and productivity are greatest during middle age.

The urgent demands of careers and growing children can put a strain on intimate relationships in middle age. But patience and tenacity during rough times can pay off in later life, because older married people are generally more satisfied than single ones.

Once the nest is empty, middle-aged couples can turn attention back to their relationship, and intimacy and satisfaction generally increase. Relationships with children also tend to improve, and both parents and children seem to be happy with intimacy at a distance.

At midlife, career development plateaus, but a good match between personal interests and job characteristics helps ensure satisfaction. Some people cope with career stagnation by becoming more involved, some by changing careers, and others by deciding to devote more time to other areas of their life.

As men in middle age enter "new cultures" through volunteer work and informal participation in community groups, they develop a capacity for guiding the next generation. Women, on the other hand, tend to become more independent and assertive in their middle years.

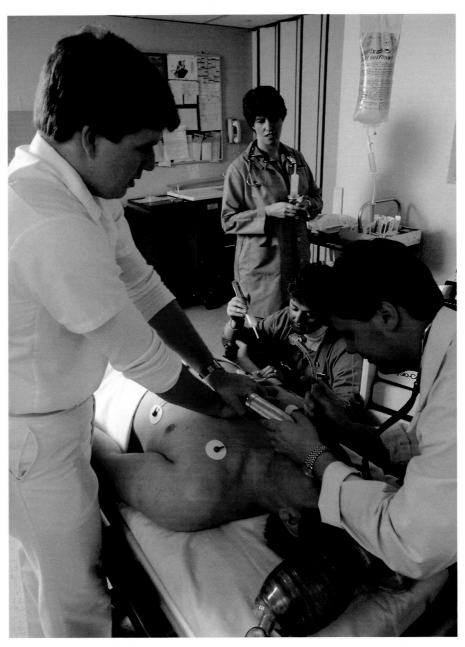

Awareness of vulnerability to the chronic, universal diseases of age increases in middle age, especially among men, who are more likely than women to be the victims of premature death.

Box 3.3 Principled reasoning

In one of Kohlberg's classic dilemmas, the interviewer asks the subject how he or she might respond to the following situation:

Heinz's wife is fatally ill, and the only cure for her condition is a drug that is quite expensive. Heinz goes to the druggist and tries to make arrangements to pay for the medication, but the druggist refuses. Does Heinz have the right to steal the drug?

The following is a stage 5 response given to the Heinz dilemma by one of Kohlberg's subjects:

Should he steal the drug?

Yes, he should. His obligation to save his wife's life must take precedence over his obligation to respect the druggist's property rights.

Which is worse, letting someone die or stealing?

Letting someone die. Because the value of human life is logically prior to the value of property. That is, property can have no value unless human life is protected.

SOURCE: Kohlberg & Candee, 1984, p. 61.

---

nature of the sixth and highest stage but believes that these two principles are definite components of the most mature judgments (Kohlberg, 1986; Levine, Kohlberg, & Hewer, 1983). Notions of stage 6 continue to be actively investigated (Sonnert & Commons, 1991; Sonnert & Commons, in preparation). Box 3.3 presents an example of reasoning thought to illustrate the higher stages in this case, stage 5.

Kohlberg's work probably has been studied more thoroughly than any other contemporary thinker, yet a number of questions remain. For example we don't know the relationship between Kohlberg's and Piaget's stages or the stages proposed by those studying postformal thought. Many researchers now align moral stage 3 with beginning formal operations (abstract operations) and moral stage 3/4 with formal operations (Alexander & Langer, 1990; Commons & Grotzer, 1990; Richards & Commons, 1990; Rodriguez, 1989). Kohlberg (1990a, 1990b) aligned moral stage 4 with advanced formal operations (systematic operations) and stage 5 with metasystematic reasoning. Box 3.4 presents definitions of these four stages along with examples of the thinkers and the kinds of developments that might be said to characterize each stage.

Kohlberg thought that reflective moral judgment controlled moral action. However, Kohlberg's measures of moral judgment may underestimate the general moral development of most people, including children. In one study of

Box 3.4 Four post-formal stages of cognitive development

The work of Thomas Kuhn (1970) on the idea of paradigm in the sciences has recently inspired one of the authors and his associates (Commons, Stein, & Richards, 1988; Commons, Stein, Richards, Trudeau, & Galaz-Fontes, in preparation) to elaborate the idea of structural analytic thinking (Commons & Richards, 1978; Stevens-Long, 1979) into four distinct stages of adult development. Each stage represents a proficiency to perceive, think, judge, reflect, and communicate at a more complex order, and to create new ways of combining and applying knowledge through reflection.

Many of us successfully deal with tasks at the first postformal order of hierarchical complexity, requiring the systematic stage of thought. Such tasks require an understanding of multiple abstract relationships. Thinkers who perform at this systematic stage separately describe each system of multiple relationships. They do not relate the systems to one another. For example, our discussion of theory in Chapter 2, and the matrices that were developed for the last part of the chapter represent systematic thinking. Systematic thinking focuses on various systems within an arena of knowledge (in this case, developmental psychology) and offers an integrated way of thinking about relations within those systems.

Few of us successfully operate on tasks at the next order of hierarchical complexity, requiring the metasystematic stage of thought. Such tasks require an understanding of a supersystem that arises from the consideration of relationship among systems. Thinkers who perform at the metasystematic stage form supersystems by seeing how different systems might be related. For instance, supersystems in mathematics might integrate systems within algebra or integrate systems within geometry. The development of rather impressive supersystems such as group theory, ring theory, and set theory in mathematics are examples of incredibly superb metasystematic thinking. The work of B. F. Skinner on operant conditioning and Jean Piaget on human de-

preschoolers, 90 percent of the children said they would not hurt someone or steal something, even if there were no rules against it (Nucci & Turiel, 1978; Turiel & Smetana, 1984). In fact, one researcher believes that the sophisticated reasoning evidenced by preschool children is obscured in middle childhood by a new appreciation for convention and in early adolescence by the need to live up to the standards and expectations of others. The resurgence of abstract morality in late adolescence and early adulthood may then only reflect the final mastery of social norms, according to this view (Hoffman, 1980, 1984).

Finally, questions as to whether men and women have a different orientation to moral questions and reason at different stages has been of great interest. Carol Gilligan (1982) claimed that Kohlberg's dilemmas often seemed unrealistic and irrelevant to women. She asserted that women tend to score consis-

Box 3.4 *(continued)*

velopment give us examples of this kind of thinking in the social sciences. Obviously, few of us will ever create a supersystem, although we may be perfectly able to comprehend metasystematic thinking when it is presented to us.

Even fewer of us successfully operate on tasks at the next order of hierarchical complexity, requiring the paradigmatic stage of thought. Such thinking requires the coordination of supersystems. One has to see the relationships between very large and often disparate bodies of knowledge, as Marx did when he began to describe the relationships between economics and politics. Einstein and Darwin were paradigmatic thinkers. Paradigmatic thinkers often affect fields of knowledge that might appear quite unrelated to the original field of the thinker. For example, Darwin affected not only the study of biology and psychology but also the fields of economics, political science, and theology. Paradigmatic thinking may have, and usually does have, important social implications. Galileo, for instance, not only described the orbit of the earth, he quite literally snatched man from the center of the universe.

At the fourth and final stage for which we have examples, cross-paradigmatic thought changes the very way we are able to think, the basis of knowledge, the way we view the universe and ourselves. It not only crosses fields, like mathematics and physics or biology and economics, it discovers—or perhaps creates—relationships between them. Descartes' invention of analysis (how to think back from the answer to the question), and Newton's melding of mathematics and physics created a completely different, more rational, knowable universe than had existed before. Descartes has even been credited with inventing the ego and the notion of the reflex, and Newton has been said to have created the idea that the universe could be understood as if it were a giant machine (Capra, 1982).

tently lower than men on Kohlberg's scale, despite impressive growth in the articulation and sophistication with which they approached moral dilemmas through the years of early adulthood. A number of reviews of possible sex difference followed, almost all finding no differences (Colby & Kohlberg, 1987; Walker, 1986).

Gilligan argued that women have an orientation toward morality that relies on responsibility and caring, rather than justice and the general welfare. She contends that women see what is moral in terms of the integrity of relationships and in terms of minimizing hurt, whereas men (including Kohlberg) assume that autonomy and an orderly system for the adjudication of rights defines what is right. For men, what is right is what is just. For women, what is right is taking responsibility for others. Kohlberg (1969, 1990) himself was deeply committed to the necessary role of moral attachment. After the controversy, Gilligan's work stimulated Kohlberg to reframe stage 6 to include the integration of both orientations.

For all these reasons, one of the more important alternative conceptions of moral development is the notion that different people develop different moral orientations, that these are based in experiential differences, and do not represent a series of stages but simply a set of equally valid alternative systems. One such scheme (Walker, 1986) includes four different adult orientations:

- *Normative:* What is right is what fulfills one's duties and roles and upholds one's rights and the rules of society.
- *Fairness:* What is right is what is just and equitable and what ensures liberty and reciprocity in society.
- *Utilitarian:* What is right is what ensures the welfare of the self and others.
- *Perfectionist:* What is right is what ensures the dignity and autonomy of human beings and harmony in social relationships.

Walker has been unable to replicate Gilligan's finding that there are sex differences in moral orientation (Walker, 1984, 1986). Instead, he has reported that his subjects do not exhibit a consistent moral orientation but apply different principles to different situations. Some of the situational factors that determine the nature of moral decisions include the likelihood of negative consequences, the severity of those consequences, the perceived relative importance of another's merit, and the perceived importance of another person's need (Kurtines, 1984).

In one rather radical environmentalist formulation of moral development, Robert Liebert (1984) argues that what occurs in moral development is moral sophistication, which he defines as the ability to pursue one's own self-interest more effectively (also see Commons, 1991). What people learn, according to Liebert, is how and why to apply social standards. Moral maturity, from his point of view, is the expression of increasingly farsighted efforts to live pragmatically, efforts which are more effective over time as one gains knowledge and experience about the long-term consequences of judgments and behavior. In support of this view, Liebert points to the evidence showing that moral conduct is situationally determined. That is, people do not behave in consistent ways, regardless of the kinds of judgments they make.

The connection between moral judgment and moral conduct is a continuing problem in the literature on moral development. Whereas Kohlberg argues that honesty, resistance to temptation, and altruism are associated with relatively high levels of moral judgment (Blasi, 1980), it is the case that the relationship between moral cognition and moral conduct is by no means a simple matter. Kohlberg argues that responsibility develops with judgment. He defined responsibility as consistency between words and actions. In other words,

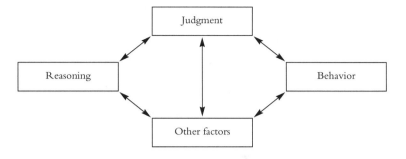

Figure 3.8 Relationships among factors influencing moral judgment.

the higher people's stage of judgment, the more likely they are to be responsible, to be committed to principles. As suggested in the matrix of theoretical concepts, the first truly principled, committed behavior probably emerges in young adulthood.

Some studies of moral conduct do show an increased correlation between word and deed as judgment becomes more mature, in Kohlberg's terms. People reasoning at higher stages are more likely to return questionnaires, to join demonstrations they say they support, to ignore an experimenter's instructions to desist from helping another subject in distress (Locke, 1983), and to keep their tutoring commitments when faced with academic problems of their own (Barnett, 1985; Commons & Barnett, 1984).

A number of formulations attempt to account for the complex relationship between judgment and action (Commons, Brodrick, Gewirtz & Kohlberg, in preparation; Kurtines & Gewirtz, 1984). But even when word and conduct are consistent, the same form of reasoning can lead to different judgments about the best behavior. Judgments can also be simple rationalizations for planned behaviors, and judgments may be modified by conduct as a person begins to act. Figure 3.8 presents one representation of the complex interactions possible among reasoning, judgment, behavior, and the situational factors suggested by Kurtines.

Both theory and research present some important challenges to those interested in moral development. The emergence of moral feelings, such as guilt, shame, and empathy, and the acquisition of responses to transgression, such as confession, lying, and reparation, have scarcely been addressed (Hoffman, 1984).

It is particularly interesting that no large-scale studies of the development into adulthood of honesty and lying exist, given that students so often say that the most important characteristic they can think of in a close relationship is honesty. The Internal Revenue Service might be interested as well. Furthermore, most of the studies of principled behavior that are quoted in the literature are rather old, like studies of the 1960s free-speech and peace demonstrators at Berkeley (Haan, Smith, & Block, 1968). Again the study of the behavioral component of development lags far behind the study of cognition. It is much easier to study what a person says than what that person actually does in life beyond the laboratory.

Creativity

What people mean by creativity (Guilford, 1950, 1959; Maltzman, 1960) varies with whom they are studying. For example, Howard Gardner (1981) has studied the professional acts of artists, writers, musicians, and scientists. Smith, Gudmund, Carlsson, and Sandstrom (1985) studied all kinds of artists and found that the "important" ones, as determined by art historians' evaluations, were quite different from the rest of the professional artists. They were more open to identification with both sexes and on the whole characterized by freedom of expression.

Much of what is identified as creativity is actually childhood creativity and may not apply to any behavior after late adolescence or very early adulthood. As David Feldman (1986) illustrates, for the preadult person, behavior is usually limited to technical expertise in a relatively narrow area (for example, dance or chess or piano). This type of "creativity" does not extend to all aspects of the individual's life. For example, a child may be a great gymnast but a terrible dancer. Preadult "creative" behavior is generally associated with performance or competition. Child prodigies usually benefit from much parental support.

There are three aspects of adult creativity lacking in child creativity. Precociousness is often seen as originality, but the products might not be viewed as original in the adult world. Even if the products are original, they might not be programmatic. This means that the products are local and specialized. For instance, a child may produce a wonderful painting as a one-time-only event. It is not a part of a larger creative program and is unrelated to other creative work in the field. The music of Mozart or Beethoven represents the kind of programmatic creative work that is suggested here. Last, even if programmatic and original, they might not be much of a social contribution (Maltzman, 1960). The behavior is not truly generative in nature, whereas adult creativity is.

Creativity means learning everything that is available on a subject and then transcending that knowledge. The creative individual must learn what information and ideas are available but cannot completely accept them. During childhood the possibility for such transcendence does not exist. By adolescence and early adulthood, there is a degree of activity that is not only predictive of creative activity, but also highly predictive of adult creative success in some areas. The best predictor of winning the Nobel prize seems to be winning or placing in the Westinghouse Talent Search for High School students.

Looking Ahead: The Tasks of Young Adulthood

Young adulthood is not only a time of new optimal biological capacities and intellectual achievements. It is also an important period of social and interpersonal growth. One of the most popular approaches to this interpersonal context involves the description of new developmental challenges. For instance, as noted in Chapter 1, R. J. Havighurst (1972) approached the study of adulthood through the description of developmental tasks, which he defined as "bio-socio-psychological" in origin. Success at these tasks at the proper, critical moment in the life course leads to happiness for the individual as well as to improvement of one's chances for success with later tasks.

Developmental tasks dominate a particular phase of the life cycle, and emerge through the interaction of a biological ground plan, individual psychological forces, and the structure of the social system. Havighurst proposed that the tasks of young adulthood include:

1. selecting a mate
2. learning to live with a marriage partner
3. starting a family
4. establishing an occupation
5. finding a congenial social group

This description may not apply to many other cultures, but these tasks seem fairly representative of central concerns for most young adults in Western industrialized cultures. The literature on each of these topics will be reviewed in the next two chapters.

Erik Erikson (1968b) offered a more abstract formulation than did Havighurst. For example, he wrote about the "crisis of intimacy: a counterpointing as well as a fusing of identity." Sexual intimacy is only a part of the general task of intimacy. Intimacy goes beyond sexual relationships and includes all companionship and communion with others, both as individuals and as groups. From Erikson's perspective, intimacy is not exclusive or destructive as relationships in adolescence sometimes are. The growth of identity in adolescence permits mature acceptance of differences among people, eventually heightening one's own sense of identity.

Just as intimacy is the central theme of young adulthood from Erikson's point of view, love is its major virtue. One must find something or someone to be true to. Erikson writes that young adults must test the extremes in order to find a deep commitment, to develop a sense of choice, and to experience loy-

"The sense of self becomes extended when the welfare of another person, a group enterprise, or some other valued object becomes as important as one's own welfare." Robert White

alty. He argues that the core problem of this stage is discovering how to take care of those to whom one becomes committed upon emerging from the identity period, and to whom one now owes his or her identity.

Some of the same thoughts were echoed and expanded in the work of Robert White (1975). White focused on young adulthood and believed that the important trends of young adult life continued throughout the life span. Writing of the deepening of interests and the "freeing of personal relationships," White contended that young adults begin to respond to people as individuals, free of much of the egocentrism and anxiety characteristic of adolescence. Adults can make allowances. There is room for warmth, respect, and criticism.

The deepening of interests in early adult life is similar to Erikson's notion of commitment, but White phrases the idea in terms of commitment to something rather than to someone. The deepening of interests always includes wholehearted activity and the progressive mastery of knowledge and skills, according to White.

Robert Kegan (1982) has made similar observations but provides a stage framework for how these issues are addressed. Armon's (1984, 1990) extensive longitudinal data on the development of relationships both at work and with one's partner supports the developmental stage progression like those of Kohlberg's and Kegan's. As Levinson (Levinson, Darrow, Klein, Levinson, & McKee, 1978) points out, early adulthood includes not only commitment but also tentativeness as to direction as our first example illustrates. Young adults do not see choices as final. Although older adults think they can still make up for lost time, they no longer think they are immortal. They no longer take such large chances.

In young adulthood, satisfaction is derived from the activity, not from the social gains that may accompany the activity. Social gains, approval, and attention from others may spark interest, but finally it is the experience of competence that becomes the most important source of reinforcement for a committed individual.

Three other growth trends in early adulthood are suggested by White:

- *Stabilization of identity.* Identity becomes more consistent and freer from transient influence. Judgments arise more often from one's own experience rather than from what others think.
- *Humanization of values.* The young adult becomes increasingly aware of the human meaning of values and their relationship to social purposes. The individual moves from an absolute to a personal system of values based on life experience.
- *Expansion of caring.* The young adult develops a sense of common humanity. There is an extension of the sense of self to the community and a growing dedication to the welfare of others.

White, Erikson, and Havighurst all touch on the same concerns: caring, commitment, and mastery. All of these themes are important throughout adult life. But they seem to be most critical in early adulthood, the period when most people are actively engaged in finding mates, establishing families, developing social circles, and becoming committed to long-term occupations and interests.

Summary

I. Physical Functioning
    A. Peak strength is achieved between twenty-three and twenty-seven, but aging is apparent in the decline in maximum work rates after age twenty.
    B. The vital functions show some declines, especially among current cohorts of young adults.
        1. Cardiac output decreases due to decline in the strength of the left ventricle and increased resistance in the arteries.

       2. Vital capacity and ventilation rate in the lungs begin to decline, along with basal metabolic rate, functioning in the lymphatic system, the adrenals, and the number of cells in the central nervous system.

       3. Regular exercise can improve cardiac function and produce increases in vital capacity, although its effect on longevity is unclear.

       4. Exercise is thought to improve body image and, therefore, self-concept, producing feelings of competence and improved mood tone.

  C. Reproductive and sexual physiology

       1. Male and female cycles of sexual arousal are surprisingly similar, including four phases: excitation, plateau, orgasm, and resolution.

          a. Excitation is characterized by vasocongestion and myotonia in both sexes, as well as lubrication.

          b. Plateau is an extremely high state of arousal during which the testes become elevated in men and the orgasmic platform develops in women.

          c. Orgasm is defined in both sexes as rhythmic contractions of the pelvic musculature that produce intense physical sensations. Most men define orgasm in terms of ejaculation. The idea of multiple orgasms is not yet well defined.

          d. The resolution phase includes a refractory period for males that may not appear in females.

       2. Young adults are more active and sexually uninhibited than earlier cohorts. Sexual activity of all kinds has increased across sex, race, religious, or ethnic groups, and for teenagers to senior citizens.

          a. As sexual behavior has become less inhibited, sexually transmitted diseases of every kind have become more common. AIDS, of course, is the most alarming of these.

          b. Other sexually transmitted diseases include chlamydia trachomatis, nongonococcal rethritis, gonorrhea, and herpes, together thought to infect over 27 million Americans.

  D. Pregnancy and childbirth

       1. Pregnancy may be characterized by a series of unique developmental tasks, which include bonding with the unborn child and which may be experienced as a vulnerable time. The postpartum period may be especially difficult, even negative.

       2. A recent study identifies four periods of pregnancy: disruption, adaptation, centering, and anticipation, each characterized by its own anxieties and developmental tasks.

II. Sensation, Perception, and Psychomotor Skills

  A. Sensation is the awareness of simple stimuli, whereas perception is thought to include recognition and interpretation of stimuli.

1. Threshold values begin to decline after twenty-five, including values for visual acuity and adaptation to the dark.
2. The ability to detect high-frequency sounds is most acute in late childhood and adolescence.

B. Tests of part-whole differentiation, perceptual closure, and speed of recognition suggest young adulthood is a time of optimum function.

C. Psychomotor skills are those that require dexterity and agility. They show minimal decline in young adulthood, although psychomotor reaction time increases between twenty and twenty-five.

III. Intelligence and Cognition

A. The quantitative approach to the study of intellectual function relies on the use of standardized intelligence tests.

1. A series of studies by Schaie employed the Thurstone test of Primary Mental Abilities and demonstrated little decline in intellectual function in sequentially designed studies of the adult life span.

2. Intelligence in adult life may be more strongly influenced by history-graded events and nonnormative life events than age-graded influences.

3. A dual-process model of adult intelligence may best fit the available data, with increases occurring in the pragmatics of intelligence and declines apparent in the mechanics.

4. The work of Horn and Cattell on crystallized and fluid intelligence illustrates how a dual-process model might account for declines in abilities that seem to reflect the ability to hold and manipulate information in memory and account for increases in more formal types of knowledge.

B. The qualitative approach to the study of intelligence is illustrated by the work of Piaget and his students on the universal characteristics of logical reasoning.

1. Westernization and industrialization are important predictors of the emergence of formal operations.

2. Formal operations may not be adaptive in certain cultural settings, and most people do not appear to use formal operations in their day-to-day lives.

3. Recently, formal operations have been redefined to include beginning formal operations as well as the traditional stage of formal operations. Beginning postformal operations, or systematic thinking, has also been proposed.

4. Some researchers have also proposed that there are four postformal stages, beginning with systematic thinking and developing through metasystematic thought to paradigmatic thinking and cross-paradigmatic thinking.

IV. Moral Reasoning and Behavior
   A. The work of Kohlberg has been especially influential in the study of moral reasoning. He has presented a series of stages that include the use of the principle of justice and the utilitarian principle at the highest stages.
      1. Recent longitudinal research shows that stages 5 and 6 do not develop until after age twenty-seven although moral judgment may continue to develop until age sixty-five.
      2. Although development at the highest stages as defined by Kohlberg does not appear in traditional cultures, it has been identified in leaders of several other modern cultures.
      3. In his last work before his death, Kohlberg outlined a four-step transition between one stage and another.
      4. Kohlberg's work may underestimate the moral thinking of most people, including children, and it has been claimed that Kohlberg's dilemmas often seem unrealistic and irrelevant to women, who may base their moral judgments on responsibility and caring more often than on justice and the general welfare.
   B. It has been suggested that what occurs in moral development is moral orientation, including an orientation dependent on duties and roles (normative), or justice (fairness), the welfare of the self and others (utilitarian), or dignity and autonomy (perfectionist).
      1. There do not appear to be sex differences in moral orientation.
      2. People do not exhibit consistent differences in moral orientation but do use different principles, depending on the situation presented for judgment.
   C. The behaviorist position suggests that what develops is moral sophistication, and it relies on data showing that judgment is not a good predictor of behavior.
      1. There is a dearth of good research on moral conduct and the connection between conduct and reasoning.
      2. There is some evidence that increasingly mature moral judgment, in Kohlberg's terms, is related to responsibility, that is, to the consistency between words and actions.
      3. Situational factors as well as reasoning and judgment affect behavioral outcomes.
V. Creativity
   A. Much of what is identified as creativity is actually childhood creativity and may not apply to any behavior after late adolescence.
   B. Technical expertise in a relatively narrow area, like chess or dance, is not fully adult creativity.
   C. Adult creativity is characterized by originality rather than precociousness, is programmatic rather than local and specific, and makes a social contribution.

VI. The Tasks of Young Adulthood
   A. Havighurst first proposed the notion of developmental tasks and described them as bio-socio-psychological.
   B. Erikson offered a more abstract formulation of tasks and emphasized intimacy in young adulthood.
   C. White identified three trends in psychological development during young adulthood: the stabilization of identity, the humanization of values, and the expansion of caring.

4

Young Adulthood: The Personal Context—Intimacy, Marriage, and Alternatives to Marriage

Love is that strange bewilderment which overtakes one person on account of another.

—James Thurber

ROBERT LOVES JANET. There is no doubt about it. They have everything going for them. Robert's got a great job. He's just been promoted to foreman at the mill. Janet's a secretary there. Doing pretty well too. She's more like an administrative assistant. But she says she'll give it up when they have children. Take some time off; maybe go back to school. That's important to Robert. He wants a real family. So, they've set a date. They chose the Baptist Church where Robert's parents go. Janet and Robert don't go to church much, but it'll please their folks. Robert's parents are still together, even though they've seen their troubles. Robert's really proud of his parents for being married thirty years. He knows the odds against black families in his parents' generation were tremendous. Janet's Dad won't be at the wedding because he lost his job years ago and the family couldn't hold together. Robert's fondest hope is to be able to support his family as well as his father did.

Janet loves Robert. There's no doubt about it. He's handsome and funny and easy to be around. They can share everything and Robert seems to love the fact that she's doing well at her job. Well, she might have to give it up for a while when the kids are small. But Janet's mother always looked after her kids when the chips were down. So Janet knows whatever happens she can make a family work. Even if Robert loses his job, as her Dad did, Janet can help out. They have everything going for them. They understand each other. Robert really knows how to be romantic. They've lived together for a whole year now and he still brings her flowers. Janet loves flowers.

Three years later, Janet and Robert are in the biggest crisis of their lives. The mill is closing. Robert needs to find a new job. Janet offers to take a promotion and let Robert go back to school. Robert doesn't want to give up being the breadwinner. If he's not bringing home a paycheck, well, it just won't feel right. If he goes back to school, they'll have to put off having kids. Janet wants kids. He wants kids himself. Could he take care of the kids and go to school? It's a totally new idea for Robert. Janet seems behind it. But she's an incurable romantic. What will happen when he can't bring her flowers anymore unless he spends her money?

ROBERT AND JANET ILLUSTRATE the tasks that psychologists have described as the central developments of young adulthood: intimacy, commitment, fidelity, and caring. But each of them sees the situation rather differently and, like the psychologists and sociologists who spend their time studying people like Robert and Janet, they may not agree on what decision would work best for them either as individuals or as a couple. They may not even agree on what "work best" means. Is the best decision the one that gives them the best chance of staying together? Is the best decision the one that enhances their intimacy and caring? Is the best decision the one that will promote their growth as individuals? Is it possible that a really good decision could do all three things?

This chapter is concerned with the abstract, elusive facets of the emotional bonds between people as well as the more accessible aspects. The discussion includes intimacy and commitment, attachment, loving and "being in love," as well as courtship, mate selection, divorce, and remarriage. Types of marriage, satisfaction in marriage, and the particular problems of the two-paycheck marriage are also examined.

Finally, the emerging literature on alternative lifestyles, including studies of singlehood, cohabitation, and homosexuality is considered.

Intimacy, Love, and Being in Love

Some say love it is a river that drowns the tender reed.
Some say love it is a razor that leaves your soul to bleed.
Some say love it is a hunger, an endless, aching need.
I say love it is a flower, and you its only seed.

—"The Rose"

If love is a mystery for everyone personally, it is no less enigmatic to those who study it professionally. Predictably, there are almost as many definitions of love and intimacy as there are writers and researchers. Love is different for everyone: a warm puppy for some, a cold fish for others.

Fifteen years ago, a search of the literature on love revealed next to nothing. Only the psychodynamic theorists had much to say, and of these, only Erikson had placed intimacy and loving in a developmental context. Erikson had defined love as the primary virtue of an intimate relationship, a product of sharing oneself; but he had little to say about how love actually feels. In fact, few psychologists have tried to describe the feeling of love. Generally, they confine themselves to labeling or listing the attitudes and behaviors that people exhibit when they love someone. Distinctions have been made between companionate and passionate love (Hatfield, 1988; Berscheid, 1988). Love has been defined in terms of passion, commitment, and intimacy (Sternberg, 1988). The trouble is that the terms used to define love are themselves poorly defined.

It is helpful, at least in understanding the literature if not the phenomenon, to distinguish three broad categories of study: intimacy, love, and mate selection. Each of these categories has been handled by researchers in slightly different ways, producing different kinds of data.

Elements of Intimacy

Several attempts have been made to define the elements of intimacy in relationships between people. As is evident later in this chapter, Erikson and other writers have stressed the importance of commitment in intimate relationships. Reciprocity, similarity, and compatibility have also been offered as defining attributes (Lowenthal & Weiss, 1976); a third approach has emphasized the concept of attachment (Kalish & Knudtson, 1976; Troll & Smith, 1976). Yet another interpretation stresses the importance of affiliation and dependency (Rubin, 1973).

All intimate relationships are not alike, of course. Moreover, the nature and conduct of such relationships probably change significantly with age (Lerner & Ryff, 1978; Reedy, Birren, & Schaie, 1982). For example, in children, **proximal,** or contact, behaviors like wandering around holding mother's skirt gradually give way to **distal** behaviors such as eye contact, vocalizations, and the like.

Most writers do agree that intimates engage in self-disclosure—that is, they talk to each other, especially about personal matters. In fact, intimacy is often said to exist and develop to the degree that self-disclosure occurs between two people. Self-disclosure must be mutual, of course, and must occur at a comfortable rate (Rubin, 1973). If self-disclosure is one-sided, the relationship resembles a therapist-client situation. If self-disclosure occurs too rapidly, people feel embarrassed and withdraw. People are unlikely to be strongly attracted to strangers who stop them on the street and begin to describe the details of their personal lives.

Assuming self-disclosure is a defining characteristic of intimacy, we might also expect a fairly strong relationship between intimacy and *identity*. Meaningful self-disclosure requires a strong sense of self. How can you tell someone else about who you are if you don't really know yourself? One research study did indeed report that young adult subjects who possessed a strong sense of identity, or who appeared to be struggling hard with identity issues, were likely to have a variety of intimate relationships with both males and females (Orlofsky, Marcia, & Lesser, 1973). In contrast, subjects who had adopted the identity outlined for them by their parents, and those who had not developed any sense of self at all, were likely to possess only superficial relationships or to develop commitments out of a sense of social convenience rather than mutuality, love, respect, and understanding (Orlofsky, 1976).

The ability to develop intimate relationships in young adulthood has been traced to earlier events as well. The fact that children, in their own way, possess intimacy (or at least its precursor) is of special interest to researchers who take a life-span approach to developmental issues. Concentrating on the importance of the parent-child bond, these researchers are particularly interested in how family relationships differ, if at all, from the intimate relationships of adulthood. The life-span perspective is especially interesting because of its consideration of negative as well as positive interactions in intimate relationships and because of the implication that intimacy may be expressed differently at different points in the life span. Most frequently, authors who are working from a life-span viewpoint use the term **attachment** for relationships characterized by feelings of intimacy and commitment (Kalish & Knudtson, 1976; Lerner & Ryff, 1978; Troll & Smith, 1976; Skolnick, 1986; Bergmann, 1987).

The Concept of Attachment

A life-span view of attachment as the basis for all intimate relationships tends to emphasize the importance of the parent-child bond. Troll and Smith (1976) contend, for example, that parent-child bonds may form the basis for all two-person relationships. This is not a particularly radical point of view and has been favored by many psychodynamic theorists. In *The Anatomy of Love,* for instance, Martin Bergmann (1987) argues that every time people fall in love, they transfer love from the opposite-sexed parent (what he calls the incestuous object) to the new partner (the nonincestuous object). In happy love, Bergmann believes that the best the parent had to offer the child is found again. What makes love so intense for some people is the fear of losing the sense of aliveness that comes from this refinding process.

In Robert and Janet's case, we might make the argument that Janet is the more romantic of the two because she has experienced loss of the cross-sexed parent. We might be concerned about whether her view of Robert was realistic enough to produce good prospects for the future of the relationship. On the other hand, Bergmann would suggest that if Janet has made a realistic choice, her love of Robert may be able to make up for what she missed from her father in childhood. Bergmann believes that love can be a healing experience if someone like Janet does not want too much from it.

Part of the problem with this point of view, however, has been difficulty in accounting for why feelings of love tend to become less intense over time. We know, for instance, that attraction decreases as attachment grows. Those to whom one becomes attached lose their novelty; they are no longer fascinating (Taylor, 1968; Troll & Smith, 1976). Another question arises about whether people who had really poor relationships with their parents can ever have rewarding intimate relationships. The psychoanalytic view suggests these early relationships may be the prototype for all later love relationships. To test this idea, Arlene Skolnick (1986c) reviewed the data from a very long-term and important longitudinal investigation, the Berkeley Guidance Study. Throughout this book, we will be looking at the data from this particular work. Box 4.1 focuses on Skolnick's study. Her overall conclusion was that there is no powerful link between the quality of the parent-child bond and adult relationships. Each period of the life span presents opportunities and problems that may allow a person to develop the emotional skills required in close relationships.

Those who study attachment tend to believe that intimacy is relative. Not all intimate relationships are the same. Intimate relationships may differ in intensity and depth and in degree of self-disclosure or compatibility. A person may have several intimate relationships that are very different from one another, including some that involve little current compatibility or self-disclosure. These kinds of intimate relationships—for example, those between relatives who know each other "all too well"—might best be termed attachments. If attachment is considered a form of intimacy, one can extend the definition of intimacy to cover feelings about groups, ideas, and objects. The idea that love, as well as other intimate relationships, is both relative and based on frequency of interaction has been most strongly developed by the social-learning theorists in a controversial and intriguing interpretation of intimate relationships called **social exchange theory.** Intimacy, they claim, is the product of a reward-cost history in the interaction between two people (Huston & Burgess, 1979; Kelley et al., 1983).

Box 4.1 Focus on Research: Early attachment and personal relationships across the life span

Over forty years ago, a group of researchers at the University of California, Berkeley, began studying a sample composed of every other child born in the Berkeley area during a particular period. Those children are now in their forties and fifties and the huge amount of data that has been amassed on them includes measures of parent-child relationships in early childhood; school performance data; personality measures; intelligence scores; clinical interview data; peer, teacher, and parent perceptions as well as spouse perceptions in adulthood; and much data have now been collected on the lives, personalities, and aging of their parents. As we shall see, these data have influenced how researchers and theorists think about many aspects of adult development and aging as well as child development.

Arlene Skolnick used the data base to create a test of the hypothesis that the quality of the mother-child bond in early childhood would predict the quality of relationships in adult life. Using infancy, childhood, adolescence, and adulthood as the major stages of life, Skolnick reviewed the data from the Berkeley subjects, scoring the quality of their relationships as either "above" or "below" average for each of those periods. This method generated sixteen possible "pathways," from a completely negative path, with poor relationships in all four periods, through various combinations (such as above average followed by below average in all three later periods, or below average in infancy followed by below average in childhood, to above average in adolescence and adulthood).

Skolnick reasoned that if attachment theory was correct, there should be many more subjects that would be expected by chance (which is one in sixteen) in the extreme sequences. That is, attachment theory would predict that most people with above-average relationships to the mother in infancy would have relationships of above-average quality throughout the rest of their lives. Conversely, people who experienced below-average relationships to the mother in infancy should exhibit below-average relationships for all three later periods. Skolnick did find that those two paths were among the three most heavily traveled. But, interestingly enough, the other most frequent path was below-average relationships in infancy followed by above-average relationships for all three later periods. Skolnick concluded that a child's sex, intelligence, talent, and physical attractiveness as well as certain personality characteristics may produce opportunities for positive relationships after infancy, compensating for the problems of early childhood.

Other interesting findings Skolnick reported included the fact that males were overrepresented among those who experienced below-average relationships throughout life, that it was possible to have below-average relationships throughout life and still be occupationally and financially successful, and that some people who had above-average relationships in infancy exhibited below-average relationships for all three later periods.

SOURCE: Based on Skolnick (1986).

Social Exchange Theory

Social exchange theory represents an attempt to explain all intimate relationships, not as irrational or selfless, but as a product of the fact that people love those who offer more rewards and fewer punishments than others. The loved one must not only be desirable but also must reciprocate one's attentions. Robert has pursued Janet (and she him) not only because he was attracted to her but also because he thought he had a reasonably good chance of catching her. She must have had that same perception (Berscheid, 1982; Berscheid & Walster, 1974; Burgess & Huston, 1979).

Ultimately, the most interesting part of the theory rests on the assumption that people who fall in love begin by engaging in a kind of bargaining process wherein assets and debits are evaluated and matched. Looking for love means searching for a rewarding (attractive, intelligent, wealthy) mate without aiming so high that one risks rejection, for rejection is punishment. In one important version of social exchange theory, the idea of a balance between rewards and punishments is especially important. The **equity theory** suggests that people seek relationships in which the rewards outnumber the punishments but in which the rewards for both people are approximately the same (Hatfield, Utne, & Traupmann, 1979). So Robert loves Janet because he sees her as a suitable mate. She is attractive (he is handsome), she has a good job (so does he), she is intelligent enough to think about going back to college (he also considers this).

Equity could also predict a very different pairing for Robert and Janet. Robert might choose a woman who was not nearly as intelligent as he but outrageously beautiful. Janet might choose a man who was much more intelligent than she but not very attractive. Even though these other mates might bring quite different assets than Robert or Janet does, the total of each person's assets minus the sum of their liabilities is equal. In an inequitable relationship, someone gets the "short end of the stick," and both the winner and the loser feel distressed. The person who offers fewer assets and more liabilities feels guilty and fears rejection or retaliation. The partner who has more to offer is angry and resentful.

Research does seem to support both social exchange theory, generally, and the equity hypothesis, specifically, at least as explanations for the first phases of pair formation. For instance, several survey studies (Berscheid, Walster, & Bohrstedt, 1973; Walster, Walster, & Traupmann, 1978) demonstrated that both members of an inequitable relationship were unhappy.

Not surprisingly, however, social exchange theory and equity theory have provoked heated debate. Is there no such thing as unconditional love? Some writers believe that social exchange theory and equity theory cannot explain the persistence of love in long-term relationships (Douvan, 1977; Murstein, 1982, 1988; Rubin, 1973). Of course, equity is difficult to calculate over the long term. People's assets and liabilities change over time, and individuals may be willing to put up with periods of inequity if they believe the deficit will eventually disappear. For instance, Janet may happily support Robert while he finishes school if she thinks he will be successful (and loyal).

It seems unlikely, moreover, that all equitable relationships are alike. If Donald is a man of few assets but few liabilities, for example, and Frank, who has numerous assets, has terrible liabilities, is Linda likely to feel the same about them? A relationship with someone who is extremely intelligent but very insensitive is quite different from a relationship with someone who is only moderately bright but is also kind.

Neither does equity theory explain why some equitable relationships are passionate while others are not, nor why some inequitable relationships seem passionate as well. Different relationships have different qualities. Many people enjoy a number of intimate, mutual, and long-term relationships. Some are passionate, and some are not. Some are joyful, some serious, others just comfortable. Yet, which is more valuable? Are some apparently equal relationships more equal than others? Most mysteriously, why do we "love" some people but feel "in love" with others?

Romantic Love

Love demands the impossible, the absolute, the sky on fire, in-exhaustible springtime, life after death, and death itself transfigured into eternal life.

—Albert Camus

Liking, loving, and being in love: social exchange theory probably does the best job of explaining liking rather than loving. As Ellen Berscheid (1988) points out in one of her latest works, we know the most about the kind of love friends have for one another, not lovers. We know that people tend to like other people who are like themselves (opposites don't attract), that absence doesn't make the heart grow fonder. In fact, as Berscheid writes, "out of sight, out of mind" is a better description of what goes on between friends. Absence and differences all add costs to the relationship. What we don't know is why people who fall in love put up with so much more misery than they would in a friendship. People love

rather thoroughly unreliable scoundrels, and conversely, we see persons giving the most glowing appraisals to a person they have just decided to dump in the divorce court—"a prince of a fellow," she says, "but I no longer wish to associate with him." We see people approaching and maintaining contact with others whom they SAY they despise and with whom, we observe, they experience emotions that are predominantly negative in quality. We see people, curiously enough, terminating relationships with another NOT because they experience negative emotions in association with the other, but rather because they experience no emotion at all—that is, we see some people regarding the absence of emotion as a bad thing and the occurrence of even negative emotion as a good thing, signifying that the relationship is alive and vital. (Berscheid, 1982, p. 42)

Berscheid (1988) argues that it's important to begin to understand romantic love better because it is increasingly the reason for which people marry. It has always been the reason men chose to marry, but women used to report more "practical" reasons. Today, 80 percent of all college students say they want to marry for love and over half of them consider falling out of love a reason for divorce.

Berscheid, and most other theorists on the subject of love, believe that romantic love is very different from liking or friendship. "One can like the other so hard one's nose bleeds, but that still does not, and seemingly cannot, cause the liking state to be transcended and romantic love to appear" (Berscheid, 1988, p. 369). Romantic love doesn't arise from the same origins as friendship, which include familiarity with another person and predictability in the relationship. In fact, novelty and uncertainty seem to increase feelings of romantic love.

Love is defined by the presence of passion, by the unfulfilled feelings of yearning to be with the other. Passionate love appears to be a mixture of elation, despair, joy, and even depression and anger. The electric, chemical quality of passionate love has led researchers to look to physiology for answers to the question "What is love?" (Hatfield, 1988). Some of the most interesting research on romantic love shows its relationship to other kinds of intense emotional arousal based on a classic study done nearly thirty years ago.

In 1962, Schachter and Singer proposed that all true human emotional experience was based first on physiological arousal, and, secondly, on the interpretation of that arousal as a particular emotion. In Chapter 2, we saw that many theories of emotional development propose that emotions develop as people learn how to interpret arousal in ways that society deems appropriate to the situation. Fear is the interpretation of arousal as a sign of danger. Berscheid and Walster (1974) have suggested that love is simply the interpretation of arousal as passion.

In one clever study of male college students the researcher reported that men who were physically stimulated by a two-minute jog and then shown videotapes of a neatly groomed, well-dressed college woman rated her more attractive and thought she had a better personality than men who had not been so aroused. On the other hand, joggers who saw tapes of a poorly groomed woman found her significantly less desirable and attractive than men who had not jogged at all (Bridgwater, 1982). In a similar experiment, men who had just walked across a narrow, shaking walkway, swaying in the wind 230 feet above a stream gave many more sexual associations to a photograph depicting a scenic attraction than men who had crossed on a low, solid bridge (Dutton & Aron, 1974).

Work on brain chemistry has suggested that love is linked to processes in the brain that produce elation and depression. Chemically, love, anger, and fear are all associated with reactions of the sympathetic nervous system. So, chemically, passion could be a response to either pleasure or pain. Arousal from other sources can intensify passion, just as passion intensifies people's experience of many facets of life—nature, art, music, and sexual experience for instance (Hatfield, 1988; Bergmann, 1987).

Romantic feelings may actually be an arousal response to the novel aspects of another person. However, intense emotional arousal and excitement cannot be sustained over the long term and the reduction of uncertainty leads to declining passion (Livingston, 1980; Tennov, 1980). As two people get to know each other well, uncertainty approaches zero, and their attention drifts to other things. Dorothy Tennov (1980) has argued that the romantic phase of love, feelings she has labeled **limerance,** lasts about two years.

Tennov's work is interesting because it represents one of the few attempts to define romantic love in terms of what it feels like. Tennov believes that limerance can be distinguished from other kinds of love, from sexual attraction, and from liking. On the basis of questionnaire responses from over eight hundred people, and interviews with more than three hundred, she concluded that "being" or "falling" in love is different from "loving someone." Being in love, or limerance, occurs in the first phases of a relationship, grows to enormous intensity, and eventually declines to zero, according to Tennov (although at least one of her interviewees seems to have preserved those feelings over a very long-term marriage of thirty years). Tennov outlined eleven basic components of limerance:

1. Intrusive thinking about the love object. Some of her subjects reported thinking about their beloved 60 to 100 percent of the time during the most intense phases of limerance.

2. Acute longing for reciprocation. What a limerant person wants is the reciprocation of feeling, for the other person to declare that he or she is also madly in love.

3. Dependency of mood on the perceived probability of reciprocation. If it seems likely that the other will reciprocate, the limerant one feels ecstatic; if it seems unlikely, he or she may feel miserable.

4. An inability to react with limerance to more than one person at a time. Limerance is an exclusive phenomenon.

5. The fear of rejection and shyness in the presence of the love object. Some people even reported sweaty hands, trembling, heart-pounding and the like.

6. Intensification through adversity. At least up to a point, limerance seems to grow if there are obstacles to the relationship.

7. Acute sensitivity. Limerant people display acute sensitivity to any act that can be interpreted favorably (as a sign of potential reciprocation), and manifest the ability to explain acts that might seem neutral to others as signs of potentially passionate feelings.

8. The aching of the heart when uncertainty is strong. People actually located negative feelings in their chests.

9. Buoyancy when reciprocation seems evident. Love is, after all, like "walking on air."

10. An intensity of feelings that leaves other concerns in the background. Limerant people say that nothing else, none of the day-to-day problems of life, seem very important.

11. Positive thinking. A final component is the ability to emphasize what is truly admirable about the love object and to avoid thinking about what is negative, even to see negative attributes with great compassion.

Tennov believes that most people experience at least some form of romantic or limerant love in the beginning stages of a close relationship, but she admits that not everyone does. She thinks some people are simply incapable of it, and others learn to avoid it or repress it, because it is obsessive and causes so much fear and anxiety. Other writers (Lasswell & Lobsenz, 1980; Lee, 1977, 1988; Livingston, 1980) distinguish between healthy romantic love and an unhealthy dependence. True romantic love does not, according to these views, diminish the lover. Fears of rejection or pain or loss of control may be associated with a weak sense of self in close relationships and can create a constant need for adulation and praise, a need that interferes with honest communication and commitment (Erikson, 1968a & b; Lowenthal & Weiss, 1976; Rubin, Peplau, & Hill, 1976).

Obviously, when two people say "I love you" to each other they may not mean the same thing. There may be different types of love and different patterns that dominate various periods of the life cycle. One study (Reedy, Birren, & Schaie, 1982) reported that passion and sexual intimacy were more important for young adults, whereas affection, emotional security, and loyalty appeared more significant to older people.

Generally, the literature now suggests that love may take various forms at different times, not only over the life span, but at different phases of a person's own life course. Love may also be defined and experienced differently by different people. Some people may not value passionate feelings. Others may find affectionate companionship relatively boring. In fact, one group of researchers (Lasswell & Lobsenz, 1980; Lee, 1974, 1977, 1988) distinguish six different styles of loving.

Styles of Loving The idea that there are different types or styles of loving has appeared in work by a variety of authors. Ellen Berscheid (1988) talks about four categories:

1. **Agape:** altruistic love without passion or even intimacy. This is close to empathy or the ideal of Christian love in which one might love a stranger.

2. **Affection:** attachment or the kind of friendship associated with familiarity. People who feel affection for one another enjoy and seek each other's company.

3. **Philias:** friendship based on the exchange of rewards. This kind of friendship is likely to disappear when people live at a distance from one another.

4. **Eros:** romantic love. The most important aspect of this kind of loving is its passionate component. Romantic love is built around feelings of sexual desire.

Bernard Murstein (1988) believes that we ought to talk about stages of love rather than types. He thinks that love in close relationships moves from passionate love (which is very intense and has a strong base in feelings of sexual desire) to romantic love (which is also intense, but more focused on the idealization of the other rather than sexuality), to conjugal love (the basis for a stable and permanent bond of affection and trust). Berscheid might also acknowledge that most close relationships move from eros to affection. But other authors believe that there are real and continuing differences in the ways that people define and experience love. According to John Lee (1977, 1988), for instance, the basic styles of love (the words are from ancient Greek or Latin) include **storge,** the love of best friends; **eros,** or romantic love; **ludus,** game-playing love; and **mania,** possessive love. He also described two styles he considers combinations of these.

As for Robert and Janet, in Lee's terms it sounds as though they may have different styles of loving. Robert talks a lot about the importance of family, the similarity of values he and Janet seem to have, and his desire to take care of Janet and whatever children they may have. Robert's style sounds like storge love, a deep, abiding affection. Storge lovers enjoy each other's company and are able to be communicative and mutually caring. The passionate phase of the relationship is not considered essential. In fact, storge lovers, according to Lee, may view an explosive, passionate relationship as exhausting and bewildering, an unnecessary drama.

Janet's view sounds more like eros, or romantic love. She tells us how handsome Robert is, how funny, how easy to be around. She talks about how important it is to her that he does little things like bring her flowers. The whole problem of supporting the family doesn't seem nearly the issue to Janet that it is to Robert. For erotic lovers, once their love is under way, there is no obstacle too great. Like Diana Ross sang years ago, "Ain't no mountain high enough, ain't no valley deep enough to keep me from you." Erotic lovers want to share everything, the dreams, the desires, even the pain. If there are these kinds of differences in the way Robert and Janet experience and express their love for each other, it may complicate the resolution of their current dilemma. Robert feels that if he loves Janet, he needs to be able to care for her and their family properly. Janet is more interested in the excitement of sharing new experiences and new solutions together.

Among the other styles Lee describes, neither mania (possessive love) nor ludus (game-playing love) would seem to produce intimate relationships. Lee describes mania as an intense form of limerance and argues that it derives from poor self-esteem. The possessive lover suffers from a consuming, despairing desire for the other, marked by jealousy and fear. Even an otherwise confident person may experience a manic relationship at one time or another, especially during periods of low self-confidence. Or a relationship with a game-playing, ludic partner might produce mania in an otherwise stable erotic lover or even a person whose basic style is storge.

Nearly the polar opposite of mania, ludus is a style that is essentially unattached. Ludic lovers appear to be in love with love. Charming and infuriating, they play at love as a game. Ludic lovers shun commitment and are often involved in more than one romantic relationship at the same time.

Social exchange theorists seem to have captured Lee's sixth style of love, **pragma,** or "love with a shopping list" (Lee, 1974). Believing that a proper relationship is the product of practical compatibility, the pragmatic lover sets out to find and preserve the correct match. A pragmatic relationship may become intimate, of course. If self-disclosure and affection grow out of basic compatibility, a pragmatic match may become a storge love affair, for instance. Such developments are common in countries where marriages are prearranged.

Ideas like Lee's or Berscheid's suggest that any one of several styles might produce a long-term, satisfying relationship. It is important, these authors contend, that people understand any differences they possess in their definitions of love, but there is no one best kind of love. Eros may be fashionable, but storge or Berscheid's idea of affection may actually produce more satisfying relationships for many people. As is usually the case in the study of human development, however, experts disagree about the issue of "one best kind." But a number of theorists, the psychodynamic thinkers in particular, have spent much time outlining the characteristics and determinants of "mature love."

Triangular Theory of Love

In an intermediate position between the psychodynamic theorists who describe mature love and authors like Berscheid and Lee, Robert Sternberg (1988) has offered a **triangular theory of love.** Sternberg maintains that love is shaped by three basic forces: intimacy, passion, and a decision/commitment component. He defines intimacy as feelings of closeness, connectedness, and bonding. Intimacy includes the desire to promote the welfare of the other, the desire to experience happiness with the other, and high regard for the other. People in intimate relationships share themselves and their possessions, receive emotional support from each other, give emotional support, and have intimate communication. Passion is the romantic component. It is based on physical attraction and feelings of sexual desire. The decision/commitment component of love is both short-term (one or both parties decide they are in love) and long-term (one or both parties decide to try and maintain that love). All the

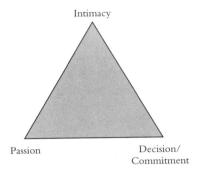

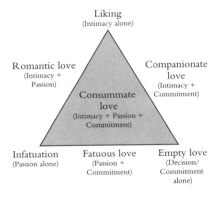

Figure 4.1 Components of love and kinds of loving.

SOURCE: Sternberg, 1988, pp. 121, 122.

possible combinations of these three elements may occur, according to Sternberg. Figure 4.1 presents his vision of the different kinds of loving that might arise from different combinations of passion, intimacy, and commitment. Sternberg doesn't believe that the pure forms at the corners are very likely to occur in close relationships, but they are not impossible. (Strictly speaking, liking is not a type of love.) He describes the types of love as follows:

1. **Infatuation:** Love at first sight or love that turns toward obsession with an unrealistic ideal of the partner. This kind of love only lasts if the relationship with the partner is never consummated or is frustrated in some ways.

2. **Empty love:** Empty love occurs most often in a stagnant relationship where mutual emotional involvement and physical attraction have been lost. Often, empty love signals the final stage of a long-

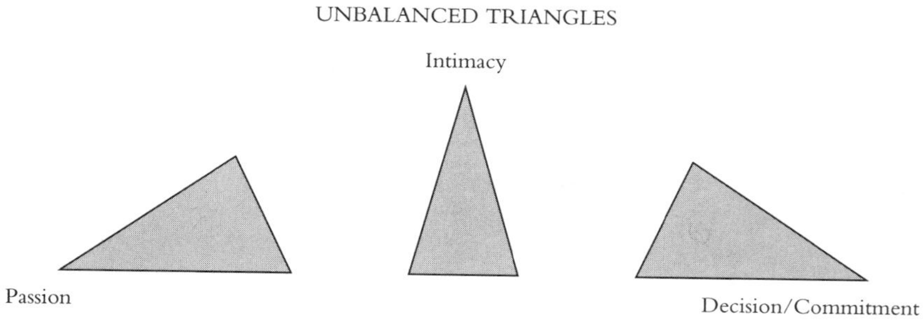

UNBALANCED TRIANGLES

Intimacy

Passion

Decision/Commitment

Figure 4.2 Differing shapes of relationships emphasizing (a) commitment and intimacy, (b) high levels of intimacy, (c) passion and intimacy but not commitment.

SOURCE: Based on Sternberg, 1988, p. 133.

term relationship although it is not always terminal. A relationship can be empty from one partner's view but not the other's.

3. **Romantic love:** Romantic lovers are drawn to each other emotionally and physically. Commitment is not a necessary part of romantic love. Permanence may be unlikely. Sternberg believes that his idea of romantic love is unlike that of Berscheid, who he thinks is talking about infatuation. Infatuation can become romantic love or friendship may become romantic in Sternberg's view.

4. **Companionate love:** Companionate love is intimacy plus commitment. In this relationship, the physical attraction has waned. This concept is similar to both Berscheid's and others' (Hatfield, 1988) idea of conjugal love.

5. **Fatuous love:** Passion and commitment in the absence of intimacy. This is the Hollywood romance or the whirlwind courtships. Fatuous love is highly susceptible to distress. When the passion fades, all that is left is commitment or empty love unless intimacy develops along the way.

6. **Consummate love:** This is love in which all three elements of intimacy, passion, and commitment are strongly present. Sternberg argues that consummate love is difficult to attain and hard to keep.

Sternberg also argues that the shape of love may be different for one person in the relationship than for the other. Figure 4.2 presents some of the shapes that love might take for different people. Relationships are disappointing, Sternberg writes, when the triangles of the partners are very different or when the triangle that represents the ideal shape of a love relationship for one or both of them differs dramatically from the triangle that best represents their actual relationship. Sternberg does believe that people can come to understand their differences and take actions that will change the shape of their relationships so that it represents something closer to what they hoped for. Sternberg also argues that people need to understand that their relationship is dynamic. It will not stay the same over time. Passion will fade, intimacy will be challenged. "The theory suggests we must constantly work at understanding, building, and rebuilding our loving relationships. Relationships are constructions, and they decay over time if they are not maintained and improved" (1988, p. 138).

Mature Love

Both Sternberg's last statement about the dynamic nature of love and his notion that there is a consummate love are close to the psychodynamic conception of mature love. In this view (Bergmann, 1980, 1987; Kernberg, 1976, 1980) the inability to fall in love constitutes a grave abnormality, and the capacity for falling in love depends on a number of developmental milestones.

For instance, Kernberg writes that parents must allow a child the opportunity for separation if the child is to develop the capacity for love. The experience of independence eventually ensures that one will be able to maintain his or her own identity in an intense relationship. As Martin Bergmann (1980, 1987) puts it, love depends on early learning about how to regulate the distance between oneself and the objects one cares about, primarily the mother. When a child cannot bear separation, realistic love cannot develop. Distance provides the opportunity for a realistic evaluation of the loved one as a person separate from the self, with shortcomings as well as good features. Bergmann and Kernberg agree that there is no love without missing. In other words, people who experience mature love may feel extremely close to one another, and very special to one another, but they are always aware of a basic separateness. Therefore, Kernberg says, mature love always has a quality of sadness as well as joy.

From this point of view, mature love involves the rediscovery of early childhood feelings of closeness. It returns to adults some feelings of the joy of being one with another person, a joy that was renounced in order to develop. In happy love affairs, there is actually an improvement on these early feelings because the adult can choose a person who can give what the parent of the child could not. Furthermore, mature love allows one to express fully sexual desire toward the loved person.

Kernberg and Bergmann even offer some tentative answers to the old question, "How will I know if I'm in love?" According to these writers, love produces a "normal idealization" of the partner, which includes cultural and social ideals as well as personal and sexual ideals. In other words, lovers see each other as representing the best of everything in regard both to cultural standards and personal ones. Normal idealization also includes a commitment to the type of life that the other person represents. There is the feeling that they are special as a pair—different from the group.

In terms of sexuality, mature love is characterized by the ability to enjoy the orgasm of the partner as well as of the self, and by the capacity to provide gratification to the partner. Kernberg writes of an intense double identification during orgasm, and even argues that this capacity represents a transcendence of the ordinary boundaries of the self.

Finally, mature love is marked by an ability to tolerate ambivalence, since one is, after all, still separate within the pair. Mature love requires confidence that anger and rejection can be included in an overall loving relationship. Kernberg (1976) believes that this combination of longing to be with the other and the renunciation of fusion adds depth and complexity to mature relationships. He warns that maturity does not guarantee conflict-free stability.

Kernberg (1980) goes on to argue that the denial of the intense, ambivalent aspects of love leads to marital boredom. He believes that the society encourages the death of romantic love because an intense couple relationship is outside the control of society. In fact, as Tennov has noted, couples in love do withdraw from society. Kernberg argues that others envy this intensity and create pressure for the conventionality and conformity that promote marital boredom. A couple that maintains its cohesion becomes a target for the anxiety and envy of others. Therefore, Kernberg suggests, love is maintained through the preservation of private forms of unconventionality.

Bringing together the cognitive and psychodynamic views of love allows for a tentative answer to the question of how love may be maintained in a long-term relationship. Remember that the cognitive view suggests hot emotion dies as uncertainty about the other declines to zero. Consider this in light of the idea that marital boredom or the loss of passionate feelings occurs because people are likely to deny the intense, ambivalent aspects of a relationship. Finally, add the notion proposed by a number of sociologists and backed by some feminist thinkers (Collins, 1985; Hochschild, 1983; Safilios-Rothschild, 1977), that mature love can be called "informed caring." This means that lovers desire the well-being and growth of the other while preserving their own honesty and respecting their own rights.

We also know from the last chapter that mature thought is characterized by an appreciation of conflict and change, although few people think in very mature ways most of the time. The tendency in thinking about relationships, in fact, is to assume that once one finds the right person, the rest will take care of itself. In reality, of course, people develop throughout adult life (at least that is the premise of this book), and in that sense, there never is a right person. People change. A person can be the right person for one phase of life, but not right for another. There is always uncertainty if we allow ourselves to perceive change in ourselves and in the other person. Uncertainty prevails if we actually encourage the growth and development of the other.

The cognitive or social exchange theories do not explain why anyone

According to an object-relations point of view, mature love is a kind of "special" or "gentle" identification in which the interests, wishes, feelings, and shortcomings of the partner attain about the same import as those of the self.

should stay in love or love someone who provides no immediate rewards. The psychodynamic thinkers cannot explain why people fall out of love. Is it because they deny their own ambivalence or because society pressures them to conform? If they do deny the intense, ambivalent aspects of the relationship, how is the person who goes on experiencing mature love different from one who does not? Furthermore, why should a person who is really mature and can completely accept the other feel ambivalent?

The problem occurs because maturity and mature love are usually conceptualized as an achievement, or a state, rather than an ongoing process or struggle. If development occurs in adult life, then the self and the loved one are always changing. If Levinson (1986) is right, major changes in needs, plans, the whole structure of one's lifestyle, occur every five to seven years. Change implies the need to reevaluate and reintegrate one's view of both the self and the other. Integration is not something one achieves; it is something one struggles to maintain.

While this process may sound difficult, it may also be the key to maintaining a loving relationship. Development produces something unknown or uncertain in the other. Uncertainty maintains the experience of love. To remain aware of and to encourage the development of the other as well as the self ought to maintain the experience of love, although the form of the relationship may change from time to time. As long as the changes in the self and the other support the plans and needs of both people, the relationship may be relatively stable. When changes in the other produce obstacles to one's own plans and needs, the pair may become more separate. But, theoretically, an appreciation of those changes might maintain feelings of love through less stable times.

Returning to the saga of Robert and Janet for a moment, we might predict that the maintenance of their love will be related to how they cope with change. If they are able to see that the growth and development of the other person is a critical value in an enduring relationship, they will be able to develop a way of dealing with the problems they are facing that might be good for each of them as individuals as well as for the marriage. It seems likely that enduring, happy relationships are those in which both people feel that their own growth and development have been supported by the other. In a similar vein, Elaine Hatfield (1988) outlines some of the advice she has found successful in helping couples learn to cope with love in intimate relationships:

1. Accept yourself; be who you are. Take pleasure in the diversity between yourself and your partner.

2. Accept your partner.

3. Express yourself. Let your partner know who you are.

4. Be prepared to deal with your partner's reactions to your honesty and expressiveness. Don't expect that your partner is going to be able to accept everything you want or everything you are without any negative reactions.

As Kernberg (1976) put it, a mature love relationship is one in which the interests, wishes, feelings, and shortcomings of the partner attain about the same import as those of the self. Those interests and wishes and even shortcomings change from time to time and it is necessary for people who want to maintain a close relationship to be aware of, appreciate, and even welcome change in the self and the partner.

Whether or not relationships are happy or mature, however, many do endure for surprising lengths of time. Although very little is really known about what makes a good long-term marriage, certainly a large amount of information is available about who marries whom, how long it lasts, why partners choose each other in the first place, and the variety of forms that marital communication, interaction, behaviors, and values may take in a complex society.

Marriage

"It is better to marry than to burn," noted Saint Paul, the Apostle (which, taken out of context, could be interpreted as a choice between two equally distasteful alternatives). He saw marriage as a kind of preventive medicine given by God to save man from immorality. "In other words—the words of these theologians—if either spouse is tempted to commit adultery or to masturbate, failing any better alternative, he can have recourse to the antidote to temptation that marriage provides" (Flandrin, 1985, p. 115). For most of human history, and certainly in Saint Paul's time, marriage was a business partnership and a reproductive arrangement—not a vehicle for companionship, love, or intimacy. Until the massive changes brought about by the Industrial Revolution, the family existed primarily as a unit of production, rather than a context for the development of intimacy. Households produced domestic goods and services, provided settings for professional activities, and functioned as cottage industries. The marital contract set forth specific religious obligations concerning sexual and parental matters, including the training and education of children. Clearly, modern life in the industrialized world has transformed the meaning of marriage. Marriage is no longer considered primarily a practical financial arrangement or a framework in which to rear children. It is viewed today as the central source of emotional gratification in people's lives, and as a context for self-actualization (Melville, 1988; Skolnick, 1986b).

Formally, traditional marriage may be defined as a "socially legitimate sexual union, begun with a public commitment and undertaken with some idea of permanence" (Stephens, 1963). It includes reciprocal rights and obligations between spouses, which have been dictated by society and may be institutionalized either in statute law or in case law. Such laws may specify who owns the property shared by married partners, who has responsibility for the welfare of children, and even the acceptable emotional and sexual behavior of partners in a marriage (Melville, 1988). Such are the formal aspects of marriage in the Western world.

Informally, however, expectations of marriage are far greater, and it may be that marriage cannot possibly meet the great number of personal, social, and sexual needs expected from it in today's complex, rapidly changing society (Libby, 1977). The institution of marriage, it has been argued, evolved to meet social demands that have little in common with needs like intimacy and commitment.

Yet, in spite of such high and diverse expectations, society also perpetuates a rather long-standing tradition of hostility toward marriage. Skolnick (1978) has pointed out two strains of ambivalence about marriage. The first is cynical, reflected in the old ball-and-chain school of humor, which pictures marriage as benefiting only the woman: "Every man is plotting seduction and every woman is plotting marriage. No woman ever remains unmarried voluntarily" (Skolnick, 1978). Skolnick believes that such jokes express male resentment of women. In an alternative interpretation, the ball-and-chain tradition is seen as a harmless form of rebellion that actually protects stable family life from disrupting impulses (Orwell, 1946).

Ambivalence also finds expression in more sophisticated humor. From the French bedroom farce to magazines like *Esquire* and *Playboy,* "the main source of humor is adultery, and the complications arising from deception and discovery." This brand of humor, Skolnick notes, "reflects the moral order of the Continental, upper-middle class, where separation of love and marriage is assumed, love affairs are expected of both spouses, but especially the husband, and conjugal love, particularly of long standing, is perverse" (1978, p. 239).

For the huge majority who do marry, the ideal is long-standing conjugal love for which romantic love will be the most important motivating force. In fact, most Americans claim that love is the only acceptable reason for marriage. Despite this belief in the primacy of love, however, and despite the fact that people are theoretically free to fall in love across social, racial, ethnic, educational, and age boundaries, most Americans tend to marry "the right kind of person"—which usually means someone of similar race, religion, education, and socioeconomic background, one's "own kind."

The Selection of a Marriage Partner

This tendency to marry someone like oneself is called **homogamy** and it explains the choice of partners in close relationships besides marriage as well as predicting which couples will develop greater commitment to courtship in the process of finding a mate. The leading advocate of the "birds of a feather" hypothesis is Bernard Murstein (1982, 1988), who has been fairly successful in putting to rest the notion that "opposites attract" (Winch, 1974), at least for most people, when it comes to choosing a spouse. However, even Murstein admits that homogamy alone is not adequate as an explanation for mate selection because one meets so many people over the life span who are basically like oneself. Most of these people become one's friends. Why does someone fall in love with one particular person and not another? This is probably the point where the literature fails us most completely. Even if romantic love begins as arousal (Berscheid, 1988; Hatfield, 1988), why do we feel aroused by one person and not another? What creates that special chemistry?

"As a general thing, people marry people most happily with their own kind. The trouble lies in the fact that people usually marry at an age when they do not know what their kind is." Robertson Davies

Elaine Hatfield (Hatfield, Utne, & Traupmann, 1979; Hatfield, 1988) believes that people are vulnerable to passionate or romantic love when their lives are especially turbulent. Martin Bergmann (1988) has argued that love is likely to come along just when we need it—when we have experienced a loss, either of another love object or a disappointment in the self, and when we are not excessively involved with a parent, another partner, or a child. So, although homogamy and certain more rational decisions are probably important in filtering through the available candidates, mate selection may often occur when people are actually quite vulnerable.

People may go through many potential partners before finding "the one," however, so Murstein (1982) has proposed that there are at least three phases of courtship and mate selection. In the first stage, he argues, people are most concerned with establishing an **equitable relationship.** That is, they look for a relationship in which the outcome for both partners is about the same. Homogamy helps people achieve equity, although there are trade-offs in most relationships. Partner A may be more intelligent, but partner B is a harder worker (or more beautiful or more sociable). Once a reasonably equitable relationship is established, Murstein argues that the couple moves into a phase he calls **value matching.** Ongoing self-disclosure allows each member of the pair to assess the value structure of the other. For instance, how important does he feel work is? Is she ambitious? Does he go to church? What are her politics? The importance of this stage varies from one culture to another, of course, because there is more social, political, and religious disagreement in some cultures than others. On the other hand, Murstein believes that value consensus is extremely important to members of the American middle class.

In the final phase, couples try to assess whether they will be able to achieve **role compatibility.** She tries to discover whether his behavior as a spouse, worker, father, or son-in-law will complement her performance as a spouse, worker, mother, or daughter-in-law. (He, of course, does the same thing from his perspective.) If communication is an important part of her expectations about how a spouse behaves, but he doesn't have much to say, there may be significant incompatibility. If he believes that she should stay home with the children when they are young, but she intends to take a job as soon as possible after the children are born, trouble will ensue.

The problem at the final stage of mate selection is twofold: First, it takes a long time to find out how people behave in the variety of roles they must play as adults. Second, no one's expectations are static. One's ideas about what makes a good husband or wife, lover, parent, or in-law change. Twenty years ago, few men considered the career ambitions of a potential mate. Today, it is a central issue in mate selection. If Robert and Janet are having difficulty in their relationship it may be due not only to the problems presented by Robert's unemployment but also to the unexplored differences they have about the role of Janet's career in their lives. Janet has a different conception of herself as a spouse and a worker than Robert may have assumed from her willingness to stay at home with their children when the children were young.

Figure 4.3 presents one scheme for thinking about the phases of mate selection (Rice, 1990). In this conception, Murstein's first phase is elaborated. **Propinquity** refers to physical proximity. We tend to choose people that live near us. Propinquity both reflects and increases homogamy since people who live near one another tend to be of similar background and to have similar everyday experiences. Attraction and homogamy are included in Murstein's first phase. The order in Figure 4.3 is approximate, although it is most likely that attraction plays a significant role very early in the relationship because of the time involved in sorting out social and cultural factors like education, intelligence, socioeconomic class, and religion. In the second stage where Murstein emphasizes value compatibility, Rice also includes temperament, attitudes, needs, and roles.

Ideas about filters and stages and matching (as presented in Figure 4.3) make mate selection sound like a terribly rational process that should even produce acceptable results. Why do so many people eventually feel they've made a mistake? That is certainly one of the most important questions Murstein raises. The discussion of love provided one answer. People become bored because they deny the ambivalent, intense aspects of a relationship. They grow away from each other because they are unaware or unappreciative of the devel-

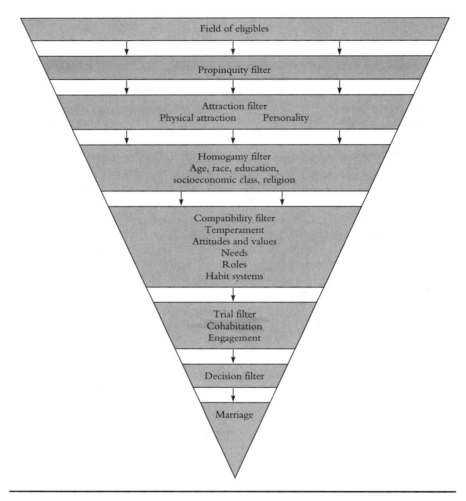

Figure 4.3 The filtering process of mate selection.

SOURCE: Rice, 1990, p. 181.

opment of the self or the other. Murstein adds to these ideas that many, if not most, romantic difficulties arise when people actively seek someone who is very much different from the self, that is, not homogamous. He believes that people usually do this because they do not accept themselves as they really are. They search for someone who represents an *ideal self* that may be quite different from their own *real self*. Murstein argues that people who do not exhibit much self-acceptance are likely to project their ideal self onto the partner. This means they tend to see in the other person qualities they wish for in them-

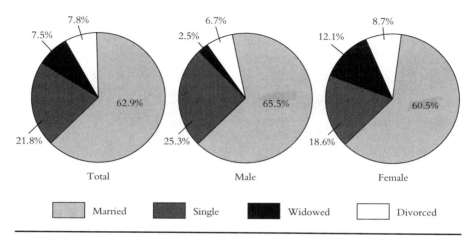

Figure 4.4 Marital status of the population, eighteen years old and over, 1987.

SOURCE: Adapted from U.S. Bureau of the Census. (1989). *Statistical abstract of the United States, 1989* (109th ed.). Washington, DC: U.S. Government Printing Office, 42.

selves—whether or not the other person possesses those qualities. Over time, projection fades, and it becomes disappointingly clear that the partner does not measure up any more than the self did. Disenchantment sets in.

There are many theories about why marriages work and don't work. What is clear, however, is that despite the pitfalls, not only do Americans marry, they believe, by and large, that family is the most important source of life satisfaction available to the average person, and the most influential socializing force of adult life. Figure 4.4 illustrates the marital status of the U.S. population, eighteen years of age and older. Although the percentage of single persons has been rising, overall, nearly 63 percent are currently married and about 22 percent are single. The remaining 15 percent or so are either widowed or divorced. If you add the number who will be married at any point in their lives, the figure approaches 95 percent.

Philippe Ariés (1985) has argued that marriage in the United States today has supplanted all other contexts in which emotional ties might develop:

> Today sentiment has been taken over by the family, which earlier had no such monopoly. . . . Social life was formerly organized around personal ties, dependence, patronage, mutual help. Relations at work were man-to-man relationships which could evolve from friendship or mutual confidence into exploitation and hatred—a hatred that was close to love; but they never settled down to indifference or impersonality. To relationships with dependents were added those with clients, fellow citizens, clan members, one's own circle. One existed in the middle of a web of sentiment

Americans believe that family is the most important source of life satisfaction. Philippe Ariés argues that marriage and family have supplanted all other contexts in which emotional ties might develop.

which was at once vague and haphazard, only partially arising from birth or locality, quickly affected by chance encounters. (pp. 70–71)

Even though marriage has come to play a central role, if not the central role, in the socialization of adults, we are only beginning to understand how that socialization occurs. Like styles of loving there are varieties of marriage. In fact, no two marriages are probably much alike. Yet it is useful to generalize about the major attributes of various marital relationships, a task undertaken some years ago in a classic study of over four hundred men and women from middle-class, enduring marriages (Cuber & Harroff, 1965).

Types of Marriage Although a number of subtypes have been described, the most general distinction emerges between **instrumental marriages** and **companionship marriages.** Enduring marriages in the Cuber and Harroff study were about equally likely to fall in either category, but people in instrumental marriages wanted very different things from the relationship than did people in companionship marriages. This distinction is still useful in beginning to understand the variety of arrangements people make in creating primary relationships (Fitzpatrick, 1988; Scanzoni, Polonko, Teachman, & Thompson, 1989; Blumstein & Schwartz, 1983).

The **instrumental marriage** is the most traditional form of marriage, because it is based on generally accepted role distinctions and cultural standards for males and females (Cuber and Harroff, 1965). The best predictor of marital satisfaction for instrumental marriages is the husband's performance in his vocational role. The marriage serves as a base of operations for the couple, making it easier for them to seek gratification in other roles. For the husband, work is a major source of satisfaction, and for the wife, the mother-housewife role is most important. While this arrangement may seem a bit old-fashioned, it characterizes many upper-middle-class marriages today, marriages in which the egalitarian ideals of the partners remain essentially unfulfilled because of the income differential between husband and wife (Blumstein & Schwartz, 1983). Imagine an instrumental marriage in a two-career situation. When both people are strongly focused outside the marital relationship, their performance in those outside roles is quite likely to predict their satisfaction with the relationship that serves as home base.

In the **companionship marriage,** on the other hand, the quality of the emotional relationship between husband and wife, as well as the frequency and breadth of their communication, predicts satisfaction with the marriage. The emergence of the companionship marriage as a major style reflects how modern marriage has been transformed from an economic and practical relationship to a framework for emotional and personal growth (Melville, 1988; Skolnick, 1986b). The people involved in a companionship marriage are highly concerned with all common aspects of family life, including the economic, emotional, recreational, educational, and social aspects. A few share a profound sense of mutuality in every aspect of each other's lives, from work and leisure through moods, thoughts, and even dreams (Hicks & Platt, 1970).

Whereas economic success and the vocational performance of the husband predict success in the instrumental marriage, and communication is the key to the companionship type, there are also some general rules for success, or at least for avoiding failure, that seem to apply across the board. For instance, marriages formed after late adolescence appear to be more stable. While the precise reason for the instability of youthful marriages remains unclear, the effect of early marriage on educational attainment seems to be an important issue. In other words, one of the reasons people who marry early risk divorce more often than those who marry later is not because of age itself, but because early marriage is likely to prevent the completion of high school or college (Doherty & Jacobsen, 1982).

For a male, the most common sequence of events in later adolescence and early adulthood requires that he finish school, find a job, and then marry. For those who buck the tide and marry before they complete their education, the rate of divorce is about 30 percent higher than usual. For females, later marriages are also more stable, perhaps because later marriage is likely to enhance a woman's social status, even for those who only finish high school (Doherty & Jacobsen, 1982).

Since interest in adult life is so recent, little current research on marriage is truly developmental. Usually, researchers begin with personality as a given and try to predict marital satisfaction from the traits different subjects display, or from socioeconomic status, age, or educational attainment. Rarely is any attempt made to assess how marriage affects personality. Ideally, such a study would be based on longitudinal or sequential designs. Although the ideal situation may be a distant prospect, some fascinating and controversial points have nonetheless been made, especially about how marriage affects men and women differently.

Marriage: His and Hers

In general, survey research has demonstrated that married people report greater life satisfaction and better mental and physical health than single people, although single women are happier and healthier than single men. However, single people report higher life satisfaction and better mental health than those who are divorced. Some evidence suggests that singles do experience some severe problems more often than other people, as they are more likely to be institutionalized than either married or divorced adults. Perhaps single people are institutionalized more often, however, because they do not have spouses or children to look after them. On the other hand, people who are healthier in the first place tend to marry, whereas those who are vulnerable remain single (Collins, 1985; Doherty & Jacobsen, 1982).

Although researchers have focused some attention on the problems and pleasures of singlehood, the most intense scrutiny has been given to the sex differences that exist even among marrieds. Married women are less satisfied than men, and some studies have even reported that single women are happier and healthier than married women. On the other hand, married women working outside the home are less depressed than married men, and the women who remain at home appear more depressed than their husbands (Rosenfield, 1980).

In their analysis of this literature, William Doherty and Neil Jacobsen (1982) have contended that the dissatisfaction of married women is strongly related to the presence of children, especially young children, in the family. Certainly, one of the best documented trends in the study of marital satisfaction over time is seen in the reduction of satisfaction during the years when there are likely to be preschool children at home. Women are especially likely to report stress over the loss of freedom that accompanies rearing young children, whereas men seem concerned that their wives have so little time left for the marital relationship once children arrive. Dissatisfaction does not necessarily mean divorce, however, and many marriages endure through lengthy periods of stress and unhappiness.

In spite of the bad news, grounds for optimism exist. Some marriages not only endure, they also fulfill. Men who do well in their vocational roles, who are able to remain open to conflict and to confront the problems of midlife transition, are particularly well satisfied with marriage (Farrell & Rosenberg,

1981). Among those in more traditional, instrumental marriages, women who become involved in the community and in educational enterprises; who form close ties with other women; and who possess a fair degree of education, initiative, and administrative ability are likely to experience great satisfaction with themselves and their marriages (Lopata, 1971).

The presence of important sex differences in satisfaction with marriage has led some investigators to suggest that how people deal with sex-role issues may be the most critical aspect of marriage today. At least two sets of researchers have argued that marriages can best be understood if we classify them with regard to how the partners perceive their roles as husband and wife. Based on a ten-year study of 700 couples, Mary Anne Fitzpatrick (1988) contends that marriages can be usefully classified in terms of the amount of conflict couples experience, the degree of interdependence they report, and the gender-role ideologies they hold. Gender-role ideology refers to how people view the role of husband and wife. Couples who hold conventional ideologies believe that the husband should play the role of traditional head of household, the wife the helpmate. Those who hold unconventional ideologies (the **independents** in her study) believe in an equal sharing of both household and decision-making responsibilities. They believe that the wife should be an equal partner.

Fitzpatrick was able to discern three basic types of marriages: traditional, independent, and separate. In the traditional marriage, the couple describe themselves as highly interdependent. They believe they rely on and communicate with each other often. However, they also report high levels of conflict and hold conventional gender-role ideologies. The independents also report high interdependence and high levels of conflict but hold unconventional ideologies. The final category, called **separates,** hold conventional ideologies but report low levels of conflict basically because they also experience low levels of interdependence. These people are not very invested in their marriages, and although they hold conventional ideologies, they do not see themselves as "doing a good job" of being husbands and wives. Using these three categories, Fitzpatrick then describes a variety of "mixed" marriages, in which one partner is traditional and one independent, or one partner is separate and one traditional, and so on. About 40 percent of her sample was composed of mixed marriages, most of which contained one person who was a separate—that is, one person was divorced from the marriage and did not feel he or she was doing a good job of the spousal role.

Fitzpatrick reported that general marital satisfaction was highest among pure-type traditional couples. This finding is consonant with most of the literature in the field at this point. However, all of the pure-type marriages, whether independent, separate, or traditional, showed fairly high levels of satisfaction. So did couples in which one partner was traditional but the other was separate. Low levels of satisfaction were reported by couples in other types of mixed-type marriages.

Contrary to her expectations, traditional men reported that they shared many feelings, including positive emotions as well as anxiety and worry with their wives. They believed their wives helped "draw them out." Fitzpatrick concludes that even traditional couples have accepted the notion that men ought to share their feelings with their wives and have adopted this notion as a new aspect of the traditional relationships. However, Fitzpatrick points out, these men were very circumspect about sharing any negative feelings they had about their wives. They did not criticize their wives directly. Among independents, a much wider range of emotional experience was shared, including the husband's feelings of vulnerability and the wife's anger. Independents tend to value the communication of both negative and positive disclosure, which may be responsible for lower levels of satisfaction. Fitzpatrick warns against assuming that open communication and self-disclosure will lead to satisfaction with marriage. In this way, she might well argue with Hatfield's (1988) advice that lovers be who they are and share everything in a relationship. For the traditional in Fitzpatrick's sample, it was inaccurate to assume that open communication produced satisfaction.

Another recent study of sexual relationships (Scanzoni, Polonko, Teachman, & Thompson, 1989) makes the same kind of distinction between conventional and other forms of male/female sexual relationship. These authors argue that conventional family norms are based on obligation and that new forms are emerging based on **individualism** and the view of love as a therapeutic exploration of self and other. People engaged in such new forms, according to Scanzoni et al., need the freedom to renegotiate the arrangement at any time rather than rely on the order and predictability of the conventional family form.

Scanzoni et al. believe there are two basic types of relationships: the conventional relationship and the **equal-partner relationship.** These two types of relationship are profiled in Box 4.2. In an equal-partner relationship, the husband and wife share equal responsibility for decision making and hold less conventional sex-role ideologies. These authors also describe an intermediate form they call the **junior-partner relationship** in which one of the partners (usually the wife) is allowed some decision-making responsibility and typically brings in some share of the family income.

Scanzoni et al. argue that the movement from junior partner to equal partner can be a very difficult transition for any couple and is usually a result of the woman's efforts. They believe that commitment is a process in a long-term relationship. As people become more involved, they begin to make more explicit decisions and bring up conflicts in the relationship. If they can find a satisfactory way to negotiate such conflicts, the rewards in the relationship continue to be high enough to support commitment. When partners feel that a number of issues have been negotiated successfully, they will demonstrate high levels of commitment to the relationship.

Both the Fitzpatrick and the Scanzoni et al. studies bring into focus a dialectical view of relationships. Both emphasize the presence of conflict in satisfactory relationships. Both report that how couples deal with conflict may be the most important thing in determining the outcome of their relationship. Fitzpatrick reports that the most critical aspect of this negotiation occurs when

---

Box 4.2 Norms for conventional and equal partner marriages

Some Basic Elements Underlying the Conventional Family Paradigm

"The elements of the previously dominant paradigm (which we call the conventional model of the conjugal family) are as follows:

1. The male head of the household, the father, is the sole economic provider.

2. The female head of the household, the mother, is the homemaker, and is responsible for domestic care and the socialization of the children. She is a help-mate to the husband providing support for him in his struggle for the family's survival.

3. The children are helpless and dependent, vulnerable and malleable. They must be nurtured full-time by the mother (or mother-surrogate) only, as emotional stability is essential.

4. The family is a private institution and within it individuals can fulfill their most important needs. This fulfillment is based on the foundation of the economic income provided by the husband (where necessary, supplemented by the state). Only when economic and material needs have been met do expressions of psychological and social needs for love, esteem, self-expression, and fulfillment emerge within the family.

5. Healthy families produce healthy individuals, who adjust to social roles.

Moral Norms for Equal Partner Relationships

1. Everything is negotiable except the principle that everything is negotiable.

2. The ultimate goal of joint decision-making (negotiation) processes and outcomes is justice and caring.

3. Each partner cultivates the capability to function effectively in both home place and marketplace.

4. The prime objective of child-socialization is to actively involve the child in age specific participatory decision-making stemming from the three preceding norms, and resulting in positive self-image and a strong sense of control of h/h own destiny, i.e., human agency."

SOURCE: Scanzoni, Polonko, Teachman, & Thompson, 1989, p. 79.

---

conflict deteriorates into personal attack. She also reports that conflicts inevitably deteriorate into personal attacks, and the important event is not the attack itself but how the partner responds. One partner must be able to disengage and not respond to a personal attack with a personal attack. In happy marriages, whether traditional or independent, one partner is able to disengage from the personal attacks that emerge in conflicts.

Like Scanzoni et al. Fitzpatrick reports that independents are committed to uncertainty and change, both partners constantly struggling to define the marriage. Therefore, she reports, independents experience conflict over even minor matters, whereas those in traditional marriages tend to report conflict only about important things. Nonetheless, both types experience conflict and how they deal with it becomes a basic predictor of satisfaction. Both of these studies would suggest that people in long-term relationships may need good conflict negotiation skills above all else.

Returning to Robert and Janet, Scanzoni et al. might argue that they are about to make the transition from junior partner to equal partner, and it will be a very difficult phase of their relationship. They will need to move away from simple decision making toward more explicit negotiation. If they are going to be successful, both partners will have to contribute to the negotiation. In a recent study, Godwin and Scanzoni (1990) reported that couples who experienced strong feelings of control were able to negotiate stable decisions among a group of 188 couples who were observed in discussion of actual marital disputes. **Control** was defined as number of attempts by the partners to influence each other. Both husband and wife must be strongly committed to their own view of the argument to reach a satisfactory conclusion. Couples were more successful where the husband was viewed as having a history of cooperation and where the wife's income was more nearly equal to the husband's. At this moment in their marital lives, Robert and Janet might well take Elaine Hatfield's (1988) advice and be very honest about who they are and what they want. It may be their best chance of reaching a decision they can really live with. It may also mean that they have to live with high levels of conflict for a while and put up with a sizable number of personal attacks.

Each couple has its own style of conflict management. There may be no one best way to argue. Fitzpatrick reports that traditional couples engage in conflict by giving each other orders, whereas independents rely on challenges and counterchallenges. Separates tend to attack and then withdraw, assert and retreat. Each type of couple may need a different form of help in dealing with their particular conflict negotiation style. Since Robert and Janet started out with somewhat traditional ideas of what marriage was about, they are likely to show a mix of exchanging orders and making challenges. If they engage a therapist or counselor in their negotiation, that person might do well to focus on how well they engage in the conflict, how easily one of them can disengage when the argument becomes a personal attack, and whether they are both able to feel they have reasonable control over the outcome of this crisis in their relationship.

Robert and Janet are faced with some of the very difficult decisions people have to make in the attempt to balance work and family in the two-paycheck family. Because nearly 60 percent of all female, married Americans work, the dual-career marriage has received some special attention over the last two decades.

Dual-Career Marriages   Rhona and Robert Rapoport (1971), who coined the term "dual-career marriage," described several potential sources of difficulty in this sort of marital arrangement. Time for shared leisure and social activities usually diminishes as the wife takes on a full career and the husband develops relationships with his children. Limited time and escalating responsibilities produce **role overload.** Women often experience intense conflict between the demands of the wife-and-mother role and the expectations they have developed in a fairly egalitarian educational system. This study suggested that there might be an optimal balance or relationship between the demands in each of the careers and demands at home. The Rapoports referred to this problem of timing as **role cycling.** If one spouse is forced to delay family concerns because of career events, or to delay peak performance at work because of family responsibilities, dissatisfaction may follow.

In a later analysis (Rice, 1979), a distinction is made between couples who married with the idea that the wife would have a career and couples in which the wife embarked on a career after the couple had been married for some time. In this study, success seemed to depend, in part, on presence of very little or no ambivalence toward the wife's career. Rice also notes that when the wife is invested in a full-scale career (as opposed to a job), both people in the relationship may well be classified as high achievers. Highly achievement-oriented people usually expect to be successful and often blame themselves when they are not, compounding whatever stress and difficulty they encounter.

Achievement-oriented people are usually quite persistent, even in the face of much stress, but they do require high levels of approval and support. Without support, high achievers often suffer from self-esteem problems, withdrawing from the relationship and thereby also withdrawing support from the spouse. A vicious cycle results, and both partners can turn to work for gratification and give up on the marriage. Since wives in dual-career marriages continue to do about 80 percent of the housework and child care (Walsh, 1989), a husband's willingness to share these tasks determines whether or not the marriage is "at risk" (Suchet and Barling, 1986).

Rice also points out that dual-career couples cannot often rely on society's conventional wisdom for marital success. These couples must create their own special structures over the years, particularly with regard to three areas: the management of time, the treatment of outside social relationships, and the raising of children. Without detailed scheduling and conscious planning, working partners often find it hard to spend meaningful time together. If their time is unorganized, one or the other partner will experience inequity. High achievers are especially sensitive to the issue of equity, or the fairness, of the marital situation. A careful assessment of how the couple uses time, Rice suggests, can help a therapist or social worker identify many of the problems the couple is facing.

Often when husband and wife both work, there are substantial rewards as well as problems (McBride, 1990). A study of some 15,000 McCall's readers (Jacoby, 1982) reported that only 6 percent of these working wives felt that their jobs were threatened by their marriages, and more than 67 percent felt their husbands were supportive and proud of their wives' work. Women in dual-career marriages appear to experience higher levels of life satisfaction than the difficulties of their role might suggest (Holder & Anderson, 1989; Scarr,

Child care is the most important problem that plagues the dual-career marriage during the years when the children are young.

Phillips, & McCartney, 1989). Although creating stress at various points in the life course, multiple roles may also buffer women against feelings of failure. When something doesn't go well at home, there is still satisfaction at work and vice versa.

Importantly, the McCall's survey showed that satisfaction in the two-paycheck marriage increased over the life span. Women over thirty-four were more satisfied than those aged twenty-one to thirty-four, and women over fifty were the most satisfied of all. This finding is in agreement with more general research on satisfaction over time. Whether because those who are most unhappy tend to get divorced, or because changes in family and personality permit more opportunity for satisfaction, older married couples tend to be happier than the young (Troll, Miller, & Atchley, 1979).

Conventional One-Career Marriages The data suggest that men and women living in more conventional marital arrangements experience stress too. Although married men live longer, experience greater occupational success, and show lower suicide rates than never-married men, they also die younger than women, commit suicide more often, and suffer more frequently from stress-related health problems such as heart attacks and peptic ulcers (Bernard, 1973; Melvill, 1988). These statistics might well reflect the emphasis placed on a man's performance as a breadwinner in the conventional marital situation. After all, a man's socioeconomic success was the most important determinant of marital satisfaction in several studies of the conventional, one-career marriage (Brenton, 1976; Hicks & Platt, 1970).

Women in conventional marriages become more submissive and conservative than they were before marriage, and they experience more neurosis and depressive symptoms than married men or single women (McBride, 1990; Bernard, 1981; Murstein, 1973). They are often quite dependent on their husbands for emotional and financial support as well as for their social and even personal identity.

Still as we have seen (Fitzpatrick, 1988), a great number of people seem not only to be satisfied but to thrive in the conventional one-career marriage. Moreover, these couples generally report that, despite the stresses, they find their marriages quite rewarding. Obviously, a review of the problems reveals only half the story.

One final point about sex differences over the family life cycle: the bearing and launching of children seem to be the most important predictors of marital satisfaction for women. Events before and after the child-rearing years have the more profound influence on many responses by male subjects. For example, husbands tend to report dissatisfaction during the years immediately prior to retirement; wives seem more dissatisfied with marriage during the parental years, from the time children are toddlers to the departure of the first child (Rollins & Feldman, 1970).

Researchers who have looked at the attitudes and feelings of older couples often find evidence that marital satisfaction recovers as children leave the home. In fact, the married couples with empty nests may be among the happiest (Campbell, 1975; Miller, 1976; Rollins & Feldman, 1970).

The presence of children probably represents a barrier to the kinds of communication and interaction associated with high levels of marital satisfaction (McBride, 1990). Evidence has been found of a positive correlation between marital satisfaction and frequency of companionship, and other data indicate that the number of children and the socioeconomic class of the family are important predictors of marital satisfaction. Children demand much time and energy as well as money. Family size and the ability to pay for child care are probably factors that facilitate or interfere with positive interaction between husband and wife (Miller, 1976). Children may also have a negative influence on the sexual life of married people.

Sexuality and Responsiveness

Sex in Marriage In her novel *Fear of Flying,* Erica Jong complained that sex in marriage, like processed cheese, grows bland and boring. Was she right? Does sexual enjoyment decline over the course of married life? Certainly, the frequency of physical affection, from kissing to sexual intercourse, declines over years of marriage, but quantity doesn't indicate quality. In fact, evidence suggests marriage today may fulfill its sexual promise far better than it ever did (Reiss, 1980).

In the late 1940s and early 1950s, a pioneering series of studies of human sexuality was published, based on personal interviews. These became known as the Kinsey reports. In 1974, Morton Hunt again asked many of the same questions Kinsey and his associates had posed. Hunt (1974) wrote that "Western civilization has long had the rare distinction of contaminating and restricting the sexual pleasure of married couples more severely than almost any other." He was able to conclude, however, that sex in marriage had become steadily more acceptable, more pleasurable, freer, and more egalitarian since Kinsey published his first findings (1948). According to Hunt, part of the reason for the elaboration of sex in marriage lies in the general closeness of married partners compared with those in Kinsey's sample. Quicker access and great social acceptance of divorce may mean that those who remain married are more satisfied in a number of ways than used to be the case.

The average American married couple reports having sexual intercourse two or three times a week through young adulthood, tapering off to about once a week after the age of fifty (Masters, Johnson, & Kolodny, 1991). Large individual differences occur in every age range, however, and some couples seem to become more active with age rather than less so.

Hunt (1974) reported substantial gains among married couples since Kinsey's studies on every measure of sexual activity and pleasure he used, including frequency of orgasm during sexual activity, median duration of intercourse, and number of married persons who described marital sex as "pleasurable" or "very pleasurable," as well as frequency of sexual intercourse. Hunt also found that the sexual techniques used by married couples today are much more varied than those Kinsey reported and include increased amounts of sexual play and a wider variety of coital positions. Not surprisingly, from this evidence he has concluded that marital sex is more pleasurable for contemporary couples than for those responding to Kinsey's survey.

People today, especially the youngest cohorts, come to marriage with greater sexual experience than in Kinsey's day. Women show more assertive and experimental attitudes. More external sources of information and stimulation are available today. So, too, are practical, accessible contraception and sexual therapy. All these conditions might be expected to facilitate the experience of sexual satisfaction in marriage.

Finally, as one might predict from the current data on increases in sexual behavior, there is evidence of a trend toward increased extramarital sexual activity (that is, more married people report having sex with someone other than their spouse). For instance, Hunt (1974) found that among younger subjects, although nearly all extramarital sexual experience was suffused with guilt and conflict, three times as many women reported such experience as did in Kinsey's sample.

Extramarital Activity One year after Hunt's report, a survey of *Redbook* readers reported that one-half of married respondents eighteen to thirty-four years old and nearly 70 percent of those over thirty-five claimed to have had extramarital sexual experience (Levin, 1975). A few years before, in 1970, a survey of *Psychology Today* readers indicated that 80 percent of respondents approved of extramarital sexual activity under some conditions. Admittedly, the readerships of these magazines are not representative samples of the American population, and more carefully designed research is clearly needed in this area. The figures reported are sufficiently dramatic, however, that one should not overlook their significance.

More thorough research seems particularly important if Hunt as well as Masters and Johnson are right in assuming that extramarital sex produces significant changes in both the marital and sexual behavior of the individuals involved (Hunt, 1974; Masters, Johnson, & Kolodny, 1991). Hunt argues that such activity, if discovered, always has negative consequences for the marriage. On the other hand, Masters and Johnson have commented that certain people become fully responsive for the first time in their lives as a result of extramarital sexual experiences (1966, 1970). Masters, Johnson, and Kolodny (1982) note that "some people find exactly what they're looking for: a release of pent-up tension, a means of getting even with their spouse for something, a way of satisfying their curiosity, a change of pace from their ordinary sexual diet, or a temporary form of escape." These authors also observe, however, that other people "find the experience to be empty, guilt-provoking, awkward, or frightening" and may develop significant sexual difficulties as a result of extramarital sexual involvement (p. 308).

Box 4.3 presents two examples of the types of reactions Masters and Johnson find common. What is the difference between an experience that benefits the individual and one that is harmful? How does extramarital sex affect marriage?

Scanzoni et al. (1989) have argued that we shouldn't try to talk about marriage and family per se but that we should simply look at extramarital sexual activity as a form of "sexually bonded relationship." They believe that many of the same dynamics that apply to marriage apply to all sexually bonded relationships. They argue that the emergence of the *new* other woman is evidence for their position. The new other woman is a professional or career-oriented individual who is interested in a relationship with a married man that provides equity of social and emotional support without the constant demands of marriage. They maintain that the same mechanisms of conflict negotiation that make marriages work are involved in the establishment, maintenance, and deterioration of extramarital relationships.

Although there is very little information about how people who consider themselves happily married handle extramarital sexual relationships, deceitful adultery is not the most satisfactory of adjustments, and a distinction should be made between **infidelity** (clandestine adultery) and **comarital sex** (consensual adultery) (Libby, 1977; Thompson, 1984). Consensual adultery is extramarital sex about which the other partner knows and gives consent prior to the in-

---

Box 4.3 From the files of Masters and Johnson

Masters, Johnson, and Kolodny use the following comments to illustrate the variety of ways people respond to extramarital sexual experiences. These married people were involved in sexual one-night stands, which Masters and Johnson believe are much more common than extramarital affairs. A one-night stand is, of course, easier to accomplish without the knowledge of one's spouse. People also seem to agree that a one-night stand poses less of a threat to the marriage since they do not generally see it as a love relationship.

A thirty-one-year-old woman: "I'd been married for almost ten years and had always been faithful, but I kept wondering what it would be like to have sex with someone else. One night I was out with some friends, and we met a few guys who bought us drinks and talked with us awhile. One of them was real good-looking and flirting with me, and I sort of flirted back. We went off to a motel for three or four hours, and it was beautiful sex, fantastic sex, just like in a novel. But that was the end of it, and it just felt good to know that I'd had the experience. I never told my husband and I don't plan to" (Author's files).

A thirty-six-year-old man: "My wife and I have very old-fashioned values and we both took our marital vows seriously, meaning no screwing around with anyone else. I never worried about it too much, since I wasn't the type to be running around anyway. But one night when I was working late a secretary asked me for a ride home, and then invited me in for coffee. Well, she was just divorced a few months, and she wanted more than coffee, and I was perfectly happy to oblige. But it was a stupid thing to do—not much fun, and lots of guilt about it afterwards—and I don't think I'd do it again" (Author's files).

SOURCE: Masters, Johnson, & Kolodny, 1991, p. 308.

---

volvement (Rice, 1990). Comarital sex may or may not involve an emotional relationship, but the affairs that are most threatening to a marriage are ongoing ones that include emotional as well as sexual involvement (Thompson, 1984).

One intriguing possibility remains totally unexplored in the literature on extramarital sexual activity. Extramarital sex may have significant historical and developmental aspects. As the attitude of the culture changes, the impact of extramarital sexual activity on marriage will probably change. Moreover, extramarital involvements may mean very different things to couples at different stages of the family life cycle. Consider this passage from *A Month of Sundays* by John Updike (1975, pp. 137–138):

Adultery is not one but several species. The adultery of the freshly married is a gaudy-winged disaster, a phoenix with hot ashes, the revelation that one has mischosen, a life-swallowing mistake has been made. Help, help, it is not too late, the babies scarcely know their father, the wedding presents are still unscarred, the mistake can be unmade, another mate can be chosen and the universe as dragon can be slain. . . . The adultery of the hopelessly married with slowly growing children and slowly dwindling mortgages, is a more stolid and more domestic creature, a beast of burden truly, for this adultery serves the purpose of rendering tolerable the unalterable . . . not often understood as such by the participants, who flog themselves with blame while they haul each other's bodies into place as sandbags against the swamping of their homes. The adultery of those in their forties recovers a certain lightness, a greyhound skittishness and peacock sheen. Children leave; parents die; money descends; nothing is as difficult as it once seemed. . . . And then, in a religious sense, there is no more adultery, as there is none among schoolchildren, or slaves, or the beyond-all-reckoning rich.

Dissolution

Few people solve their marital problems extramaritally, however. Most Americans choose exclusivity at the expense of permanence. Americans move gingerly from one monogamous relationship to the next, from when they go steady in high school to when they marry for the second or third time. Apparently, people learn the pattern of serial monogamy as adolescents and continue it in adulthood.

This propensity for changing partners has become most apparent over the past thirty years. At midcentury, a larger percentage of the population married than ever before or since, and people married younger than at any other time in recent history. The divorce rate, which spiked just after World War II, declined significantly, and the birth rate was extraordinarily high. Much of the American working and middle class moved to the suburbs. Women left the work force and the rigors of collegiate and professional education. For middle America, the Eisenhower years were marked by felt skirts, ducktail haircuts, and Sid Caesar.

With the end of the fifties, the situation began to change dramatically. In the last thirty years, singlehood has regained some of its earlier popularity; the trip to the altar typically occurs later in life for couples in the 1990s than it did in the late 1950s; motherhood seems to have lost some of its luster; and the suburbs are strewn with the wreckage of lifelong monogamy gone awry.

Today, about 50 percent of all first marriages end in divorce, compared to about 38 percent in 1960, and 11 percent around the turn of the century. Almost every Western country has experienced the same phenomenon over the last half of the twentieth century.

Although marriage and divorce rates are affected by economic trends, the overall increase in divorce during the last 100 years is most often attributed to changing expectations and changing roles of women. People expect marriage to provide an opportunity for development and self-fulfillment, and women have continued to progress toward financial and emotional independence. Increases

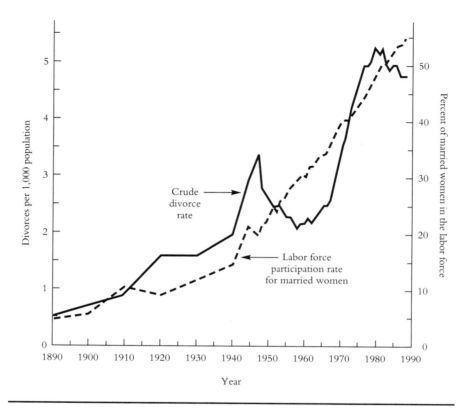

Figure 4.5 Labor-force participation rates for married women and crude divorce rates, U.S.A., 1890–1988.

SOURCE: Greenstein, 1990, p. 658.

in divorce rates probably reflect both the rising expectations of both women and men about the benefits of marriage, and the increasing ability of women to support themselves. Figure 4.5 presents the crude divorce rate for the last 100 years along with the labor-force participation rates of married women.

As Theodore Greenstein (1990) summarized the data in Figure 4.5: "We find that both indicators have been generally increasing since the late nineteenth century; that both indicators have increased sharply since the 1950s; and that the relative increases in the indicators are approximately equal" (p. 659). Greenstein has studied the effects of wife's employment on marital disruption for a national sample of women first married between 1968 and 1982. He found that the rate and timing of marital disruption was negatively related to a wife's income and positively related to the number of hours she worked along with the amount of premarital work experience she had had.

Women with less premarital work experience were somewhat less likely to experience marital disruption. Women who had averaged fifty weeks per year of premarital work experience were about half again as likely to experience disruption. Although the number of weeks per year a wife worked did not predict marital disruption, women who typically worked over thirty-five hours per week were estimated to be at the greatest risk for it. Furthermore, this effect was stronger for blacks than whites.

This last bit of data is particularly distressing because black women are so much more likely than white women to be primary breadwinners. In fact, one group of researchers (Hatchett, Veroff, & Douvan, 1990) have concluded that the conditions that foster black marital instability have probably become worse over the years. In this study of young married couples, a black husband's perception of the adequacy of the couple's finances was an important predictor of disruption. It was not low income level per se (for low income is a predictor of disruption for both blacks and whites), but the anxiety of black husbands about their continued capacity to provide for the family that seemed to be most strongly related to marital instability.

Robert and Janet are an example of the problem. Even if Janet can provide for the family quite adequately, Robert may not be able to deal with his inability to maintain his role as head of household. According to Hatchett, Veroff, and Douvan (1990), Robert may decide that leaving the family is the best way to maintain some sense of personal control. They conclude that the "position of black males in the economic opportunity structure of the United States makes them quite vulnerable to developing weak commitments to the institution of marriage" (p. 34).

These researchers also argue that black husbands and wives are less likely to deal with conflict directly and speak more often of seeking someone other than the spouse in whom to confide about the problem. Black culture seems to induce a wariness about confronting conflict that may contribute to marital instability. However, as Veroff, Douvan, and Hatchett (1990) point out, if structural factors like unemployment and discrimination are responsible for much of the conflict in black marriages, then it may be the better part of valor to avoid confrontation.

Among these young couples, both blacks and whites reported that the most common source of conflict was money. For husbands, the second most troublesome area had to do with the use of their leisure time—whether to spend it with family or friends. For wives, in-laws were placed second. Close kin networks seem to cause problems for both blacks and whites, but among blacks, interference from the husband's family was especially unwelcome (Veroff, Douvan, & Hatchett, 1990).

Divorce was also likely to occur among poorer, less educated, and younger respondents. Premarital pregnancy increased the frequency of divorce, as did unemployment. Divorce rates in this particular study were better for whites and worse for blacks than the national average in the 1980 census. Eight percent of the white couples and 11 percent of the blacks were divorced in the first two years. In this sample, the black couples were eight times more likely than whites to have total incomes below $10,000. Furthermore, black men had lower levels of education than any other group. This disadvantage more than anything else might contribute to the negative marital interactions that underlie instability among blacks. In this study, education was a strong predictor of destructive conflict, which, in turn, was a reliable predictor of marital unhappiness. Veroff and Oggins (1988) emphasize that this is basically not a race effect but an education effect. The results were present for white couples as well.

For whatever reasons, many couples finally decide that they can no longer live together as husband and wife. Although authorities agree that divorce rates are leveling out at about 50 percent, the frequency of divorce belies the pain of separation. Even though the decision to divorce is rarely a complete surprise to either party, both experience trauma, although one partner may have a more difficult time than the other. In most cases, the decision evolves over a number of months, or even years, but it is often not a mutual decision. Usually one partner wants the divorce much more than the other.

One important study of divorce reported that nearly 50 percent of the men were totally opposed to the divorce and another 20 percent or so were very reluctant to proceed. Only 34 percent of the women in this study expressed strong opposition (Wallerstein & Kelly, 1980). Furthermore, the impact of divorce was very great for the rejected partner, who was rarely prepared for the shock, even though he or she may have been through previous separations and may have considered the possibility of divorce a number of times. The rejected spouse seemed to experience a profound sense of humiliation expressed as pain and shattered self-esteem. Although initiators often reported feeling guilty or stressed, they also were more likely to make an adequate adjustment after the divorce.

Sources of stress in this study ran the gamut from incompatibility of interests and goals to outright violence. Some important sex differences were apparent. Many more women than men described intense conflict accompanied by violence; the children involved in such marriages usually supported the perceptions of the mother. Evidently, men underreported violence or perceived it as less frequent and less intense than either wives or children (Kelly, 1982).

Gender role conflicts also seemed to be a growing source of discontent among those who sought dissolution. Women most often complained of feeling unloved; men most often felt neglected and tended to blame the women's movement. Elsewhere, women also report that their husbands have insufficient respect for their intelligence or that their husbands are just generally denigrating (Kitson & Sussman, 1982). Although the reasons people give may not be as specific or elaborate as researchers wish, it is also clear that few people divorce for trivial reasons. As Joan Kelly attests, most of the marriages included in the *California Study* of divorce (Wallerstein & Kelly, 1980) were "awful," a morass of unmet needs, dishonesty, and abuse, with little or no mutual respect and only the most rudimentary communication skills.

Kelly also describes the responses of divorced people to separation and the postdivorce period in terms of six common patterns. An individual might experience more than one of these over a period of time, or might even feel some of the characteristics of two or more patterns simultaneously:

1. Anger: Anger was the most common reaction to the divorce experience in the California study. For most, conflict escalated after the separation, especially where children were involved. More than 20 percent of the men and nearly 45 percent of the women in this study were judged to be extremely and intensely angry following the separation. Most of the rest were labeled moderately angry. About 10 percent of the men and 17 percent of the women continued to be so angry even months after separation that they could not function effectively. Kelly calls these individuals the "embittered chaotic," and notes that they were likely to engage in childnapping, violence, and prolonged battles over the division of property and the custody of children.

2. Depression: During the years of the marriage, more women than men experienced chronic depression and even attempted suicide, but equal numbers of males and females responded to separation with severe depression (30 percent). Most of the men were unhappy about losing custody of the children. For the women, anxiety over their economic situation and the problems of living alone seemed to contribute heavily to depression. Women who divorce and do not remarry typically experience a substantial decline in family income, despite the fact that many go back to work. On the other hand, divorce typically improves a man's financial status.

3. Disequilibrium: About one-quarter of the men and a similar number of women experienced a period of profoundly disturbed behavior for at least a few days. Even among successful, well-controlled men and women, a bout of spying or hysterical and primitive behavior was not uncommon in the first few days or months. Vandalism, violence, and childnapping occurred among the men. All of this was much more frequent among those who had been rejected. The initiators of the divorce, as well as those who did not really care much, were far more likely to escape the postdivorce adjustment period without experiencing intense disequilibrium.

4. Attachment: A great many people reported a lingering sense of attachment to the ex-spouse despite the divorce decree. Although the attachment might well have been more strongly related to the loss of an important role than an important person, it created conflict, especially in females who had initiated the proceedings. On the other hand, in time, attachment allowed many couples to establish a kind of "quasi kin" relationship, which carried some trust and friendship once the initial disorientation eased.

5. Relief: Women were especially likely to report a sense of relief from fear, tension, and indecision. This response was most common among those who had reported long-term irritation with the spouse.

6. Feeling of having a new chance: The feeling of having a new chance in life was also common among women, especially if they felt the marriage had been bad for the children. Men rarely experienced the feeling of beginning again, perhaps because they seldom had custody of the children.

Despite the ordeal of divorce, most people eventually recover completely enough to remarry, often within two or three years. Eventually 75 to 80 percent of all divorced people remarry, and people in second marriages report being about as satisfied as people do the first time around. Sexually, people in second marriages report being more satisfied than they were the first time although divorce rates are somewhat higher than for first marriages (Rice, 1990).

Some people, perhaps a growing number, do choose less conventional solutions, at least for a while, if not forever. While the study of nontraditional arrangements lags far behind the study of marriage, some progress has been made in understanding singlehood and in particular, cohabitation.

Alternatives to Traditional Marriage

The possible combinations and permutations of living arrangements are virtually endless in this highly diverse society. You can live alone, with another person of the same or opposite sex, in a group, or in a crowd. Some people want to write down all the rules, and some prefer to work them out as a relationship develops. Social, financial, sexual, and emotional arrangements occur in contemporary America in great variety. Some are more socially acceptable than others; some more enduring; some provide great freedom; some offer financial security; and in some, people may starve to death. The rest of this chapter looks briefly both at the possibilities and at some of the important questions encountered in studying and evaluating the development of an alternative lifestyle.

The Single Life

Over the past two decades, the number of never-married persons has increased dramatically. Although many writers argue that young adults are not consciously choosing to remain single for life, there is some reason to believe that a slightly larger proportion of young people will remain single, if only because they cannot find appropriate partners. Because many babies were born in the 1950s and early 1960s, women who are now at a marriageable age encounter a shortage of men two to three years older, the usual differences between the ages of men and women who marry (Glick & Carter, 1976; Glick, 1977). Males born at the end of the baby boom face a shortage of women a few years younger.

Demographic realities aside, more people today are probably choosing the single life for positive rather than negative reasons. Historically, marriage has

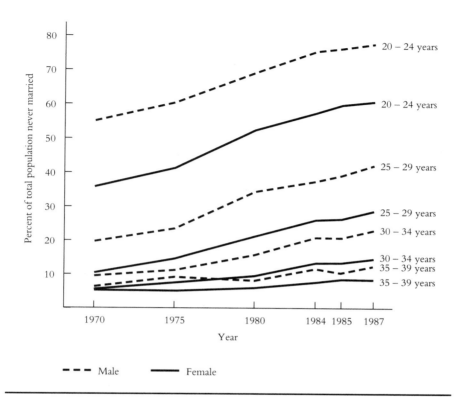

Figure 4.6 Never-married persons as percent of total population eighteen years old and over, by age and sex: 1970–1987.

SOURCE: Adapted from U.S. Bureau of the Census. (1989). *Statistical abstract of the United States, 1989* (109th ed.). Washington, DC: U.S. Government Printing Office, 43.

not always been available to everyone. In the Middle Ages, for example, marriage was a privilege generally reserved for the upper classes; much of the population never married (Ariés, 1985). At the turn of the century, the single life was far more common than it was in the 1950s. Recent trends toward postponement of marriage and the increasing popularity of the single life may simply represent a normalization of choice.

Figure 4.6 presents the rate of singlehood for various age groups in the population. As you can see, most people will be married at least once by the age of forty, but a small minority will be permanently single. In one survey of 3,000 singles, about one-third of the men and one-fifth of the women stated that they were single by choice (Simenauer & Carroll, 1982). Some were members of religious orders who had taken vows of chastity. Some saw marriage as incompatible with their careers. A small minority were homosexual in orientation.

Singlehood is not only a tolerable way of life today but a highly satisfactory way for many. Women, in particular, seem to find the single life to their advantage: single women of all ages report being happier than single males. Singles do, however, report feeling lonely more often than marrieds, although single women believe that the loneliness and anxiety is preferable to living in a relationship that does not meet their expectations. Many professional single women choose singlehood because they have found it very difficult to develop the kind of relationship that is compatible with their work and emotionally supportive enough in a world of changing gender role expectations (Jensen, 1989).

In one important study of singles (Cargan & Melko, 1982), a variety of myths about single life are explored and exploded. Single men and women do not appear to have relationships with their parents that are stronger than the relationships of marrieds. Singles are not better off financially, nor are single men happier than married men. These authors conclude that although the single life is becoming more rewarding and less frustrating than it used to be, the alternative of marriage does not appear to have become less attractive.

Like every other social arrangement, singlehood has its advantages and disadvantages. Single people are able to explore some kinds of opportunities for personal growth and self-fulfillment in a less restricted way than marrieds. They have the opportunity to meet and enjoy more varied friendships than marrieds, to be more economically independent and self-sufficient, and to develop opportunities for career change and expansion (Rice, 1990). On the other hand, singles must learn to live with the tenacious cultural attitude that failure to marry is tantamount to failure as a person or that it represents a pathological state. (The image of the so-called spinster in this society is not an attractive one; the bachelor over thirty-five is often suspected of being homosexual or neurotic.) Even more crucial is the difficulty of establishing an adequate social network as a single person, with the related problems of finding a congenial, trustworthy sounding board when one is often denied access to traditional lines of communication (Adams, 1971).

Mileski and Black (1972) argued in the early seventies that the single lifestyle would expand as housing, social groups, magazines, newspapers, and a host of material goods designed for the single life, from small-portion cans of soup to Mediterranean cruises, became available. Moreover, changing cultural values, they believed, would allow single people the opportunities to meet their sexual and social needs outside of marriage.

It is not clear whether the trends that Mileski and Black applauded will produce increasing numbers of singles in a culture that is threatened by sexually transmitted diseases, and especially, of course, by the presence of AIDS. It has been repeatedly suggested in the popular media that the AIDS crisis is changing the world of singles, but little concrete research exists on the matter. It seems extremely important for those who are interested in sexual behavior as well as marriage and family to begin to examine the ways in which AIDS may have already changed or be changing the nature of single life in America.

Nontraditional Arrangements

Inadequate definitions complicate the study of the alternatives to marriage. When does a couple become a couple? At what point does a relationship become a courtship instead of a friendship? When does a sexual relationship become cohabitation?

Heterosexual Cohabitation   The term **cohabitation** can be applied to a wide range of alternative lifestyles, including weekend marriage between two people who live in different cities, term-contract marriage, common-law marriage, and homosexual marriage. Some of these relationships are little different from traditional marriage, save for the legalisms. Others are scarcely more committed than going steady, only one step removed from a casual date.

On the basis of the limited research available, one can scarcely draw firm conclusions, but Skolnick (1986b) has suggested that the advantages and disadvantages of a cohabitation arrangement can be understood in terms of the tension between commitment and freedom. If the emotional bond between two people is the only basis for continued cohabitation, if they maintain the freedom to form other emotional and sexual relationships, how does either know where freedom ends and disengagement begins? If the commitments of the individuals involved in such a relationship are not clear, they may find themselves doing constant battle with insecurity and jealousy.

According to the Bureau of the Census (1987), there are currently 2,334,000 persons of opposite sexes sharing living quarters. This represents a 40 percent increase since 1980, and nearly 31 percent of these couples had children under the age of fifteen living with them. Fifty-six percent had never been married and about a third had been divorced. Another 11 percent were married to someone else or were widowed. Most of these couples were between the ages of twenty-five and forty-four (61%). Twenty-three percent were under twenty-five, 11 percent were between forty-five and sixty-four, and 6 percent were over sixty-five.

A major study of cohabiting couples published in 1987 (Tanfer, 1987) reported that cohabiting women in their twenties tend to be white, to be less educated and less likely to be employed than noncohabiters, to be concentrated in large metropolitan areas in the western United States and are one-third more likely than noncohabiters to have grown up in a single-parent family. Cohabiters have intercourse at a relatively young age and are more likely to have had a pregnancy than noncohabiters. Cohabiters are more likely than noncohabiters to engage in unconventional behavior and to perceive themselves as liberated from traditional sex-role characteristics and to describe themselves as introverted, assertive, and independent. However, a significantly larger proportion of cohabiters than noncohabiters want to get married. They are no more likely than noncohabiters to perceive their singleness as permanent.

The data from the Tanfer study seem to substantiate the notion that cohabitation is not a substitute for marriage but an advanced form of courtship (Reiss, 1980; Rice, 1990). In another study, most cohabiting couples stated that they planned to marry someday, although the women in these relationships expected to marry more often and sooner than did the men (Risman, Hill, Rubin, & Peplau, 1981). On the other hand, the men saw fewer problems with the cohabitation than did the women. In this study, cohabiting women seemed to feel less powerful than noncohabiting women but also expressed greater satisfaction with their relationships than noncohabiters.

Cohabitation does not appear to pose a threat to marriage but, rather, to represent a step in the courtship process. In fact, many couples report that they are living together to learn how to relate to others in an intimate relationship. Premarital cohabitation is unrelated to marital satisfaction for whites in the first few years of marriage (Crohan & Veroff, 1989) but is negatively associated with marital satisfaction for blacks. In other words, black couples who had cohabited before marriage in the Crohan and Veroff study were less happy with marriage than black couples who had not. The authors of this study were unable to say why there were racial differences, but it may be that marriage is so much more difficult for black couples, especially for black men who are less educated and underemployed, that the transition to marriage is experienced as very stressful.

Of course, cohabitation has its problems. Unstructured relationships produce the same conflicts over division of labor and role behavior that one might expect in a married household, especially when the woman sees herself as unconventional about sex-role issues (Stafford, Blackman, & Dibona, 1977). Both married and cohabiting females do the lioness's share of the housework, even when holding full-time jobs. Although cohabiting men help with the laundry and dishes more often than do married men, cohabiting women do more gardening and home repair than married women and so lose some of the benefits they gain from assistance at laundry and other housework. A traditional ideology produces traditional behavior even in an unconventional relationship, creating traditional problems from decision making to sexual functioning.

In addition to the problems everyone else experiences, of course, cohabiting couples have to cope with guilt and with pressure from others, especially parents, to enter a more traditional arrangement. In fact, one study suggests that cohabiting couples decide whether or not to marry sooner than dating couples do, in part as a response to parental pressure (Risman, Hill, Rubin, & Peplau, 1981). The effects of social pressure and guilt, which must be considered in the evaluation of any alternative lifestyle, are even more evident in the cohabitation of people who express a sexual preference for someone of their own sex.

Homosexual Cohabitation Perhaps the least accepted form of cohabitation is the homosexual marriage, although in many ways homosexual marriage is similar to heterosexual cohabitation. Homosexual relationships have been subject to the ravages of instability and guilt, just as are other socially ill-defined

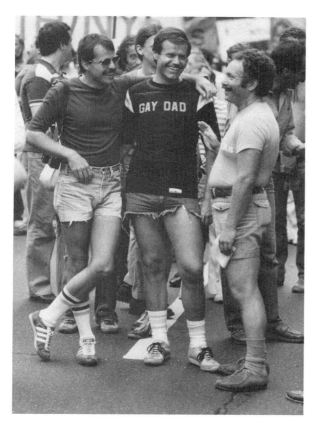

Public acknowledgment of homosexuality is a key force in the acceptance of this once alternative lifestyle as part of mainstream culture.

types of cohabitation. In ill-defined arrangements, the obligations and responsibilities of the partners are neither institutionalized—as are sex-role distinctions—nor legally defined. The ambiguity of the relationship and the disapproval of society can combine to produce much guilt and instability.

Although Hunt's (1974) study of sexual behavior did not show any increase in homosexual behavior since Kinsey's day, it is clear that homosexuality is far more visible today than it was in the 1950s. As Melville (1988) has written, probably not many homosexuals wish to change their sexual orientation, and homosexuality is no longer regarded as a mental illness by most psychologists and psychiatrists. Homosexuality is a part of modern life, probably a permanent part. But homosexuals still suffer the special difficulties associated with intense legal and social pressure to give up their lifestyle and conform to sexual and social norms.

Yet, one study of older homosexual men (Kimmel, 1982) points out that a number had been in relationships for as long as several decades. In this relatively small sample (fourteen men), two had experienced the death of a lover and gone on to establish a new, long-term relationship. Other research suggests that lesbian couples are even more likely than homosexual men to establish long-term, close relationships (Bell & Weinberg, 1978). What is more, Masters, Johnson, and Kolodny (1991) report that homosexual couples were able to communicate better and share more information about their sexuality than heterosexual couples. Homosexual couples also appeared more relaxed about sex, whereas heterosexual couples seemed to focus on achieving orgasm.

Publicly acknowledged homosexuality and homosexual cohabitation and marriage have become a much more prominent part of the contemporary social scene. Many urban areas now provide environments conducive to the development of a normalized homosexual subculture. Yet the Kinsey Institute (1989) reported that throughout the seventies American attitudes toward homosexuality continued to be extremely negative. Undoubtedly, the AIDS crisis among homosexual men has contributed to some reentrenchment of conservative attitudes.

One of the reasons why attitudes toward homosexuality may continue to be so negative, according to Virginia Sapiro (1990) is that our culture holds that any homosexual feelings are deviant and one homosexual experience makes you a homosexual (although one heterosexual experience does not make you a heterosexual). Therefore, heterosexual men and women may deny or be afraid to express any feelings of attraction they have for members of their own sex, making homosexuality yet a greater taboo.

As Gagnon and Greenblatt (1978) point out, it is only since the 1960s that a public, open homosexual culture has emerged. Openness means talking about one's sexual preference with others, disclosing those preferences to parents and friends, shaping loving and caring relationships in an atmosphere of acceptance, and solving problems of identity and ideology. Through the early 1980s, one of the most striking features of contemporary society had been the easing of the ban on homosexuality (Ariés, 1985). Whether this trend has been affected by heterosexual concerns over the spread of AIDS is not apparent. It may be that the AIDS crisis has created fear in some, empathy in others. In any event, it has certainly brought the homosexual lifestyle into cultural awareness and that alone is certain to have important effects.

Acceptability and Endorsement In *Family Systems in America* (1980), Reiss made the point that every new social philosophy creates a new potential for dogma, a new tendency to state an opinion as if it were a fact. Those who experiment with new social forms, like cohabitation or premarital sex or extramarital sex, begin to think of those who are more traditional as narrow-minded and thoughtless.

In sorting out the dogma on both sides (that is, the traditional dogma versus the unconventional dogma), Reiss makes two distinctions: one between discrimination and inhibition, and the other between acceptance and endorsement. Although the experimenters, according to Reiss, are likely to see the traditional people as "inhibited," there is a difference between inhibition and discrimination. "The difference centers [on] being *unable* to allow oneself to do something because of the inability to even entertain certain thoughts and, on the other hand, the *desire* not to do something because one *has examined* a behavior and decided that it is not appropriate for oneself. Discriminating people and inhibited people can be found on *both sides* of this debate over new family forms" (Reiss, 1980, p. 464).

Moreover, Reiss argues, one can accept a possibility for other people without offering the endorsement that leads to dogma. "Rather than any increase in real freedom," endorsing a certain behavior as "*the* right way for everyone" restricts freedom. "Freedom involves choice, and choice is more in line with the concept of acceptance and . . . [in line] with the concept of discrimination rather than the concept of forced choice or endorsement of some lifestyle simply because it is old or new" (p. 465).

This era is one in which expanding diversity of choice is viewed with great alarm by some and with unbounded delight by others. The discriminating person seems unlikely to take either of these positions with regard to change. Discrimination implies the serious consideration of all possibilities, an understanding of the antecedents and consequences of new forms, and deliberate, conscious selection of the form best suited to the self. Discrimination also suggests no fear of change, but a welcoming of the opportunity to exercise choice, yet an awareness that not all possible choices are equally appropriate. Reiss (1980) has written:

> If I had to pick one characteristic that was a trademark of the family in twentieth-century America, I would pick the *legitimation of choice*. There is no question in my mind that as I write these words, the range of truly legitimated choices is far greater than it was in 1950, 1960, or even in 1970. . . . We must learn to live with this, and we must learn to arrive at a judgment of our own preferences if we are to adjust to the type of society that has developed at this point in time. This does not necessarily call for a relativistic type of ethic in the sense of denying common values. What it does call for is the realization that although people feel that they can agree upon values such as integrity, honesty, concern for other human beings, happiness, and so forth, they may still disagree as to how best to achieve those values in their personal lives. (p. 466)

Summary

I. Intimacy, Love, and Being in Love
    A. Intimacy has been defined in terms of commitment, reciprocity, similarity, compatibility, attachment, and dependency.
        1. Self-disclosure is required for intimacy to occur.
        2. There is a strong relationship between intimacy and identity.
    B. Attachment is a life-span concept that permits the possibility of negative interaction in intimate relationships.

1. Attachment suggests that adult relationships may reflect the quality of the parent-child bond.
2. Recent research has not supported a strong attachment theory view of relationships.

C. Social exchange theory posits that all relationships are the product of the rewards and punishments people offer each other.
   1. The equity hypothesis suggests that people seek relationships where the outcome for both parties is approximately the same.
   2. Research supports the idea that both the winner and the loser in an inequitable relationship feel uncomfortable.
   3. Critics have raised questions about social exchange theory and equity theory in terms of whether they can explain the persistence of love in long-term relationships or the fact that various equitable relationships may have different qualities.

D. Romantic love appears to be a kind of love that differs from either the love one has for friends or the attachment in long-term relationships.
   1. Romance may wear off as uncertainty declines to zero in a long-term relationship.
   2. Some people experience limerance in the first stages of their relationships. Limerance includes intrusive thinking, acute longing, dependency of mood on the other, exclusiveness, and a general intensity of feeling tone.
   3. The aspects of a relationship that people say they value change over the life span.
   4. Different styles of loving may exist, which determine what a person means by "being in love."
      a. Six styles have been defined including eros, storge, ludus, pragma, agape, and mania.
      b. Eros, storge, and agape all meet the criteria for intimacy. From this point of view they are orientations; no one type of love is best for everyone.

E. Some theorists have tried to define mature love.
   1. Robert Sternberg talks about a balance between intimacy, passion, and commitment.
   2. The psychodynamic thinkers believe the capacity for mature love develops from early childhood and depends on the opportunity for independence.
      a. Mature love may involve the rediscovery of early childhood feelings of closeness but also includes an inevitable sadness with the acknowledgment that adults are really separate beings.
      b. Mature love requires the ability to tolerate ambiguity and to accept rejection and anger as part of a loving relationship.
   3. Enlarging the idea to say that mature lovers support and encourage each other's development may explain both why love can

persist in close relationships and why it continues to be an ambivalent experience.

II. Marriage
   A. The meaning of marriage has changed over the last 100 years from a context for economic activity and child rearing to a concept for self-development and emotional gratification.
   B. The selection of a partner appears to be homogamous, that is, people choose people like themselves.
      1. Equity and social exchange theory may best explain the first stage of partner selection.
      2. Value matching takes place in the second stage of courtship and may be most important among members of the middle class.
      3. In the last stage of mate selection, partners try to determine the degree of role compatibility they have, but such a determination is difficult, since it may require years and may change over the life span.
   C. Over 95 percent of all Americans will marry at one time or another, and marriage plays a central role in the socialization of adults. Two major types of marriage have been described.
      1. In an instrumental marriage, always characterized by traditional role distinctions, satisfaction is best predicted by the husband's performance in his occupational role.
      2. In a companionship marriage, the quality of the emotional relationship between the husband and the wife and the frequency of their communication predicts satisfaction.
      3. Regardless of the type, early marriage, especially one that interferes with educational attainment, is less stable.
      4. Although married people seem to be happier than single or divorced people, marital satisfaction is strongly correlated with the presence of small children in the home, especially for women.
      5. Men seem more satisfied with marriage, and at midlife successful men who have remained open to conflict are particularly well satisfied with marriage.
      6. The traditional wife who becomes involved in the community, has strong ties to other women, and has a fair degree of education and initiative is also likely to be satisfied.
      7. Women in two-paycheck marriages do not feel their jobs are threatened by their marriages and report feeling supported and admired by their husbands, although this trend is strongest among women over fifty.
         a. Dual-career marriages are often characterized by role overload, especially for women who experience strong conflict between working and the wife-mother role.
         b. Dual-career marriages are more successful if there is no ambiv-

alence toward the wife's career, and if both partners feel high levels of support and approval.

8. Recently, researchers have begun to classify marriages in terms of the couple's view of sex roles.

   a. Traditional, independent, and separate marriages may all be more satisfying than marriages in which one partner has a different view than the other.

   b. How couples negotiate conflict may be the key to continuing commitment.

D. The average American married couple is more satisfied with their sexual relationship than was the case at the time of the Kinsey report.

   1. Frequency of intercourse, variety of sexual techniques used, and frequency of orgasm have all increased among married couples since the 1940s.

   2. Extramarital sexual experiences have also become more frequent, at least among women.

   3. No consensus exists about whether extramarital sex is always harmful to a marriage; nor is there information about how extramarital sexual activity may change over the life span.

III. Dissolution

A. Divorce rates have increased dramatically over the past twenty-five years.

   1. The increase in divorce is a long-term trend that began at the turn of the century. It probably reflects changing expectations about marriage and the life span as well as the continuing emancipation of women.

   2. Women who work over thirty-five hours a week are subject to the highest divorce rates.

B. Divorce is usually very difficult for both parties, although the one who is rejected has more trouble adjusting.

C. More women complain of intense conflict accompanied by violence, and gender role conflicts appear to be a growing source of discontent.

D. The California Study reported that most divorcing couples were in extremely unhappy marriages and described six common patterns of response to divorce including anger, depression, disequilibrium, attachment, relief, and the feeling of having a new chance.

E. Despite the ordeal of divorce, 75–80 percent of all divorced people eventually remarry.

IV. Alternatives to Marriage

A. Singlehood is increasingly popular, perhaps because of recent trends toward the postponement of marriage.

   1. The relevant social organization for a single lifestyle has developed, making single life more satisfactory today than it was twenty-five or thirty years ago.

    2. Single people do still report feeling lonely, however, and have problems establishing an adequate social network and finding congenial, trustworthy friends.

B. Heterosexual cohabitation is an increasingly common alternative lifestyle and often includes children.

    1. The advantages and disadvantages of cohabitation can be understood in terms of the conflict between commitment and freedom.

    2. At least among younger people, cohabitation may represent a form of courtship and may be characterized by many of the same problems as marriage, including gender role conflicts.

C. Homosexual cohabitation has been studied in recent years and is far more visible today.

    1. Some homosexuals, especially lesbians, are able to establish long-term relationships, and most have more information about sex and are able to communicate better about their sexuality than heterosexual couples.

    2. As the relevant social organization for homosexuality emerges, homosexuality is likely to become a more prominent part of modern life. It remains to be seen how the AIDS crisis will affect the homosexual lifestyle.

D. The distinction between discrimination and inhibition, acceptance and endorsement is important in dealing with the legitimation of choice about family and sexuality in the twentieth century.

5

Young Adulthood: The Expanded Context—Work and Family

There is time for work. And time for love.
That leaves no other time.

—Coco Chanel

AMY IS THIRD-GENERATION: Sansei, Japanese American. She learned what Japanese she knows from her grandmother. Her parents were trying too hard to fit in. They seemed to have given up everything that was Japanese, except for their traditional ideas about women. Amy got a good education, but they never expected her to have to work, at least not while she had children. Oh, they might have imagined that she would help out in a store or a restaurant if her husband had a business, but it probably never occurred to them that she would be facing the problem of finding a job for the first time at thirty-five. Dennis left her a couple of weeks ago and it looks as though he really isn't coming back. Amy thinks he'll probably let her live in the house with the kids for a while, but she knows from watching the divorces of her friends that she will have to be ready to sell the house sometime in the next couple of years.

She's going to need help and she's got precious little money to find it with. Dennis has been giving her what she needs for groceries and paying the bills, but that won't last long. Besides, she hates going to him for every little thing. She can't very well ask him to foot the bill for her perm or a new dress. With two little kids, she isn't thinking of a "career." Careers take a lot of time and energy. She hopes she can make it on an ordinary job. But what kind of job? When she took all the vocational tests as a teenager, they said she'd make a good doctor or a forest ranger. That's about as useless as information gets! She knows they don't exactly pay top wages at the Jack-in-the-

Box, but at least there'd be medical coverage. Dennis will probably agree to cover the kids, but she won't have medical if there's a divorce.

Sales, maybe sales. Maybe residential real estate. That's a way to make some money without going back to school. But there's a long period when you're just building a business and you have to live on commissions. Amy never had to think about finances before. There was always a steady paycheck. How do people make it on commission? Do real estate people have medical insurance? What kind of test will she have to take? Where could she find out how much money real estate agents are making these days? It's too much. Amy starts to cry. She'd go home to her parents, but she can't imagine living under her father's thumb again. On the other hand, her mother would be able to take care of the children while she got some of this straightened out. Maybe she'll just tell Dennis he can have the house and the children. How come she got stuck? Stuck! She didn't really mean that. She loves the kids. She'd never abandon them. How did she end up so unprepared, so unready to fend for herself? That doesn't matter now. What matters is getting out of this house and getting started.

ADULTS ARE THE CARETAKERS, THE ONES who are responsible. We assume that adults have the skills to care for themselves and to care for others when choice, chance, or circumstances require. To care for someone implies both emotional and physical support. In today's world, providing physical support means choosing, finding, and maintaining a job, whether one works at home or in a factory or an office, in a store or in the great outdoors.

Caring also implies a special closeness: the closeness of friends, lovers, and children. This chapter explores the literature on work and family in young adulthood. Beginning with a survey of theory and research about vocational choice and job satisfaction, we will examine how people choose jobs, why they become committed to them or why they change, and how they come to consider themselves successful or satisfied. The discussion will address the special problems of women and minorities in the job market.

The second half of the chapter deals with the other central developmental task of young adulthood: the establishment of a family. This section encompasses not only the traditional choices but also the growing trend toward alternative family careers, from single parenthood and stepparenting to the decision to forego childbearing. Of course, such issues and decisions are not limited to that part of the life cycle called young adulthood. But, for most of us, these matters are central during the young adult years, whether or not they are permanently resolved.

Work, Occupation, and Career

Almost all adults work. Unless you are lucky enough to be wealthy, you will have to labor to produce the goods and services that make possible personal, cultural, and species survival, as well as improvements in the quality of life. The chances are that most people would choose to work even without financial necessity, for work is a major social role of adult life. One's *occupation* or *vocation* identifies a significant aspect of the self. An occupation provides an important social and personal anchor, a stronghold of identity. It is impossible to understand adult life without understanding the role of work.

Whereas the terms *occupation* and *vocation* are both generally applied to all forms of work, the word **career** is often reserved for prestigious occupations. Some writers believe that career is a minority, elite institution in Western society. From this point of view, people who have careers stay in one occupational field and progress through a series of stages associated with upward mobility, achieving ever greater mastery, responsibility, and financial remuneration (Krause, 1971; Ritzer, 1977). Constructs such as being "on time" and "getting ahead" are central to the study of careers. Insurance executives and university professors have careers; carpenters and domestic workers do not.

This discussion probably explains why Amy is having so much trouble seeing herself in a career. She believes that a career requires a specialized education, a high degree of commitment, and too much outside responsibility for a woman with two small children. Adopting a different approach, other authors have defined a career as any organized path across space and time—as consistent ongoing involvement in any role (Van Maanen & Schein, 1977; Greenhaus, 1988). In this sense, a doctor, a plumber, or a homemaker may have several concurrent careers: one as a worker, one as a spouse, one as a citizen, and so on. From this perspective, the study of careers is the study of change through the life cycle.

The concept of career as involvement over time is especially useful for a life-span psychology. The study of an individual's occupational career can be expected to yield rich information about important life events that accompany progress in one's role as worker. Events like being hired, promoted, fired, or retired are critical milestones in overall adult development. Amy's reentry into the labor force will undoubtedly change her life very dramatically. Plumbers, letter carriers, bookmakers, doctors, lawyers (as well as criminals), and police officers all experience changes in occupational status-career changes.

Careers over Time

A number of writers have offered stage models of career development (Ginsberg, 1972; Super, 1957, 1984; Wanous, 1980; Van Maanen & Schein, 1977;

Table 5.1 Characteristics of different career stages

1. Preparation for Work
Typical Age Range: 0–25
Major Tasks: Develop occupational self-image; assess alternative occupations; develop initial occupational choice; pursue necessary education.
Significant Information Needs: personal values, interests, talents, lifestyle preferences; different occupational fields and their education and training requirements.

2. Organizational Entry
Typical Age Range: 18–25
Major Tasks: Obtain job offer(s) from desired organization(s), select appropriate job based on accurate information.
Significant Information Needs: personal values, interests, talents, lifestyle preferences; characteristics, duties, rewards, and pressures of job(s) under consideration; outlook, resources, human resource practices, culture of organization(s) under consideration.

3. Early Career
Typical Age Range: 25–40
Major Tasks: Learn job and organizational rules and norms; fit into chosen occupation and organization; increase competence, pursue Dream.
Significant Information Needs: personal values, interests, and talents; requirements of new job; organizational policies, practices, expectations, norms, and culture; level of performance on current job; desired balance of work and nonwork involvements; presence/absence of a match with chosen occupation and organization; availability and appropriateness of alternative career paths; opportunities for additional learning experiences; appropriate career strategies; accessibility of mentor.

Greenhaus, 1988). Table 5.1 presents Greenhaus's scheme along with a list of both the major occupational tasks of each phase and comments on the kinds of information a person might need at each.

Although all individuals will not necessarily proceed through these stages at the times indicated, the age ranges provide what might be considered typical for a person who stayed in a single career throughout the life span. If Van Maanen and Schein (1977) are correct, even jobs that offer little prestige, like domestic service or assembly-line work, and deviant occupations, like prostitution or burglary, can provide a context for the development of skills and the opportunity to be a mentor one day instead of a novice.

The first two stages in Greenhaus's scheme, *preparation* and *organizational entry,* have been more thoroughly researched than any of the other stages of career development. In particular, the process of exploration and career choice in preparation for work has attracted much attention, both from researchers who are trying to help people make successful choices and from those who

---

Table 5.1 *(continued)*

---

4. Midcareer

Typical Age Range: 40–55

Major Tasks: Reappraise early career and early adulthood; reaffirm or modify Dream; make choices appropriate to middle adult years; remain productive at work.

Significant Information Needs: emergence of new talents; possible changes in values, interests, and desired balance of work and nonwork involvements; organization's future plans and needs; advisability of midcareer change; level of performance on current job; availability and appropriateness of vertical or lateral mobility opportunities; feasibility of improving current job
if mobility is unavailable or unwanted.

5. Late Career

Typical Age Range: 55–Retirement

Major Tasks: Remain productive in work; maintain self-esteem; prepare for effective retirement.

Significant Information Needs: possible changes in values, interests, and desired balance of work and nonwork involvements; level of performance in current job; feasibility of lateral or downward mobility or improving current job; opportunities for part-time employment or other employment opportunities involving reduced level of involvement; options for timing of retirement; personal resources required for retirement; required psychological transition between work and retirement.

SOURCE: Adapted from Table 5.4 (Five Stages of Career Development) in Greenhaus, 1988, p. 87.

---

are helping organizations select individuals who will be productive, committed employees.

Exploration and Vocational Choice

*No other technique for the conduct of life attaches the individual
so firmly to reality as laying emphasis on work; for his work
at least gives him a secure place in a portion of reality, in the
human community.*

—Sigmund Freud

The period of **exploration** has attracted so much attention, in part because people receive more professional and family advice at this stage of career development. Parents, teachers, and adolescents require information on the subject, as well as do those adults who make career changes or begin careers relatively late in life. Unfortunately, most of the data are, once again, cross-sectional rather than longitudinal. The data may indicate what kind of person is a successful doctor, airline pilot, or teacher, but not what sort of young adult becomes successful in later years at a particular kind of career or what kind of characteristics enable career change. Traditionally, vocational choice has been approached as a problem of match. The underlying assumption is, "If person A is successful at job X, then anyone who has the same characteristics as person A is also likely to become successful at job X."

Differentialist theories rely on the assumption of matching, emphasizing the measurement of personality characteristics and job characteristics through paper-and-pencil tests. Typically, the test taker is asked to choose between pairs of occupations (Would you rather be a taxicab driver or a police officer?) or between pairs of activities (Would you rather read a book or watch television?). The pattern of responses a person makes is then compared with the patterns typical of several different major vocational types (Holland et al., 1973; Osipow, 1990). Typically these include:

1. Conventional workers: Secretaries, receptionists, bookkeepers, typists fall in this category. Efficient, conforming, and even inhibited people seem to do well at conventional jobs.

2. Enterprising people: Sales, management, business ownership, even running a small farm might fall in this category. The personal requirements include energy, the ability to dominate the situation, and an outgoing, ambitious personality.

3. Artistic individuals: People holding jobs in fashion, architecture, or design, as well as the traditional artistic pursuits are likely to be imaginative, expressive, original, creative, and introspective.

4. Social types: Teachers, social workers, psychologists, counselors, and personnel managers are likely to appear cooperative, helpful, understanding, and gregarious.

5. Investigative workers: Scientists, researchers, perhaps even creative mechanics, or people who are "trouble-shooters" in larger companies usually possess such traits as curiosity, intellectual interests, and a rational approach to problem solving.

6. Realistic individuals: Engineers, most mechanics, and some computer programmers who are mechanical, practical, materialistic, and not very sociable belong in this category.

The evidence shows that the kinds of tests differentialists use do a good job of predicting whether or not a particular person will be successful at one type of career or another, particularly if that person is a white male (Osipow, 1990; Cairo, 1982; Lunneborg & Lunneborg, 1975; Carter & Swanson, 1990). In fact, the rational, problem-solving approach suggested by the differentialists may well be the optimal way to choose a job, or to change jobs. As Greenhaus (1988) points out, career exploration is a lifelong process, and the more information one has about one's self, the environment, and the options, the more likely one will be able to fulfill one's needs and utilize one's talents. People who make such conscious choices are probably more productive and satisfied in their jobs. However, very few people develop vocational choices in this manner. In the first place, luck and circumstance often play an important role in vocational choice, as they are likely to do for Amy in making her choices after a divorce. The best choice a person can make (e.g., artistic) may not coincide with the opportunities available (checker in a local grocery store). Second, socioeconomic conditions, both at the time someone looks for a job and during his or her childhood, are critical determinants of both aspirations and opportunities (Neff, 1985).

More recent versions of the differentialist position (Davis & Lofquist, 1984) consider the match between a person's vocational needs and skills and the task requirements of a job, along with the degree to which a particular job might fulfill that individual's job needs. These factors are then used to predict job satisfactoriness and tenure. Again, however, this very rational approach has relatively little predictive value. Correlations between a person's skills and needs on the one hand, and task requirements and the ability of the job to fulfill vocational needs on the other account for less than 20 percent of the differences among people in the matter of job choice. People too often choose jobs and stay in them because they lack any other realistic opportunities, not because they like the job (Neff, 1985).

The differentialists view vocational choice as a rational, cognitive process and are interested in developing measures that predict a successful career. More interested in what actually happens than what ought to happen, the **developmentalists** (Ginsberg, 1972; Super, 1957, 1963, 1984) propose that career choice proceeds through an orderly sequence of stages. One version (Ginsberg, 1972) suggests a series of stages representing successively more realistic choices. This version of the developmental position assumes that occupational choice is a process that is largely irreversible, since early choices eliminate many possible occupational paths. Compromise is assumed to occur between internal factors like skills, traits, and interests, and external forces like opportunities and socioeconomic circumstances (Neff, 1985).

This view suggests that fantasy ambitions, unleavened by a realistic assessment of job requirements and personal assets, are slowly eliminated through childhood, becoming more realistic by adolescence. Unfortunately, the research has demonstrated that few people progress in such a predictable way. In fact, many children are almost too realistic in their choices. Little girls rule out business careers and professional athletics very early, whereas blacks and Latinos give up most of the prestigious professions long before adolescence (Barclay, 1974; Vigod, 1972; Werts, 1968). On the other hand, many older **adolescents** seem unaware of vocational realities. As many as 65 percent of all high school students indicate a strong interest in the professions, yet only 14 percent will ever become professionals (Cosby, 1974; Hutson, 1962).

In another version of the developmental position, Donald Super used the development of self-concept as a primary explanatory concept (Super, 1957, 1963, 1984). Vocational choice, he argued, proceeds from the implementation of ideas about the self formed in childhood. These ideas include beliefs about what is comfortable and appropriate, and what kinds of skills, abilities, habits, and patterns are most suitable to the self as well as the cultural, social, and economic realities that shape the options one pursues.

Super formulated four stages, each characterized by growing clarity about the self: crystallization, specification, implementation, and stabilization. In early adolescence, ideas about work *crystallize,* but a particular occupation is not *specified* until sometime between eighteen and twenty-one. In the years between twenty-one and twenty-four, people generally *implement* their decisions, obtaining the necessary education and experience for the jobs they have chosen. Then from twenty-five to thirty, vocational choices *stabilize.*

In a series of important longitudinal studies, Super's students have produced results that demand substantial theoretical revisions. These studies have demonstrated that career choice is rarely a stagelike process, and permanent decisions are often not reached in early adulthood. In fact, even among the older subjects in these studies (aged thirty-six), job commitment often remained provisional. Nearly 40 percent of the older subjects were still involved in career exploration and almost 20 percent exhibited cycles of exploration, implementation, and stabilization over the course of the research. Furthermore, although a high level of job attainment was associated with early decisiveness and commitment, job satisfaction and success seemed to be more strongly related to flexibility in vocational development than to stabilization (Phillips, 1982a,b).

One recent study of women's careers (Ornstein & Isabella, 1990) has even suggested that Super's stages may not be useful in describing women's careers at all. From a life-span point of view, both developmental stage theories underrate a number of significant forces. First, both ignore the possibility of vocational development and change in adult life; second, neither captures the way in which the historical and social context changes and alters the plans and goals of individuals at any age. For instance, men's lives may be more orderly and stagelike than women's because women tend to move in and out of work and family roles depending more on life events than do men (Ornstein, Cron, & Slocum, 1989; Ornstein & Isabella, 1990). Stage theories are also challenged by the way people discover their calling fortuitously, or even as a product of random behavior. Some people look for a career in a fruitful, flexible way, some run around in circles and get stuck in an unrewarding spot. Some people just stumble into jobs (Vondracek & Lerner, 1982).

Developmental theories do a good job, however, of pointing out how vocational choice is a process that begins in childhood and is shaped by many of the same forces that shape other kinds of behavior. For example, research on

"The child was diseased at birth—stricken with an hereditary ill that only the most vital men are able to shake off. I mean poverty—the most deadly prevalent of all diseases." Eugene O'Neill

vocational choice among Black Americans (Carter & Swanson, 1990) indicates that blacks who are successful in their careers often show different patterns of interests than do whites in the same career. Blacks express stronger interest in business, sales, verbal-linguistic, and social service occupations than whites, who tend to show more interest in the biological and physical sciences, technical and skilled trades, as well as aesthetic-cultural occupations. Developmental theory would emphasize the role of cultural differences and values in shaping one's self-image in childhood as well as the importance of limited opportunity among less privileged groups.

Because developmental theories emphasize the role of self-concept and self-esteem, they also help explain why certain kinds of attitudes about the self have been recently found to predict career decisiveness. One recent study of college women (Taylor & Popma, 1990) concluded that feelings of **self-efficacy** were important in predicting which women were having the most difficulty making decisions about their vocations. Self-efficacy was defined as the confidence that one can successfully make the decisions involved in selecting a career. Along with other researchers, these authors have argued that we need to study whether teaching self-efficacy to people in late adolescence or adulthood can create greater career decisiveness (Betz & Hackett, 1987).

There is little doubt, however, that many important forces that shape career

Table 5.2 Summary of factors facilitative of women's career development	
Individual Variables	**Background Variables**
High ability	Working mother
Liberated sex role values	Supportive father
Instrumentality	Highly educated parents
Androgynous personality	Female role models
High self-esteem	Work experience as adolescent
Strong academic self-concept	Androgynous upbringing
Educational Variables	**Adult lifestyle Variables**
Higher education	Late marriage or single
Continuation in mathematics	No or few children
Girls' schools and women's colleges	
SOURCE: Betz & Fitzgerald, 1987, p. 143.	

choice are present in childhood. Strong relationships have been reported between self-concept and school ability as well as self-concept and eventual educational attainment and occupational status (Bachman, O'Malley, & Johnston, 1978; Betz & Fitzgerald, 1987). Table 5.2 presents some of the factors Nancy Betz and Louise Fitzgerald reported in their extensive work on the career psychology of women. These factors, or variables as they are labeled in the table, are both internal (individual abilities and values) and external (family, educational, and work experiences).

We also know, however, that a data base for explaining vocational choice may not be reasonably limited to adolescence and young adulthood, especially if it is to include the vocational decisions of many women. Susan Phillips (1982a,b), one of the researchers working in Super's lab, has proposed that a cyclical model of decision making is necessary to describe vocational development over the life span. Perhaps career stages should not be considered age-linked at all, since the consideration of stages often leads researchers to overlook exploration or new beginnings after a certain age (Peacock, Rush, & Milkovich, 1980; Ornstein & Isabella, 1990).

Of course, whenever we choose a career path, the act of choosing alone is not enough. We must also look for a job, choose an organization, be recruited by that organization or develop the resources to be an independent contractor or business owner. Unfortunately, little available research focuses on the career development of individuals who work for themselves. Obviously, it is easier to study people in organizations, and most organizations provide formal procedures for job search and recruitment, making it easy to study how people are selected for entry and how they adapt once they are chosen.

Job Search and Recruitment

Part of what is amazing, given the amount of research we have on vocational choice, is that so little attention has been paid to how people choose an organization. We do know that about 50 to 80 percent of all blue-collar workers use informal sources, like referrals from a friend, to find a job. White-collar workers use formal channels more often, but research indicates that people who find jobs through informal channels are more likely to be satisfied than those who learn of a job through an ad in the newspaper or an employment agency. Overall, however, turnover rates for new employees are extremely high. One study has estimated that 50 to 60 percent of all new recruits can be expected to leave within the first seven months (Wanous, 1980).

Why do so many people make choices that they regret so soon? John Wanous (1980) has argued that individuals and organizations are both to blame. During the search and recruitment process, recruits hope to maximize opportunities and organizations hope to develop a large pool of applicants. Therefore, both the recruit and the recruiter put their best foot forward. Rather than enabling job applicants and organizations to gain a realistic picture of each other, the situation promotes unrealistic expectations. Therefore, it is hardly surprising that the attitudes of new recruits become steadily more negative over the first few months and even years of employment.

As Georgia Chao (1988) points out, it is not that new recruits don't have the qualifications to do the job they were hired to do. In fact, organizations often focus too strongly on whether recruits are qualified in terms of skills and attitudes. The problem is that the "fit" with the organization is wrong. Every organization has a **culture,** a set of assumptions, beliefs, attitudes, and ways of doing things that are unique. Most often, however, people in organizations do not consciously understand how their own **organizational culture** works (Schein, 1987), so they are likely to make errors in selecting recruits that will be satisfied and productive in their particular culture.

Even within the same industry, cultures vary dramatically from one company to another. Let's say Amy decides she's going to try her hand at real estate and applies to two different companies doing business in her area. One is a small, family-owned business where the agents are on a first-name basis with the owner. People in this office dress casually unless they are taking clients around to see property. They often go out to lunch with each other and even include the owner. They value their personal relationships at work and think it is extremely important to keep the office running harmoniously. They help each other out all the time, even taking care of calls from another agent's client or holding houses open for each other.

Amy also has applied to a large, national real estate company with branches in thirty states. There is a manager on site in the office she applied to, but there is no owner and all procedures and **organizational policies** come down from the main office in another state. The manager of this office is very busy working with the national network and the main office and has little time for social interaction with the agents. Everyone wears the same company jacket and skirt or pants. People in the office are very competitive and one agent or another is always complaining that someone else in the office has "stolen" a client.

The cultures of these two organizations are very different. A person who would be happy in one would probably feel like a fish out of water in the other. To reduce the very high initial turnover rates in organizations today, Chao (1988) believes it is necessary to choose applicants who fit the organizational culture, which means more realistic recruitment procedures and better programs that train or socialize people in the ways of the organization once they are hired. **Socialization** refers to all the formal and informal opportunities the organization provides for learning about culture. What is suggested by Chao (1988) and others is that organizations should focus on recruiting people who they will be able to socialize successfully. This process begins by asking the right questions. Aside from the usual questions about qualifications, past experience, and personal life, companies also need to know what kind of culture the applicant is seeking. Does the applicant expect a friendly, informal working situation? Is she or he only interested in earning a top salary? Do flexible working hours appear to be important? Does the organization offer child care? Is the potential for advancement a significant consideration for this applicant? What about independence on the job?

Corporate culture includes how organizations use space (office allocation, office space), time (actual working hours, tempo, punctuality), things (dress, furnishings, symbols, logos, etc.), and language (repeated phrases, words, body language). Vijay Sathe (1985) suggests the following seven questions for the potential recruit trying to check out organizational culture:

1. What are the most important agreements the members of the organization seem to have about work (It is very important, it is very hard, it is only a part of one's life), human nature (human beings can be trusted, they have to be told what to do, they are easy to motivate), and human relationships (competition makes a business healthy, cooperation is the most important thing)?

2. What does the organization stand for? What is its motto? ("At Ford, quality is job 1." "Better living through science." "We don't want to change your life, we just want to change your oil.")

3. What does it take to be highly successful in the organization? What kind of person is respected? What is considered heroic? (The founder really cared about people. The founder had a great new concept. The founder beat the competition hands down.)

4. What company folklore, rituals, symbols, and ceremonies best reveal the essential character of the organization? (The best producers in the company all have special plaques and trophies that are awarded at the yearly banquet. The person considered most helpful or friendly is pictured on the front of the newsletter.)

5. What is considered serious punishment in this organization? What kinds of mistakes are not forgiven? (Conflicts with the manager result in firing. Making a mistake on a contract meant the last person in this position was demoted.)

6. Make believe this organization is a person. How would you describe that person? (Is the organization fat or sleek, is it short or tall, well dressed, or down at the heels?)

7. What are the main rules that everyone has to follow in this organization? (People always show up at 8:00 A.M. on the dot and try to look busy all day. Does anyone ever question what the manager says or are people expected to make suggestions and attend all the office meetings with new ideas and plans?)

Informal hiring practices probably work as well as they do because the applicant who is referred by a friend is likely to have some idea of what the culture is really like. Getting a job through a friend is at least informative. On the other hand, such methods tend to be discriminatory. In many places, affirmative-action guidelines mandate the use of formal procedures; thus, realistic recruitment and the formal assessment of culture have become more important than ever.

Acceptance, Reality Shock, and Commitment

Although unrealistic expectations inevitably produce disillusionment about one's new job and organization, not all of these expectations are created in the search-and-recruitment process. In many occupations, great disparity also exists between the image we gain of a job from education and anticipatory socialization (informal training) and the reality of the day-to-day demands of the job. Especially in those occupations for which the education or training is idealistic and principled but the job itself involves knowing and maintaining established procedures and routine bureaucratic functions, **reality shock** is a common entry phenomenon. For instance, the realities of teaching and social work are quite different from the images of the teacher or social worker as transmitted by a college or university curriculum.

The idealistic occupations are not the only shocking jobs. Reality shock is common among homemakers, secretaries, and truck drivers. Entry information is almost always positively biased, and anticipatory socialization is most often unrealistic. Playing house and baby-sitting are not adequate preparation

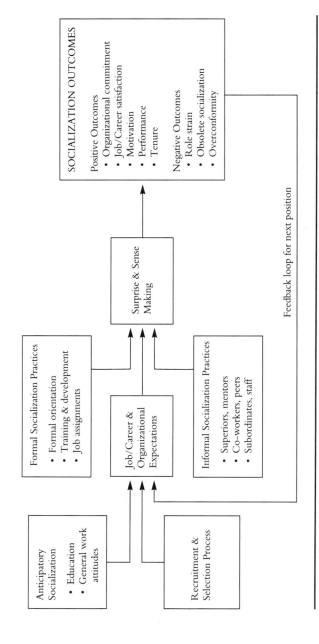

Figure 5.1 Organizational socialization model for newcomers.

SOURCE: Chao, 1988, p. 33.

for the overwhelming and irrevocable responsibility of a career as a homemaker and parent. Typing classes and television comedies don't offer a realistic picture of life as a medical receptionist or secretary, and law school provides at best only meager contact with the realities of being an attorney.

Reality shock is worst where there is little upward mobility in jobs like nursing or teaching, and where the rewards for settling down after the shock wears off are minimal. If shock is very deep, individuals may feel disoriented and need to reevaluate their original career decision (Ritzer, 1977). Furthermore, the stronger the organizational culture, that is, the more control it exerts over the lives of employees, the stronger reality shock is likely to be (Sathe, 1985).

Again, it is through the process of socialization that newcomers are protected from excessive feelings of shock and disorientation. Socialization begins with the ways people learn general work attitudes and behaviors in families and continues through formal education. Organizations try to influence this process by influencing the kinds of coursework and projects that are offered in schools and colleges. Recruitment and selection also offer an opportunity for socialization, although it is not often seen that way by either the organization or the individual.

Figure 5.1 presents one version of what happens in the socialization of newcomers. It depicts how the job, career, and organizational expectations of newcomers are influenced by anticipatory socialization (family, friends, and education) as well as recruitment and selection. As soon as the recruit enters the work environment, however, the formal and informal socialization practices of the organization begin to create surprises. The newcomer finds that his or her expectations are not going to be met or that they have been exceeded. Newcomers respond to these surprises by trying to make sense out of the environment (e.g., they decide that the company is poorly managed or they feel they were in the right place at the right time). Chao (1988) believes that it is very important for the organization to monitor whatever surprises the newcomer experiences, for it is at that point that the organization can have great influence on how the newcomer perceives the company, the work, and his or her place.

Too often, formal socialization practices are vague and general, present too much information, or are too outdated to be informative. Organizations often mistakenly assume that new employees will read written materials or figure things out as they go along. Really good orientation programs, for instance, focus on such issues as what the supervisors are really like, what to expect in terms of initiation from the other employees, and what the organizational culture is like. Such information can reduce other kinds of training people need by as much as 50 percent (Chao, 1988). Successful socialization ensures that employees develop commitment, job satisfaction, and high levels of motivation; perform well; and stay on the job. Poor socialization may produce role strain or overconformity and may be outdated very early.

Socialization generally takes from six months to a year as new recruits learn technical jargon and special terminology, then the business and technical aspects of the job, and, finally, the secrets of the culture and the social and political systems (Sathe, 1985). Sathe contends that the faster a new recruit can learn the ins and outs of organizational culture, the faster adjustment will occur. Listening to how people use language, watching traffic patterns, learning who spends time with whom, trying to discover the informal structure of power in the organization as well as the formal one are all ways to learn about organizational culture. The informal power structure of an organization—who influences decisions, who has access to higher authorities, who controls resources—is a central feature of culture and can make the difference in organizational survival (Snodgrass, 1986).

Sathe also stresses how important it is to handle early encounters well, and to begin contributing to organizational productivity by handling the first assignment well, which means understanding what the assignment really means. He recommends new recruits ask for a little history. Questions like, Who did this assignment last and what happened, What has experience taught us are the obstacles, Who opposes this assignment and why, Who supports it, and why, are usually considered reasonable by older members of the organization and can give the new recruit much insight into the job and the culture.

Of course, some organizations use the first assignment to test the mettle of a new recruit. A first assignment can be phony or "Mickey Mouse." On the other hand, it can throw new recruits in over their heads, deliberately exposing them to failure. The point of such a method is often not to teach skills but to establish commitment (Chao, 1988).

Feelings of commitment are the product of one's investment in an organization or profession. Education constitutes an investment and so does the learning of specific skills acquired on the job. Learning the ropes—the informal workings of the organization, the shortcuts, and the problematic situations—contributes to growing occupational commitment. Moreover, the organization's investment in the individual increases commitment. Pension plans, fringe benefits, stock options, promotions, and salary increases all serve to deepen such feelings (Ritzer, 1977) as well as programs like child care or flextime (Zedeck & Mosier, 1990). Similarly, the interests expressed by unions—medical and dental insurance, job security, and cost-of-living increases—foster commitment to the union and to unionized companies.

Investment is also increased by the personal bonds of sponsorship. Sponsorship does occur in most jobs within organizations and may even be an explicit part of the entry phase, as it is in occupations that involve apprenticeships. A sponsor, or mentor, takes a personal interest in the progress of the recruit, offering knowledge, help, support, providing recommendations or referrals, and assisting the novice in establishing contacts in the trade, business, or professional community. Success often depends on the acquisition of an appropriate sponsor. In academic life the power of one's sponsor, or major professor, can significantly affect one's professional attainments (Crane, 1965; Lips, 1988). In film, music, and the other arts, as well as politics, the role of protégé is a common one in the lives of successful individuals—for example, the French director François Truffaut is considered a student of Alfred Hitchcock. Recall, too, that Jung studied under Freud.

In an article titled "The Mentor Connection" (1977), Gail Sheehy reviewed a study of twenty-five female executives done at Harvard by Margaret Hennig (1970). Hennig's research underlined the significance of women in the business world. Each of the most successful of these women had developed a close relationship with one powerful, successful man, and each was guided up the first rungs of the ladder by her sponsor. Because there were so few female executives in high places, all of the women discussed had male mentors. And all experienced the concomitant confusion of relationships laden with sexual and erotic implications as well as social and intellectual opportunities. A cohort effect may be present in these data: all of the women in the study were unmarried and under thirty-five at the beginning of the investigation. Attitudes may change enough to allow different kinds of work relationships to develop between men and women (Colwill & Lips, 1988).

Success, Job Satisfaction, and the Life Cycle

The new recruit, riding the white stallion of commitment and guided by a gentle but powerful mentor, gallops off into the sunset pursuing fame and fortune. At least that is the way this story is supposed to end. Yet it has become increasingly clear that Americans at all levels of society are dissatisfied with work in this bureaucratic, affluent society, and that many are not placated by the traditional economic incentives. Labor, management, and professional organizations are searching for ways to make work more meaningful and less autocratic within organizations of every kind. Gradually emphasis is being shifted to the noneconomic rewards of work, and efforts are being made to increase the challenge and value of work (Miernyk, 1975; Wanous, 1980).

The nature and organization of work is changing. Concepts like participatory management have evolved from our desire for less autocratic work environments. Workers are frequently organized into teams that make their own management decisions, sitting down with administrators to develop goals and objectives as a common project. Transitory groupings of individuals who are task-oriented, rather than standing groups that perform the same function over and over again on every task, can provide a satisfactory solution to the problems of both worker and management (Toffler, 1970; Peters, 1987). Organizing employees in task-oriented groups allows workers to follow a project through each phase to completion. Instead of tracking the costs of several projects, for example, one accountant might be assigned to all phases of a specific project and be acquainted with all the workers assigned to a project. Sometimes this is called a team approach.

Other favored innovations are flexible scheduling, which allows workers to set their own hours (within limits) and even to pursue some occupational activities at home (Zedeck & Mosier, 1990), and support for continuing education, through programs to provide both leave time and economic assistance. Indeed, support for continuing education is far more common today than ever before, and education seems to be a more important part of work at all levels. The revolution in work values and attitudes has contributed to an emphasis on learning and improving the quality of one's work (Peters, 1987).

Most of those who are contemplating the future believe we must move from a fixed to a flexible life cycle—designed to meet the needs of workers. As Robert Butler wrote in an article appropriately titled "The Burnt Out and the Bored" (1970), one approach to creating more productive and satisfying work environments is to reshuffle the life cycle. If people could schedule periods of work, leisure, retirement, or education throughout life, rather than being forced into long, boring blocks of the same activities for twenty, thirty, or even forty years, they might feel that all activities are more meaningful. People also need time to work through the conflicts among self, family, and work at different stages of the life cycle, returning to work refreshed and recharged. Butler made five recommendations:

1. Employees should be allowed to accumulate leave for as long as they like and to use it in long, uninterrupted blocks.
2. Organizations should make greater provisions for employees to return to school, whether their course of study is job-related or not.
3. Adolescents should be encouraged to work if they wish, rather than being forced to continue an education that seems meaningless.
4. Compulsory retirement should be abolished.
5. The rules of tenure, promotion, and seniority that encourage people to stay in the same job for forty years or more should be reassessed.

The American worker wants more than a paycheck. Workers are demanding job satisfaction, fair treatment, and involvement in decisions that affect their lives, as well as challenge, interest, and value in life both in and out of the occupational role.

Social consciousness is increasingly apparent in business, industry, and the professions. It has been said that this society is in transition, from a culture based on unconscious agreements to one based on conscious ones (Babbie, 1977). As a result of that increasing consciousness, many workers are demanding promotion based on performance rather than on arbitrary decisions determined by race, sex, or the whim of a supervisor. Yet, clearly, race, sex, and other forms of discrimination are still firmly on the scene.

Socioeconomic Level, Race, Sex, and Work

In a classic longitudinal study of adolescence and young adults by Bachman, O'Malley, and Johnston (1978), one conclusion emerged with great clarity. "In many ways, the most basic predictor variable in the Youth in Transition study is family socioeconomic level (SEL). SEL is related to most other background measures; indeed, there are times when what appears to be effects of other factors can be attributed equally well (and with greater parsimony) to SEL" (p. 21). Some of the background factors to which these authors refer include intelligence, vocabulary skill, reading comprehension, grades, college plans, attitudes toward school, citizenship, and even personal perceptions of academic ability. All these variables were predicted by socioeconomic level. Within a few years after high school graduation, Bachman, O'Malley, and Johnston also demonstrated a strong relationship between socioeconomic level and occupational as well as educational attainment.

It is said that those who have, get, and these data illustrate the point. People who have few resources in the first place are unlikely to encounter the models, the early training, or the later emotional and financial support that promote high aspirations. While there is evidence that such blue-collar occupations as carpenter, heavy machine operator, and electrician provide greater satisfaction as they become more lucrative, there is still a positive bias toward the professions among both middle- and working-class young adults. Relegation to less prestigious jobs may be disappointing and have a negative impact on self-esteem.

In addition to limited opportunity, however, Bachman, O'Malley, and Johnston have argued that young adults from less affluent families face overt discrimination. Working-class people usually have less education than members of the middle class, and employers often refuse to give someone who has dropped out of high school a job with potential for promotion or prestige. Even when the job does not really require a high school education, a dropout may be considered an unfit employee because dropouts have been stereotyped as unambitious, unintelligent, and beset by behavioral problems. In America today, despite many years of gradual change, discrimination of many kinds still affects the lives of millions and discrimination based on SEL is widespread. It is also subtle, however, because it cuts across sex, race, and ethnic group. Institutional and personal discrimination against women, blacks, and other minorities is more apparent and far better publicized.

Sex and Occupation

No one should have to dance backward all their lives.

> —Jill Ruckelshaus, former officer,
> U.S. Commission on Civil Rights

October, 1990: *Time* Magazine releases a special issue, one of only twenty such issues it has released in its history. It is called *Women: The Road Ahead,* and it begins with this statement: "A generation from now, if all the dreams of reformers have come true, a special issue devoted to women will seem about as appropriate as a special issue on tall people." The issue reveals that today's young women both want and believe that they can have it all. They want families and careers and the flexibility and support to balance them. Although more women than men still say that a happy marriage is the most important goal in their lives (39% vs. 30%), fully 27 percent of the women listed a successful career as the most important single goal of their lives. This proportion was not far behind that for men (32%) (*Time,* Fall 1990, p. 14).

The writers argue that women are knocking at the door of equality in the workplace. In the next ten years, there will be changes that may have been hard to imagine ten years ago. Much of this change may come because the work force in this country is changing dramatically. While the labor force will grow slowly over the next decade, most of the increase will be the product of women starting or returning to work. Only 9.3 percent of the new workers will be white, non-Hispanic U.S.-born men (*Time,* Fall 1990, p. 50).

Some of the changes are already reflected in the growth of women in the professions. Nearly 18 percent of doctors are now women, as are 22 percent of lawyers, and 32 percent of computer systems analysts. On the other hand, women make up only about 3 percent of the managers holding the top five positions below CEO in Fortune 1,000 companies. Almost 30 percent of all working women in the United States are still classified as "administrative support, including clerical" by the U.S. Bureau of the Census. Nearly 18 percent are employed in some form of service-oriented work, including private household help. Figure 5.2 presents the distribution of employed men and women by occupation for the year 1987.

Overwhelmingly, women are employed in "pink-collar" jobs, jobs that often require looking feminine, wearing attractive clothing, and being well groomed. Pink-collar workers are expected to be self-effacing and submissive rather than ambitious, which is the standard in the more upwardly mobile world of male blue-collar workers. Pink-collar workers tend to value the opportunity to work and the social connections they make at work (rather than a specific job) and to see their stint in the workplace as temporary (Sapiro, 1990; Colwell & Lips, 1988). Many women with college educations still get stuck in pink-collar jobs. An average male high school dropout earns more than a female college graduate partly because there is overt sexual discrimination against women and partly because women are segregated into the pink-collar and semiprofessional occupations. Women are more likely to be nurses than doctors, paralegals than lawyers, teachers than principals (Betz & Fitzgerald, 1987).

Even when women do achieve a place in a man's world, they do not earn equal pay, nor can they look forward to equal opportunity for a promotion. Women earn less than 60 percent of what men do—the same percentage that was the case in 1959. Figure 5.3 presents some of the data on male and female income.

One of the problems reflected in such statistics is that traditional female occupations tend to be dead-end jobs. That means they offer little hope of advancement. Few sales clerks become department store executives. Cooks, not

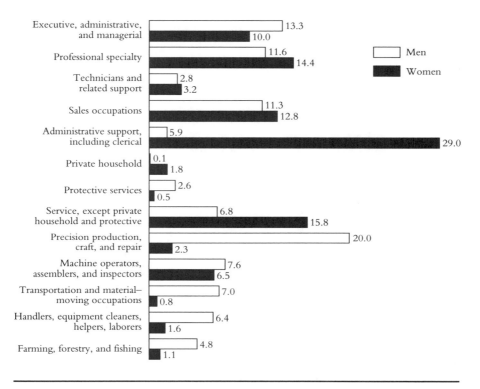

Figure 5.2 Distributions of employed men and women, by occupation, 1987 (in percent).

SOURCE: U.S. Bureau of the Census, 1989, p. 31.

waitresses, become restaurant managers. Nurses cannot be promoted to doctors, and secretaries are routinely overlooked for promotion to managerial or supervisory positions. Women are overrepresented in the lower ranks of the professions. They are lawyers, yes, but not judges, professors, not college presidents, doctors, but not chiefs of staff. Why is this? What are the barriers to the progress of women?

These statistics are the result, in at least some cases, of the personal decisions of individual people who have the power to hire, fire, and promote. People are far more likely to see a woman as a subordinate than a supervisor, and to evaluate effective power strategies more favorably when they are used by men than women (Sapiro, 1990; Lips, 1990). But much of the situation is the result of **institutional discrimination.** That is, the nature of work and family are simply not conducive to the employment and advancement of women. Both men and women expect to have families, but women are expected to, and do, carry the major burdens of child care and homemaking.

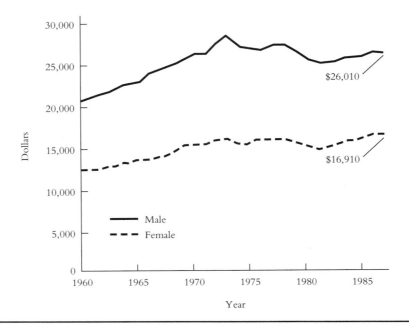

Figure 5.3 Median earnings of year-round, full-time workers: 1960 to 1987 (in 1987 dollars).

SOURCE: U.S. Bureau of the Census, 1989, p. 33.

Work is conducted outside the home. Children are not allowed in the workplace. Many women believe that such conflicts are more significant career obstacles than either professional and social stereotyping or explicit job discrimination (Jacoby, 1982; Melville, 1988; Betz & Fitzgerald, 1987).

In 1985, 58 percent of all married women were in the work force. Nearly 70 percent of these between twenty-five and forty-four worked outside the home, and over 68 percent of all women with school-aged children worked. A majority of intact families are now two-paycheck families, and a majority of women of all classes express a preference for combining work and household roles. Furthermore, 67 percent of married men in at least one recent study (Hiller & Philliber, 1986) expressed a preference for a wife who did or would like to work and agreed that husbands ought to help with household chores and child rearing. Yet, 30 percent of all working wives still say they do all of the household chores, and another 44 percent say they do nearly all such tasks. Only about 25 percent of wives in two-paycheck families report that their husbands share equally in housework (Roper, 1985).

Generally, employed women make time to do housework by reducing their leisure time, buying more prepared meals, and purchasing child care (Nickols & Fox, 1983). Husbands of employed women contribute about thirteen hours per week of family work whereas wives contribute twenty-eight hours. These husbands contribute only about fifteen minutes more per week on the average than husbands of women who do not work. On the other hand, employed wives contribute about fifteen hours per week more family work than employed husbands (Mortimer & London, 1984).

What attitudes underlie these numbers? Why haven't we made more progress toward the equalitarian distribution of work and income? Although women have entered the work force in unprecedented numbers, men have not taken over much if any of the work at home. Traditional attitudes still predominate in American marriage. For one thing, women themselves continue to attach less significance to their own jobs than they do to the jobs of their husbands. Only 10 percent of all married women believe a husband should turn down a better job in another city so a wife can continue her job. Both men and women continue to see the husband's income as the prime determinant of family socioeconomic level, and we know this is an accurate perception because of the general disparity between male and female incomes (Hiller & Philliber, 1986; Roper, 1985).

Furthermore, although married men express gratitude for their wives' contributions to the family coffers, they also report fear, anger, and envy as women enter traditionally masculine occupations. Many men still feel that the wives of truly successful men do not work and feel inadequate as providers when their wives enter the work force. Most central to our discussion, men express the notion that female employment will end male dominance, that work is the last bastion of masculine advantage (Astrachan, 1986).

Though men do have more respect for working women than for traditional homemakers, they are unwilling to do the family work that might make it possible for women to be successful (Blumstein & Schwartz, 1983). Not one study has ever shown that a substantial number of husbands do half of the household chores or child care. And women appear reluctant to ask for help for several reasons. First, it may be that men simply don't do household tasks well enough, either because they have not been socialized to do them well or because they don't care to do them well. Second, men who do housework express less satisfaction with their marriages than men who do not, so wives may be unwilling to create more tension in the already difficult two-paycheck marriage (Melville, 1988; Thompson & Walker, 1990). Until these attitudes change, it is unlikely that parity in employment will be a part of the American scene. As Mirra Komarovsky summed it up: "The right of an able woman to a career of her choice, the admiration for women who measure up in terms of the dominant values of our society, the lure, but also the threat that such women represent, the low status attached to housewifery, but the conviction that there is no substitute for the mother's care of young children, the deeply internalized norm of male occupational superiority pitted against the principle of equal opportunity irrespective of sex—these are some of the revealed inconsistencies" (1973, p. 884).

At work, a family is seen by employers as a hindrance to a woman's career, whereas it is considered an asset for a man to have a family (Valdez & Gutek, 1987). In 1986, Secretary of Labor William Brock observed:

> It's just incredible that we have seen the feminization of the work force with no more adaptation than we have. . . . It is a problem of sufficient magnitude that everybody is going to have to play a role: families, individuals, businesses, and government. (Matthews & Rodin, 1989, p. 1392)

Recently, researchers report that women are increasingly opting to leave their jobs (Deutsch, 1990) rather than carry the load. Yet the preponderance of married women in all kinds of jobs shows high levels of occupational commitment, despite the fact that their abilities are often underutilized and they are consistently paid less than their male counterparts (Betz, 1984).

If the United States is to continue to have a competitive labor force in the world market, women will have to be rewarded and supported in developing and maintaining careers. Nancy Betz and Louise Fitzgerald (1987) have outlined the enormity of this task in a pioneering work on the career psychology of women. They believe that the educational system must begin to counteract social stereotypes. Career counseling for females should include the encouragement of nontraditional interests and competencies, especially continuation in math and the sciences. Teachers, counselors, and parents must learn how to help young women deal with realistic issues and fears (e.g., Can I survive as the only woman on this job?). We must begin to use nonsexist materials in schools and colleges and help young women locate the support systems, role models, and mentors they will need to become successful. We must also help them learn how to deal with sexual discrimination and sexual harassment. These authors believe that the key to improving the status of women is education.

In the workplace, women have to learn how to overcome stereotyped perceptions of their performance and coping styles. They have to figure out how to deal with role overload and conflict as well as sexual harassment. A number of studies have reported that as many as 90 percent of all females claim that sexual harassment is a problem in their workplace, and 40–50 percent report that they themselves have been a target of such harassment. These reports describe everything from a negative work atmosphere in which unpleasant, inappropriate sexual behavior occurs, although the women are not expected to cooperate, to workplaces in which there are severe negative consequences for refusing sexual advances. The problem is so widespread as to affect virtually every woman, and the consequences include a wide variety of symptoms from poor work performance and emotional difficulties to physical disorders and leaving the job or being fired.

And the very solution that Betz and Fitzgerald offer, education, is not free from discrimination and harassment. Betz and Fitzgerald have estimated that as many as 70 percent of all female college students experience sexual harassment in one form or another, from repugnant remarks and unwanted touching to sexual advances, invitations, and even bribes. The most reliable estimates suggest that about 30 percent of all college women are subjected to serious sexual harassment. These women are likely to respond by forfeiting a class, a research opportunity, their personal comfort, and even their career choice. Table 5.3 presents some of the figures on sexual harassment in higher education.

If the door to equality is to open wide, these issues will have to be addressed by parents, educators, corporations, and government. So too, the system will have to address other forms of discrimination. As the workplace becomes increasingly diverse, American business and government will have to view workers of a different sex and of varied cultural and racial backgrounds as a new and flexible resource, rather than an unmanageable and imperfect lot (*Time,* Fall 1990, p. 52).

Race and Occupation

Discrimination against lowerclass workers is a fact of American life, but even the problems of females are overshadowed by the prejudices against minority workers in the American workplace. As one group of social psychologists records the result of racial discrimination:

> Racial prejudice against blacks by whites has been one of the most tenacious social problems in American history. It has resulted in an enormous catalogue of social ills, ranging from the deterioration and near bankruptcy of large cities to poverty, shorter life expectancy, high levels of crime and drug abuse, and human misery of all kinds among blacks themselves. (Freedman, Sears, & Carlsmith, 1981, pp. 460–461)

Minority workers include blacks, Puerto Ricans, Mexican Americans, other Latinos, Native Americans, and smaller groups of recent immigrants from undeveloped countries. Many of these individuals are plagued by failure from childhood on, beginning with early school failure. School is a place where cognitive skills are transmitted and work personality is acquired. Early school failure compounds intense discrimination against minority workers. Slowing economic growth and increasingly sophisticated technology have made it more and more difficult for immigrants and unskilled or semiskilled laborers to penetrate the American economic system (Neff, 1985).

Figure 5.4 presents income figures for blacks, whites, and Hispanics. As one can see, there has been little improvement in the income of minority groups relative to whites. In fact, whereas incomes of white families have been increasing since 1980, those for both Hispanic and black families have remained almost unchanged (U.S. Bureau of the Census, 1989).

There are some hopeful signs. Differences in levels of education have been

Table 5.3 Percentage of graduate and undergraduate student women who endorsed items concerning sexual harassment

Item	Under-graduate Women	Graduate Women
1. Treated "differently" because I am a woman	47.5	47.3
2. Suggestive stories and offensive jokes	42.3	38.0
3. Sexist remarks about women's career options	38.0	36.0
4. Crudely sexual remarks	31.0	26.0
5. Staring, leering, or ogling	27.0	23.8
6. Seductive behavior (requests for dates, drinks, backrubs, etc.)	20.0	20.6
7. Seductive remarks	17.2	21.6
8. Unwanted sexual attention	16.0	19.0
9. Suggestive or pornographic teaching materials	16.0	15.0
10. Unwanted discussion of personal or sexual matters	10.0	12.1
11. Attempts to establish a romantic sexual relationship	8.0	12.0
12. Unwanted stroking or fondling	8.0	8.6
13. Propositions	7.5	8.6
14. Subtle offers of reward	5.0	3.8
15. Subtle threats	5.0	3.7
16. Forceful attempts to kiss or grab	2.5	3.7
17. Punished for refusal	2.5	2.0
18. Direct bribes	<1.0	<1.0
19. Rewarded for social or sexual cooperation	<1.0	<1.0
20. Direct threats of punishment for refusal	<1.0	<1.0
21. Engaged in unwanted sexual behavior due to promise of reward or threat of punishment	<1.0	<1.0

Note. Five items, each describing situations of extreme physical harassment, were not endorsed by any of the sample. $N = 903$ (graduate = 351, undergraduate = 552). From Fitzgerald, Shullman *et al.* (1986).

SOURCE: Betz & Fitzgerald, 1987, p. 241.

In spite of limited opportunities due to overt discrimination, most urban Mexican-American families remain intact and will experience less divorce than either Euro-Americans or black Americans.

decreasing for blacks and whites aged twenty-five to thirty-four years old, and have been doing so since the 1960s. In 1988, 80 percent of all black adults had completed a high school education. The proportion for whites was 87 percent; however, the proportion of young black adults completing four or more years of college has not changed over the last ten years.

Unemployment rates tell another part of the story. Of blacks over sixteen years old, 13 percent were unemployed in 1987 compared with only 5.3 percent of the white population over sixteen. Unemployment rates for black men and women are similar, although the rate for men is slightly higher than that for women. About 30 percent of all black families were below the poverty level in 1987, up from 28 percent in 1979. This rate is about three times that for white families. More distressing, however, is the fact that 46 percent of all black children under the age of eighteen live in families considered poor by the Bureau of the Census while only 15 percent of white children live in poor families.

Among Hispanic families, almost 30 percent are classified as below the poverty level based on 1987 income: about 2.5 times the rate for non-Hispanics.

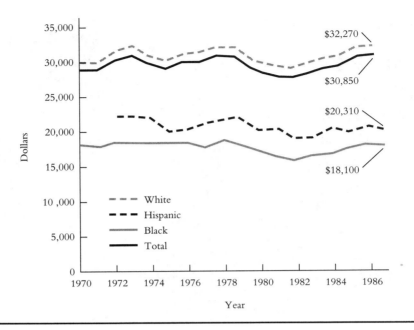

Figure 5.4 Median family income, by race and Hispanic origin, 1970 to 1987 (in 1987 dollars).

SOURCE: Insel & Roth, 1991, p. 193.

Furthermore, the unemployment rates for Hispanics sixteen years and older (8.5%) is higher than that for non–Hispanics (5.8%). Only 10 percent of all Hispanics over the age of twenty-five have completed four or more years of college, and although this is quite an improvement over the percentage doing so in 1970 it is still less than half the rate for non–Hispanics. About 51 percent of all Hispanics complete high school, compared with 78 percent of non–Hispanics.

Furthermore, things do not seem to be improving. The income gap between blacks and whites, for example, was as large in 1980 as it was in 1960 (Center for the Study of Social Policy, 1983). The principal reason for the continuation of this large discrepancy was a sharp drop from 1960 to 1980 in the percentage of black men who are employed (from 74% in 1960 to 56% in 1980). Second, there was also a very sharp increase in the number of black families with dependent children headed by a woman (from 20% to 47%). Among Hispanics, family incomes were 71 percent of Anglo-American family incomes in 1972. By 1982, Hispanic incomes had fallen to 68 percent of Anglo-American incomes, and 30 percent of all Hispanic families were living below the poverty level (Taylor, 1984).

From a psychological standpoint, one of the critical aspects of discrimination is its negative effect on the development of self-image and self-esteem. Negative social attitudes and stereotypes create self-fulfilling prophecies. To illustrate, consider two intriguing studies by Snyder and Swann (1978a, 1978b). In the first experiment, subjects were told how a "target" person with whom they were to interact would behave. Some were informed that the target was hostile, cruel, and insensitive; some were not. The target was never told of the experimenter's description. Nonetheless, the informed subjects perceived the interaction as hostile, and the target actually began to act in a hostile way. In the second experiment, the target was introduced to a new, uninformed person. In this second interaction, targets who had been described as hostile before continued to act hostile and were perceived that way by the subjects.

In these studies, the stereotype the experimenter gave the subject affected not only how informed subjects perceived the target, but also how the target perceived the situation and how the target behaved. People who were stereotyped as negative and hostile began to see themselves in that way and to act in accord with that perception. Research has demonstrated that people who are the objects of negative social attitudes tend to internalize those attitudes, perhaps without realizing it. For example, when compared to the self-ratings of whites, blacks seem to consider themselves less valuable citizens, less important human beings, less able, and less responsible. They also tend to view the environment as hostile and threatening (Ziajka, 1972). Mexican-American children born in the United States are more likely to describe themselves as emotional, unscientific, authoritarian, proud, lazy, indifferent, and unambitious than are Mexican-American children born in Mexico (Derbyshire, 1968).

Wendall Oswalt (1986) has described deep-seated differences between white Americans and Native Americans that may be instrumental in discrimination and unemployment. Native Americans have great tolerance for idiosyncratic behavior and disdain persons who are greedy or selfish or concerned with material wealth, particularly in the manner of whites. However, it is almost impossible to find any psychological research on the self-image of Native Americans and many other, smaller ethnic minorities, a disturbing situation at best. A useful analysis of the effects of discrimination seems a long way off at the moment. This area is certainly one in which almost any serious attempt at systematic investigation might constitute an extremely valuable contribution to the literature.

Mainstream White Males

An analysis of the problems of women, blacks, Hispanics, and Native Americans raises some questions about what it means to be a white male in this country. Whereas others may have problems finding employment, white males have jobs. There are no excuses. They must be aggressive, brave, successful, and ambitious. Love and nurturance are not part of the job of the breadwinner.

Most Americans expect to experience parenthood as joy-giving and fulfilling. But knowing what constitutes a positive role model for children is no longer a simple, rigidly defined stereotype.

The breadwinner must win, must dominate, and, with luck, must keep his wife out of the labor market if that is her choice (Bernard, 1984).

Jessie Bernard (1984) has argued that the role of the good provider has always been a burdensome one for many men but that recent changes in sex-role expectations have resulted in a sharp increase in dissatisfaction with marriage among men. The proportion of working men who said marriage was primarily restrictive and burdensome doubled between 1957 and 1976. Bernard believes that these men need desperately to find new social connections, reassert control over their own lives, and regain some sense of freedom. Women have begun to demand nurturance and intimacy as well as financial security and social success. They also want their husbands to share more of the household tasks and the child care. But most middle-class men are very poorly prepared to meet these demands even if they agree, as they often do (Roper, 1985), that men ought to participate in household work.

The primary social and self-identification of the middle-class and working-class American male is derived from his occupation or from sports, friends, and machines. Men often find themselves ill-equipped for retirement and leisure. They die early of stress-related diseases. They are often isolated from the emotional rewards and support of family life.

Unemployment or underemployment in any form or for any reason is a major, if not the major, psychological and social crisis for the white male. Unemployment and underemployment probably affect most would-be workers, white and nonwhite, in this way; but the white, middle-class male who is unemployed is probably the most socially isolated of all Americans from individuals with similar experience and from people who can understand and sympathize with his dilemma.

Although the pressures and constraints imposed on white males by our society have been of concern to literary and artistic minds for some time, these issues have received wider attention only recently. Still, interest in exploring the consequences of the masculine stereotype seems sporadic and tentative at best. More attention has been given to comparing the attitudes of men and women or trying to decipher whether men are living up to the changing image women seem to be demanding.

Figure 5.5 presents some information about differences in attitudes between men and women. Although these data are for nonwhite males as well as white males, the conflicts are probably representative. Men place much more emphasis on physical attractiveness than women do. They are far more interested in finding a mate who exhibits traditional feminine traits than women are in masculinity. Yet they want an intelligent, hardworking spouse, and although a large number of them (48%) say that they would be interested in staying home and raising children if they had the chance, only 9 percent report that well-adjusted children are the single most important goal in their lives compared to 23 percent of all women.

It seems inevitable that some of the conflicts in attitudes between men and women will affect their futures as husband and wife, mothers and fathers, workers and citizens. Researchers will undoubtedly spend a lot of time observing the struggle and reporting the outcomes. Aside from the workplace, the focus of most of this interest will be the family and in particular in the institutions of marriage and parenthood. In the last chapter we discussed the selection of marriage partners and the development of other intimate relationships. Now we turn our attention to the decision to have children, to the effects of children on parents as individuals, and to the effect of children on marriage.

Parenthood

Parenthood provides a special opportunity for loving, nurturing, and guiding the next generation. Children give people a unique stake in the shape and direction of their society. Thus, Erikson (1963) has argued that we feel more investment in the betterment of the world of human beings when we are making

WHAT YOUTH THINK

LOVE & MARRIAGE

Which of the following is an essential requirement for a spouse?

	Females	Males
Physically attractive	19%	41%
Masculine/feminine traits	41%	72%
Well-paying job	77%	25%
Intelligent	95%	88%
Ambitious and hardworking	99%	86%
Faithful	100%	97%

How difficult is it to have a good marriage today?

	Very difficult	Difficult	Easy	Very Easy
Females	18%	56%	23%	3%
Males	22%	55%	18%	4%

Will couples in your generation be more or less likely than those in your parents' generation to get divorced?

More likely	85%		Less likely	14%

BRINGING UP BABY

If you had the opportunity, would you be interested in staying at home and raising children?

	Females	Males
Yes	66%	48%
No	33%	51%

Would you raise your own children the same way you were raised?

Yes, the same		56%
No, very differently		43%

THE MORE THINGS CHANGE . . .

Do you think it is easier to be a man or a woman?

	Females	Males
To be a woman	30%	21%
To be a man	59%	65%

Which of the following is your single most important goal?

	Females	Males
A successful career	27%	32%
A happy marriage	39%	30%
Well-adjusted children	23%	9%
Contributing to society	6%	16%

From a telephone poll of 505 Americans aged 18 to 24 taken for TIME on Sept. 5–11 by Yankelovich Clancy Shulman. Sampling error is plus or minus 4.5%.

TIME Chart by Joe Lertoia

Figure 5.5 What youth think.

SOURCE: Adapted from *Time* Magazine, Fall 1990, p. 14.

a place for our own progeny. From this perspective, the evolution of the species is ensured not only by the birth of children but also by the caring evoked by children.

According to Erikson, children also fulfill important emotional needs, including the need to be needed, the need to be important to another person, and the need to be creative in an objective way—a way that makes a real difference in the world. Children can be a legitimate source of pride and of emotional growth not available to those who choose not to parent. Intense, fundamental experiences that can best be described as moments of great tenderness, awe, and wonder are often reported by parents who feel strong bonds with their young children. Finally, parenthood often enhances one's sense of a common human heritage, of universal kinship with other people and their children. As Ann Roiphe (1975) wrote:

> I remember the moment, now some twelve years ago, when I suddenly knew my child was being taken care of. I was bathing my daughter—who was trying to put soap in her mouth—and felt this sudden kinship with all other women who had done the same thing—this feeding, cleaning, disposing of urine and feces, smiling, hugging, and touching. And with this sense of a common bond, I entered a new phase in my life. I had grown to value my wonderful individuality a little less and my common humanity more.

For years, the literature on parent-child relationships described, explained, predicted, and otherwise concerned itself with the effects that parents have, or are presumed to have, on children. Then, in a seminal article, Robert Bell (1968) brought into clearer focus some important questions about the direction of these effects. Does parental use of punishment cause children to be more aggressive, or do the parents of an aggressive child finally turn to punitive measures? Do autonomous children have warm, permissive parents, or do the parents of an autonomous child feel more confident and positive about the child? Slowly but persistently, researchers and writers have turned their attention to the serious examination of how children affect parental personality development and self-perception (Zeits & Prince, 1982). Now, there is a burgeoning literature in this area, as well as research on attitudes toward parenting and the impact of changing cultural expectations.

Clearly, the effect of child rearing on adult self-perception is profound although the effects may be greater for women (Thompson & Walker, 1990), who still engage in more intimate relationships with children than do men (Maccoby, 1990). Nonetheless, men as well as women consistently refer to the birth of children as a turning point in their lives (Lowenthal, Thurnher, & Chiraboga, 1975). In one major study of 1,500 couples, for example, most people described the birth of children in terms of the establishment of adulthood (Hoffman & Manis, 1978). Both men and women viewed parenthood as a source of maturity and as a growth experience. Furthermore, the birth of children seems to effect changes in existing relationships with one's own parents. Often people express a more empathic view of their parents during a woman's pregnancy, although they may also still feel a need to "do better" than their parents did (Lamb, 1978).

Bernice Neugarten (1968a) has argued that parenthood affects self-concept, self-esteem, and most other aspects of identity quite profoundly. In that sense, the birth of children constitutes a crisis in the dialectical sense, an opportunity for development: a turning point.

Parenthood as Crisis

Most Americans feel that it is normal, necessary, and natural for individuals to replace themselves by bearing children. They expect to experience parenthood as joyful and fulfilling and tend to assume that good parents will be guided by instinctual love in the proper care of children. Anxious to demonstrate good, natural parenting, people often become secretly guilty when they don't know exactly what to do.

According to Arlene Skolnick (1986b), Americans seem to expect a "natural fit" between the needs of infants and the needs and behaviors of parents, reflecting a belief in *maternal* (and, perhaps, paternal) *instinct*—a belief that denies the enormous role of culture and learning in all human behavior. In fact, there is little evidence that humans have any innate abilities as parents. Consider, for example, that for over two thousand years male psychologist-philosophers (and even politicians at times) have been trying to convince mothers of the importance of breast-feeding their babies; and for two thousand years, many mothers all over the world have rejected or resisted the idea (Kessen, 1965). Would this be the case for such a basic behavior pattern if so-called maternal instincts directed the mothers' choices?

In the late fifties and early sixties, a number of researchers reported that most people were so poorly prepared for parenthood that the birth of a first child was experienced as a crisis. In two of these studies (Dyer, 1963; Le Masters, 1957), 50–80 percent of the new parents interviewed expressed feelings of moderate to severe crisis when their first child was born. Later studies (Hobbs, 1965; Hobbs & Cole, 1976; Russell, 1974) suggested that the birth of a first child might more adequately be conceptualized as a "moderately stressful transition" rather than a crisis.

Recent work (Wallace & Gotlib, 1990; Belsky & Rovine, 1990; Belsky & Pensky, 1988) has shown that many couples do report declines in marital satisfaction after the birth of the first child, and some are at more risk than others for experiencing a crisis. In one study of ninety-seven couples during the first six months of parenthood (Wallace & Gotlib, 1990), declines in satisfaction occurred for all couples after the first month or so of parenthood. The best predictor of how much decline the couple reported depended on their marital adjustment prior to childbirth. Couples who had been least satisfied before the birth of the child were most likely to report decline. This is a clear argument against the notion that the birth of a baby can "save" a marriage that is on the rocks.

Some of these researchers (Belsky & Rovine, 1990; Belsky & Pensky, 1988) have argued that the problems creating declines in satisfaction are the same problems the couple had before the birth of the baby. Problems are simply magnified by childbirth. These researchers also report, however, that there are several patterns of response to childbirth when one looks at data for individual families. They describe four such patterns, two in which marital satisfaction decreases, one in which no change occurs, and one in which modest increases in marital satisfaction are evidenced.

Overall, Belsky and Rovine (1990) reported declines in feelings of love for the spouse for both men and women as well as increases in feelings of ambivalence and conflict for women. This study followed 124 couples over a period of four years. In households where declines occurred, husbands and wives were younger, less educated, and married for fewer years. These couples also had lower incomes; the husbands were less interpersonally sensitive, and the wives had lower self-esteem.

Paradoxically, these authors reported that planned pregnancies appeared to be associated with stronger declines in marital satisfaction than unplanned ones. Perhaps, the authors argue, people who planned their pregnancies had higher expectations that the outcome would be positive and the difficulties few.

Finally, women whose babies were described as irregular in eating and sleeping habits showed greater declines in feelings of love and more ambivalence. These authors felt that the baby's temperament interacted with the mother's existing problems. That is, marital problems may contribute to the baby's difficulties and these, in turn, increase marital discord.

A final recent study (MacDermid, Huston, & McHale, 1990) cautions against assuming that childbirth is necessarily the cause of declining satisfaction. In studying 98 couples over the first two and one half years of marriage, these authors found that marital satisfaction declined for the couples who did not become parents as well as those who did. For the couples who became parents, those who had the most difficulties were those who had disagreed about appropriate sex-role behaviors. Perhaps the reason that the results of this later study seem to challenge the conclusion that parenthood is experienced as a crisis is that all of the couples in this study were newlyweds. Marriage may be a crisis too.

Both mothers and fathers repeatedly lament that children tie them down so completely. Parenting has the quality of "alwaysness": one loses the freedom to do things on the spur of the moment. Children are perceived as career-limiting by women (Hoffman & Manis, 1978; Jacoby, 1982; Roper, 1985), and both parents experience financial pressures and worry over the children. Worries increase with the age of the children, culminating in the teen-aged years, when mothers and fathers outline long lists of troublesome areas from accidents to drugs, alcohol, sex, and self-doubts about how they have performed as parents. Despite these later pressures, however, the demands of preschoolers may well have the biggest impact on adults and are most likely to evoke paradoxical feelings (Hoffman & Manis, 1978).

As psychological theories of child rearing have reached the public, and as the society becomes more complex, many have concluded that the rearing of children is too difficult, too risky a business. The stresses have become more apparent, the joys less so. Although parents report that children offer them a feeling of maturity and the opportunity for unreserved love and caring, they are also more sensitive to the losses and constraints due to parenting (Alpert & Richardson, 1980; Hoffman & Manis, 1978; Melville, 1988). Certainly, the economic burden children pose is significant. As shown in Figure 5.6 the costs of bearing and raising a child have swelled in the last thirty years.

Parenting is a twenty-four-hour-a-day, seven-day-a-week job, with no time off for good behavior. In the transition to parenthood, the family becomes a *continuous-coverage* institution, like a hospital. People are both surprised and bothered by the complete change of lifestyle that parenthood demands (Alpert & Richardson, 1982; La Rossa & La Rossa, 1981; Sapiro, 1990), although the effects are somewhat different for fathers than for mothers.

Mothering "Motherhood is inevitable; every woman will or should be a mother. A woman's identity is tenuous and trivial without motherhood. A woman enjoys and intuitively knows what to do for her child; she cares for her child without ambivalence or awkwardness. . . . A mother is all-giving and all-powerful" (Thompson & Walker, 1990, p. 860). Many authors believe that, as dated as it may seem, this image of motherhood is still with us. Americans still believe that full-time mothering is critical for the successful development of children, especially during the early years. It is assumed that substitute mothering, multiple mothering, and part-time mothering are inadequate (Birns and Hay, 1988). A mother must devote herself to her children, above everything else, certainly above her career. It is the mother who is ultimately held responsible for the outcome of child rearing. The sins of the father may be visited on the child, but the sins of the child are visited on the mother. Sapiro (1986) writes about the burden of motherhood:

> He fathered that child. She mothered that child. The connotations of these two sentences are different. Fathering a child generally refers to the act of conceiving a child, and mothering a child refers not to conception or even to birthing, but to caring for a child and the style of care given. The common-sense difference between mothering and fathering is also illustrated in these two sentences: Don't mother me! Don't father me! The second of these sentences doesn't even make sense. (pp. 348–349)

$5,774

THAT'S HOW MUCH A BABY COSTS IN ITS FIRST YEAR OF LIFE . . .

That's a national figure, one that includes material goods and some services, but excludes such additional costs as trips to the pediatrician for illnesses.

Food	$855
Diapers	$570
Clothes	$352
Furniture	$995
Bedding	$223
Medicine*	$396
Toys	$199
Day care	$2,184

*Vitamins, personal care products
Sources: U.S. Bureau of the Census, National Center for Health Statistics, U.S. Department of Agriculture, American Baby

Figure 5.6 How much does a child cost?

SOURCE: U.S. Department of Commerce, 1979, p. 12.

In the United States, a mother has the full burden of responsibility for child rearing and little or no support from the society, great pressure to work as well as raise children, and little recognition for the difficulties of meeting these demands. In a recent survey of 1,100 mothers aged 18–80 (Genevie & Margolis, 1987), the huge majority of women reported that parenthood had created negative changes in their marriages and that they felt discouraged and frustrated with their husbands, maintaining that problems arose because fathers remained so uninvolved with parenting and family. About 20 percent of these mothers felt predominantly negative about their experiences as mothers. About a quarter felt very positive. The vast majority were ambivalent. Although, on the whole, they felt the positive outweighed the negative, the joys did not negate the tremendous difficulties, pain, and heartaches of the role.

Furthermore, only about 3 percent of these mothers reported feeling negative about motherhood before their children were born. Nearly 70 percent said they had been brought up with unrealistic fantasies of being able to have perfect children and perfect families. They felt they had underestimated the responsibilities, and the difficulty of combining work and parenthood in particular. Many of these women felt "duped." They felt they had been lied to by society in general, if not their own mothers in particular.

The responsibilities of motherhood come hard and fast, according to this report. Many of the women reported feelings of drowning or being stretched to their limits, especially if they worked, or if the children were sick or if they were single. Many of them talked about their own rage and anger over the defiance of their children or about being ignored and rejected by their children. Even mothers who were generally loving and accessible reported feeling they had to leave at times, they were so angry and frustrated.

These authors found that harried mothers didn't feel more negative, but, interestingly, more positive toward mothering. Women who had the most difficulties tended to be those who had more time but still felt overburdened. Perhaps, the authors suggest, women who put the most time into mothering were most likely to feel harried but also most likely to be getting something out of the role.

Consistent with most of the literature, these authors reported that although working mothers reported a good deal more conflict than full-time mothers, working did not affect their feelings toward their spouse or the children. Mothers who worked full-time more often expressed the desire to stay home with their children. But being at home full-time and not liking it was the most devastating situation for a woman. Unhappy full-time mothers suffered from low self-esteem, felt more negatively about motherhood, and were more likely to criticize their children.

These authors also reported that whether or not a mother likes a child (as opposed to loving that child), makes a big difference in how the mother felt about mothering. Mothers found it very difficult to mother a child they did not like, although they might feel quite positive toward other children in the family.

In a comprehensive study of the literature on mothering, Thompson & Walker (1990) conclude that many women feel ambivalence about mothering. Based on their findings, the authors conclude that about one-third of all women experience motherhood as both enjoyable and meaningful. One-third report they derive no meaning or enjoyment from it. The rest give the role mixed reviews. Women report that looking after small children is unsettling and irritating because of the constant need to be vigilant and the tedium of watching. Children interfere with a mother's other activities, confine her to home, and require routine. Yet most mothers also voice feelings of fulfillment and commitment.

Most authors agree that women experience considerably more change with parenthood than do men, especially working-class women (McBride, 1990; Thompson & Walker, 1990) and women with difficult infants or health problems. Many working women feel that the demands are higher than either they or their spouses prefer. And the stress is higher if the spouse is not supportive or the mother is unable to find adequate child care (McBride, 1990).

Despite all the woes, however, women in their twenties place as much value on mothering as women in their seventies, and there is no relationship

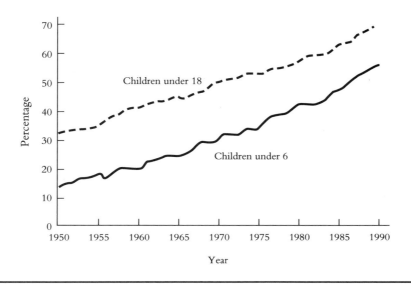

Figure 5.7 Percentage of mothers in labor force, 1950–1990*.

SOURCE: Coleman, 1988, p. 280.

between education and the value a woman places on mothering (Genevie & Margolis, 1987). The institution of motherhood may have changed dramatically, but, as Genevie and Margolis point out, women's feelings about motherhood have not.

Today, a majority of women of all classes express a preference for the combination of work and household roles (Melville, 1988; *Time,* Fall 1990), and they are entering the work force in ever increasing numbers, regardless of the age of their children. Figure 5.7 presents data for the percentage of families with employed mothers and fathers.

It seems essential to the study of motherhood that we begin to examine the combination of work and family more carefully. Angela Barron McBride (1990) has suggested that we need to look at how the number of hours a mother works affects her experience and the child's. What kind of career makes motherhood and work an easier combination? What kind of family? What kind of child? What are the kinds of social support and coping strategies that are associated with the successful combination of work and mothering?

In recent years, researchers have also begun to question the strong, almost exclusive focus on the role of the mother that has long characterized the literature on parenting. They have begun to ask how men interact with their children, how they respond to the problems of combining work and family, and how they feel about the role of father.

Fathering Men do not come through the early years of parenting unscathed either. Many husbands experience strong role conflicts between fatherhood and occupation. For fathers, the establishment of a coherent family role is a complex problem, and a critical predictor of life satisfaction. In fact, overall, survey research suggests that life satisfaction for males is more strongly related to the quality of family life than to occupational achievement (Alpert & Richardson, 1980; Biller, 1982; Lamb, 1978).

Yet the impact of fathering on the development of personality in adulthood is essentially unresearched. Even the function of the father in the context of the modern family is still obscure, although some researchers have begun to break ground in this area. For example, researchers now see the behavior of fathers as critical in the development of sex-typed behavior in small children. Dramatic changes in the behavior of fathers during the second year of an infant's life have been reported. Fathers begin spending less and less time with their daughters and more time with their sons, when children reach age two (Lamb & Goldberg, 1982).

In another pioneering report, Parks and Swain (1976) concluded that although both parents were sensitive to the cues offered by infants, fathers were more likely to respond to an infant visually. Other studies have confirmed that infants show attachment to both parents by seven to nine months of age and that infants greet their fathers as heartily as they do their mothers, showing distress when separated from either parent (Lamb, 1981). The kinds of interactions infants have with their fathers are, however, clearly quite different from the typical mother-infant exchange. Whereas mothers spend some time playing with their babies, almost all of the time fathers spend with infants can be characterized as play. Data from one study show, for instance, that mothers spend 10 percent of their time playing with an infant, whereas fathers play 50 percent of the time (La Rossa & La Rossa, 1981). Fathers are more directive than mothers with older children and, although they are perceived by adolescents as more autocratic than mothers, they report fewer conflicts (Thompson & Walker, 1990).

Why do mothers and fathers display different kinds of behavior in their parental roles? Is parenting behavior determined biologically to any significant extent? Such questions have provoked considerable controversy among researchers. For example, Michael Lamb contends that any biological predispositions directing sex differences in parenting are probably slight but exceedingly complex. He believes that social pressures exaggerate biological influences and that, given the opportunity and training, males and females can be equally good parents (Lamb & Goldberg, 1982). Coming from an entirely different point of view, David Gutmann (1964, 1969, 1977, 1990) has argued that a powerful biological phenomenon, which he labels the **parental imperative,** not only directs parenting behavior but also serves to organize much of adult personality development and provides an ultimate source of meaning as species needs intersect personal needs (Gutmann, 1975).

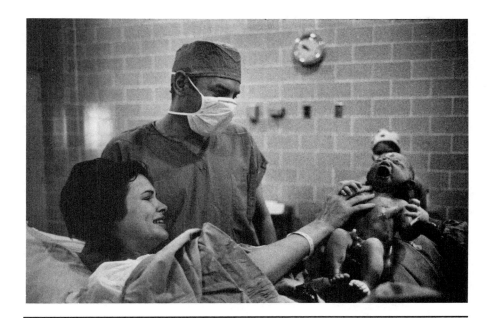

When fathers participate in the birth process, they are able to ease the pain and discomfort of labor and share in the deeply moving emotional experience of childbirth.

Certainly, the research suggests that the impact of parenthood on both parents may be characterized as a traditionalization of sex-role behavior. Research has demonstrated that women experience a loss of power in the marital relationship and that they receive less help with housework from fathers after children are born. Compared to women in the same age group without children, mothers are more likely to think husbands should make all the decisions and provide money for the family (Hoffman & Manis, 1978). Fathers tend to react to the birth of a child with greater concern about their performance in the role of provider (Alpert & Richardson, 1980; Farrell, 1986).

Gutmann (1975) has reported that sex-role distinctions are heightened in a variety of cultures during the childbearing years. He has maintained that these distinctions are critical if the emotional and physical needs of children are to be adequately met. One parent, the father, must play the instrumental role, leaving home to slay dragons or sell refrigerators. The instrumental parent is expendable in emotional terms. Women, according to Gutmann, provide the emotional security that men cannot offer their children.

Gutmann's point of view presents a number of problems, even given the rather sparse data we have on parenthood. First, a growing body of literature shows that fathers do form close, affectionate relationships with their infants

Some studies indicate that people who become parents later in life are less likely to regret their decision or the timing than those who have children in late adolescence or early adulthood.

(Biller, 1982; Melville, 1988; Parks & Swain, 1976). We also know that fathers experience real and enduring distress when they are separated from their children (Kelly, 1982). Finally, little if any evidence shows that the children of working mothers are developmentally disadvantaged by the more instrumental behavior of their female parents, and much evidence indicates that infants who are emotionally well fathered show greater curiosity, more exploratory behavior, and react better to strangers and other novel stimuli (Biller, 1982; Field & Widmayer, 1982; Sapiro, 1990). If anything, the research suggests that the woman who works because she wants to will be a far better parent than the one who forces herself to stay at home.

Eleanor Maccoby (1990) has argued that the subcultures boys and girls are reared in ensure that sex differences will emerge in families. Women's ways of influencing others tend to create the kind of sex differences one sees in parents. Men learn to joke and compete and use rough-and-tumble play. Women learn more intimate, verbal styles.

Work on couples who become parents late in life also challenges the notion of a biological parental imperative. People who delay parenting are far less likely to regret their decision or the timing of it than those who have children in late adolescence or early adulthood (Daniels & Weingarten, 1980). Yet, one would suppose that the parental imperative would lead to problems for older people who typically have less stereotyped sex roles in their relationship at the time their children are born. This research has also demonstrated that the traditionalizing impact of childbearing is less significant among couples who choose to have children late than among the young. It is little wonder, given the responsibility of parenthood and the enormous changes in family and sex-role behaviors, that more and more people are deciding to postpone parenthood until both partners have established personal identities and careers. It is also the case that some of these postponers, and a larger and larger number of early deciders, will not have children at all.

The Decision Not to Parent

Once a controversial decision, the lifestyle some call "child-free" is becoming increasingly acceptable. People who choose not to bear children feel growing social support for that decision. College women, for instance, have been reporting for more than a decade (Houseknecht, 1977) that people they know would support such a decision. Social approval makes it more likely that a couple will be able to develop a satisfying childless marriage. From 5 to 10 percent of all married couples have no children by choice, but 14 percent of all women who have graduated from college are child-free. Childless couples tend to be more independent and to enjoy being with each other more than do other couples. Some couples may be choosing the child-free life for erotic reasons; that is because the relationship between the couple is paramount to them. As we know from earlier parts of this chapter, the birth of a first child may well present a major challenge to marital satisfaction and feelings of love (Belsky & Rovine, 1990). Furthermore, women consider childbearing the biggest obstacle to their own career advancement (Betz & Fitzgerald, 1987), and there is little doubt that the woman who desires to invest in her career will find it much easier if she does not have children.

More and more couples may also be making this decision for political reasons. Some are concerned about the problem of overpopulation, while others feel that it doesn't make good sense to bring a child into a world that is beset by the problems of crime, drugs, pollution, and war that are a part of twentieth-century life. In addition, as Philip Rice (1990) points out: "Judging from the thousands of cases of child abuse in the United States each year, large numbers of people should not become parents. *Many people have neither the interest nor the aptitude to be parents;* the resultant performance is at best marginally competent

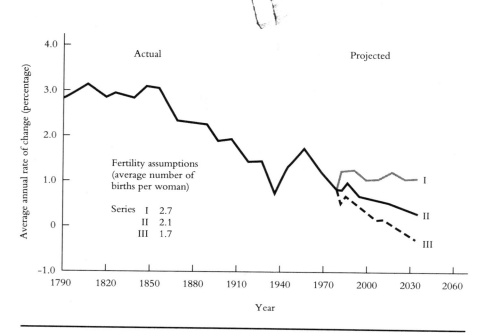

Figure 5.8 Average actual and projected annual rate of population change, selected years, 1790–2040.

SOURCE: U.S. Bureau of the Census, 1989, p. 32.

and at worst blatantly irresponsible" (p. 455). Data for the birth rate in the United States over the next century suggest continuing declines as illustrated in Figure 5.8.

Yet many of these couples still report that they feel a good deal of pressure to change their minds and have children, especially the wives (Veevers, 1980). The idea that women are not complete without the experience of motherhood or that motherhood is the ultimate demonstration of a woman's mature nature (Genevie & Margolis, 1987; Thompson & Walker, 1990) creates the impression that the woman who decides against childbearing is selfish, irresponsible, immature, or, worse, immoral. Pressure from friends and family to have children tends to build through the first few years of marriage, not diminishing until sometime in the fourth or fifth year (Veevers, 1980).

In what has become the last word on the matter, Jean Veevers (1980) followed fifty-two child-free couples over a period of years, exploring how they had become aware of their decision and begun to cope with it. She distinguished two types of couples: those who were **early articulators,** knowing from childhood that they preferred not to have children, and **postponers,** those who simply put off the decision again and again until they became aware that they had, in fact, actually made a decision.

About one-third of the couples she interviewed included an early artic-ulator, nearly always the wife. For these women, childlessness had become a characteristic of the self. No matter what kind of relationship they had estab-lished with a spouse, they did not want children as part of their lives. Some felt that children had an inevitably debilitating effect on a marital relationship, while others were simply unwilling to give up other pursuits for parenthood (especially those women with very ambitious career plans). A 1986 follow-up of the Harvard Law School Class of 1974 seems to support Veevers' findings about career women. Among these 71 women, only 38 had had children, and of those, one half had lowered their vocational sights since graduating from law school (Abramson & Franklin, 1986).

Some early articulators felt that only incompetent women choose to mother, whereas others argued that motherhood leads to female incompe-tence. A few saw children as demanding and expensive or expressed an active dislike of children and childish things. Veevers points out that some early artic-ulators had very unpleasant experiences with unattractive or repellent children who were monstrously spoiled or, in some cases, deformed or retarded.

Veevers labels one group of early articulators **rejectors.** In general, rejec-tors disliked children, were committed to a childless lifestyle, and would de-mand that an accidental pregnancy be terminated or that the child be placed for adoption. More common than rejectors were **aficionados.** Aficionados tended to like children but to have developed a deep appreciation for the op-portunity to be spontaneous and to pursue novel experiences. They delighted in the freedom to work hard or to quit if they felt like it. They were particu-larly fond of activities like travel that are difficult, if not impossible, after children are born. However, aficionados were not nearly as committed to childlessness as rejectors. Often, the decision had been negotiated between husband and wife over a period during which the major strategy had been simply to postpone making a decision. Aficionados give the kind of erotic reasons Collins (1985) outlined.

Postponers seemed to progress through several stages, first putting off childbearing for a definite time, later becoming less and less definite, and fi-nally, consciously deliberating the pros and cons and adopting a child-free life-style. Such couples were also far more likely to see the decision as related to the particular relationship they had established. Often, they said that if they had married someone else, they might have made a different decision.

The kind of longitudinal research Veevers has conducted offers an un-usually rich source of information. This is precisely the kind of work that is required in so many other areas of developmental research. Other family con-figurations, including single parenting and stepparenting, deserve this kind of attention. Most of the data we currently have on such arrangements are demo-graphic: how many, how old, what race, and what income. Such data gener-ally give little insight into the day-to-day psychology of family, offering only a starting place for closer scrutiny.

Single Parents and Stepparents

The family is the nucleus of civilization.
                    —Will and Ariel Durant

*As long as the family and the myth of the family have
not been destroyed, women will still be oppressed.*

                    —Simone de Beauvoir

Single-Parent Families Available information about single-parent families is badly in need of clarification. It is particularly difficult to sort out the effect of single-parenting from the economic, social, and often racial or ethnic differences that set these families apart from the usual nuclear family. As you can clearly see in Figure 5.9, over 34 percent of families with a female householder and no spouse present are considered poor. Women may be discriminated against in both the job and the housing markets *because* of their children and their divorced or separated status. Employers often feel that a woman with young children is unreliable. Apartments and condominiums in better areas may refuse to rent or sell to families with children, especially to single-parent families.

In 1987, 27 percent of all families with children living at home were maintained by one parent. Eighty-eight percent of these were maintained by mothers, only 12 percent were maintained by fathers. Between 1970 and 1987, the number of one-parent families grew by 142 percent. The median income of families headed by women is 50 percent of the income of families headed by a male. These problems are critical for black families since 55 percent of all black children under eighteen are currently living with a single mother as compared with 17 percent of white children under eighteen (U.S. Bureau of the Census, 1989). Children in black-female-headed families are the poorest of all children. They are three times more likely than white children to be poor and their mothers are more likely to have to work full-time and less likely to receive child support than children in white single-parent families (Washington, 1988).

Even when single-parent families have sufficient economic resources, there are special problems with important psychological implications. The single parent must cope with the social isolation and loneliness of singlehood that we discussed in Chapter 4. These problems may be of even greater magnitude for the single parent, who is tied down by the care of young children and cannot take advantage of the opportunities that are available. Often, single parents are completely cut off from most of the channels of communication in society.

In one study of single parents in Great Britain (Schlesinger, 1977), parents consistently reported feelings of loneliness and alienation. They also expressed frustration about the need to forego sexual gratification because of the potential effects on the children or adverse reactions of neighbors. Difficulty in

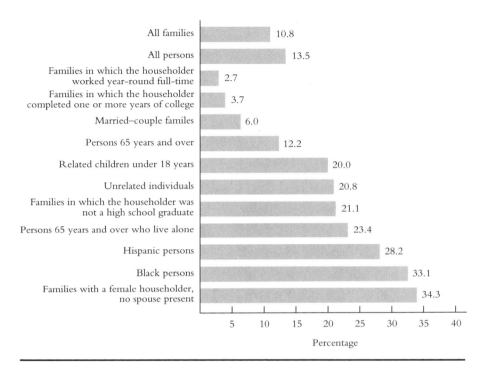

Figure 5.9 Poverty rate for persons and families with selected characteristics, 1987 (in percent).

SOURCE: U.S. Bureau of the Census, 1989, p. 35.

meeting the physical demands of young children was a major problem for these parents, who also reported difficulty in finding ways to help the children cope with feelings of being different from "normal families."

Family relationships are often conflicted and problematic. For example, in a longitudinal study of 180 families during the first six years after divorce (Hetherington, 1987), researchers found that mothers who did not remarry had more emotional problems and were less satisfied with life than those who did. They complained of intense, ambivalent, and coercive relationships with their sons, although the relationships they experienced with their daughters were generally more positive.

Since the rate of divorce among remarrieds is about 60 percent, many children will live in one-parent families at several points in their lives. Furthermore, 35 percent of all divorced women never marry again, and there is a growing number of women who are choosing to raise children alone, having never been married. Single-parenting must be considered an emergent lifestyle, not a "temporary" situation (Brown, 1989).

Fredda Brown (1989) has argued on the basis of clinical evidence that first, and foremost, single mothers need to realize that they must become emotionally as well as legally divorced. They should not blame their situation on the spouse and they need to salvage themselves from a difficult situation. Like Amy, many single divorced mothers have never lived alone before. They went right from their families' homes, from living with their mothers and fathers, or from a college dormitory, to a marriage. They have to establish themselves as independent people, to renegotiate their relationships with their own parents as well as their in-laws, and to establish a balance between dependence and independence again.

Brown contends that there are three phases in the adjustment of single-parent families following divorce: aftermath, realignment, and stabilization. Establishing independence is the primary task of the first phase, and this may be extremely difficult, for, like Amy, many single divorced mothers have been out of the labor force. Their income may decrease by as much as 73 percent in the first year. Still, many women don't tackle the problem of career in the first phase because they don't know what they want to do and they don't want to leave their children. Many of these women fill the vacuum in their daily lives by returning home or calling on their own mothers or fathers for assistance. Amy is considering this move, but Brown warns that often problems arise when the daughter returns home or becomes the mother's friend and confidante, then rebels if and when she finds a boyfriend. Similar difficulties can occur when the grandfather becomes overinvolved in a single mother's family and cannot back out when the time comes.

In Amy's situation, she may have particular difficulty during this phase in dealing with her husband's parents, because in Asian families the couple often joins the husband's family. The problems of this phase will be complicated by ethnic and racial values around parenting and family (McGoldrick, 1989).

Brown maintains that it is critical for a woman to develop her own friends and social support system in the first phase, to solve her financial and legal problems, and to think about her career even if her lawyer recommends not going back to work until the divorce settlement is completed. The single mother needs to define what kind of help she needs and to "employ" that help, whether it is the grandfather or the grandmother or hired help. She should retain a sense of control. Therapy is often less useful in this phase than a support group or a group of friends who have "been there too."

Realignment, according to Brown, is a two- or three-year roller coaster ride to regrouping. The marriage terminates emotionally at the end of this second phase, often marked by grieving and sadness, or the couple may stay overinvolved with each other and never fully negotiate the legal problems. During this phase, women often find they have to sell the family home, and most will have to get a job. Children usually experience the loss of the home as the major loss. They need continuing contact with both parents, which may be an extra strain on a single mother trying to find and establish herself in a career, make a new home for her children, and develop a social support network.

Brown insists that women must establish their power in the family during the realignment phase, or the temporary arrangements made in the first phase may overwhelm their ability to parent. A triangle may develop between the children, the mother and the grandmother, the grandfather, or the father. To avoid this, the mother must learn how to manage and discipline the children by herself.

Parents also start to date during this phase, and children lose the fantasy that they will be able to get their parents back together, although they may attempt to break up the new relationships their parents are trying so hard to establish.

In the final stage, any problems that remain unresolved from the realignment phase may threaten a remarriage or the stabilization of the mother's lifestyle. Brown feels very strongly that women must accept their status as a single parent and begin to cope as though it were a permanent lifestyle. In this way, they are more likely to establish the independence and power that goes with a successful life whether or not they remarry. Amy would be well counseled to begin to look realistically at her career alternatives. She might find that her own parents could assist her in whatever temporary arrangements she needs to make, but she should continue to see these as temporary and to stay in charge of them rather than letting her parents or her husband's parents establish themselves as primary forces in the children's lives. She would do well to join a self-help group or any group of women with children in which the mothers are likely to be divorced. Being able to share some of her problems with other people who have been through it and survived will probably be a great relief.

Although there is a great deal of literature about the effects of divorce on children, and at least some literature about the effects of divorce on the lifestyle of parents, there is very little information about the single-parent family created by the unmarried individual who adopts a child or who has decided to have a natural child without marrying. The practice is not widespread in adulthood, although adolescent pregnancies are common. Research on these new family forms would seem to fill an important niche.

Perhaps the biggest difficulty faced by all single-parent families is how to provide an adequate model for the behavior of the absent parent. Jane Burgess (1970) has pointed out that many single mothers manage to provide adequate models of male sex-role behavior through relatives and friends. Peers may also compensate to some extent for the absence of a father figure. For many of the children of single parents, the problem is eventually solved by remarriage; with remarriage comes the problem of stepparenting.

Stepparenting   It has been estimated that approximately 35 percent of all children under eighteen will live with a stepparent for some period during their lives (McGoldrick & Carter, 1989; Furstenberg, 1987). Given such dramatic figures, some authors are calling for an entirely new way of understanding what it means to be a family. It has been argued that even the term *stepparent* is too negative to use when referring to families created by remarriage. These same authors (McGoldrick & Carter, 1989) also believe, however, that the term *blended family* tends to underestimate the problems of remarried families.

These families vary in complexity from a couple that brings only one child to a new marriage in which only one of the partners has ever been divorced, to families in which both adults have custody of children from one or more former marriages and the newly formed family will have children of its own. Although it is difficult to make generalizations over such a wide range of forms, certain characteristic problems seem to occur frequently in remarried families of many types. Although divorce rates are the same for remarrieds who have children and those who don't, stepchildren are the primary source of strain in families with children (Furstenberg, 1988).

First and foremost, perhaps, remarried families are plagued by the fantasy of the "blended" family, the idea that a nuclear family can be recreated after the remarriage. The idea that stepparents and children will be able to form the kinds of bonds children have with their biological parents, while not unheard of, is certainly unrealistic for most remarried families and creates severe problems when it is held as a standard for family success (McGoldrick & Carter, 1989; Stinnet & Walters, 1977). Happiness, love, and togetherness are not automatic results of the creation of a new family. Children continue to admire their absent biological parent, often more than their stepparent, often producing feelings of inadequacy or rejection in a stepparent.

The problems are likely to be easier to overcome when the children involved are young (or adult) males. Relationships between stepfathers and stepdaughters appear to be particularly difficult, especially where the daughter is an adolescent. Many people find that result surprising, but it can be predicted from the more general rule that relationships between stepparents and stepchildren seem to work best when the stepparent and the child are of the same sex and when the relationship is friendly but not intense. It appears that stepdaughters and stepfathers may have some difficulty forming friendly, rather distant relationships because girls are socialized to push for more intimate, positive relationships (McGoldrick & Carter, 1989).

In one of the few studies of remarried families who were not in family therapy, one group of researchers (Dahl, Cowgill, & Asmundsson, 1987) made the following observations:

1. It takes about three to five years for a sense of "belongingness" to emerge in remarried families, even longer if the children are adolescents.

2. Both spouses preferred to maintain courteous but distant relationships with the ex-spouses of the new partner.

3. Serious disciplinary problems and arrangements for visitation are generally handled by the biological parent. This is so even when the custodial parent is the father.

4. Childhood experiences in large families appeared to help people adjust to the complexities of remarriage.

5. Marital satisfaction was associated with the stepparent's ability to develop good relationships with steppchildren and respect the special bond that children maintain with their biological parents.

6. Remarried families emphasize the role of communication, negotiation, and compromise in their relationships as well as the ability to accept what cannot be changed.

In general, stepmothers appear to have the most difficult time adjusting to remarried families, although stepfathers and stepdaughters may have the most problematic relationships. First, perhaps because it is rare for women to join families in which men have custody of children, stepmothers experience much ambivalence about the role. Given the myth of motherhood we have been discussing throughout this chapter, it seems quite predictable that stepmothers might have difficulty finding the right distance in a family where the father needs to be very active in parenting. John Santrock and Karen Sitterle (1987) note that stepmothers spend less time with stepchildren in everyday activities than do biological mothers. From the children's point of view, they appear more detached, yet they are seen as more active and involved than the majority of stepfathers. These authors conclude that one of the primary problems a stepmother faces is the struggle over how involved to be. Box 5.1 presents a list of do's and dont's for remarried families based on the problems that family therapists encounter in their work.

The role of stepparent is essentially without social definition, although most Americans hold a negative stereotype of stepparents (Fine, 1986). It is a role for which we receive no preparation, just as we receive no preparation for biological parenting. Little social consensus exists about how stepparenting should differ from or be the same as parenting. New stepparents have no clues about how their duties, obligations, and rights might vary with the age, sex, or number of children in the family, or how they might best interact with the biological parent not residing with the child. Guilt about one's performance under these circumstances may well inhibit the spontaneity needed to build loving relationships.

The number of stepparent adoptions is increasing rapidly. Legal adoptions open the possibility for denying the biological parent visiting rights to the child. In fact, all official records of one of the biological parents may be expunged at adoption—an event that seems filled with important and unresearched implications. We are used to change, and we are ready to institutionalize it in many different forms. However, if the new wave of adoptive parents or, for that matter, the less formal stepparent arrangement, is to be successful, better information will be needed as well as more support from the legal, educational, and familial institutions of society. The rights and obligations of stepparents should be clarified, and the status and problems of stepparents should receive greater attention.

Box 5.1 Focus on Application: Forming a remarried family

With the warning that no list of do's and don'ts can take the place of a clear theory or experienced clinical judgment, Monica McGoldrick and Betty Carter provide the following outline of some attitudes and procedures that have helped them understand remarried families. Generally, in working with these families, they have tried to establish the following:

1. Working, open relationships between former spouses who are sharing the custody of children.
2. A resolution to the emotional divorce between former spouses so that they can operate without continuous conflict, which would intrude in the present marriage and affect the children.
3. Clear parental responsibility for remarriage, custody, and visitation, with more input from older children than younger ones, but with the parent retaining ultimate authority.
4. Parental acceptance of divided loyalties among the children and ability to help the children express the full range of their feelings.

As more specific rules of thumb, the authors suggest the following:

1. One must try to understand the entire history of each spouse's original family and previous marriages to grasp current household problems.
2. It's important to keep in mind that families have different needs at different points in the life cycle, that women carry the central emotional role in most families, and that families will be hard put to maintain the myth of being perfect.
3. One must beware of families struggling to attain closeness without allowing time for relationships to develop.
4. Families need to learn to tolerate ambiguity and not "overtry" to make things work out. Negative feelings, conflict, ambivalence, and divided loyalties are quite predictable.

Race, Ethnicity, and Family

Figure 5.10 shows the population of selected racial and ethnic groups in the United States. Clearly, black Americans constitute the largest group, with Mexican-Americans next, followed by those of Puerto Rican heritage, Native Americans, Japanese, Chinese, and Filipinos. Little information is available aside from statistical portraits for many of these families, but some beginning statements can be made.

Black Families

There is a way in which we might argue that black families are leading the way for the rest of the population. Black families have the highest rates of single-

Box 5.1 *(continued)*

5. A spouse may need professional coaching in how to deal with an ex-spouse, and the new spouse ought to be included in these coaching sessions.

6. One has to take the characterization of the ex-spouse as "crazy" with a grain of salt. Crazy behavior may be a product of provocation.

7. When a remarriage ends a close single-parent/child relationship, the feelings of loss, especially for the child, have to be dealt with and the shift to the new system will take time.

8. If the child is having problems, all the parents and stepparents should probably be involved in therapy. Joint sessions should focus on the child's difficulties, not marital issues.

9. When a child is the focus of an uproar, the natural parent should be put in charge of the child. When the uproar subsides, the natural parent may benefit from professional coaching on how to "move over" and include his or her spouse in the system—first, as a spouse only. The family will need to understand that it takes several years to shift to active stepparenting.

10. Therapists should consider the "hidden agenda" behind any sudden proposals to rearrange custody, visitation, or financial arrangements. They should also include work on the spouses' families of origin as early in treatment as possible.

SOURCE: From McGoldrick & Carter, 1989, pp. 426–427.

parent female-headed households, and this has too often been taken as evidence that the black family is matriarchal or mother-centered. Yet blacks believe strongly in the institution of family and generally have stronger ties to kin than white families (Demos, 1990).

Generally, the literature has demonstrated a problematic view of black family life, reinforced by studies of poverty and social problems. Only recently have we begun to take the view that black families present a different but equally valid form of family life (Demos, 1990). What is that form? There is little evidence to suggest that it is matriarchal, although the fact that so many black women are rearing families alone has been used as an explanation of the poverty and unemployment that plagues blacks (Washington, 1988).

As Valora Washington (1988) points out, black women work more years, have lower incomes, and experience greater unemployment than white women.

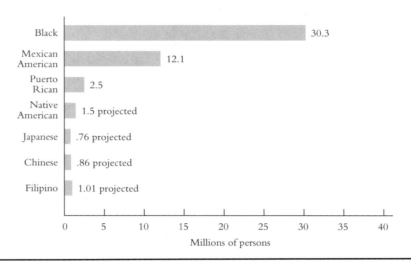

Figure 5.10 Size of selected minority groups in the United States, 1988.

SOURCE: Adapted from U.S. Bureau of the Census. (1989). *Statistical Abstract of the United States, 1989.* Washington, DC: U.S. Government Printing Office, 39. U.S. Bureau of the Census (1988). The Hispanic Population in the United States, March 1988. *Current Population Records,* ser. P-20, no. 431. Washington, DC: U.S. Government Printing Office.

They are also more likely to have dropped out of school because of pregnancy. Many more black females participate in the labor force when their children are young, and more black females with children work full-time than white. Unlike whites, the higher the family income, the more likely that the mother works. Among black families in the highest income brackets, 94 percent of the women work in contrast to 57 percent of white women.

Black families tend to have stronger relationships with the extended family, especially the wife's mother. The maternal grandmother often has a profound effect on the children, because the mother is so likely to be working full-time. Black husbands are more accepting of maternal employment than are whites and are active parents because the mother so often works. Black fathers, of course, are plagued by problems of poverty and joblessness, which often interfere with their ability to provide for their families. Such problems threaten family stability among blacks more often than among whites (Veroff, Dovan, & Hatchett, 1990).

Black mothers tend to have strong relationships with their children and high aspirations for them. They tend to emphasize the physical care and development of their children and to practice stricter discipline than is characteristic of white mothers. Black mothers demand respect and obedience more often than their white counterparts, and this is especially true for black grandmothers (Washington, 1988).

Valora Washington (1988) makes the following recommendations in our attempt to understand the black family:

1. We must withdraw the notion that mothers are totally responsible for the outcomes of their mothering. They are not isolated from social forces and social change.

2. We need to be more realistic about black females, careful to neither denigrate nor idealize the black mother.

3. Black mothers have been in the vanguard of family trends.

4. Poverty must be addressed as an integral aspect of black family life.

5. We must reexamine what work means to black mothers and fathers. Work has been oversold as black motherhood.

6. We must make greater efforts to understand the black father. The view of the black family as a matriarchy has underemphasized his role.

Mexican–American Families

The majority of Mexican-American families live in urban areas and most live in intact families. Family values are very strong among Mexican Americans and are held to be more important than those of the individual. Like the black family, the Mexican-American family has strong ties with the extended family, including grandparents, uncles and aunts, brothers, sisters, cousins, nieces, and nephews.

A much smaller percentage of Mexican-American families are headed by females than is true for black, Native American, or Puerto Rican families. Only 19 percent of Mexican-American families are headed by a female with no spouse present. Divorce rates are lower for Mexican-American families than for all other ethnic groups except for Asian Americans (U.S. Bureau of the Census, 1989).

Mexican-American families have, historically, been traditional or conventional as defined in Chapter 4. However, research has suggested that family forms are often quite equalitarian among Mexican-American families, and the most prevalent patterns are those in which the husband and wife share in decision making although the role of the wife is still seen as one of the conventional homemaker. The husband-wife relationship among Mexican Americans tends to be based primarily on procreation and the expression of love rather than companionship (Stromberg & Harkess, 1988; Rice, 1990). It is difficult to know, however, how much these values are driven by socioeconomic patterns rather than ethnic values because it is also true of working-class families that husband and wife enjoy minimal companionship. More specific research on the variety of Mexican-American family styles and the influence of socioeconomic forces and education on family values is needed before we can draw a definitive picture of the Mexican-American way of family life.

Asian-American Families

Most Asian Americans place a strong emphasis on family life, although certain kinds of immigration patterns have made it difficult for members of the Asian community to live out those values.

For example, for the first half of the twentieth century, Chinese females were not allowed to immigrate to the United States, whereas their husbands could. Although the overall sex ratio is now nearly equal, there are many older Chinese men who are isolated from intimate family ties (Rice, 1990; McGoldrick, 1989).

Chinese families tend to include their ancestors and descendents in their conception of family and believe that their own behavior affects other generations. Traditional Chinese families practice very strict child rearing and limit the social interactions of their children. They rely on commands or scolding in dealing with the problems of their children and expect clear obedience and conformity. Families who have been Americanized are more likely to use verbal praise with their children and offer some freedom and choice, although they still expect everyone to work for the welfare of the family and assign children a good deal of family responsibility (Young, 1972; Sih & Allen, 1976).

In Asian families, the young married couple often joins the husband's family, creating difficulties for the young wife, who must join the triangle now formed between her husband and her mother-in-law (McGoldrick, 1989). To understand an Asian family, however, it is critical to know how long it has been since the family immigrated as well as why they did so, what stage of the family life cycle they were living at the time of immigration, and whether they had any language difficulties at that time. This is true for all immigrant families, of course (McGoldrick, 1989), but especially so for Japanese Americans, who often refer to themselves by the Japanese words corresponding to first, second, or third generation. Children who were born in this country may need to reconnect with their culture of origin, particularly if the first generation cut itself off from the old country in an attempt to accelerate assimilation. Furthermore, young Asian-American immigrants may reverse the traditional flow of generational power in the family if they become the primary interpreters of the new culture to the immigrant generation. Cut off from their own parents and the extended families they grew up revering, parents may suffer multiple losses in newly immigrated families when their children leave home.

Asian families also have to struggle, as do other immigrant families, with what it means ultimately for children to become assimilated. This may be especially difficult when the family is faced with the marriage of a child to a member of the new culture, a person who may have a very different view of the meaning of family. Families may also deplore their children becoming too "Americanized," as in the case of Asian women who seek equal opportunities and reject the traditional image of Asian women as docile or submissive (Sih & Allen, 1976). Often the second generation has the most difficult time finding a balance between the "old" country traditions and the new. By the third generation, efforts are made to reconnect with lost traditions and preserve ethnic heritage (McGoldrick, 1989).

Native American Families

It is fairly difficult to say anything coherent about Native American families because they represent a wide variety of subcultures. Tribal identity is extremely important among Native Americans; family values and traditions vary from one tribe to another. Family forms vary as well and include some matrilineal groups. For most, however, there is an emphasis on the extended family, with members of different generations often sharing the same housing facilities (Keshna, 1980).

Native Americans have made very strong efforts to preserve and transmit cultural values to their children. For instance, the Northwest Indian Child Welfare Association has mounted a program aimed at reinstating traditional values and methods of child care as a way of preventing the abuse and neglect they believe to be a product of the intrusion of modern American society. They point out that:

> within the extended family network, child rearing was, and often still is, shared among several persons. This is a natural system of protecting children. . . . It is up to the entire community to nurture and protect our children so they can become healthy and productive adults. Members of Indian communities and tribes must share the responsibility of creating an environment in which children can thrive. By drawing upon the experience of our elders, and the wisdom passed down through generations, we can insure the survival of our culture and our way of life. (Northwest Indian Child Welfare Association, 1990, p. 3)

The Northwest Indian Child Welfare Association honors traditional Native American values in drawing on the experiences of elders to develop programs. They encourage community involvement, tribal direction, and a belief in the superiority of natural systems. They emphasize respect between children and parents, stress the importance of obedience to tribal teachings, and promote self-discipline and the extended family system as solutions to child abuse and neglect, seldom problems in traditional tribal settings.

Native Americans suffer from the highest death rates of any ethnic group in the country. They also have the shortest life expectancies, suffer more hunger and malnutrition, and have a lower standard of living than any other minority group. Unable to adjust to the alien culture of the classroom, many Native Americans experience inadequate schooling. Classes are usually conducted in English, though many Native American children speak only limited English at best. Despite these problems, the number of Native Americans getting a college education is increasing. Today, one in four Native Americans has at least some college (U.S. Bureau of the Census, 1989). As is the case for black, Hispanic, and Asian–American families, we have very little sense of the degree to which family life among Native Americans is a product of socioeconomic conditions, education, and tribal traditions and teachings. A great deal of work must be done if we are to become a multicultural society that respects, appreciates, and understands the strength of its own diversity.

Summary

I. Work, Occupation, and Career
   A. Career is defined as any organized path taken by an individual across space and time—as consistent involvement in any role over time.
      1. Careers have both external and internal paths that have been discussed in terms of stages such as exploration, establishment, maintenance, and later career development.
      2. People develop over time in both the external and internal aspects of career path.
II. Exploration and vocational choice have been studied in some depth because of the interests of teachers, counselors, and young adults in this phase of career development.
   A. The differentialist school assumes that optimal matching between personality characteristics and job characteristics will produce successful career development.
      1. Vocational types (e.g., conventional, enterprising, artistic, social, investigative, and realistic) form the basis for person-job matches.
      2. The differentialist position tends to ignore the role of socioeconomic conditions, opportunity, and chance in the selection of a job.
   B. The developmentalists propose that career choice proceeds through a series of stages.
      1. One version assumes that these stages represent increasingly realistic perceptions of the possible career paths available. However, the evidence tends to suggest young children are more realistic and older adolescents less realistic than this position requires.
      2. In another version, the self-concept is seen as a primary explanatory device and the stages are specified as crystallization, specification, implementation, and stabilization.
      3. Longitudinal studies of vocational development suggest that vocational choice is not nearly as rational as the developmental position suggests and that people do not proceed through any series of stages in a simple, straightforward way, stabilizing in young adulthood.
      4. Women's careers may fit stage models less well than men's because their work force participation tends to be discontinuous.

C. Job search and recruitment often proceed most successfully through informal channels. Formal recruitment often produces turnover rates in excess of 50 percent during the first seven months.
1. Unrealistic selling of the organization to the best-qualified recruits may produce later disenchantment.
2. Consideration of organizational culture, and matching of the personal and professional needs of the individual to the job as well as his or her skills and abilities might increase retention and job satisfaction.
   a. Culture is the set of important assumptions shared by community members including ideas about the use of time and space, and reflected in objects and use of verbal and nonverbal language.
   b. Recruits might be well advised to ask questions and make observations to determine the type and strength of organizational culture.
   c. Organizations should develop more formal orientation programs that teach culture.
D. Acceptance, reality shock, and commitment to the organization are entry phenomena and are affected by the type of socialization process offered in the organization.
1. Reality and cultural shock are strongest where training has been idealistic and organizational culture is controlling.
2. Socialization takes six months to a year and occurs in phases. Knowledge of culture is usually gained in the final phase of socialization. Careful observation can speed the process.
3. Commitment is a product of personal investment, and the opportunities and benefits organizations provide. Sponsorship also increases commitment.
E. More flexible organizational policies and an emphasis on fair treatment are increasingly important to long-term job success and satisfaction, especially for women and minorities.
III. Socioeconomic level (SEL), race, and sex all affect career aspirations and attainment.
A. SEL appears to be one of the most important predictors of educational attainment, occupational aspirations, and eventual occupational attainment.
B. American women are still relegated to the ranks of the pink-collar occupations, and equal pay for equal work is not a social reality although representation in education, the professions, and management is increasing.
1. Institutional discrimination is probably not as important as the fact that women are expected to, and do, carry the major burdens of child rearing and housework.

2. Traditional attitudes about the importance of a husband's job and the fear that men express about losing the last of the traditional male advantages are important forces maintaining the occupational dominance of men.

3. Men have not taken up household and child care responsibilities commensurate with the exodus of women to the labor force. Family is still considered a hindrance to a woman's career.

4. Career counseling for women should emphasize nontraditional choices and encourage interest in math and science.

5. Sexual harassment in the workplace and higher education must be acknowledged and addressed.

C. Racial discrimination is still clearly a fact of American working life. Unemployment, underemployment, and underutilization are characteristic of work life for blacks, Latinos, Native Americans, and recent immigrants of other ethnic groups.

1. Differences in education have been decreasing for most minorities, but income differences remain high as do unemployment rates.

2. The negative effects of discrimination on self-esteem contribute to the perpetuation of unemployment and underemployment among minorities.

3. Deep-seated differences in cultural values, especially among Native Americans, may also contribute to discrimination, but we do not have a clear idea of what the differences are and how they affect development.

D. The role of the good provider is a central sex-role expectation for white males and may contribute to general dissatisfaction with marriage as well as stress-related disease and emotional isolation.

IV. Parenthood is one important way in which adults achieve a sense of generativity and also constitutes one of the principal socializing events in adult life.

A. Children and parenthood affect adult development in a variety of ways. Many adults experience the birth of the first child as a developmental crisis.

1. Recent studies suggest childbirth is associated with declining marital satisfaction, especially among younger couples with less education and lower income, and those with difficult infants.

2. Parenthood has a paradoxical quality—both joyful and stressful. Parents believe it strengthens a marriage, but they also mourn the loss of personal freedom and the increase in stress that children bring.

3. With the birth of children, the family becomes a continuous-coverage institution, and the effects appear to be strongest for women.

4. Mothers experience much conflict and stress, partly because of the

dogma of full-time mothering and the stress society places on the role of the mother in child development.

    a. About one-quarter to one-third of all women find little meaning or joy in motherhood.

    b. Today's young women consistently want to combine work and family. Working mothers experience more stress and conflict but do not feel more negative about marriage and children.

    c. Full-time mothers who do not wish to be appear to have the most negative experiences of motherhood.

    d. Despite the problems, women still extol the joys of motherhood, including the increased closeness they feel in their marriages after the birth of children.

4. Fathers may also experience intense role conflicts between career and family since they are expected to perform as the good provider, but life satisfaction is strongly related to family involvement.

    a. Fathers are instrumental in the sex-role development of male and female children, and they can develop intense bonds with infants.

    b. Bonds between fathers and children tend to be based on visual interaction and play more often than are mother-child bonds.

    c. Fathers are more directive with older children and experience less conflict with adolescents.

B. Parenthood does seem to be accompanied by a traditionalization of sex-role behavior.

  1. A biological basis seems unlikely, since older couples do not experience increased stress, and fathers can play an important role in the emotional development of children, whereas the mother's instrumental activities do not appear to affect development adversely.

  2. The subcultures boys and girls grow up in may strongly influence their behaviors as parents and spouses.

C. The decision not to parent has been more popular in recent years with increased acceptance of the child-free lifestyle. Child-free couples include early articulators and postponers.

  1. Early articulators experience child-freeness as a characteristic of the self.

  2. Early articulators include rejectors and aficionados, the latter group often coming to the decision not to have children through continual postponement.

D. Single parents and stepparents are more and more frequent faces on the American scene, but there is relatively little research on the psychological aspects of single parenting and stepparenting.

  1. Single parents are overwhelmingly female and often black. Many of these families live below the poverty level.

        a. Even single-parent families with economic resources must cope with social isolation and loneliness.

        b. The problem of providing an adequate model of the absent parent is a special difficulty faced by every single-parent family.

        c. Single mothers are likely to experience several phases of family development after a divorce. It is important for them to begin to establish themselves as independent people and take charge of their children.

2. Although the number of children living with stepparents constitutes nearly one-third of all children, there is not a great deal of recent research.

        a. Evidence suggests that stepparents are more easily accommodated by very young children or adult children and by males, although stepfather-stepdaughter relationships appear to be problematic for many.

        b. Children continue to miss their biological parent, causing stepparents to feel inadequate or rejected.

        c. Stepfamilies often have unrealistic expectations about instant love and togetherness. Combined with a lack of social norms and a general negative social stereotype of stepparents and stepchildren, stepfamilies experience a great deal more stress than intact families.

        d. It takes three to five years to establish feelings of togetherness in stepfamilies, and establishing good relationships between stepparents and children is crucial.

        e. Stepmothers have the most difficult time, for they experience trouble deciding how involved to be in a society that expects high maternal involvement.

E. Little information exists on minority families except for statistical portraits and a few tentative research studies.

1. Black families have been viewed as problematic and this view is too often reinforced by studies of poverty and social problems. Recently, however, researchers have begun to look at black families as an alternate but valid family form that includes a strong network of extended family and emphasizes achievement, physical care, and respect.

2. Mexican-American families exhibit very strong family values and have lower divorce rates than the population in general. The husband-wife relationship tends to be based on love and procreation rather than companionship, but husband and wife still share in the decision-making process.

3. Asian-American families place a strong emphasis on family life and are characterized by traditional relationships between husband and wife; however, patterns and recency of immigration may be

more important in understanding Asian Americans than any other set of variables. The same is true for any recently immigrated family.

4. Native American families are hard to characterize because family values and patterns vary from tribe to tribe. In general, however, most groups emphasize a respect for tribal teachings and community and the importance of the extended-family network.

Middle Age

6

The Personal Context:
Physiological and Psychological
Changes at Midlife

*Middle age is when your classmates are so old and wrinkled and bald
they don't recognize you.*

—Bennett Cerf

SOMETIME IN THE MIDST OF OUR THIRTY-SEVENTH or thirty-eighth year, most of
us notice that middle age has arrived. We greet the news with mixed feelings.
One day in the mailbox you find the invitation to your twentieth high school
reunion. Where did the time go? What has happened to all those people?
Does it really matter? What to wear?

You stumble into the bedroom and stare into your closet. The problem,
you confess, cannot be solved at Bloomingdale's. All the signs of middle age
have crept up on you: wrinkles, gray hair, and extra pounds around the
middle. And the whole bag and baggage seems to be sagging at the seams.
At least you are not alone. Around age forty everyone begins to feel the
effects of age, and though not all unpleasant, they do change one's perspective in a variety of ways.

IN THIS CHAPTER, WE EXPLORE THE PHYSICAL CHANGES that are typical of biological development in middle age. We discuss the contribution these may make to
psychological and social life. We will review data on changes in skin, hair, and
bones, as well as more general information on health and physical well-being,
sensation and perception, and psychomotor performance. In the next section
of the chapter we will examine the cognitive and intellectual developments of
midlife. Finally, a review of the developmental tasks of middle age is included
as a transition to Chapters 7 and 8.

Physiology and Biology at Midlife

Some of the most dramatic and obvious changes first appear in the mirror. Faces and bodies begin to show the effects of several important physical phenomena. These phenomena include a redistribution of fatty tissues, and an atrophy of muscles and certain proteins that make up various tissues, including the skin and internal organs. The lips, breasts, eyelids, and often the lower portion of the face seem to shrink, whereas the nose, ears, and middle of the body seem to grow. A layer of fat disappears from the face and another develops around the middle. This layer of fat appears in the trunk rather than the legs as is the case for younger people (Kleemier, 1959). The skull, as well as the nose and ears, continues to grow. Bones increase in size throughout the normal adult life span, although they become more brittle and less strong with age (Garn, 1975).

Furthermore, the protein tissues of the body change in ways that affect one's appearance. The changes also have critical implications for health and well-being. Underneath the wrinkles and bags in the skin, the tissues become progressively less elastic. The **ground substance** that surrounds individual protein cells changes. Water is lost and tissues become drier (this has been going on since birth not just since age forty). Waste products build up in the cells and affect the exchange of nutrients across the membrane. Often cells are unable to maintain the chemical balance they need for optimal function (and appearance) (Finch, 1978).

Finally, the protein molecules age. The two major proteins that make up most of the tissues of the body are **collagen** and **elastin.** With age, both of these proteins become cross-linked. **Cross-linking** occurs when one cell becomes attached to another. As cross-linking becomes more frequent, tissues become less flexible. An example of this would be that leather is produced by the process of tanning, which induces cross-linkage. Leather is much less flexible than natural cowhide. Though superior as a purse or shoe, leather is not so nice as skin (Bakerman, 1969). Cross-linking occurs in all the internal tissues too. Eventually, it limits the elasticity of the muscles and tendons, affects the heart, lungs, intestines, glands, and the entire circulatory system down to the tiniest arteriole and venule. Along with changes in the immune system and the buildup of waste products in cells, the stiffening of internal tissues is responsible for dramatic increases in the incidence of chronic and life-threatening disease during middle age. In the next few pages, we'll look at how these general changes affect a number of organs and organ systems.

Appearance

The earliest physical sign that one is approaching midlife is increasing body weight and change in girth measurements. Body weight increases from one's twenties through one's fifties, declining thereafter (Whitbourne, 1985b). Weight gain is particularly rapid for women (Kleemier, 1959), and the pounds are less harmoniously distributed. The extremities and the face lose subcutaneous fat, and the excess appears in the trunk of the body. The fat seems to be distributed in two forms: apple-shaped and pear-shaped. Apple-shaped is the tire around the middle. Pear-shaped is weight on the hips and nonstomach areas.

Changes in the skin are especially apparent in the face and hands, forearms, and the V-shaped area at the junction of the neck and the chest because of constant exposure to the weather and the rays of the sun (Whitbourne, 1985b). Although these changes are progressive, of course, and neither begin nor end in midlife, people seem most conscious of them during the middle years.

Bone and Connective Tissue

Changes in the outer layer of the skin, or the epidermis, become apparent as the cells of this layer flatten. The arrangement of epidermal cells becomes less orderly with age, and the skin becomes drier as the production of natural lubricants declines. Darker complexions are less affected by the sun, and the most dramatic changes occur in blue- or green-eyed blonds and redheads. Black skin retains a youthful appearance longer than white skin (Selmanowitz, Rizer, & Orentreich, 1977). Figure 6.1 presents an example of changes in the face over the years of adult life.

After the age of thirty, the weight of the bones begins to decline, at about 6 to 8 percent per decade. Spongy bones are particularly vulnerable, and the rate of bone loss is greater for women, especially women in their fifties, than for men. The depletion of estrogen may be implicated in declining bone weight among late middle-aged women (Heaney, 1982).

Changes are noticeable in even the smallest ways. For example, the rate of nail growth declines by 40 percent during the adult years. The nails also become opaque and sometimes yellow or gray with age. Nails may also take on a ridged appearance and begin to split in layers. Age or "liver" spots proliferate and accumulate, especially on the hands (Selmanowitz et al., 1977).

Psychological Reactions

Naturally, these developments affect how people feel about their physical appearance. Women are especially likely to interpret the changes in a negative way. Middle-aged women see themselves as less attractive than do any other age group. They are worried about whether or not they will continue to be sexually attractive. Neither women nor men in other age groups view middle-aged women so negatively (Nowak, 1977), but social support for middle-aged women who have these concerns is easy to find. Even a brief glance at the magazines on the supermarket checkout stand or half an hour in front of the television suggests that female aging is not an attractive phenomenon. Despite Linda Evans and Jane Fonda, double standards of aging exist in North America. Older women are often considered unattractive and sexually undesirable, if

Age 25   Age 59

Figure 6.1 Changes in the face between youth and late middle age.

not completely sexless (Troll, 1977). Lieblich (1986) reports that those women who do withstand the attrition of the aging process develop more androgynous personalities during their adult development and thus avoid the crises more "feminine" women face.

Part of the problem in researching these issues is there is not much information about what is sexy in this culture or other cultures. Casual observation would suggest that youthful good looks are sexy, as exemplified by popular figures from Jean Harlow to Madonna. However, the marks of experience, power, and prestige are also attractive. Older men are much more likely than older women to evoke these images. Men like Paul Newman are considered sexy although they can certainly not be considered young. Time will tell whether power, experience, and prestige will ever be thought sexually attractive in women. Today, it is more common to see women dating, even marrying, men who are five to ten years younger than they are. Still, this is much less frequent a social phenomenon than the older-man/younger-woman pair. Furthermore, the physical attractiveness of a middle-aged woman is critical if she is to attract the attention of a younger man. The physical attractiveness of middle-aged men, however, is not nearly as important to younger women (Masters, Johnson, & Kolodny, 1991).

Health

It should be the function of medicine to have people die as late as possible.

—Ernst L. Snyder, M.D.

At middle age, one's awareness of vulnerability to the chronic, universal diseases of age increases, especially among men. Men are often victims of premature death. It is quite common for middle-aged men to engage in a good deal of "body monitoring." This continual, if low-key, concern about health and well-being (Neugarten, 1968b) is often shared by the wives of these men. James Fries and Lawrence Crapo (1981) point out that the chronic diseases are the major threat to human health in developed countries.

> Atherosclerosis and other arterial diseases, cancer, diabetes, arthritis, emphysema, and cirrhosis cause over 80 percent of all premature deaths and over 90 percent of all disability. . . . These diseases tend to (1) be incremental, (2) be universal, (3) have a clinical threshold, and (4) be characterized by a progressive loss of organ reserve. In many ways, these diseases are similar to normal processes of gradual loss of function with age, but the disease processes cause such loss to occur at an accelerated rate. (pp. 79–80)

These conditions are not generally responsible for premature deaths until after age forty-five. All of them, however, begin relatively early in adult life as minor changes occur in the cells of particular organs. The clinical threshold, or the point at which symptoms appear, is reached rather late in many disease processes. For instance, Figure 6.2 presents the clinical course of **atherosclerosis.** The figure shows that heart disease is something that starts early and may grow worse in a slow, steady way (solid line) or erupt and become visible suddenly (dotted line). The symptoms begin without conscious awareness (high cholesterol) and proceed through chest pains (angina pectoris) and deficits in blood flow (transient ischemic attacks) to events that are fatal.

Beyond a doubt, cardiovascular diseases are the most threatening chronic diseases of middle age. Cardiovascular disease accounts for 40 percent of all premature deaths in this age group. However, cancer takes its toll as well. In cardiovascular disease, the process for atherosclerosis (Figure 6.2) includes undetected progression toward severe illness or death. According to Fries and Crapo (1981), the key to preventing chronic illness is to be found in delaying

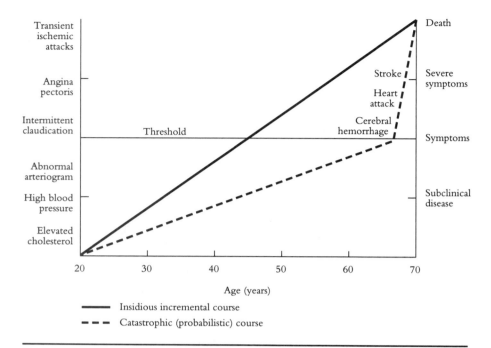

Figure 6.2 The clinical course of atherosclerosis. Atherosclerosis may progress relatively evenly, or it may result in a sudden catastrophic event such as heart attack or stroke. Both the decrease in vessel caliber and flow and the probability of catastrophe proceed incrementally and progressively. The other major chronic illnesses show similar progressions.

SOURCE: Fries & Crapo, 1981. Copyright © 1981 W. H. Freeman and Company. Reprinted with permission. Note: This figure was created from data of U.S. Bureau of Health Statistics.

the time of clinical appearance, so "symptoms will not develop during the natural life span, and the disease will have been 'prevented'. Actually, the disease process will not have disappeared, but its accelerated characteristics will have been lost, and, from the standpoint of the affected individual, it is as if it never occurred" (pp. 85–86).

Several assumptions underlie Fries and Crapo's position. They believe the natural life span is not likely to exceed eighty-five or eighty-six years of age in this century or the next. They argue, as do a number of important biologists, that there is a predictable limit to the extension of the life span through medical technology. They point out that most recent increases in the life span have been primarily achieved through the dramatic reduction of infectious diseases like pneumonia and influenza. They also assume that death and aging occur because cells cease to function in late life. They believe that rapid, terminal decline at or about the age of eighty-five would be predictable even if all of the chronic diseases were to be eliminated.

Whether or not you accept these assumptions, the preventive health strategies Fries and Crapo describe make sense. Many environmental and lifestyle factors are instrumental in accelerating disease processes. Diets high in fat, especially saturated fat; use of drugs, alcohol, and tobacco; exposure to pollution and radiation; the proliferation of chemical agents in food, water, and the atmosphere; a sedentary lifestyle; and certain personality traits have been consistently associated with the major health problems of middle age. In recent years, educational efforts seem to have borne some fruit. Mortality due to heart disease may be declining as people become more aware of the importance of diet, exercise, and staying away from cigarettes. Awareness is also increasing about the importance of stress management in the progress of the chronic diseases. In the last fifteen years, research in a new area called *behavioral medicine* has suggested some important psychological strategies for improving physical health (Siegler & Costa, 1985). One approach focuses on the behavioral treatment of diseases. Behavioral programs have successfully helped people quit smoking— a behavior that causes heart disease, stroke, cancer, and emphysema, diseases that dramatically shorten the life of smokers and the people around them.

Change in diet, especially the reduction in fats, also seems to have a large effect. Such changes reduce cardiovascular diseases in men and women, and some forms of cancer such as colon cancer (Willett, Stampfer, Colditz, Rosner, & Speizer, 1990) and breast cancer (Knekt, Albanes, Seppanen, Aromaa, Jarvinen, Hyvonen, Teppo, Pukkala, 1990). Reducing the fat content of what we eat and alcohol in what we drink seems to have the largest effect. Weight loss is also very important. Behavior programs have found exercise to have long-term benefits in reducing weight. Crash dieting per se seems to have no positive long-term effect. However, some long-term behavioral programs have promise (Lavery, Loewy, Kapadia, Nichaman, Foreyt, & Gee, 1990; Lovibond, Birrell, & Langeluddecke, 1986). Weight loss and exercise not only reduce the high blood pressure that causes cardiovascular disease; in addition, they reduce the severity of the disease for non-insulin-dependent diabetics (adult-onset diabetes). The limits of behavioral medicine have also been recognized. Separated-twin and adoption studies suggest much weight gain is inherited. Energy utilization may play a major role (Ravussin & Pogardus, 1989).

Another approach in behavioral medicine focuses on personality characteristics and lifestyle. For example, Friedman and Rosenman (1974) first outlined the compulsive, highly stressed Type A personality. They showed its association with elevated serum cholesterol level, accelerated blood coagulation, and high levels of some of the hormones associated with stress (Rosenman et al., 1970; Siegler, Nowlin, & Blumenthal, 1980). In these studies, premature heart disease rarely if ever occurred among those who exhibited an easygoing, non-aggressive (Type B) personality style.

Fortunately, people who exhibit a Type A personality can often be taught to manage their high stress levels. This is done by recognizing the conditions that cause high blood pressure and by relaxing. Such intervention may prevent catastrophic episodes of stroke or heart attack. These individuals can also learn behavioral interventions that punish aggressive, explosive behavior. These interventions can also reinforce or reward a more relaxed, patient style (Siegler, Nowlin, & Blumenthal, 1980). Such procedures have been used to treat tachycardia (rapid heart rate), hypertension, muscle-contraction headaches, and a variety of other ills associated with stress.

A second approach to disease prevention emphasizes how life stresses affect us all, regardless of personality type. Whether stress is positive (eustress) or negative (distress) (Selye, 1976), the body undergoes a wide variety of accompanying physiological changes. The totality of these changes has been called the **general adaptation syndrome,** a term that describes the mobilization of the sympathetic nervous system (SNS). Whether you win the Academy Award (**eustress**) or find yourself in an automobile accident (**distress**), SNS mobilization produces changes in the cardiovascular, hormonal, respiratory, and temperature systems of the body. Such changes result in more acute audition and vision (as you either wait for Robert Redford to announce your name, or career toward the open area on the right shoulder of the road). Glycogen is transformed into glucose for quick energy, and endorphins, the natural painkillers produced by the body, are released (just in case you lose the award or miss the shoulder). It has been argued that the continuous stimulation of urban life produces so much stress and so little opportunity for physical release that people are constantly "overmobilized." This overmobilization often eventuates in stress-related diseases of all sorts (Insel & Roth, 1991; Selye, 1976).

Heart attacks are not the only expression of cardiovascular disease, of course. The heart is only one part of the system. Changes in the blood vessels are also apparent by middle age. The large arteries become markedly less elastic with time. Stiffness of these blood vessels doubles between the ages of twenty and sixty. This is related to the rising incidence of high blood pressure among subjects in longitudinal studies (Kohn, 1977). A practical dietary prescription for those suffering from hypertension includes a decreased intake of sodium (2 grams per day), less saturated fat, more fiber, no more than two ounces of alcohol per day. The Joint National Committee on Public Health (1984 report) has supported this dietary approach and advocates nonpharmacological therapy (of hypertension) with careful medical monitoring.

Arteriosclerosis and atherosclerosis are diseases of the blood vessels that have in common the thickening of the arterial walls. Often the words *arteriosclerosis* and *atherosclerosis* are used interchangeably (Robbins, 1967). Although both are related to high blood pressure and high serum cholesterol levels, the exact relation among blood pressure, cholesterol, and changes in the arteries remains something of a mystery (Robbins, 1967). The incidence of atherosclerosis increases in men after the age of forty, leveling off around age fifty-five; rates for women continue to rise until about age sixty-five.

In atherosclerosis, lesions or injuries to the arterial walls appear. The number of lesions increases with the passage of the years. Fat, cholesterol, collagen, and small capillaries build up on the site of the lesions, forming plaques. The elastin fibers that make up the walls of the blood vessels are split and fragmented at the site of the lesion. Plaques can be pictured as reefs in the bloodstream that restrict flow through the arteries.

Arteriosclerosis involves the same kinds of events as atherosclerosis but occurs in smaller blood vessels and does not usually involve the formation of plaques. It has been said that the changes in the large arteries and other blood vessels constitute a basic aging process. This process is intrinsic to the cells and tissues and is progressive, universal, and irreversible (Kohn, 1977).

The role of stress or environmental factors in the progress of arterial degeneration has not yet been clarified. We do know, however, that the general adaptation syndrome becomes less efficient with age. According to Hans Selye (1976), this nonspecific biological response has three stages. The first, called alarm, is accompanied by all the physiological mobilization changes just described. The second stage, resistance, permits the body to repair whatever damage has been done during the first stage. If stress continues unabated however, adaptation is lost and the final stage, exhaustion, occurs. If Selye's stages are an accurate description, resistance may require more time in later life, and exhaustion may occur sooner.

Older persons recover from stress more slowly because they require more hormones and other chemicals to produce alarm. Therefore, researchers have been particularly interested in how aging of the endocrine system affects one's response to stress and disease (Timiras, 1972). However, no one has yet pinpointed the endocrine changes that are critical in the decreased efficiency of stress reactions. Relatively little is known about the action of individual hormones, and even less about the complex interactions among these chemicals as they circulate in the bloodstream. Most of the available literature is descriptive and suggestive rather than experimental. It is especially sparse on the subject of adrenocortical and pituitary hormones, although these appear to play a very important role in the general adaptation syndrome.

New and important theoretical ideas about how people learn to cope with stress have come from the study of critical life events and illness (Lazarus, 1981). How people evaluate stress appears to be at least as important as the event itself. Also, coping with the stress of illness may require a different mechanism than coping with other life events (Siegler & Costa, 1985). Coping with the illness of a loved one has also inspired a great deal of research.

Zarit (1989) argues that the burden a caregiver feels depends on the stressor or life event; the perceptions or appraisal of that event; the coping skills and resources a caregiver can bring to bear; and the outcomes for the caregiver, such as level of morale.

Research on stress and illness along with information on physical fitness and other good health habits seems to be making substantial changes in the health behavior of many Americans. Per capita, tobacco consumption has decreased 26 percent in the years since the Surgeon General's report on the harmful effects of tobacco. National body weight has declined by about five pounds per person and a huge number of adults have entered regular programs of exercise. The incidence of lung cancer may have peaked in the early 1980s. Declining rates are predicted because the rate of smoking in the U.S. is decreasing among men (Centers for Disease Control, 1989). The same is expected for emphysema.

In current work on heart disease, it has been discovered that 60 percent of men who live beyond sixty years of age have a 75–100 percent **stenosis** (narrowing) in at least one coronary artery. Even with such high rates of stenosis, the overall incidence of cardiovascular disease has declined about 25 percent since 1968 (Fries & Crapo, 1981). People are eating less fat—especially animal fat—in their diet and high blood pressure is treated more often.

As Fries and Crapo conclude: "The health and aging problems of the present time are not intractable. The postponement of chronic diseases and the retardation of aging through fundamental research and collective personal effort are realistic strategies for the near future, entirely consistent with our health gains up to the present" (p. 142). Perhaps we shall soon see the day when, like Oliver Wendell Holmes's wonderful one-hoss shay, we go

. . . to pieces all at once,
All at once, and nothing first,
Just as bubbles do when they burst.

For the foreseeable future, however, one notable exception to "all at once" can be expected: the reproductive system. This area of physical change is one in which no disease process is evident.

The Reproductive System

Involution means retrograde development, the return of an enlarged organ to its original size. It refers to the period of the **climacteric** in men and women when the reproductive organs decline in function. In women, the climacteric is far more marked than in men, beginning sometime late in one's thirties and continuing through the fifties. Still, even among females, the changes are much more gradual than those that mark the onset of fertility in adolescence. Decrease in the production of estrogen is relatively gradual, and involution of the breasts, genital tissues, and uterus is slow.

For most women, the critical aspect of the climacteric is the menopause, or end of menstruation. Menopause usually occurs in women between the ages of forty-eight and fifty-two (Masters, Johnson, & Kolodny, 1991). However, this event does not occur in one day. It is more reasonably considered a process of many months or even years. Sometime around age forty, there is a noticeable decline in the number of oocytes (eggs) that mature and erupt from the ovaries. Those that do develop often fail prematurely, producing increased irregularity of the menstrual cycle. Usually, only after a long period of irregular or skipped cycles, menstruation ceases altogether (Neugarten, 1967; Newman, 1982).

Because the developing oocytes produce much of the hormones estrogen and progesterone in the female body, the level of circulating estrogens declines at the climacteric. This affects the entire genital tract and sometimes sexual function. The walls of the vagina often become thinner and do not lubricate as quickly or as completely among older women. If these developments are extreme, sexual intercourse can become uncomfortable. Usually, however, the use of a lubricant jelly eliminates the discomfort (Masters, Johnson, & Kolodny, 1991).

Menopause itself is surrounded by as much mystery, misinformation, and often anxiety as the onset of menstruation. For instance, some argue that only neurotic women experience symptoms during menopause. Many women find their symptoms cause for grave concern. Some even indicate that they fear a mental breakdown or the loss of their sexual attractiveness (Neugarten, Wood, Kraines, & Loomis, 1963). A large body of research has demonstrated that certain physical symptoms are common. These include hot flashes, night sweats, pelvic or breast pain, and feelings of suffocation or shortness of breath. These symptoms appear to be hormone-related because estrogen-replacement therapy (ERT) can alleviate if not eliminate such menopausal symptoms (Insel & Roth, 1991).

There has been controversy over the use of estrogen-replacement therapy (ERT). Some data indicate that ERT can increase the risk of uterine cancer. Other data show that if progesterone is added to estrogen at the end of the menstrual cycle, the risk of cancer with ERT is minimal. Furthermore, evidence shows that ERT decreases the risk of osteoporosis, an extreme form of bone loss (Bruce & Stevenson, 1990; Gennari & Agnusdel, 1990) and may even protect menopausal and postmenopausal women from certain forms of heart disease. Principally, of course, ERT is prescribed because it relieves the symptoms of the climacteric, which can be quite distressful if extreme (Masters, Johnson, & Kolodny, 1991).

Hot flashes are probably the most common symptom of the climacteric. About 75–80 percent of all menopausal women experience hot flashes. Some women report hot flashes as often as every few hours, but most experience them once a week or less. Hot flashes can last a few seconds or, in extreme cases, a few minutes and have been attributed to a malfunction of the temperature control mechanism in the hypothalamus. Hot flashes cease in a few years after the menopause in most women, although a few continue to report them longer (Masters, Johnson, & Kolodny, 1991).

Studies have also shown that natural menopause leads to few changes in psychological characteristics, with only a decline in introspectiveness and discomfort due to an increase in hot flashes being apparent. Researchers have concluded that natural menopause does not have negative mental health consequences for the majority of middle-aged women (Matthews, Wing, Kuller, Meilahn, Kelsey, Costello, & Caggiula, 1990).

Generally, attitudes toward menopause are good predictors of the severity and duration of reported symptoms. Women who feel positive about the cessation of fertility, who are not anxious about growing old, and who possess ample information about the climacteric and menopause seem to experience less concern. Postmenopausal women often feel quite positive about menopause, experiencing increased feelings of vigor and well-being and reporting an upswing in sexual desire and activity (Neugarten et al., 1963). As Barbara Newman writes:

> It appears that as a young woman views menopause she confuses the physiological phenomena with all the negative connotations of growing old. The importance of physical beauty may be heavily weighted in a woman's definition of femininity. Further, the younger woman may be still quite invested in her role as mother and fearful of a potential end to her years of childbearing. The older woman, on the other hand, is likely to be glad to have reached the end of the years of childbearing. She may be eagerly awaiting a future of new roles and new freedoms. (1982, p. 623)

The climacteric means something quite different for men than it does for women. There is really no male biological equivalent to menopause, in spite of a recent rash of media images of "male menopause." Changes in the male reproductive system actually occur gradually. Production of sperm, for example, declines only 30 percent over the period between twenty-five and sixty. In fact, at age eighty, most men are still producing about one-half the sperm typical of twenty-year-olds.

Yet males are not unaffected by the climacteric. There are other changes in the reproductive system that can have important effects. Most often, the involution, or degeneration, of the prostate gland causes concern, it being one site of semen production. The degeneration of the veins and arteries in the penis as well as the stiffening of these tissues contributes to changes in sexual function (Talbert, 1977). Erection and ejaculation occur more slowly with age. The refractory period that follows orgasm and ejaculation is also longer (Masters, Johnson, & Kolodny, 1991). The effects of the male climacteric are not all negative, however. Age does alleviate the primary American male sexual problem: premature ejaculation. It may open a whole new range of sexual pleasures and activities if men can approach sex with greater patience and humor.

Sexually, both middle-aged men and women experience less muscle tension during arousal and plateau than they did in young adulthood. Declining muscle tension may account for the reduced intensity of orgasm people report in middle age. After fifty, women experience fewer contractions during the orgasmic phase, and lubrication takes longer. There are also fewer vascular changes during excitement and plateau.

In men, especially over the age of fifty-five, erections are less firm, the volume of semen is diminished, and the need to ejaculate feels less intense. Typically, young men experience orgasm in two phases. The first is marked by regular contractions of the prostate and the feeling that orgasm is inevitable. The second commences with contraction of the penile musculature. Older men show only irregular contractions of the prostate and may not really experience stage 1 at all (Masters, Johnson, & Kolodny, 1991).

The best predictor of sexual activity in later life is previous sexual activity. Most sexually active people report only a modest decline in the frequency of sexual activity from age fifty-five on into their seventies. Continued sexual function is of course more likely to occur when people have the opportunity to remain active. That is, access to a sexual partner, a positive body image, and positive feelings about sexuality are important predictors of sexual function in middle and later life. Although Masters and Johnson (1966) may have overstated the case (as we shall see in Chapter 9) when they summed it up, "Use it or lose it," their advice remains basically sound.

Sensation, Perception, and Psychomotor Performance

When that invitation to your twentieth high school reunion arrives, you may have to put on your new glasses to read it. Other subtle changes as well mark the beginnings of sensory aging. For example, you may find that you don't want to attend a play or concert unless you can get very good seats. And you may fiddle constantly with the graphic equalizer on the stereo because the bass seems too loud.

Once again, the changes of age strike in insidious ways. Deterioration of the arteries and veins and increasing stiffness or fibrosis of all the tissues of the body slowly affect many functions throughout adult life. Often, the threshold of noticeable symptoms is reached in middle age, especially for functions requiring fine discriminations. These functions include vision and hearing, or those that demand rapid, complex actions and decisions, such as the psychomotor skills.

Vision

By middle age, two important changes usually reach a stage at which they become a nuisance if nothing else. First, the lens, which has become less elastic throughout adulthood, may be rigid and compacted enough that objects placed too close or too far away appear blurred. This blurring happens because the lens loses its ability to accommodate or change focus. Moreover, the lens becomes increasingly opaque and yellow. Light scatters as it enters the pupil

Glasses:
"I wear them. They help me. But I
Don't care for them . . .
My gaze feels aimed. It is as if
Two manufactured beams had been
Lodged in my sockets—hollow, stiff
And gray, like mailing tubes—and when
I pivot, vases topple down
From tabletops, and women frown." John Updike

and sensitivity to the blue-green end of the spectrum diminishes (Corso, 1981; Fozard, Wolf, Bell, McFarland, & Podolsky, 1977). See Figure A.5 in the Appendix for the major structures of the eye.

The lens of the eye is rather like a piece of skin; and as is the case with the skin on the arms, legs, or face, new cells are constantly emerging. The difference is that cells cannot be sloughed off from inside the eye, as they can from our external layer. Thus, the cells of the lens become more and more com-pacted and the weight of the lens increases with age. At seventy, the lens weighs about three times more than during infancy (Spector, 1982).

During adulthood, the vitreous humor also begins to break down, and old cells and blood vessels collect, producing "floaters"—the dark spots that ap-pear before the eye during rapid ocular movements (Corso, 1981; Klein & Schieber, 1985). Sometimes the changes in the vitreous humor produce blurred vision, or flashes of light that have no outside stimulus source.

As the lens is compacted and opacities appear, light from the external en-vironment becomes scattered as it enters the pupil. Many of the problems of the aging eye, such as increasing sensitivity to glare, are produced by such scat-tering. Other difficulties, for example, depth perception, are related to the in-creased weight and stiffness of the lens. Another cause of visual deterioration is glucose metabolites building up on the lens because of diabetes. Beswick and Harding (1987) have demonstrated glucose 6-phosphate (a glucose break-down product that persons with diabetes mellitis cannot metabolize) will cause changes in the lens.

Depth is judged in part by the accommodation of the lens to near versus far objects and by subtle distinctions based on brightness and contrast. The nearest distance at which an object can be seen clearly without blur is called the **near point of vision.** "As a person grows older, the near point of vision recedes so that the range of accommodation decreases markedly between the ages of ten and thirty, more slowly for the next ten years, and then at a rapid pace between forty and fifty, slowing again after fifty. Accommodation requires more and more effort to achieve, not because the muscles deteriorate, but because the lens is so much less flexible (Kline & Schieber, 1985).

There is a huge loss of cones, the receptor cells in the center of the retina, in the years between forty and sixty. The retinal capillaries may atrophy, perhaps because of prolonged exposure to the ultraviolet rays of the sun. There is also a loss of neurons in the visual projection areas of the brain. However, researchers have not yet been able to show how this type of aging is related to cognitive or perceptual performance (Ball & Pollack, 1989).

However, there is general evidence that changes in the retina and nervous system are important in the deterioration of depth perception and reduced **vi-sual acuity** between forty and fifty. Morrison and McGrath (1985) show that depth perception declines with age. They make a convincing case that the ret-ina and postretina nervous system are responsible for the discrepancies seen in spatial vision with age. Furthermore, vascular changes in the retina are thought to cause a decline in function of the rods, the cells that govern vision at low levels of light (Fozard et al., 1977).

Decreasing efficiency in the transportation and utilization of both sugar and oxygen combines with muscular changes to affect adaptation to the dark (**dark adaptation**), and to cause shrinkage of the visual field. Interestingly, a smaller visual field can be produced in young subjects by reducing the amount of oxy-gen in the air they breathe.

Older men exhibit reduced visual sensitivity and poorer performance on a variety of measures that reflect the efficiency of cognitive neural function. However, this research also shows differences that depend on aerobic fitness. Compared to men judged poorly fit, physically active men exhibit more efficient cognitive neural activity and better visual sensitivity (Dustman, Emmerson, Ruhling, Shearer, Steinhaus, Johnson, Bonekat, & Shigeoka, 1990). These authors speculate that the performance superiority of the physically active men may be partially due to more oxygen being available for the metabolism of the brain.

Continued breadth of visual field is related to total vital capacity (Corso, 1981). There is also some evidence that lifelong physical fitness, good diet, and a sensible lifestyle can be instrumental in the maintenance of good vision. That makes sense when you consider that fitness is associated with improved cardiovascular and respiratory function. Also validating that idea, most of the sensory decline that occurs in middle age has been attributed to decreasing blood supply and declining efficiency in the transportation and utilization of both sugar and oxygen (Corso, 1981).

All these changes are noticeable by the age of fifty. Most people begin to wear glasses when they want to see something clearly, but alterations in the sensory processes are probably not an important source of limitation in daily life until at least age seventy (Birren, 1964). Visual perception and the processing of visual information do not appear to change much during middle age. Unless subjects are tested under extremely adverse conditions, like reduced illumination or poor contrast, performance on tasks of visual perception is remarkably stable throughout the middle years (Comalli, 1970; Pitts, 1982).

Audition

Many of the same culprits responsible for changes in vision, such as vascular problems, are also responsible for changes in audition (hearing). Starting as early as ten or twelve, the ability to hear high-pitched sounds declines. Tones over a frequency of 1,000 Hz (cycles per second) must be presented at significantly greater intensity (volume) if middle-aged people are to hear them, especially men. In daily life, this means that many of the overtones of musical instruments can no longer be appreciated without special amplification. Overtones are the harmonic vibrations of an instrument that occur along with the fundamental tone. They account, in part, for why a sax and a clarinet sound different when they play the same note. All of the overtones of the human voice in the soprano range occur above 1,000 cycles per second, as do the overtones of many soprano instruments like the piccolo and the flute. In fact, hearing is affected for most of the wind instruments and the common stringed instruments (Cohen, 1969). Figure 6.3 presents the fundamental and overtone frequencies of some common instruments and animal sounds.

Although 20 percent of the population between forty-five and fifty-four have some hearing loss for high-frequency tones (Olsho, Harkins, & Lenhardt, 1985), they do not lose the ability to hear high-frequency sound altogether. If

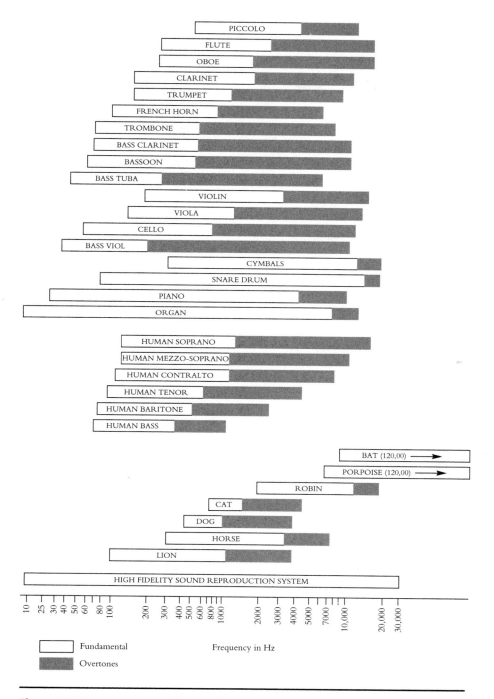

Figure 6.3 Frequency range of musical instruments and human and animal voices.

SOURCE: Cohen, 1969, p. 10. Reprinted by permission of the author.

they are to detect tones above 1,000 cycles per second however, the sound must be presented at greater volume than is necessary for younger subjects. Important sex differences also exist, with men suffering the worse losses at high frequencies.

Men may be subject to greater auditory loss because they are exposed to damaging levels of noise more often at work and in recreation. Work noises include jet engines, electric and pneumatic saws and hammers, musical instruments, guns, and other forms of blasts. Indeed, the ubiquitous noise of modern life is clearly responsible for some of the auditory problems older people suffer. There is evidence, however, that even in isolated, preindustrial groups, the ability to hear high-frequency noise declines throughout adulthood (Timiras & Vernadakis, 1972; Corso, 1981). Four different forms of **presbycusis,** a progressive, perceptive hearing loss that occurs with age, have been identified, each of which is associated with a different kind of hearing problem among the elderly (Rupp, 1970; Schuknecht & Igarashi, 1964):

1. **Sensory presbycusis:** a loss of hearing for high-pitched tones that seems to result from atrophy of the hair cells in the inner ear

2. **Neural presbycusis:** problems of speech discrimination that suggest progressive loss of auditory neurons

3. **Metabolic presbycusis:** loss of pure tone hearing attributed to atrophy of the striavascularis

4. **Mechanical presbycusis:** loss of high-frequency hearing caused by decreasing flexibility of the basilar membrane

These four categories of auditory change occur in the spiral organ (organ of Corti) within the cochlea of the inner ear (see page A-8 in the Appendix). In addition, as the individual ages, impacted wax builds up in the ear canal and usually contributes to some of the hearing problems older people experience. Moreover, fluid often obstructs the eustachian tubes, and the bones in the middle ear become rather spongy, limiting their ability to conduct sound (Corso, 1977).

Degenerative changes in the auditory system are clearly present by the early years of middle age, but few people will be greatly affected by them. Many never even notice. One can simply turn up the stereo or buy better seats for a concert. Auditory deficits, like those of the visual system, are troublesome only under stressful conditions. For example, when words are made to overlap or are frequently interrupted, subjects over forty have difficulty hearing sentences. Otherwise, speech discrimination is only minimally affected until very late in life (Corso, 1957, 1977, 1981).

For biologists and psychologists interested in sensory aging, the deficits of middle age are important not because they affect people's daily lives (they don't really), but because they raise significant research issues. Is damage to the sensory organ—for instance, the loss of hair cells in the inner ear or the stiffening of the lens—responsible for all the deficits associated with age? Or are changes in the central nervous system implicated? Questions about central versus peripheral mechanisms abound in the literature on sensation, perception, and cognition; but perhaps nowhere have they received more serious attention than in the study of psychomotor performance and response time.

Psychomotor Response and Reaction Time

Typing, dancing, tying shoe laces, skipping, and jumping rope are all examples of psychomotor skills. Playing games at the video arcade is a good example of using psychomotor skills under pressure. Psychomotor skills involve dexterity and finely coordinated patterns of movement; one must be prepared to release and execute responses at a particular time even within a complex sequence.

Research leaves little doubt that the slowing of psychomotor responses is one of the hallmarks of middle age and may account for declining performances on timed intelligence tests, tasks requiring information processing, or problem solving. As Timothy Salthouse wrote in his 1985 review for the *Handbook of the Psychology of Aging:* "Seldom in psychology is a researcher at a loss for new adjectives to describe the reliability of a particular behavioral phenomenon. The phenomenon of a general slowness of behavior with increased age may be one such case, however" (p. 400).

In its most basic form, psychomotor slowing has been documented by research on choice or disjunctive response time. In these studies, the subject is asked to make a swift response ("pull the lever as quickly as you can") when one stimulus but not another occurs ("when you see the green triangle, but not when you see the red square") (Birren, Woods, & Williams, 1980; Welford, 1977). The differences between young and old people are greatest when both a complex decision and a rapid response are required (Hoyer & Plude, 1980).

Osborne (1986) points out that even in tasks that depend on simple responses, if the task is made more complex, age differences will appear in simple reaction time that did not occur when a less difficult task was performed. Furthermore, when a task requires two movements not easily performed together (response-response incompatibility) age decrements increase (Light, 1988, 1990). Performance on cognitive and sensory-motor tests declines with age from the early twenties. The decline is most marked for tasks requiring complex muscle coordination or complex memory and least marked for sensory-motor tasks requiring simple responses to simple stimuli. Educational attainment provides a greater advantage in the cognitive than in sensory-motor tasks (Pacaud, 1989).

The typical experiment on psychomotor performance might report that middle-aged people copy digits and words far more slowly than younger people. In fact, between the ages of twenty and sixty, there is a 97 percent increase in the time required for tasks like copying digits (Birren & Botwinick, 1951). Such performance decrements are not universal, however. Occupation influences performance on this type of test. For example, clerical workers tend to finish such tasks quickly throughout adult life.

If a psychomotor skill is used on a daily basis (like buttoning a shirt), decline is not so noticeable. People who hold jobs such as air-traffic controller, computer technician, surgeon, or court reporter may not show decrement in performance because, after a lifetime of practice, such skills no longer require attention. The skills have become automated. In controlled research where automated responses are required in the detection and processing of information, age differences diminish and sometimes are not found at all (Hoyer & Plude, 1980). However, in any novel task that requires a great deal of effort and does not rely on automated responses, older adults will perform poorly when compared to the young.

Of course, we have to ask whether laboratory findings that show decline have much significance for everyday life. Experience and confidence help to compensate for whatever slowness appears over the years. Certainly, the experienced court reporter, no longer rattled by the presence of several fast-talking attorneys, may work more effectively than a young reporter facing the situation for the first time. Poor performances in young and old people may well be determined by different aspects of the same situation. The middle-aged court reporter may be affected by a decline in sensory acuity (hearing) or psychomotor slowness. The younger person on the other hand may put in a poor performance because anxiety or lack of familiarity interfere with psychomotor automation. As another example, traffic accidents that involve older people tend to involve deficient psychomotor skills, whereas the accidents of the young suggest poor judgment (Welford, 1977). For reasons like these, one cannot assume that the young will necessarily do better outside the laboratory.

Beyond limited data on traffic or industrial accidents, we have very little objective information about daily life. Most of the discussion of psychomotor performance has not focused on the practical implications, but on the search for underlying physiological mechanisms. To this end, researchers have examined a variety of physiological evidence, including **electroencephalograph** (EEG) records, measures of **galvanic skin response** (GSR), as well as patterns of **event-related** potential, or ERPs (an increase in electrical activity in the nervous system as a response to stimulation).

Physiology of Psychomotor Slowing

Using the EEG records of young and elderly subjects, researchers have demonstrated a very general change in the alpha rhythm of the brain over the adult years. **Alpha rhythm** is the regular pattern of brainwaves recorded during relaxation. It usually has a frequency of 9 to 12 Hz (cycles per second). A strong association has been demonstrated between both simple and complex response times and the frequency of the alpha rhythm. In fact, correlations between age and response time have been shown to be insignificant once the frequency of the alpha rhythm is taken into consideration.

In young adulthood, the mean frequency of the alpha rhythm is about 10.5 cycles per second. By age seventy, the mean may fall by as much as 2 cycles per second. If it is true that information can be processed only during a specific part of the alpha cycle, then older subjects, who exhibit fewer cycles per unit of time, may require longer to perceive the onset of a stimulus (Marsh & Thompson, 1977).

In addition to the data garnered from studies of the alpha rhythm, Simpson et al. (1985) suggest event-related potential (ERP) as another index of brain stimulation. ERPs reflect specific brain activity synchronized with the onset of a stimulus. Unfortunately, the measurement of such specific activity is plagued by technical and methodological problems. Simpson et al. among others have used the ERP to provide evidence of a general slowing of brain wave activity at all structural levels of the brain.

Preliminary investigation suggests that ERPs reflect deficits in reaction time even among extremely healthy older people (Ford & Pfefferbaum, 1980; Harkins, 1980; Salthouse, 1985b). In an intriguing study, Woodruff (1972) reported that increasing the alpha rhythm of older subjects through biofeedback produced faster response times. The elderly were still not so quick as the young even after increases in the frequency of the alpha rhythm; other important forces must be at work as well. Moreover, even if we accept the importance of alpha-wave slowing, there is still no reason to believe that alpha slowing causes response time to slow. Quite possibly, changes in the vascular system are responsible for both slowed response time and slowed alpha-wave activity. Nutrition may also be related to cognitive performance (Tucker, Penland, Sandstead, Milne, Heck, & Klevay, 1990). A decrement in alpha-wave activity is noted in people with low thiamin levels, suggesting that neuropsychological impairment can occur with even mild deficits in nutritional status. Other findings indicate the frequency of brain wave responses among older subjects with high-iron status is similar to that of younger persons; however, these data are more difficult to interpret. Further research on nutrition and neuropsychological function will undoubtedly lead to a better understanding of the role of nutrition in maintaining the functional integrity of the aging brain.

Certainly, there is evidence that cardiovascular diseases, especially atherosclerosis, reduce psychomotor speed. Reaction time can actually be manipulated in cardiac patients with pacemakers. Lowering the pulse rate by adjusting a pacemaker produces significant slowing of reaction time and gives other indications of poor mental performance (Birren, Woods, & Williams, 1980). The importance of cardiovascular health is also implicated by the data on physical fitness. Habitual exercisers have faster reaction times than do people who lead sedentary lives or exercise only sporadically. Some improvement has been produced in motor performance and related noncognitive psychological tasks by programs of regular exercise.

For people over age sixty, low- or moderate-level exercise programs have been shown to improve self-reported sleep (sleep quantity and dream recall), mental status (attention/concentration, short-term memory, and higher cognitive functioning), health perceptions (health outlook, health worry, rejection

As we age, physical fitness may improve the quality of life, both prolonging the life span and delaying the onset of problems related to cardiovascular health—from reaction time and vision to the function of the central nervous system.

of the sick role), and cardiovascular fitness indicators (Stevens & Topp, 1990). Maximum oxygen uptake has also been correlated with reaction time (Birren, Woods, & Williams, 1980). Self-assessed health status, however, does not significantly affect age trends in several measures of cognitive functioning (Salthouse, Kausler, & Saults, 1990).

Other research emphasizes the aging of neural cells. For example, **neural noise,** or random activity of the neurons, is thought to increase with age. If so, sensory signals may be more difficult to discriminate if the activity produced by one decision or response begins to interfere with the next cognitive activity because it is producing a long after-effect. Studies of **perceptual masking** have given substance to the idea that duration of after-effects increases with age.

Perceptual masking occurs when the presentation of one visual figure is followed (after a short interval) by another stimulus known to "erase" the perception of the first figure. Older subjects take longer to recover the perception of the first figure after perceptual masking. In fact, it takes 24 percent longer to overcome the masking of a visual stimulus at the age of sixty-five than it does at twenty (Birren & Renner, 1977).

The neural-noise hypothesis has been refined to include the possibility that older people spend more time monitoring incoming signals before they execute a response. Older people may be less willing or less able to cease monitoring previous responses and move on to the next part of a task. Increased monitoring may represent an attempt to compensate for increased neural noise and reduced signal strength (Welford, 1977). It has been suggested that neural noise increases because the axons of nerve cells degenerate with age (Cerella, 1990).

After reviewing many studies of neural change and performance, Timothy Salthouse (1985b) concludes that the most productive research is likely to occur in the testing of the "**Birren hypothesis.**" James Birren has consistently written that all neural events become slower with age. He has maintained that adults experience an electrical "brown-out." All the processes are the same in young and older adults, according to Birren, but they simply become slower the older we get. Salthouse admits that his preference for the Birren hypothesis is not the result of convincing evidence but simply a preference for ideas that are easily researched. As an earlier article concluded: "The basic problem with these hypothetical notions about physiological bases of age changes . . . is that they are difficult to test. It is probably best to think of them as interesting, but oversimplistic" (Elias, Elias, & Elias, 1977).

Ultimately, research on speed and timing leads to a consideration of more general cognitive performance and intellectual behavior. For even when speed is not a requirement, the elderly do not do so well as the young on a variety of intelligence measures and tests of problem solving.

Cognition

Longitudinal and sequential studies of intellectual behavior through the adult years often report that the performance of the middle-aged represents a kind of plateau of competence (Arenberg & Robertson-Tchabo, 1977). As we discovered in Chapter 3, however, there is some evidence from cross-sectional studies that particular kinds of performances improve during middle age while others decline. The sheer power of reasoning, as represented by developmental stage, reaches its peak during middle age (Armon, 1984; Commons, Armon, Richards, & Schrader, 1989). What John Horn calls crystallized intelligence also seems to peek during that period. On the other hand, cross-sectional studies but not all longitudinal studies show decline in what Horn calls fluid intelligence. As noted in Chapter 3, fluid intelligence entails the portions of the abstract capacity for problem solving.

Changes in the flexibility of attention may be implicated in the decline of fluid intelligence (Stankov, 1988; McDowd & Birren, 1990). The literature reveals age-related deficits in divided attention performance—the process by which attention is controlled to perform successfully two simultaneous tasks. Additionally, attention switching—altering the monitoring of two or more sources of input—requires more time with age and, since the work of short-

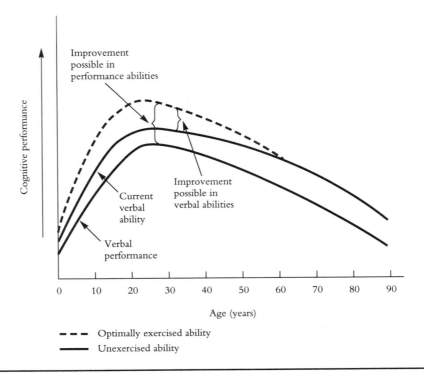

Figure 6.4 Amount of improvement possible in both verbal and performance abilities at ages thirty and fifty.

SOURCE: Denney, 1982, p. 820.

term memory is normally reduced by attention switching, impairment in short-term memory occurs with age.

The ability to filter out irrelevant information from the environment and to focus on the relevant information also seems to deteriorate with age. The research suggests that older people are more distracted by irrelevant information. Finally, overall levels of performance tasks requiring sustained attention seem to decline with age.

In understanding how all of this affects daily performance, Nancy Denney (1982) and her colleagues (Denney & Palmer, 1982; Denney & Pearce, 1982; Selzer & Denney, 1980) make an important distinction. They have demonstrated that aging differs for exercised and unexercised abilities. Denney believes that the intellectual and problem-solving abilities one exercises throughout adulthood will show long periods of stability through the lifespan and that peak performances in these abilities occur later. Figure 6.4 presents hypothetical curves representing the course of exercised and unexercised abilities over the life span.

In her research, Denney has compared the performances of young, middle-aged, and elderly people on two basic kinds of problems: those found on traditional tests of problem solving and a series of questions she believes reflect the practical problems of everyday life. Researching the traditional tasks, Denney asked her subjects to play a game of "twenty questions." In this task, the subject is required to discover what object or person the experimenter is thinking of. The winning strategy eliminates as many alternatives as possible with each guess. One starts, for example, with the question, "Is it animal, vegetable, or mineral?" Say the answer is "animal." You might ask, "Vertebrate or invertebrate?" The objective is to ask as few questions as possible, and the strategy is called **constraint seeking.**

In the course of the game, however, you sometimes play a hunch. So, instead of asking if the animal is vertebrate or invertebrate, you say, "Are you thinking of a human?" Of course, playing a hunch (Denney calls it hypothesis testing) is not always the most rational strategy. Denney gave lower scores to individuals who played this way. She found the greatest number of constraint seekers in the thirty- to thirty-nine-year-old group, even when young and old subjects were matched for educational level. People over forty were more likely to engage in hypothesis testing.

Two nagging problems come to mind at this point. First, people in the thirty- to thirty-nine-year-old cohort group have the greatest amount of experience with the game. Raw data from one of these studies (Denney & Palmer, 1982) is interesting in this regard. Among twenty- to twenty-nine-year-old subjects, 68 percent were constraint seekers, and the average subject in this group asked 16.86 questions. Among forty- to forty-nine-year-olds, 65 percent were constraint seekers, but the average number of questions was only 15.07. Even among sixty- to sixty-nine-year-olds, of whom only some 41 percent were constraint seekers, subjects asked only 17.86 questions on the average. Is it possible that people develop better hypotheses with experience?

On the practical problems, middle-aged people did seem to exhibit the benefits of experience. Not only did they do better on practical problems designed for their own age group but also, when compared with the young, they did better on problems designed for the elderly. Examples of these problems appear in Box 6.1.

In scoring responses to these problems, Denney assigned more points to those who produced good solutions that did not require the intervention of others. For instance, the solution "pour flour on a grease fire," would be considered a better solution than "call the fire department." Denney's results are compatible with the results of many other researchers (Poon, Rubin, & Wilson, 1989; Sinnott, 1989).

Generally, deficits in response quality on problem-solving tasks do not occur during middle age; often midlife is a time of optimal performance (Elias, Elias, & Elias, 1977; Kangas & Bradway 1971), especially on tests of verbal ability and "everyday problem solving" (Cornelius and Caspi, 1987).

Under extreme, distracting conditions, especially where very rapid, novel responses are demanded, important age differences in the performances of

---

Box 6.1 Practical problems in adult living

Two Problems for Young Adults

1. Let's say that a twenty-five-year-old woman comes home to her apartment, where she lives alone, at 1:00 A.M. When she gets to the door she notices that the front door is unlocked and standing open. It is dark inside. The woman is surprised because she usually locks her door when she leaves her apartment. What should she do?

2. Let's say that a college student wants to go home to another state for Christmas but finds that he does not have enough money for the plane ticket. He also does not own a car. What should he do?

Two Problems for Middle-aged Adults

1. If a middle-aged man is on vacation in a foreign country and he loses his wallet, which contains all his money and all his credit cards, what should he do?

2. The parents of a teenage daughter told her that she should be home from her date at 12:00 midnight on Saturday night. Although the daughter is usually very responsible, at 4:00 A.M. she is still not home. What should the parents do?

Two Problems for the Older Adult

1. Let's say that a sixty-year-old man who lives alone in a large city needs to get across town to a doctor's appointment. He cannot drive because he doesn't have a car, and he doesn't have relatives nearby. What should he do?

2. What should an elderly woman, who has no other source of income, do if her Social Security check doesn't arrive one month?

SOURCE: Denney & Palmer, 1982.

---

young and middle-aged people may emerge. It is not surprising to find video arcades populated by children, adolescents, and young adults. It is also wise, however, to remember Horn's suggestion that, with age, certain performances may simply not be compelling. Winning at the game of "twenty questions" or a high score at Nintendo or Pac Man may not matter to one's sense of self-esteem or may not be interesting. One may be more likely to use strategies that are successful in everyday life (like hypothesis testing) in situations that demand the development of novel or more rational modes of operation.

Hayne Reese and Dean Rodeheaver (1985) warn that there are many other pitfalls in evaluating any documented age differences in performance. We do not know how memory, attention, or familiarity with the problem influences these performances. If older subjects experience more anxiety, lower self-esteem, or greater cautiousness in making responses, these factors might also influence performance. Researchers have tried to create improved performance among older people. In these studies, interventions have been aimed at increasing motivation, confidence, and familiarity, as well as at providing increased time to plan. These interventions have all produced positive results, and very quickly. Sometimes, simply instructing older people about how to improve their responses is sufficient.

Reese and Rodeheaver have also suggested that Nancy Denney's data on exercised and unexercised abilities may be influenced by familiarity. Middle-aged adults may have encountered problems like being stranded on a highway in bad weather, more often than other age groups. Familiarity does make an enormous difference in problem-solving performance. For instance, one study of highly skilled chess players (Charness, 1981) demonstrated that age did not make a difference in overall performance. Although older players showed some memory deficits, they also knew how to take shortcuts on some problem-solving steps. This compensated for the deficits attributed to memory.

Other work has demonstrated that problem solving and other kinds of abstract thinking, including the ability to solve problems that require formal operations, is more strongly related to education and occupational achievement than to age. Reese and Rodeheaver conclude that since intervention is so successful in improving problem-solving performance, people of all ages must have the capacity to solve experimental problems efficiently. Older people, however, often do not use that competence. They may simply prefer, for whatever reasons, whether motivational, historical, or biological, to use less efficient strategies.

Timothy Salthouse (1990) offers yet another perspective on the problem of aging and cognitive functioning. First he differentiates between cognitive competence and cognitive ability. Psychometric tests and experimental tasks tap cognitive ability in the form of intellectual level. The results of these tests reveal age-related declines. Cognitive competence, on the other hand, is defined as the "utilization of one's abilities—cognitive, interpersonal, and others—in adapting to particular situations" (p. 311). The degree to which one *utilizes* an *ability* determines **competence** on a task. From his perspective, cognitive competence seems to increase at least through middle adulthood, whereas cognitive ability is thought to decrease from early adulthood. According to Salthouse, the two act independently: it is possible for a person of low cognitive ability to be highly competent by maximally utilizing available abilities for functioning in specific situations. This view can account for why older people continue to function well in familiar environments despite the declines in cognitive ability measured by psychometric tests.

Finally, it is important to emphasize that differences do not necessarily imply deficits. The matrix introduced in Chapter 2 notes differences in the thinking of young and middle-aged adults but certainly does not imply the appearance of developmental deficits among older people. If Edelstein and Noam (1982) are right, the fact that middle-aged or older people problem-solve differently than the young reflects the need to reconcile logic with reality, to reunite logic and emotion. In this view, mature thinking is more contextual than the formal operations that develop in adolescence (Labouvie-Vief, 1990). It co-ordinates the demands of logic with social interaction. Wisdom allows one to discover the adequate solution, the one that will work, as opposed to the one that is the most logical. In the social world, unlike the world of logic, statements can be both true and untrue depending on one's point of view. Formal operations will therefore not be sufficient for resolving the contradictions of day-to-day life.

By early adulthood, many people know that the linear logical solution is not always the workable one in everyday life, and two kinds of response to this problem have been described. The first is to acquire a good deal of conjectural knowledge, expertise, and wisdom. The second is to transcend formal operational logic with the logic of systems. As described in Chapter 3, the logic of systems allows one to consider many possible arrangements of relationships. Not only the simple effects of actions but also the unintended side effects are considered. In the fuzzy everyday domains of life (Brabeck & Wood, 1990), such a logic makes it possible to see that one set of truths may work in one system but not in another (Richards, 1990; Richards & Commons, 1990). Higher-order analogies (Sternberg, 1984) between what is fact and what we know may be helpful.

In the laboratory, researchers present problems that have one best answer. In life, paradox and uncertainty often prevail. Life is more like a horse race than an intelligence test. The winning bet is a matter of calculating possibilities.

Creativity

Generativity is a central characteristic of adult creativity. Generative acts lead to something new in the society. Interest in adult creativity has enjoyed a renaissance in the eighties and nineties (Gardner, 1982; Perkins, 1981). Creativity, according to one view, is due largely to the insightful use of knowledge-acquisition components and to extremely sensitive feedback between the various components of intelligence (Sternberg, 1985). Knowledge has to be organized in serviceable and richly interconnected ways. Commons (in preparation) identifies some of the factors that may be involved in producing creative works:

1. Standing at a cultural crossroads for a period of time (frontier) where there are clashes between apparently unreconcilable views of reality.

2. Having an imagination, a curiosity, and a vague vision about what the creation might be like and what its importance may be before it is worked out.

3. Being dogged by and overcoming adversity in conquering the problems the development of the creation presents. Some researchers call this ego-strength.

4. Being involved with the ideas or activities. Being turned on by the creative work and loving it—a passion in the innovation and work-ing-out process. In addition, the idea that the creation is the "cat's meow" and an interest in promoting the creation. This includes being a founder by organizing the enterprise and the people necessary to develop the creation. It includes the marketing of the idea to obtain funds and recruit the people necessary for its development.

5. Facing risks with a sense of challenge rather than upset, for example, the risk of not knowing the details or the direction of one's enterprise. Furthermore, creative people aren't stopped by disconfirmation or failure at a particular step in the enterprise because the passion is for the enterprise, not for the self or the particular act.

6. Being independent of social approval. This usually means that crea-tive people are somewhat unconventional and don't compete for traditional forms of power. They are not overly concerned with ap-proval, social position, and status.

7. Reasoning at least at the metasystematic developmental stage in the domain of the creation and having reasonably high intelligence.

We think of artists and scientists as creative. However, both social and per-sonal factors affect creativity. Feldman (1986) and Skinner (1953) point out that original acts may be reinforced by people in society. Whether the original act is just a chance event and the creator is its midwife as Skinner suggests, is of in-terest to the sociologist and historians of art and science. From a social perspec-tive, creative people have to do more than create. Creative acts overturn or go against what is now accepted. This puts the creators in conflict with other people in the professions, many of whom have extensive power. In most in-stitutions there is a tension between people who produce versus those who col-lect and distribute creative products. For example, in higher education, the respected teacher and scholar is a dutiful promoter of the treasures of the cul-ture and not necessarily innovative and creative. One is not necessarily re-warded with power (published, tenured, or given grants) for being original. This is because people in professions hire, fund, publish, and display the work of and reward people who act like themselves and hold the same values (Kuhn, 1972). The tendency for those in power to choose assortatively people like themselves seems to be a basic human tendency (Trudeau & Commons, 1991). Many creative people are at the margin. They are not mainstream but are not isolated. They are more likely to be between cultures and classes and may not be in the middle of mainstream institutions.

A society that promotes as well as tolerates creativity produces more crea-tive acts. In a study of originality in word associations the researchers found that subjects exposed to persistent minority views tend to reexamine issues and engage in more divergent and original thought (Nemeth and Kwan, 1985). On the other hand, subjects exposed to persistent majority views tend to concen-trate on the position proposed and to be less original.

Both the social reasons mentioned above and personal reasons restrain personal creativity. Many people are in professions we think require creativity, but not many practitioners are very creative. Indeed, Smith, Carlsson, and Sandstrom (1985) tested thirty-two adult professional artists and found that not all were creative. Other kinds of proficiency seem to be part of creativity. To be really creative, people have to do original things and have those things be complex enough to contribute to society. Khatena (1983) found that originality is correlated significantly with creative analogy and image complexity, a finding that is consistent with earlier thought on the relationship between creativity and a preference for complexity. This preference for complexity has to withstand social pressure toward conformity.

Stage of cognitive development also constrains creativity. This constraint delays the emergence of creativity more in some fields than others. Even during middle age, few individuals think at the highest levels of cognitive development.

In highly formalized fields like mathematics and theoretical physics, important creative works often occur during early adulthood, perhaps because these fields are highly symbolized and systematized and the logic articulated. Individuals do not have to represent and interpret the language. Russell and Gödel (1977) are examples of early creativity in mathematics and Einstein (1950) and Planck in physics. Newton's (1666) notebooks, written in his twenties, during the plague, reveal the early emergence of most of his ideas, although he was older when he formed the arguments and published his Optical Theory. In nonmathematical science, Darwin's creation of evolutionary biology and paleontology first appeared in his notebooks, written in his thirties. Yet, only in his fifties did he publish *The Origin of Species* in 1842.

In many fields, creativity and scientific productivity peak during middle age (37 to 55 years old). Funk (1989) has argued, for instance, that Beethoven's most creative work was his last—the Ninth Symphony. In a review of research on creativity, Gruber (1985) concluded that the person doing creative work is a complex, many-faceted system that is continuously evolving. Gruber's view is rather like the view presented in Chapter 2, where we argued that cognition, emotion, motivation, and behavior are all developing subsystems that may be only loosely connected. According to Gruber, this "restless" organization accounts for the long duration of numerous creative enterprises through cycles of activity and dormancy in the life of one person.

The type of creative effort possible during middle age probably differs from that of young adulthood. Literary texts, such as *Catch-22* by Joseph Heller and *Invisible Man* by Harlan Ellison, which were written relatively early, tend to detail and analyze problems but do not offer solutions. The creation of realistic solutions, especially in the social realm, may await middle age.

The solution to tasks the society deems creative quite often requires a new synthesis of systems of thought (the metasystematic stage) or even a whole new way of viewing the world (paradigmatic state). For example, before Darwin, geology and biology were considered separate fields. The fossils in the lower layers of earth were not known to be the ancestors of the ones in the layers above them. Evolution provides a mechanism for putting together geologic notions with economic and biologic notions. These were: (a) the geologic notion of the ages of layers in the earth, (b) the biological notion that different species were found at different layers, (c) the economic notions of scarcity and survival of the fittest. This formed the new paradigm of evolutionary biology that synthesized and transformed previous paradigms.

Generally, researchers have reported that a certain kind of high-level thought is necessary for the sort of creativity we have been discussing. Most studies have suggested only 10–15 percent of the population is capable of systems thinking or high-level moral reasoning (Colby & Kohlberg, 1987).

Great creativity may require certain emotional developments as well as cognitive maturity. Truly creative people may not be much concerned with other people's opinions of them or with how their "successes" compare to others. Studies of field independence (the ability to make certain perceptual judgments independent of the orientation of one's own body), dogmatism, and internal locus of control (the feeling that one is in charge of one's own life) suggest that creative people must function in independent ways and must love, believe, and be focused on their own ideas.

Creative people may also be relatively free from anxiety and fear of rejection. Smith, Carlsson, & Sandstrom (1985) found that creative people exhibited fewer compulsive or depressive defenses and little anxiety. They also found that creative individuals had access to their dream life and their early childhood more often than noncreative subjects and tended to remember both positive and negative qualities. Furthermore, they have argued that "important" artists (based on an art historian's evaluation) were more open to identification with both sexes and were generally characterized by freedom of expression and a high level of functioning.

Finally, ambiguity and risk taking are necessary components of creativity and may be more tolerable for older adults. Gisela Labouvie-Vief (1985) noted that older adults were at ease when working with ambiguity creatively (also see Arlin, 1983; Labouvie-Vief & Blanchard-Fields, 1982). Younger adults focus on reaching a conclusion that makes sense when presented with logically inconsistent statements. Older adults concentrate on the problems inherent in the premises. They ask questions and point out inconsistencies that go beyond the information presented in the problem based on their own personal experience and knowledge. Finding ambiguity, conflict, and inconsistency is probably crucial to highly creative work.

Finally, creativity requires one to separate one's self from one's products. Otherwise one would never be self-critical of one's creative products; there would be no development, no reaching for more. Older adults are more aware of the self as an interpreter and are able to separate their own views from other possible interpretations. For instance, in one study (Labouvie-Vief, Adams, Hakim-Larson, & Hayden, 1983), social situations were described and subjects were asked questions about them. In one, a woman threatens to leave her drunken husband if he comes home drunk one more time. Subjects were asked what the woman would do if he did come home drunk one more time. Older subjects were far more aware of the ambiguities in the situation, the bias of the person supposedly telling the story, and how context might influence the behavior of the characters.

Labouvie-Vief contends that the idea of adult intelligence must be redefined in light of the developmental tasks of middle age and later life: responsibility, generativity, and integrity. It may be wise to enlist the services of the young if one needs to receive and decode fast-paced messages, transmitted at high frequencies, especially if the messages are constantly interrupted by CB radio transmissions and masked by static noise. On the other hand, one might be well advised to have a middle-aged person on hand to decide how the information should be used. Experience can be an asset. And that leads to the final topic for consideration in this chapter: the developmental tasks of middle age.

Developmental Tasks

Erikson (1963, 1968a) discusses the central developments of middle age in terms of a conflict between generativity and stagnation. Generativity is an "expansion of ego interests and a sense of having contributed to the future" (1968a, p. 85). Erikson believes that the mature man or woman needs to be needed and to receive guidance and encouragement from what he or she produces. Generativity is reflected by a deep concern for the establishment and nurturance of the next generation. In the words of McAdams et al. (1986): "Generativity implies a blending of agency and communion in human experience." The central achievement of the generative stage is the direction of one's creativity and energy in a way that produces a lasting accomplishment worthy of sustained effort—a legacy. Impoverishment and self-indulgence are characteristic of individuals who fail to develop a generative personality and lifestyle in middle age.

Havighurst (1972) expanded the concept of developmental tasks to include middle age. In middle life, he argued, achievement of adult civic and social responsibility and the establishment and maintenance of a standard of living are arenas of major growth and development. Teenagers must be assisted in becoming responsible, happy adults. The middle-aged adult must develop appropriate leisure-time activities and learn to relate to his or her spouse as a person. Middle-aged people must also meet and accept the demands of physiological change during these years. Added to the physiological reminders of aging are generational, contextual, and mortality cues. All of these combine to determine age consciousness of the individual (Karp, 1988). People at this age must also adjust to the aging of their own parents.

The outline of developmental tasks for middle age has also been explored in

"All strengths arising from earlier developments from infancy to young adulthood . . . now prove, on closer study, to be essential for the generational task of cultivating strength in the next generation." Erik Erikson

the work of Robert Peck (1968), who elaborates four sets of important developmental challenges for the middle-aged:

1. The individual must come to value wisdom over physical strength and attractiveness. One must accept inevitable losses of physical prowess with age and learn to use one's experience. Wisdom is defined as making "effective choices among the alternatives which intellectual perception and imagination present" (p. 89). (Notice that Peck is speaking not of speedy choices but of effective ones.) People who do not make the transition from physical prowess to wisdom in middle age often become bitter and depressed.

2. Socializing must replace sexualization as the major focus for male-female relationships. The middle-aged person redefines people as individuals and companions. Note the similarity of this suggestion to

the belief that the middle-aged person comes to relate to the spouse as a person (Havighurst, 1972).

3. The individual must demonstrate cathected flexibility: the capacity to shift one's emotional investment to new people, activities, and roles as old ones lose their potential for satisfaction. During middle age, children are launched from the home, and one experiences the death of one's parents, friends, and relatives. It becomes critical to participate in a wide range of relationships and events to experience personal meaning and fulfillment.

4. Mental flexibility must become a central personal characteristic. In the middle years, the ability to use personal experience as a provisional guideline must emerge and replace the tendency to rely on experience as a rigid, automatic basis for rules of thought and behavior.

These four developmental patterns seem to imply a tendency toward increasing rigidity and withdrawal with age. As we will see in the next chapter, questions about rigidity and withdrawal have been central concerns in the study of personality throughout adult life.

Summary

I. Physiology and Biology at Midlife
   A. Changes in the connective tissues include the loss of water from ground substance and the cross-linking of protein molecules.
   B. Changes in appearance include weight gain and the redistribution of fat.
   C. Bones and connective tissues show signs of aging after thirty.
      1. The weight of bones declines at about 6 to 8 percent per decade.
      2. Wrinkles and sagging of the skin appear.
      3. Middle-aged women are especially concerned about changes in appearance and consider themselves less attractive than other groups perceive them to be.
   D. Chronic diseases like arteriosclerosis, cancer, diabetes, arthritis, emphysema, and cirrhosis are the major health concerns in developed countries.
      1. These diseases are incremental, universal, have a clinical threshold, and are characterized by a progressive loss of organ reserve.
      2. Cardiovascular disease and cancer are the most frequent causes of premature death among adults.
      3. Fries and Crapo believe preventive health strategies can ensure that the clinical threshold of chronic diseases is not reached during the normal life span.

4. Behavioral medicine may provide important preventive health strategies, such as modifying the aggressive Type A personality.
5. The effects of stress on health are being researched. Although the exact role of stress in the course of chronic disease is unclear, we know the general adaptation syndrome becomes less efficient with age. Also, how people evaluate stress may be as important as the nature of stressful events.
6. As the prevalence of smoking and obesity declines, the incidence of cardiovascular disease should decline, along with the rate of lung cancer and emphysema.

E. Involution refers to the period of the climacteric in men and women when the reproductive system declines in function.
1. Menopause is the cessation of menstruation and usually occurs between forty-eight and fifty-two.
   a. Levels of female hormones decline at the climacteric in women, and there are changes in the genital tract.
   b. Symptoms like hot flashes and night sweats are related to declining levels of estrogen and can be alleviated by estrogen replacement therapy (ERT).
   c. Attitudes toward menopause are a good predictor of severity and duration of symptoms, and young women may view menopause in unnecessarily negative ways.
2. Males experience a gradual decline in sperm production at the climacteric, and the involution of the prostate gland, a gland which contributes to semen production.
   a. Erection and ejaculation occur more slowly with age and the refractory period lasts longer.
   b. Erections are less firm, there is less semen and less need to ejaculate. Contractions of the prostate are less regular, and older man may experience only one stage during orgasm rather than two.
   c. The best predictor of sexual activity in later life is previous sexual activity. Continued sexual function depends on the opportunity to remain active, a positive body image, and positive feelings about sexuality.

F. Sensation, perception, and psychomotor performance
1. Changes in vision include the compacting of cells in the lens, the buildup of waste materials in the vitreous humour, the loss of cones and rods, and changes in the retina.
   a. The lens loses some of its ability to accommodate and the near point of vision recedes.
   b. The visual field shrinks, and dark adaptation is prolonged.
   c. Lifelong physical fitness can be instrumental in the maintenance of vision, and the sensory change apparent at midlife does not greatly affect daily function.

       2. Hearing of high-frequency tones is affected as early as age ten or twelve.

          a. There are four forms of presbycusis that occur with change in the organ of Corti; sensory presbycusis is the loss of hearing for high-pitched tones.

          b. Degenerative changes in the auditory system are apparent by middle age, but hearing for speech and everyday sounds is minimally affected.

   G. Psychomotor response and response time

       1. Psychomotor slowing is a reliable phenomenon of aging especially under conditions of choice or disjunctive response where people must make complex decisions.

          a. This slowing may not affect people who use psychomotor responses on the job, because such responses become automated.

          b. We don't know how slowing affects everyday performances. Most of the research has focused on the physiological mechanisms of psychomotor slowing.

             i. Slowing of the alpha rhythm appears related to response time.

             ii. Neural noise and perceptual masking or slowing of specific brain activity may be implicated in psychomotor slowing.

             iii. The Birren hypothesis that there is a general neural slowdown or "brown-out" may be a productive direction for current researchers.

II. Cognition

   A. Longitudinal and cross-sectional studies of intelligence suggest that middle age is a period of plateau.

       1. Exercised abilities may fare better than unexercised abilities over the adult life course.

       2. Middle-aged people do better than the young or the old on tests that include practical problems of everyday living.

       3. Middle-aged people may show some deficits when rapid, novel responses are required or when a task relies heavily on fluid intelligence.

   B. The interpretation of age differences in cognition is problematic because we usually do not know whether differences are influenced by memory, attention, motivation, and/or familiarity.

       1. Differences need not always imply deficits. Older adults may solve problems differently because they are more influenced by the need to reconcile logic with reality and emotion.

       2. Middle-aged and older adults work easily and creatively with ambiguous situations and are able to use different perspectives to evaluate social problems.

       3. It may be necessary to redefine intelligence in light of responsibility, generativity, and integrity.

III. Developmental Tasks of Middle Age
   A. Erikson defines the central conflict of middle age as a battle between generativity and stagnation, generativity being the sense of having contributed to the future.
   B. As tasks of middle age, Havighurst included the achievement of adult civic and social responsibility and the establishment and maintenance of a standard of living.
   C. Peck added four arenas of development to the tasks of middle age.
      1. The ability to value wisdom over physical strength
      2. The desexualization of male-female relationships
      3. The ability to shift one's emotional investments to new people, activities, and roles
      4. Mental flexibility in the use of personal experience as a basis for thought and behavior.

7

Middle Age: The Personal Context—Stability, Change, and Challenge

Life's afternoon is brighter, warmer, fuller of song, and long before the shadows stretch, every fruit grows ripe.

—Walter B. Pitkin

"BERNADINE DOHRN SPENT ELEVEN YEARS as a fugitive from justice. Back in the early 1970s, she was virtually a household name; as one of the leaders of the Weatherman faction of the SDS (Students for a Democratic Society), she was wanted for conspiracy to bomb several places throughout the United States. The core of the Weatherman's philosophy was 'Kill all the rich people. Break up their cars and apartments. Bring the revolution home, kill your parents, that's where it's really at.' . . .

"In 1980, Bernadine Dohrn surfaced, surrendering to the authorities to face other charges. (The bombing conspiracy charges had been dismissed because of illicit federal surveillance.) Dohrn was given three years probationary sentence. But by 1985, she had passed the New York State bar exam and was employed by the Manhattan office of Sidley & Austin, a Chicago law firm. (She had graduated from the University of Chicago Law School back in 1967.) One of her bosses describes her as 'very mature, hardworking, and quiet'; a colleague says, 'She acts like a perfectly typical lawyer in a big firm'; another claimed 'She's so conservative she's dull.'" (Quoted in Wrightman, 1988, p. 135)

PSYCHOLOGIST ZICK RUBIN (1981) HAS REMINDED US of the changes in other famous figures of the sixties and seventies. Jerry Rubin, who was an outspoken member of the Chicago Seven, the group who protested police brutality at the 1968 Democratic Convention, eventually became a perfectly ordinary member of the so-called establishment: "Jerry Rubin enters the 1970's as a screaming, war-painted Yippie and emerges as a sedate Wall Street (stock) analyst wearing a suit and tie" (p. 18).

People change in the other direction as well. Richard Alpert, "an ambitious assistant professor of psychology at Harvard, tunes into drugs, heads for India, and returns as Baba Ram Dass, a long-bearded mystic in a flowing white robe who teaches people to 'be here now'" (Rubin, 1981, p. 18). Today, as Baba Ram Dass, Richard Alpert divides his time between working for peace and stability in Nicaragua (trying to learn how to do good well) and riding the lecture circuit speaking about enlightenment to a mostly middle-aged crowd of New Agers and running Nobody for president, pointing out that Nobody "got more votes combined than anybody else" (Baba Ram Dass, 1989). But, Wrightman asks, "Do these changes in appearance reflect *personality* change?" David McClelland, a colleague of Richard Alpert at Harvard, after spending time decades later with Baba Ram Dass claims that it was the "Same old Dick—still charming, still as power-oriented as ever" (Rubin, 1981, p. 27).

In this chapter we will consider various forms of the question, Is there personality change in adulthood? And we will be particularly concerned with whether such change occurs in middle age. For it is only in the past fifteen years or so most people have begun to think that personality change may occur in adulthood and that middle age, in particular, has been recharacterized as a time of changefulness rather than a long, stable plateau marked only by slight drifts in the direction of conservativism or rigidity.

The great popularity of Gail Sheehy's books *Passages* (1976) and *Pathfinders* (1981) brought with it a complete turnabout in the attitudes of many toward midlife. Many people began to see middle age as a time of inevitable discomfort, even crisis. In some ways, the culture exchanged one set of stereotyped ideas about middle adulthood for another equally unrealistic, if more romantic, set. In the classic variation of the new myth, the middle-aged, middle-class man abruptly abandons his wife, his family, and his friends for a new Porsche and a twenty-year-old blonde. Although the wife is, of course, devastated at first, she soon finds that the single life has its advantages and so is unwilling to take him back when the fling is over.

In another variation on the same theme, the gray-suited, gray-haired executive in his forties or fifties, chronically depressed and sexually bored, wastes away on alcohol and pills. And, of course, there is the stereotype of the menopausal woman, tearfully watching soap operas or sitting in an empty kitchen longing for the days when the floor was constantly marred by little footprints. In the more modern version of the middle-aged fairy tale, she decides to attend law school, in the face of opposition from her family, friends, and teachers.

Still, in the back of our minds is the legacy of the years before midlife crisis became an issue. There is the successful, middle-aged doctor, graying at the temples, president of the AMA, powerful, controlled, self-satisfied, with his smiling, competent wife at his side. They were always pictured on the society page, dancing at a benefit for the mentally retarded. The caption under the photo praised her skills as an organizer and administrator. To us they embodied the notion that middle-aged people are successful, confident—in charge.

The conflicting stereotypes contribute to confusion about the experience of middle age. In this chapter we will explore that confusion. We will examine the evidence for both midlife crisis and for life satisfaction in middle age, as well as research that depicts fairly high levels of adjustment and productivity among people in their middle years. The attempt to make some sense of the contradictions will lead to a discussion of stability, change, and personality in middle age. Finally, we will consider the available evidence on sex-role changes and sex differences, as we search for clues about how midlife crisis is engendered, experienced, or evaded.

Midlife: Crisis, Challenge, or Consolidation?

Mainstream America is not without professional company in its confusion over middle age. Throughout the last fifteen years, there have been a variety of studies designed to explore whether there is such a thing as a "midlife crisis"; if so, whether it should be considered universal and inevitable; and what the content of the experience is for those who have reported it. Generally, the idea that there is some important adjustment or series of adjustments that characterize midlife, especially the years from forty to forty-five, has been more often supported by data from clinical studies and in-depth interviews than by survey research.

As case studies report evidence of personal disorganization first appearing at midlife, clinicians have focused on the incidence of low marital satisfaction among middle-aged people as well as reports of stress and psychosomatic illness (Chiriboga, 1989; Rosenberg & Farrell, 1976).

The Case for "Crisis"

By some accounts, midlife constitutes a nadir of marital satisfaction (Collins, 1985; Rollins & Feldman, 1970; Tamir, 1982). The rate of alcoholism is highest during this period of the life span (Chiriboga, 1989). Peptic ulcers, hypertension, and heart disease are most often first diagnosed in middle age (Rosenberg & Farrell, 1976) and case study data over the past fifteen to twenty years has repeatedly suggested that middle-aged participants, especially males, consider their early forties a difficult time. Among those who have claimed there is at least a problematic transition, if not a full-blown crisis, are Roger Gould at the University of California, Los Angeles (UCLA), Daniel Levinson at Yale, and George Vaillant and Charles McArthur at Harvard. Sheehy's successful *Pathfinders* (1981) was largely based on the work of Gould and Levinson, as was *Passages* (1976).

For most men, the life cycle may well be defined at work by such terms as "new recruit," "assistant representative," "manager," and "retiree." Even participation in social clubs can define a man's place in the life cycle.

Gould's studies (1972, 1980) contained interview and questionnaire data gathered from individuals who were being seen at the UCLA clinics as well as a large number of nonclinical subjects. Levinson (1986) and his associates (1974, 1978) have presented very detailed descriptions of the life course for forty middle-aged men over a four-year period; and Vaillant and McArthur (1972; Vaillant, 1977) have outlined the data from a forty-year longitudinal follow-up study of 268 men from the Harvard University classes of 1939–1941 and 1942–1944.

Taken together, these three studies have suggested the existence of a definite transitional period of adult life occurring at about age forty. This transition is said to be characterized by feelings of turmoil, a heightened awareness of aging, and a sense of the finiteness of time.

The following generalization from Vaillant and McArthur (1972) is typical of the observations contained in all three of these studies as well as in the books by Sheehy:

In any case, around forty a change occurred in the men. They appeared to leave the compulsive calm of their occupational apprenticeship, so reminiscent of grammar school days, and experience once more the *sturm und drang* [storm and stress] of adolescence. In fact, most subjects consciously perceived their forties as more tumultuous than they had their adolescence. . . . Just as adolescence is a time for acknowledging parental flaws and discovering truths about childhood, the forties are a time for reassessing and reordering the past. (p. 423)

The Harvard graduates described by Vaillant and McArthur experienced much more overt depression in their forties than they had in young adulthood. They often felt disenchanted with life and experienced agonizing bouts of self-appraisal and instinctual awakening. Yet these men had been selected for study as young adults because they were considered healthy and well adjusted. The Harvard Grant Study had been designed to illustrate how the male adult life cycle proceeds under the most favorable circumstances. On the average, men in the Harvard study had the income and social standing of a successful businessman or physician and the political viewpoint, intellectual tastes, and lifestyle of a college professor. By all ordinary standards, these men were successful, well-adapted adults.

Gould's data from UCLA supported the notion that in the period "between forty and forty-three there is a series of temporary excursions from well-established lifelong baselines on statements dealing with personal comfort, indicating an acutely unstable period with a great deal of personal discomfort" (Gould, 1972, p. 530). From interviews with patients in early middle age, Gould crystallized their concerns as a definite tendency toward the existential questioning of "self, values, and life itself . . . quiet desperation and an increasing awareness of time squeeze" (p. 526).

Finally, Levinson (1986) and his associates (1974, 1978) identified a period called **midlife transition** in their subjects too. They defined some of the major issues as (1) bodily decline and a vivid recognition of one's mortality; (2) the sense of aging; and (3) the emergence of the more feminine aspects of the self. Middle-aged men in this study seemed to be confronting their own mortality and struggling with youthful illusions of omnipotence. They focused on healing old psychic wounds and learning to love formerly devalued aspects of the self. According to Levinson and his associates: "It is the changing relation to the self that is the crucial issue at midlife" (1974, p. 255).

In several other recent studies, evidence for some degree of crisis has emerged (Mulvey & Dohrenwend, 1984; Reinke, Ellicott, Harris, & Hancock, 1985; Offer & Sabshin, 1984; Tamir, 1982, 1989), but each of these studies suggests that the phenomenon may be strongest among certain individuals and under particular sets of circumstances.

First, conflict may be more intense among midlife men than women. Levinson (1986) contends that women as well as men experience a series of five- to seven-year phases in which a life structure for each of the major periods of adult life is constructed, lived out, and revised. Another major project

(Reinke, Ellicott, Harris, & Hancock, 1985) reports that women describe important transitions in their lives at thirty, forty, and sixty. For these women, however, the most important turning point occurred between twenty-seven and thirty. Among women in their thirties, 80 percent of those with preschool children experienced a major transition. Of these, 50 percent were between twenty-seven and thirty. Those most likely to report this transition had worked outside the home in their mid-twenties, before having children. The transition lasted an average of 2.7 years, and most women experienced increases in life satisfaction at the end of this unsettling phase.

Many women in their forties also indicated a transition that included decreases in marital satisfaction and increases in assertiveness, but it was not as widespread as the transition of the thirties. These later changes seemed to be tied to the launching of children and were especially likely to occur for women who had reared large families and were young when the last child was ready to leave home.

Based on these data, the authors conclude that the major transitions in women's lives are tied to the family life cycle. More particularly, one of the authors (Hancock, 1985) claims that the real challenges in women's lives are precipitated by changes in significant interpersonal relationships rather than age. The challenge can occur at thirty, or forty, or fifty, according to Hancock: "Women who could forge a new framework for living in which the self became the subject of experience and the object of care credited their maturity to this process. The decisive maneuver in this developmental pivot sprang from a person's ability to seize autonomy and wield initiative on her own behalf" (p. 278).

Daniel Offer and Melvin Sabshin (1984) agree that the lives of women are much more strongly tied to family and less strongly tied to work than those of men. In their data on midlife, subjects reported feelings of strain, conflict, and overload that were unique to the thirties and forties. For women, depression because of conflicts between work and family was common throughout the middle years. For men at midlife, work played the central role in self-definition and life satisfaction. Not that career success always produced high life satisfaction. In fact, Offer and Sabshin argue that men who experience very high and very low career success may have the most difficulty at home, whereas men in middle-level occupations with no severe time constraints may be free to enjoy their marriages and families.

Along these same lines, Anne Mulvey and Barbara Dohrenwend (1984) have reported that middle- and late-middle-aged men report feeling less control over the events of their lives than do women or older men. They suggest that as men fall from the highpoint of success and dominance at midlife, they may feel greater loss of power or control than do women who have never experienced the fall.

Finally, one more large-scale study of men at forty conducted by Lois Tamir (1982, 1989) offers an interesting perspective on crisis. Her results,

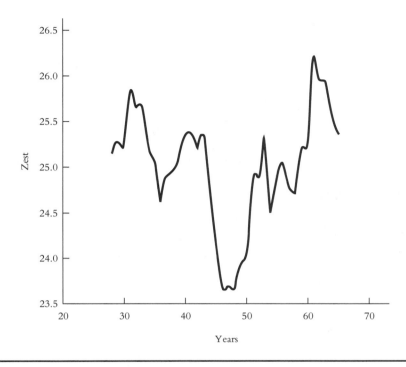

Figure 7.1 Zest for life among college-educated men, by age.

SOURCE: Tamir, 1982, p. 45.

based on the lives of 155 men aged forty to forty-nine, showed few changes in reported happiness and life satisfaction over the life span from twenty-five to sixty-nine but did suggest that some special difficulties are experienced by men in their forties, although as Tamir puts it: "Crisis is optional" (1989, p. 161). Tamir analyzed data for college-educated and non-college-educated men separately, which proved quite informative. Both groups reported a number of problems in their forties, but the types of problems differed.

College-educated men between forty-five and forty-nine reported low levels of what Tamir labeled "zest for life," whereas the difficulties of non-college-educated men were reflected in low levels of self-esteem. Figure 7.1 presents the data for college-educated men regarding their experience of zest for life. These men also reported feeling psychologically immobilized and admitted to more drinking than other age groups. They were more likely to use drugs to cope with worries, nervousness, and tension than were other groups, including the non-college-educated men in this sample. More than 20 percent of the college-educated group reported feeling at some point that they were on the verge of a nervous breakdown. Only 12.8 percent of all other men reported this experience. Tamir considered these data an indicator that psychological distress at midlife is most likely among the college-educated.

Non-college-educated men were less expressive and more likely to report amorphous feelings of dissatisfaction and vague yearnings. Tamir believes that these men were more rigidly defended against the feelings of anxiety and instability the college-educated group reported. She also notes that this group derived more satisfaction from their work than the college-educated, yet showed low levels of self-esteem despite job satisfaction. She contends that job satisfaction does not contribute substantially to overall life satisfaction for men at midlife, and that marriage becomes a more important focal point of well-being at this stage.

She has also argued (1989) that her data are evidence against at least two major myths about midlife men. First, she points out that these men appeared to have good judgment, the ability to delegate, to be able to see the big picture, to manage contradiction, and to be functioning at peak cognitive capacity. She believes that midlife represents a state of high achievement rather than a period of rapid obsolescence or a time when people's skills become so outdated that they are left behind in the dust.

She also feels that her data show the vision of the midlife man leaving his wife and family for the Porsche is also a myth. There is no upsurge in the divorce rates for people in their forties and men over forty become more emotionally invested in their relationships and families. Self-perceived happiness and self-esteem are highly related to marital happiness during these years, and, if a man leaves his marriage, he is likely to remarry very soon.

Theoretically, several viewpoints might be used to support the "crisis" position. Erikson (1963, 1968a, 1968b) would, of course, predict that men and women at midlife experience crisis as a normal product of adjustment to the new biological, cognitive, and social demands of middle age. As the issue of generativity becomes ascendant a "normative crisis" arises. Generativity involves "an expansion of ego interests and a sense of having contributed to the future" (1968a, p. 85). The generative person develops a deep concern for the establishment and nurturance of the next generation. The pivotal expression of this concern occurs as middle-aged people direct their energies toward establishing a legacy.

Erikson's position seems to fit the work of Levinson, Gould, or Vaillant; but Tamir's suggestion that career contributes little to overall life satisfaction at midlife brings the issue of generativity into question, at least as we might ordinarily define it. The suggestion that men and women become more concerned with the self might be more easily explained by the framework of Carl Jung (1933, 1960), who wrote a great deal about changes in personality at middle age.

Jung defined personality as a collection of conflicting forces. For example, he argued that there were two forces in the unconscious, the **collective un-**

conscious, a repository of memories from the entire human experience, and the **personal unconscious,** where primitive ideas, thoughts, and feelings from one's own personal history were stored. He thought that the personal unconscious was often in conflict with conscious desires and goals and that conscious desires and goals might also be in conflict with the collective unconscious. Every man, according to Jung, possesses **anima,** or the primitive female force, as a part of the collective unconscious. Every woman possesses **animus,** the primitive male force. Furthermore, Jung posited a part of the personality called the **shadow,** which he thought embodied the animal instincts that are a part of being human. At midlife, the **Self** (a unifying force in personality) is finally able to appraise and evaluate these conflicting aspects of personality, and the first real opportunities for integration present themselves.

The work of Gould and Levinson seems compatible with Jung's ideas. Gould (1972) emphasizes midlife confrontation with the unconscious images of childhood that lead one to question "self, values and life itself" (Gould, 1972, p. 530). Levinson (1986) and his associates (Levinson et al., 1974, 1978) are quite explicit about how men in their study had to confront and integrate the more feminine aspects of the self as well as come to terms with youthful illusions of omnipotence. The contribution of Reinke, Ellicott, Harris, and Hancock (1985) on the lives of women suggests the importance at midlife of growing assertiveness and independence, ordinarily considered masculine traits. Whether such changes actually constitute a "crisis" or whether they should even be considered true personality change is a major issue for those who believe that the evidence for crisis or for even a major transition at midlife is unconvincing (Kogan, 1990; McCrae & Costa, 1987; Haan, 1989).

The No-Crisis Position

Those who take the no-crisis position are likely to be social and developmental psychologists, armed with paper-and-pencil tests and inventories. On checklists and rating scales, midlife men and women rarely report crisis or even distress that is much greater than at other periods of the life span. Norma Haan (1989) believes that one of the reasons why clinicians are likely to find evidence for crisis in in-depth personal interviews and case studies is that people have a tendency to dramatize their lives when they are asked to tell their stories. Haan believes that the only kind of data one can really trust is found in the reports of trained observers who tend to report certain kinds of change in personality over the adult life span but who do not see much evidence for an inevitable, universal crisis at midlife.

Taking a similar position, David Chiriboga (1989) has pointed out that rates for suicide actually decline after age forty-four or so until later life, when rates for men begin to rise again. Furthermore, mental health admissions decline for the years from forty-five to sixty-four. Chiriboga contends that only about 2 to 5 percent of the population experience serious problems or "crisis" at midlife. In fact, most people report that early adulthood is a period of greater emotional strain and stress (Chiriboga, 1989; Veroff & Feld, 1970).

Certainly, there is little reason to believe that the normal events of middle age inevitably precipitate a serious crisis. Even as dramatic an event as menopause does not appear to be universally experienced as traumatic. Although older women do often find the symptoms of menopause disagreeable, they also report some degree of control over the extent and severity of their symptoms. In general, they see the climacteric as a temporary inconvenience but do not regret losing their reproductive capacity. To the contrary, they emphatically welcome the freedom from pregnancy (Neugarten, Wood, Kraines, & Loomis, 1963; Neugarten & Datan, 1974; Newman, 1982).

In fact, the evidence that midlife women experience a transition is even more tentative than that for men (Kogan, 1990). A number of studies have suggested that even when women show some of the stages that Levinson reported for men, the issues are different because women much more often live with the **split dream** that they can be successful in both family and occupational roles (Roberts & Newton, 1987). Perhaps because they are invested in both family and career, there is evidence that even such critical events as the launching of the last child from the home is unlikely to precipitate strong feelings of distress for most women. In fact, the research shows that most women do not view the departure of their children as an unhappy prospect. Instead of dread, forerunner to the **empty nest syndrome,** they look forward to the empty nest with some eagerness, experiencing a new sense of freedom and delight in having the time to use latent abilities and talents in ways that were impossible with a houseful of children (Reinke, Ellicott, Harris, & Hancock, 1985). Furthermore, many field studies have shown improved functioning and psychological health for a large number of women in late middle age (Livson, 1981a, 1981b; Lowenthal, Thurnher, & Chiriboga, 1975).

In general, middle-aged men also describe themselves as satisfied and tend to see middle age as the prime of life. They want to feel young, but they do not want to be young again. They experience a heightened capacity to manage their environment, an increased sense of authority and autonomy, and feelings of expertise. Upper-middle-class men, such as those in the Harvard sample, are particularly positive. They take pride in their own objectivity, polish, ease of operation, and incisiveness (Neugarten & Datan, 1974). Overall, like middle-aged women, they describe these years as an improvement over the "life-cycle crunch" of young adulthood, when one must meet extensive familial and occupational demands (Harry, 1976; Chiriboga, 1989).

Studies of fun and happiness fall in line with the rest of the data presented by the no-crisis school of thought. For example, in one series of interviews with nearly seven thousand males and females from ages 4 through 103, one researcher found few relationships between age and mood or degree of current happiness and opportunities for fun (Cameron, 1972, 1975). Longitudinal data from Duke University (Busse & Maddox, 1985; Palmore & Luikart, 1974) confirm that reported life satisfaction neither rises nor declines as subjects pass through the middle years of life. In the Duke study, perceived health—not age—was by far the strongest factor predicting life satisfaction. Perceived health was more important than either objective health, as rated by physicians, or income and education.

In recent years, Robert McCrae and Paul Costa, Jr. (1984, 1987, 1989) have taken the most radical stand among those who support the no-crisis position. In an extensive longitudinal study of men at midlife, these authors report no evidence of any important personality changes over the adult years, and no support at all for the notion of a midlife crisis. Using an instrument called the *Midlife Crisis Scale,* based on the work of Roger Gould, as well as several major personality inventories and intensive interviews, these authors conclude: "We see little basis for adopting the model of development proposed by Levinson and his colleagues, or the more widely held theory of a midlife crisis, and we are skeptical that the processes described by Gould are universal, developmental changes in personality and consciousness" (1984, p. 106).

Combining data from the personality inventories they employed, McCrae and Costa have defined five major personality traits. Three of these, called **neuroticism, open-mindedness,** and **extroversion,** reflect six different factors each. Figure 7.2 presents a diagram of these three dispositions and the subfactors or facets of each. Two more traits, **agreeableness,** and **conscientiousness,** are considered **global personality traits,** that is, they have not been broken down into various aspects; however, McCrae and Costa (1989) define agreeableness as sympathy, trust, cooperativeness, and altruism while arguing that conscientiousness reflects organization, scrupulousness, persistence, and achievement motivation. Together, these five factors make up the NEO-AC Model of personality (McCrae & Costa, 1987; Costa & McCrae, 1988).

According to Costa and McCrae, people do not change appreciably on these major personality traits despite aging or major life events like marriage, parenthood, divorce, or career changes (Costa & McCrae, 1988). These authors maintain that habits and behaviors may change over the life span as well as attitudes, opinions, social roles, and interpersonal relationships, but "life does not lead to change or growth in personality" (1984, p. 108). That is, "personality is one aspect of the self that does not change in adulthood" (1984, p. 115). Other authors have also found substantial stability in extroversion and neuroticism over periods as long as fifty years (Conley, 1985).

McCrae and Costa admit that some people experience midlife crisis, but they do not believe that most people do, and they argue that the experience of crisis at midlife may be better predicted by personality predispositions than age. For example, poor self-esteem is associated with neuroticism, and those who exhibit high levels of neuroticism are likely to be dissatisfied with life and to report low scores on measures of recent mood. There is some evidence, according to McCrae and Costa, that these individuals use ineffective coping

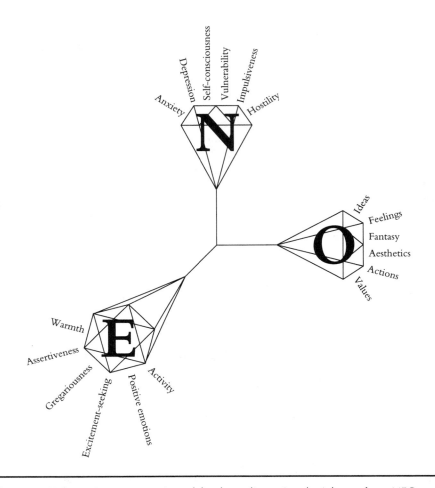

Figure 7.2 Schematic representation of the three-dimensional, eighteen-facet NEO (neuroticism, extroversion, openness) model.

SOURCE: McCrae & Costa, 1984, p. 33.

mechanisms such as hostile responses, passivity, and self-blame. Perhaps these are the people most likely to experience midlife crisis, or, for that matter, crisis during any significant life transition.

And so, we have come full circle from the argument that middle age is a critical stage of life, perhaps the most stressful period in the life cycle, to the contention that there is no relationship at all between age and personality development. How can we make some sense out of these two competing sets of results?

Denial and Crisis

A number of writers and researchers have addressed this conflict in the literature. For instance, some of the more clinically oriented believe that middle-aged people tend to rationalize and to deny the experience of crisis. In a psychiatric interview, the experimenter is able to see through the apparent calm to the real inner turmoil. But the questionnaires of the survey researchers simply pick up what the subject believes to be the socially desirable response—not how life is really going but how it should be going (Rosenberg & Farrell, 1976).

Two major proponents of the denial hypothesis, Michael Farrell and Stanley Rosenberg, published a study of personality development based on a sample of 500 men in young adulthood and middle age. In their book, *Men at Midlife* (1981), Farrell and Rosenberg point out that the literature on midlife crisis is plagued by the use of differing methods and quite different samples of men. They also reiterate the notion that questionnaires are likely to reflect denial and a reluctance to report negative experience. They do not, however, believe that all middle-aged people, or even most, will experience a crisis.

Farrell and Rosenberg discovered that a variety of resolutions were achieved when the men in their own sample encountered the central tasks of midlife development—tasks such as assuming the role of "patron" of the family, becoming a source of financial and emotional stability for both the older and the younger generations, learning to live with increasing physical vulnerability, and accepting one's inability to achieve the unfulfilled dreams of youth. In assessing different responses to these tasks, Farrell and Rosenberg developed a four-part typology of their subjects. They pointed out that the men differed along two major dimensions: the ability to confront stress and the degree of life satisfaction reported. Table 7.1 outlines the four types and shows how they are defined along these two dimensions of stress confrontation and life satisfaction.

About 12 percent of the Farrell and Rosenberg sample fell into the **antihero** type. These individuals appeared to be alienated from the community and the mass culture. They expressed little satisfaction with their occupational careers, and they seemed to possess little or no sense of the future. Often, they talked about wanting to "start all over again." More of the antihero subjects were married to working women than in any other group. But the men were not dissatisfied with their marriages, although they often expressed disappointment about the way their children were turning out. More often than any other type, the antihero was likely to experience a strong personal sense of midlife crisis, and unlikely to deny or project these feelings. Men in this group also tended to suffer from physical as well as psychological symptoms.

The largest group in the sample, 32 percent of the men, classified as **transcendent-generative,** appeared to negotiate the midlife transition with no experience of crisis or turmoil, but rather with a deep sense of personal satis-

Table 7.1 A typology of responses to middle-age stresses	
Ability to Confront Stress	
Denial of Stress	*Open Confrontation with Stress*
Degree of Life Satisfaction	
Dissatisfied	

Punitive-Disenchanted
   Highest in authoritarianism
   Dissatisfaction associated with
   environmental factors
   Conflict with children
	Antihero
	   High alienation
	   Active identity struggle
	   Ego-oriented
	   Uninvolved interpersonally
	   Low authoritarianism

Satisfied	

Pseudo-developed
   Overtly satisfied
   Attitudinally rigid
   Denies feelings
   High authoritarianism
   High on covert depression and
   anxiety
   High in symptom formation
	Transcendent-Generative
	   Assesses past and present with
	   conscious sense of satisfaction
	   Few symptoms of distress
	   Open to feelings
	   Accepts out-groups
	   Feels in control of fate

SOURCE: Farrell & Rosenberg, 1981, p. 32.

faction in marriage, family, and work, along with good health, continuing faith in the future, openness, and feelings of confidence and self-assurance.

About 26 percent of the sample fell into the **pseudo-developed** group, who also reported satisfaction and showed few psychological or physical symptoms. Farrell and Rosenberg believe, however, that these men simply deny the stress they experience. They do not report any real hopefulness about the future and seem to have problems thinking and deciding. They just can't get going. They admit to dissatisfaction with their sex lives and experience their children as a source of trouble. They are ethnocentric and authoritarian and likely to accept the social prescription that middle age is a comfortable, successful time in the life cycle. The pseudo-developed man copes with the problems of the period by sticking his head in the sand.

Finally, nearly 30 percent of the sample were classified as **punitive-disen-chanted.** The vast majority of these men were in crisis, despite their ability to deny any problems. They were likely to be dependent and unhappy, to feel restless and irritable, and to use alcohol to alleviate their symptoms. They were unhappy with their wives and their children and showed very low tolerance for ambiguity, often appearing bigoted as well as authoritarian. Farrell and Rosenberg classify Archie Bunker as a member of the punitive-disenchanted group.

Obviously, since over one-half of the Farrell and Rosenberg sample used denial as a major coping mechanism and since another 32 percent reported that they did not really experience what has been described in the literature as crisis, survey and questionnaire research is unlikely to show high levels of psychological discomfort among middle-aged men as a group. Nevertheless, as Farrell and Rosenberg put it: "Though we do not find 'crisis' in the sense of conscious disruption of identity to be a common pattern as men confront middle-age, we do find a range of responses, some of which may be just as problematic as a crisis" (1981, p. 208).

Of special interest is Farrell and Rosenberg's finding that the overwhelming majority of the transcendent-generative men in their sample came from affluent, middle-class areas. They often began life with a wealth of economic and emotional resources and by young adulthood had been able to develop multiple coping strategies. Farrell and Rosenberg believe disappointment and insurmountable crisis in middle age may be, in good measure, an injury of class. In this culture, male vocational failure is most likely to be accompanied by a devastated self-concept and feelings of estrangement from the society and even the self. Consider the fact that a great many of the punitive-disenchanted men were the sons of semiskilled or unskilled laborers, or had suffered a childhood of abuse and neglect. Farrell and Rosenberg argue that our society establishes criteria for success that most men will never be able to attain. As a result, the majority end up as psychological casualties, experiencing their failure as a personal deficiency, and seeing themselves as inadequate.

Farrell and Rosenberg's emphasis on the importance of socioeconomic class and the opportunities of childhood suggests a related hypothesis. Midlife crisis may be more likely under certain cultural, historical, and generational conditions. Perhaps some groups or even whole generations of people are more likely to encounter crisis than others; changing social and historical conditions in postwar Germany provide a dramatic example (Bradbury, 1975). For those whose adult lives were shattered by World War II, middle age was a very different experience than it was for those who entered middle age in the economic boom years of the 1960s. Certainly, the experience of middle age in this country may be different for those who entered the prime of life in the boom of the 1960s when compared to those who entered it in the economic slump of the late 1970s and early 1980s.

It is also possible that midlife crisis emerges only in those cultures and historical times that offer the basic affluence required for extensive introspection or concern for the psychological quality of life. As a society becomes wealthier and more leisure time is available, people have the opportunity to pursue more narcissistic concerns, especially introspection and self-expression (Cytrynbaum et al., 1980). This cultural-historical hypothesis may explain why midlife crisis does not seem to occur in some parts of the world. It is more frequent in highly industrialized, affluent nations, but it is also more apparent in the United States and England than in Germany and France (Bradbury, 1975).

Undoubtedly, important cohort influences affect the experience of middle age (Elder, 1985). Yet, such forces cannot explain why some individuals in a given cohort report crisis and some do not. Even when people from very similar economic and social circumstances enter middle age in approximately the same time frame, there are those who make the transition with little or no difficulty, and those who experience midlife as a difficult time indeed. Furthermore, careful evaluation of personal reports even suggests that within the same individual, midlife is often experienced in a paradoxical way—as a period of both difficulty and opportunity.

Defining Crisis

It may also prove helpful to focus on the word *crisis*. Our ordinary understanding of the term may not be a satisfactory definition for the uncertainties of middle age. A midlife crisis is not necessarily a catastrophe. Take into consideration, for instance, the Harvard Grant Study subjects who described their forties as more tumultuous than their adolescent years. "Despite this turmoil, the best-adapted men tended to perceive the period from thirty-five to forty-nine as the happiest in their entire lives" (Vaillant & McArthur, 1972, p. 423).

These men saw their forties as a time for reordering their lives and for reassessing the past. They experienced more overt depression during middle age than during other periods of adult life, but at the same time they seemed able to acknowledge and accept depression and turmoil as a part of the lifestyle of a successful man. Among the men Levinson followed, midlife transition was also characterized by feelings of vitality and by the freedom to express compassion and reevaluate formerly suppressed aspects of the self.

A crisis need not be defined as a terrible problem or a total catastrophe. Although social scientists tend to emphasize the pathological and fatalistic implications of the term, stability and crisis do not have to be seen as positive and negative poles. Positive development can emerge from crisis—from upheaval, uncertainty, and change. As one writer has noted, the notion that crisis is always negative would lead us to "emphasize sexual satisfaction but not excitement" (Riegel, 1975b, p. 336). Or, as Washington Irving observed: "There is a certain relief in change, even though it be from bad to worse; as I have often found travelling in a stagecoach, that it is often a comfort to shift one's position and be bruised in a new place."

New behavior, attitudes, and solutions often arise out of conflict. Even in the view of learning theorists, conflict creates variability in behavior, offering the possibility for discovering new solutions. Solomon Cytrynbaum and his associates (1980) offer a systems approach to the study of midlife as a way to integrate and understand the existing research. They assume that personality differences affect one's capacity to adapt at midlife, when the coping and defensive strategies one has learned are pitted against a variety of challenges. The biological changes of middle age combine with cultural and social transitions such as launching children, career changes, and the death or illness of family and friends, as well as with a growing sense of time running out and of personal confrontation with one's own mortality, to demand a new integration of personality and lifestyle. Box 7.1 outlines the phases of destructuring and reintegration that Cytrynbaum and his coauthors have described.

Cytrynbaum et al., along with a growing number of researchers engaged in work along similar lines, do not believe everyone is able to seize the creative opportunity of a life-span transition. Some individuals do not experience middle age as a period of positive growth. Some become disenchanted with life. Some are unhappy and dissatisfied. For some, middle-age *is* a catastrophe and they do not adapt. When the time comes to reassess the life course, some count themselves failures and are unable to accept the accounting. Failure or perceived failure may precipitate dissatisfaction and despair. Individual differences are clearly of central importance.

Personality, Timing, and Midlife Transition

Clearly, social and economic circumstances might insulate one from the experience of disillusionment in middle age. There is also evidence that, as with most developmental phenomena, timing is important in negotiating the midlife transition. Those who progress through the adult life course in a normal, expectable way are able to anticipate and predict the life course more accurately. They experience fewer difficulties than those who do not follow the normal sequence and rhythm—the **social clock**—of adult life (Neugarten & Datan, 1974; Kogan, 1990).

In one recent study of adult women from young adulthood to midlife (Helson & Moane, 1987), for example, the authors defined three different "social clock patterns." Women who had started families by age twenty-eight were said to have adopted a Feminine Social Clock, whereas those who had begun to advance in a career field at the same age were said to be using the Masculine Occupational Clock. A third group of women followed neither clock. Members of both of the first two groups, whether having adopted a feminine pattern or a masculine one, became more dominant, independent, self-controlled, tolerant, and psychological-minded with age, even if they failed at the project that they had initiated at age twenty-eight.

In a related piece of research, Sara McLanahan and Aage Sorensen (1985) examined data from a representative sample of American families followed in what is known as the Michigan Study, since 1968. They were interested in how life events like employment changes, having children, a relative moving in or out of the house, residential moves, and so on affect people of different ages. Overall, they found that younger people report more events of all kinds but that middle-aged people report more changes in household composition than other groups. Their study showed that people who experience events **off-time** almost always experience those events as producing negative effects.

Box 7.1 Developmental phases in midlife

Precipitators of the
Destructuring Process ⟶

Conscious			
	Biological change and decline.	Death and illness of significant others.	"Time left to live."
	Life-threatening illness.	Cultural and social structural transitions such as "empty nesting," parental imperative, early retirement, status loss.	

Confrontation with death, mortality, death anxiety.

Unconscious

SOURCE: S. Cytrynbaum et al., 1980, p. 469.

Box 7.1 *(continued)*

Reassessment →	*Reintegration and Restructuring* →	*Behavioral and Role Change*
Reassessment of primary relationships and current identity and life structure.	Testing in reality, and/or rehearsing in fantasy different visions of primary relations to men, women, and children.	Recommit, modify, or dramatically change behavior and/or relationships to primary family and/or work systems.
Denial and externalization leads to defensively premature role change (in family or work).	Integration of the more creative forces in personality in the form of a revised dream or legacy and of existing and emergent masculine and feminine components of personality.	Act on creating legacy, sense of community, mentoring, or other expressions of generativity.
Emergence of real or fantasized transitional partners.		
Mourning and grieving losses: dream, mentors, idealism, legacy.	Realignment of defenses and consolidation of primary polarities, such as male-female and destructiveness-creativeness.	
Oscillate between depression and elation.		
Internal distress, reemergent contrasexual and other suppressed components of personality.		
Reactivation of mother-son, mother-daughter separation individuation struggle.		

People who are off-time, that is, who are going through events like marriage or parenthood or widowhood either early or late, may be isolated from the common knowledge or wisdom of the culture, making it difficult for them to use the normal lines of support and communication available to those in transition. They may not have gone through the anticipatory socialization process that society offers to those who experience events at or about the same time as everyone else in their cohort. **Anticipatory socialization** includes all the formal and informal ways we learn about how to perform the roles society offers us from being a child to being an elderly person.

Being off-time is not always an inevitable disaster, however. As we learned in our discussion of parenthood, people who become parents relatively late do not necessarily regret their decision (Daniels & Weingarten, 1980). Moreover, at least 7 percent of the best-adjusted men in the Harvard studies had marched to a different drummer, whereas 23 percent of those who were the least well adjusted were considered on-time.

Why are some people able to cope with the untimely, while others are dissatisfied and poorly adjusted even when things proceed in normal, timely ways? If upheaval, turmoil, and conflict provide the opportunity for new solutions, they also offer the prospect of failure. If one is unwilling to risk failure, the necessary adjustments may not emerge. As Sir James Barrie summed it up, "We are all failures—at least the best of us are."

The best-adjusted men in the Harvard studies were able to "accept their own tragedy" (Vaillant & McArthur, 1972, p. 424). The transcendent-generative men in the Farrell and Rosenberg study were able to acknowledge and confront conflict in their lives. Here the psychiatric literature and the social sciences converge. "As a result of the life history with its accumulating record of adaptations to both biological and social events, there is a continually changing basis within the individual for perceiving and responding to new events in the outer world" (Neugarten et al., 1964, p. 194). Not the events of midlife themselves, or age alone, or timing, can explain individual responses to the challenges of middle age. Rather, it is the perceptions of those events, the personal context in which they are experienced that is central.

Personality: Change and Sameness

Personality research is rarely done from a developmental point of view. That is, because many researchers define personality as a set of stable and enduring traits or dispositions, they tend to create tests and measures that reflect the most stable attributes of personality. If there were no such stable traits or capacities or skills, if human beings changed radically over the life span, then the study of personality would be pointless. In a sense, people would have no personalities.

Most personality tests, like the ones used by McCrae and Costa (1984,

1987, 1989) to establish the NEO-AC model (Figure 7.2), are designed to exhibit **reliability.** That means that people are not supposed to change their answers from one time of measurement to another. If too many people do change their response to a particular item, that item is most often removed from the test and the opportunity to study change is lost. Klaus Riegel once wrote that "since human beings are changing all the time, they cannot be appropriately described by instruments that are supposed to reflect universal and stable properties" (1975b, p. 357). Of course, stability is not just an illusion created by personality tests. People do exhibit enduring characteristics, or at least characteristics that do not change radically for many. Extroversion, open-mindedness, neuroticism, agreeableness, and conscientiousness count among those characteristics. Other researchers have reported that twins reared apart score more alike on measures of emotionality, activity, and sociability than people who don't share genetic similarity (Plomin, Pederson, McClean, Nesselroade, & Bergeman, 1988).

As Nathan Kogan (1990) suggests: "Personality change is observed only when the measures employed in the study are of developmental relevance" (p. 596). Those who see changes tend to focus on different constructs and use different measures than those who find stability. Kogan contends that what we need to do is to try to understand which traits generate high levels of stability and which yield change across the life span. Furthermore, we need to look for those conditions that produce stability or change.

Change need not imply complete unpredictability or crisis. Change may be predictable and positive even when it is relatively dramatic. For instance, the scores people achieve on various traits may change in a consistent direction. That is, everyone in a sample may show a decrease in a trait like extroversion over the life span.

Genotypic Continuity

There may also be **genotypic continuity** of personality without **phenotypic persistence.** Phenotypic persistence means that either absolute or relative consistency occurs. Genotypic continuity means that individuals who share certain kinds of personality characteristics may all change in the same kinds of ways, even though some of them are quite unexpected. For example, people who were happy, dependent, anxious youngsters may become independent, dissatisfied, assertive adults. In this instance, no single trait or characteristic has remained stable, but the course of change was the same for everyone who fit the original description. If one expects genotypic continuity, it might be necessary to develop a typology: a description of groups of individuals with the same personality traits.

One of the earliest and most influential multidimensional, longitudinal studies of personality and aging to suggest changes in personality was carried out over thirty years ago at the University of Chicago (Neugarten, 1964). Information from interviews, projective tests, and questionnaires was collected from a large and representative sample of people aged forty to eighty over a period of ten years.

Although the Chicago researchers found evidence of stability for some processes—styles of coping, life satisfaction, and strength of goal-related behavior—important areas of change were discovered as well. In particular, they were impressed by a shift from **active** to **passive mastery** among male members of the sample. At forty, the men in the sample felt in charge of their environment: they viewed risk taking in a positive light and perceived themselves as wellsprings of energy and change. By sixty, all this had been transformed. These same men began to see the external environment as dangerous and threatening, and the self as passive and accommodating (Neugarten, 1973; Neugarten et al., 1964).

Movement from active to passive mastery has been observed in cultural groups as diverse as the Navajo, Lowland and Highland Mayans of Mexico, and culturally isolated groups in Israel. Over time, people show an increasing tendency to accommodate the self to outside influences (Gutmann, 1964, 1977, 1978). Throughout middle age, both men and women become more preoccupied with their inner lives. They pay greater attention to their feelings, experiences, and cognitive processes. Increasing interiority is among the best-documented phenomena discovered in the developmental study of personality. **Interiority** is defined by some of the traditional aspects of introversion, but it also refers to decreasing attachment to persons and objects in the external world (Neugarten, 1973).

The Chicago group was also intrigued by changes in the way people think about time. Sometime during middle age, people stop perceiving their life cycle in terms of time since birth and begin to view life in terms of time left to live. In another major multidimensional study of personality at the Institute of Human Development in Berkeley, Florine Livson (1981a, 1981b) found that changing time perspective and an increased awareness of death is one of the main forces behind the kind of personality change she and her colleagues observed over the middle years of adult life.

Over the forty years or so of the Berkeley study, evidence accumulated that psychological health and well-being does not draw on the same resources at different phases of the life cycle. For this reason, psychological health is not particularly stable over the years of adult life, and different individuals have difficulty at different points. For instance, in the Berkeley study, responsibility and intellectual competence in adolescence predicted psychological health in men subjects at age forty. At age thirty, however, such adolescent traits had not predicted psychological health well at all. This evidence confirms that the concept of genotypic continuity may be very useful in understanding development over the life span (Livson & Peskin, 1981; Peskin & Livson, 1981).

The Berkeley researchers have also reported some rather interesting sex differences. For women, the process of predicting psychological health from adolescence was almost the inverse of the process for men. Women seemed to draw heavily on adolescent traits during early adulthood. By age forty, however, women who had been described as independent, bright, and interesting in adolescence were depressed, irritable, and conflicted (Livson, 1981a, 1981b). By age fifty, these women had rebounded.

In a more detailed analysis of women who were among the best adjusted by age fifty, Livson (1981a) found that it made sense to divide all the subjects into two distinct groups: **traditionals** and **independents.** Traditional women were described as gregarious, nurturant, conventional, charming, and cordial. They exhibited a tendency to handle anxiety by repressing it and to show rather frequent signs of **somatization**—the expression of anxiety in terms of physical symptoms like headaches or indigestion. Independents were ambitious, skeptical, and unconventional. They seemed to be able to cope with anxiety through insight and other, more direct forms of expression. One-third of the independents were divorced or widowed; many held full-time jobs. Traditionals tended to be primarily committed to the role of housewife.

Traditionals moved through the years from forty to fifty without difficulty. They did not experience midlife crisis and, at forty, appeared close and trusting, giving and poised. By fifty, they had a strong protective attitude toward others and were very nurturant. At forty, in contrast, the independents were quite dissatisfied and in the midst of what looked like a crisis. Out of touch with their own creativity and intelligence, they were bothered by demands of work and family and exhibited low levels of psychological health. By fifty, they had survived the transition and seemed much more able to trust and to be close. Livson feels that the change in these women occurred as they were able to respond to unfulfilled needs for achievement when the children began to leave home (Livson, 1981b).

In a parallel analysis of psychologically healthy men, Livson found a similar pattern. Men who improved in psychological health between forty and fifty were described as expansive, sensuous, outgoing, and gregarious, but less controlled and more unrealistic than their stably adapted counterparts. At forty, the former had chosen to suppress their emotionality and impulsiveness, adopting a sort of macho exaggeration of the masculine stereotype—angry, hostile, defensive, and ruminative. At fifty, the improvers were able to give up this dubious adaptation and move toward greater closeness and intimacy in their interactions with others. In sum, Livson suggests that for both men and women, inability to conform to the conventional gender stereotype is often associated with unhappiness and dissatisfaction as one enters middle age, but over the years from forty to fifty, it is possible to learn to cope with stereotyped, external demands in a more personally gratifying way.

A final example of genotypic continuity from the Berkeley researchers is found in their work on intelligence and personality (Eichorn, Hunt, & Honzik, 1981). Using the Stanford-Binet, the Terman-McNemar, and the Weschler Adult Intelligence Scale as measures of intelligence, the Berkeley researchers have found no evidence of decline in IQ over the years of adolescence and adulthood to age fifty. Neither did they find any reason to make a distinction between verbal and nonverbal skills.

Often people are not socially prepared to cope with events that occur in their lives at times very different from when their cohorts had the same experience.

The Berkeley group did, however, find evidence of an average gain of about 6.2 IQ points, and one report focused on the personality characteristics associated with changes in IQ. This report described IQ gainers as balanced people—well socialized but not timid or conforming, and highly but not extremely independent, adaptable, and self-confident. Of special interest is their observation that people who as adolescents were "highly controlled (perhaps especially in sexual expression), dependable, calm, and somewhat aloof from their peers," had higher IQs in middle adulthood as well as at adolescence, but that by adulthood (even young adulthood) they had changed in many other significant ways. In fact, by middle age, the men who increased in IQ showed a whole new list of personality correlates including insightfulness, rebelliousness, and the tendency to have interesting, unusual thoughts. Another victory for genotypic continuity!

Again and again, it appears that the intellectual aspects of personality tend to be more stable and better predictors of the direction of personality change than other aspects of personality. For instance, data from the Oakland Guidance Study (part of the larger Berkeley sample) show that intellectual capacity is a much better predictor of late-life adaptation than is either psychological health in early adult life or a variety of other personality measures (Kuypers, 1981). In this study, the people who seemed to cope best with the challenges of aging were objective, logical, flexible, tolerant, and able to concentrate. Those who showed greater personality disorganization with age appeared unable to appraise life realistically and demonstrated a definite tendency toward tangentiality and confabulation in thinking. They also showed withdrawal, delusion, and preoccupation. Joseph Kuypers concludes that self-actualization is rooted both in intellectual capacity and in the limitations or advantages one's environment offers in using that capacity.

The Berkeley Mothers Both work- and group-centered mothers experienced positive changes of lifestyle over the years from thirty to seventy. At thirty, the work-centered mothers were dissatisfied with their marriages and reported more financial problems than the other mothers. By middle age, however, these women had ventured into new and, apparently, highly gratifying lifestyles. They had developed adequate economic rewards, independence from marital ties, and a new circle of friends.

The group-centered mothers also seemed to be able to lead more fulfilling lives with the advent of middle age and the end of child rearing. On the other hand, uncentered mothers (those who focused almost exclusively on the role of mother), who had been happy and healthy at thirty, had the lowest economic status at the age of seventy and were in poor health. Many of these women were widowed in their seventies, too late to change the course of their lives. Most had lost their homes, and few of them even had much interest left in their children or grandchildren. These were the same women who "were completely and very contentedly engaged as wives and mothers all through their early and middle adult years" (Maas, 1985, p. 171).

In terms of predicting life satisfaction at seventy, the personality data for the Berkeley mothers have been less useful. The life satisfaction of this group of women was not well predicted by early adulthood personality, or by combinations of their own and their husbands' personality traits (Mussen, 1985). Although there is some suggestion that a buoyant, positive, responsive attitude toward life is predictive of later life satisfaction for women, it was obvious that the qualities of the early marital relationship and other life circumstances (like income and availability of leisure time) was an overriding force in the lives of these women. Paul Mussen (1985) has suggested that the reason why circumstances were so powerful is that older cohorts of women have had very little personal control over their lifestyles.

The Berkeley Fathers The most dramatic shifts for male subjects were predicted by personality type rather than lifestyle, as exemplified by the "conservative-ordering" fathers. As young adults, these fathers were described as withdrawn, shy, distant, and conflicted, and they seemed to have many marital problems. At seventy, although their marital problems had declined in importance, the men had become conventional, controlling, and even more distant.

Active-competent fathers also showed some noteworthy development over the years. As older men they were conforming, direct, capable, and charming, if somewhat critical of others and rather distant in their personal relationships. They saw themselves as active in the role of friend, despite the fact that they spent much of their leisure time alone. As young adults, these same men had been demonstrative and outgoing and had felt a strong sense of personal adequacy. But they were also described as explosive and irritable, tense, and nervous. Over the years, most of them had been occupationally successful, and the personal and economic rewards of success seemed to allow them to develop the charming, attractive personalities that characterized their later years.

What is remarkable about this study is the degree to which people who were alike as young adults were also alike in later life, despite change in many personality traits and lifestyle characteristics. Different types developed along the same track, lending predictability to the course of change. If the authors of this study had averaged scores over all the people in different groups, few patterns might have emerged. As we know from McCrae and Costa, the overall stability of personality traits might have been substantial in this study, but the variability of development within groups turned out to be one of the most interesting aspects of the data.

Does life affect personality? The Berkeley parents study suggests some interesting answers to this question when the data for the mothers and fathers are compared (Mussen, 1985). The lifestyles of the fathers showed greater continuity than lifestyles of the mothers. In other words, women experienced more changes of lifestyle than men did, and for women, lifestyle was a more important predictor of life satisfaction at seventy than personality. For men, who experienced relatively few changes in lifestyle, personality was a better predictor of late life satisfaction. The most satisfied elderly men had been relaxed, emo-

Perhaps the most significant change that has been reported in the lives of men at midlife is a growing appreciation of and desire for increased intimacy and caring in their relationships with others.

tionally stable, and in good physical condition as young adults (Mussen, 1985). When circumstances change often or dramatically, it appears that personality, at least as it is measured by life satisfaction and the kinds of descriptions offered by the Berkeley group, is affected. When circumstances are continuous, there seems to be more continuity in personality from early to late adulthood.

Most multidimensional studies of personality, like the Berkeley studies, reveal that development is characterized both by stability and change over the life course. In general, however, the greatest changes seem to take place in how people perceive their lives and how intensely involved they are in the external world, its demands and roles. These dimensions of personality, which have been called the **executive processes,** refer to changes in one's sense of self, in the way time and the life cycle are conceptualized, and in the way emotions are experienced.

Change in the Context of Stability

"People change, but slowly, while maintaining some continuity," so concludes Norma Haan (1985, p. 25) whose work has also come out of the Berkeley data. She has also written that "the life span seems typified by movement toward greater comfort, candor, and an objective sense of self" (1976, p. 64). Figure 7.3 presents the developmental curves she has found for the Berkeley Guidance Sample (GS) and the Oakland Guidance Study (OGS). Data for males and females are presented separately. Generally, this work supported the conclusion that the intellectual aspects of personality are relatively stable. That is, the people who were interested in intellectual matters as adolescents were also more interested in intellectual matters as adults. For example, in Figure 7.3 the data for **cognitive investment**—the value subjects placed on intellectual matters, ambitiousness, breadth of interests, fluency, dependability, and the propensity for introspection—remained quite stable between the ages of fourteen and forty-seven. On this measure, everyone maintained approximately the same rank order.

On the dimension labeled "open/closed to self," however, females remained stable but males did not (Haan, 1985). People who were rated as very open appeared insightful, introspective, interesting, and able to think unconventionally. People who were described as closed were also conventional, uncomfortable with uncertainty, defensive, fastidious, and power-oriented. Haan has suggested that men are less stable than women on this dimension because they are so focused on career achievement through the early years of the adult life span. Adolescent males had appeared more open than females but by adulthood had become closed. Perhaps, Haan speculates, adult life, at least through age forty-seven, is more difficult for males.

In an earlier analysis (Haan, 1981), the strongest overall finding in the study was the development of greater openness among those of the highest socioeconomic status. It may be that career success permits men the luxury of personal openness. In 1981, Haan concluded that adaptation at midlife appeared "to re-

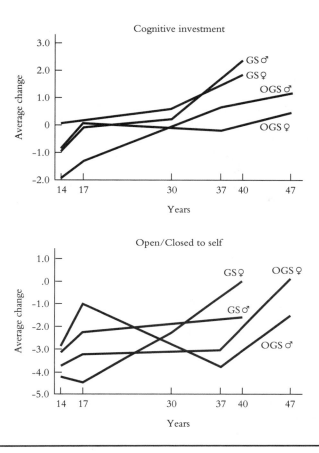

Figure 7.3 Average scores on personality dimensions for four time periods.

SOURCE: Haan, 1985, pp. 30–31.

flect the accrued wisdom of people who have grown tolerant and become instructed, socially and psychologically . . . our middle-aged had also become considerably more giving and self-extending . . . as well as interpersonally predictable and accountable to others—or generative, to use Erikson's terms" (pp. 150–151).

In 1985, Haan went on to analyze the data in terms of clusters of traits that she labeled "possible personality organizations," such as "self-confident and cognitively invested." She then looked at whether people tended to use the same personality organization over the entire course of the life span from adolescence to middle age or whether they changed from time to time. Her analysis strongly suggests that people do use different organizations at different times in their lives. Only 9 percent of the sample was classified in the same way at each time of measurement. Furthermore, certain types were more likely to shift organizations than others. People who were initially classified as "open to self/cognitively invested" were more likely to be classified in another way at subsequent times of measurement, whereas people who were classified as "self-confident/cognitively invested" were likely to be classified the same way each time. Finally, Haan found that some personality organizations did not occur at every time of measurement. No one was classified as "open to self/cognitively invested" until adulthood, and "nurturant/cognitively invested" was an exclusively female personality organization.

It is easy to see that the more precisely a researcher defines what he or she means by personality, and the more carefully a group of subjects is described, the richer the information the researcher is likely to discover. Haan does not believe that stage-specific theories like those of Gould and Levinson can account for her data; moreover, she does not find evidence for a midlife crisis. Adults do undergo impressive changes in personality, but, these studies suggest, there is no compelling reason for the definition of tightly organized stages. On the other hand, obviously Haan does not agree with McCrae and Costa that personality is generally quite stable. Even in McCrae and Costa's work, many people exhibited changes, although the overall results demonstrated significant stability (Kogan, 1990).

In her most recent work, Haan (1990) argues that personality is *less* stable over the years of adulthood than it is through childhood. According to her analysis, the biggest changes occur during early adulthood on measures of assertiveness, outgoingness, and dependability. Among middle-aged participants, self-confidence and warmth increased, and the biggest changes on these measures occurred for men in the transition from early adulthood to middle age. Middle-aged women seemed to become more confident and warm slightly later and to show change also in the direction of greater intellectual commitment and dependability. During this period, half of the participants began a new line of work, one-third experienced a major illness, one-third the death of a close friend, and one-fifth reported the death of someone in their immediate family. Overall, women showed about twice as much change as men in this sample.

Haan concludes that personality changes occur in response to definitive experiences with clear, unalterable consequences. She believes this accounts for the greater change among female participants, which she attributes to the shifting, conflicting roles that most women play over the adult years. She did also find, however, that toward the end of middle age, vigor, self-certainty, and efficient problem solving began to decline. Why these changes take place is not clear and whether they continue is of great interest.

Other researchers have demonstrated clear areas of change in middle age (Kogan, 1990). For instance, there appears to be a decline in certain kinds of motivation over the life span (Veroff, Reuman, & Feld, 1984). Women show less need for achievement and affiliation with the passing years while the hope of power peaks for men at middle age. In the study in question, the women subjects were mostly high school graduates and the researchers attribute the fall in achievement motivation to the fact that many of them were stuck in dead-end jobs throughout adulthood.

Evidence also exists that middle-aged men develop "a definite capacity for establishing and guiding the next generation, beyond raising their own children" (Snarey, Son, Kuehne, Hauser, & Vaillant, 1987, p. 596). However, the question of stages is not clearly answered by such shifts. Evidence for declines or increases in levels of reported motivation does not constitute proof of some general, stagelike change.

In an intensive, if small, study of generativity in men and women, John Kotre (1984) makes an interesting suggestion about the problem of stages. He reported that among his subjects both men and women experienced several different chances for the expression of generativity. As these people entered new "cultures" in adulthood, like the culture of grandparenting or the culture of retirement, they often discovered an opportunity to be fertile in a new way. His data did not fit the notion that there is one long, continuous stage of generativity that occurs after the dilemma of intimacy has been resolved. He contends that generativity is more reasonably considered an impulse and that various types of impulses toward generativity are felt at different moments. He does not believe that there is a proper age or a necessary foundation for these moments or episodes of generativity. People may experience them regardless of their ability to form intimate relationships, or of the degree to which they have resolved identity issues favorably. Kotre even argues that some people are able to draw energy from the transformation of an earlier deficit in intimacy or identity development to seize an opportunity for generative behavior. Only in a few rare individuals, Kotre contends, does generativity really motivate a general state.

In the final pages of this chapter, we will tackle one final, hotly debated area of study in personality development, the degree to which sex-role stereotypes dominate personality organization over the adult life span.

Personality and Sex-Role Behavior

To understand current theory and research in the area of personality and sex-role behavior, we must return to the original work of the Chicago group (Neugarten, 1968a, 1968b). The finding that middle-aged people tend to move from active to passive mastery has formed a context for much subsequent work in personality and sex-role behavior, because such movement is more characteristic of male than of female development. Men appear to become less aggressive and domineering with age and also more in touch with the sensual and familial aspects of life. At the same time, evidence indicates, women move toward greater independence, less sentimentality, and greater dominance in middle age (Gutmann, 1975, 1990).

As is discussed in Chapter 5, Gutmann attributes the "normal unisex of later life" to the resolution of the parental emergency and tends to see the sex-role changes of middle age as part of an inevitable, genetically based process. Other authors (Self, 1975) adamantly disagree. However, whether or not there is a biological imperative that directs sex-role behavior, there is little doubt that the course of personality development differs in important ways for men and women over the adult years.

For example, we have seen in several studies that men appear to progress toward greater sensuality and openness in middle age, although, in the Haan studies, men remained less open than women through age forty-seven. All the males in the Haan studies showed greater sexuality over time, more markedly so than did the females, but only the older cohort of males showed much progress toward increased nurturance with age. Even in the older cohort, however, the women continued to be much more nurturant than the men at all ages.

Livson (1981b) indicated that many of the men in her sample who displayed a macho, exaggerated, angry, defensive style at age forty, moved toward more nurturant, intimate styles later on. However, both the independent and the traditional women in her sample also showed greater nurturance with age; the independents, in particular, were able to demonstrate greater intimacy and closeness at age fifty than at forty. In this study, it appears that those who did not conform to conventional gender roles, whether male or female, were more likely to develop real intimacy and tenderness as they moved toward old age.

Another researcher studying the Berkeley sample (Brooks, 1981) discovered some interesting relationships between sex-role behavior and **social maturity,** which she defined as the ability to live comfortably with others, to respond appropriately to both ordinary and extraordinary stress, and, when necessary, to depart from the conventional mores and institutions of a society. As men and women pass through middle age, they become more and more similar in social maturity. Brooks goes on to speculate that as women in their late fifties and sixties take responsibility for heading the household, they will begin to function like men in their thirties, while the men, withdrawing from the work force, function more and more like young women.

Brooks' speculation fits the notion of "**contrasexual transition**" as outlined by Gutmann (1990) (Box 7.2). In other words, Gutmann expects women to begin to function in more and more masculine ways, whereas men adopt more feminine modes of responding. The process eventually results in complementary roles but reverses the dominance-submission patterns of the parental years.

The evidence for sex-role reversal in the later years is scant. Even Gutmann's work has been roundly criticized on procedural grounds and because his samples have been very small (McGee & Wells, 1982). Generally, research in this area suggests that men and women move toward **androgyny**—the acceptance of both male and female personality characteristics—rather than contrasexuality. Haan (1981, 1985, 1989) clearly demonstrated increasing openness and nurturance for both sexes. Furthermore, women may not actually become more aggressive or achievement-oriented with time but simply may have greater opportunities to express themselves in instrumental ways. Over the

Box 7.2 Focus on Research: Interpretive science

Recently, researchers have begun to argue that developmental psychologists interested in the adult years ought to make more and better use of autobiography and biography as a research tool (Wrightman, 1988). In a brilliant example of how a biography can become a case study for the developmentalist, David Gutmann (1990) writes about the life of Ernest Hemingway, arguing that Hemingway's story shows how the contrasexual transition of middle age may predict disastrous events in the lives of men who cannot accept their feminine side.

Gutmann argues men reared by destructively domineering mothers and passive fathers are unable to deal with the midlife transitions of their wives toward greater assertiveness and active mastery just at the time they themselves may be feeling more passive and emotional. Wealthy men, Gutmann argues, may try to stave off the consequences by divorcing and remarrying a younger woman. Men who are less well-off may try to prevent the wife's transition, producing depression and unhappiness in her life instead of his own.

For Gutmann, Hemingway's life demonstrates how this particular set of life circumstances can be played out. Hemingway's mother was a very angry, demanding woman who often humiliated his father, even bringing a lover into the household. Moreover, she dressed the young Ernest as a girl long past the age when boys are expected to start wearing more masculine clothes. Ernest, according to Gutmann, said his mother was more dangerous dead than most people were alive. He did not attend her funeral. Gutmann believes that Hemingway's tragic preoccupation with the dilemmas of manhood arose from his peculiar family circumstances. In the course of his adult years, Hemingway married four times. His third wife was quite young and a successful journalist herself. After marrying her, however, Hemingway attempted to keep her at home and prevent her from continuing her career as a foreign correspondent. She left him.

His last wife was again much younger than he, living out her life in a series of crippling illnesses, accidents, and depressions that made it possible for Ernest to have the traditional, compliant wife he apparently needed. Even so, Hemingway progressed through increasing alcoholism to paranoia and finally committed suicide at the age of sixty-one. Gutmann points out that one of the last novels Hemingway wrote was the story of a wife who becomes explicitly masculine and tries to destroy her husband's manhood. Gutmann has described a number of middle-aged men hospitalized for psychiatric problems who have had childhood family constellations similar to those of Hemingway and who appear, like him, to be unable to make the sex-role transitions of adulthood.

adult years, women with the highest need for achievement tend to go back to work. The experience of employment may have more to do with the direct expression of achievement needs and aggression than the decay of parental roles (Baruch, 1967).

Finally, although personality traits may change with age, there are more overt aspects of gender typing to be considered in addition to the subjective experience we have been discussing. People develop a **gender identity**—that is, a self-concept that is masculine or feminine. They also hold certain beliefs about what is appropriate behavior, and they behave in more or less traditional ways. Research has focused on how well a person's verbal report of his or her self-concept matches the cultural sex-role stereotype or how closely scores on tests and in interviews match this stereotype; but little work has been done on other kinds of overt behaviors or on beliefs.

The research that does exist suggests that contrasexual transition, or even androgyny, does not occur in the everyday behavior of men and women. When men retire, for example, they do not begin to help out with the house-work; women continue to do it and often complain of less leisure and independence with the husband's retirement. The wives of retired men report a loss of privacy and less time for their own social network because they must begin to cater to the needs and desires of their retired husbands. Furthermore, inequalities of language, both verbal and nonverbal, continue in old age. Women speak when spoken to in old age as in youth. They lower their gaze and generally behave in more submissive ways. Men retain control of the conversation at senior citizen's centers, just as they did at the Rotary Club in their youth (Keating & Cole, 1980; McGee & Wells, 1982). Clearly, more research along these lines seems warranted before we can speak of contrasexuality.

Summary

I.   Midlife: Crisis, Challenge, or Consolidation?
     A. Two distinct points of view, the crisis school vs. the no-crisis school, emerge in the literature on midlife.
         1. Clinicians and psychiatrists tend to support the view that there is a midlife crisis.
             a. The work of Roger Gould at UCLA, Daniel Levinson at Yale, and George Vaillant and Charles McArthur at Harvard have been important sources of data for those who believe a crisis occurs.
             b. These studies suggest a nearly universal transitional period of adulthood occurring around age forty.
             c. Other studies show some degree of crisis, but of a more limited sort. Men seem to experience greater crisis in their forties,

women in their thirties, and middle-aged men report feeling less control over life events than younger men.

   d. College-educated men may experience more turmoil than non-college-educated men. The college-educated report less zest for life, more drinking and drug use, feelings of immobilization, and more often say they have felt on the edge of a nervous breakdown.

   e. Erikson and Jung have both proposed theories that might explain the emergence of a crisis at midlife, although Erikson's description of a conflict between generativity and despair may not reflect all the dimensions of change the clinicians have reported.

2. Sociologists and research psychologists using questionnaires and rating scales have not found strong evidence of a universal, critical transition at midlife.

   a. The climacteric and the "empty nest" do not appear to be traumatic life events. The launching of children seems to be experienced by most women as a positive transition.

   b. Occupational satisfaction and career progress do not predict crisis. Most men see themselves in the prime of life at forty.

   c. Studies of fun and happiness show no age-related trends.

   d. McCrae and Costa have taken the radical stand that there are no age-related changes in personality and there is no evidence of midlife crisis. Their model identifies five stable major aspects of personality: neuroticism, extroversion, openness to experience, agreeableness, and conscientiousness.

3. Michael Farrell and Stanley Rosenberg have suggested that some middle-aged men experiencing crisis may deny that experience. They present a typology of responses to middle-age stress that includes punitive-disenchanted type, the antihero, the pseudo-developed type, and the transcendent-generative type.

   a. Transcendent-generative and pseudo-developed men do not experience crisis, whereas punitive-disenchanted men tend to deny their problems. The antihero type was most likely to report crisis.

   b. Socioeconomic class seemed to be central in predicting how men would negotiate the middle years.

4. It may be that crisis has been defined in too negative a way to fit the data on the middle-aged transition. It represents a challenge to development and a possible opportunity for creativity as well as a difficult period.

B. Timing is an important predictor of satisfaction at midlife. People who are off-time seem to have more difficulty than those whose lives progress in a normal, predictable way.

1. Which social clock people follow may predict whether they experience personality development.
2. Not all people who are off-time are poorly adjusted, however. Some are able to cope with off-time events more easily than others.
3. Neither age nor events alone seem to explain individual responses to the challenges of midlife. It may be that the perception of those events is what is central.

II. Personality: Change and Sameness
   A. Dozens of studies have shown the existence of relative consistency in personality.
      1. Neuroticism, extroversion, psychopathology, openness to experience, occupational interests, egocentrism, dependency, and many other traits appear to be relatively stable over the life span.
      2. Not only the perceptions of subjects but the perceptions of independent judges and spouses confirm that there is much stability of personality in adulthood. However, there is also change in behavior and habits, attitudes and beliefs, as well as relationships and social roles.
   B. The Chicago study was one of the earliest to indicate arenas of change in personality, suggesting movement from active to passive mastery.
   C. The Berkeley studies have also indicated change, especially when subjects are divided into groups based on personality type or lifestyle. This type of change is called genotypic continuity.
      1. Livson's study of women suggests that independents move from dissatisfaction to trust and closeness over the years of midlife, whereas men who have not conformed to gender stereotypes are also more dissatisfied at forty, moving to better adjustment by fifty.
      2. Studies of those who gained IQ points over adulthood suggest that those who gain points have many personality characteristics in common.
      3. Maas and Kuyper's study of the Berkeley parents showed that lifestyle type was a good predictor of life satisfaction among women at seventy, whereas personality type was more predictive for men.
      4. Taken together, these studies suggest that change is more likely to emerge when subjects are divided into groups or types and researchers look for genotypic continuity—that is, for patterns of change that are typical of groups.
   D. Studies of the executive processes, that is, of one's sense of self and how time and life are conceptualized, also show areas of personality development.
      1. Haan's analysis of the Berkeley data suggests that most age-related changes in perception are positive.

2. Haan's data also suggest that people may actually use different types of personality organizations at different stages in the life span.

E. None of these data support the idea of tightly organized stages but perhaps a model that predicts moments or episodes of generativity or opportunity throughout adult life.

F. There has been much debate about sex differences in personality over the life course, and there is some evidence for a contrasexual transition.

1. Men may move toward more nurturant, intimate styles in later middle age, while women become more independent and assertive.

2. It may be that this trend is better described as androgyny than contrasexuality.

3. There is little evidence of changes in gender-role behavior that might be related to any trend toward androgyny or contrasexual transition.

8

Middle Age:
The Interpersonal Context

Grow up as soon as you can. It pays. The only time
you really live fully is from thirty to sixty.

— Hervey Allen

ON MANY DAYS IT SEEMS as though there is so much going on that John doesn't actually have a life at all. Just a series of demands. There is the usual management by crisis at work, but he is used to that now after years in the business. In fact, work is the least of his worries and sometimes even seems like a vacation from the rest of his life. At least people at work respect his opinion and do what he asks them to do. It's his family that's causing the big headaches at this stage of his life. Just when he thought things would be getting easier, they seem to be falling apart.

John's dad died a number of years ago, and his mother insisted on maintaining her usual bull-headed independence. She stayed on at the house his dad built to retire in. It's out in the middle of nowhere, sixty miles from the nearest real city and fifteen miles from a doctor. Now her health is in question and John is trying to decide how to deal with the situation. He's spending half his time on the weekends making the hour-and-a-half drive to the desert to visit his mother in the hospital, talk to real estate agents, and try to cajole her into selling and moving closer to his sister. His sister's kids are gone and she's probably the one who is able to handle his mother best. They'll all have to take a turn, of course, but it may not come to that for a while. The doctor says his mother may recover completely. It was a small stroke. You never know about these things. One thing for sure, though. They have to get her closer to a hospital.

On top of making all those decisions, John's twenty-four-year-old son, Todd, has moved back into the house. They thought he was gone for good when he went off to college. It never occurred to either him or Gloria that Todd might not be able to make it on his own with a college education. But the job market in banking is really bleak right now and Todd just hasn't been able to find anything besides offers as a teller, and he can't really get along on that by himself. John's going to talk to him about finding a roommate. Maybe he and Gloria will even subsidize the deal if they have to. It's not that they don't love Todd. Of course they do. It's just that they were used to their privacy and Todd seems to think that the only one having problems with the arrangement is him. If they ask him where he's going or what time he's going to be home, he acts just the way he did when he was seventeen. He doesn't seem to realize how hard it is on them, having another person in the house again.

And Gloria . . . well, who knows about Gloria. She's having a great time at the new job and getting more and more involved all the time. They eat out most nights now. Gloria's just too busy to cook, and, heaven knows, she deserves whatever she can get at this point. She did a great job with the kids, even if Todd is a pain. It's just that John didn't imagine that just as he was climbing off the career ladder, she'd be getting on. He was looking forward to some long, pleasant evenings in front of the fire when the kids were gone. He'd been thinking Gloria might learn to play golf and they could spend weekends in places like Palm Springs or Florida. Now Gloria's working most Saturdays and traveling by herself to places like Detroit and Omaha, not really places he's dying to visit.

You never know. You think you've got everything under control and it turns out that nothing is ever under control even partially. There's a bright spot though. Ann's going to have a baby. John's really looking forward to being a grandpa. He never had a grandfather and this baby is going to have one of the best grandfathers there ever was. John never had enough time with his own kids, but now it's different. He'll spend all those weekends he thought he would be golfing with Gloria helping Ann out. Life is really weird sometimes. Who would have thought he'd be looking forward to changing diapers at fifty-four?

IN AN AFFLUENT MODERN SOCIETY LIKE OURS, the middle generation acts as the load-bearing wall. Middle-aged people take responsibility for the stability of the structure and the welfare of both the younger and older generations. People in their middle years run the government, manage the work force, pay the bills, and hope to leave a better world behind them when they are ready to pass the privileges and obligations of power on to the next generation.

Furthermore, middle-aged people do all of this at a time when their own personal lives are beset by change. As one moves through the years from forty to sixty-five, the experiences of family, marriage, work, and leisure are all altered. Children leave home, and families revert to being a two-person system again. Aged parents become problematic as the years take their toll, leaving older people less and less able to care for themselves. One moves from the highpoint to the final stages of a career and must begin to prepare successors. Leisure assumes new significance once children leave and retirement looms in the not-so-distant future.

In the next few pages, we will discuss how the social world of the middle generation changes and how those changes affect the attitudes and adjustments of people in their middle years. Researchers have only begun to examine the problems and rewards of this period in social terms. Midlife crisis may be a personal, subjective event, but life in middle age is related in a million ways to every conceivable aspect of the social environment. The multiple interactions that characterize all human development are most profoundly evident in the lives of human beings in their most active and powerful years as adults.

Marriage and Family

They were a happy family once, she thinks. Jeffrey and Melinda were beautiful, healthy babies; charming toddlers; intelligent, lively, affectionate children . . . Then, last year, when Jeffrey turned fourteen and Melinda twelve, they had begun to change; to grow rude, coarse, selfish, insolent, nasty, brutish and tall. It was as if she were keeping a boarding house in a bad dream, and the children she had loved were turning into awful lodgers—lodgers who paid no rent, whose leases could not be terminated.

—Alison Lurie

When Charles Dickens wrote, "It was the best of times; it was the worst of times," he could have been describing marriage at midlife: full of promise and disappointment, satisfactions and turmoil. For some, the transition from parent of an adolescent, through launching, to the empty nest comes as a relief. For others, the exit of children means looking across the empty nest at a stranger. Our discussion begins with a look at marriage and family in the stage of family life when parents are confronted by the adolescence of their children.

Middle-Aged Parents and Adolescent Children

Sometime between the ages of twelve and fourteen, most children begin the transition from childhood in ways that can be exasperating and difficult but that are, nonetheless, a hallmark of adolescence in this society. Like physical growth, social and personal development undergoes uneven but accelerated change. Between parent and child, the process generally looks like a series of zero-sum (nobody wins) challenge matches characterized by bickering, nagging, and quarreling.

Despite all this unpleasantness, surprisingly few core issues are at stake. Most adolescents feel much the same way about marriage and family, religion and politics as their parents. The value teenagers place on achievement, idealism or materialism, and their political orientation is well predicted by how their parents stand on these issues (Troll, 1989). The real struggles are over much less abstract, even trivial everyday issues. Twelve-year-olds don't want to go to bed at eight o'clock. They want to ride their bikes after dark. By thirteen, they want to take a spin with a friend's sixteen-year-old brother. They want to take the bus to the movies on Saturday night. At fourteen, they don't want to report their whereabouts all the time, and they don't want to be told when to do their homework. They want to turn up the stereo, go to "R"-rated movies, and stay up all night playing computer games and drinking Coke. These may not be the issues that try one's soul, but they do try one's patience (on both sides of the generation gap).

Day-to-day interaction between parent and child may be downright disagreeable, especially if Mom and Dad start making split decisions. Friction increases between all members of the family (siblings usually have opinions about family conflicts). The research indicates that family relationships reach an all-time low point just as the first child leaves home (Anderson, Russell, & Schumm, 1983; Rollins, 1989). Marital satisfaction is lower in middle age than in early adulthood or later life, probably because of the role overload and strain that is described in John's story. There is just too much to do to do it all well, and some of the criticism that takes place between spouses probably is promoted by the fact that most middle-aged people find themselves performing less than optimally in one role or another much of the time (Rollins, 1989).

Eventually, the overt battles taper off, but parents still worry, even though there is less overt conflict. By the time children are sixteen or seventeen, parents are more concerned about sex and drugs and whether they have equipped their children to deal with a world so different from the one they knew (Miller, 1976). Most psychoanalytic thinkers believe that family tensions are heightened during a child's adolescence by a "striking reappearance of the oedipal drama" (Adelson & Doehrman, 1980). That is, the psychoanalysts argue that sexual feelings toward the parent of the opposite sex (feelings repressed since the age of sex or seven) resurface in adolescence when hormonal changes pave the way to adult sexual status. Between mother and son or father and daughter, continual "picking at each other" may reflect oedipal tension. "The boy may suddenly turn surly or sullen or cocky or competitive or scornful vis-à-vis his father; the girl may treat her mother with withering scorn or her most patronizing, brittle 'friendliness,' or may be overcome with dark, inexplicable rages" (Adelson & Doehrman, 1980, p. 278).

Other writers have suggested that the problems of midlife, the evaluation of one's career status, the rethinking of the marriage and one's sexuality, correspond to the problems adolescent children are facing. This parallelism may aggravate the parent's attempts to cope with his or her own internal psychological changes. Furthermore, the kinds of decisions adolescents make can be very expensive (the decision to go away to school) or exceedingly complex for the parent (the decision to enter into a sexual relationship coupled with a request for assistance with birth control) (Rollins, 1989). How parents react to these events depends on a variety of social, economic, and personal forces, but one of the most important factors is the sex of the parent.

Mothers and Adolescent Children

Whether or not oedipal issues are at stake, the psychoanalytic description often rings true. However, the degree to which these normal hassles become personal disasters for parent or child depends on the lifestyle and personality of the parents. For example, among women who are full-time homemakers, especially the college-educated wives of high-status men, middle age and the children's adolescence is likely to be a stable, happy period. These women possess high morale and self-esteem and are giving and warm despite the troublesome transition their children face (Stroud, 1981). Working women who are very committed to their careers are quite likely to have been divorced and to have remained single during this period; and, in at least one study, these women were judged to be as warm and giving as the homemakers, and the least negative of any group in the study (Stroud, 1981). Gloria, John's wife in our opening anecdote, is most likely experiencing a very positive phase of her own life course.

The women who seem to have the greatest difficulty negotiating this phase are those who are equally committed to work and family. These **dual-track women** appear assertive and independent but report low morale, low self-esteem and seem rather cold. Livson (1981) refers to dual-track women as **independents.** Her results suggest this group is very uncomfortable in the traditional feminine role during their children's adolescence. Another group, identified as **unstable workers** by Stroud, became hostile, angry, depressed, and negative in early middle age. They had worked off and on again throughout their married lives but did not really enjoy either their marriages or their children. Still, they had no sense of satisfaction in their work lives.

Dual-track women and independents may well include a good many dual-career women who delayed childbearing in order to establish themselves in careers and, therefore, are those most likely to have younger adolescents during middle age. Having adolescents might seem to ease some of the strains of child rearing, since teenaged children do not require as much physical care and supervision as younger children. On the other hand, as Lucia Gilbert and Sherwin Davidson (1989) point out, women often feel more pressure to be available during the teenaged years of their children, especially if the children are having trouble in school or beginning to experiment with sex or drugs. Working women also have a tendency to blame themselves and their careers when problems arise in the family.

"Oh, to be only half as wonderful as my child thought I was when he was small, and only half as stupid as my teenager now thinks I am." Rebecca Richards

In one large-scale study of middle-aged women (Baruch, Barnett, & Rivers, 1983), mothers were classified as either **autonomous** or **coupled.** The autonomous mothers viewed their children as individuals and seemed to feel rewarded by their growing independence and maturity. Autonomous mothers liked their children as people and were proud of their development. Coupled mothers were more likely to refer to the rewards of feeling special and irreplaceable in the lives of their children. For the coupled mothers, children provided a sense of meaning in life. Coupled mothers felt needed by their children but appeared anxious and depressed and exhibited low self-esteem when compared to the autonomous group.

As Alice Rossi (1980) has pointed out, there is little doubt, regardless of what kind of mother a middle-aged woman is, that children and the family life cycle are still the central concern. Women's lives are shaped by family events and women in their thirties and forties mention children in listing the best and worst events of the last year twice as often as men do. In their late forties, women are three times as likely as men to mention children on their best- and worse-event list. Nonetheless, a growing body of evidence points to the importance of satisfaction and involvement with family in the overall life satisfaction of men as well (Tamir, 1982, 1989).

Fathers and Adolescent Children

For middle-aged fathers, Farrell and Rosenberg (1981) report that personality type is a critical determinant of family outcome. Of the four types described, in *Men at Midlife* (see Chapter 7), the transcendent-generative man was most likely to be satisfied with marriage and fatherhood, whereas the punitive-disenchanted man often reported problems with his children and said that, after twenty years or more, marriage just was not rewarding anymore.

Farrell and Rosenberg believe middle-aged men use their families to express their needs for both love and control. As the children reach adolescence, fathers frequently become more authoritarian, acting as if the maturation of their children threatened them personally. They may even view the child as a traitor or an enemy when the child moves away from the family. Mothers are usually closer to the children than fathers, and in many families, mothers form alliances with their adolescent children as they try to prevent more trouble with the father and to protect him from experiencing loss of control. The alliance keeps Dad in the dark; he never really knows what's going on. Of course, he is a conspirator too. He pretends as if nothing is happening, although his wife and children may seem alien at times, even dangerous. Mom gives Suzie money for birth control pills, and Dad never notices the expense. Mom covers up Billy's poor grades, and Dad never asks to see report cards.

To complicate matters, in the Farrell and Rosenberg study, both parents often exaggerated how much family values and customs differed from those of the outside world. In some families, parents saw violations of family codes as "concrete proof of criminal tendencies," in the child (1981, p. 146). Parents feel a heightened distrust of the social system over which they have so little power. They really believe an adolescent who is two hours late may have met with foul play. To ease their personal discomfort, they try to slow the child's growing independence just when it should be encouraged. The child rebels, causing more anxiety until the son or daughter leaves home in the midst of open warfare.

Farrell and Rosenberg think it possible to ward off the worst catastrophes. When a father confronts the conflicts generated by his own declining power and by the wife-child alliance, refusing to pretend that all is well until things blow up, the situation can often be redeemed. Fathers in the Farrell and Rosenberg study had a greater difficulty letting go of their children than did their wives. Fathers experienced a stunned sense of loss while mothers managed to persevere. Although the father's role frequently appeared to the outsider to be peripheral, his emotional involvement was considerably more intense than outward appearances suggested, even though he was unable to see what was going on or to evaluate his own contribution to it.

Certainly, the battle between parents and children, the formation of secret

For some middle-aged parents, the lives of their children represent the only opportunity for the fulfillment of their own youthful dreams.

alliances, the conflict between ties to the past and the need to move on, as well as the physical and emotional changes of midlife have implications for the middle-aged marriage. It is not hard to see why middle age may represent a low point of marital satisfaction compared to other stages of life. In a way, it is remarkable that so many middle-aged people stay together. For, despite recent increases in separation and divorce, divorce occurs less often in middle age than earlier in marriage; and, when marriage survives midlife, relationships with children usually improve and satisfaction with marriage rebounds.

The Empty Nest

Let us not be too particular; it is better to have old second-hand diamonds than none at all.

—Mark Twain

In a number of studies, a U-shaped curve has been found to best represent the course of marital satisfaction over the family life cycle (Anderson, Russel, & Schumm, 1983; Rollins, 1989). Although declines are gradual, feelings of satisfaction with marriage reach an all-time low during the adolescence of the children and recover significantly only after the last child has departed. Furthermore, the more children a couple has and the longer the marriage, the greater the midlife slump.

Since the overall decline is relatively small, however, it is undoubtedly the case that some couples may actually show increases in satisfaction over time while many couples experience large changes in a negative direction. However, most middle-aged couples stay together anyway. The divorce rate continues to decline between forty-five and fifty-four despite high levels of stress and low levels of satisfaction (Rollins, 1989). Why don't more middle-aged people get divorced?

Perhaps they see few viable alternatives. Financial pressures and the presence of children may make it difficult for middle-aged people, especially women, to envision a single lifestyle that makes sense. However, couples may also stay together in anticipation of the rewards of the empty-nest marriage. Tensions ease in the empty nest, partly because the attitudes of late-middle-aged men change toward interpersonal relationships, and the amount and quality of time women have for their own interests or careers increase. Couples also have more time to spend together. On the other hand, couples without children also show increases in marital satisfaction during late middle age (Barber, 1989), so it may be that the personal and career changes that characterize middle age are more conducive in general to marital satisfaction. Like John, in our opening vignette, the middle-aged man may be ready to share more of his life with his wife and to be more available to his family at the same time that his wife is feeling less strain about living her life in a way that suits her.

Middle-aged men feel less compelled to be highly involved at work (Tamir, 1982; Gutmann, 1990), whereas women may feel more comfortable with their

After the last child leaves home, couples in middle age reassess and readjust their lifestyles, many continuing a vigorous lifestyle well into their old age.

career roles whether they have children or not. It may be that the social pressure to pursue one's traditional sex role is experienced as less important during late middle age, allowing people to express themselves more freely and choose their activities in less restricted ways. Figure 8.1 presents data for women's perceptions of the equity of their marriages and their contentment at different stages in the life span. Increases in contentment beginning in middle age may be related to increases in women's perception that the marital arrangement is fairer after children leave home and men become less involved in their own careers (Traupmann & Hatfield, 1983). It may also be, of course, that many of the most unhappily married people are divorced by middle age, although the few longitudinal studies of those who do not divorce also suggest the kind of changes presented in Figure 8.1

Of course, not all empty-nest marriages improve. If circumstances produce a loss of income, or if significant health problems arise, or if one or more children continue to be dependent after leaving home, marital satisfaction may not recover (Skolnick, 1981). About one-quarter of all married men continue to feel unhappy in their marriages after the children leave, especially older men who have fewer children, a strong nurturing orientation and who lack feelings of companionship with their wives (Barber, 1989).

One of the more interesting literatures developing in the study of the un-

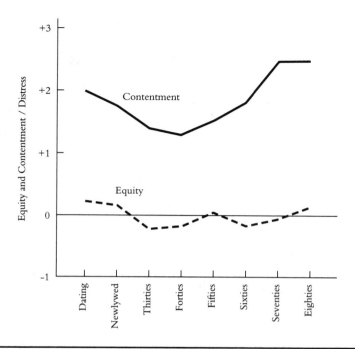

Figure 8.1 Women's perceptions of the equity of their marriages, and their contentment/distress at different stages in the life span.

SOURCE: Traupmann & Hatfield, 1983, p. 96.

happy empty nest is the study of what happens when children return home unexpectedly. Most often, parents are unhappy and surprised by their children coming home (Barber, 1989). They complain about the children coming and going all hours of the day and night, the increases in cleaning and maintenance, and the problems of entertaining the child's friends. Returning to our opening anecdote, John's son Todd would be well advised to help out around the house and keep a reasonable schedule if he wants to get along with his parents.

It's not likely that Todd will see it that way, however. In one study of fifty-five young adults living at home (Shehan and Dwyer, 1989) the researchers report that young men are likely to believe that their parents have a responsibility to provide them with a home and they see themselves as providing companionship for their parents. "Apparently, some college-aged children believe the myth of the empty nest syndrome" (Shehan & Dwyer, 1989). That is, they believe their parents were unhappy they left and are glad to see them home again. According to these authors, Todd is likely to focus on his own problems. He will complain about the lack of privacy he feels at home and his own lack of freedom but is unlikely to mention the financial burden on his parents.

It's interesting to note that if Todd were a girl, he would be less likely to live at home and more likely to have a job. Fifty-two percent of all men ages twenty to twenty-four are living at home, whereas only 33 percent of the women in this age bracket are doing so (Shehan & Dwyer, 1989). This may be because women this age are more likely to be living outside the home with an older man who may be established in a career. It may also be that women in this age range are more likely to take less well-paid entry-level positions in order to leave the parental home because they do not intend to pursue their initial career as fully as men in the same age range.

Because older married people are generally more satisfied than single elderly people, the resolution of marital problems in midlife may make all the difference later on. Arlene Skolnick (1986b) has speculated that recent cohorts have too often chosen divorce, unaware that even longstanding problems can ease later in life. Of course, remarriage offers continuing companionship too. It would be helpful to know if remarriages in middle age are as satisfying as the long-term variety. We can also expect some spectacular cohort effects over the next few years, as younger cohorts (already marked by high divorce rates) begin to renegotiate midlife commitments to marriage and family. How will people react to such negotiations when the wife has a longstanding career? What happens when a midlife marriage is a second or third marriage? What happens when stepchildren refill the empty nest or the wife's grandchildren from the daughter of a former marriage become a focus of her attention?

One thing we do know is that the middle generation has always cared, in many different ways, for the younger one even after the nest is quite bare. Through the exchange of gifts, the loan of money, and the support of social institutions like education, middle-aged people help younger generations. Furthermore, as children reach middle age, they contribute more heavily to the welfare of their aging parents, through state-supported institutions like Social Security and Medicare and through direct financial gifts, as well as by offering physical and emotional support.

The Lineage Family

Designing good research on family relationships presents a variety of complex problems. For one thing, researchers often fail to induce members of various generations of the same family to participate, and it is not easy to keep the data sorted out by family. Analyses that allow one to maintain family relationships and also provide one with information about how families operate as a whole are very complex and, therefore, infrequently used.

Even the terminology for family relationships presents problems. Writers talk about the **lifetime family,** consisting of parents and one set of offspring (sometimes referred to as the nuclear family), and the **lineage family,** consisting of a middle generation, their parents, and their children. The latter defini-

Maintaining a fit body helps to ensure a long and vigorous life. Whatever advances medicine may achieve by the year 2000, the quality of an older person's life will still depend largely on personal habits.

IF THE U.S.
WANTS FREEDOM
FOR KUWAIT,
WHY NOT
LITHUANIA

Elderly people who remain socially and physically active continue to demonstrate high levels of cognitive performance.

In old age, creative output is more likely in works that synthesize a lifetime of experience—such as history and philosophy—than in works that require cognitive audacity—such as pure mathematics and theoretical physics.

A network of friends and family is a mainstay of support through the losses of later adulthood. Although the family plays the central role in times of crisis, a strong social network seems essential for the maintenance of a positive self-concept.

Marriage seems to be the most satisfying in later life, and both men and women perceive greater equality in their relationship. Perhaps the later years of marriage are particularly precious because the couple knows that widowhood will end their life together before long.

Many people continue working past sixty-five, some out of economic necessity but others for the satisfaction of being productive. Their psychomotor capacities may be less, but older workers are more reliable and more accurate than younger ones.

For many older people, retirement may mean no longer earning a living, but it does not mean inactivity. Retired people are free to pursue their special interests, and many invest their energies in promoting the good of their community.

It's normal for the older person who is dying and
the family members to experience a kaleidoscope of
emotions: acceptance, denial, resistance, anger,
sorrow. An "appropriate death" is one in which all
these emotions can flourish alongside personal
identity and independence.

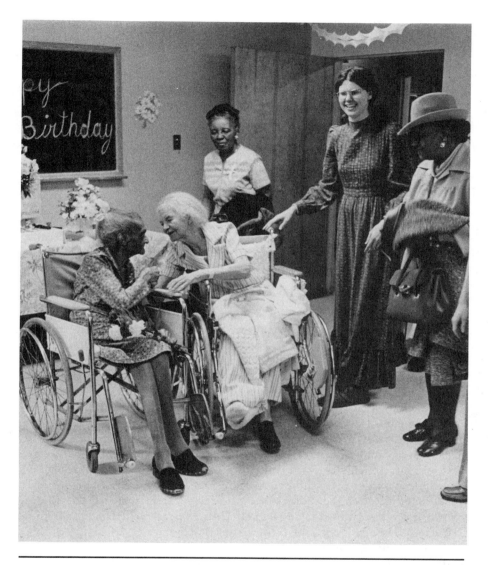

The American family is linked through its women; the emotional heritage flows from mother to daughter rather than from father to son.

tion tends to ignore the growing number of four- and even five-generation families, and no terms are available that apply to blended families. Increasingly, Americans are parenting children that belong to several lineage families. Divorce creates two sets of parents and four sets of grandparents. What do you call your stepfather's mother? Obviously, the relationships in these new forms of extended families are going to be difficult to track but should make interesting copy.

Currently, family research focuses on the traditional three-generation family, and much of it addresses the transmission of values from one generation to the next, or the exchange of goods and services across generational lines. Overall, the evidence indicates that influence, comfort, and support flow easily from generation to generation, particularly from the middle generation to the younger and older ones (Bengston, Cutler, Mangen, & Marshall, 1985; Bengston, Mangen, & Landry, 1984; Troll, 1989; Gatz, Bengston, & Blum, 1990). Middle-aged children are an important resource for the lineage family, and the norm of filial responsibility is strong. Filial responsibility refers to the care that children take of their parents.

Core Values in the Lineage Family

A great many researchers, especially those working since the era of the so-called generation gap, have been interested in what values are transmitted across generations and what values change from one generation to another. Others have looked at the transmission of personality characteristics and behaviors over generations, usually from the middle to the younger generation.

After the rocky years prior to launching, parent-child relationships improve, often quite dramatically. By the time children are of college age, only a small minority (10 percent) do not feel close to at least one parent. Over the years, young adults perceive greater closeness and more family solidarity; however, attachments between daughters and their families are more intense than those between male children and their parents. American families tend to be linked through the mother-daughter relationship, which is usually described as positive and rewarding by both parties once the child enters adult life (Baruch & Barnett, 1983; Troll & Bengston, 1982).

Generally, one finds similarity in intergenerational values although children tend to exaggerate the differences between themselves and their parents and parents tend to underestimate the differences (Troll, 1989). This phenomenon has been called the **generational stake** because the younger generation has a stake in establishing its unique identity and the older one is invested in creating generational continuity (Bengston, Cutler, Mangen, & Marshall, 1985). Certain core values, like political and religious affiliation, are handed down fairly regularly from one generation to the next in all families. In fact, this process happens regardless of closeness or the quality of family relationships (Bengston, Cutler, Manger, & Marshall, 1985; Troll & Bengston, 1982; Troll, 1989). Some researchers have even shown surprising similarity between grandparents and grandchildren in values like orientation toward materialism and humanitarianism. However, Vern Bengston reminds us that period effects can be mistaken for generational transmission. It might well be that the historical influences on grandparents and grandchildren have created a similarity in values rather than teaching or modeling of values. Nonetheless, as Bengston has written: "There is no marked indication of conflict in orientations between aged parents and their children or grandchildren. In short, the 'generation gap' perceived at both the cohort and lineage levels turns out, on closer inspection, to be a dubious set of contrasts reflecting more consensus than cleavage" (Bengston, Cutler, Mangen, & Marshall, 1985, p. 325).

Although there is substantial continuity in certain core values, there are often changes in how these values are expressed. For instance, parents may contribute to the campaign of a favorite antiwar candidate. Meanwhile, their children join a peace demonstration at the university: same belief, different expression. The need to achieve is also transmitted rather strongly, although attitudes toward work per se (such as agreement with the statement "Hard work pays off") are not. The younger cohort may place more faith in creativity, for instance, than hard work.

Cohort differences are also powerfully influential in the development of sex-role orientation and attitudes toward sexual behavior. Research on these issues usually shows that values are not strongly transmitted from parent to child. One study of femininity even reported a negative relationship between femininity in mother and daughter dyads (Troll & Bengston, 1982). Other values like libertarianism, egalitarianism (a belief in the importance of equality in human relationships), and dedication to causes are only moderately transmitted; and, again, specific attitudes vary from one generation to another. For instance, the middle generation may be labeled "liberal" because it supports racial integration, whereas the most important liberal issue for the younger generation is the freedom to live an alternative lifestyle (Troll & Bengston, 1982).

Despite the many similarities, parents and children have very strong feelings about one another—feelings that often erupt in conflict and probably account for the American family's preference for "intimacy at a distance." Parents continue to see children as very high on the list of stressful forces in their lives even when they feel very positive about their adult children. As Lillian Troll (1989) points out, we get most upset about the people who are really important to us.

The study of whether personality characteristics are transmitted across generations is even more complex than the study of attitudes. In one of the Berkeley reports (Clausen, Mussen, & Kuypers, 1981), for instance, parents and children were judged most alike in personality when the parent-child relationship was warm and involved. The personality traits most likely to be transmitted had a rather intellectual flavor, like insightfulness, fluency, and interest in intellectual matters—not surprising since we know that intellectual traits are among the most stable aspects of personality. However, negative parental traits also influenced children in significant ways. If parents were distant, for example, rebelliousness or negativism was more likely in the child.

Intergenerational Exchange

Most frequently, the middle generation is the giving generation, and the recipients are both the older and younger generations. Typically, exchanges occur through the women in the family, from a middle-aged mother to her daughter or to her own mother. Of course, general social institutions, like education and welfare, ensure family well-being and are heavily subsidized by the middle generation. In addition, the middle generation provides cash gifts or loans for college, for buying a home, or for paying medical bills. Social support (about 70 percent of all young adults see their parents weekly) and physical help occur frequently too. Grandma sits for the kids or Dad drops by to lend a hand painting the house or planting the garden (Troll & Bengston, 1982; Sussman, 1977).

Once grandchildren are born, relationships between middle-aged people and their adult children become more complex and the rate of exchange increases. About 75 percent of all older people have grandchildren and most visit them about once a week. Extended-family interaction is even more extensive among black and Mexican-American families. Figure 8.2 presents data on weekly family interactions for people aged sixty to seventy-four.

Interpersonal contact between generations is a source of important emotional and social support. Often, the younger generation interprets and helps the older generations make sense of the technological changes that shape our lives. The middle generation tries to influence both the older and younger generations, and the oldest generation exerts pressure on the middle-aged. There are frequent attempts to influence the dress and grooming of other generations and to change their health-related behaviors. Middle-aged children try to give their parents practical advice on the use of money and time. Middle-aged people also try to influence the younger generation on issues like work, education, money, personal lifestyle, dress, and grooming. Young adults try to change the leisure behavior of their parents and try to change their attitudes on social issues, politics, and sex-role ideology. Interestingly, children tend to see their parents as being more influential than the parents see themselves (Hagestad, 1984).

Middle-aged men most often try to influence their young adult children than their parents. Young women try to change their mothers more than their fathers. All generations try to influence the health of the others from concerns about diet and smoking to seeing the doctor and taking medicine. Young adults see themselves as trying to help their parents and grandparents "keep up with the times" (Troll, 1989).

Women tend to be the **kin keepers** in the family. They are the ones who arrange the family get-togethers, alert others that a family member is in need, and offer help when necessary. Men are more often the advice givers. They

1. "When was the last time you saw your adult children?"
   (Percent responding "within the past week")

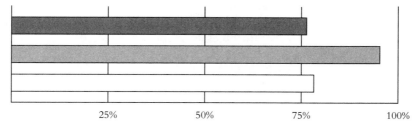

2. "When did you last see your grandchildren?"
   (Percent responding "within the past week")

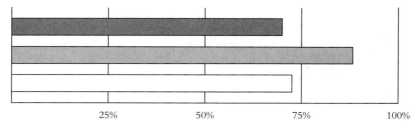

3. "When did you last see any other relatives?"
   (Percent responding "within the past week")

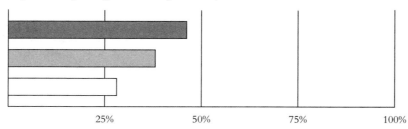

Black respondents ($n = 404$)

Mexican–American respondents ($n = 416$)

Anglo respondents ($n = 416$)

Figure 8.2 Family interactions for blacks, Mexican Americans, and Anglos, age 60–74.

SOURCE: Bengston, Cutler, Mangen, & Marshall, 1985, p. 320.

make recommendations to other family members on taxes, investments, and housing. Mothers and daughters are much closer than any dyad, a close, warm relationship in childhood predicting a close, warm relationship with an adult child. Middle-aged mothers tend to expect a lot from their daughters but tend not to give them credit when they live up to those expectations. On the other hand, these same mothers are likely to lavish praise on their sons. The father-daughter dyad is the most unbalanced in the average family, with the adult daughter giving more than she receives. Nonetheless, adult daughters tend to be more pleased with their relationships to their fathers than to their mothers (Troll, 1989).

All of this contact and pressure takes its toll, of course. Women are especially affected by the difficulties of cross-generational interpersonal relationships. Women are likely to use family members as confidants and are especially likely to see their own children as helpful, particularly when there is a divorce in the middle generation (Hagestad, Symer, & Stierman, 1983). On the other hand, middle-aged women are likely to feel overloaded with family responsibility, particularly if they are trying to care for elderly parents and have children who are off-time—going to school or living at home in their late twenties and thirties (Hagestad, 1984).

Ursula Lehr (1984) has noted that middle-aged women are more exposed to stress in family relationships than men. Especially after the grandchildren are born, women often become more involved with family and less satisfied with intergenerational relationships. Among the older women in her study, those who continued to participate in activities outside the family experienced the highest levels of well-being. Those who were family-centered exhibited increasingly negative attitudes toward family after the last child left home, and experienced increased stress and conflict. The less family-centered women enjoyed family interactions more. Lehr has argued that family-centered women are actually at psychological risk in the three-generation family. Family-centeredness appears to restrict one's life space and glorifies the traditional female role.

Today, however, fewer first-time grandparents fit the stereotype of the sweet old man or woman. In fact, most people become grandparents for the first time in their late forties, when they are still very active outside their own homes. It is becoming commonplace for grandmothers to hold full-time jobs.

Nonetheless, most grandparents take their new role seriously, increasing the role complexity of middle age. Middle-aged people continue to work; to fulfill the role of spouse; to be responsible children, members of the community, citizens, and tax payers; to have a large social network; to volunteer their services to the church, the club, or the local city council; and to take on some share of the rearing of grandchildren. A huge majority (80 percent) of the grandparents polled in one study of Chicago families reported numerous attempts to influence their grandchildren, especially with regard to values and lifestyles. Furthermore, grandparents are often an important factor, for good or bad, in the emergence or resolution of conflict between grandchildren and their parents (Troll, 1980). Speaking of grandparents as a group is somewhat meaningless, however. Their influence varies with age, sex, lifestyle and the expectations they have from the role.

Grandparenting

Grandmothers have been the focus of more research than grandfathers, perhaps because grandmothers have more direct contact with their grandchildren, often providing child care, acting as a surrogate parent when death or divorce strikes the family, or offering rest and recuperation for parents in crisis (Robertson, 1977).

Not all grandmothers are so involved, of course. Most research has described several general types of grandmothering. For instance, Joan Robertson found three common styles. The **symbolic grandmother** functioned as a guardian of the child's moral development, whereas the **individualized** type focused on the emotional satisfaction in her relationship with her grandchildren. Robertson also described an **apportioned** type who found both of these kinds of rewards important.

In an earlier study of grandparenting, Neugarten and Weinstein (1964) had also reported that many grandparents wanted emotional self-fulfillment in their role and tended to focus on companionship and good times with the children. Perhaps because their study included grandfathers as well as grandmothers, they noted several motives not mentioned by Robertson. A summary of the results from this study appears in Table 8.1.

About one third of the Neugarten and Weinstein sample appeared remote from the family. Many of these grandparents, both men and women, felt uneasy about the distance but rationalized it in terms of their own busy lifestyles or strained relationships with their children. Neugarten and Weinstein did not describe any of their female subjects as symbolic grandmothers.

More recent work (Kivnick, 1982, 1985; Miller & Cavanaugh, 1990) has suggested some of the same themes that Neugarten and Weinstein first noted. In these recent samples, grandparents were described in terms of whether the role of grandparenting was central to their lives, a dimension similar to "remoteness" as described by Neugarten and Weinstein. The theme of biological renewal was expressed in statements about carrying on the family line through the clan. The theme of fun-seeking in the new samples was labeled "indulgence." Vicarious accomplishment also appears, but with a more personal flavor, as the reliving and reworking of earlier experiences. These recent studies also suggest that most grandparents derive multiple meanings from the role.

The meaning of grandparenthood and its centrality as a role are very much affected by the age, lifestyle, and sex of the grandparent and the grandparent's relationship to his or her own children (Peterson, 1990). Younger grandchildren feel closer to their grandparents, and in general younger grandparents are more likely to be fun-seeking rather than formal types. Most grandchildren are closest to their maternal grandparents, although there may be a special

Table 8.1 A typology of grandparenting	
Style	**Characteristics**
Formal	Always interested in child, provides special treats, indulges child, may even babysit; but leaves parenting to the parent, does not interfere or give advice
Fun-seeker	Informal, playful relationship like a playmate; authority is irrelevant, expects mutually satisfying emotional relationship; sees grandparenting as leisure
Surrogate parent	Grandmother assumes actual care-taking responsibilities, as when the mother is working
Reservoir of family wisdom	Distinctly authoritarian grandfather dispenses special skills or resources; parents are subordinate to him as well as the child
Distant figure	Visits on holidays and special occasions; contact infrequent and fleeting; benevolent but remote

SOURCE: Based on Neugarten & Weinstein (1964).

bond between paternal grandparents and grandsons. Grandmothers tend to feel closer to all their grandchildren. Grandfathers often report feeling peripheral. Middle-class grandfathers have more contact with their grandchildren than do working-class grandfathers.

Among grandchildren, granddaughters spend more time worrying about, talking to, and visiting their grandparents, but parents influence and help maintain the relationships between grandparents and children. If they are close to their parents, the grandchildren are likely to be close as well. Grandchildren do not feel very close to grandparents they don't see at least several times a year (Peterson, 1989).

In one interesting study of the grandparent role in divorcing families, Colleen Johnson (1989) has reported that divorce loosens the boundaries between generations, affording parents more influence with their adult children than they had during the marriage. Contact between paternal grandparents and grandchildren declines sharply after divorce, partly because about half of all divorced fathers have no contact with their children after the first year of divorce. Divorcing women tend to have custody of the children and turn to their own parents for help.

Grandparents can help ease the strain of a divorce (Johnson, 1989), and the mothers of divorcing sons are likely to maintain contact with their ex-daughter-in-laws to retain the relationships with grandchildren (Johnston & Barer,

1987). This may weaken their relationship with their own son. In Johnson's opinion, divorce strengthens all of the female links in divorcing families. Remarriage, she points out, makes things exceedingly complex. The distance between grandparents and their children increases again, and the remarriage of a son is very problematic because he is even less likely to offer a link to the grandchildren of the former marriage. A close relationship between a son's parents and his former wife can strain the relationship with his new spouse.

Grandparenting is only one side of the generational tug of war for the middle-aged, however. As the years pass, the oldest generation needs more assistance too, and the middle-aged may find themselves pulled in both generational directions.

Filial Responsibility

In time, the oldest generation can become more and more fragile, and eventually so dependent upon their children that a **role reversal** occurs. Middle-aged children take on some of the obligations and responsibilities of a parent, and elderly parents must accept not only their own faltering health but also their growing inability to function without help. If the situation progresses to the point where parents cannot live independently, family relationships usually deteriorate. Whether the problems are created by the illness of the parent or by physical proximity and emotional conflict, no one has yet been able to say (Johnson & Bursk, 1977; Sussman, 1977, 1985; Troll, 1971).

Undoubtedly, the future of the American family will be strongly shaped by the growing number of extremely elderly Americans. Can the middle generation afford to continue as caretakers of the lineage family when there are four or five living generations? Although most researchers see the visiting and helping across generations as a sign of the vitality of the family, some authors (Hess & Waring, 1978; Kruse, 1984; Lehr, 1984) have begun to question the meaning of such assistance. Caring for failing parents and continuing to support the extended adolescence and youth of the younger generation might be more of an emotional and financial burden than anyone should be expected to shoulder. Can John reasonably be expected to look after his mother's affairs, offer his grown son a home, and learn to change his grandchild's diapers? His situation is becoming more and more common as the American family becomes a long-lived "bean pole" with more living generations, each of which has fewer members.

Filial responsibility appears to have especially important consequences. In addition to imposing emotional and financial burdens, caregiving is often associated with physical demands that cause people to neglect their own health. Most studies show elevated levels of depression among caregivers, who have been called the "hidden patients" (Schulz, Visintainer, & Williamson, 1990). Seventy percent of all caregivers attribute the declines they report in their health to their role in caregiving.

A spouse is most likely to be the caregiver for an elderly person. Next

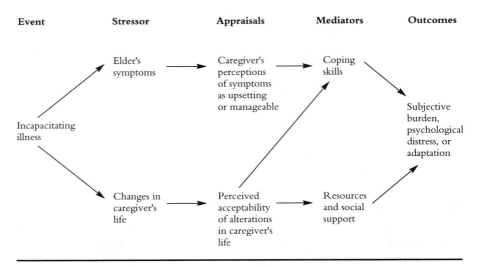

Event   **Stressor**   **Appraisals**   **Mediators**   **Outcomes**

Incapacitating illness → Elder's symptoms → Caregiver's perceptions of symptoms as upsetting or manageable → Coping skills → Subjective burden, psychological distress, or adaptation

Incapacitating illness → Changes in caregiver's life → Perceived acceptability of alterations in caregiver's life → Resources and social support → Subjective burden, psychological distress, or adaptation

Figure 8.3 Conceptual framework for caregiver stress and coping.

SOURCE: Gatz, Bengston, & Blum, 1990, p. 412.

in line, however, is the middle-aged adult daughter. In the USC study of three-generation families (Gatz, Bengston, & Blum, 1990), 18 percent of the caregivers were spouses, 38 percent were adult children, 3 percent were grand-children, 4 percent siblings, and 6 percent nieces or nephews; 31 percent of the caregivers were assisting a spouse's relative.

Neither the absolute amount of assistance an elderly person needs nor the severity of the cognitive deficits they are suffering predicts whether the care-giver sees the job as difficult or burdensome. What does make the job difficult, if not impossible, is disruptive behaviors on the part of the patient, especially difficulties in dressing or bathing the patient or incontinence. Sleep distur-bances, repetitive questions, and the tendency of the patient to follow the care-giver around or to be agitated or combative are all associated with high levels of caregiver stress. However, whether the caregiver feels he or she can cope with the symptoms and how much social support the caregiver has are also important (Schulz, 1988).

Figure 8.3 presents a model of stress that has been used to explain caregiver feelings of burden and difficulty. Those caregivers who do best under difficult circumstances are those who are able to reframe their task as an opportunity for growth and those who have the social and financial resources to have help when they need it and time off for vacations, rest, and recuperation themselves.

Many of the social changes we have discussed seem unlikely to make things easier either. With the extension of the life span and the postponement of marriage and childbearing, we may well be talking about a future middle generation in its seventies or eighties taking care of elderly parents who are in their nineties or past the century mark. The health of that elderly middle generation itself becomes an issue. Who will care for the caretakers? Can a middle generation in its fifties or sixties bear the responsibility for two older generations as well as young adult children? These are some of the hard questions that are posed by the social realities of an aging population at a time when the society is not yet prepared to handle the problems in a systematic, humane way.

General social changes can be expected to alter many of the institutions of adult life. Families are changing. Parenting and marriage are influenced and one's role outside the home is likewise affected. Especially for men, progress through the normal steps of career life are important landmarks in the definition of the life cycle, and middle age is accompanied by important changes in the role and meaning of work. As Marjorie Fiske (1980) has pointed out, although there are many changing patterns of commitment throughout the life cycle, the most basic commitments of all, to love and to work, must be renewed at midlife if personal growth is to continue.

Work

Like many people at midlife, our friend John, in the opening anecdote, has reached the stage of career development called **maintenance** (Van Maanen & Schein, 1977; Williams & Savickas, 1990) or **plateau** (Hall & Rabinowitz, 1988; Bardwick, 1990). John is likely to be in a position to achieve maximum productiveness and to be privy to occupational and organizational secrets. He may share these with some of the younger people he knows, taking the role of mentor. He is a valuable asset to the organization. But internally he feels less involved and motivated. The danger of stagnation inherent in strong feelings of security may create a need for renewal on the job. On the other hand, the danger posed by younger, more ambitious recruits must create fears about holding on (Super, Thompson, & Lindeman, 1988).

In a study of 380 upper and middle managers between the ages of thirty-five and sixty-four, Caitlin Williams and Mark Savickas (1990) found much concern for updating and holding on. They describe many of the younger men in this range as shifting their focus to develop new competencies and expand. Yet, within a few years, many were also partly in the next stage showing signs of deceleration and disengagement, like John. These researchers even found some evidence for deceleration and disengagement among men as early as forty-five. Overall, however, they did not find that the tasks of renewal and holding on or deceleration and disengagement were very well related to age. In fact, Williams and Savickas don't even think they form a sequence. Rather, these authors argue, the concerns of the maintenance stage reflect responses to changes in one's personal and work life. Overall, they conclude, adapting to change was probably the core concern of the maintenance stage for most of these men.

Between forty and sixty, most people reach the pinnacle of the occupational careers, accepting jobs as administrators, managers, supervisors, and members of the board. Recently, however, this progression has become somewhat less predictable. The new "lean, mean" corporation of the nineties has less room at the top (Peters, 1987) and many middle-aged men are less willing to sacrifice their health, family lives, and peace of mind for power or money (Tamir, 1982, 1989).

At midlife, many men and women who have been in career tracks since early adulthood feel burnt-out or depressed on the job (Korman, 1989). They report that their dedication to their careers has hurt their relationships with spouses and children. Men are especially likely to have jettisoned friends and family for work. The "affiliative" costs of success may be very high for those on the fast, upwardly mobile track. Furthermore, the track is narrower than it used to be. In middle age, fear of loss of job and constricted job opportunities are high on the list of job stressors (Hall & Rabinowitz, 1988).

When people first experience career plateauing, they are likely to feel a certain amount of shock. There is less movement and change, fewer surprises, pay levels off, and one finds oneself defending one's position without the learning and growing of earlier career stages. Plateau is often accompanied by feelings of low marketability and lower job involvement, but not necessarily declining performance. People who show high performance and have few prospects for advancement may make up as many as 80 percent of organizational members (Hall & Rabinowitz, 1988). Obviously, corporations and businesses need to attend to how to maintain the loyalty and commitment of these workers.

Among middle-aged workers, a good match between personal interests and job characteristics helps ensure satisfaction. In addition, autonomy and the freedom to be creative are important as well as the chance to do nontrivial tasks and to be involved in decision making. High-involvement organizations offer the opportunity to participate in self-managed teams, and education not only about one's job but about the whole industry so that employees can make meaningful contributions to decision making (Peters, 1987).

Of course, not everyone wants to become more involved in the organization at midlife. Some workers may need the opportunity to develop other areas of their lives, to take more time off or to have a flexible schedule. Douglas Hall and Samuel Rabinowitz (1988) have suggested a **two-path career model** presenting employees with the kind of choices that will maintain commitment and decrease turnover and dissatisfaction at midlife or, for that matter, as things change at any stage of the life course. Figure 8.4 suggests how these paths might run based on an experiment at a Motorola assembly plant in Fort Lauderdale.

People in the higher-involvement path choose jobs that offer more responsibility, autonomy, opportunities for learning and creativity, for lateral movement in the organization, and for participation in decision making and

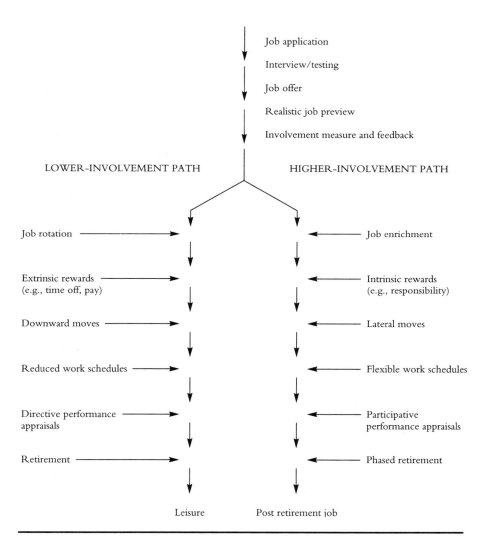

Job application

Interview/testing

Job offer

Realistic job preview

Involvement measure and feedback

LOWER-INVOLVEMENT PATH   HIGHER-INVOLVEMENT PATH

Job rotation ──────────→   ←────── Job enrichment

Extrinsic rewards ──────→   ←────── Intrinsic rewards
(e.g., time off, pay)   (e.g., responsibility)

Downward moves ─────────→   ←────── Lateral moves

Reduced work schedules ──→   ←────── Flexible work schedules

Directive performance ───→   ←────── Participative
appraisals   performance appraisals

Retirement ─────────────→   ←────── Phased retirement

Leisure   Post retirement job

Figure 8.4 Two-path career model.

SOURCE: Hall & Rabinowitz, 1988, p. 74.

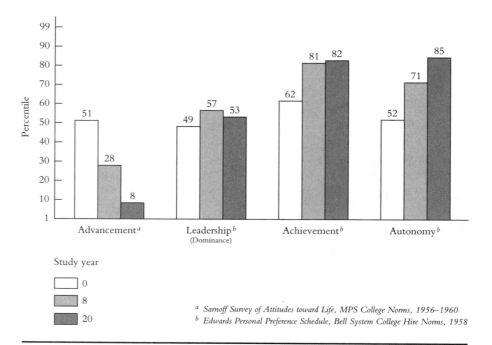

Figure 8.5 Key motivators for managers at entry, eight and twenty years later.
SOURCE: Bray & Howard, 1988, p. 9.

performance appraisals. People who choose the lower-involvement path choose different work experiences, ones that stress extrinsic rewards like pay or time off, and are offered the chance to rotate jobs, as jobs on this track are likely to become too routine. Hall and Rabinowitz also suggest that people be allowed to switch from a high-involvement track to a low-involvement one, or vice versa. "By not having everyone in the organization in the same track, it should be possible to provide more of the activities in each track to just those people who choose it. With resources becoming scarcer, it is becoming increasingly important to get maximum mileage from the rewards we do have to offer" (p. 75).

In a thirty-year longitudinal study of telephone company managers, Douglas Bray and Ann Howard (1988) have shown that the need for advancement is likely to decline quite dramatically over the years from young adulthood to middle age, while the need for autonomy increases. Figure 8.5 presents some of their data.

By midlife, many of the people (both men and women) in this study began to see that their chances for increasingly higher positions were poor. These authors have also identified a similar trend over cohorts. That is, younger people showed lower needs for advancement at the time they were hired than older cohorts did. Bray and Howard argue that younger cohorts have lower expectations for advancement even though they still show high levels of need for achievement. It may be that younger people are adapting to recent trends in downsizing organizations and decreases in the number of management positions available.

Of course, another way to deal with the issue of plateau is to change organizations or even careers, and there are an increasing number of people who do just that. Some move because they are dissatisfied, others because early retirement affords them the opportunity, or because they must leave jobs reserved for young adults (like police officer or athlete). There is little serious research about career change, but growing interest in how and why people change jobs at midlife, how successful they become, and whether or not they are happy may soon pay off in new work on this matter.

Career Change at Midlife

There is a proverb, "As you have made your bed, so you must lie in it," which is simply a lie. If I have made my bed uncomfortably, please God, I will make it again.

—G. K. Chesterton

In one study of blue-collar workers (Kay, 1974), the author reported that as many as 35 percent of those interviewed wished they could begin new careers. People in white-collar professions and management also appear interested in change. There are even men who are willing to take less prestigious jobs at midlife to avoid stress or to attain greater job satisfaction (Stagner, 1985). On the other hand, many middle-level managers and white-collar workers are reentering school in order to develop professional skills. At some eastern colleges, where the enrollment of older students is encouraged, as many as 20 percent of the graduate students are over the age of thirty-five. At California State University, Los Angeles, the average graduate student in psychology is over thirty. Despite these statistics, however, only about 10 percent of all established male workers ever actually change careers (Havighurst, 1982). The desire for change may be satisfied by a shifting emphasis or transfer to a different position in essentially the same line of work.

What data we have indicate that a growing number of people feel dissatisfied with their jobs and think their abilities are underutilized (Havighurst, 1982). Remember, the challenge and interest value of a job are primary rewards at midlife; most jobs are not all that challenging. Today, the average American is over twenty-five; there are more and more middle-aged and late-middle-aged people in the work force. Perhaps in the nineties we will see the number of people making real career changes increase, especially if the economy prospers. Throughout the 1970s and early 1980s, poor economic conditions may have discouraged career change (Stagner, 1985).

What forces encourage a second career? Not everyone who is dissatisfied changes, and not all changes are a product of dissatisfaction. Sometimes an unexpected opportunity arises—an offer that's hard to refuse. A growing company offers a professor a job heading the research department. The children leave or a spouse returns to work, opening up new doors. A salesman tries running his own business. Of course, some people become so bored or burnt-out with their jobs that they have to leave. Others try something new because they have not achieved anything substantial: a dissatisfied school teacher moves on to a job as a computer programmer. People stay in jobs they dislike for a wide variety of reasons as well, from fear of failure to fear of success, and all the emotional and economic fears that tie people down.

Furthermore, older workers are aware that it is harder to find a job in a new occupation after forty. Older people stay unemployed longer when they lose a job. Employers argue that it is less cost-effective to hire an older person. They believe an older worker is less likely to return costs of training and organizational entry. Furthermore, older men and women are generally considered less fit for work than the young and are thought to require closer supervision.

Such arguments are simply not justified. At least 85 percent of all workers are still physically fit for work at the age of sixty-five or more. Working days lost due to incapacity actually decline with age, perhaps because those in poor health retire earlier (Parker, 1982). Besides, people consciously seeking a second career in middle age are unlikely to be in poor health. Intellectually, as we saw in Chapter 6, the middle-aged perform like young adults throughout the working years. In fact, they turn in superior performances on practical problem solving, even when the problems are typical of another stage of the life cycle (Denney, 1982). Performances that require great speed or agility, especially under stressful conditions, deteriorate beginning in midlife, but middle-aged people rarely seek jobs that demand speed or agility as second careers. Even when they do, however, experience or dependability may compensate for declining speed. For instance, compared to the young, older workers arrive on time more often, require less supervision, and are more likely to work right up to the normal finishing time.

The attitudes, personality, and behavior of older workers are generally rated superior, particularly their reliability, conscientiousness, tolerance, reasonableness, and loyalty. Turnover and absenteeism decline with age. All in all, the benefits of hiring middle-aged workers seem to outweigh the problems. Yet occupational mobility declines with age, and both individuals and organizations probably suffer in ways that reinforce negative attitudes. Bored, dissatisfied workers are less productive, are absent more often, and need closer supervision. Cooperation and enthusiasm decline, and people develop hostility toward the organization when dissatisfaction becomes long-term. Studies that focus on the number of years a person has been employed at the same job, rather than on age, would be very useful in this area. No one seems to have asked how years on the job affect people of different ages, although it has been speculated that if a person stays at the same job for fifteen to twenty years, he or she may be immune to burnout (Stagner, 1985). How does a fifty-year-old person with ten years on the job differ from a thirty-year-old with the same amount of experience?

Over the next two decades, the way may be paved for second careers if those now approaching middle age demand changes at the organizational level. The postwar baby boom may have an interesting impact on work, as the baby-boomers enter the ranks of the middle-aged. This cohort will spend more years in the labor force simply because there will not be enough younger people to support the massive pension and retirement system that would move them out of the work force. Older workers become more valuable as the number of younger workers declines; age discrimination may disappear of necessity. Most probably, discrimination will ease as the level of education among workers rises, especially if retraining or returning to school becomes common.

Women and Work at Midlife

Obviously, much of the literature on careers at midlife has been built around data collected on the work lives of men. What data we do have suggests that working women have higher self-esteem at midlife and experience less anxiety and better physical health than homemakers (Coleman & Antonucci, 1983). The middle-aged woman seems to reap substantial benefits from employment unless she also has a small child or encounters opposition from a spouse. And it is the work, not the money, that seems to deliver the benefits, for there is little relationship between income and reported positive effects in the data we have.

There may be some relationship to education, however, as the benefits of work seem to accrue most consistently to well-educated women (Stroud, 1981). At midlife, single women are most advanced in their careers and married college graduates are the next most advanced. Once the empty nest permits these women to divest themselves of the more demanding aspects of maternal responsibilities, they may become more satisfied with their lives. We know that working women are the most satisfied when they are well past the child-bearing years (Jacoby, 1982).

At midlife, women in dual-career marriages appear to make a shift from using coping strategies that focus on understanding the problem (e.g., adopting a different attitude) or managing the stress (e.g., by working more efficiently), to actually changing the situation by rearranging their work hours, their responsibilities, and by hiring out some of the tasks they least enjoy (Gilbert & Davidson, 1989). Decreasing financial responsibility for the children as well as declining child-rearing obligations may make it possible for the dual-career woman to really begin enjoying the wider scope of possibilities she has maintained for herself by continuing to work through young adulthood and early middle age.

On the other hand, middle-aged women just entering the work force are often struggling with unfulfilled goals and values. Middle-aged women want a great deal from work, including increased status and self-esteem as well as help in adapting to aging. Susan Zuckerman (1981) warns that "these intrapsychic forces exist in the context of a rapidly changing, fluctuating, but increasingly accepting social attitude toward working women. The result of the intermixture of these personal and cultural factors can be emotional upheaval, doubt, depression, and a sense of being unfulfilled" (p. 187). We don't know whether women who reenter or become strongly recommitted to work at midlife succeed and are satisfied. In fact, there is very little narrative clinical work about women of the kind done by Vaillant (1977) or Levinson et al. (1978). However, consider these thoughts from Erica Jong (1973):

> Though she is quick to learn
> & admittedly clever,
> her natural doubt of herself
> should make her so weak
> that she dabbles brilliantly
> in half a dozen talents
> & thus embellishes
> but does not change
> our life.
> If she's an artist
> & comes close to genius
> the very fact of her gift
> should cause her such pain
> that she will take her own life
> rather than best us.
> & after she dies, we will cry
> & make her a saint.

The function of work at different points in the life cycle and the meaning of work in individual lives are poorly understood. Most of what we know is expressed in terms of statistics about who does what, for how long, and for how much money. Why has this activity, to which most of us will devote more than a third of our lives, sparked so little interest among psychologists? Perhaps because professional people tend to value work without questioning its meaning or its usefulness. Similarly, the work ethic of the middle class, and upper middle class, may account for the lack of psychological research on the role and meaning of leisure. Given a relatively predictable future, leisure will undoubtedly play an increasingly important role in an extended life span. Already as the work week declines and the number of years spent in the empty nest and retirement increase, leisure is an increasingly prominent feature of the adult life cycle at midlife.

Leisure

The definition of leisure is not really a simple task, although it might seem straightforward until you give it some special thought. Like the old saw about one man's meat and another man's poison, one man's leisure is often another man's work. Jack Nicklaus makes his living doing what millions consider the ultimate in leisure: golfing. Artists, especially writers, moan about how hard they work, how much they suffer, and so on, yet a growing number of Americans participate in the arts and crafts as a form of relaxation, although they may not be averse to selling their products at the local fair or festival. However, if that same person *had* to sell something in order to eat that day, the activity would cease to be leisure.

Certainly, leisure is an economically optional activity. Still, the work of an artist seems more leisurely than that of an assembly-line worker. The notion that work and leisure are the opposite of each other or that they are strictly separated in people's lives is not very helpful. People prefer complex relationships between work and leisure, and combine the two whenever they have the opportunity. Are the doctor and the psychiatrist who refer patients to each other at work or at leisure on the golf course? Is the line supervisor who bowls on the company league working or playing? In her review of midlife issues, Marjorie Fiske (1980) questioned the traditional dichotomy between work and leisure. As she noted, "Confronted with a checklist, [most people] have difficulty in deciding whether a particular undertaking is work or nonwork. On a strictly behavioral level, they can tell us how much time they spend 'on the job,' but this is a geographic rather than a functional allocation ('I was working' equals 'I was *in* the office' or 'I was *on* the job'.)" (p. 249).

Unfortunately, many researchers have looked only at what people do when they are not on the job, how they spend their free time. The results of such surveys are dismaying indeed. Most people spend their free time watching television. Few report having any special hobby or participating in sports or the arts, even as a spectator. Almost no one spends any time engaged in volunteer or civic activities.

This kind of information has led some writers to conclude that Americans simply do not possess a **leisure ethic** (a set of beliefs about how leisure contributes to life). Leisure is seen only as a vacation from work or a reward for working hard. Leisure activities are not valued in and of themselves. This argument assumes that some leisure activities are valuable, of course, and others are not.

After all, watching television is a leisure activity; it just does not gain the approval of those who study leisure. So again, what is leisure? One systematic attempt to treat these issues (Neulinger, 1980) refers to leisure as time when one is free to choose whatever activities one enjoys and to participate in them at one's own pace. In this sense, the opposite of leisure is **constraint.** Some activities must be done in a particular way, at a particular time or speed. Constraints may be imposed by other people (a teacher, for instance) or by the activity itself (video games, for example). Furthermore, some things are fun to do, and we would enjoy them whether or not we were paid. Other activities are so noxious no one will do them for love or money.

Neulinger defines **pure leisure** as an activity that provides freedom and intrinsic motivation. **Pure job** is activity that offers constraint and high extrinsic motivation (like factory work). **Pure work** lies in between leisure and job, offering constraint but also intrinsic motivation. A dancer who loves to dance, an actor who adores acting (and makes a living at it) are engaged in pure work. Leisure and work, then, are not mutually exclusive (Neulinger, 1980).

Something is still missing from our discussion, however, because we have not identified why it is that television watching is considered a poor use of leisure time. It is not strongly constrained (as long as you don't really care what you watch), and if you like it, it is intrinsically rewarding. The usual criticism has to do with passivity; that is, television watching is not an active pursuit. Table 8.2 presents a scheme of leisure that classifies activities by the level of involvement and energy they require. Television watching, along with sleeping, resting, and reading require relatively little energy. Forms of leisure that offer more involvement generally command more approval in the literature. Yet acceptable leisure activity is not defined by involvement alone, for those activities at the highest level of intensity, like sex and the use of psychoactive drugs, are often not even considered leisure.

Some writers contend that only those leisure activities that retain some of the meanings associated with work are considered acceptable (Gordon, Gaitz, & Scott, 1977; Cutler & Hendricks, 1990). A leisure career may be considered legitimate only if it contributes to one's development (like physical exercise, learning, and travel), or offers potential economic rewards (like the arts and crafts). However, most Americans are so work-oriented that they see leisure almost exclusively as compensation for working hard or as "spill-over" from work. Spill-over leisure involves activities, such as the physicians' Wednesday afternoon golf game, that parallel or complement work (Burrus-Bammel & Bammel, 1985).

Perhaps because of the close connection between work and leisure, people believe that one must be good, or at least not awful, not only on the job but at leisure as well. Over the life span, people tend to choose less active pursuits, and although health drives some of this change, it is also possible that older people choose low-involvement activities because of the **portent of embarrassment,** that is, because they are afraid they will make fools of themselves through poor performance. Older people don't take up football or ballet not only for physical reasons but also because they may look or feel awkward.

Middle age is a time when some of these shifts in activities begin to appear (Atchley, 1988; Kelly, 1987a), although a number of factors besides age appear to influence the type and continuity of leisure pursuits. Higher socioeconomic class is associated with the choice of higher-involvement activities although less strongly than one might suppose, and type of occupation as well as education affects leisure choices. People who have strong social support networks continue to remain involved in the leisure activities they pursued in young adulthood and middle age. Gender differences also predict certain effects. Men participate in discretionary activities more often, particularly in outdoor recre-

Table 8.2 Leisure activities according to intensity of expressive involvement

Intensity of Expressive Involvement	Forms of Leisure Activity
Very high	Sexual activity
	Psychoactive chemical use
	Ecstatic religious experience
	Aggression, "action" (physical fighting, defense or attack, verbal fighting)
	Highly competitive games and sports
	Intense and rhythmic dancing
Medium high	Creative activities (artistics, literary, musical, etc.)
	Nurturance, altruism
	Serious discussion, analysis
	Embellishment of instrumental activity (art or play in work context)
Medium	Physical exercise and individual sports
	Cognitive acquisition (serious reading, disciplined learning)
	Beauty appreciation, attendance at cultural events (galleries, museums, etc.)
	Organizational participation (clubs, interest groups)
	Sightseeing, travel
	Special learning games and toys
Medium low	Socializing, entertaining
	Spectator sports
	Games, toys of most kinds, play
	Light conversation
	Hobbies
	Reading
	Passive entertainment (as in mass-media usage)
Very low	Solitude
	Quiet resting
	Sleeping

ation, including hunting, fishing, spectator sports, and travel. Women tend to prefer cultural and home-based activities (Cutler & Hendricks, 1990).

Although leisure activity outside the home declines with age, solitary activities (such as cooking for men) remain steady or may even increase for some individuals (Kelly, 1987b). Membership in certain types of organizations also changes in middle age since peak membership in youth groups and school organizations occurs in families with school-aged children. However, longitudinal studies of leisure do suggest basic continuity over the life course in level and types of activities. There is even some evidence that childhood leisure predicts leisure in adulthood to some extent (Cutler & Hendricks, 1990).

Most studies of leisure over the life span treat age or sex or socioeconomic class as an independent variable and look for effects on type or amount of activity. Very few studies look at leisure as the independent variable, but we do know that satisfaction with leisure activities (not amount, but perceived quality) is associated with higher levels of general life satisfaction (Cutler & Hendricks, 1990). Other questions might include whether leisure contributes to the maintenance of identity in later life and how it affects family and social relationships. We know that health predicts level of involvement in leisure, but it is also possible that leisure promotes health. There is evidence that exercise reduces several types of mortality (Schnurr, Vaillant, & Vaillant, 1989). Other forms of leisure like meditation or participation in self-development groups may also contribute to mental and physical well-being.

Stephen Cutler and Jon Hendricks (1990) have suggested that we need to study leisure as a form of consumption as well. People buy all sorts of objects in the pursuit of leisure from cameras and video equipment to golf clubs and tennis balls. What part do these objects play in the definition of self over the life course? Are they associated with status differences? What does it mean to have a terrific bowling ball as opposed to a pool cue or a wonderful set of golf clubs? Do these meanings change over the life course? For instance, a person who is a great bowler may be treated very differently at thirty-five than at seventy-five.

We simply don't know much about what effects leisure has on people. Perhaps we have neglected the study of leisure because of the tendency to equate work with goodness and leisure with evil. Idle hands are the devil's workshop. Great social systems decayed, we are told, because people did not work hard and long enough. Until we are able to examine and understand our own attitudes toward work and leisure more clearly, it seems unlikely that we will even ask the right questions. Yet many economic and social changes are likely to increase the leisure time in our lives. The average number of hours people work each week is declining and flexi-time presents many workers with the opportunity for a four-day work week. Industries are choosing locations with an eye to leisure and recreational facilities, and the shift of jobs from blue-collar to the service industries and white-collar work may leave people with more energy for leisure (Cutler & Henricks, 1990).

There are also cohort changes in attitudes toward work and leisure. Younger people are not nearly as concerned about what is and is not work.

They are more willing to include some features of work in their choice of leisure activities, as one does in volunteer and civic activities, and to bring their leisure to work. The very elderly, on the other hand, have rarely made the transition from valuing work to valuing leisure and are, therefore, unable to mix the two (Kaplan, 1979). However, the young-old, the middle-aged, and the young appear to place far more value on leisure as an end in itself.

In this chapter, we have seen that the meanings of both work and leisure appear to be changing and that today's middle-aged and those who are about to become so seem to be demanding very different things than those who have moved through the labor and leisure force before them. People want interesting, significant work that is well integrated with the rest of their lives. People want more time to pursue leisure in an effective way, including longer blocks of time, and the right to choose from a wider range of activities. It is possible that a leisure ethic is developing as the conditions of work and the course of the adult life span change.

Summary

I. Marriage and Family
   A. Parenting and marriage in middle age change with the age of the children involved.
      1. Between ages twelve and fourteen, typically, there is a struggle over the rules for everyday living.
      2. By ages sixteen or seventeen, the issues are more serious and may represent a reappearance of the oedipal drama.
      3. Marital satisfaction reaches an all-time low as the last child is launched.
   B. There are sex differences in the response middle-aged people make to parenting an adolescent.
      1. For women, commitment to work and family plays an important role in how marriage and family are experienced, with those committed to both areas having the more difficult time.
      2. Men seem to use the family to express their needs for both love and control and often become more authoritarian and threatened with the adolescence of their children.
      3. Alliances between mothers and children are common in the attempt to prevent fathers from experiencing loss of control.
   C. During the stage of the family cycle when the children are adolescents, marriage generally reaches a nadir of satisfaction. Yet most middle-aged people stay together.
      1. As children leave home, satisfaction in marriage often rebounds, especially for those who have fewer children and marriages of shorter duration.

2. The increasing emphasis men place on the quality of interpersonal relationships and the movement of middle-aged women from the home to the outside world may contribute to the rebounding satisfaction of marriage at middle age.

3. Increased time together, especially time spent in joint or shared leisure activities, may be important in the improvement of middle-aged marriage.

4. The impact of refilling the empty nest is generally negative for middle-aged parents, who feel a loss of freedom and privacy.

   a. Young adults who live at home feel they should be provided with room and board. They fail to see the problems their parents are having.

   b. More research is needed on the impact of divorce, remarriage, and stepchildren in middle age.

II. Research on the three-generation family has made it clear that both financial and emotional support as well as influence flow from one generation to another, particularly from the middle generation to the older and younger ones.

   A. Values, especially religious and political affiliation, achievement motivation, and attitudes toward work are handed from one generation to the next although the particular expression of those values may change.

      1. Warmth of family relationships seems to have little influence on the transmission of values.

      2. Despite familial similarities, strong feelings often erupt into conflict. Adult children and their parents prefer intimacy at a distance.

   B. Sex-role orientation and attitudes toward sexual behavior are not strongly transmitted over generations, whereas liberalism and egalitarianism are moderately transmitted.

   C. The intellectual side of personality shows the strongest continuity from one generation to the next. The transmission of other characteristics is affected in complex ways by feelings of warmth and closeness.

   D. Financial and physical support flow from the middle generation to the old and young in many ways, including the care of grandchildren and the care of infirm elderly patients.

      1. Each generation makes many and varied attempts to influence the others.

      2. The birth of grandchildren increases exchange and contact. Studies of grandparenting stress the importance of emotional fulfillment for grandmothers, as well as their desire to set an example. When grandfathers are added to the survey, such rewards as biological renewal, the experience of vicarious accomplishment, and service as a resource person become important.

3. Maternal grandparents have the closest ties to their grandchildren and divorce tends to strengthen all the female links in a family.

4. As elderly parents become more and more dependent upon their middle-aged children, role reversal may occur.

5. The ability of generations to live independently is probably very important in predicting how family relationships proceed, and the dependence of both the elderly and young adults on the middle-aged has led some to question whether this does not constitute a financial and physical burden that may be almost impossible to carry.

III. Work

A. During middle age, people enter the stage called maintenance, or plateau, during which they are expected to reach their maximum productiveness and to assume the role of mentor as well as to cope with the plateauing of their occupational lives through remotivation.

B. There is some evidence that middle-aged men are not as willing as they once were to struggle to the top of the corporate ladder.

1. Need for advancement declines rapidly after the first few years of work.

2. Midlife transition and a new emphasis on interpersonal relationships may be involved in the decision of middle-aged men to be less competitive.

3. Organizations are finding that they must offer more interesting and challenging work, more freedom, and less stress if they are to retain productive employees. Some authors have suggested a two-track career model to accommodate both those who need challenge at work and those who wish to pursue areas of life outside the work environment.

4. Today it is estimated that only about 20 percent of all middle-aged men make true career changes at midlife; however, this may be due to current economic conditions and stereotypes about aging that can be expected to change as today's young adults move toward middle age.

C. A strong commitment to work seems to have beneficial effects for women at midlife, regardless of salary, and this effect is seen among a broader section of the sample as the children leave home.

1. In several studies, single, work-committed women were the best adjusted and most satisfied middle-aged women surveyed.

2. Dual-track women committed to both home and work have the most difficult time in early middle age but appear to be better adjusted and more satisfied as the children leave home.

3. At least one author has suggested that reentry into the work force at midlife may be much more disappointing than is generally believed; however, there is no systematic research yet available on the course of reentry at midlife for women.

IV. Leisure
   A. Leisure is difficult to define, especially in a society that draws a strong distinction between work and leisure, often classifying leisure as "time not spent at work."
      1. This problem has led to the conclusion that Americans need to develop a leisure ethic.
      2. Pure leisure is characterized by low levels of constraint and high levels of internal motivation. It is not the opposite of work.
      3. The portent of embarrassment, or the need to perform at socially acceptable levels whether at work or leisure, along with changes in health, may lead to declining levels of active leisure with age.
   B. In middle age, some changes in leisure activities appear, although education, occupation, and sex are also important predictors.
      1. There is evidence that satisfaction with leisure contributes to over-all life satisfaction.
      2. Evidence exists that younger cohorts may be able to handle leisure time more comfortably, because they are demanding more of it.
      3. The development of a leisure ethic may depend on freedom from guilt about not working, as well as the freedom to choose activities and levels of intensity based on one's personal preferences rather than social approval.
      4. The distinction between work and leisure may disappear in a social system where people demand more leisure at work and the opportunity to work at leisure.

Later Life

9

The Personal Context: Biology and Cognition

Age only matters when one is aging. Now that I have arrived at a great age, I might just as well be twenty.

—Pablo Picasso

WHY BOTHER TO STUDY OLD AGE, especially if you are young? Oh sure, somebody has to work with the elderly, or deal with them on the job, but why would anyone else be interested? Questions like these come up all the time in the classroom. Few people consciously plan for old age; in fact, most people try to avoid thinking about it. How many times do you hear someone say, "I stopped having birthdays last year?" Why do people lie about their age? Why do they want to look young? Why do they find the subject of gerontology depressing?

The image of aging most people harbor is obviously not a positive one. As Alex Comfort (1976) put it, people become "unintelligent, unemployable, gray, and asexual" in old age (p. 10). And yet, unless we are old already, the next "old people" will be us. Negative bias about aging is, perhaps, the most mystifying of all prejudices, because everyone grows old. If you are a man, you don't suddenly become a woman. If you are born white, you die white. But everyone is born young and almost everyone these days will die old. We know that more and more people are dying later and later in the life cycle, and in the first two or three decades of the twenty-first century, the postwar baby boom will join the ranks of the elderly. In 1977 in the United States, there were 23 million people over the age of sixty-five, more people than have ever in the history of the world reached sixty-five. By the year 2000, there will be 31 million people over sixty-five; and by 2030, 52 million. Figure 9.1 presents a

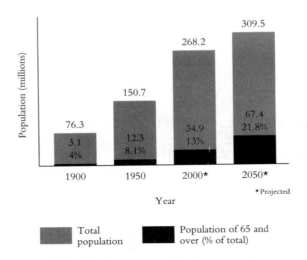

Figure 9.1 Growth of the U.S. population: sixty-five and over.

SOURCE: Insel & Roth, 1991, p. 531.

graphic representation of the growth of the elderly population. The outlook is even more interesting after 2030, for it has been estimated that 80 percent of the children born in the early 1980s will live past the age of seventy (Scott, 1981).

Certainly, some important social, economic, and political changes will occur as the population grows old. The leading edge of this change is already apparent in social policies such as the end of mandatory retirement. But this only hints at things to come. How will this mushrooming elderly population be supported? What will they do with themselves? How will they relate to the rest of the society, a diminishing proportion of young people? In 1945, the ratio of workers to retirees was thirty-one to one. Today, it is about three to one, but by the year 2035, it is estimated that there will be fewer than two persons at work for every retiree (Kaplan, 1979). And, finally, how will it feel to be a member of the burgeoning group of old people? These are some of the questions addressed in the next two chapters.

Beginning with the biological and cognitive correlates of age, we will review the work on the physical aspects of aging and discuss some hypotheses about why people age. Changes in physiological functions are discussed, and the psychological disorders associated with extreme age change are described.

Age differences in sensation, perception, learning, and memory are also covered in this chapter, although often it is difficult to discriminate among these processes. We will also discuss whether the changes observed in elderly people are inevitable, or whether they can be corrected or delayed.

"We grow neither better nor worse as we get old, but more like ourselves."
May Lamberton Becker

The Biology of Aging

"We grow neither better nor worse as we get old, but more like ourselves."

—May Lamberton Becker

The study of aging is not so much the study of why people grow old as it is the study of why human beings become vulnerable and die. Is it a miracle that a person lives to be eighty, or should that be commonplace? Why do certain diseases like arteriosclerosis and pneumonia increase with age, and why do people respond less well to stress when they are old? Human beings live to about seventy or eighty on the average. An olive tree survives for thousands of years. Why the difference? Figure 9.2 presents some typical maximum life spans of various primates. As you can see, even among nearest relatives of *Homo sapiens,* there is great variation in the life span.

Any acceptable comprehensive theory of biological aging would explain this variation as well as a number of other well-established facts. For example: radiation accelerates aging, whereas fasting appears to slow its effects; the life span of every species is related to its brain and body weight ratio; cells that

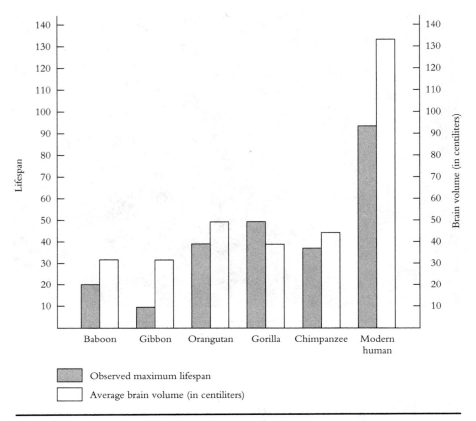

Figure 9.2 Maximum life span and average brain volume in primates.

SOURCE: After Cutler (1975) and Relethford (1990).

reproduce themselves do so only a limited number of times; cells transplanted from an old organism to a young one tend to live longer than the donor organism. A complete theory would encompass these disparate facts (Brash & Hart, 1978).

Current Theories

At present, the most popular theories of biological aging are those that emphasize events at the cellular level. These theories can be reasonably divided into two basic schools of thought. The first focuses on degenerative processes occurring both within individual cells and between cells. The second posits the existence of a genetic program whereby the death of the organism is predetermined and suggests human beings must accept that the maximum life span is about a hundred years, at least for the foreseeable future.

Process Theories The observation that events occurring within different kinds of cells change over time is basic to our first set of theories. For example, consider cells that reproduce themselves to produce new cells containing genetic errors.

With age, the total number of cells containing errors increases and the number of errors in an individual cell may also increase. Eventually, cells become so inefficient that death ensues. One process theory suggests that cell death, and eventually the death of the organism, is the result of an **error catastrophe.** In support of this notion, data exist that suggest there is probably at least one error in every cell in the human body by the time a person is ninety (Brash & Hart, 1978; Curtis, 1965; Orgel, 1963).

Error theories of aging detail species-specific life spans and attempt to correlate these with heart rate, metabolic rate, and a variety of other functions, as well as the effect of radiation. Cellular vulnerability to disease and stress is also explored, one hypothesis suggesting that as the number of well-functioning cells drops, those that do perform well become fatigued prematurely without the usual backup.

However, many biologists believe that cellular error is insufficient to explain the whole story behind aging. Other processes must contribute to the general loss of vitality that occurs with age.

Immune theory is often discussed in combination with error theory. Cells that make up the immune system may function less and less satisfactorily as errors accumulate. Basically, the immune system is designed to attack and destroy foreign elements that enter the body. With age, however, the system goes awry in a variety of ways. It may eventually lose its ability to distinguish between the self and foreign elements as errors build up. Or, when it attacks cells that are full of errors, healthy surrounding tissue may be damaged. The system may also become less effective in eliminating infected or cancerous cells (Adler, 1974; Beaubier, 1980). Again, however, other processes must be at work too, because even organisms without immune systems age.

A third possibility, collagen theory, is based on the observation that collagen and elastin, the proteins of which cells are made, undergo certain important changes with age, as discussed in Chapter 6. Of particular importance is the fact that they become cross-linked or joined to their neighbors, and skin becomes stiff and tough with age. Internal tissues like the muscles, arteries, and organs are similarly affected, becoming less elastic and slowing the diffusion of gases, hormones, and nutrients, and the exchange of waste materials between cells.

How does this all happen? What causes errors to emerge and cells to cross-link? Some theorists believe that aging and death are natural outcomes of the most basic acts of living: eating and breathing. During ordinary body metabolism, molecules are regularly produced that have fewer or greater than the usual number of electrons. Such molecules are called **free radicals,** and they will bond with just about any other available molecule. If they bond with the protein molecules in cells, cross-linking may result. If they bond with chromosomal materials, mutations occur. Free radicals may even provoke the destruction of the immune system (Beaubier, 1980; Hershey, 1974).

Pehaps, by modifying metabolism, the normal life span might be extended past that magical 100 years. It has been suggested, for instance, that fasting may extend the life span because the oxidation of food is slowed, and, therefore, fewer free radicals are produced. A diet rich in fish, vegetables, wheat germ, eggs, yeast, and fruit may inhibit the production of free radicals; vitamins C and E are thought to suppress oxidation and to slow cell metabolism (Hershey, 1974). In fact, a variety of chemical therapies might inhibit the production of free radicals or slow the process of cross-linking. Furthermore, some evidence (Hausman & Wekster, 1985) has implicated the decline of the thymus gland in the aging of the immune system, suggesting a large number of experimental interventions that might eventually produce some effective antiaging regime (Videk, 1982).

Many biologists think that the essentials of aging will be understood as early as the year 2000, and one writer (Strehler, 1979) offers the following optimistic picture.

1. An 80 percent probability of extending the healthy life span by 20 percent
2. A 40 percent chance of extending it 50 to 100 years
3. A 5 percent chance of an indefinite extension

Before we get carried away with the possibility of increased longevity, however, it is only fair to note that many biologists do not believe oxidation, cell metabolism, or the production of free radicals explains biological aging. Some argue that the underlying events that trigger cell changes are actually programmed into cellular material, that there is a genetic death clock. Death, they contend, is essential to the evolution of the species, and they note that all organisms having two sets of chromosomes also exhibit natural aging.

Death-Clock Theory With the appearance of **diploid organisms** (those that have two sets of chromosomes), evolution exploded. It took about three million years for organisms with only one set of chromosomes to produce one organism with two sets, and only about one-sixth of that time for the rest of evolution to occur. Perhaps the elimination of individuals past the reproductive age is one part of the evolutionary process (Sonnenborn, 1978). If death is linked to evolution, should we, or could we, substantially alter the maximum life span? Leonard Hayflick, one of the most productive students of biological aging (1974, 1979, 1981), was the first to demonstrate that human cells cultured in the laboratory cease to replicate themselves at a certain point. After about fifty replications, they simply run out of genetic material, and, according to Hayflick, shut off the organism. Hayflick maintains that death is programmed into all complex organisms and that we are a long way from changing the process—from knowing how to reset the **death clock.**

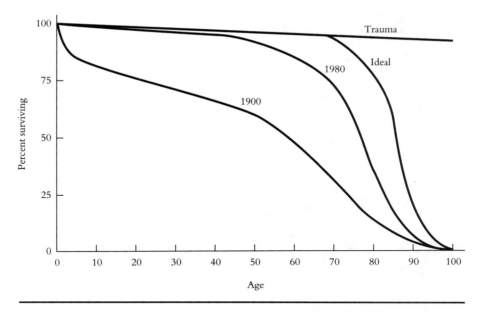

Figure 9.3 Ideal survival curve resulting from the elimination of premature disease in the United States. By 1980, over 80 percent of the area between the curve for 1900 and the ideal curve had been reduced.

SOURCE: Fries & Crapo, 1981, p. 73.

The Rectangular Society

Still, even Hayflick admits that many processes probably contribute to the signs and symptoms of age and that we can intervene in some of these. There appears to be no reason why most of us cannot live to the age of 80, 90, or 100 with health and vigor. Theoretically, we ought to be able to extend the average healthy life span whether or not we extend the maximum span. Van-Benzooijen (1987), a biomedical gerontologist in the Netherlands, believes that advances in the field of molecular biology could soon extend healthy life span. The most important research would have to address **Alzheimer's disease** and **osteoporosis.** Whatever the "ultimate cause of aging at the molecular level, the ideal aging process for the individual is represented by a rectangular curve" (Fries & Crapo, 1981; Fries & Vickery, 1989). A rectangular curve is depicted in Figure 9.3.

In what Fries and Crapo call a "rectangular society," modern medicine and wise personal choices make it possible for nearly everyone to live 85–100 years. Death will come quickly and "all at once." As Fries and Crapo put it, "What a way to go! A celebration of life!" A long life of vigor and vitality

In spite of the problems of thinning bones and stiffening joints, many active adults fear the loss of mobility and independence even more. How much benefit can regular exercise be in delaying or lessening the effects of the aging process?

ending suddenly, a decline-free process, and death a natural end to a natural life. The maximum life span is not prolonged, but the period of maximum vitality is. What are the chances that a rectangular society can be achieved? Certainly, the evidence today is encouraging. As we review the literature on health and cognition, personality and environmental issues (in the next chapter), we will come across many successful attempts to understand and optimize the aging process.

Physiological and Cognitive Change

Skin and Bones

Older people complain that their bones creak and that they no longer recognize the old person peering back at them from the bathroom mirror. The skin no longer snaps back (marks left by the elastic in your clothes last for hours) and wrinkles are no longer limited to those caused by the use of facial muscles. Laugh lines are joined by more general wrinkling, and in the very old, the skin may even take on a cross-hatched appearance (Rossman, 1977). Very old skin also becomes blemished by senile warts, age spots, and black-and-blue marks that occur when fragile blood vessels break (Rockstein, 1975; Whitbourne, 1985b).

As for those creaky bones, changes in the joints as well as the tendons and muscles contribute to the sensation. The weight of the skeleton declines because the bones become more hollow. The probability of bone fractures increases because hollow bones are weak and brittle. Vertebral collapse can occur, and if muscles and tendons are weak, postural slump may appear (Garn, 1975). The head is aligned slightly in front of the body and the upper limbs are bent. Figure 9.4 shows the loss of bony material over the course of adult life and the related probability of bone fracture.

Bone loss is greater if the diet is poor in calcium, and women appear to lose more bony material than do men. Menopause, pregnancy, and breastfeeding may be responsible for this sex difference, along with the fact that many older women do not get enough calcium. Postmenopausal women need about 800–1000 milligrams of calcium per day, the equivalent of one quart of milk. Calcium supplements initiated prior to menopause may slow bone loss, but it can take several years for the benefits to appear (Barzel & Wasserman, 1987; Worthington-Roberts & Hazzard, 1982).

Bone loss is not the only process responsible for the increased incidence of fracture, however. Bone stress studies show that older bones become increasingly mineralized, losing their resistance to impact as they become brittle. When bone loss and mineralization are extreme, osteoporosis may be diagnosed. Osteoporosis is not a separate disease of old age, just an extreme form of the bone loss and mineralization that ordinarily occur with age (Whitbourne, 1985b). In its most extreme form, the bones become quite porous and may even appear moth-eaten. The exact point where normal bone loss becomes osteoporosis is unclear, and the causes of severe bone loss are unknown (Tonna, 1977).

Finally, age-related changes in the bones cause any fracture that does appear to heal more slowly. The bones of younger people generally break in small, multiple fractures, whereas older bones suffer larger, cleaner breaks. Susan Whitbourne (1985b) offers the following analogy: Breaking a young bone is like trying to snap a green twig. It takes a lot of bending and creates many fracture lines. An older bone tends to snap completely, like a dry stick. Such complete fractures are more difficult to treat.

Changes in the cartilage at the joints are also typical of old age, and many, if not most, elderly people have some degree of arthritis, either osteoarthritis (caused by the stiffening of cartilage and bone) or rheumatoid arthritis (rheumatoid arthritis develops earlier but can be crippling in old age) (McKeown, 1965). As cartilage becomes thin and less resilient, it may also fray, crack, and

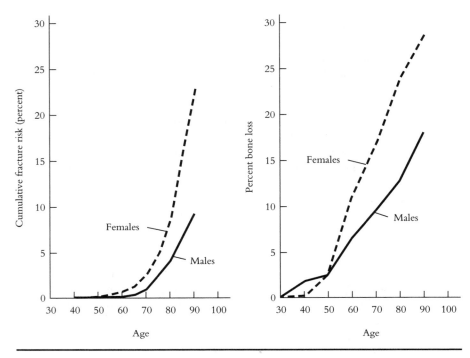

Figure 9.4 Cumulative fracture-risk curves and cumulative percent bone-loss curves.
SOURCE: Garn, 1975, p. 43.

shred. The bones may begin to rub against one another. As is the case for bone loss, however, the point where normal wear and tear becomes the disease arthritis is hard to pinpoint (Whitbourne, 1985b).

Almost all elderly people notice changes in their skin and bones, but similar processes go on in every other tissue as well. Loss of weight and stiffening occurs in every organ and organ system, and these internal changes often affect health and vigor.

Internal Organ Systems

Heart, lungs, kidneys, and intestines are affected. In old age, each beat of the heart is less effective, and the maximum blood flow declines by as much as 35 percent. However, most heart failure in old age is caused by vascular degeneration, or arteriosclerosis, whereby the arteries and veins become less elastic, clogged with fat and other debris. In very old age, blockages can produce gangrene of the lower limbs and are the most common reason why older people have high blood pressure (Rockstein, 1975).

The heart is primarily a muscular structure, and the changes that take place in all aging muscles affect cardiac function. Muscle weight decreases relative to general body weight late in life. Significant changes occur in the structure and composition of the muscle cells, including shifts in chemical balance and the accumulation of collagen and fat. Both the number and the diameter of muscle fibers decrease in later life, and sometimes the remaining fibers **hypertrophy** (become enlarged) (Gutman, 1977).

As it is usually defined, the basic **motor unit** consists of a single motor neuron and all the fibers it innervates. Age brings occasional fragmentation of the myelin sheath that surrounds the neuron, and other structural irregularities occur. The transportation of protein through the axons may be disturbed, the membrane may become thicker, and the synaptic cleft (the gap between axons of different neurons) may become larger.

The time it takes for a muscle to relax or contract and the time required before it can be restimulated increases in later life. The maximum rate of tension development, the rate at which tension develops in a muscle that is contracting, decreases. These changes probably account for some of the decline in motor function that is observed in older people. However, most researchers agree that one must postulate changes in other parts of the nervous system to account for the magnitude and variety of age differences in motor performance. In addition, Offenbach et al. (1990) report that poor physiological condition may contribute to reduced cognitive ability on tasks that require rapid responses.

In later life, cardiovascular problems are more often related to changes in the muscle of the heart than in middle age. The valves become thicker and less flexible, and the aged heart has more fat tissue. The left ventricle may atrophy while the left atrium and the aorta enlarge. Despite these changes, the evidence does not support the view that heart failure in old age is a direct result of deterioration in the muscle. Instead, heart failure is more likely to be caused by the advance of the arterial changes discussed in Chapter 6 (Harris, 1975).

Heart failure is also related to the function of the lungs. The muscles that lift the ribs weaken, and the number of air pockets through which gases are exchanged in the lung decline. The small tubes that carry air to the lungs become less elastic, and the amount of air one can inspire in a single breath decreases.

Some degree of emphysema is almost always present in elderly people. Smoking causes most of the serious emphysema that leads to death, with airborne particles in coal dust, silicon in mining and dusty winds, asbestos, cotton dust, and smog all being large contributors. Combinations of these various airborne particles are much worse than any single source. Airborne-particle emphysema is a particularly severe form of the disease.

The kidneys filter the blood more slowly with age, and injured renal cells are no longer replaced. Decreased blood flow through the kidneys is probably responsible for much of the change, but some is also due to the loss of nephrons, the tiny units that filter blood in the kidney (Lindeman, 1975). It has been estimated that decline in the function of the kidneys occurs at the rate of about 6 percent per decade. Loss of nephrons is most often attributed to vascular changes that cause an insufficient supply of blood to reach these tiny filters (Whitbourne, 1985b).

The intestines of older people are also plagued by a loss of cells, especially in the mucosa that lines the gastrointestinal tract. Furthermore, there is a decline in the amount of gastric juice secreted, causing general intestinal distress and constipation. Intestinal distress can cause poor nutrition and contribute to other health problems. Of all internal changes, however, the ones most often misinterpreted and least well understood are those that characterize the brain and other parts of the central nervous system. These are the changes that most people equate with aging, the ones people refer to as **senility**.

The Central Nervous System

As is the case for skin and bones and other internal organs, brain weight declines over the adult years. Perhaps 40 percent of the cells in some cortical areas are lost by the age of eighty or ninety. Even if the losses are more selective, chemical differences between old and young brains suggest significant changes in the cortical environment. The aged brain contains less water and protein, and more fatty tissue and inorganic salt. Furthermore, blood circulation to the brain declines over the adult years (Brody & Vijayashankar, 1977; La Rue & Jarvik, 1982; Ordy, 1975).

For most of us, changes in the brain raise the specter of senility. Unfortunately, the word *senility* is abused so often that it has little meaning beyond evoking anxiety and suggesting the aged are "aimless, apathetic, disruptive, . . . out of control" (Smith, 1979, p. 333). Often, people use the word to sum up all their worries and fears, applying it to a wide variety of changes, some of which are related to social and economic conditions, others of which are treatable, even reversible, and only a few of which are the result of degenerative changes in the brain.

People even use *senility* to refer to purely psychiatric problems, as though poor mental health were a symptom of aging. Actually, the term *senescence* simply refers to changes that accompany age, but it is clear that its connotations are very negative indeed.

Aging, Brain Physiology, and Behavior

There is no evidence that normal aging produces mental disorders. Psychiatric disorders are not more frequent among the elderly; however, as one group of authors (La Rue, Dessonville, & Jarvik, 1985) concluded: "The hypothesis of age differences in the nature and expression of psychopathology in adulthood is supported" (p. 692). Diagnosis of the psychiatric problems of the elderly is confounded by negative attitudes and by the social and economic disenfranchisement of the old. Elderly people are depressed more often than other age groups when they do seek psychiatric help (Srole, Langner, Michael, Opler, & Rennie, 1962). Moreover, it is often difficult to say whether the depression of elderly people is a "normal demoralization" or a psychiatric disturbance. After all, people of great age often suffer many losses and grave difficulties. Barry Gurland and John Toner (1982) estimate that about 10 to 15 percent of the elderly are clinically depressed and 20 to 30 percent of them demoralized.

Elderly people are also likely to be admitted to institutions for the first time because they suffer from dementia, drug-related problems, or paranoid ideation (La Rue, Dessonville, & Jarvik, 1985). However, the differentiation of each of these problems is also complicated by the general confusion over senile brain disorder. There are several different brain disorders of age, not just one called "senility." **Organic brain syndromes** are caused by the physical damage of brain tissues, and there are two major kinds: **acute brain syndromes** and **chronic brain syndromes.** Both are marked by mood changes, irritability, fatigue, agitation, and, later, deficits of memory and learning. Severe forms of either can produce great disorientation, confusion, and bewilderment. Important differences between them exist, however. Acute syndromes are caused by metabolic malfunctions like diabetes or renal toxicity and by vitamin deficiencies or alcoholism. They are essentially reversible but often seem identical to irreversible brain damage. Here, the word *often* is critical. Patients with the acute syndrome show fluctuating awareness. Even when hallucinations, space and time disorientation, and memory loss are present, lucid periods occur, however brief. People who develop chronic brain syndromes exhibit more predictable symptoms. Still, chronic brain syndromes are usually treatable; that is, substantial improvement can occur, although full recovery is not possible. One chronic syndrome has received much recent media attention, probably because it often occurs as early as one's late forties or early fifties. Alzheimer's disease is caused by the degeneration of brain cells, although no one knows exactly why these cells should begin to die in such great numbers. Symptoms range from forgetfulness and confusion to disorientation and the impairment of speech and concentration. Although drugs can relieve the agitation or depression of an Alzheimer's victim, there is no known cure at present (U.S. Public Health Service, 1979).

Nationally, Alzheimer's is the fourth leading cause of death among the elderly, affecting nearly three million Americans a year, and 20 percent of those over sixty-five. Eventually, most Alzheimer's victims enter institutions because they lose the ability to communicate, to reason, or to care for themselves. Although there have been no breakthroughs in the treatment of the disease, there has been some progress over the last few years in the treatment of Alzheimer's patients. New facilities, specifically designed for these patients, have sprung up. One of the major problems in dealing with Alzheimer's disease has been controlling the wandering of advanced patients. New facilities offer enclosed gardens where patients can wander without danger. Respite care for families is also increasingly available so that caretakers or relatives can take

Diagnosis of the psychiatric problems of the elderly is confounded by negative stereotypes, by the expectation of disability, and by the social and economic disenfranchisement of the old.

a break to rest or deal with other problems. In addition, many more adult day-care centers are now willing to accept these patients and to provide the services and security Alzheimer's victims require.

The symptoms of **senile dementia** are similar to Alzheimer's, and it is also caused by the dissolution of brain cells. However, Alzheimer's is more common among males, whereas dementia tends to occur in females. The average age at onset of dementia is later than Alzheimer's, usually about seventy-five. As with Alzheimer's disease, victims become less rational, more anxious and depressed, less able to think clearly or make judgments. In the end, people are unable to perform the daily tasks of personal care. There may be some involvement of the autoimmune system in senile dementia or Alzheimer's, but the precise cause is still largely a mystery (La Rue & Jarvik, 1982). Both are fatal, the average patient living about five years after the disease has been diagnosed, which brings us back to the problems of diagnosis.

Alzheimer's and dementia must be differentiated from other chronic disorders. For example, two kinds of brain syndromes are caused by vascular disease.

Multiple strokes and arteriosclerosis cause injuries to brain cells by blocking or damaging blood vessels in the brain and thereby preventing oxygen and nutrients from reaching individual cells. Furthermore, because so many of the problems of elderly people are demoralizing and anxiety-provoking, there is a tendency to confuse depression with brain syndromes, physical illness, and psychological problems (La Rue, Dessonville, & Jarvik, 1985).

Gurland and Toner (1982) even identify a condition they call **pseudodementia,** in which the patient exhibits all the symptoms of dementia although no physical brain damage actually exists. The onset of pseudodementia is different than it is in dementia, however, the intellectual symptoms appearing suddenly in people who are usually severely depressed.

Depression itself is an important problem. Many elderly people are beset by physical illness, experience the loss of close friends and family, and suffer economic and social deprivation as a result of retirement. Such conditions are certainly demoralizing, and when demoralization and physical illness or drug effects are present, it may be very difficult to discriminate between a brain syndrome and a functional depression. **Functional mental disorders** do not have any identifiable physical basis.

A special note should be made of the role played by drugs. In recent years discussions of geriatric medicine as a separate discipline have emerged. Its distinction is considered necessary because of physiological effects of drugs, diseases, and disorders special to the elderly. The overprescription of drugs, and the use of alcohol or over-the-counter preparations and prescriptive drugs are a major cause of acute brain syndromes among the elderly (Levy, Derogatis, Gallagher, & Gatz, 1980).

Elderly people respond to very low dosages of drugs, and about 95 percent of the elderly use them in one form or another. Over 80 percent of all elderly people take two or more drugs on a continuing basis, only 8 percent take no drugs at all, and about one-third take medications that they cannot even identify (La Rue, Dessonville, & Jarvik, 1985). The combined effects of several drugs or over-the-counter preparations can cause severe confusion and disorientation. Obviously, these syndromes are reversible but often go undiagnosed.

Finally, some researchers have identified a syndrome called **paraphrenia,** which appears to be more frequent among elderly people (La Rue, Dessonville, & Jarvik, 1985). Paraphrenia is characterized by paranoid ideation and hallucinations without any signs of dementia or any primary emotional disorder like depression. Paraphrenia occurs in about 10 percent of first admissions of patients to mental health facilities after age sixty, and it is more common among women. People who have never married, have few or no children, live alone, have hearing losses, and have a family history of schizophrenia are more likely to be diagnosed as paraphrenic. Many of these people are first admitted after many years of effective coping, and no one knows why they develop such vivid symptoms late in life. Paraphrenia can be treated with the major tranquilizers, but many paraphrenics never seek treatment because they are suspicious of the medical establishment.

Despite the fact that the elderly respond to a wide variety of interventions, from simple visiting programs to sophisticated psychiatric and psychological therapies, mental illness is all too often considered a natural outcome of aging and, therefore, untreatable. The full range of possible interventions is seldom considered in treating elderly patients, and factors like health, economic resources, the patient's social network, and even physical illness are ignored. Gerontological researchers rarely assess the health of their subjects (La Rue & Jarvik, 1982).

Despite the stereotype, brain damage is usually treatable. Curiously, the severity of psychiatric symptoms is not strongly related to the amount of apparent damage. Constitution, personality, heredity, and environmental conditions all predict how a patient will respond to and cope with the degree of physical damage. Some elderly people experience extensive damage, respond well to treatment, and seem relatively free of psychiatric symptoms. Others are gravely affected by what appears to be relatively minor physical damage.

The mysterious boundary between physiology and psychology confounds the study of age in many ways. If researchers are unsure how brain damage is related to behavior, they are less confident still about how normal changes in the nervous system affect cognition. Nonetheless, the questions are being asked, and the issues outlined in the study of sensation, perception, learning, memory, and even creativity.

Cognitive Function

If you are smart and manage to stay healthy, you'll also stay smart, although it may take you longer to demonstrate that fact at sixty-five than it did at twenty-five, and the print in which the questions are written may need to be larger.

—Ward Edwards

Sensation and Perception

After the age of sixty, most people notice sharp declines in vision and hearing. Again, poor blood supply and the progressive stiffening of tissues in the eye and ear (including changes in the bones of the middle ear) are prime determinants of the decline. Yellowing and stiffening of the lens of the eye continue after middle age. The retina or the brain centers that process visual input may be damaged by arteriosclerosis. As the pictures in Figure 9.5 illustrate, vision becomes blurred and fuzzy. It takes elderly people about ten times longer than young adults to find a gap in the drawing of a ring presented for a fraction of a second. Color discrimination is also affected, and by the age of seventy people are able to perceive colors as accurately as the young only about 76 percent of the time (Corso, 1981). Identification of various shades of blue and green is more difficult than perception in the red-yellow range.

Researchers often use the visual illusions to study aging perception. Some typical figures are presented in Figure 9.6. Generally, such investigations demonstrate that the elderly tend to perform more like teenagers than adults in response to visual illusions.

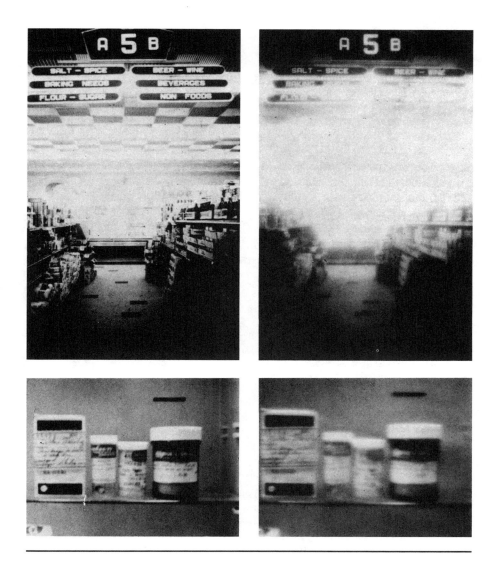

Figure 9.5 Photographic simulation of scenes as seen by people in their late seventies or early eighties is shown in the right hand member of each pair. The increased susceptibility to glare by the elderly is illustrated in the upper panel, while problems of acuity associated with poor contrast are illustrated in the lower pair. The prints were made from color slides prepared by Dr. Leon Pastalan.

SOURCE: Fozard et al., 1977, p. 516, ©1977 by Litton Educational Publishing, Inc. Reprinted by permission of Van Nostrand Reinhold Company.

Are the center dots in both figures the same?
Tichner's Circles

The Müller-Lyer illusion

Do you see an old lady or a young girl?

Do you see two profile faces?
Or a wine glass?

The Necker Cube. It can be seen as projecting up or down in three dimensions in the first cube. In the other two cubes the perspective is stabilized.

Figure 9.6 Common visual illusions.

Elderly people are strongly affected by the Müller-Lyer illusion (see Chapter 6). They see a line without arrow tips as longer than one of the same length with tips (McCarthy, 1991). On the other hand, they fail to reverse the Necker cube or the old/young figure (Comalli, 1970; Kline & Schieber, 1985) or to identify figures embedded in more complex forms (see Figure 9.7 for an example of an embedded-figures test). These data have been used to argue that

Instructions: This is a test of your ability to find a simple form when it is hidden within a complex pattern.

Here is a simple form which we have labeled "X":

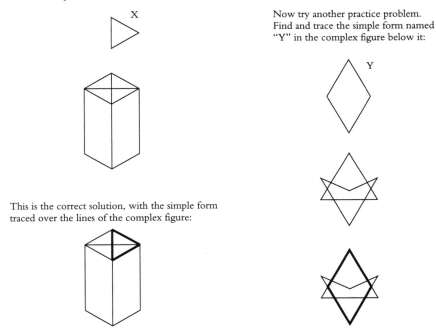

Now try another practice problem. Find and trace the simple form named "Y" in the complex figure below it:

This is the correct solution, with the simple form traced over the lines of the complex figure:

Figure 9.7 Group embedded-figures test.

SOURCE: P. K. Ohman, E. Raskin, and A. Witkin. Copyright 1971 by Consulting Psychologists Press, Inc.

---

older people regress, that they behave more like children or adolescents than adults. The **perceptual regression hypothesis** has not been popular, however, because there are so many other plausible explanations for the evidence. For instance, older people are not as familiar with the perceptual illusions as young adults. Young or middle-aged adults have seen the Necker cube or the old/young woman more often than either children or the elderly. The elderly are also more vulnerable to the stress created by unusual variations in what they see or hear (Fozard & Thomas, 1975). Finally, elderly people may be unwilling to spend the energy it takes to reverse an illusion or find an embedded figure. Differences in motivation may account for some of the cognitive performances that distinguish the elderly from younger adults.

Later Life Turning our attention to audition, we find the evidence also shows substantial, widespread decline. About 13 percent of all older people need hearing aids, and all older people make more errors identifying single-syllable

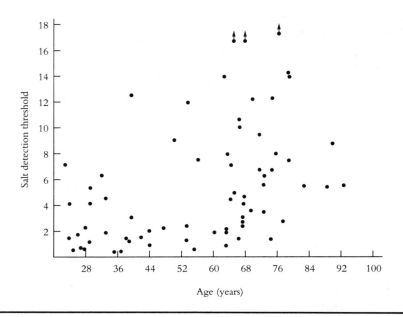

Figure 9.8 Comparison of age differences in thresholds for salty tastes.

SOURCE: Grzegoczyk et al., 1979, p. 837. Copyright 1979 by The Gerontological Society. Reprinted by permission.

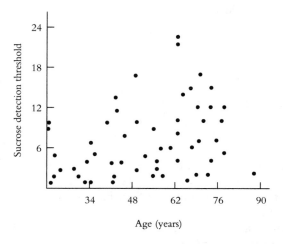

Figure 9.9 Comparison of age differences in thresholds for sweet tastes.

SOURCE: Moore et al., 1982, p. 65.

words than do young adults, especially under stressful conditions (for instance, if speakers interrupt each other or speak quickly) (Brooks & Impleman, 1981; Corso, 1977, 1981). Speech discrimination is critical in social exchange. Hearing losses interfere with personal relationships and cut one off from important information, from door bells to sirens. Depression and even paranoia may be linked to moderate or severe hearing loss. People with undiagnosed hearing problems can develop the impression that others are deliberately whispering or talking behind their backs.

Although not as noticeable to most people, gustation and olfaction also decline. Sensitivity for the primary tastes (sweet, salty, bitter, and sour) deteriorates, and the ability to identify complex tastes seems less keen, especially for vegetables like corn, celery, carrots, beans, and broccoli; and fruits like lemon, pineapple, and strawberry (Corso, 1981; Whitbourne, 1985b). Figures 9.8 and 9.9 present some data on gustatory changes. The dots in the scatter plots represent data for individual subjects. The overall patterns indicate an increase in the threshold for tasting sugar in the early fifties and for tasting salt in the early forties.

Older people are less sensitive to odors as well as tastes. Taste buds are lost with age. So are sensory cells in the nose. Nutritional problems may be partly explained by these losses. When things begin to taste and smell alike, people may become less interested in food.

Clearly, there are definite, wide-ranging changes in sensation and perception during the last part of the life span, but the reason for such change is not entirely clear. We know that the bones stiffen (for example, those in the ear), muscle strength declines, as does blood supply. The question is, are such changes inevitable? John Corso (1977, 1981) believes that they are caused by a variety of problems, including damage to receptors, nerve fibers, and brain projection areas. But he also asserts that proper environmental planning makes it possible to use information from several senses to compensate for loss in any one. For instance, directions can be labeled and color-coded. Eating habits, smoking, drug use, health habits, and even such general changes as environmental pollution may also determine the degree of impairment a person experiences. Furthermore, education, experience, intelligence, as well as economic and social resources allow one to compensate for sensory losses. In a society where people take better care of themselves, exercise their abilities, and stay involved with the world around them, no doubt fewer sensory and perceptual changes will occur.

Learning and Memory

If I'd known I was going to live so long, I'd have taken better care of myself.

—Leon Eldred

One of the most complicated problems in the study of cognition rears its thorny head in the literature on learning and memory. Good research in this area disentangles developmental change from generational change, and various situational effects. It also distinguishes learning from memory and competence from performance. In addressing this problem, Salthouse (1988) suggests that the time has come to develop and investigate formal, physiological models of cognitive aging. He himself has presented a model based on the metaphor of the **associative network,** or neural network (Commons, Grossberg, & Staddon, 1991). Such networks simulate the functioning of networks of neurons in the brain. Cerella (1990) has suggested that the problem of age-related deficits in memory may best be explained by neural noise. With age, the axons of local networks of neurons become degraded and attenuated, creating noise in the system and making it more difficult to process the information necessary to remember something.

Most of the tentative models we have deal with the deterioration of memory, but obviously people must learn something before they can remember it. Therefore, there is no way to test memory without testing the effects of previous learning. Furthermore, poor performance on a test in a laboratory may or may not have anything to do with either learning or memory. Performance does not always reflect "absolute ability" or learning. Competent people may be unmotivated by some situations, or may be unable to perform in a way that demonstrates their competence because laboratory conditions interfere. For instance, we know that there are correlations between cognitive performance and how much a person feels in control of the situation (Winocur, Moscovitch, & Freedman, 1987). Programs that incorporate the elderly as active participants may stimulate highly competent cognitive performances (Babins, 1988). Such programs treat cognitive function as the outcome of a complex interaction among social, affective, and physical factors.

Despite the complexity of the problems, however, various attempts have been made to outline basic distinctions between learning and memory. For instance, Fergus Craik defines **learning** as the acquisition of rules and information about the world, and **memory** as the recall of events that occur at a given place and time. One can learn what will result from an action, how to perform that action, and when and where to act (Commons & Hallinan, 1989). You learn that 2 plus 2 is 4 or that the lights go out when a circuit breaker trips or a fuse blows. You learn to reset the circuit breaker or replace the fuse after locating where the electrical box is. The time and place in which these things are learned is not important. You can use what you learn in a variety of situations (for example, you realize that a circuit breaker serves the same function in any house). Memory, on the other hand, is specific. You remember what you did yesterday or who your teacher was in the fourth grade. Memory is the reconstruction of a particular event (Craik, 1977). Both learning and memory require the encoding, storage, and retrieval of information. For this reason, many researchers use the term **information processing,** which emphasizes *how* people store and retrieve ideas rather than *how well.*

Research on Learning For years, traditional learning research has focused on the acquisition of associations. In one classic testing format, two words or syl-

"It's a man's own fault, it is from want of use, if his mind grows torpid in old age."
Samuel Johnson

lables are paired and the subject is asked to recall one word when the other is presented. The subject sees both words or syllables together during a period called the **inspection interval.** After a complete list of pairs has been presented, one member of a pair is presented and the subject is given a brief period, called an **anticipation interval,** in which to recall the other member of the pair. Nearly all studies of paired associates report that older subjects require more time to learn the pairs (Arenberg, 1983; Arenberg & Robertson-Tchabo, 1977; Willis, 1985).

More interesting than the study of general age differences in learning, however, is the question of why they arise and whether they are universal. The earliest attempts to answer these questions showed that prolonging the anticipation interval improved performance among elderly subjects more than young ones. Prolonging the inspection interval does not affect performance in either group. Such evidence has led researchers to believe that memory, not learning, is most strongly affected by age and that the basic problems with memory occur during the process of retrieval, although at least one researcher (Bowles, 1989) has argued that delayed response time in older adults may be due to longer decision-making time rather than prolonged retrieval.

Yet older people have little trouble retrieving association between two meaningful words (for example, the pair "chair-table"). It is only when mean-ingless syllables are used that older people do very poorly. For a while, re-search seemed to suggest that motivation might be the cause of differences in performance on tests involving meaningless, or nonsense as they are called, syllables. When given the chance, older people refuse to participate in experi-ments using nonsense syllables instead of words because they find such re-search "silly" (Hulicka, 1967). Recent research has shown, however, that older people also have difficulty abstracting meaningful material (Botwinick, 1981; Hultsch & Dixon, 1984, 1990; Light, 1990). Moreover, one group of re-searchers (Cohen & Faulkner, 1986) have suggested that elderly people experi-ence certain very specific cognitive deficits that may be overcome by certain linguistic strategies. They have shown that **elderspeak,** a pattern of speech de-signed to place stress at locations optimal for linguistic processing, improved the performance of elderly people. Longitudinal data on normal aging have also led to the conclusion that aging affects specific cognitive functions more than it affects others (Schludermann, Schludermann, & Brown, 1983). In other words, normal aging produces distinct patterns of cognitive deficits.

Evidence for this position also comes from data on **concept learning.** To demonstrate concept learning one must identify an instance of some well-defined class of objects and explain how to discriminate between members of that class and nonmembers. For example, a cocker spaniel is an exemplar of the class of objects we call dogs. The spoon is an eating utensil, a chair is a piece of furniture, and so on. Younger people make these kinds of abstractions more easily; however, education predicts this kind of learning better than age, so it is possible that age differences in concept learning are really generational differ-ences. After all, fifty years ago, abstract ideas were taught in high school and college, not elementary school. The education of the average person over sixty-five ended at the age of twelve or thirteen (Giambra & Arenberg, 1980).

Sherry Willis (1985) believes that much of the age-related decline demon-strated by people who are now in their sixties and seventies may be due to the negative cohort effects. Studies of inductive reasoning and vocabulary show that current cohorts of elderly people function at a lower level than the young. Willis argues, on the basis of some longitudinal data, that current elderly people also functioned at lower levels when they were young than do today's young people. She believes that when today's middle and young adults become elderly, they will show less decline and greater training effects because they have functioned at a higher level throughout the adult life course. This cer-tainly fits Denney's (1982) notion that the abilities we exercise will show less decline than those we do not. If people who are middle-aged and younger con-tinue to use their intellectual capacity through a greater portion of the life span, they may well show less decline. More schooling and a more complex set of job market skills may require one to exercise a larger number of intellectual abilities over a longer part of the life span.

Older people may also organize and process information in a different way than the young (Hartley, Harker, & Walsh, 1980). An interesting illustration was first presented by Irene Hulicka and her associates (Hulicka & Grossman, 1967). Hulicka demonstrated that young people use more mediators, especially visual mediators, than the elderly. **Mediators** are internal, unobservable responses (like thoughts or images) that influence observable responses. For instance, if you meet Mrs. Byrd and you imagine her with a bluejay on her head, you are using a visual mediator. When Hulicka taught older people to use mediators, performance improved substantially. However, this discussion blurs the distinction between learning and memory, leading us to look more closely at the latter.

Research on Memory

Despite the fact that memory is one of the most intensely researched of all subjects in gerontology (Poon, 1985), a review of the current literature makes it apparent that we do not really know what memory is; however, we do know something about what it is not. Memory is not stored in a place the way it is in a computer. In fact, it is probably not a single, unitary thing at all. You might think of it, instead, as a collection of processes that may occur in many different places in the nervous system. Present neural network theories of memory see memory as localized to sets of networks but not to individual cells.

In one important model of memory, three such collections of processes are described: **sensory memory, short-term memory,** and **long-term,** or **secondary memory.** Sensory memory is a label for the processes by which we collect data from the environment. Everything that happens in the environment may be registered in sensory memory, but information decays and is replaced by new information very rapidly. If information is to be maintained, it must be moved to short-term memory. The process (or group of processes) by which the movement occurs is called *attention*. That is, when a person attends to something in the sensory register, movement occurs from sensory to short-term memory. A sensory trace lasts up to approximately two seconds; hence most older people probably register fewer pieces of data available per unit of time in sensory memory, although the differences between age groups are small. Decline in sensory memory might be due to decline in the sense organs also. For instance, older people are not able to discriminate fine visual details as well and may, therefore, not pick them up in sensory memory (Craik, 1977; Craik & Lockhart, 1972; Elias, Elias, & Elias, 1977; Poon, 1985; Walsh, 1975). Most researchers do not believe age differences in sensory memory are responsible for the most important age changes in memory.

Primary, or short-term, memory refers to the ephemeral, limited capacity we have to hold things "in mind." Although attention automatically moves information from sensory to short-term memory, short-term memory has a limited capacity. Only about 5 to 7 digits can be held in short-term memory at a time, for example. Remembrance for events in short-term memory decreases inversely with the number of events (Commons, Mazur, Nevin, & Rachlin, 1987; Commons, Woodford, & Trudeau, 1991). Therefore, information acquired in short-term must change or be transferred to long-term memory if it is to be retained over time. For example, when driving to a new place, one sees various landmarks along the way, such as a Shell gas station. Each image of a landmark is in sensory memory. If one attends to these images, they may be remembered until a number of other landmarks have appeared. However, one needs to remember to "turn left at the Shell station" if these images are to be of use the next time one plans to go to the same place. That means a tendency to drive straight has to be modified. Quite often we change our responses or choices without remembering why. For instance, we may not remember who told us to turn left at the Shell station. McIntyre and Craik (1987) asked younger adults and older adults to recall facts and the origin of those facts as taught to them the previous week. It was discovered that the older subjects showed significantly poorer performance in recalling the source of their knowledge.

Because there seem to be few differences between the old and the young in the capacity of short-term memory (Poon, 1985), it is the transfer from short- to long-term memory that has received much attention. Many investigators believe that this is the point at which age most affects memory processes.

Studying this transfer, however, is no small task. As David Hultsch and Roger Dixon (1984) have written: "Memory performance depends on the characteristics of the subjects we study (e.g., education, age), the kinds of materials we ask them to remember (e.g., digits, texts), the nature of the acquisition conditions under which we ask them to remember it (e.g., incidental, intentional), and the kinds of criteria tasks we use to determine performance (e.g., recall, recognition)" (pp. 82–83). Further complicating the task of memory assessment are subjects' erroneous self-assessments. Dobbs and Rule (1987) report negative correlation between **metamemory** scores and prospective memory performance. Metamemory scores attempt to measure how well people think they remember something. Dobbs and Rule suggest that either people have poor knowledge regarding their own memory abilities, or their concept of memory is different from that of the psychologist.

Nonetheless, strong evidence indicates that, even under optimal conditions, elderly people do not do as well as the young on almost every kind of memory task. For example, David Arenberg (1983), in summarizing data from an important series of longitudinal studies, concludes that data for paired associates, serial learning (learning a list of words in order), and memory for visual images all decline. The number of errors on the paired associated task doubled between ages seventy and eighty, and was nearly four times as great as the error rate for thirty-year-olds. Moreover, as detailed by Hultsch, Hertzog, and Dixon (1987), older adults, in comparison to younger adults, report the perception of having less memory capacity and more decline in memory functioning. They believe they have less control over their memory ability. Data from some of the studies summarized by Arenberg (1983) appear in Figure 9.10.

Given data like these, much recent research has been devoted to the issue of why these differences occur and whether or not the memory of elderly people can be improved by various types of interventions. The leading hypothesis has

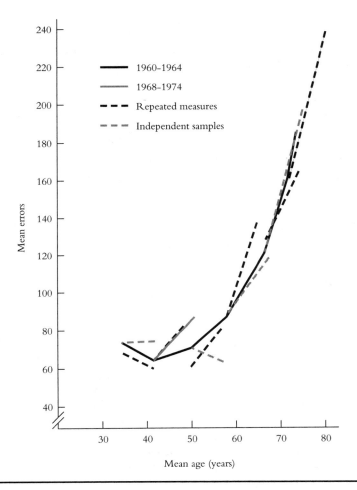

Figure 9.10 Paired-associate learning—short interval.

SOURCE: Arenberg, 1983, p. 314.

been that older people must process incoming information differently than do the young. Most researchers agree that one must do something fairly active to move information from short- to long-term memory. People must process information in some direct way. For example, they may employ a simple process like repeating the spelling of a new word. Or, the process may be much more elaborate, as for example, when you learn the spelling of new words from their Greek or Latin roots. One must also have some rehearsal of the act reinforced (Commons & Hallinan, 1989). In developing a hypothesis about differences in process, Fergus Craik has suggested that older people manipulate information in less complex ways when they transfer it from short- to long-term memory (Craik, 1977; Hines & Fozard, 1980).

This hypothesis assumes that when a process requires more effort it will produce better retention. The memory deficits of age, Craik has argued, reflect *shallow processing*. The failure to use mediators as demonstrated by Hulicka is an example of shallow processing. Poor processing results in the storage of less information and makes it hard to retrieve what information is stored. It may be useful to think for a moment about storing information in a file cabinet. Consider the difference between having twenty-six file tabs (one for each letter of the alphabet) and only nine file tabs (one for A–C, one for D–F, etc.). If twenty-six are available and each entry is alphabetized as it is placed in the file, information storage is harder, but later retrieval easier, than with just nine file tabs.

Some serious questions have been raised about the concept of "poor" processing, however, when it is defined as less elaborate, or shallow, manipulation. Perhaps the most interesting problem is presented by data that show that repeated shallow processing improves memory (Fozard, 1980; Hines & Fozard, 1980). This should probably not occur if Craik is correct.

In another challenge to Craik's work, David Hultsch (Hultsch & Dixon, 1984) was able to show that elderly people remembered meaningful text better if they were simply instructed to read and recall the text than if they were given elaborate instructions that led to deep processing, but were not informed that they would be tested for recall. Hultsch's data show some improvement under conditions that required deep processing when compared to shallow processing, but the greatest improvement occurred for the "intentional" recall condition, in which subjects were simply informed that they would be tested later.

However, the young still do better than the old when intentional recall is tested. Generally, present evidence suggests that aging is accompanied by frequent and pronounced decrements in **explicit** versus **implicit memory** (Hultsch & Dixon, 1990; Light, 1988; Schacter, 1987) as well as a decline in **working memory.**

Explicit memory is intentional. It occurs when you set out to remember something. Implicit memory involves no conscious awareness of trying to remember. If there are age decrements in implicit memory, they appear to be small. Implicit memory is measured by exposing people to some stimulus and not telling them that they will be required to remember it later.

Working memory involves the ability to store recently presented material while continuing to process additional information. There appear to be substantial age differences in favor of the young in working memory (Craik, Morris, & Gick, 1989).

Interestingly, elderly people show very accurate long-term memory for names and faces and remember information relevant to their own cohort (for instance, "Who was Clark Gable's first wife?") better than young people who have learned it secondhand. In one such study, Hultsch and Dixon (1983) demonstrated that cohorts remember stories about figures from their own histori-

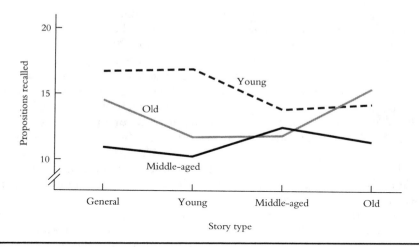

Figure 9.11 Mean number of propositions recalled as a function of age and story type.
SOURCE: Hultsch & Dixon, 1983.

cal periods best. In this experiment, young, middle-aged, and elderly adults were given brief biographical sketches of Mary Pickford (a figure best known to the old), Susan Hayward (best known to the middle-aged), Steve Martin (known to the young), and Bob Hope (a general figure well known to all three cohorts). The elderly performed the best of all three cohorts on recalling the details of the Pickford story. Data for this experiment are presented in Figure 9.11.

If differences in processes were all that was involved in recall, the elderly should not outperform the young in the way Hultsch and Dixon have demonstrated. Perhaps most importantly, as James Fozard has pointed out, Craik never clarifies why he considers one process more elaborate or deeper than another. Craik implies that more elaborate processes take longer, but it is possible to construct a very time-consuming shallow process. For instance, thinking about how words are related is a deep process for remembering words on a list. Looking to see if the words have the letter *d* in them is considered shallow. Fozard notes that looking for a *d* followed by the letter *e* or the letter *s* is very time-consuming, but it is still a shallow process.

Fozard believes that there exist a wide variety of useful memory codes. Some are visual, some are auditory, some may be based on meaning rather than sensory information. Different codes may be processed and stored in different areas of the brain. Some of these processes may become easier to use with age while others become less accessible. For example, elderly people require longer to decide whether an uppercase letter is the same as its lowercase counterpart (*Aa*), but older people make fewer errors. Perhaps the elderly are more cautious and therefore slower. On the other hand, processes that young people activate easily may be relatively unavailable to the elderly.

Furthermore, there are a variety of conditions besides those that involve deep-process training that attenuate the deficits of the elderly. In the study of memory for text materials, for instance, "age differences appear to be attenuated when the text is well organized, when there is prior knowledge about the topic, and when the subjects possess superior levels of semantic abilities" (Hultsch & Dixon, 1984, p. 103). Memory for text or discourse is poorest among the elderly when working memory is taxed by the presence of large amounts of material, or by the interpolation of irrelevant material. Under such conditions, the elderly are likely to forget the earlier part of the material and be unable to draw correct inferences that require them to think about all of the information presented (Light, 1990.)

Certainly the issue of prior knowledge is an important one in understanding everyday memory. Researchers most often study memory using unfamiliar materials, nonsense syllables, and text materials that the subjects have never seen before. But most of the information we commit to memory in everyday life is related to and builds on what we already know. People who have played bridge for years can master a new bidding convention in the time it takes a beginner to arrange a hand of cards. If you already play Pac Man, you can learn Ms. Pac Man faster. The integration of new and old information has received little attention in the traditional study of memory, yet it is critical in everyday life (Charness, 1989; Hartley, Harker, & Walsh, 1980).

Outside the laboratory, memory is always a transaction between incoming information and what one already knows (Meacham, 1977). When people are young, they may be better at treating novel information. Over the years, certain processes may become automatic because they are effective in relating new information to old. As these processes become automatic, it may become difficult to handle information that does not relate well to what we already know (like the nonsense syllables researchers often use). Young people are frequently required (in school and on the job) to deal with novel information, so they may use processes that are better suited to the typical laboratory test (Hultsch & Pentz, 1980; Labouvie-Vief & Schell, 1982).

For years, many researchers have assumed that information is processed "from the bottom up": the individual perceives incoming information, finds a way to organize it, and then processes it for storage. The research on such bottom-up processing implies that age changes in the brain make it more difficult to use elaborate forms of processing. An alternative view describes "top-down" processing. As certain modes become automatic, flexibility may decrease because less useful modes become inaccessible. Top-down processing might explain why elderly people do so much better at recalling dated material (like the story about Mary Pickford). They are able to hang the story on existing "memory pegs" (Hultsch & Pentz, 1980; Labouvie-Vief & Schell, 1982; Meacham, 1977).

Finally, some researchers have been looking at the notion that what a person knows about memory processes may actually affect the quality or nature of memory (Perlmutter, 1983), and young people may know more about how memory works than do the elderly. Metamemory is a term that refers to what people know about their own memory, to their understanding of how memory works. In one study (Dixon & Hultsch, 1983), the authors measured the degree to which subjects used memory strategies (i.e., mnemonics), knowledge of memory tasks, knowledge of their own memory capacities, attitudes toward their own memory and the perception of change in their own memories, activities supportive of memory, memory anxiety, memory motivation, and locus of control in memory abilities. Locus of control is a measure of whether people believe they can control their own memory processes. They found that knowledge of general memory processes, knowledge of how memory develops, and locus of control were the best predictors of memory performance among young, middle-aged, and older adults. Knowledge of memory strategies seemed to be more important in the performance of the young than the elderly subjects. In other words, young people who knew a good deal about memory strategies did better than young people who did not, whereas older people who knew about memory strategies were not much helped by that knowledge. Marion Perlmutter (1983) has argued that even when older people know as much about memory as the young, they simply don't have the surplus energy for deep processing under less than optimal conditions.

Other researchers have reported that there are few age-related differences in metamemory and it is, therefore, unlikely that metamemory accounts for much of the memory declines that emerge in the research data. On the other hand, older people appear to have poor evaluations of themselves as "rememberers." It is possible that poor performance on memory is something of a self-fulfilling prophecy. If you do not expect to do well, you may not be motivated to try (Hultsch & Dixon, 1990).

It seems important to note at this point that in all of this research there are always those older individuals who do not appear to exhibit any decline in memory function. For instance, in the Baltimore studies, although the vast majority of elderly subjects made many more errors than younger subjects, 28 percent of those in their seventies did not make more errors over the years. As Arenberg (1983) suggests, we might do well to look more closely at the factors that predict healthy memory function in old age, as well as the variables associated with decline.

Problem Solving and Creativity

The nature of artistic attainment is psychologically inaccessible to us.
—Sigmund Freud

Psychologists have tried to plumb the depths of the creative mind and, if not explain it, at least identify when and how creativity emerges. A somewhat more prosaic but related enterprise is the study of problem solving. After all, problem solving is a creative activity, and although more creative problems may exist than those studied in the laboratory, laboratory problems usually call for both abstract thinking and some degree of imagination.

Problem Solving Like studies of concept learning reviewed earlier, most research on problem solving has demonstrated a decline in performance with age (Arenberg, 1968; Giambra & Arenberg, 1980; Rabbit, 1977). Generally, investigators find that older subjects are slower to solve complex problems. Furthermore, elderly subjects make more uninformative inquiries and treat information they are given a second time as though it were new and different. Older people also have difficulty handling negative information. For instance, if A and B are given as examples of a particular concept, and C is given as an example of what does not fit the concept, they treat C as an example of the concept anyway. This is also somewhat true of all people. Even when the elderly are testing their own hypotheses, they do not always discard ideas they have already proved to be incorrect (Giambra & Arenberg, 1980).

Several explanations for these observations have been advanced over the past few decades. First, and fairly obvious after considering memory and aging, studies of problem solving are complicated by the fact that the elderly are adversely affected by memory requirements. The more information one must remember to solve a problem, the more difficulty elderly subjects will have. Furthermore, more difficult problems take everyone longer to solve, so people have to remember all the relevant information longer. As Patrick Rabbit has pointed out: "It is important to recognize that a 'vicious spiral' effect will here result. The greater the memory load, the greater the time for each operation. The greater the time, the greater the probability of memory inaccuracies. The greater the probability of memory inaccuracies, the greater the probability of incorrect decisions which have to be modified by extra operations. The greater the number of extra operations, the greater the elapsed time and interference by this extra activity, and the greater the probability of inaccuracies, etc., etc." (1977, p. 619). Based on Rabbit's description, one might conclude that memory requirements explain all poor problem solving among elderly subjects. But, as Rabbit notes, not all the data can be handled this way.

Consider again the work of Denney and her colleagues (Denney, 1982; Denney & Palmer, 1982; Denney & Pearce, 1982). Denney has shown that the performance of the old can be improved through the use of rewards. Rodeheaver and Datan (1988) also used the game called "twenty questions." They found that older people may perform poorly on "twenty questions" because they have less opportunity to exercise the abilities involved or have lower motivation. Strategy hints and memory aids help too; however, given time and practice, the elderly show improvement without any assistance. In fact, practice alone seems to have as long-term an effect as any other training procedure. This practice effect is quite puzzling, really, considering research results on processing, teaching strategies, and the like (Giambra & Arenberg, 1980).

Clearly, we need to know more about how simple experiences affect learning, memory, and problem solving.

Creativity   As was true of problem solving, learning, and memory, early research on creativity also demonstrated a decline in creative production over the adult years. In one famous study, Harvey Lehman (1953) analyzed the life work of prominent artists, scientists, scholars, and technicians from the fifteenth century to the present. He concluded that most major creative achievements occur between the ages of twenty and forty.

Later researchers discovered two major flaws in Lehman's approach. First, Wayne Dennis (1966) challenged Lehman's subject selection. Many of Lehman's subjects had died before they attained great age. Dennis repeated the analysis, including only long-lived subjects, and concluded that creative productivity continues well beyond middle age. Lehman retorted that Dennis had only counted how many contributions people made at different ages, without evaluating each work.

The most important contributions people made occurred early even for those who did not die young, according to Lehman's original study. Other writers, including Jack Botwinick (1981), have challenged Lehman's evaluations. Lehman included only creative people who had achieved prominence, and Botwinick argued that prominence is too often accompanied by leadership roles like teacher, advisor, and administrator, roles that leave one less time for more creative work. In a fascinating personal account, the writer May Sarton (1981) argued that psychic energy is the most important element in late-life creativity. However, she acknowledged that the concurrent problem of dealing with public responsibility was overwhelming. How to respond to the thousands of letters she receives? Which invitations to accept, which to reject? What teaching posts should she consider?

Dean Keith Simonton (1988a, 1988b, 1988c, 1990) has extensively studied and reviewed creativity of both famous individuals such as Shakespeare (Simonton, 1986) and ordinary professionals (Simonton, 1985). If one counts the number of contributions (e.g., publications, paintings, compositions, and so on) per time unit, the resulting longitudinal fluctuations tend to rise early in adulthood and then decline gradually (Cole, 1979; Dennis, 1966; Horner, Ruston, & Vernon, 1986; Lehman, 1953; Simonton, 1980, 1988a). The magnitude of the postpeak decline varies depending on the domain of creative achievement. Again, as discussed in Chapter 3, the peak for lyric poetry, pure mathematics, and theoretical physics is in the early thirties and even the late twenties, with a somewhat steep decline thereafter. On the other hand, in novel writing, history, philosophy, and general scholarship, there is a slow rise to a relatively late peak in the late forties and early fifties with a minimal drop-off, if any.

Part of this decline may reflect the fact that creative people are affected by the stereotypes of age, just like everyone else. Arguing that passion and sexual drive are important to creativity, John McLeish (1981) maintains that five "myths of aging" are antithetical to creativity: (1) senility, (2) sexual impotence, (3) rigidity, (4) the decline of learning, and (5) the loss of creative power. Such beliefs might convince anyone that creative activity in later life would be not only futile but an embarrassment as well. Thomas Jefferson, for example, seemed convinced he was becoming an imbecile at the age of sixty-eight when he wrote: "Had not a conviction of the danger to which an unlimited occupation of the executive chair . . . [made it my] duty to retire when I did, the fear of becoming a dotard and of being insensible to it would of itself have [caused me to have] resisted all solicitations to remain" (Comfort, 1976).

A final point about cohort differences may also be important in explaining declines in creative production. McLeish has noted that today's elderly may be less adventurous or bold partly because they were reared in a society and a school system that did not value the development of unusual ideas. Despite this prejudice, Blackburn and Lawrence (1986) have found that in the academic setting, as measured by the three functions of the professor—teaching, scholarship, and service—there is no significant decrement in performance with age.

McLeish, Botwinick, and Sarton agree, however, that the really interesting question may not be why some people seem less creative, but how so many display great talent well into later life despite the odds. Creativity flourishes when people are free to change, to reinvent the world and the self. Creative people remain more autonomous and independent; more open to the irrational; more self-accepting, adventurous, bold; and yet more stable than other people. Stability is a key characteristic; one must have the discipline to harness the creative energy (McLeish, 1981). In an analysis of 200 creative older people, McLeish concluded that exuberance and tenacity were paramount.

Inspired exuberance and tenacity are found in every arena of creative enterprise. M. M. Kaye wrote *Far Pavillions* between the ages of sixty-five and seventy-five, fighting cancer through those ten years as well. To be able to go on painting, Renoir built a machine to move his hands, which were so crippled by arthritis he could no longer move them. At sixty, Clementine Hunter, the painter, was able to afford her first set of paints. She overcame all odds: age, lack of training, poverty, being black, and being a woman. These are the people who could not live without creating. What sets them apart?

Julia! Never grow old. Whenever you think you cannot do something, get up and do it.
    —Excerpt from letter to Julia Ward Howe

Box 9.1 presents a list of enormously creative older people and lists ages at which they made significant accomplishments, but it only suggests the creative possibilities of later life. Evaluation of the quality of accomplishments adds an important dimension to the discussion.

Among the great painters, sculptors, and architects, Leonardo produced his masterpiece, the *Mona Lisa,* in his sixties. Titian finished *Christ Crowned with Thorns,* considered by many his most important statement on light and

---

Box 9.1 Some late great events

George Bernard Shaw writes his first play	Age: 48
Karen, Baroness Blixen writes her first book	Age: 49
Clementine Hunter paints her first painting	Age: 60
John Wayne wins an Oscar	Age: 62
LeCorbusier creates Notre Dame du Haut	Age: 64
Michelangelo finishes painting *The Last Judgement*	Age: 66
Cervantes writes *Don Quixote*	Age: 68
Charles de Gaulle returns to power in France	Age: 68
Konrad Adenauer wins the election that allows him to lead West Germany to reconstruction	Age: 72
Mahatma Gandhi launches the Quit India movement, which leads to India's independence	Age: 72
Coco Chanel comes back into the world of fashion	Age: 72
Benjamin Dugger discovers antibiotic chlortetracycline	Age: 72
Claude Monet begins his *Water Lily* series	Age: 73
Verdi produces *Otello*	Age: 74
Von Benden discovers the reduction of chromosomes	Age: 74
Mary M. Kaye writes *Far Pavillions*	Age: 65–75
Cecil B. DeMille produces *The Ten Commandments*	Age: 75
Sophocles writes *Oedipus Rex*	Age: 75
Pope John XXIII is elected	Age: 77
Benjamin Franklin invents the bifocal lens	Age: 78
George Burns launches a new movie career, winning an Oscar for *Sunshine Boys*	Age: 80
Verdi produces *Falstaff*	Age: 80
Goethe finishes *Faust*	Age: 82
Freud writes his last book	Age: 83
Bertrand Russell forms the Committee of 100, a radical organization devoted to nuclear disarmament	Age: 88
The Durants write the *Age of Napoleon*	Age: 89
Michelangelo creates St. Peter's Church and frescoes the Pauline Chapel	Age: 71–89
Frank Lloyd Wright completes the Guggenheim Museum	Age: 91
Georgia O'Keefe masters pottery skills in her nineties Picasso paints until his death at	Age: 91

SOURCE: Based on Van Moose & Worth, 1988, p. 93, and on Schaie & Geiwitz, 1982, pp. 415–419.

---

color, when he was eighty-two. Rembrandt painted two master works, *The Polish Rider* and *Christ Preaching,* just a few years before his death at sixty-three. The bust of Balzac, perhaps the most daring work of August Rodin, was a product of middle age. And, as an architect, LeCorbusier created what has been called "the most revolutionary building of the mid-twentieth century" at

At age 72, Mahatma
Gandhi launches the
Quit India movement,
which leads to India's
independence.

the age of sixty-four. Notre Dame du Haut defies analysis; its irrationality reflects the "spiritual condition of Modern Man—which is a measure of its greatness as a work of art" (Janson, 1962, p. 545).

It is possible that certain creative works are more likely in later life. Could an architect create a building mirroring the spiritual condition of modern man much before middle age? The great works of Sigmund Freud were a product of the last half of his life. Works that synthesize a lifetime of experience, works that reflect a deep understanding of the human condition, and works that draw upon wisdom and maturity are likely to be the products of later life.

Summary

I.   The Biology of Aging
     A.   Certain basic facts must be explained by any adequate theory of the
          biology of aging. These include:
          1.   species–specific life spans
          2.   the acceleration of aging by radiation
          3.   the extension of the life span by fasting

      4. the relationship between species-specific life spans, brain, and body weight

      5. the limited number of times cells appear able to reproduce themselves

      6. the fact that cells from an old organism outlive the donor if transplanted to a younger organism

  B. Biologists do not agree on whether the maximum life span of human beings can be extended by any significant amount.

      1. Process theories focus on processes within and between cells that may ultimately be controlled.

         a. Error theory stresses the accumulation of genetic error in individual cells when they are reproduced.

         b. Error theory is usually combined with the theory that emphasizes that declining immune system function plays an important part in aging.

         c. Collagen theory focuses on why cells become attached to one another, causing the tissues to stiffen and become less elastic.

         d. Free radicals, produced during oxidation, may contribute to cross-linking, the production of genetic errors, and declining immune system function.

      2. Proponents of death-clock theory state that death is a product of evolution and is programmed into human cells.

  C. Biologists do agree that it is possible to extend the average, healthy life span through medical technology and increasingly wise personal health choices.

II. Biological and Cognitive Change

  A. Skin and bones undergo significant changes.

      1. Skin becomes less elastic and wrinkling no longer just follows the pattern of muscle use.

      2. As bony material is lost, especially in females, fractures become more frequent.

      3. Changes in the joints produce arthritic conditions in most elderly people.

  B. All the internal organs are affected by stiffening of tissues, loss of muscle tone, and inadequate circulation.

      1. The efficiency of the heart declines, and vascular problems increase.

      2. Air pockets are lost in the lungs and some degree of emphysema usually appears.

      3. The filtration rate of the kidneys declines because of loss of nephrons and decreased blood flow.

      4. Digestion is affected by the loss of mucosal lining and declining production of gastric juices.

  C. The changes people fear most are associated with aging of the central nervous system. These changes tend to be linked with words like *senile*.

    1. The normal course of aging is not associated with increasing frequency of functional mental disorder.

    2. Problems of diagnosis obscure the differentiation of organic brain syndromes from functional disorders.

        a. Acute brain syndromes are characterized by fluctuating levels of awareness and are reversible.

        b. Chronic brain syndromes are progressive and often terminal, but with treatment partial recovery is possible.

III. Cognitive Function

  A. Sensation and perception

    1. Reduced blood supply in the lens and weakened muscle tissues produce changes in visual acuity and color discrimination.

    2. Older people often respond to the visual illusions more like adolescents or children than like young adults. However, this may be a cohort difference in familiarity with the illusions or may be related to a declining ability to handle new or unusual information.

    3. Hearing disorders requiring professional intervention increase with age and may be related to some of the emotional problems of the elderly.

    4. Gustation and olfaction decline with age and may be related to poor nutrition.

  B. Learning and memory

    1. Learning is the acquisition of information and rules, whereas memory is the ability to reconstruct events.

    2. Research on learning has often relied on the presentation of paired associates. The elderly benefit from increases in the anticipation interval more than the inspection interval in this type of research.

    3. Older people are able to learn meaningful material more easily than nonsense material, but research on concept learning suggests that they may process information differently than do the young.

    4. Elderly people tend to use fewer mediators than younger subjects.

    5. Using a three-process model of memory, many researchers have concluded that the difficulties of the elderly lie primarily in the transfer of information from short- to long-term memory.

    6. Fergus Craik has argued that depth of processing differentiates elderly performance from that of the young.

    7. James Fozard contends that the concept of deep processing is poorly defined and obscures the importance of cohort differences. Fozard believes that there may be many different memory codes and that memories are stored in many different areas of the brain.

    8. Studies of everyday learning and memory, especially studies of how people relate new information to information they already have, are rare.

B. Problem solving and creativity
1. Studies of problem solving show declining performance among the elderly on a variety of laboratory tasks. Much of this decline appears to be related to memory load, the opportunity to exercise the necessary abilities, and cohort differences in familiarity with the kinds of problems investigators use.
2. Early research on creativity also suggested a decline with age, but many of the subjects were not long-lived, and others had achieved prominent positions that might well have interfered with their productivity.
3. The myths of aging are likely to affect the perception of the self as a creative person, especially since creative people must be free to invent and reinvent the self.
4. Nonetheless, examples of important late-life creativity abound, even where great pain was associated with the creative process.
5. It may be that different forms of creativity are most likely at different points in the life cycle.

10

Old Age: The Interpersonal Context—Social Roles, Work, Family, and the Physical Environment

To be seventy years young is sometimes far more cheerful and hopeful than to be forty years old.

—Oliver Wendell Holmes

GORDON IS GETTING MARRIED FOR THE SECOND TIME at the age of seventy. Diana is forty and this will be her first marriage. In June they'll be married in Africa, where Gordon will be returning for his second stint as a Fulbright scholar. Gordon met Diana on tour in the Middle East last year. During his first Fulbright in Uganda, Gordon climbed Kilimanjaro. Made it to the top. A lot of the younger men on the trip didn't. They were racing their way up the mountain and just ran out of steam. Gordon feels as though he relived the story of the tortoise and the hare. Anyway, he fell in love with Africa: the wildlife, the people, the opportunity to be useful. He built a medical clinic at a village near the university, funded entirely with money he'd raised through his connections back home. And, of course, best of all, if he hadn't gone to Africa, he wouldn't have met Diana.

Meanwhile, Gordon's ex-wife Marta is going great guns in her first real career at the age of fifty-five. She's learning banking law and hopes to develop a consulting practice as a "compliance officer." With banks in their current crisis, she knows there are plenty of opportunities. When she and Gordon sold the house they built, she was able to take her capital gains forgiveness and use the money to buy a condominium in Hawaii. The man she has been dating for several years loves Hawaii. Marta's not so sure she wants to be married again. There was so much trouble about money in the divorce and that's only been final for about a year. Furthermore, Milton has children from a previous marriage and Marta's got two children. It's probably best to leave their estates just as they are. Actually, it's kind of nice when you don't own everything together. Marta can retain control over her own money and nobody ever questions anything she buys.

THESE ARE NOT THE ORDINARY VISIONS we have of older people. We don't think of seventy-year-old men climbing Kilimanjaro or the wife, divorced after fifty, making a really good life for herself. Yet both of these stories are about real people that are friends of one of the authors. They aren't examples culled from newspaper accounts or secondhand reports. These are just some examples of the way people can take advantage of the events of later life. There is much opportunity and freedom in aging if we only take advantage of it, especially as people become more affluent and healthier in their later years.

In this chapter, we will look at both sides of old age, the negative, constraining forces and the other, less obvious side, the possibility of freedom and integration. We begin by examining attitudes toward aging, the aged, and the self as an elderly person. Here, most clearly perhaps, the duality characterizing the last stages of life emerges. Few elderly people want to *be* young, but almost everyone wants to *feel* young.

We will also review the literature on later life adjustment and consider the concept of adjustment itself. A problematic concept, adjustment has been measured in numerous ways, few of them either very useful or creative. Work on personality in old age, and the possibility of measuring subjective changes in how people experience the life span will be covered as well. Leaving abstractions like attitudes and adjustment, we then tackle the concrete realities of the social world, reviewing research on marriage and sexual behavior in old age and relationships between elderly people and their family and friends.

Attitudes and Adjustment in Old Age

In the last few years everything I'd done up to sixty or so has seemed very childish.

—T. S. Eliot

Researching attitudes is one of the most complex tasks psychologists and sociologists attempt. First, while the researcher's goal is to determine how people perceive issues or objects or other people, such generalizations are based on what people *say,* which may or may not describe their feelings and beliefs accurately. Secondly, the questions researchers formulate often evoke feelings and attitudes that are far more complex than originally assumed. Questions designed to measure attitudes and feelings about one subject may evoke responses about a completely different subject. In the study of aging, these considerations arise because the attitudes people have toward age are not only complex but also conflict-ridden and only partially conscious.

In most studies, for example, it is difficult to tell whether the researcher has

"When I was younger, I could remember anything whether it happened or not; but I am getting old, and soon I shall remember only the latter." Mark Twain

tapped attitudes about aging, elderly people, or a particular cohort of elderly people. At the time a researcher sets out to do a study, attitudes toward elderly people reflect attitudes toward a particular group of elderly people. Negative, prejudicial responses to elderly people also reflect fears about aging, fears based on limited contact with the elderly and/or misinformation.

Box 10.1 presents an opportunity for you to determine whether misinformation affects your own attitudes about aging. This quiz first appeared in 1977. Since then, it has been used with a variety of subjects in many settings, permitting some interesting generalizations.

Overall, most people know the facts of aging. Among undergraduate psychology students, the average score is about 70 percent correct. Graduate students answer 80 to 90 percent of the questions correctly; social workers average 64 percent; medical students, 70 percent; and groups of adults in the general population are right more than half of the time. But certain items are missed more consistently than others. People underestimate the percentage of the population that is elderly. They also overestimate how many elderly live in institutions and assume (incorrectly) that elderly people usually become more religious. Generally, people associate old age with poverty and boredom more often than the facts support (Lutsky, 1980; Prado, 1988). On the positive side, most subjects reject the idea that elderly people are asexual, senile, or intractable.

Box 10.1 Facts on aging

Before proceeding further, you are encouraged to try out the quiz to find out which facts you may be unaware of. Circle "T" for True or "F" for False.

T   F   1. The majority of old people (past age sixty-five) are senile (i.e., defective memory, disoriented, or demented).

T   F   2. All five senses tend to decline in old age.

T   F   3. Most old people have no interest in, or capacity for, sexual relations.

T   F   4. Lung capacity tends to decline in old age.

T   F   5. The majority of old people feel miserable most of the time.

T   F   6. Physical strength tends to decline in old age.

T   F   7. At least one tenth of the aged are living in long-stay institutions (i.e., nursing homes, mental hospitals, homes for the aged, etc.).

T   F   8. Aged drivers have fewer accidents per person than drivers under age sixty-five.

T   F   9. Most older workers cannot work as effectively as younger workers.

T   F   10. About 80 percent of the aged are healthy enough to carry out their normal activities.

T   F   11. Most old people are set in their ways and unable to change.

T   F   12. Old people usually take longer to learn something new.

T   F   13. It is almost impossible for most old people to learn new things.

T   F   14. The reaction time of most old people tends to be slower than reaction time of younger people.

Ageism is discrimination based on age, especially discrimination against middle-aged and elderly people. It is reflected in the language we use, the way we treat people, the expectations we have. For example, words like *mature, mellow, sage,* and *venerable,* words that present a positive image of age, are relatively rare. Terms like *old bag* (*bat, biddy, battle ax*) and *dirty old coot* (*codger, fogy, fossil, fuddy-duddy, geezer, goat*) dominate the linguistic picture (Nuessel, 1982). Clinical psychologists evaluate the mental health of older people more negatively than that of the young. Ageism may even be reflected in some of the research in this chapter. As Douglas Kimmel (1988) has pointed out: "Ageism in psychological research is a concern because of the ubiquitous nature of conflicting ideas about age in our society. It may manifest itself in the way the research question is asked, in the respondents selected, in the data analysis, or in the interpretation of results" (p. 177).

Ageism appears about the same time as racism and sexism (sometime be-

---

Box 10.1 *(continued)*

T   F   15. In general, most old people are pretty much alike.

T   F   16. The majority of old people are seldom bored.

T   F   17. The majority of old people are socially isolated and lonely.

T   F   18. Older workers have fewer accidents than younger workers.

T   F   19. Over 15 percent of the U.S. population are now age sixty-five or over.

T   F   20. Most medical practitioners tend to give low priority to the aged.

T   F   21. The majority of older people have incomes below the poverty level (as defined by the federal government).

T   F   22. The majority of old people are working or would like to have some kind of work to do (including housework and volunteer work).

T   F   23. Older people tend to become more religious as they age.

T   F   24. The majority of old people are seldom irritated or angry.

T   F   25. The health and socioeconomic status of older people (compared to younger people) in the year 2000 will probably be about the same as now.

The key to the correct answer is simple: all the odd numbered items are false, and all the even numbered are true.

SOURCE: Palmore, 1977.

---

tween six and eight years old) and is present even among the elderly, who often complain that they don't want to be around "old people." Negative stereotypes can produce low motivation among the elderly as well as behavioral decline and even poor physical health, as older people may be less likely to take good care of themselves or to receive good care from the health care system (Kimmel, 1988).

Negative attitudes toward the aged are certainly not a new phenomenon, however. Attitudes toward the elderly have always been ambivalent, although through most of history there has been reverence for as well as dread of great age (Achenbaum, 1985). In the biblical culture of the Jews and early Christians, age was considered a reward from God for leading a good life. The Bible says Noah was 600 years old at the time of the deluge. Among the Greeks and Romans, conflicted attitudes were more apparent. Geras, the god of age, for example, was portrayed as a wrinkled, dwarflike monster, despite the fact that many important Greek poets, lawyers, historians, and statesmen were over sixty.

In the last decade, some sociologists (Achenbaum, 1985; Von Kondratowitz, 1984) have gathered evidence that a shift from ambivalence tempered by respect, toward more strongly negative feelings about age probably began sometime around the American Revolution, with the decline of patriarchy and the emergence of more egalitarian family structures. Sometime during this period, the veneration of age ended, and Western societies became quite youth-oriented. Hans-Joachim Von Kondratowitz (1984) gives an interesting example. He points out how the powdered wig and long coat of the eighteenth century gentleman was replaced by the tight-fitting tunic and natural hairstyle of the nineteenth century. Furthermore, sometime during the nineteenth century, expressions of ridicule for the aged crept into the language.

W. Andrew Achenbaum (1985) believes that the negative posture of the nineteenth century has been reinforced by modern medical advances. Over the past 100 years, death has become reserved for the end of the life cycle, and Achenbaum has argued that the elderly are now excluded from the mainstream of a youth-oriented society by a "general reformulation of previously held notions about death and dying, which reinforced negative images of age" (p. 141).

Research on attitudes is not without its silver lining, however. It has been demonstrated, for instance, that lively older people who act young are more valued than young people who act the same way. A speech or piece of writing is not devalued when it is attributed to an older person, and people look forward to the freedom and leisure of retirement (Lutsky, 1980). Despite the fact that most people fear aging and usually prefer younger friends and advisors, the context in which a choice is presented can change the response. One can create an attractive, young-at-heart older person, and people will prefer the exceptional older person over a young person with the same attributes (Kalish, 1982).

Research also shows that given opportunity to make exceptions to their generalizations (generalizations like "older people need more time to learn something than do the young"), people make many exceptions. In fact, subjects indicate that as many as 50 percent of the elderly may not fit the stereotypic image (Schonfield, 1982). Stereotypes are essential tools in a complex society where many difficult decisions must be made. Think how much time it would take to contemplate thoroughly every decision you make in the course of a normal day. What brand of aspirin is really best? What television program is honestly worth your time? Which birthday present would really please your son's friend (whom you do not know too well)? We develop stereotypes just to survive. All aspirin are the same, we say. I like adventure series best. Seventeen-year-old boys don't want Barbie dolls. But are you absolutely certain? There are always exceptions, and we have to avoid using stereotypes to define what is normal (older people who are very sexually active are not crazy). Furthermore, we have to remember a stereotype does not necessarily reflect some biological force (waning sexuality is not inevitable). There are people like Gordon and Marta everywhere and we must be careful not to impose our own fears or prejudices on older people we encounter. After all, everyone becomes an older person someday, if he or she is lucky. Negative attitudes toward aging and the elderly limit our own future in a way that no other stereotype we hold may do.

It may also be important to sort out just what it is we feel so negative about. The literature is unclear as to whether people are negative toward elderly people, aging, the stereotype itself, or particular elderly individuals they know. Elderly people themselves have a fairly optimistic view of themselves and of life as an older person, but even they doubt that other old people are as well off. It is possible that the confusion contributes to low self-esteem. The elderly may not take care of themselves and demand the support and services they need to stay fit and satisfied. The more positive aspects of aging must be clearer if self-esteem is to be maintained or improved in the last part of the life course.

As Von Kondratowitz (1984) reminds us, even the most negative attitudes toward old age are the products of long-term but mutable forces. Attitudes toward age are historically transitory. They can and do change and are not necessarily related to the physical or biological realities of age. "Being old in the United States today thus has positive and negative features that result from the interplay of broad historical vectors, which are themselves independent of any intrinsic features of senescence" (Achenbaum, 1985, p. 144). Ageism may needlessly magnify our own fears of aging.

All of which spotlights issues of stability and change in later life. Does personality change in ways that might support the stereotype? Are life satisfaction and adjustment negatively affected by whatever changes take place in personality, biology, or circumstance?

Personality and Adjustment

Erikson maintains that the dominant theme in later life is expressed in a conflict between **integrity** and **despair**. He believes that integrity consists in maintaining a sense of coherence and wholeness at supreme risk—under the threat of physical, psychological, and social loss. Integrity is an appreciation for the meaningfulness of one's own life cycle, a timeless love for those "others" who have played a significant role in one's life, and an understanding that all human history is related to individual integrity. The virtue born of the conflict between integrity and despair is **wisdom**, which he defined as "informed and detached concern with life itself in the face of death itself," and the antithesis of wisdom is **disdain**, "a reaction to feeling (and seeing others) in an increasing state of being finished, confused, helpless" (Erikson, 1982, p. 60).

In the last stage of the life cycle, people confront the proposition "I am what survives of me." One must find a narrative line in one's own life; make sense of the passing years; finish the puzzle; discover the will, purposefulness, competence, love, care, and wisdom one has been able to contribute to society (Erikson, 1968a). If these tasks prove impossible, despair develops, and a person cannot accept his or her own fate, cannot accept death, and is victimized by feelings of regret, frustration, and discouragement. Death becomes the ultimate destroyer, ending any hope of fulfillment in life.

As is usually the case in things theoretical, some important criticisms of Erikson's formulation have been advanced. For instance, a number of writers argue that Erikson's concepts are **ethnocentric**, that he speaks of attributes and traits that are valued in Western societies as though they were universally optimal. Of integrity, in particular, it has been said he ignores the continuing importance of rebellion and doubt throughout the life cycle. As Allan Buss (1979) suggests, Erikson's emphasis on accepting one's life implies an end of questioning and stresses acceptance at the expense of continuing development. Some people are never content to rest on their laurels. Zorba the Greek said, "Men like me should live a thousand years." Was he right? Or, more to the point, was he mature?

The whole question of individual differences is largely ignored by most stage-type theories of development, but there is good reason to believe that older people are more different from one another than are the young. In any group of twenty-year-olds, you are likely to find that some are married and some are not, most have finished high school, a few have been divorced, and almost all are in good health. In a group of eighty-year-olds, think of the variety of experience. Some are married, some divorced, some widowed, some lifetime singles. Some are in good health, some very ill. Some have childen, grandchildren, great-grandchildren, and some have no kin at all. Some live alone, some with family, some in institutions. The possibilities are nearly endless, and different lifestyles are probably optimal for different personalities. Nonetheless, many researchers and writers have yet to adopt a pluralistic point of view about the aged personality and adjustment to old age. The impact of life events on personality in old age has only recently become a focus of concern.

Personality, Age, and Adjustment

In a major review article for the second edition of the *Handbook of the Psychology of Aging,* Vern Bengston, Margaret Reedy, and Chad Gordon (1985) conclude that "cohort membership, sex, sociocultural trends, and life stage experiences have more significant impact on self-conceptions than does maturation" (p. 587). These authors argue that personality or self-concept should be studied in groups of people categorized by life stage rather than age. They believe that life events have a more important impact on variables like personality traits, self-esteem, sociability, assertion, achievement, and the like, than age itself.

As the population ages, particularly if the life span is much increased, people will undoubtedly be forced to spend a greater proportion of that increased span as active members of the labor force in order to maintain some measure of economic security.

Most recently, James Birren and Candace Stacey (1988) have concluded that personality and coping styles seem to show considerable stability with age, although there is evidence of increased introversion among the elderly (Costa & McCrae, 1989, 1990). They also point to research showing greater neuroticism and lower psychological well-being among older women but believe that this may be explained by the greater percentage of women who are widowed (compared to men) and the lower economic status of older widows.

Birren and Stacey write that among persons aged seventy to eighty, there may be some decline in personal involvement for men and mental energy for women, but the changes are minimal. Small increases may also occur in the need for order and conformity and lower needs for exhibition and dominance among both men and women. Overall, however, the picture is one of stability on the usual measures of personality. Slight increases in rigidity are better explained by cohort differences, according to Birren and Stacey, than by age.

Yet there is a widespread assumption that older people become narrow in their views and inflexible in their responses. They are viewed as primarily having and posing problems. Most importantly, these problems are considered worse than, not merely different from, the problems of people at other ages (Prado, 1988).

As for the evidence, most elderly people report few changes in their self-concept even through the age of eighty (Eisenhandler, 1989). They do not even report many health problems, despite a wide variety of diseases from arthritis to diabetes, so long as their daily activities are not greatly restricted. "Elders who remain engaged with life are more likely to see their own old age as unproblematic. Old age does quite literally sneak up and into a coherent identity" (Eisenhandler, 1989, p. 176).

The most frequent kinds of changes people report have more to do with values than with self-concept or personality. For instance, middle-aged women report that instrumental values such as being active and controlling are more important than intimacy, the necessity for which they found more salient in young adulthood. Both men and women in middle age experience generativity as most significant, whereas older people talk more about the value of reflecting and contemplation (Ryff, 1984). In Chapter 7, we reviewed data on sex-role convergence in middle age; however, evidence exists that certain other changes may be sex-specific among the elderly.

Sex Roles and the Aging Personality

A number of authors have cast sex-role changes in later life in terms of **androgyny**, that is, the acceptance of both male and female characteristics of the self. One researcher reported that most of the nearly four hundred older adults in his sample could be classified as androgynous (Sinnott, 1982); other writers have found that older women appear more dominant, whereas older men show increased expressiveness and nurturance (Skolnick, 1986b; Turner, 1982). In these reports, however, the changes are not usually described as sexual convergence, David Gutmann's term (1964, 1975, 1977, 1990) used in the discussion of personality in middle age in Chapter 7. Healthy older men continue to be assertive, even pugnacious, and healthy older women lose none of their nurturant caring qualities (Lieberman, 1981; Turner, 1982; Huyck, 1990). Men and women who exhibit the masculine traits associated with being instrumental are likely to experience higher levels of well-being in old age (Huyck, 1990).

These attitudinal or personality changes are not necessarily manifest in the behavior of older people, however. In fact, there is some indication that behavior remains essentially unchanged. In old age, men report a greater desire for closeness, but few may have developed any real capacity for it. Although they say they feel an increased interest in friends and family, they actually spend most of their time alone, and their wives, who are usually their closest confidants, continue to complain that men lack the ability to communicate (Turner, 1982).

"Nothing is inherently and invincibly young except spirit. And spirit can enter a human being perhaps better in the quiet of old age and dwell there more undisturbed than in the turmoil of adventure." George Santayana

Reviewing these data, Lillian Troll and Vern Bengston (1982) concluded that some of the sex-role changes older people report are probably due to failing health among the men. Postmenopausal females are often healthier than they were earlier and are usually healthier than older men (Huyck, 1990). Furthermore, since many women continue working after their husbands retire, a shift in power and dominance seems inevitable. In addition, Troll and Bengston argue, years of living together make people think and act more alike. The androgyny of later life may reflect growing similarity based on continuing interaction. Finally, they note that young people tend to treat the elderly as though they were asexual, encouraging the development of androgyny. In all, Troll and Bengston conclude, the changes are more internal than external, involving the expression of dependence and autonomy. "Where resources are less," they have written, "flexibility helps" (1982, p. 138).

We might wonder if these data will change as the cohort currently reaching middle age moves into the last stages of the life cycle. These people were young adults and adolescents during the women's movement of the 1970s, and sex-role behaviors are not very strongly transmitted across generations. Can we expect some real changes in the sex-role behaviors of elderly people as younger cohorts move through the life cycle? The study of personality development is never complete, for historical change affects attitudes, values, and, eventually, behaviors. The evolution of the human personality at every stage of the life course is endlessly fascinating. Personality is a complex mosaic of traits and characteristics, having continuity and predictability, but also alive with constantly changing forms and patterns.

Adjustment and Life Satisfaction

In this section, we turn from the issues of specific traits and personality to more general measures like *life satisfaction, morale,* and *happiness.* As Linda George (1981) wrote in her article for the *Annual Review of Gerontology and Geriatrics,* such phenomena as happiness and life satisfaction lie in the mind of the beholder. A life situation that is unacceptable to one person may be just the ticket for another. Keeping this in mind, she defines life satisfaction as the congruence between goals or expectations and achievements. In other words, people feel satisfied when they accomplish what they set out to do. Life satisfaction, according to George, is an intellectual evaluation. Of course, it is strongly associated with some fairly objective factors like health, personal resources, social support and involvement, financial assets, coping capacity, and one's own stereotype about aging, and is stable over rather long periods of the life cycle (Lee and Markides, 1990; Busse and Maddox, 1985).

Happiness, George points out, is a more ephemeral phenomenon. It is an emotional or affective assessment of an inner feeling state, and it is shorter-term. People may be happy for a day or a week and not expect it to continue. Generally, happiness is not more likely at one period of the life cycle than another. However, researchers have not studied cohort differences on how people define happiness or how much happiness they expect. It is quite likely that members of younger cohorts expect to be happy more often than older cohorts do. It might be interesting to see how that expectation affects the experience of middle age and later life.

Finally, George contends that the word *morale* has very little meaning. At times, researchers use psychiatric symptoms like anxiety, worry, dependence, fear, sleeplessness, and tension as measures of morale. At other times, such symptoms are used as measures of life satisfaction. Furthermore, she argues, surveys usually elicit very general assessments of morale or life satisfaction, ignoring the potential for specific statements about different arenas of life: marriage, family, work, income, leisure activity, friends, housing, community.

Terms like *morale* also appear frequently in the study of social roles. Most often, it is assumed that role loss (children leaving home, retirement, widowhood) produces stress and has a negative impact on self-concept and therefore on morale. If society provided meaningful roles for the elderly, the argument continues, morale would improve. Yet, as we know, neither the launching of children nor retirement is strongly associated with poor morale or low life satisfaction. In addition, as Leslie Morgan (1982) affirms in another volume of the *Annual Review of Gerontology and Geriatrics,* it is not clear that role activity in and of itself produces higher morale. For instance, deviant roles like the role of criminal, or victim, or patient don't seem to support morale. And, finally, the available data showing that role activity is related to higher morale and life satisfaction do not permit us to assume that activity produces high morale. Perhaps people who have high morale and life satisfaction continue to be active, whereas those who are discontent withdraw from social roles as soon as possible. Historically, the issue of activity and withdrawal has played a very important part in the study of adjustment. The investigation of these questions began with the hypothesis that normal aging might be universally characterized by declining lack of interest or engagement in the outside world.

Disengagement Theory

In the early sixties, the notion that mutual withdrawal in later life between the individual and the society was normal, in fact optimal, was developed as **disengagement theory** (Cumming & Henry, 1961). The sloughing off of roles and activities was said to produce high levels of satisfaction and adjustment.

As critics soon noted, however, disengagement is often forced on the elderly. There is nothing voluntary about it. Society devalues the aged and requires them to resign their roles and activities. When the opportunity arises, many older people choose continued activity and involvement and derive satisfaction from a variety of lifestyles (Havighurst, 1969; Palmore, 1979). On the other hand, continued engagement itself does not predict satisfaction for everyone. Most probably, the opportunity to express one's basic personality pattern at each stage of the life cycle is important. People who were always active and involved will be happiest if they remain engaged. For those who have never loved the busy, active life, however, late life may offer a welcome opportunity to shed unwanted roles and activities (Neugarten & Hagestad, 1977).

Critics still speculate, however, that disengagement is natural and adaptive only for the self-protective and emotionally bland, or perhaps for people trapped in stressful circumstances (Lowenthal, Thurnher, & Chiriboga, 1975; Palmore, 1968). Marjorie Lowenthal theorizes that many people respond to loss by lowering their goals and limiting their behaviors, that is, by becoming disengaged; however, other patterns are normal too. What about Renoir building the machine to move his hands? Some people expand their behavioral repertoire when they encounter loss. Some find new ways to continue in cherished roles, others substitute new roles and relationships for old ones. Lowenthal calls these assertive patterns **transcendence**. Of course, Lowenthal reminds us, there are also the dreamers or escapists who always expand their goals but not their behaviors, who plan the book that never gets written, the golf lessons that never quite materialize. Furthermore, we all recognize the behavior of *deniers,* who change neither goals nor behaviors in the face of loss but act as though nothing has changed.

Unfortunately, Lowenthal observes, the circumstances of later life encourage disengagement, escapism, and denial. In a major study called *The Four Stages of Life,* she concluded that the most complex personalities, those who are happiest as young adults, are most likely to be dissatisfied as elderly people. She has argued that the unhappiness of complex elderly people reflects reduced opportunities for meaningful engagement and self-expression. Complex people who might otherwise transcend their losses, lack the resources to continue being productive, creative people.

Disengagement is probably an economic necessity for many. Income is still the most important predictor of life satisfaction among the elderly (Shanan & Jacobowitz, 1982). Intellectual traits are also predictive of adjustment (Kuypers, 1981), and these characteristics tend to be fairly stable over the life span. Even if personality is stable, however, certain traits become more important with age.

Certainly, the evidence for the notion that some traits become more important to adjustment and life satisfaction seems more consistent than the data on personality change. Flexibility and self-directedness, tolerance for ambiguity, empathy, and logical thinking appear to be especially important (Kuypers, 1981). Joel Shanan and Jacob Jacobowitz (1982) sum it up as the ability to draw on internal resources in response to loss. In part, the importance of internal resources may derive from the withdrawal of society, but it can also be understood as a response to the normal physical and social losses of later life, losses of energy, health, and significant others.

More recently, Ewald Busse and George Maddox (1985) have presented extensive data on life satisfaction from the Duke Longitudinal Studies of Normal Aging. They report that leisure and group and social activities did contribute to both health and happiness among their subjects, and that group activities and work satisfaction were actually associated with longevity among the men they studied, whereas female life satisfaction improved if friends and family lived nearby. They also found that sexual activity predicted health, happiness, and longevity among all the participants.

Generally, however, these researchers found few changes in life satisfaction or happiness over the course of the study, the exception to this rule being a decline in satisfaction following the death of a spouse in middle age. Patricia Gurin and Orville Brim (1984) confirmed this finding when they studied sense of control over the adult life span. They concluded that rare off-time events were much more likely to produce change in life satisfaction and sense of control than those that occur at the anticipated point in the life cycle, regardless of the nature of the event. Early widowhood and early retirement are examples of the kinds of events that affect people most strongly if they are off-time.

Both the Gurin and Brim study and the Duke Longitudinal Study present a fairly optimistic view of aging and adjustment. Gurin and Brim report data suggesting that people actually feel a stronger sense of control and self-efficacy over sixty. Busse and Maddox found their panelists exhibited the capacity to adapt to retirement, widowhood, children leaving home, and even serious illness. None of these events appeared to produce long-term negative events. Even major medical traumas that produced declines in health and activity had no major effects on life satisfaction. Older people appear to have an amazing ability to bounce back from the most trying times, and Busse and Maddox expect that younger cohorts will do even better as they age than the people studied so far, as better diet, health habits, and medical care; more physical exercise; less poverty; and higher levels of education should increase the adaptive resources of the future elderly. As Gurin and Brim put it, people learn to live with fewer arrows, less corn, and poorer eyesight.

Activity, social roles, and life satisfaction appear to be similar among elderly Mexican Americans as well (Lee & Markides, 1990; Markides & Lee, 1990). An eight-year longitudinal study of 508 older Mexican Americans and Anglos (Markides & Lee, 1990) found that activity itself does not predict mortality or life satisfaction. The researchers write that "activity theory is the layperson's theory of aging, and many elderly persons explain their longevity in terms of their continued high activity level" (p. S39). Yet their findings are in agreement with Busse and Maddox and with Gurin and Brim. Despite declining activity with age, they found only minor overall declines in functioning and well-being. The most important variable related to life satisfaction in this study is functional health. Markides and Lee (1990) also report that Mexican Americans show less increase in psychological distress with age than do Anglos. However, Palmore et al. (1985) reported the reverse finding for blacks. It is not clear why such ethnic and racial differences occur. Overall, however, continuity of life satisfaction seems typical of most groups in our culture.

All of these data appear to agree with Susan Eisenhandler's (1989) observation that old age does not much influence one's experience of life or self-

As society evolves and needs and expectations change, so will the possibilities for adjustment and satisfaction later in life. For those elderly who are forced to retire or stop work without adequate financial security, the role of income in determining life satisfaction becomes extremely important.

concept until significant health problems arise. Thus, as we might expect, changes through the last part of the life cycle represent continuing adaptation and adjustment rather than discontinuity. In the studies by Markides and Lee (1990), the strongest relationships for life satisfaction and psychological distress were found between ratings taken at the beginning of this eight-year study and ratings for life satisfaction and psychological distress taken at the end of the eight years. People who are satisfied tend to continue to be satisfied and those who are distressed continue to be distressed. Preliminary data even suggest that successful aging can be predicted from early adult adjustment, especially for women. In a continuing analysis of the data from the Berkeley studies, Joseph Kuypers (1981) has defined adaptation in later life in terms of a fluid responsiveness to both the external and the internal world. The well-adapted subjects in his sample appeared self-directed, empathic, and firm but flexible. In addition, they were able to suppress their own anxieties when necessary or redirect anxiety into productive activities (**sublimation**).

Kuypers also describes subjects who tended to rationalize and were haunted by doubt as **defensive adapters**, whereas **disorganized personalities** exhibited tangential thinking and often appeared immobilized. Repression characterized defensive individuals, whereas withdrawal, preoccupation, and even delusional thinking were characteristic of the disorganized personality.

Adaptation in women, according to Kuypers, showed greater stability than adaptation in men from early to later adulthood, and it seemed more strongly related to family life events. Overall, for both men and women, socioeconomic class and intellectual ability were the best predictors of adjustment in later life. These findings may ultimately mean that success in one's major life roles is in fact the best predictor of late-life satisfaction. Socioeconomic class is usually a reflection of occupational achievement for males, and marital disharmony is related to the success a woman experiences in the traditional female role. Is it possible, Kuypers wonders, that certain individuals, especially certain women, are "locked" into ego failure from the earliest years of adulthood because they are unsuccessful at the major life roles? If it is accurate to hypothesize that adult role fulfillment is important in determining adaptation, then we might also expect historical changes in the determinants of adaptation. If roles change substantially from one generation to the next, there may be concomitant changes in the factors that best predict adjustment.

Like the study of personality, the exploration of successful aging may be an endless project. As the society evolves and needs and expectations change, the possibilities for adjustment and satisfaction later in life may be continuously altered. Futurists like Alvin Toffler (1970, 1980) predict enormous increases in cultural diversity in the next generation, and these trends can be expected to influence adults of all ages. It may be that such concepts as "adjustment" are too general to yield valuable information, particularly in the context of rapid social change. The conditions and circumstances that favor one pattern of aging over another may not be static long enough for anyone to make even temporarily definitive statements about optimal patterns. Studies like those of Lowenthal and her associates are most provocative when they address circumscribed phenomena. For example, substantial age differences have been found in some aspects of time perception.

Time Perspective

The study of time perspective has offered some productive research about the ways in which our perception of time may be related to other attitudes and behaviors. Children in Western cultures learn to associate time with distance, for example, and have a strong tendency to view time in a linear way. Time is perceived by most of us to pass, moment by moment, each second disappearing as it is ticked off by the clock. Americans, in particular, grow up with the notion that time passes in a definite, measurable way, just as the miles fly past in a speeding car. In America, time marches on. It may come as some surprise, then, to learn that time evidently passes quite differently for people of different age groups. Although we know that "time flies when you are having fun" or that the days before your birthday party drag when you are six and race when you are thirty-nine, the subjective experience of time holds a mystery for most of us. Why does time seem to go faster as one grows older?

It has been suggested that time passes faster for adults because each moment represents a smaller proportion of one's total life. If this were so, old men and women should perceive time as passing more swiftly than the middle-aged. In actuality, however, more middle-aged men describe time as passing quickly than do members of any other age group. Could it be, then, that one's orientation toward the present or the past, rather than the future, best predicts the experience of time pressure? Middle-aged men spend a good deal of time rehashing the past, reworking and reorganizing their lives. Perhaps people experience a sense of time pressure at transition points throughout the life span rather than at one point or the other (Lowenthal et al., 1975).

Older people too may spend a lot of time thinking about the past. There is evidence, however, that older people evaluate the past in a positive and satisfied way more often than do young adults or middle-aged people (Cameron, 1972; Lieberman, 1970). Older people also report less experience of eventfulness, or density of time, than those at the threshold of middle age. Subjects in their fifties and sixties report fewer turning points and fewer frustrations in their lives than do people in their forties. They also express less involvement in the events they do experience. Perhaps changes in the experienced density of time may eventually explain age differences in the sense of time pressure people feel.

The healthy elderly may live more in the present than any other age group (Eisenhandler, 1989). Healthy elders tend to focus on what they still have rather than what they have lost and to find new and more realistic aspirations as time passes. They express relief at not having the worries about children and their marital situation that they did when they were younger. They don't say they want to be young again. Most simply say that they do not think of themselves as old and they try to live life one day at a time. Although older people may engage in more vigorous life review, no existing data indicate that older people dwell on the past and younger subjects live in the future.

It does seem true, however, that the future is seen as better than the present or the past throughout the first half of the life cycle. Sometime around the age of fifty, the past, present, and future are all perceived as about equally negative or positive. After the age of seventy, the past is evaluated as better than the present, and the present is seen as better than the future (Bortner & Hultsch, 1972).

Most older Americans do not believe the future is likely to be the best period in their lives. Many young people do. Younger subjects project much farther into the future than do the old. About 75 percent of the high school students and newlyweds in the Lowenthal study (1975) projected into their eighties, but only 66 percent of the middle-aged subjects and only 46 percent of the preretirement group did so. Interestingly, the happiest of the preretirees were found in that 46 percent. In the oldest group, two-thirds of those individuals who were rated as "impaired" in adjustment showed limited ability to project themselves into the future. Thus, although the happiest group might not have a rosy vision of the future, they appear willing to plan for and accept it anyway. As Arthur C. Clarke quipped about Robert Browning's lines "Grow old along with me / The best is yet to be": "I think he's whistling in the dark, but I'm going anyway."

One last finding about time perception from Lowenthal and her associates has some interesting implications. Time perspective may have more predictive value for the old than for the young. We have seen that in older groups the ability to project into the future is associated with adjustment. There are also data to support the notion that the most competent older people are those who are *not* heavily invested in the future. They may plan for the future, but they do not live in it. Neither do they dwell in the past, although they have learned to consider the past as well as the present and future. Older people may actually be in a position to achieve balance in time. An older person has a past long enough to be a history, to contain triumphs and defeats, to be as exciting as the future; and so the future becomes less demanding and less impressive.

The alteration of one's perspective on time may be part of the process by which integrity develops. In describing integrity, Erikson (1963, p. 268) says that it is in part "the acceptance of one's one and only life cycle." This acceptance is accompanied by a diminished need to rush toward the future to achieve unfinished goals and tie up loose ends. Again, we are standing at a juncture of developmental trends and social structure. The social structure dictates acceptable goals and achievements, which are also defined and interpreted in the context of a particular personality. These social and personal events combine with a changing sense of time to determine the developmental course of later adulthood. Ruth Benedict expressed the interaction eloquently when she wrote that "society in its full sense . . . is never an entity separable from the individuals who compose it. No individual can arrive even at the threshhold of his [or her] potentialities without a culture in which he [or she] participates. Conversely, no civilization has in it any element which in the last analysis is not the contribution of an individual" (Peter, 1979, p. 92).

The Social Network

It has been argued that all present theoretical frameworks for the study of adult development underestimate the importance of the interaction between biological and environmental forces. Even more specifically, some contend that, unlike the first seven stages of Erikson's scheme, the eighth stage is too often described almost exclusively in terms of internal, developmental factors. Too little consideration is given to the influence of external, environmental experience and the problems of coping constructively with the physical, psychological, and social losses of the later years (Glenwick & Whitbourne, 1978).

In this section, we begin to consider some important environmental events in relationship to the general development trends we have discussed so far. What effect does the lifestyle of an elderly person have on adjustment, satisfaction, health, morale, and survival? In this chapter, information about marriage, family, and friendship is surveyed. Economic, ecological, and work-related issues will be covered in Chapter 11.

Marriage and Family

Many studies suggest that marriage is most satisfying in the last years of the life cycle, but it is not always clear why this is so. It is unlikely that the divorces of unhappy couples explain why marital satisfaction increases, for even now, relatively few older people divorce. However, a contrast effect may be at work since nearly eight out of ten males over sixty-five are married, whereas only four of ten females are. Since married middle-aged women are, by and large, least satisfied with marriage, old age may bring greater satisfaction in contrast to the plight of widowed friends. Furthermore, because the chances of remarriage for women are very poor (the remarriage rate for men over sixty-five is seven times that of women), widowhood is pretty much a permanent state of affairs. Over age sixty-five, one half of all females are widowed, but only 14 percent of men are (Kalish, 1985). By age eighty-five, there are only 44 men for every 100 women (Aizenberg & Treas, 1985).

Older women perceive marriage as more equitable than middle-aged women do. Between thirty and seventy, most women feel slightly under-benefited in marriage, but, after seventy, they feel more benefited than even newlywed young women. Perhaps the shift toward greater androgyny in both men and women encourages a more positive feminine evaluation of marriage in the later years (Traupmann & Hatfield, 1983).

Men also perceive greater fairness in marriage in later life and both sexes experience more positive interactions and fewer negative sentiments than younger couples (Treas & Bengston, 1987). In one study of couples married fifty years or more (Condie, 1989), the authors note that couples reported the greatest amount of marital satisfaction in the last stages of the family life cycle. Figure 10.1 presents data on the marital satisfaction of wives and husbands from the Condie study. The stages of the family life cycle refer to various events, such as birth of the first child (stage II) or launching of the last child. Stage VIII corresponds to the celebration of their fiftieth wedding anniversary.

Of course, late-life marriage is not entirely trouble-free, especially where there are health problems. When women must begin to function more like mothers or nurses and less like spouses, resentment usually ensues. Retirement can create difficulties too, if wives experience a loss of freedom and an increase in demands (Keating & Cole, 1980; Turner, 1982).

Nonetheless, most older couples describe their relationships as "very happy" or "happy" and most believe their marriages have improved with time. Even sex may improve with age. Longitudinal data from the Berkeley and Oakland studies show a resurgence of heterosexual interest during middle age (Haan, 1981, 1985), and men in the empty-nest stage have even been described as hedonistic. Figure 10.2 presents Norma Haan's data on heterosexual interest from young adulthood through middle age.

Right now, we don't know whether this increased sexual interest continues into later life; however, most older people are unlikely to speak of romantic or passionate love (Decker, 1980). The meaning of sexuality probably changes over the life cycle, becoming less specifically genital with age. In later life, sex

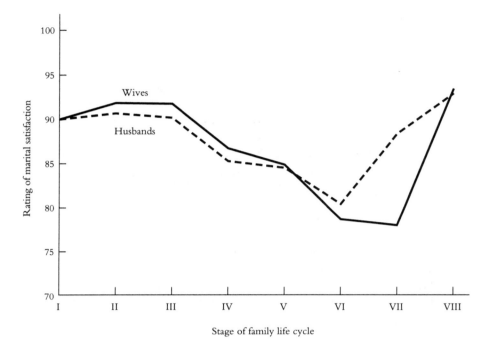

I. Couple marries.
II. First child is born.
III. First child enters school.
IV. Last child enters school.
V. Children reach adolescence.
VI. First child leaves home.
VII. Last child leaves home.
VIII. Couple celebrates fiftieth wedding anniversary.

Figure 10.1 Marital satisfaction throughout the family life cycle.

SOURCE: Condie, 1988, p. 147.

may leave the bedroom and become more strongly associated with everyday affection. Of course, among today's elderly, marriage is a very important predictor of sexual activity. Those who are widowed or divorced are often sexually stranded. Still, we must not overemphasize the importance of sexual activity in the lives of elderly people. In recent years, sexual activity has been touted as though it were a prescription for health in later life. Although there is an association between sexual activity and life satisfaction (Busse & Maddox, 1985), sex is not essential to happiness, nor is it prerequisite to mental health.

As L. Eugene Thomas (1982) quips, sex is like popcorn. Nobody says,

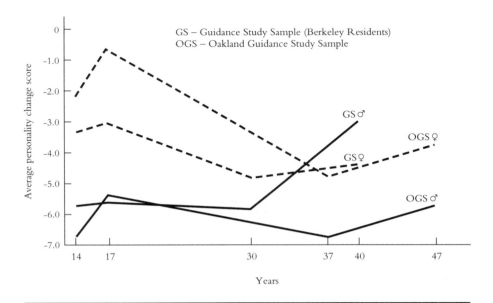

Figure 10.2 Heterosexual interest from young adulthood to middle age.

SOURCE: Haan, 1985, p. 31.

Marriage may be more important in the emotional lives of men than women, especially in old age, because men derive feelings of intimacy almost exclusively from their wives, whereas women are connected to a broader network of significant others.

"Eat your popcorn, it's good for you," or "Don't eat popcorn! It will ruin your teeth." Popcorn is not serious business, and psychologists and sociologists probably ought to stay out of it. Too much attention could bring on such plagues as popcorn anorexia or "popcornoholism." A critique of popcorn takes the fun out of it, and perhaps sex in old age, like popcorn, is best left to the individual preference.

As the more sexually liberated young and middle-aged in recent cohorts reach the ranks of the elderly, they are bound to change both marital patterns and sexual behavior outside of marriage. Younger cohorts are more sexually active whether married or single. If Masters and Johnson are right when they insist that one "use it or lose it," it seems likely that more elderly people will use it in the years to come. However, the way people lead their lives may have to change substantially, since one of the most important facts about sex in later life is this: Widowhood, for either a man or a woman, can remove one permanently from the ranks of those who have a lover, a spouse, or even a close companion.

Widowhood

For two years (after my husband's death) I was just as crazy as you can be and still be at large. I didn't have any really normal minutes during those two years. It wasn't just grief. It was total confusion. I was nutty, and that's the truth.

—Helen Hayes

Widowhood is not the exclusive province of the old. In fact, the average age of recent widows in this country is fifty-six, but data on widows and widowers tend to come from older groups, and so the discussion seems appropriate for this chapter. Between sixty-four and seventy-five, 81 percent of all Americans males are married, but only about 49 percent of the females. After seventy-five, the figures drop to 69 percent and 22 percent, respectively (Kalish, 1985). The average life span for males is shorter, of course, but one must also remember that women tend to marry men who are older than they. Furthermore, women may have lower remarriage rates than men because they are reluctant to marry and care for another man they may very well outlive (Kalish, 1982).

Widowhood at any age brings a special kind of social stigma. Widows and widowers are tainted by death. Widowhood may evoke fear or embarrassment in friends and family. No one knows quite how to help a bereaved person, and people often decide it is best to leave the grieving individual alone. There is even an exonerating mythology that grieving people want to be left alone.

As a consequence, someone who loses a spouse also loses those friends and family members who are unable to deal with bereavement or with the bereaved's new status as a single person. After the pain of loss begins to recede, a new kind of discomfort arrives. A single person is a fifth wheel or even a threat to married friends.

Bereaved men and women must learn to deal with all the ways in which widowhood embarrasses or threatens others. Some societies go to great lengths to exclude the widowed. Many practice the seclusion of widows; some have even encouraged ritual suicide by the surviving spouse. We are certainly more tolerant, but there are many obvious signs of strain. It is common, for example, to separate the widow or widower and the immediate family from the rest of the mourners at a funeral. At times, the mortuary secludes the family behind a curtain. The bereaved are driven in a separate car, often a limousine with tinted windows. The family enters and leaves the funeral home and the gravesite before or after the other mourners.

Embarrassment and fear are only two of the emotional responses the bereaved encounter. Grief is often viewed as a kind of self-indulgence, rather than as a psychological necessity. Samuel Johnson wrote: "Grief is a species of idleness." Johnson died in 1794, but his attitude is still part of our chin-up, stiff-upper-lip, pull-yourself-together heritage. The show must go on. Grief is seen as self-pity rather than as a response to loss, to loneliness, and to deprivation. Feelings of grief are the natural consequence, the price, of committing oneself to another human being. Grief derives from the need for interaction and intimacy, feelings of danger and insecurity, and the loss of comfort, information, and financial security that follow the death of a spouse.

Mourning—the feeling of a sense of duty to the dead—may last a lifetime. But acute grief occurs within a few days of bereavement and is severe for several months. Recovery usually takes place in twelve to eighteen months, although several turning points are ordinarily experienced within the first year, times when a major change for the better in feelings, attitudes, and behavior occur. Positive changes can be seen in such mundane activities as moving the furniture around, as well as more obvious steps such as getting a job or going on a holiday (Parkes, 1972).

Acute grief is accompanied by physical symptoms as well as emotional distress. About one-half of all widowed people complain of headaches, digestive upsets, rheumatism, asthma, and other stress-related disorders. Health is generally poorer than before the bereavement. The number of widows and widowers who die during the first year of bereavement is substantially higher than the death rate for individuals of the same age who are not bereaved. The most frequent cause of death during this period is heart disease. To date, no adequate explanation for increased mortality has been found. It may be that widowed individuals alter their personal habits too dramatically, from smoking and eating to sleeping and exercise. Ultimately a physiological explanation may be provided by those who study stress and health. For the moment, however, the old notion that the surviving spouse dies of a broken heart is at least as good as any that science can offer (Parkes, 1972).

Surprisingly, young adults who are widowed are most likely to be categorized as health risks and to suffer from prolonged or delayed grief. It is among the young that grief is most likely to interfere with work or social life for several years rather than months. The younger a widowed person is, the more likely he or she is to express ideas of guilt or self-reproach about the circumstances surrounding the spouse's death (Glick, Weiss, & Parkes, 1974).

Younger people most probably suffer extreme disorganization in bereavement. They are likely to be left to raise children alone, and they are less likely to have friends who have been widowed. The spouse is likely to have died unexpectedly and to have left financial and personal accounts disorganized or to have made no provision for surviving family members. Young adults are unrehearsed. Older people, especially women, seem to spend a substantial amount of time rehearsing for widowhood, thinking about how they will act, what they will do, how they will get along. Preparation, anticipatory socialization, and planning ease the way through any transition (Lowenthal, Thurnher, & Chiriboga, 1975).

Almost all the evidence supports the idea that widowhood is more difficult for the young. But there is some controversy about whether it is harder for men or for women. Widowhood may have different meanings for males and females.

Widows Some contend that because the male role is more prestigious than that of the female, the loss of a husband is more devastating than the loss of a wife. Furthermore, it is harder for a widow to find a new husband than it is for a widower to find a new wife. A widow loses a friend, a companion, and a sexual partner. She also loses an escort and a provider. Usually, her socioeconomic status plummets. Many widows are unable to support themselves. In every age category, widowed females earn less than widowers. The poorest widows are older than sixty-five, even though they may be receiving social security or pensions of some kind. Black and other minorities in rural areas or urban ghettos are the most impoverished (Rice, 1990).

In the age range sixty-five through sixty-nine, 34 percent of all females are widowed. By age eighty-five, 82 percent have lost their husbands. Widows depend heavily on their children for emotional, social, and financial support, which may cause family conflict and generate negative feelings between parent and child. Middle-class widows tend to be economically advantaged and therefore to make better adjustments (Bengston, Rosenthal, & Burton, 1990). However, the middle-class widow may have to struggle to make that adjustment, given that so many of the activities and friendships of the educated middle class are built around couples, at least in the current cohort of elderly people. If a middle-class woman's income is dramatically affected by the death of her spouse, she may have to move to less expensive housing, sacrificing all the stable, day-to-day relationships and informal activities based in the old neighborhood. Many married females lose their major roles in life with the death of the spouse, and there are no comparable roles to assume as a widow.

More traditional societies, and some preindustrial cultures, have well-defined roles for the widow. Later life can even be characterized as a matriarchy in some settings. The role of shaman or sometimes witch is ascribed to widowed women in older cultures; more modern traditional societies emphasize the roles of grandmother and mother-in-law (Gutmann, 1977, 1990; Lopata, 1975). In most of American society, however, the role of the widow is not a major feature of the social landscape. It is assumed that the younger widow will marry again and the older one will become inactive. Widows are forced to choose between these limited options, because they seldom are affluent enough to be independent with style.

Still, there are examples of successful styles of widowhood at all socioeconomic levels and among all social and ethnic groups. In a classic study of more than three hundred widows living in the Chicago area, Helena Lopata (1973) described three particularly adaptive but widely divergent styles. First, **self-initiating widows** maintained those aspects of old roles that were appropriate to their new status; related freely and independently with their children; and moved away from couple activities and friends, often entering into or strengthening involvement in community roles. Gradually, these women took over, reassigned, or gave up the role functions of their husbands, and engaged in a conscious reexamination of life and society in an attempt to adjust to their new position in the social network. Lopata's second category consisted of women who were members of an ethnic group and had lived in a sex-segregated world all their adult lives. Often relatively unaffected by their loss, these widows became immersed in family, peers, and neighbors, and continued their daily habits and routines with little disruption. The third style of widowhood was embodied by women who became downwardly mobile social isolates, unable to maintain the social interactions and activities typical of marrieds. These widows suffered substantial loss of status, believed that old friends could not be replaced, tended to see people as hostile and unhelpful, and withdrew from family, peers, and friends. Probably always marginal members of society at best, they appeared fearful and possessed few skills and little confidence. Paradoxically, adjustment to the role of widow was relatively easy for them, because isolation and loss of status fulfilled the expectations they had of widowhood and society.

Lopata points out that active, engaged, self-initiating widows were found most frequently among the highly educated, upper socioeconomic groups. The isolated, downwardly mobile widow was actually closer to the norm. Many American women spend their lives committed to home and family and cannot develop an active, socially engaged lifestyle after a spouse dies. Lopata reported that upper-middle-class women experienced the most acute grief but were also the most likely to make excellent recoveries because they had greater resources, including money, education, contacts outside the home, and so on. Recovery was related to resources. Depth of grief was related to the centrality of the spouse in the individual's married lifestyle.

Studies of widowhood repeatedly refer to economic and role losses in the lives of bereaved women (Kastenbaum, 1981a). The meaning of widowhood for men has been approached in a different way. The literature shifts from the detailing of social and economic consequences to more personal and interpersonal dimensions.

Widowers Those who argue that widowers have more difficulty adjusting to the loss of the spouse believe that a man may experience his wife as a part of the *self,* "my flesh and blood." A wife may well be a man's only close friend and confidante, the only one who really knows him (Glick, Weiss, & Parkes, 1974; Pitcher & Larson, 1989).

Moreover, men are relatively unprepared to live out their lives alone. Fewer men than women are widowed, and men are usually widowed at a later age than women. The death of a spouse may ruin a man's plan for life in retirement. He never imagined what life might be like as a widower (Atchley, 1980).

Widowed men often find themselves emotionally estranged from other family members but dependent on them for the necessary tasks of daily life—cooking, shopping, and keeping house—as they lack these mundane skills. Nor do they have the social skills that permit the development of meaningful new relationships with family and friends, a new confidante, or sex partner (Bernardo, 1968, 1970).

Men are usually widowed at a later age than women. Therefore, if men do have more difficulties in developing a single lifestyle than women, some of these problems are probably attributable to their greater age. If age is controlled, widows report greater anxiety than do widowers, but widowers seem to suffer from greater feelings of **anomie**, or loneliness (Atchley, 1980).

Although men have more options available to them for new heterosexual relationships, women seem to have the advantage in developing significant same-sex confidantes and friends. Men are less likely to form new, significant relationships after bereavement than are women, but they also tend to have had fewer close relationships prior to bereavement.

The loss of a spouse is traumatic regardless of one's sex, and our culture is not organized in a way that facilitates recovery and reintegration for the recently widowed. It has been said that Western society has deinstitutionalized the rituals of mourning and bereavement to such a degree that they are not adequate for the individual faced with the shock, confusion, and grief that follow a great loss (Lopata, 1975).

Services Over the last fifteen years, however, some new resources have become available for bereaved people. Perhaps the best known of these is an organization called Widow-to-Widow, a group of widowed people who provide comfort and services to those in bereavement. Widow-to-Widow tries to create a safe environment in which grief can run its course. Helpers offer companionship and acceptance (Silverman, 1977). They wait out the ambivalence, the demanding or irritating behavior, even the paranoia that accompany grief, and they let the bereaved person decide what is best for herself or himself.

Widow-to-Widow usually initiates contact without being asked, and each helper is matched for socioeconomic level, education, and other characteristics with the bereaved person. The helper is there to assist in the transition from being married to being a widowed person, to help the individual learn the new role. No effort is made to minimize mourning or to cheer up a grief-stricken person.

The organization stresses that most people are unprepared for widowhood, because most of us are reluctant to face dying or death. Bereaved people are often surprised and frightened by the overwhelming intensity of their feelings. They sometimes believe they are going crazy or having a nervous breakdown. They are unprepared for the degree of emotional distress and disorganization that accompanies widowhood.

Sometimes a person from outside the family can be more helpful than kin in situations that threaten self-esteem, especially if the family has no traditions for the expression of grief. An outside helper who has lost a spouse is not alarmed, frightened, or surprised by the intensity or duration of the grief process, and that alone can provide great reassurance (Silverman, 1977; Parkes, 1972).

Widow-to-Widow was designed to create a social network where none existed before or to strengthen an existing network where it is inadequate. Friends and family are often too unfamiliar with death and bereavement to fill the need.

In the midst of all this concern, however, it is important to remember that widowhood is a predictable event of married life in late adulthood. In that sense, there is much anticipatory socialization, so it is not surprising to find that despite great bereavement and all of the accompanying social and financial problems, older people are generally able to adapt to the loss of a spouse. Widowhood in later life is not accompanied by long-term negative effects on adjustment and, in fact, may signal an increase in life satisfaction if the dying spouse was extremely ill (Gurin & Brim, 1984).

Less predictable, and perhaps, therefore, even more difficult is the prospect of divorce in later life. Although divorce rates among married people decline over the years of adult life, divorce after age forty is not an uncommon event. The significant personal and societal consequences probably merit more attention than researchers have currently given them.

Divorce

Between 1975 and 1985, the proportion of divorces involving women over the age of forty increased from 19 to 23 percent, and although most of those divorces involved women in their forties and fifties, perhaps 2 percent involved women over the age of sixty. As the baby-boomers begin to age, bringing with them into later life more liberal attitudes toward divorce, it is expected that the divorce rates for the population over age fifty will continue to grow until they

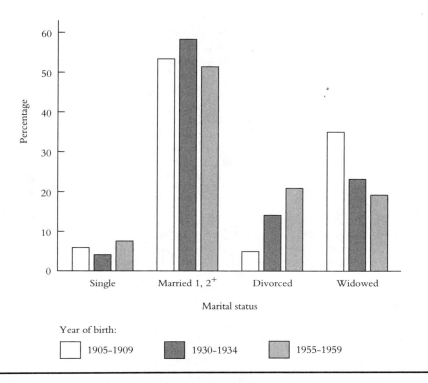

Figure 10.3 Marital status distribution at age sixty-five to sixty-nine by cohort.

SOURCE: Uhlenberg, Cooney, & Boyd, 1990, p. S7.

reach a level about 50 percent higher than in 1985 (Uhlenberg, Cooney, & Boyd, 1990). Conservative projections show that less than half of women born from 1955 to 1959 will be in first marriages at midlife, and almost a third (32%) will be living outside of marriage as singles, divorcees, or widows. Figure 10.3 shows the increases in divorce and decreases in numbers of married women expected for the cohort born between 1955 and 1959 when compared to women born in the early thirties and at the turn of this century. Four times as many women are expected to be divorced in the youngest cohort as in the oldest.

In middle and old age, recently divorced women are less likely to be living independently than are the widowed, and they are much less likely to own their own homes than are married women. Widowed women sustain economic levels closer to those of married women than do the recently divorced. Divorced older women are much more likely to be working than are married or widowed women. About one-fourth of recently divorced women over sixty-

Box 10.2 Focus on Research: Remarriage among middle-aged and elderly women

In recent years, a great deal of controversy and misinformation has arisen about the probability of marriage and remarriage among middle-aged and elderly women. A recent analysis of survey data by I-Chiao, L. F. Bowmer and Stephen J. Bahr (1989) offers some of the more reliable information available. Two national surveys formed the basis for their research: (1) the Current Population Survey, which is conducted in approximately 57,000 randomly selected households in the United States on a monthly basis and which includes data for the June 1985 Marital History and Fertility Survey, and (2) the General Social Survey conducted by the National Opinion Research Center for 1982 through 1987.

The data show that remarriage is infrequent among the elderly when compared to remarriage among younger persons. Remarriage rates for women who divorce before age thirty hover around 77 percent compared with 55 percent for those who divorce during their thirties and only 16 percent of those who divorce after age sixty. Of those widowed before age thirty, 73 percent remarry, as do 50 percent of those widowed in their thirties. Only 3 percent of those widowed after age sixty remarry.

A comparison of remarriage rates for men and women by age and previous marital status shows that, overall, 69 percent of all divorced men remarry along with 65 percent of all divorced women. Among those who are widowed, 47 percent of the men remarry but only 22 percent of the women do so.

five are working compared to about 5 percent of widowed and married women. Statistical comparisons of these kinds of indicators suggest that "although widowhood and divorce have negative consequences for women's socioeconomic well-being, the effects of divorce are generally more severe" (Uhlenberg, Cooney, & Boyd, 1990, p. S7), the differences being greater for nonwhite than white women. Furthermore, as these authors point out, "high rates of divorce could jeopardize family supports for elderly persons, if divorced daughters, faced with their own economic problems and the pressures of single parenthood, are unable to assume additional responsibility for their aging parent(s)" (p. S10). In terms of these statistics, our opening vignette about Martha is not atypical. Although she owns her own home, she is working, unlike many of her married peers. Obviously, she is better off than most, but she lives with a friend and does not plan to remarry. However, both of these are positive choices from her point of view. Researchers have yet to tell us how older women actually experience their situation. More detailed information is required before we conclude that older divorced women are in great distress.

Among divorced men in later life, the primary focus of researchers has been

---

Box 10.2 *(continued)*

These data suggest that gender differences in remarriage rates are not very significant. Even when only persons over age fifty are considered, the remarriage rate for men is 77 percent, whereas 72 percent of older divorced women remarry. Among divorced persons between the ages of fourteen and twenty-nine, remarriage rates are considerably higher for women than men. Fifty-three percent of all young women remarry, but only 42 percent of young men do so.

Using the CPS data, the authors were also able to report figures for the stability of remarriages. The data show that remarriage among elderly people is much less likely to end in divorce. About 53 percent of all remarriages for women under fifty end in divorce. Only 22 percent of women remarried after fifty are divorced again. The marriage survival rates for first marriages is somewhat greater than for remarriages. However, the differences in the divorce rates for first and second marriages decrease with age. The authors report that: "The older the age at the second marriage, the higher the probability that the second marriage will endure" (p. 91). Furthermore, the general and marital happiness of elderly remarried people is just about the same as for younger remarried persons. Finally, these researchers report that they found no evidence for significant differences in the general or marital happiness of remarried men and women.

---

on the interpersonal and social effects rather than economic factors. Peter Uhlenberg and Teresa Cooney (1990) in another study of divorced persons in later life point out that men's contacts with their adult offspring decline dramatically after divorce, and they cease to perceive their children as potential sources of support in times of need. Although almost 90 percent of never-divorced older men have weekly contact with at least one of their adult children, only one-half of never-divorced men do and one-third have lost contact entirely with at least one of their children. These findings lead Uhlenberg and Cooney to predict that divorced men will be at greater risk than never-divorced men for reduced well-being and low morale in later life. They also question the extent to which older men who have no contact with their adult children will be able to meet their own physical and health care needs.

Although frequent interaction with adult children is not consistently related to greater psychological well-being among the elderly, troubled relationships are known to have a negative impact on life satisfaction. For most people, a network of friends and family is a mainstay of support through the losses of later adulthood, the family playing a central role in the support system of the elderly.

Friends and Family

Can you imagine us
Years from today
Sharing a park bench quietly?
How terribly strange
To be seventy.
Old friends.

> —Paul Simon

Nearly all older people are connected to society by a complex web of close and distant kin, as well as by friendships, acquaintances, and associates. Eighty-one percent of the elderly have children; 75 percent have grandchildren; 4 percent have living parents; and those who never marry are usually aunts or uncles, siblings or cousins. Perhaps 5 percent of the elderly have no family ties. However, since 4 percent of males over sixty-five and 10 percent of females live with unrelated persons, familylike bonds may be available even to those without blood relations (Sussman, 1985).

Fifty percent of people over sixty-five are members of four-generation families and 20 percent of females over eighty are part of five-generation families. Because of increasing longevity, people will spend more time in family roles than ever before in history. Over the last 100 years, the time women spend in the role of daughter has increased fourfold. Declining fertility has also led to the beanpole family we discussed in Chapter 8, with more generations but fewer members of each. "With fewer family members per generation, individuals have a greater opportunity to invest themselves heavily across a group of kin that is more manageable in size" (Bengston, Rosenthal, & Burton, 1990, p. 267). Of course, this greater opportunity may only occur for women, as the significance of family roles is declining for men, who spend less time with children or as spouses than they have in past generations.

Nonetheless, intergenerational bonds may be stronger than ever because so many people will spend so long a period of shared years, or "cobiography" (Hagestad, 1988) with other family members. Not only are there more shared years, but also a very strong norm holds that families should be together, that they should visit each other, particularly on special occasions, and that they should provide assistance and support across generations (Hamon & Blieszner, 1990).

Eighty-five percent of all elderly parents live within one hour of their middle-aged children, whereas only 33 percent of all young adults live that close to their parents. This suggests that older people relocate in retirement to be near their middle-aged children (Atchley & Miller, 1980). Despite the physical proximity, however, helping tends to be very specific: when there is a need. Parents want to live independently as long as possible. With greater affluence, elderly people are also likely to continue helping out their middle-aged children. Parents give to children for as long as they are able. In fact, it has been suggested (Lee and Shehan, 1989) that people of all ages are much more willing to give than to receive. Receiving may raise fears of dependency or helplessness especially among the most independent elderly.

To date, most of the research on elderly people and their families has focused on the extent and frequency of contact. From this research, it is clear that children do not abandon their elderly parents. Over half of all middle-aged children live within ten minutes of a parent and as many as 75 percent see that parent at least once a week (Aizenberg & Treas, 1985). Contact is especially frequent between elderly women and their daughters. However, the fact that people see each other does not mean that they enjoy each other, and a number of researchers have called for more work on the quality of family ties in later life.

As most families prefer "intimacy at a distance," even if it is only a one-hour distance, critical problems may arise when parents become less independent. Optimal relationships seem possible only when generations are physically separate; the parent–child bond is jeopardized when an elderly parent needs assistance (Decker, 1980). Current cultural norms do not allow parents to demand much from their children. In fact, Lowenthal and Robinson (1977) have argued that even when older people say they see their children as often as they like, they may only be expressing "superficially assimilated norms." Most elderly parents might benefit from more genuine interaction with their children. Congenial intergenerational relationships are widespread, but real intimacy is rare.

In a study of the quality of family relationships, Kees Knipscheir (1984) reported that neither frequency nor type of contact with family predicted the self-evaluations of elderly people or whether parents felt they could turn to their children for help. Generally, elderly people in this study seemed unsure how much they "counted" with their children socially. Elderly people who had no contact with anyone except their children exhibited negative morale. Knipscheir contends that ambivalence is a hallmark of the parent–child bond in adult life, a relationship highly regulated by unwritten social norms. Children see their parents out of a sense of duty, and parents feel that they must stay out of the affairs of their children. Middle-aged children feel their parents should ask them for help, but the parents don't see much willingness to help in their children. As for the emotional aspects of the relationship, most of the children in this study emphasized the need for distance, whereas the parents talked about the need for contact. Parents were more positive about visits from their children than children were, and the parents knew that their emotional need for contact made them relatively dependent on their children.

On the basis of this data, Knipscheir argues that there are clear limits to the quality of the parent–child relationship. Certainly, this may be the case in later life, but the distance or lack of intimacy does not originate there. It is a rare adolescent or young adult who bares his or her soul to a parent, and it is certainly a rare parent who is completely honest with a child of any age. Throughout the life span, intimacy between parents and children is discouraged by the duties and obligations inherent in the bond. During the child-rearing years, parents are not supposed to burden children with their problems, and by adolescence, children are supposed to learn to handle their problems themselves. It is not surprising to find that friendships are more predictive of general life satisfaction or morale than family associations (Aizenberg and Treas, 1985). Furthermore, few friendships form across generations. People of different ages have different roles and responsibilities, different values and attitudes; there is always a certain tension over autonomy where there are large age differences (Kalish, 1982).

In the most recent work on the matter (Lee and Shehan, 1989), researchers have reported that it is wrong to say that older people value interaction with their children. Some do; some don't. It is also wrong to suggest that all older people value their independence. Again, attitudes of the elderly people in this sample of 750 families in Washington state varied widely, and those who were most dependent were not always negatively affected. Lee and Shehan believe that older people are able to accept dependency and support when they feel that the exchange is an equitable compensation for what it cost them to rear their children.

Other researchers (Long & Mancini, 1989) have also reported that most older people feel their exchanges with their children are equitable. They report giving their children love and nurturance as well as material things. Most felt their children would provide for their needs and this understanding increased their own feelings of security. Such balanced exchanges of resources engender positive feelings between parent and child and lead to greater frequency of interaction (Roberts & Bengston, 1990). The problems arise, of course, when elderly parents begin to need more care and support than adult children can provide without feelings of inequity and stress.

Some have argued that communal living arrangements among the elderly may be part of the answer to the problem of care, an answer that would support the continuation of intimacy at a distance between parent and child. However, as Martin Sussman (1985) points out, communal arrangements assume a kind of equality. Everyone is expected to pitch in. Unrelated people living together in groups are not often willing to handle crises, dependencies, and disabilities. While these arrangements may work for the 72 percent of the elderly who have no difficulty performing everyday activities, it seems unlikely that the bonds between unrelated people will be strong enough to persist through the difficulties of long-term care.

Sussman believes that the problems of an increasingly elderly population can only be met if social services become an ally of the family; if we begin to involve the family in the planning of care for the elderly; and if we make it economically feasible for the family to maintain some kind of independence while providing long-term care. He suggests that families might be given direct monthly subsidies, tax write-offs, low-cost loans, and property tax waivers during the care of an elderly family member. He also argues for the provision of specific services, like medical visits, meals, and day care, that would support families trying to deal with the frail elderly. Recent research from his laboratory suggests that as many as 80 percent of all families are willing to take on an elderly person given the financial assistance and service support that would make it less burdensome. Interestingly, the youngest generation expressed the greatest willingness. Sussman believes society must be willing to remove the sacrifice and deficit living from family care, and replace it with reward.

The Social Convoy It is probably true that peer relationships will never replace family ties in times of crisis. Nonetheless, the kind of social network an older person possesses outside the family can be an important predictor of good adjustment, high life satisfaction, and a positive self-concept (Busse & Maddox, 1985). However, it is not clear whether one needs to have frequent or high-quality contact with friends. It may be that the perception of continuing friendship rather than the frequency of association or the intensity of involvement promotes well-being. In other words, if you think you have enough friends, you will be happy. You may not even need to see those friends (Tesch & Whitbourne, 1981). People who have always been social isolates do not report unusually low life satisfaction. It is people who want frequent associations and intimacy that may be the most disappointed by the losses of later life. Those who expect less may be content with less, or even pleasantly surprised by any continued involvement with friends.

Toni Antonucci (1985, 1990) refers to the changing members of a person's social network as a **convoy** of social support. She writes that there are few differences in the size of that convoy between middle age and later life. In fact, it is young adults that are the most likely to see their convoy as inadequate, perhaps because they want more friends than elderly people do, at least the current generation of elderly people. Most adults have two to five close relationships in their convoy, although women have significantly larger convoys than men. Women are also more satisfied with the friends they have and provide more support to the members of their convoy than men do. On the other hand, men are more satisfied with marriage than women and see themselves as providing more support within the marriage than women do.

Women also tend to have more different types of relationships in their networks than do men (multiplex relationships). These differences hold up across cultures too, among blacks, whites, Hispanics, French, Italians, Israelis, and Japanese (Antonucci, 1990). Social support is related to a wide variety of well-being measures and is associated with feelings of efficacy, social competence, and mastery (Sarason, Sarason, & Pierce, 1989).

A large social network has its price, of course. Caregiving is one of them and is more likely to fall to women. Women are also more negatively affected by events in the lives of the people in their convoys; those with larger convoys may experience more ineffective, unwanted, or unpleasant interaction than people with smaller ones (Rook & Pietromonaco, 1987). The strong obligatory component of relationships with family probably makes for more negative or unwanted interaction. Ties with friends are more strongly related to well-being than family ties (Crohan & Antonucci, 1989).

Antonucci believes that one's social network may be critical to well-being in later life because successful aging depends on the ability to define and pursue areas that allow one to maintain a positive self-image (Baltes & Baltes, 1988). A strong social network may help people maintain positive self-regard and optimism, even in the most dire of circumstances. However unrealistic, positive self-regard correlates with happiness, contentment, the ability to care for others, and the capacity for creative work (Antonucci, 1990). As long as you and your friends agree that you are doing OK, perhaps you are, regardless of how the situation looks to an outsider.

Education is associated with richer support systems that include more non-kin. The poor elderly have less education as well as smaller convoys than older people who have better financial resources. High socioeconomic status is also associated with a more positive perception of the social convoy. Relationships between the elderly and their confidants, their closest friends, and family deserve more detailed attention. What kind of contact do elderly people have with their friends? What do close friends talk about? Does it make a difference in terms of feelings of support or life satisfaction whether one goes bowling with a friend or spends the afternoon talking over coffee? What kind of support do friends generally provide in times of crisis? It may be that family members are more reliable, but if friends come through, does it make a difference? The type and quality of contact among elderly people, their friends, and close family members is only just being examined; the role of more distant kin and more casual associates has not been investigated at all. We know very little, for instance, about sibling relations in later life, although there is some evidence that frequency of contact decreases despite continuing feelings of closeness (Cicirelli, 1980).

What we do know is that children, siblings, and other relatives are more predominant in the confidant network, whereas friends and spouses are more likely to act as companions. That is, older people tend to confide in their family and to do things with their friends and spouses (Connidis & Davies, 1990). In the networks of widowed people, friends, children, and other relatives tend to take the place of the spouse. Childless women tend to develop ties with friends as both companions and confidants more than any other group. Siblings are also a more critical component of the networks of childless women. Childless men also place greater emphasis on friends, although they use them more as companions and less as confidants than women. These men cultivate ties with other relatives as confidants more than any other group of older people. According to Connidis and Davies (1990): "Single women are a unique group in their focus on siblings as both companions and confidants. Perhaps due to having fewer demands from other relationships, single women appear to negotiate particularly strong and diverse ties with their siblings" (p. S148).

Researchers have begun to look at the effects of siblings on development in childhood, and the information strongly suggests that development is deeply affected by the birth of a sister or brother. The most long-term relationship in one's convoy is likely to be a sibling, as siblings usually outlive parents. Over the age of sixty, 83 percent of all elderly report that they feel close to at least one sibling, such closeness being a long-term feeling, originating in childhood and adolescence with shared family experiences (Dunn, 1984).

Ties between sisters are the most intimate and durable, and sisters are the primary providers of emotional support among adult siblings (Cicirelli, 1980). Closeness, envy, resentment, instrumental support, emotional support, acceptance, and psychological involvement as well as frequency of contact appear to be critical to understanding sibling relationships (Gold, Woodbury, & George, 1990).

In a recent study of elderly siblings (Gold, Woodbury, & George, 1990), four types of sibling relationships in old age were identified. Type I was characterized by unusual closeness, frequent emotional support, and weekly contact. Psychological support, acceptance, and frequent instrumental help unaccompanied by feelings of resentment or envy were also associated with Type I, which was found primarily among women and among participants not currently married. Less educated women who were divorced or widowed were most likely to report Type I relationships.

Type II was defined by moderate levels of closeness, psychological involvement, instrumental assistance, and emotional support. This type was found likely to occur between sister/brother dyads and to be associated with currently married siblings. Most of the pairs in the study had some level of college education and were from small families of origin.

In Type III relationships, only partial acceptance of the sibling and modest levels of resentment, envy, and instrumental support were shown. Both dyad members were well educated and either married or widowed. Type III was not strongly associated with either gender or gender mix.

Feelings of rejection, resentment, rare contact, intense envy, and no psychological support were characteristic of Type IV. Type IV siblings were typically described by male respondents, who could be referring, however, to relationships with either a brother or a sister. Most often, however, Type IV pairs were brothers. Middle- and upper-class respondents were more likely to report Type IV relationships.

Gold et al. also report that the triangle phenomenon seems to have some effect on siblings in old age. "Families in which there are three siblings still alive fall into the less intimate relationships more frequently than do other family constellations" (p. S50).

Studies of more distant kin relationships are almost nonexistent, although elderly people quite often maintain ties with favored nieces, nephews, or cousins. Particularly for the never married or the individual who loses both spouse and children, extended family may play an important role. There is clearly much room for more focused studies of the social convoy, its membership, function, and maintenance in later life.

Summary

I. Attitudes and Adjustment in Old Age
  A. Attitude research is complicated by the necessity of discriminating between attitudes toward age, aging, and the particular cohort of people who are elderly.
    1. People tend to overestimate the problems and passivity of the elderly.
    2. Attitudes toward the old have always been conflicted but usually tempered by respect for age.
      a. Since the late eighteenth century, the demise of the patriarchal family and the increasing association between age and death have produced more negative feelings about and less reverence for age.
      b. *Ageism* refers to discrimination against middle-aged and elderly people.
    3. The elderly who act young at heart are more valued than people at other ages who act the same way.
    4. Attitudes toward age are long-term historical trends, but they are not immutable.
II. Personality and Adjustment
  A. Integrity has been identified as the main personality development of later life. Erikson argues that the conflict between integrity and despair may produce wisdom or disdain, but his theory has been criticized as ethnocentric.
  B. Personality researchers tend to ignore the problem of individual differences in personality and the impact of life events.
    1. Cohort membership, sex, sociocultural trends, and life stage experience probably have more impact on personality in later life than does maturation.
    2. Objective studies of personality traits tend to show stability over the adult life course. Studies of self-concept and self-perception also suggest little change with age although health may be an important influence.
    3. Recent research tends to cast this hypothesis in terms of growing androgyny, the acceptance of both male and female characteristics of the self, in later life.

       a. Nonetheless, masculine traits related to behaving instrumentally are related to well-being for both sexes.

       b. While there is much evidence that attitudes toward sex roles may change in later life, there are few data showing that behavioral changes occur.

  C. Studies of life satisfaction, happiness, and morale tend to suggest that these variables are stable over long periods of time and are essentially unrelated to stage of life.

    1. The question of how activity and life satisfaction are related in later life forms a basis for controversy over disengagement theory.

       a. Disengagement theory posits that later life is characterized by mutual withdrawal between society and the individual, resulting in high levels of life satisfaction and adjustment.

       b. Critics have argued that disengagement is seldom mutual but more often forced by society.

       c. The freedom to withdraw from activities one does not value may be important to life satisfaction, but certain traits that allow one to cope with loss are probably more central.

       d. Recent evidence from the Duke Longitudinal Studies as well as evidence on Mexican Americans and blacks shows that elderly people are likely to be satisfied and to adjust to the losses of later life without long-term negative side effects.

       e. The conditions and circumstances that favor one pattern of aging over another may well change from one historical period to another, and studies of less general issues often yield more interesting data.

    2. Time perspective appears to change in later life and may be associated with life satisfaction.

       a. Middle-aged people experience time as passing more quickly than do other age groups.

       b. Older people often believe that the future is not likely to be the best period of their lives, but the happiest older people are able to project into the future.

       c. In later life, the prospect of being well balanced in time increases as the future becomes less impressive.

III. The Social Network

  A. Older people tend to be more satisfied with marriage than the young.

    1. This may be in part due to a contrast phenomenon among women who begin comparing themselves to their widowed friends.

    2. Sexual activity is associated with marital satisfaction and may continue into very late life, although it may become less specifically genital.

  B. Widowhood brings a variety of problems, including the social stigma of being associated with death and the problem of grief and bereavement, which may be accompanied by acute physical symptoms.

1. More older women are widowed than men, and women often lose a large share of their identity as well as their financial security with bereavement.

2. Successful styles of widowhood include the self-initiating widow, the widow who has always lived in a sex-segregated world, and the downwardly mobile social isolate.

3. Widowers are more likely to suffer from anomie and to be emotionally estranged from their families than widows, but they are also more likely to remarry.

4. Community services, like Widow-to-Widow, can help create a social network when friends and family are inadequate for the task.

5. Most elderly people are able to adjust to loss of the spouse in later life and do not suffer from long-term negative effects.

C. Researchers have begun to study the impact of divorce in later life on both men and women.

1. Women who divorce late are more likely to be working and are less likely to own their own homes or live independently than married or widowed women.

2. Older men who have been divorced are likely to have lost contact with one or more adult children, a fact that may have implications for the long-term care of elderly divorced men.

D. Most older people live within an hour of their adult children and see those children at least once a week.

1. Frequency of contact suggests that the American family is still very much intact, but it does not tell us much about the quality of family life.

2. Frequency and type of family contact do not predict self-evaluations among the elderly, and the parent-child relationship seems best characterized as "intimacy at a distance."

3. Children tend to see parents out of a sense of duty, whereas parents are more emotionally dependent on that contact.

4. However, not all older people value contact with their adult children and not all parents who have such contact seem to feel the relationship is unequitable or makes them unacceptably dependent.

5. Economic and social incentives may be necessary if the family is to function as the primary caretaker for the frail elderly.

E. Most older people have a social convoy of two to five close relationships, a figure that is no different from that for adults at other stages of the life cycle.

1. Contact with friends does not appear to be as important as the perception that one has enough friends.

2. Women have larger social convoys and are more satisfied with them than men, although larger convoys have higher costs in

terms of being affected by the negative events of other people's lives.

   3. Education and socioeconomic status predict the development of social convoys that include more nonkin and are perceived in a more positive way.

F. Little is known about the relationships between siblings in later life, but they are often close, and the closeness is related to sharing family experiences as children and adolescents.

   1. Sister–sister ties tend to be the closest sibling relationships, especially for pairs where one member is childless or single.

   2. Among older siblings, at least four types of common relationships have been described with less educated sisters reporting the closest, most affectionate bonds and men reporting hostile or distant relationships, especially with brothers.

11

Old Age: The Expanded Context—The Ecology of Aging

I could be handy, mending a fuse
When your lights are gone.
You can knit a sweater by the fireside,
Sunday morning go for a ride.
Doing the garden, digging the weeds,
Who could ask for more?
Will you still need me, will you still feed me,
When I'm sixty-four?

—Paul McCartney

AT SIXTY-TWO, AMOS WILL BE ELIGIBLE for partial Social Security benefits and he's been thinking seriously about retiring. He's worked hard all his life as a house painter and wallpaper hanger, and he could still work some even if he retired. You can make a certain amount without losing any benefits. His health isn't very good, so that's a factor both ways, really. He'd like to retire and take it easier. The arthritis in his wrists is especially hard on him. On the other hand, he doesn't qualify for Medicare until he's sixty-five and private health insurance is really expensive. If he takes Social Security and doesn't work as much, his income will be maybe half of what it was before and he'll still have those insurance payments to make.

His wife, Betsy, has been working too ever since the kids left home. Now, she really loves it. Practically runs that agency, even though they only pay her a secretary's wage. But she hasn't been working very many years, so her Social Security benefits aren't going to amount to much and she doesn't have a private pension. Betsy'll probably just keep working. She likes it and they need the money. If Betsy keeps working, there won't be anybody around the house. He'll just be there by himself all day. If she stops working, maybe she'll see him as being underfoot. Of course, they could take some of those long vacations they always planned: the Grand Canyon, maybe even Mexico. They could go on all the trips with the Fifth-Wheel Club. As long as they're both still working, they haven't got much use out of the trailer.

Amos goes over all of this a couple of times a month. But he always decides to go on working. He knows Betsy's not really ready to quit and who wants to sit in a house in the middle of an empty neighborhood all alone? Maybe when the Medicare kicks in and Betsy has a few more years of work under her belt. They can sell the house and buy something outright someplace outside the city. Not one of those retirement places. Just a place where people might like to retire, but there'd be a lot of younger people too. Maybe up at the lake. Something small, so they could just shut it down once in a while and take off in the five-wheeler. Three more years. He can probably live with the arthritis three more years, but he'd better start working on Betsy now. Otherwise, she'll work until she's seventy and there won't be enough time for the five-wheeler and the house by the lake.

ECOLOGY IS THE SCIENCE OF PLANTS AND ANIMALS as they are related to their environment. Humans are included among the animals studied by ecologists; we are part of an ecosystem, we adapt to our niche, and our niche changes as a result of that adaptation. A high-rise apartment building is as much a niche as is a fox's den. And, as is the case for other animals, the impact of the physical environment changes with age. People see and hear less well as they grow old. They become less sensitive to some aspects of the environment and more sensitive to others. The relationship between people and their physical and social world is always evolving, changing both the people and the environment (Lawton & Nahemow, 1973; Lawton, 1980).

Some of the objective changes that occur with age are explored in this chapter—changes in income, work, housing, and mobility. Some of the processes and possible outcomes associated with various patterns of adaptation are described. In a sense, however, we have been studying the ecology of aging from the first page of this book. As M. P. Lawton (1970) contends, the *individual environment* (the biological, psychological, and social conditions of a particular life), the *interpersonal environment* (the world of interactions with others), the *social environment* (the world of norms and institutions), as well as the *physical environment* (housing, neighborhoods, and transportation), must be considered in defining a human ecology.

In Chapters 9 and 10 we examined the individual and interpersonal environments of the elderly and considered some information on the social environment. This chapter focuses in greater detail on those aspects of the social environment associated with retirement and leisure, and on the physical environment. There will be facts, of course, such as how many people retire at what age, how much money they make, how they structure their time, and where they live. But we will also consider a variety of questions researchers have only begun to explore. How do people adapt to age-related changes in their social and physical world? Do most people enjoy retirement? Why do some resist it? What happens when an older person is forced to move? What physical conditions are associated with feelings of well-being and optimal physical or psychological functioning?

The Demography of Aging

During the past hundred years, the number of people over the age of sixty-five living in the United States has increased approximately sixfold. By most of the standards traditionally used to characterize national populations, the United States is an aged population. Aged populations are generally defined as those in which more than 7 percent of the residents are currently over the age of sixty-five. Worldwide, the elderly constitute the fastest growing segment of the population. In 1980, there were 57 million more people in the world over sixty-five than there were in 1970. In the United States at the present time, there is a slight decline in the number of aged being added to the population every year, because people who were born in the 1920s are entering the ranks of the elderly, and the 1920s was a period of relatively low birth rates. By the year 2000, however, the situation will change; there will be a steady gain in the net number of elderly, and that trend is predicted to continue through the early decades of the next century (Myers, 1985).

Most of America's elderly are concentrated in smaller cities, in rural areas, and in the inner cities of our great urban areas. Few live among the more affluent in the suburbs. As people moved from the plains of the Midwest to the cities, and finally to the suburbs, the oldest citizens often stayed behind. Thus, both rural and inner-city populations have become relatively aged.

Contrary to popular misconceptions, nearly all Americans over sixty-five live in community settings and in their own homes or with family members. Home ownership has risen with growing income, among older widows especially. Even the most vulnerable now tend to live in their own homes. Home ownership at ages sixty-five to seventy-four rose from 48 percent in 1940 to 79 percent in 1980. Ninety percent of the elderly who do own their own homes have paid off their mortgages (Kendig, 1990). Only about 5 percent of the aged live in institutional settings, and of this 5 percent, it is estimated that at least one-quarter could live in the community if enough financial aid were available (Lawton, 1985). Living arrangements for all persons over age sixty-five are summarized in Figure 11.1.

Through the 1970s and 1980s, the financial situation of the elderly improved steadily. Increases in Social Security benefits, growth in the availability and value of private pension plans, and increased tax benefits have all contributed to the relative affluence of the elderly in the 1990s. Poverty rates among people over sixty-five declined from around one-third in 1959 to 13 percent in 1985. This percentage dropped still further in 1986, to 12.4 percent. Poverty rates for the elderly in every major racial group and for both sexes declined even though the poverty rate of the general population rose slightly. Today, the poverty rate for the elderly is slightly below that for the general population (Bahr, 1989).

If one takes into account Medicaid, Medicare, food stamps, and public housing benefits, only about 2.9 percent of the elderly population live below

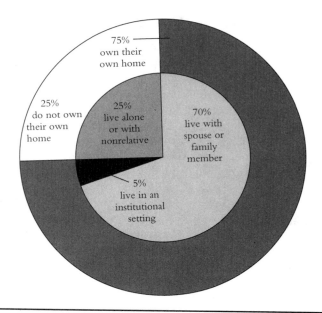

Figure 11.1 Living arrangements of the elderly.

SOURCE: Based on Lawton (1985) and Sussman (1985).

the poverty level, as opposed to 9 percent of the general population. Whites are better off than blacks and Hispanics, and black females are most likely of all elderly to be living below the poverty line. Of course, these figures tell only a small part of the story. If aging begins at birth, the disadvantages of the minority elderly must be studied in life-span perspective.

Ethnicity and Aging

The study of ethnicity, race, and aging has focused on what is called the **double jeopardy** hypothesis. According to this proposition, because older people have been relatively disadvantaged and discriminated against in the past, and members of minorities are also disadvantaged and discriminated against, the gap between members of disadvantaged minorities and whites should increase in later life. However, most of the recent evidence shows that older blacks may not be as disadvantaged as young blacks in some ways (Gibson, 1989). For example, some data show that older blacks may actually survive longer than whites. This is called the **racial mortality crossover**, and has been attributed to the fact that only the very hardiest black people probably survive to old age (Markides, Liang, & Jackson, 1990).

Although blacks experience shorter life spans and more disability at every other point in the life span, after eighty, they outlive whites. Mexican Americans show a mortality crossover sometime in early adulthood, and Asians have a lower mortality rate than the general population probably because of cultural differences in dietary, health, and risk-taking behaviors (Jackson, Antonucci, & Gibson, 1990). There is no crossover effect for Native Americans. Work on the black elderly has suggested that after age seventy-five, few differences in physical or mental health distinguish blacks from whites (Ford, Haug, Jones, Roy, & Folmar, 1990).

Despite the improvement of income and education among older minorities over the past few decades, substantial differences still exist between blacks, Mexican Americans, Native Americans, and whites. In the total population, about 58 percent of all older adults have high school degrees, 9 percent have four or more years of college. Among elderly blacks, only 27 percent graduated from high school and 2.5 percent went on to four or more years of college. Eighteen percent of older Mexican Americans graduated from high school, as did 18 percent of Native Americans. However, only 59 percent of older Mexican Americans report having completed more than five years of schooling, and 63 percent of older Native Americans never attended high school at all (Jackson, Antonucci, & Gibson, 1990).

The poverty rate among older blacks is approximately 38 percent, 31 percent among Hispanics, and 50 percent among Native Americans. Older Asian Americans also live in poverty more often than whites; about 20 percent of them are considered poor (George, 1988).

Furthermore, nearly one-half of all retired, single females receive only the minimum Social Security benefit of $1,125 per year, and about one in four black males draws the minimum. On the average, blacks receive about twenty dollars per month less than elderly whites. Elderly singles constitute another problematic group. The percentage of elderly single persons with enough income to meet what the government considers an "intermediate budget" (one above the poverty range, but only slightly) declined over the years between the 1970 and 1980 census (Chen, 1985).

On the positive side of the ledger, blacks, Hispanics, Native Americans, and Asian Americans all exhibit healthy relationships with their families, socioeconomic status being a better predictor of psychological well-being than is race (Markides, Liang, & Jackson, 1990). Some evidence exists that people (other than whites, who tend not to see themselves as a "race") develop a more positive conception of their own racial group with age (Broman, Neighbors, & Jackson, 1988).

And finally, all groups of elderly people have experienced general improvement in their circumstances since the 1970s, when six in every ten elderly Americans were classified as poor. Much of the improvement can be attributed to a 210 percent increase in Social Security benefits since 1965 (although this increment represents only about a 57 percent increase in purchasing power). At present, Social Security is the single most important source of income to the elderly, providing "40 percent of the aggregate income of all aged units, with 90 percent of aged units receiving income from it. . . . Of those receiving Social Security, two-thirds (65 percent) relied on such benefits for at least half of their income, and more than one-quarter (26 percent) relied on such benefits for 90 percent or more of their income" (Chen, 1985, p. 654).

One of the reasons why the aged of the twenty-first century are expected to be more affluent than today's elderly is that younger people are more likely to contribute to private pension funds or to set up their own retirement accounts with the blessing of the Internal Revenue Service. Even among recent cohorts of retirees, there is evidence of substantial change. Among those who retired in the late 1970s, about 60 percent of the males and 40 percent of the females have some source of income aside from Social Security. With a private pension, income is often twice that of other elderly retired people. Among those in the highest income groups of elderly, nearly 40 percent were receiving income from private pensions, whereas only 4 percent of those in the lower income group did (Atchley, 1980; Chen, 1985; Decker, 1980).

Asset income (income from interest and dividends, rental income, etc.) is also widely received by the elderly. Nearly 100 percent of those in the highest income groups receive some form of income from assets, and 70 to 90 percent of the elderly in middle-income groups receive income from assets (Chen, 1985). Figure 11.2 presents a list of income sources for the elderly and the percentage of income reported from each of these sources for the population over sixty-five.

As you can see from Figure 11.2, about 20 percent of all elderly people receive income from earnings, and those who work average twice the annual income of those who do not. Only 6 percent of those in the lowest income group (under $5,000) have earnings from earned income, whereas 58 percent of those in the highest group have some earned income. These figures have created much controversy over the Social Security "earnings test." As it currently stands, one dollar in Social Security benefits is lost for every two dollars an elderly person earns over $3,480 each year. The minimum unpenalized wage is scheduled to increase over the next few years, but many believe it will still be a major obstacle in the road toward an increased standard of living for retired persons. Others believe that the earnings test is unfair primarily because income from investments and interest is excluded, allowing relatively wealthy people to collect Social Security benefits, but penalizing those who must continue to work.

In the future, many writers believe that earnings will constitute a more important source of income for the elderly, because recent low birth rates and the low rate estimated for the future will mean fewer young workers in the labor force. Under these conditions, the aged may be permitted, even required, to remain in the work force longer. The debate is growing among sociologists

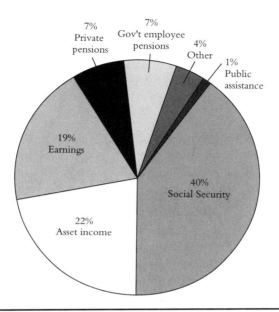

Figure 11.2 Income sources for the elderly.

SOURCE: Chen, 1985, p. 654.

and demographers about the overall economic significance of a huge increase in the number of elderly persons (Habib, 1985). Will the elderly constitute an economic burden, not only for their families but for the national economy as well? Consistently, this debate has raised the issue of retirement. What does it mean economically, psychologically, and socially? Does it make sense to encourage people to postpone the "golden years," or does the aging worker cost more to keep on the job than he or she is able to produce?

Retirement

Work is what you do so that some time you won't have to do it anymore.

—Alfred Polgar

In the last stages of the life cycle, most people can look forward to retirement from the work force and to a number of healthy, vigorous years at leisure. This phenomenon is new in the history of work, just recently perceived and expected as a normal phase of the life course. Only since the end of World War II have a large number of people retired, although pressure toward compulsory retirement started around the turn of the century. Assembly-line work, with its emphasis on speed, created demand for older workers to leave their jobs; the Great Depression then increased the pressure (Johnson & Williamson, 1987). Although the situation changed somewhat during the war years, older people have come to appreciate the possibility of retirement. In fact, younger people now worry that the Social Security system is not sound enough to guarantee them the same level of benefits elderly people enjoy today (Parker, 1982; Chen, 1989).

On the other hand, most people, including the young, are happy to see the easing of compulsory-retirement regulations. As the number of older workers grows, and the number of young people in the labor force declines, retirement will probably occur later. In the best case, the expectations of the individual and the competing economic requirements of the social system may produce a slower transition to retirement and a general reevaluation of the older worker.

Time Magazine (February 16, 1987) reported the initiation of the "McMasters" program at McDonald's, a program designed to attract the older worker to fill jobs for which there are no longer enough younger workers. It will be interesting to see whether senior citizens are willing to work at entry-level jobs in the mushrooming service sector of the economy, as there is likely to be great demand and a fair amount of flexibility on the part of employers in the decade ahead. Over time, retaining older workers in higher-level jobs may also become an important priority, because the size of the general labor force is declining.

There is little doubt that older workers are able to fulfill the requirements of their jobs well past sixty. "While capacities may decline throughout most of the worklife, productivity may not, as one's ability far exceeds the demands of the job" (Habib, 1985). In other words, most people are actually overqualified for the jobs they have and are quite capable of continuing in those jobs if they choose to do so until well into later life.

In his most recent review, Jack Habib (1990) again concludes that "every author who summarized the direct studies of productivity concluded that productivity, on the average, does not decline with age" (p. 332). In fact, there is reason to believe that older workers in a variety of occupations may perform better than the average younger worker. Studies of clerical workers, for example, show no general decline in productivity with age, and older workers are often steadier and more accurate than the young (Stagner, 1985).

Older workers also fulfill certain informal tasks in organizations, tasks that cannot be carried on effectively without them. Older workers socialize the young, teaching them the company rules and how to get along with supervisory staff; they transmit attitudes toward work and toward the organization. Furthermore, as job satisfaction has been shown to increase consistently with age, the older worker is likely to model positive interest in the work itself and less dissatisfaction with organizational policies.

The issues in studying retirement do not revolve around the problems of whether older workers ought to be retired. Most writers agree that older

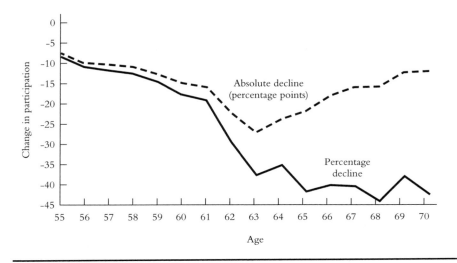

Figure 11.3 Change in male labor-force participation rates, by age, 1968–1986. From U.S. Department of Labor.

SOURCE: Quinn & Burkhauser, 1990, p. 309.

workers constitute an asset to the organization. Most of the literature concerns the current view of retirement as a right, one to which an individual is entitled by virtue of a lifetime's contribution to pension funds and the Social Security system. Before Social Security, those who could not work were viewed as a burden. The status and role of retiree is unique to modern times, for many if not most are perfectly capable of work. Today, many people actively choose to retire as early as possible, and the most important single predictor of age at retirement is income (Robinson, Coberly, & Paul, 1985; Johnson & Williamson, 1987), although the relationship is a complicated one.

Figure 11.3 shows how participation in the labor force declined for men over the years from 1968 to 1986. The largest absolute declines occurred for ages sixty-two to sixty-five. Participation for males over sixty-two dropped by 30–45 percent over the period. This drop is predicted by both Social Security benefits and private pension plan provisions. For many workers, staying on the job after sixty-five can actually result in a loss of lifetime benefits. There being no increase in benefits for working after sixty-five, people actually begin to lose money if they postpone payment of their benefits after that age. As Joseph Quinn and Richard Burkhauser (1990) point out: "Considerable research suggests that people behave as though they understand and respond to these incentives" (p. 314). Although it may look as though mandatory retirement policies or informal demands for retirement are driving people to leave the work force at age sixty-five, the design of Social Security and private pension plans probably accounts for the exodus. Most of the elderly who continue to work make clear attempts to earn less than the amount of income that might reduce their Social Security benefits, and the people who retire late tend to be those who have the most to gain economically by doing so.

Part of Amos's dilemma in the opening vignette has to do with the uncertainty he experiences in working through the calculation of his Social Security benefits. Most people don't understand in a conscious way exactly how much they stand to gain or lose from retiring at sixty-two rather than at sixty-five or later. Only about 10 percent of the population currently enrolls in any formal retirement preparation workshop or course (Ferraro, 1990). Even so, certain prominent features of the system, such as the provision of Medicare, are so clear that people behave in a way that maximizes their long-term benefits. By not considering retirement until sixty-five, Betsy is also behaving in a way that maximizes her benefits. She is in fact acting like most of her cohorts. There have only been slight declines in the proportion of older women leaving the labor force for early retirement, and most of the women who continue to work at older ages do so voluntarily. Women often take up work at a later age and are either working to increase their savings and pension contributions or simply enjoying their participation in the labor force more than men of a similar age who have been working for a greater number of years (Quinn & Burkhauser, 1990).

Current concerns over the Social Security system have led to changes that will delay full Social Security benefits until age sixty-six by the year 2009. In 1984, only one-third of those surveyed in a national sample expressed confidence in Social Security (Chen, 1989). Yet there is little reason for such pessimism for the foreseeable future. Increasing immigration, declining numbers of children who must also be supported by adult workers, phased retirement programs, and a program of partial Social Security for those who wish to continue to work part-time will probably maintain a close balance between income and outgo in the Social Security system for the next seventy-five years or so (Chen, 1989).

The people most likely to be affected by the changes in the Social Security system are single people, blacks, women who have substantially lower retirement wealth than married white males, and women who are more dependent on Social Security for retirement wealth than white males (Gohmann, 1990). Because Social Security makes up a larger portion of retirement wealth for women and blacks, they are more likely to be adversely affected by decreases in Social Security benefits. They are also more likely to find themselves in exactly the types of jobs from which people desire most strongly to retire, although older women who have been in the labor force for fewer years may participate longer for personal as well as economic reasons. These reasons may have less to do with the enjoyment of the work itself, however, than with its enhancement of the social aspect of women's lives and/or their sense of independence.

Since modern industrial technology separates workers from the products of their labor, many workers do not find their jobs intrinsically rewarding. Work is often boring and repetitious, and rarely meaningful. Michael Harrington has noted, for instance, that "more and more university students are convinced that work in American society is morally empty, aesthetically ugly, and, under conditions of automation, economically unnecessary" (Peter, 1979, p. 536). Given the fact that work has lost meaning—even to university students, who are likely to hold more prestigious jobs—older workers will undoubtedly continue to retire as early as possible from all kinds of jobs. The role of retiree is a social role, just like spouse or worker or parent, and can be defined in terms of both rights and duties, but it is also a status and a process. In the next few pages we will cover each of these aspects of retirement as it is lived in the last part of the twentieth century in America.

The Status of Retirement

What does it mean to be retired? Some older people have never officially worked and so never retire. Those with deviant careers, like gamblers, don't retire in the usual sense. And police officers, fire fighters, or photographers' models are not considered retired unless they move out of the work force completely, even though they may be retired from their first jobs. Usually, researchers define retirement as a status in which one does not hold a regular job and collects at least part of his or her income from Social Security or another pension (Atchley, 1980). However, not all researchers use the same definitions, and the situation generates conflicting results. For instance, Stanley Parker (1982) points out that half of all retired workers in Britain do not have pensions. Parker goes on to argue that no single definition is good enough, and one might even contend that retirement is, in some sense, a state of mind.

The best definition of retired may be a subjective one. That is, a retired person is one who considers him or herself retired. A secretary who stops doing office work at sixty-five but goes on to be a successful writer may consider herself retired, but may be making too much money to collect Social Security. Many older people make unreported incomes as well. There is probably a huge underground economy in both cash and traded services in which the elderly participate. Is an elderly worker who continues to work but also collects Social Security retired?

As a status, then, the distinction between retired and not-yet-retired people is a little blurred. Retirement may begin early or late, be voluntary or involuntary, be partial or gradual, or even self-perceived. This ambiguity affects many aspects of the literature, and perhaps the best research simply begs the issue and focuses on variations in role perception, motivation, and the nature of the decision to retire.

Retirement as a Role

The question "Can life be meaningful without work?" resounds in the literature. Can people be happy without the structure work provides? Of course,

There is a growing expectation in this society that healthy, relatively affluent retired people will give freely of their skills and their time to the community.

certain obligations are associated with retirement. It is not entirely without structure. Retired people are expected to manage their own resources and to remain economically and emotionally independent. More and more often, they are expected to continue to contribute their expertise and energy to the community when necessary. Associations of retired businesspeople and teachers, professionals and artisans help channel the skills of the elderly back into society.

Despite these basic agreements, however, the role of retiree is ambiguous, and many sociologists and psychologists believe that role ambiguity is associated with poor adjustment (Atchley, 1980; Sussman, 1972). They argue that one must find a reasonable alternative to work in order to adjust. As Gordon Streib (1983) has written: "Generally speaking, retirement is regarded negatively by all age strata. The retiree is usually considered to be in a slightly lower or degraded status than he occupied while gainfully employed. Retirement is associated with decreased activity and interaction and is often thought to be associated with physical and psychological maladies. Indeed, there is a prevailing attitude on the part of some persons that it is retirement itself which is the causal element in any subsequent physical or psychological deterioration" (p. 203).

Perhaps because there is this generally negative view of the retiree, much of the literature has focused on retirement as a turning point affecting life satisfaction and adjustment, and much of the theoretical literature deals with what can be done to make retirement a positive process.

Retirement as a Process: Adjustment

Most theories of retirement consider it a process that entails loss. **Substitution theory**, for example, posits that leaving work requires that one find new activities offering much the same gratification as work (Friedman & Havighurst, 1954; Shanas, 1972). However, there is little evidence that American workers miss work per se. Oh, they miss the money (Shanas, 1972), but they are unlikely to find some other activity that produces as much money as work did. Substitution theory is a variation on the more general notion that retirement constitutes some sort of crisis and that one must do *something* in order to adjust to not doing anything. From this viewpoint, retirement causes psychological, social, and cognitive changes, and even health problems.

In one version of substitution theory, Marvin Sussman argues that the central variable determining adjustment is the number of options an individual can exercise. The most successful retiree is the one who has the most choices and is most capable of matching his or her needs and abilities with the options and then taking appropriate action. Sussman advocates taking up a series of new "careers" in retirement, in the sense of career defined in Chapter 5, as a continuous involvement in a role over time. He also believes that social responsibility should constitute a major theme in the development of these careers.

As Streib (1983) points out, however, Sussman's ideas may be considered elitist. He does not acknowledge the social and economic circumstances that limit choice, and he assumes that new roles can be adopted easily, without considering the effect of a person's lifetime pattern of interests and activities. Furthermore, Sussman does not really acknowledge the role of leisure in retirement, since, Streib argues, leisure cannot be considered a career.

In one of the most influential studies of work and retirement ever undertaken, Streib and Schneider (1971) were unable to find evidence that retirement constituted a major disruption in an adult's role and had deleterious consequences for the individual. This research included both objective and subjective measures of well-being for over four thousand men and women employed in jobs ranging from production-line work to professional services. The majority of these retired subjects were satisfied and well adjusted. Retirement made no difference in health, and most saw their incomes as adequate. Only a few felt retirement was difficult and most felt the problems of leaving the work force were exaggerated.

Almost without exception, more recent research has supported these findings. Most workers see retirement as an active, busy, involved, expanding, full, fair, hopeful, relaxed, and independent state of affairs, especially blue-collar workers, although blacks and Hispanics are more dissatisfied with retirement because they are more often living near or below the poverty line (Johnson &

Williamson, 1987). Given enough money, however, most workers, even those who held white-collar jobs, feel very positive toward retirement.

It is only among professionals and highly educated men and women that substitution theory fits the data. Greater autonomy on the job is associated with less favorable attitudes toward retirement (Streib & Schneider, 1971), and professionals are among the last to leave the work force. Studies of job complexity have shown that jobs requiring independent thought and judgment usually serve as a source of self-esteem and are perceived as meaningful and challenging (Kohn, 1980). On the other hand, people who hold complex jobs develop great cognitive and emotional flexibility during their occupational lives, and so it is not surprising to find that professional people usually make excellent adjustment once they retire.

Streib (1983) contends that the impact of retirement on adjustment varies with both personality and the type of employment from which the individual retires. Retirement can offer freedom from exhausting, difficult, or stressful work; the possibility of esteem or prestige in some substitute activity; the opportunity to pursue hobbies, interests, and leisure activities; the ability to direct one's own activities; and some degree of economic security. Whether or not a person adjusts well to retirement will depend on the degree to which these rewards are available in retirement and how the person evaluates them.

Another way to conceptualize retirement is offered by Robert Atchley (1980) when he suggests that we consider retirement a series of phases, rather than one single, unitary stage of life course. Atchley defines six such phases, beginning with a preretirement phase. In **preretirement**, people who are "short-timers" in the work force (people who are close to retirement) entertain a number of fantasies about retirement, including images of how they will feel, what they will do, and how life will develop once they retire. In the second phase, the **honeymoon**, newly retired people play out these fantasies, if they are able to. Of course, the fantasies must be realistic if there is to be a honeymoon at all. If the fantasies are not really possible, or if they turn out to be unsatisfactory, **disenchantment** sets in, and the individual must begin restructuring his or her time in a constructive, meaningful way. Disenchantment is followed by a phase called **reorientation**, in which disenchanted retirees pull themselves together and discover how to become realistically involved in the world around them. With luck and effort, reorientation will produce choices that lead to a comfortable, satisfying lifestyle, ushering in a period of **stability**. **Termination** is the final phase. Retirement may end because an individual goes back to work, but more often it is terminated by illness or disability. Retirement requires that one be independent, and it comes to an end when grave disabilities begin. The transition from stability to termination is usually gradual, however, and is never complete unless the individual is institutionalized.

Not all people go through all of these stages, of course. Some individuals may have developed plans so realistic and satisfying that they proceed from preretirement to stability without a hitch. Others are more or less disenchanted throughout retirement. Perhaps as many as 30 percent or so are never really satisfied (Atchley, 1980; Streib & Schneider, 1971). What most people dislike about retirement is the feeling of economic dependence or being forced to retire because of mandatory retirement policies or health problems.

As Parker (1982) sums it up, adjustment to retirement is best predicted by two general factors: flexibility, and resources. However, he is talking not only about individual flexibility and resources but also about the flexibility and resources afforded by society. There is little doubt that adjustment is easier when there are options, both as to how retirement comes about and as to how one lives afterward.

Retirement as an Option: Flexibility

Like so many other subjects we have examined in this book, there appears to be no universally best way to retire, just as there is no best way to marry or to parent or to work. Adjustment and life satisfaction are not all-or-none phenomena either. People enjoy freedom in retirement from clocks, bosses, and boring or stressful work. But they also miss the social life, the structuring of their time, and, of course, the money. However, fewer than 10 percent say they actually miss their jobs (Johnson & Williamson, 1987). Retirement usually produces a one-half to two-thirds reduction in income, although only 17 percent of retired people report that they don't have enough money to live on (Robinson, Coberly, & Paul, 1985).

On average, women and members of visible minorities are most likely to have lower Social Security and pension benefits. More blacks and Hispanics also report retiring involuntarily because of poor health, and are likely to suffer economically (Johnson & Williamson, 1987). Blacks, Hispanics, and women are also likely to be employed in the types of jobs that are the least flexible when it comes to retirement.

The more choices people are offered in making the transition, the easier it is likely to be. Professionals may make the best adjustments when they do retire because they are so often able to "call the shots" and quit working when they want. Amos, the painter in our opening story, is also in a pretty good spot. In his trade, he may well be self-employed and able to cut down on the number of hours he works without quitting work altogether, especially if the agency Betsy works for ever gives her the kind of raise Amos thinks she's entitled to. Many older people take up being self-employed in later life and the number is increasing (Quinn & Burkhauser, 1990). Today about 80 percent of all older workers report they would prefer to stay employed on a part-time basis with their present employer if that option were available. However, it seldom is and switching employers late in life in order to work part-time usually incurs severe wage losses (Quinn, Burkhauser, & Myers, 1990).

Still, many people are partially retiring by becoming self-employed; others take new jobs that are quite different from their previous work. About one-half end up in a different industry later in life even though they experience large decreases in income. It may be that much of the decline in income of people over sixty-two may be an intentional attempt to stay under the $3,400 maximum allowed if one is to continue receiving Social Security (Quinn, Burkhauser, & Myers, 1990). Such public policies encourage early retirement and limited labor force participation.

Changes in Social Security in the nineties are expected to retain more older workers. Experiments like job sharing and the use of computers to encourage work at home, combined with partial pensions, might encourage people to stay on the job. Creating options that make work more attractive seems far more likely to have a positive impact on the elderly than discouraging retirement through changes in the Social Security system. Currently, about one-half of all retirees suffer from some form of illness or disability, like Amos, by the time they retire (Robinson, Coberly, & Paul, 1985). Public policies that are applied without consideration for individual differences reduce options and are likely to create dissatisfaction.

On the other hand, lifting the mandatory retirement age from sixty-five to seventy will probably increase the diversity of retirement options, resulting in an increased number of older workers. Increases in the numbers of married women in the labor force will probably help retain older male workers as well. As Amos's situation highlights, when women don't retire, their spouses are likely to remain working, and since married women are several years younger, on the average, than their spouses, married men may continue to work until their wives are ready to retire. Larger numbers of divorced and single older women may also add to the number of older workers in the future, as will the trend toward employment in the service and information industries, where heavy, arduous labor is not required.

Flexible work and retirement policies not only increase the likelihood that people will stay in the labor force, they also increase the probability that people will be able to take advantage of some of the options available in retirement. For example, the basic conditions for success in leisure activities include economic resources. The number of people who plan for retirement, invest in private pension funds, and qualify for Social Security will approach 100 percent in younger cohorts, especially as women become more active participants in the work force. Developing a lifestyle that relies on leisure activities usually requires that one be mobile and be able to afford the entry fees, materials, equipment, or other facilities required for the activity. Increasing the availability of meaningful leisure activities is the other side of expanding retirement options.

Retirement and Leisure

Of course, the elderly must see leisure as a legitimate source of pleasure and self-esteem or identity if they are to make use of the option. Future elderly are more likely to be educated in leisure pursuits, and finding fellow participants will be easier. Furthermore, there is little doubt that younger people value leisure activities. As John Kenneth Galbraith has observed, "The students react to my praise of toil with great applause and loud demands for a holiday from work." Young people have helped develop a tremendous variety of leisure pursuits, some of which are very recent innovations, like motocross racing, windsurfing, and ski sailing. Computer games, cable television, and video recorders contribute to the burgeoning number of leisure activities readily available at every level of intensity and involvement to nearly every rung on the socioeconomic ladder. People have developed more positive attitudes toward leisure than ever before, and they are certainly finding new and creative ways to fill their time.

Leisure education is less problematic, of course, when leisure is an acceptable source of identity and self-esteem from one's earliest years. The boy who played in the American Youth Soccer Organization from first to twelfth grades becomes a fan, maybe even a coach, especially if he retains his interest after he retires. The girl who loved gadgets as a child but ended up teaching English, buys a computer as an adult and becomes a lifelong "hacker." One need no longer wait for retirement to learn how to use leisure time. It is a normal part of the life course and, therefore, easier to structure and utilize.

Judging the role of leisure in retirement among today's elderly is very difficult, for many of them have had so little leisure education. Typically, research suggests that the older the respondent, the greater the amount of time devoted to leisure; but the range of activities is narrower and the activities are more sedentary (Gordon & Gaitz, 1983; Robinson & Peterson, 1989). Although it is possible that the narrowing of leisure interests occurs over the adult life span, it is more likely that this result is a cohort difference and that leisure will play an increasing role in the retirement lifestyles of younger cohorts. Only a very small number of individuals take up new activities after retirement. Even people who predict that they will spend more time in leisure after they retire, rarely do so (Basse & Ekerdt, 1981; Teague, 1980). Positive attitudes toward leisure do not simply arise because one suddenly has a lot of time on one's hands. The tremendous emphasis American education places on job skills has left older cohorts unprepared to restructure their time around other activities.

There is very little current literature on the impact of leisure or retirement education, but such education is becoming available through a variety of institutions, from private workshops to community colleges. It is possible in any major city to take a class in photography, jewelry making, gourmet cooking, or yoga almost any night of the week. The success of these ventures suggests the eagerness of younger people to learn and pursue new hobbies and interests over the life span; their willingness to try new activities; as well as their ability to pay for the education, materials, and facilities that make leisure possible. Preretirement education and realistic planning for retirement are associated with higher levels of adjustment among retired people and more favorable attitudes toward retirement during the work year (Atchley, 1980; Chown, 1977; Green & Tyron, 1969).

However, the response of current cohorts to the development of educational programs for the elderly has not been encouraging. Only about 9 percent of all people over fifty-five participate in such programs and only 2–4 percent of those over seventy. It may be that the design of current programs is inadequate for a number of reasons. Research shows that 70–80 percent of the elderly report participating in a self-directed learning project. Perhaps formal educational programs need to be paced to the individual to a greater extent than they are at the moment, or they may need to take the physical and motivational needs of older people into stronger consideration. Mobility may be a major issue, or it may be necessary to redesign classrooms for the use of older students (Robinson & Peterson, 1989).

The need to increase the options for elderly people and to discover their unique needs and requirements is a much repeated theme in the literature on aging. Nowhere is it more apparent, however, than in research on the physical environment. It is, in fact, probably the major concern of those who study such matters as housing, transportation, and the variety of available services and support systems in the community.

The Physical Environment

When you live on the banks of the River Pudma, you must make friends of the crocodile.

—S. Lall

A number of major themes have emerged in the rapidly growing literature on environments and aging. Some of the most important include housing choice; mobility and relocation; satisfaction with housing; and the design of special settings, especially institutional settings for those who need greater care. We'll explore all of these themes, but remember that the key to satisfactory adjustment can nearly always be summed up in one word: *options*. As Archibald MacLeish observed, "Without the possibility of choice and the exercise of choice a [human being] is not a [human being] but a member, an instrument, a thing." To lose one's options, one's choices, is to lose a significant part of the self.

Housing Choice

As noted already, most older Americans own their own homes, and nearly all Americans over sixty-five live in regular community settings. Ninety-five percent live outside institutional settings, and only about 10–20 percent live with their adult children. The percentage of old people living alone has risen steadily, as has income among the elderly, especially among elderly widows (Kendig, 1990).

Because the homes of the elderly tend to be older, however, they often are of lesser value, have fewer rooms, and have fewer amenities like central heating

Growing numbers of module and mobile homes give the elderly a housing alternative that is inexpensive, efficient, and modern and provide the opportunity to live in a community planned with their needs in mind.

or air conditioning than do the homes of younger people. Moreover, many elderly people have excessive housing costs, running as high as 35–40 percent of their income, and this is especially frequent among those who rent or have not paid off their mortgages. On the average, younger people spend about 20 percent of their income on housing. Maintenance costs are higher for older homes; an old house can be quite expensive, even when the mortgage is relatively low. Leaking roofs, incomplete plumbing and kitchen facilities, as well as problems with rodents, are common complaints of elderly homeowners (Lawton, 1985).

Older people living alone have the worst housing problems, particularly older men and blacks whether they are tenants or owners. Older women seem better at finding adequate housing, despite the fact that they make less money. Women may spend more time searching for good housing, or may have more help finding housing from family or friends.

Despite the general inadequacy of much older housing, home repairs occur less often and remodeling occurs much less often among elderly homeowners. An increase in income is less likely to go toward housing repairs among the elderly than the young, and only about 10 percent of all elderly people make any modifications to their homes, including the provision of handrails or wheelchair access, which might improve safety and convenience (Parmelee &

Lawton, 1990). Perhaps the priorities of older people lie elsewhere, but it is also possible that health problems or the inability to locate and supervise contract services prevents older people from repairing, remodeling, or modifying their homes. Possibly older people do not understand the condition of the home or what is necessary to repair whatever problems arise (Lawton, 1985).

Even so, most elderly people claim to be satisfied with their housing and rate it as satisfactory, even when outside observers assess it as poor. Some researchers have argued that older people say they are satisfied with their housing only because there are no alternatives. In other words, their reported satisfaction is a defense against anxiety (Carp, 1977; Lawton, 1985). However, stability among older homeowners is remarkable and housing adjustments usually only occur near death.

Much of the current literature focuses on how to help people "age in place" (Parmelee & Lawton, 1990). Most older people say they want to stay in their own homes and never move. Those who do are most often tenants displaced by evictions, condominium conversions, or redevelopment (Kendig, 1990). Long-term ownership probably bestows special meanings on a home, for elderly nonmovers acknowledge that nostalgia and a preference for the familiar are important in their choices to remain stationary (Howell, 1980a).

As Hal Kendig (1990) argues, however: "From a societal point of view, the housing stock could probably be better utilized and older people more appropriately housed if there were fewer barriers to moving and a wider range of housing options" (p. 297). He has proposed that the costs of moving, such as real estate commissions and taxes, be reduced or removed for older people who wish to move, and that older people be encouraged to share housing. It might also ease the problem of household maintenance if people could share larger, older homes. On the other hand, one of the most consistent complaints older people have about alternative housing is the lack of privacy in new, more modern facilities. Certainly, this would constitute a problem in sharing a house as well.

Aging in place in an older home usually means an older neighborhood, of course, and for many it means the inner city. Noise and traffic head the list of headaches among the urban elderly. Those who live in the inner city are also worried about crime and litter. A home is more than a few rooms, a bath, and a yard. It also encompasses a territory—a neighborhood, a social group, and access to the larger world. The entire community is an important ecological unit for older people, because so many depend on their immediate surroundings to supply all their needs. Public transportation is very poor in most cities in this country. Even in New York City, where public transportation is more readily available than in other cities, it does not meet the needs of older citizens. Older New Yorkers tend to be "block bound," that is, they spend almost all of their time within walking distance of their homes (Nahemow & Kogan, 1971). Walking distance for most elderly is about one-half mile, or nine blocks in any direction. Few neighborhoods, even sophisticated urban communities, provide a wide variety of services within walking distance of one's home, and so older people do without the services they cannot reach by walking.

Overall, the research suggests that elderly people do best when they live in small and midsized communities where they perceive a low rate of crime. The fear of crime is a central predictor in satisfaction with housing. Since many older Americans live in central cities, have below-average incomes, and live in the older, poorer neighborhoods, fear of crime is very common, and they are unable to take advantage of the possibilities inherent in city life (Scheidt & Windley, 1985).

Given basic adequacy of housing and community, however, "the evidence reviewed overwhelmingly supports the assertion that the great majority of older people would prefer to remain where they are" (Lawton, 1985, p. 471). For this reason, it has been suggested that programs aimed at assisting the elderly to maintain and repair current housing may be among the best ways to deal with housing needs. Moreover, it may be among the least expensive ways, since it appears that there is at least as great a need for information and assistance in locating help as there is for money.

For those who are dissatisfied, however, there is the need to cushion relocation and to ensure that a move occurs in a timely way. Often, the problem of relocation is the problem of convincing elderly people to move to more suitable housing, in a better neighborhood, near better transportation, with easier upkeep, before they become too frail to function in the inner city or in an inaccessible rural area.

Relocation and Mobility

New trends in housing seem likely to encourage more timely relocation for those who need to move. For instance, the growing availability of condominium and cooperative housing offers the elderly low maintenance along with a social setting conducive to interaction. Twenty-eight percent of all condominium owners are currently elderly, as well as 41 percent of all cooperative owners (Lawton, 1985). These housing arrangements also have the advantage of fixed monthly payments. Another promising trend can be detected in the increasing popularity of module and mobile homes, especially since the federal government has ruled that mobile homes are eligible for assistance programs. Although mobile homes depreciate, the upkeep on a new one is very modest compared with the expense of maintaining more conventional housing. Moreover, in some areas it is possible to purchase the land on which a mobile home or module home sits, thus ensuring that part of the investment will appreciate over the years (Struyk, 1981).

One interesting study of mobility identified a group of "adventurous" elderly (Kahana, Kahana, & McLenigan, 1980). Adventurers enjoyed retirement and saw themselves as "young-old." They moved away from the homes where they had reared families and pursued careers, judging life satisfaction on the basis of interest and challenge. Of course, voluntary relocation produces the best outcomes. However, often older people must resettle involuntarily. Sometimes they are caught in the renovation of older areas of the city, or the conversion of apartments into condominiums. At other times, family members take over moving an elderly person closer to a child, away from the inner city, or to a specialized living environment.

Generally, involuntary relocation has been associated with declining health and morale (Chown, 1977), but some individuals benefit if the new environment is favorable. Competent people who are moved to settings encouraging autonomy and providing warmth and support, improve. High morale among the staff in the new environment and the careful handling of personal possessions are paramount in turning transfer from trauma to therapy (Eustis, 1981).

Relocation is "virtually irrelevant to survival so long as the support system is made adequate" (Eustis, 1981, p. 494). However, some people are more vulnerable to a traumatic or poorly planned move. Of course, those who are forced to move, especially those who enter institutions, are often already very frail, and it is difficult to say whether problems develop because of the transfer or as an extension of the conditions that forced relocation in the first place (Coffman, 1981).

Relocation, itself, then, seems less important than the characteristics of the individual and, perhaps most importantly, the characteristics of the new environment. At the moment, no research exists on the comparative satisfaction of elderly living in conventional, condominium, cooperative, or mobile housing. Most of the research on housing for the elderly focuses on the impact of planned housing, specially designed for the elderly and usually constructed under the supervision of the government. Generally, studies of government housing projects and planned communities suggest that expressed life satisfaction and social behavior are affected in a positive way by such environments. Typically, statements about the effects of housing on physical health have been more difficult to interpret, with some investigators reporting positive effects and some finding no evidence of improvement (Carp, 1966; Lawton & Cohen, 1974; Parr, 1980; Sherwood, Greer, Morris, & Sherwood, 1972).

Planned Housing

Like the study of general life satisfaction, the study of life satisfaction and housing is plagued by semantic measurement problems. Some researchers have measured satisfaction; some, morale; and some, adjustment (Parr, 1980). Furthermore, researchers often assume the behavior they see in a particular environment is directly related to the features of that environment. But, as Sandra Howell (1980a) points out, the way older people behave is a product of a lifetime, and their responses can reflect the need to maintain a sense of identity in a new environment. For instance, people may miss a formal dining room not because they use a dining room but because they have fond memories of family meals and celebrations. Dissatisfaction with housing is not always adaptive or even related to the housing itself.

Most of the time, however, the responses older people give seem quite straightforward. They tend to feel most secure in high-rise, urban buildings, and generally do well in communities planned for the elderly (Carp, 1966, 1975; Howell, 1985a, 1985b). Although they want to spend more time with the

Research on congregate housing that is not characterized by high levels of control shows increases in satisfaction, morale, and involvement among residents.

middle-aged, they prefer communities that are age-segregated to those that are not controlled for age. Some researchers have suggested, however, that the optimal community would include people of all ages, if it were carefully designed. There is evidence, for instance, that when elderly hospital patients are assigned to wards with young patients they do better than if assigned to wards with only other elderly (Kahana, 1982). The young may have beneficial effects on older people, challenging them to higher levels of adaptation.

Most American communities are not designed for optimal age mixes, however. It is assumed that older people do not want anything to do with children and adolescents and that middle-aged people do not want to live with the elderly. In Europe, however, where a wider variety of age mixes have been tried, the data show that elderly people can benefit from living near other age groups (Carp, 1977).

The Victoria Plaza Project In the study of age-segregated housing, some of the most detailed and intriguing results have been presented by Frances M. Carp (1966, 1977, 1987) in a long-term follow-up study of a government-planned apartment called the Victoria Plaza in Texas. Carp concluded that the Victoria Plaza project seemed to have had favorable effects on the social and psychological well-being of its tenants. Follow-up data also suggested favorable effects on physical health. Residents of Victoria Plaza exhibited unusually low rates of death and institutionalization (Carp, 1977). Of course, certain individual differences were notable. Those who were most sociable when they came to the Plaza increased their sociability over the period of the study, while those who had little need to socialize withdrew and even became isolated (Carp, 1987). Carp argues that congruence between the needs of residents and the design of the environment becomes important once basic problems like food and shelter have been solved. Carp uses Maslow's hierarchy (see Chapter 2) to talk about the match between needs and environments.

As M. Powell Lawton (1990) points out, research in the area of housing affirms the continuity of the person as a rule over the life span. People prefer to stay in their own homes if possible, but when they move, they do better in housing that permits them to continue lifelong patterns. On the other hand, certain innovative aspects of the Plaza drew applause from most of the residents.

Residents were questioned about their likes and dislikes after they had moved into their new lodgings. Among the things these older adults liked best were the clean, modern rooms and conveniences, including stoves, refrigerators, private baths, elevators, and access to transportation and community facilities. They also appreciated the physical security in the building and the closeness of other people their own age. They praised the idea of a complete maintenance staff and seemed happy to be living in age-segregated quarters where there were no children as full-time residents.

Although the residents of Victoria Plaza liked the closeness of other old people and the absence of children, a number of residents felt that middle-aged residents would provide more interesting company and stimulation. Most studies of age segregation compare communities that are completely age-segregated with those that are not controlled for age. A few investigators have considered the effects of high **age density** (a large proportion of residents of a particular age group) versus low age density, but all of these studies present problems. Often the residents of age-segregated, specially designed environments have just moved into bright, new housing, clearly superior to what they left behind. Yet, residents in older age-dense neighborhoods may show high levels of morale because they have lived in the same area for a long time and appreciate the familiar surroundings.

The residents of Victoria Plaza seemed to prefer age-restricted housing, but they also noted some important drawbacks. Competent residents were especially concerned about living with people who could not take care of themselves or were unable or unwilling to engage in the flow of social life in the project. Residents of the Plaza often expressed high standards of cleanliness and behavioral propriety. They seemed especially dissatisfied with one older man who insisted on bringing his women friends in through the fire escape. Some residents felt that the presence of competent, proper, middle-aged people might inhibit such behavior.

A number of residents lodged design complaints that provide insight into the details of everyday life at the Plaza. The building had been constructed around one major entrance lobby, where much social activity took place. The

---

Box 11.1 Focus on Application: Human factors design for older adults

---

In the study of human factors, researchers try to optimize the design of living and working environments based on physiological, psychological, and social studies of older adults. In recent years, such applications have produced interesting results, from information about the best way to design computers to how to lay out an entire community. In a recent review of the subject, Neil Charness and Elizabeth Bosman (1990) offer some examples.

For instance, they point out that such everyday tools as the common stepstool can be redesigned to great advantage for older adults. Widening the step and adding handrails increases safety significantly. Many of the improvements recommended by human factors researchers involve safety concerns, such as how large the letters should be on traffic signs or the timing of lights at crosswalks.

Human factors designers are also concerned with how people use machines and appliances. For example, they point out that computers need to be redesigned for older adults. The characters are difficult to see and many keyboards give little auditory or tactile feedback. Researchers have found that black-on-white characters are best for middle-aged and older users and a mouse seems to speed the performance of the elderly as long as the targets on the screen are large enough. Designers also point out that older people are slower at learning a tutorial, needing 1.5 to 2 times as much exposure to new material as younger users. Charness and Bosman point out, however, that it is as yet unclear whether written menus or icons are more useful to older users.

Human factors designers also address such problems as whether people take their medications on time. For those who often forget to do so, one solution is to set a wrist watch alarm. However, current alarm wrist watches require too much dexterity for an elderly person to set and the alarm is often pitched too high for older people to hear.

If, as Charness and Bosman argue, human factors designers take into account the goals of older people as well as their capabilities, human factors applications should offer much potential for improving the quality of life in old age.

---

only elevators in the building opened into this lobby. Many residents felt the building should have had at least one private, quiet back entrance where people could come and go unnoticed. Special problems were created by the single entrance when a resident fell ill or died. Because everyone and everything had to enter and leave through the same set of elevators, residents never knew if they might be confronted by death or illness when the elevator doors opened.

Tenants also complained about the weight of the lobby doors, which had to be pushed open by hand. And they objected to the heavy window draperies, which did not provide privacy and sunlight simultaneously. There were also some curious blindspots in special areas. For instance, refrigerators had been installed high off the ground in an attempt to prevent stooping, but short residents were unable to reach the upper shelves. Bathroom doors had been widened to allow the passage of a wheelchair, but the bathroom was too small for a wheelchair to turn around in.

These problems underline the importance of consulting older people throughout the design process. Such consultation is not yet common, but it always produces interesting results. At one conference, sponsored by a builder in cooperation with a local community college and a council on aging, the elderly participants mentioned a variety of facilities that might be beneficial. Many said they would like Jacuzzi-type therapy pools in housing facilities. And, although questionnaire responses indicated that the cost of housing was the single most important concern of these older people, other possibilities also generated enthusiasm. Most insisted on being allowed to keep a pet—one woman commented that her cat was "the only warm thing that has touched me in years" (Ryon, 1978)—and the majority wanted a small piece of land nearby where they could grow flowers and vegetables, not just for recreation but also for the table. Some small, inexpensive details were also revealed as important, including sliding rather than swinging doors, extrawide tubs, seats built into showers, electric wall plugs installed eighteen inches to three feet above the baseboard, and windows placed low enough so that someone sitting in a wheelchair or lying in bed could see outdoors. Some comments emphasized the need for security and convenient transportation.

Not everyone asked for special amenities, however. One man is quoted as follows: "I believe a major problem with senior housing is the increasing tendency to provide these kinds of extras. This is the kind of coddling most of us resent, and friends of mine who live in such places object to their cost" (Ryon, 1978). The issue of whether special planning and services is tantamount to coddling brings us to one of the central points of many current theoretical formulations—the role of supportive environments.

Theory and Environment

Environmental planners commonly assume that because older people are less independent, they need supportive environments. It is possible, however, for the environment to be oversupportive, robbing the individual of the opportunity to experience a sense of mastery and the self-esteem that proceeds from successful functioning (Lawton, 1985; Lawton, 1990; Parmelee & Lawton, 1990).

Here we should distinguish between **prosthetic** and **therapeutic** environments. Prosthetic devices are permanent supports, such as eyeglasses or artificial limbs, that allow a person to function fully only as long as the devices are present. Prosthetics can encourage dependence but should also permit people to continue functioning when they become permanently impaired. Therapeutic environments offer rich and varied opportunities, even challenges, and the security and permissiveness that lead to new growth and adaptation (Carp, 1977; Birren, Butler, Greenhouse, Sokoloff, & Yarrow, 1963).

The balance between prosthesis and therapy is critical in the maintenance and encouragement of adaptive behavior. One especially sophisticated treatment of this issue was formulated by M. Powell Lawton and his associates (Lawton & Nahemow, 1973; Lawton, 1977, 1980, 1985; Parmelee & Lawton, 1990). Lawton assumed that the most adaptive outcomes would occur where the **demand quality** of the environment was within the range of the individual's competence, particularly when the demand quality approached the maximum capacity of that individual. **Environmental press** is a measure of how much demand the environment makes for competent behavior. **Competence** is seen here as the total range of biological, sensorimotor, and cognitive abilities. Performance potential refers to the individual's capacity for competent behavior. The demand quality of the environment refers to the potential of the physical setting for evoking the desired behavior. From this point of view, either very high or very low levels of challenge or stress will be associated with poor outcomes. Figure 11.4 gives a graphic representation of the relationship between demand quality, competence, and adaptation.

Lawton's presentation focused on the hypothesis that **person-environment congruence** is an important principle of housing design. Optimal person-environment congruence is found in environments that are person-specific; that is, people must be individually matched to their environments to assure the proper balance between therapy and prosthesis. Prosthesis cannot be denied when it is necessary—that would be as ridiculous as denying someone glasses if he or she needed them. The proper level of prosthesis can prolong independence rather than create dependence. Also, it isn't desirable to remove all challenge from the environment. The important consideration is the fit between the needs and abilities of the individual and the degree of support and challenge offered by the environment (Kahana, 1973, 1975; Lawton, 1975).

Many questions have been raised by Lawton's original hypothesis suggesting that a challenging environment is optimal. Some have argued that concepts like "adaptive behavior," "environmental press," and "maximum performance potential" are too vague. Environmental press, for instance, has been defined in terms of at least eleven separate dimensions (Windley and Scheidt, 1980):

1. Sensory stimulation: To what extent will the redundant cues (such as both color coding and labeling directional information) compensate for sensory decline?

2. Legibility: Is press affected by the degree to which designers use spatial organization to facilitate orientation and direction finding?

3. Comfort: How do dimensions such as the level of illumination and temperature affect either perceived press or behavior?

4. Privacy: In what ways can the control of unwanted stimulation be enhanced?

5. Adaptability: Is it possible to increase the ways in which a particular space can be adapted by its inhabitants as their needs change?

6. Control: In what ways does individual ownership and jurisdiction over space affect functioning, and how can such control be facilitated?

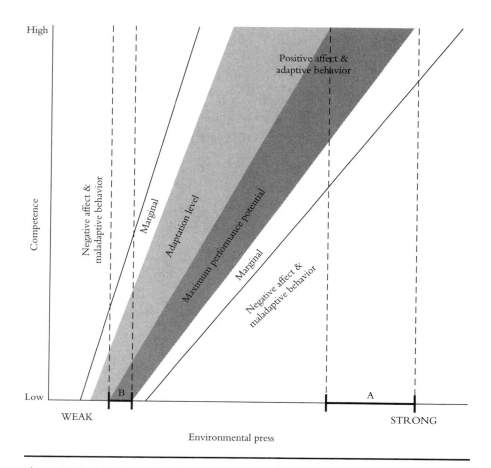

Figure 11.4 Behavioral and affective outcomes of person-environment transactions. This figure indicates that an individual of high competence will show maximum performance over a larger range of environmental situations than will a less competent individual. The entire range of optimal environments will occur at higher levels of environmental press (A) for the most competent person than for the least competent person (B).

SOURCE: Lawton & Nahemow, 1973, p. 661, Copyright © 1973 by the American Psychological Association.

7. Sociability: What kinds of spaces encourage interaction between in-habitants or interaction with the community at large?

8. Accessibility: How can mobility be enhanced within a particular space as well as making entrance and exit as easy as possible?

9. Density: How does the perception of crowding affect social inter-action and well-being?

10. Meaning: Do people behave differently in spaces that have symbolic meaning (such as the design of a church) or personal meaning (memories and social history) connected to them?

11. Quality: In what ways do the aesthetic appeal, design utility, and the size of a space affect behavior?

All of these are interesting questions, and the few partial answers offered by Windley and Scheidt are fascinating. Designers have found, for example, that reducing the size of areas set aside for social interaction but increasing their number results in greater frequency of social interaction. Even more interesting, some studies suggest that one effective way to involve people in their social setting is to design space so that one moves from private, enclosed, personal space through semiprivate space (like a front porch), to public space (like a sidewalk). The house/porch/street configuration substantially increases social interaction over more conventional designs.

In a similar article, Joyce Parr (1980) proposed that researchers might profitably choose a behavior and study how it is influenced by a variety of environmental characteristics. One might focus on the number of social interactions initiated by a particular set of people, or in a particular space. Changes in the design of a space could then be assessed in a very specific way. For example, it has been demonstrated that the location and length of the path from a front entrance to an elevator affects social interaction (Howell, 1978).

Parr also believes that researchers ought to study the meaning of environmental characteristics for individuals as well as their impact on behavior. How do people interpret the installation of rails in a bathroom? Do they see it as helpful and supportive, or do they feel it implies incompetence? Parr underscores how important it is for social scientists interested in this arena to spend more time in interdisciplinary research. In particular, the architectural literature must be considered if recommendations about the creation of space are to be developed.

Significantly, some researchers have questioned the notion that challenging environments provide more potential benefits than congruency (Kahana, 1975, 1982; Scheidt & Windley, 1985). Congruent environments provide perfect fit between individual needs and environmental stimulation. An undersupplied environment can be as inadequate as an oversupplied one, according to those who argue for congruency. Another set of concerns is expressed by Sandra Howell (1980a, 1980b), who has argued that the major motive for people in their environments is not the need to adapt at all, but the desire for continuity of identity. This desire is reflected, for example, in the way people everywhere display their personal effects in the spaces they inhabit. Often, people break institutional rules and suffer punishment in order to keep their own things around them. Such behavior is hard to explain in terms of adaptation.

In response to these issues, Lawton (1990) proposes that choice, whether provided by the external environment or created by the individual, is the key to understanding continued competence. People need to maximize their ability to provide for both security and autonomy. Security is freedom from risk, danger, concern, or doubt. **Autonomy** is the ability to pursue life goals without calling on the resources of others. An optimal balance between security and autonomy provides a sense of satisfaction, contentment, and mastery.

In developing this hypothesis, Lawton was particularly struck by the behavior of severely impaired elderly who continued to live in their own home despite the fact that many of them had to spend their entire day in a very small area, usually the living room, arranged to function as a **control center**, and reducing the need for help to getting up in the morning and back to bed at night.

> A self-created control center enabled these individuals to make maximum use of this severely constricted space for information, stimulus variety, and social integration. The control center began with a chair, usually a comfortable one, that also met good ergonomic specifications, in terms of ease of access and steadiness. The chair invariably faced the living room window, with a maximum possible view of front porch, sidewalk, and street. The same chair orientation enabled the front door to be monitored. A telephone, television set, and usually a radio extended psychological space far beyond the living room. Table surfaces on either side of the chair afforded the enriching objects of personal preference, whether photographs, letters, knickknacks, food, medicine, or reading material. The control center was completed by some arrangement for toileting, whether by a urinal, or nearby commode, or for the few who were lucky enough to have a ground-floor bathroom, a pathway to it alongside convenient places to grab while in transit. (1990, p. 640)

This description leads Lawton to argue that the ability to choose and self-direct the environment actively affects the overall quality of life. Designers must attend not only to the prosthetics that might support the older persons, from illumination to handrails, but also to the opportunity for them to fashion their environments to meet their own unique, particular needs and preferences. These ideas are especially helpful in coming to grips with the literature on institutionalization. More than any other topic in the study of aging, institutionalization carries connotations of marginal behavior, the loss of well-being, the disruption of person-place history, and the denial of choice.

Special Settings

Many people are appalled by any mention of institutional care, associating it with hopelessness and abandonment. However, it is important to make some distinctions here. Institutions that foster independence and provide personal warmth do produce positive results, especially among the most responsive elderly. Even family interactions can improve once the decision to institutionalize an elderly member has been taken, almost regardless of the care policies of the institution (Montgomery, 1982; Smith & Bengston, 1979; Timko & Moos, 1990).

There are three basic types of special setting: (1) congregate apartments that provide meals only; (2) residential care facilities that provide housekeeping, meals, and assistance with routine activities, but limited medical care; and (3) nursing homes. Each of these may differ along several important dimensions including **segregation** (the degree to which residents are isolated from the outside world), **congregation** (how often residents must perform the same activities together), and **control** (the degree of autonomy permitted to residents). Generally, the more segregated, controlled, and congregated the setting, the more often the environment is perceived as hostile (Lawton, 1977). There are exceptions, however, since the most fragile individuals require more support. Research on congregate housing that is not characterized by high levels of control shows increases in satisfaction, morale, and involvement among residents but decreases in off-site activities, suggesting that congregation leads, in a way, to segregation (Moos & Lemke, 1985). These data have also been used to argue that Lawton's ideas about environmental press are correct. An oversupplied environment may permit residents to become more passive in their adaptation.

However, many older people do need services, and residents that receive maintenance and security services, and social activities often experience high morale, good health, and satisfaction with their living quarters. Rudolf Moos and Sandra Lemke conclude, based on such data, that "the danger of premature dependency must be recognized, but we believe that the availability of physical and service 'supports' enhances [a] resident's feelings of security and independence" (p. 879). Crowding and surveillance may be more important than congregation or segregation when people need help. On the other hand, power and control are critical issues regardless of the resident's condition (Kahana, 1982).

Americans value independence, perhaps above all else. The idea that someone else controls what you do, and when and how you do it, is horrifying, even on one's death bed. It is not surprising, then, that when control and responsibility are given to residents, activity, social interaction, and well-being increase regardless of the health problems of the residents (Beck, 1982). Residents given responsibility for themselves feel happier; more alert, active, and involved. They also show lower mortality rates (Moos & Lemke, 1985). In one interesting study of a nursing home (Rodin, 1980), each resident was given fifteen minutes of nursing time per day. During these fifteen minutes, the resident could have the exclusive attention of the nurse, and could use the time with the nurse for any reason. At first, some of the residents called for trivial reasons, but over time, residents requested the nursing time less and less, but both health and sociability improved. Being able to get the attention of staff on one's own terms makes a difference. Unfortunately, institutional staff tend to define the patient's well-being in terms of physical and medical needs, whereas patients focus on personal dignity and social relationships (Gubrium, 1974).

In nursing homes, the evidence pretty consistently suggests that in addition to provision of good professional services, an emphasis on stimulating interaction, autonomy, and personal choice has beneficial effects. Higher levels of choice and resident control are associated with cohesive, organized, and inde-

Institutions need be neither inhumane nor dehumanizing if the concept of caring is extended from the physical to the social and psychological needs of the patient.

pendence-oriented social environments and high resident activity levels (Moos & Lemke, 1985). Control is associated with low levels of social interaction among patients, since competition increases dramatically when resources are scarce. One author has suggested that payments be contingent upon the progress of the patient, thus allowing patients to exchange progress or improvement for control (Schmidt, 1981–82).

In fact, it seems likely that the most important negative features of institutions are related to power and control. In one interesting sociological analysis (Schmidt, 1981–82), two different residential settings for the elderly were evaluated in terms of social exchanges and power. Both of these homes were well regarded, and both drew from white, middle-class populations with unusually high levels of education in their cohorts. Both homes had boarding facilities characterized by high levels of privacy and autonomy, and both also had nursing units where control, segregation, and surveillance were the order of the day. Eventually, all boarders entered the nursing-care facilities, becoming "patients" instead of "boarders." Part of the analysis describes how boarders were able to delay demotion to patient.

Schmidt wrote that "patienthood was at once a threat and a demotion."

Furthermore, because these homes did not take Medicare payments, patients were also threatened with being sent away to a home that accepted Medicare. Boarders who were competent enough to walk to town and to do favors for the staff were typically given prestige-enhancing jobs and were able to delay transfer to the nursing unit. The possession of a color television set or the attention of an interested relative was also instrumental in delaying transfer. Boarders' resources were many, including mobility, independence, and the freedom to renounce the care offered by the institution. Since boarders were allowed to control their own money and since they often had their own transportation, they could simply leave the institution as a protest.

Patients, on the other hand, possessed very few resources. Both homes having asked relatives to handle all monies, it was impossible for elderly patients to deploy even the most basic financial resources. Without mobility or independence, patient resources were so scarce that competition between patients made solidarity improbable. In other words, patients were not likely to cooperate in confronting staff with a grievance. For patients, the only remaining resources were emotional. Patients used guilt, anxiety, and abrasiveness to coerce staff. Patients also showed less conformity to peer or staff norms, for they were less likely to be rewarded.

Contact with families is another way in which residents in special settings maintain control. Family visits predict well-being, and families undoubtedly provide for the social and personal needs of elderly residents. It is also true, however, that residents who are visited by family members receive more attention from staff, feel less alone, and are more likely to control their own lives, especially when family members are involved in the planning of patient care (Montgomery, 1982; Tesch & Whitbourne, 1981).

People who maintain their ties with family and friends are more likely to experience good morale and life satisfaction after entering long-term care. **Density of ties** is important. Density refers to the number of ties and is related to multiple interconnections that reinforce the norm of contact. In other words, if you talk to your sister and your brother and ask them to visit, they are likely to remind and reinforce each other too. Interconnections between relatives, especially children, and between friends are associated with more friends visiting as well (Bear, 1990).

"Taken together, these findings indicate that a facility social climate that encourages supportive interpersonal relationships and self-direction is associated with better quality of care and resident functioning, and that facilities differ in the extent to which they provide this type of social climate" (Timko & Moos, 1990, p. S184). Building on all of the earlier work, Christine Timko and Rudolf Moos conducted a study of group residential facilities for older people aimed at determining which physical resources and policies created self-directedness and interpersonal support. They looked at the perceptions of both residents and staff and the impact of security, social and recreational facilities, age and gender of the staff, number of staff, size of the facility, policies and resident involvement in setting them.

They found the presence of physical features that add convenience, attrac-

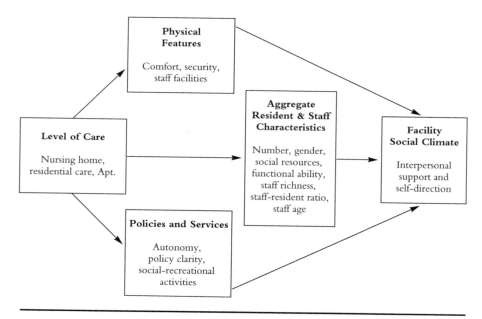

Figure 11.5 A model of the determinants of group residential facilities' social climates.
SOURCE: Timko & Moos, 1990, p. S189.

tiveness, and space, as well as designs that promote social and recreational activity, helps to create support and feelings of control for the residents. Interestingly, physically separate facilities for the staff were good for residents, perhaps because they felt their own privacy was maintained, but were associated with feelings of conflict for the staff. Timko and Moos suggest that separate facilities for staff may encourage staff members to talk about conflict between themselves and the residents more often.

Giving the residents more privacy and choice over daily routine as well as more formal influence over policy making was associated with reduced feelings of conflict for the residents. These authors argue that residents are likely to remain active and socially engaged if they exercise control over their environment. This is especially important in light of the fact that other researchers have demonstrated that care providers in such facilities tend to reinforce dependency and passivity because these characteristics make residents more manageable (Baltes & Wahl, 1987). Explicit policies that encourage choice and self-direction should help maintain competence.

Timko and Moos also report that a high staff-resident ratio was associated with lower feelings of independence and control. This is partly due to the fact that elderly residents may be prevented from acting independently by staff who see dependency as compliance. Too many staff members may mean residents do not have an opportunity to practice self-management or come to be-

Choice depends upon the availability of options. For these villagers in the Soviet Caucasus, the elderly remain a vital part of village life even beyond the age of 100 years.

lieve that they are incapable of it (Baltes & Wahl, 1987). Figure 11.5 presents a model of the major variables identified by Timko and Moos. It shows how level of care is mediated by physical features, policies, and services as well as aggregate resident and staff characteristics.

They also found that larger facilities have more conflict but do not necessarily enforce more congregate policies. Perhaps, the authors argue, the greater diversity of residents and the lesser probability of personal contact between them aggravated disagreement and incompatibility. Other studies have suggested that large, nonprofit residential care tends to be superior in other ways because larger facilities are likely to offer more options (Parmelee & Lawton, 1990).

Choice depends on the availability of options, and, as is clear from the literature, many interesting possibilities are essentially unavailable. Certainly, it behooves us to support the development of more voluntary, nonauthoritarian communities and a greater range of facilities, and to demand that meaningful, supportive social relationships be established along with good medical care. After all, looking after the interests of today's elderly is really insurance for our own future. Why study aging? Because we are going to be elderly in the not-so-remote future and will come into our own legacy.

Summary

I.   Ecology is the science of plants and animals as they are related to their environment; ecologists study how organisms adapt to their niche and how the niche changes as a result of adaptation.
  A. The ecology of aging includes an increasing number of elderly people in the population, and an increased length of stay in the elderly population.
  B. Most elderly people are concentrated in smaller cities, in rural areas, and in the central cities.
  C. Most older people own their own homes, and the financial situation of elderly people has improved dramatically since 1970.
    1. The percentage of elderly poor declined from one-third in 1959 to 13 percent in 1985.
    2. Females and blacks are relatively disadvantaged as well as elderly singles.
  D. Race and gender are important in the study of aging.
    1. Although blacks and Hispanics are disadvantaged financially and educationally, older blacks may actually live longer than older whites, and mortality crossover occurs earlier for Hispanics.
    2. The poverty rate for all visible minorities, including Asians, is much higher than for whites.
    3. Elderly single women are much more likely than men to receive the minimum Social Security benefit.
    4. It is predicted that future cohorts of the elderly will be better off because they are less likely to rely on Social Security and more likely to have income from private pensions and assets, as well as to have the potential for earned income.

II. Retirement
  A. Since the end of World War II, a large and increasing number of people have retired, although demographic factors are expected to slow this trend.
    1. As the people of the baby-boom generation retire, there may be too few young workers to support the Social Security system.
    2. Most workers can fulfill the requirements of their jobs well past the age of sixty.
    3. Many older workers are more productive than the average young worker, and most older workers have better attendance records, have fewer accidents, and switch jobs less often.
    4. Older workers also fulfill such organizational tasks as teaching and the transmission of positive attitudes.
  B. Today's elderly often view retirement as a right and do not wish to remain in the work force full-time. Labor force participation has declined steadily over the past few decades, among men over fifty-five.

1. Social Security changes may result in the retention of more older workers, especially among blacks, women and singles.
2. Retirement is defined as a status in which one does not hold a regular full-time job and collects at least some of one's income from a pension or Social Security.
   a. Some older workers never joined the labor foce and, therefore, never really retire.
   b. Retirement may be as much a self-perceived state as an objective relationship to job and pension.
3. As a role, retirement is said to be ambiguous and, therefore, to be associated with poor adjustment.
4. As a process, retirement may demand the substitution of other activities for work if adjustment is to be achieved.
   a. Many people are unable to find new substitute activities at retirement after a lifetime of limited interests and activities.
   b. There is not much evidence that retirement is extremely disruptive in people's lives. Most retirees are satisfied and well adjusted.
   c. The impact of retirement varies with both personality type and the kind of work one did prior to retirement.
5. As a process, retirement may be divided into several phases, including preretirement, the honeymoon, disenchantment, reorientation, and stability, as well as termination.
   a. Not all people go through all of the phases.
   b. Flexibility and resources within both the individual and the society support adjustment to retirement through all the phases.
6. As an option, gradual, voluntary retirement produces the best adjustment.
   a. Many people are choosing partial retirement by becoming self-employed or by changing jobs after retiring.
   b. Concepts like job sharing, the sheltered workshop, and the growth of the service sector of the economy should make retirement more flexible.
   c. Flexible retirement policies should make it possible for workers to take advantage of the possibilities of retirement, including leisure activities.
7. The meaningful use of leisure time during retirement depends on economic resources but also requires that one perceive leisure as a legitimate source of pleasure and self-esteem.
   a. Leisure may not be something one can learn to enjoy at the end of the life span but is best appreciated and employed when it is a part of the normal life course.
   b. Today's elderly exhibit a relatively narrow range of activities, and most of those in which they do engage are sedentary. Younger cohorts may show higher levels of involvement and a wider range of activities in retirement.

      c. Preretirement education should make people more aware of the options, resources, and possibilities of retirement; however, few members of current retirement cohorts have engaged in any formal educational program.

III. The Physical Environment

    A. Although most older Americans live in the community and own their own homes, they often live in less desirable housing and poor, older neighborhoods.

       1. Older people spend more on their homes than do the young, but accomplish fewer repairs and less remodeling than young homeowners.

       2. Older people more often spend an excessive percentage of their income on housing.

       3. Despite all this, older homeowners are satisfied with their housing and, although some of these feelings of satisfaction may be defensive, long-term ownership probably bestows special meanings on a home. "Aging in place" has become a major theme in current research.

    B. Older people tend to live in older neighborhoods and to worry about noise, traffic, litter, and especially crime.

       1. The neighborhood is an important ecological unit, and for most elderly, a very distance-restricted one.

       2. Research suggests that older people do best when they live in small to midsized communities where they perceive a low rate of crime.

       3. The evidence overwhelmingly suggests that older people wish to stay in place and may need assistance in maintaining and repairing their properties.

    C. When elderly people must relocate, one of the primary problems is to get them to do so in a timely manner.

       1. Housing trends like mobile homes, condominiums, and cooperatives encourage such mobility.

       2. Adventurous, mobile elderly people show high life satisfaction.

       3. Involuntary relocation is associated with declining health and morale, but competent people who are moved to settings that encourage autonomy and provide warmth may improve.

    D. The study of planned housing is difficult because the measurement of satisfaction, morale, and adjustment is problematic.

       1. Older people do well in high-rise, urban buildings and in communities that are planned for the elderly.

       2. Elderly people prefer age-segregated communities, perhaps because the optimal age mix in a community is essentially unavailable in the United States.

       3. Studies of housing projects show satisfaction with clean, modern housing; access to transportation and community facilities; secu-

rity; and high age density. But problems with design vary from privacy to convenience of design for the handicapped.

4. Research on all forms of housing confirms the continuity of the person as the rule over the life span.

E. Theories about environmental design address the balance between prosthesis and therapy.

   1. M. Powell Lawton was among the first to talk of person-specific environments and the need to match the abilities and requirements of the individual to the resources in the environment.

   2. More specific work on environmental characteristics like sensory stimulation, legibility, and comfort, privacy, control, and so forth, would be useful in evaluating theory.

   3. Researchers also need to look at the meaning of environments and to make practical recommendations about the creation of space.

   4. A major theoretical debate concerns whether the level of stimulation an environment offers should be slightly above the adaptation level of the individual, or if optimal fit is the best outcome.

   5. The historical meaning of the environment to the individual must also be considered if behavior is to be understood. People show a strong preference for continuity in their environment and for a balance of security and autonomy.

F. There are three types of special settings: congregate apartments, residential care, and nursing homes.

   1. The degree of segregation, congregation, and control varies over these settings.

      a. Crowding and surveillance may be more important than congregation or segregation when people need services.

      b. In residential care facilities and nursing homes—when residents are given control and responsibility—activity, social interaction, and well-being increase.

      c. When control is taken from residents, guilt, anxiety, and abrasiveness are the only forms of control left to patients.

      d. The involvement of families in planning patient care and family visits give patients greater control. Density of ties is important in ensuring continued contact.

      e. The presence of physical features that add attractiveness and convenience, privacy and choice, along with explicit policies that encourage self-direction, predicts resident satisfaction.

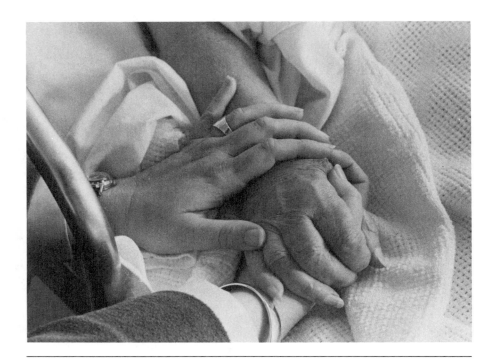

12

Death and Dying: A Final Context for Development

I'm not afraid to die. I just don't want to be there when it happens.

—Woody Allen

I IMAGINE WHEN I DIE, I SHALL BE QUITE OLD. Yes, very old, at least 90, maybe 100. I will die peacefully and quickly. I'll be at home. Maybe I'll know a week or so ahead that I'm going to go, so I'll call my friends and relatives to come and say goodbye. When I die, they'll all be there, especially the children. I'll be at home and I'll be alert and aware. I'll take the time to tell each one of them how much I love them and what wonderful people they are. They'll be OK about it. They'll feel OK that I'm going out so easily after a really long, full lifetime. The final moments will happen suddenly. I'll just close my eyes and leave with a smile on my face. They'll say I died of old age. Afterward, maybe they'll all have a big party instead of a funeral. I'd rather they had a party. I don't want anybody to be really sad.

WHEN COLLEGE STUDENTS ARE ASKED to picture their **deathbed scene**, they write scenarios like the one above (Kastenbaum & Norman, 1990). Most young people imagine they will die when they are old, even very old (more than a hundred years), and they say they will die of old age. Few describe dying in a hospital and nearly everyone expects to be alert, lucid, and aware of their coming death. Most students expect to be surrounded by their loved ones, whose attitudes are usually portrayed as accepting or even cheerful, and most say that the process will take a few minutes, hours, or days at the most. Few people picture themselves coping for a long time with an illness and hardly anyone expects to have pain or any type of distress at all.

Of course, none of this is very realistic. Eighty percent of all deaths occur in hospitals, nursing homes, or retirement homes, and most dying people suffer from a wide variety of distressing symptoms. The deathbed scene that students imagine is probably just one more example of how unfamiliar we are with death as a phenomenon in modern life. We don't experience death very often. We don't live in extended families; people we know who die, die in institutions. Professionals, from nurses and doctors to morticians and florists are called in to deal with a death once it occurs. We try to avoid the whole subject if possible. In fact, psychologists and sociologists typically avoided the subject themselves until the last two decades or so. Why? And why are we suddenly interested in a subject that we have so long avoided? Why is there a death education movement in this country now, and why is there a chapter on death and dying in almost every book on adulthood?

Herman Feifel (1990) believes that the great social issues of our time from abortion to AIDS, euthanasia, drug abuse, alcoholism, and violence are all forcing us to face death and dying. He also argues that psychology has only recently begun to cope with the study of death and dying for a variety of reasons. When psychologists began to think of themselves as scientists, they excluded the study of events that could not be objectively measured, and as we shall see, there are huge problems involved in even defining the state of death itself, much less dying. Moreover, Feifel contends, psychologists have tried very hard to separate themselves from philosophers and metaphysicians. In doing so they became preoccupied with measurable stimuli and responses (i.e., with the mechanical model) and excluded the study of love, will, values, and death in favor of such subjects as memory, response time, size constance, and perception.

On balance, Feifel argues, this preoccupation has produced positive results, emphasizing the necessity of standard evidence, intelligible communication, and clarity of definition. In the post–World War II era, however, the specter of atomic annihilation, the growth of existential psychology, and interest in alternatives to the mechanical model all contributed to a burst of writing and research on death throughout the sixties and seventies. Feifel has been an important figure in this movement since the publication of *The Meaning of Death* in 1956. His work was an important starting place for those willing to open up the last door and take a look at what it is possible to know.

Death: Personal and Professional Meanings

Many of the major research questions about death revolve around the problem of meaning. Basic issues arise. For instance, is everything we know and believe about death learned, or is there some basic, perhaps instinctual, human response to death? One important group of writers, the **existentialists**, have argued that, in a nuclear age, people must experience fear of death, for life itself has become meaningless. Existential thinkers contend that in societies where religious beliefs are not strong, and no one is certain mankind can prevent the ultimate holocaust, death anxiety will be so strong that people will deny death. That is, people will be unable to consider or encounter death, because it is viewed as a void, an end to existence (Becker, 1973; Kastenbaum, 1981b; Lifton, 1981).

In the place of spiritual immortality, modern societies have emphasized the importance of living through one's progeny, of making a contribution to society. Speaking from an existential perspective, Robert Lifton contends that the nuclear age even robs us of a belief in social immortality (Lifton, 1981; Lifton & Olson, 1974). He argues that the specter of the holocaust and the possibility of Armageddon create an indelible image of death as a senseless tragedy and an absurdity rather than a fitting end to life. If nothing can endure the atomic age, then nothing matters. Life is meaningless and so, therefore, is death.

Lifton draws his conclusions from years of working with those who survived some of the great tragedies of modern times: German concentration camps, the bombing of Hiroshima, and the war in Vietnam. He believes that all of us are, in a sense, survivors of these horrors. Those who were there personally are more extreme in their reactions, but all of us are affected. Lifton's studies reveal the following common themes among survivors, themes he contends are found in all modern cultures:

1. The death imprint: All survivors report vivid, indelible images of death as grotesque and absurd, images produced in moments of tremendous anxiety.

2. Death guilt: To a greater or lesser degree, all survivors experience guilt because they did not die. This is not moral or legal guilt; it is paradoxical. It is a product of the vulnerability and helplessness created by situations in which it is impossible to act, or even feel, appropriately.

3. Psychological numbing: Survivors also experience a paralysis of mind in moments of horror. Lifton believes that psychological numbing is an adaptive response because the intensity of feelings appropriate to such horror would cause insanity.

4. Suspicion of nurturance: Survivors often resent any offer of help. They may see the need for assistance as a sign of weakness, or they may reject help because they are in conflict between accepting the horror as reality and rejecting it.

5. Struggle for meaning: Finally, survivors often spend much of the rest of their lives and their energies in a struggle to make sense, to produce meaning from their experiences. The creation of the state of Israel and the crusade of Vietnam veterans for recognition represent this kind of struggle. Lifton believes that these missions are an expression of unrelieved mourning for those who died.

Lifton has consistently argued that these five themes all reflect an emotional denial of the reality of death. Dying and death become taboo subjects when they rob life of its meaning. Unfortunately, this is a terribly hard proposition to research. Denial is an unconscious process: People are unaware that they are denying their anxiety. Therefore, it is difficult, if not impossible to document such denial. Survey research showing that only 10–25 percent of the population feel that death is an important source of fear in their daily lives does not dissuade the existential psychologist, who believes this is simply evidence of how widespread the denial is (Greer, 1965; Kalish & Reynolds, 1976; Schmitt, 1982–83).

Another approach to the existential hypothesis explores whether people really have no belief in an afterlife or any version of immortality. One naturalistic researcher has brought several lines of evidence to bear, including the remarks of important public figures, interview material from ordinary working adults, and the responses of children. In this study (Schmitt, 1982–83), the author found that most Americans, from important figures like Hubert Humphrey and Richard Nixon to the waitresses and truck drivers described by Studs Terkel in *Working* (1974), seem to believe in some form of social immortality. Either they believe they will be immortalized through their achievements, or they believe their descendants will allow them to "live on." Even the media promote the idea of immortality, consistently using phrases like, "He will always be remembered for . . ." or "Her immortal portrayal of . . . ." Furthermore, interviews with parochial school children in this study suggested that many people continue to believe in God and in traditional spiritual immortality. In fact, Richard Kalish (1985) reports that data from his survey research show that 75 percent of all Americans believe in life after death.

It appears that a wide variety of forces shield Americans from the experience of existential crisis in the nuclear age. Nuclear weapons have no relationship to the roles people play in everyday life. Most of us do not know the facts of atomic warfare well enough to discern whether nuclear weapons might ever be relevant. The government shrouds such information in secrecy and complexity, if not fabrication. Furthermore, Americans see nuclear weapons in terms of protection rather than destruction and find it difficult to imagine their own deaths, much less the collective death of the species. The belief that one can overcome any obstacle also shields Americans from the reality of nuclear disaster. Even the antinuclear-power alliances have not focused on nuclear weapons until recently. Finally, traditional beliefs in an afterlife and in social immortality persist (Schmitt, 1982–83).

Even if such beliefs did not persist, however, there is little evidence that they form the strongest bulwark against death anxiety. In fact, some researchers have reported that the absence of religious beliefs is associated with the lowest levels of death anxiety, whereas those who have strong beliefs about an afterlife tend to show moderate levels of anxiety. People who report they are uncertain about their religious beliefs show the highest levels of death anxiety (Kalish, 1985; Kalish & Reynolds, 1976; Glass, 1990).

Relatively few North Americans spend much time thinking or talking about death. Robert Kastenbaum (1985) has argued that, in a modern society where we can expect to live well into old age, death is a "task" reserved for the old, and the rest of us are supported in our attempt to evade its reality. He believes that this complicates society's attitudes toward the aged, because old people are seen as the most suitable candidates for death. He has even suggested that the Eriksonian idea that life review and acceptance of death are components of integrity and wisdom in old age is simply another way of consigning the elderly to a powerless, devalued status and to dying. On the other hand, the fact that nearly 75 percent of children born today will live past the age of sixty-five means that death and dying are an important aspect of aging (Marshall and Levy, 1990).

Interestingly, there is evidence that older people are not as anxious about death and dying as are the young. Over the past ten years, a huge number of studies have been conducted on death anxiety (Kastenbaum, 1987–88). We know, for instance, that there appear to be gender differences in death anxiety as well as age differences, with women expressing more anxiety than men (Dattell and Neimeyer, 1990). We know that physicians show higher levels of death anxiety than the general population (Cochrane, Levy, Fryer, & Oglesby, 1990–91), that the death of a significant other or a near-death experience has little impact on death anxiety (Franke & Durlak, 1990). We know that death anxiety among health care personnel interferes with their ability to relate to dying patients and that death is less disruptive and causes less anxiety when it occurs on an expected timetable rather than unexpectedly (Marshall & Levy, 1990). All of this knowledge has very few practical implications, however. Most of the research is still descriptive rather than explanatory.

Personal Meanings

If avoidance of death and dying has not been generated, as the existentialists argue, by the great historical changes of our times, and if most of us do continue to have a belief in some sort of afterlife, why is death such an uncomfortable, unpleasant, even taboo subject for many? It has been argued that death and dying are difficult to deal with in the modern, Western world because they are inconsistent with the dominant value system. Westerners see death as defeat. Death means loss of the ability to be productive, to achieve. It represents the loss of the future (Feifel, 1990). If this is the case, then fear of death may not be a universal feature of experience. It may simply be a learned response.

The Learning of Death Anxiety   If we learn to fear death, then we must do so by analogy, for we cannot fear death from our personal experience—we have no personal experience of it. One important source of the fear, however, is the death of someone else, the experience of separation. As some have noted, people cannot make distinctions between how survivors feel and how someone who is dead feels. We have no idea how it feels to be dead, but we associate death with loss and attendant feelings of grief and anxiety. Furthermore, from the survivor's point of view, dead people are also inactive, and most Westerners value productivity and fear loss of mobility (Howard & Scott, 1965; Kastenbaum, 1981b; Feifel, 1990).

The notion that death is not threatening to all people is partially supported by cross-cultural data. To illustrate, a study of one Polynesian kin group shows a very different set of attitudes toward death than are familiar to most North Americans. Although essentially without any strong beliefs in immortality, these people believe that death must be pleasant if one is freed from work and responsibility. This Polynesian culture does not foster a strong work ethic. Kinship is broadly recognized, and most members of the group develop numerous, diffuse emotional relationships and hence rarely experience separation anxiety. They do not, in fact, seem to experience such simple forms of separation anxiety as homesickness (Howard & Scott, 1965).

A quite extensive study of death anxiety by Richard Lonetto and Donald Templer (1986) also concludes that death anxiety is learned. These researchers reported that death anxiety scores for mother-daughter and father-son pairs showed the highest correlations of any kin pairs. They also found very high correlations between the scores of spouses. They believe that such associations demonstrate the impact of experience on death anxiety and even suggest that behavior modification might be used to treat death anxiety where it has become a problem interfering with everyday life.

Given this kind of evidence, it seems reasonable to ask how our concept of death develops. What is it that people believe about death, and how do they come to hold these beliefs? Over the past forty years, a number of researchers have addressed these questions; their answers, though tentative, have interesting implications.

The Development of the Death Concept   In 1948, the first study of children's thoughts about death appeared (Nagy, 1948), and although there have been occasional additions and corrections, the original observations have been repeatedly validated (DeSpelder and Strickland, 1992). Very young children do not seem to have any sense of how death differs from life; they consider it a kind of low-level living, a long rest or waiting period. They often think that breathing or thinking go on after death and believe that the condition is reversible. Young children expect veterinarians to bring dead animals back to life, for instance. Of course, the adult culture reinforces such ideas with stories about princesses who sleep for a hundred years or the notion that death is "like going to sleep." Considering the poor quality of information children ordinarily receive, it is surprising that they finally do understand that death is permanent, a concept that Nagy found children expressing as early as age five.

Nagy reported that children often personify death as a monster or a devil one can fight or even evade. Although Nagy studied Hungarian children, and personification is not as common in other cultures, once children understand that death is irreversible and permanent, such fantasies disappear. By nine or ten, most children have a fairly mature concept of death as a final, irreversible state that can be the product of internal forces.

Before the age of nine or ten years, children do not seem to understand that death is permanent and irreversible.

But, one might well ask, how adult is an adult concept of death? Despite the evidence that nine- or ten-year-old children know death is permanent and irreversible, many adolescents behave as if natural laws did not apply to them. As David Elkind (1978) has suggested, adolescents cling to the **personal fable**, believing they are special and that what happens to other people will not happen to them. In fact, Elkind believes the personal fable explains self-destructive behavior in adolescence from drinking and drug abuse to unplanned pregnancies.

Elkind writes that the personal fable eventually fades, and one understands that death and misfortune happen to everyone. It is not clear, however, if this development is ever complete. Some people never really accept the idea that death is inevitable and permanent and most people are still struggling with the concept at midlife. As we pointed out in Chapters 7 and 8, researchers maintain that the majority of us first develop a deep sense of our own personal mortality sometime during middle age (Levinson et al., 1978; Gould, 1980). Other studies show that while awareness of death promotes the reorganization of time among some elderly, other elderly people never come to terms with their own mortality (Kastenbaum, 1985). Finally, we know that as many as a quarter of all terminally ill patients never accept the notion that they are dying (Kastenbaum, 1981a).

A mature concept of one's own death may be an impossibility, since it is something one experiences only once and since we have no reliable accounts of it from others. Furthermore, every moment of the day contradicts the idea of mortality. I wake up every morning alive. I have no personal experience of waking up dead. Death is the ultimate paradox of human existence: it occurs to every living thing, but it occurs to me only once. Death is universal, but my own death is a unique one-time-only event. The paradox affects the behavioral study of death too, for death, an event that people never experience until the end of their lives, motivates much of their behavior beforehand. All human goals and aspirations, ideas and feelings are both limited and expanded by death: limited in time, expanded in intensity (Feifel, 1990).

Given the paradoxical, mysterious quality of the subject matter, it is unsurprising that objective meanings of death are almost as difficult to establish as the subjective ones. Biologists and psychologists, doctors and lawyers, philosophers and sociologists have all tried, but professional definitions, like the personal ones, remain elusive.

Professional Meanings

. . . Death
is strictly scientific
& artificial &
evil & legal)

—e. e. cummings

Death is the cessation of all the biological, psychological, and social processes that attend the life of an individual person, but each one of these three components, the biological, the psychological, and the social, has been an object of professional debate and controversy. How do we know when all of the processes that attend a person's life have ceased? The problems are most obvious in examining the biological-medical definitions of death, but they are certainly no less complex for a psychologist or sociologist.

Historically, **biological death** was thought to occur when the body ceased to show respiration and heart function. Modern medical technology has obscured this basic idea, however, since it is now possible to sustain both respiration and heart beat mechanically, for days, weeks, months, even years. Furthermore, hope of life is possible even when respiration and heart function must be mechanically sustained. Today, the traditional criteria have been supplanted by very complex sets of measures. One such set is called the Harvard Criteria of Total Brain Death. The important part of the Harvard Criteria refers to the cessation of impulses from both the major lobes of the brain and the brain stem, as measured by an electroencephalograph (EEG). A summary of these criteria appears in Box 12.1.

To some researchers, however, the Harvard Criteria seem both too inflexible at times and too conservative under other circumstances. Stray marks produced by the EEG can be misinterpreted as signs of life, and hypnotic

---

Box 12.1 A Summary of the Harvard Criteria

1. *Unreceptivity and unresponsivity:* The individual is totally unaware of externally applied stimuli and inner need, and completely unresponsive.

2. *No movements or breathing:* Observation of at least one hour reveals no spontaneous muscular movements, spontaneous respiration, or response to stimuli such as pain, touch, sound, or light. Total absence of respiration after the patient is on a mechanical respirator may be determined by turning off the respirator for three minutes and observing whether there is any effort on the part of the patient to breathe spontaneously.

3. *No reflexes:* The pupils of the eyes are fixed and dilated and do not respond to intense light. Ocular movements, in response to head turning or irrigating the ears with ice water, and all blinking movements are absent. There is no swallowing, yawning, or vocalization and no postural activity. There are no tendon reflexes or plantar response, and the application of noxious stimuli has no effect.

4. *Flat electroencephalogram:* Given that the EEG electrodes are properly applied, the apparatus is functioning properly, and the personnel in charge are competent, a flat EEG is of "great confirmatory value," if hypothermia (temperature below 90 degrees Fahrenheit) or the use of central nervous system depressants, such as barbiturates, are excluded.

5. All of the above tests shall be repeated at least twenty-four hours later with no change.

SOURCE: Based on "A Definition of Irreversible Coma" (1968).

---

drugs can result in an EEG that mimics brain death. Robert Veatch (1976, 1981, 1989), a vocal critic of the Harvard Criteria, has argued that doctors ought to consider the capacity for consciousness and social interaction. He holds that only the functioning of the higher cortical centers permits these functions and that the idea of **total brain death** should be replaced by the notion of cerebral death. In other words, he does not believe that the presence of brain-stem reflexes is evidence of human life. He defines being human in terms of personhood as well as biological function.

In 1981, the President's Commission for the Study of Ethical Problems in Medicine and Biomedical and Behavioral Research adopted the Uniform Determination of Death Act, which essentially endorses the Harvard Criteria. Noting that no person meeting these criteria has ever regained any brain function, they argued for a whole-brain rather than a higher-function definition of death because of the difficulties in agreeing on a definition of "personhood" or "consciousness." Nevertheless, it is unlikely that doctors and lawyers will be able to turn the issues entirely over to machines. Professional judgments are still required even when the most sophisticated measures are available.

Box 12.2 A living will

TO MY FAMILY, MY PHYSICIAN, MY LAWYER, MY CLERGYMAN,
TO ANY MEDICAL FACILITY IN WHOSE CARE I HAPPEN TO BE,
TO ANY INDIVIDUAL WHO MAY BECOME RESPONSIBLE FOR
MY HEALTH, WELFARE OR AFFAIRS

Death is as much a reality as birth, growth, maturity and old age—it is the one certainty of life. If the time comes when I, _____ can no longer take part in decisions for my own future, let this statement stand as an expression of my wishes, while I am still of sound mind.

If the situation should arise in which there is no reasonable expectation of my recovery from physical or mental disability, I request that I be allowed to die and not be kept alive by artificial means of "heroic measures." I do not fear death itself as much as the indignities of deterioration, dependence, and hopeless pain. I, therefore, ask that medication be mercifully administered to me to alleviate suffering even though this may hasten the moment of death.

This request is made after careful consideration. I hope you who care for me will feel morally bound to follow its mandate. I recognize that this appears to place a heavy responsibility upon you, but it is with the intention of relieving you of such responsibility and of placing it upon myself in accordance with my strong convictions, that this statement is made.

Signed, _____

Date _____

Witness _____

Witness _____

Copies of this request
have been given to   _____

_____

_____

_____

SOURCE: Euthanasia Educational Council, New York.

Part of the reason for the heated controversy is that emergency considerations (such as the need for organs for transplant operations) may color the decisions of medical personnel. Another obvious issue is raised by decisions about the use of heroic measures for the support of life. Many people do not want to have their lives sustained when they no longer possess their "personhood." The use of a document known as a living will (see Box 12.2) is one attempt to consider the patient's wishes in the process—to make it possible for the patient to guide physicians and family members in this most difficult decision.

Yet the living will doesn't address many of the specific questions that a person ought to consider in making decisions about life-sustaining measures. In some states, it is possible to execute a Durable Power of Attorney for Health Care. This instrument invests another person with the power to make decisions for the patient should the patient be unable to decide for himself or herself. Still, the patient's wishes must be clearly known for the power of attorney to have weight. Charles Culver and Bernard Gert (1990) argue that executing a power of attorney is preferable to a living will, the effectiveness of which is undermined by the use of vague terms like "heroic measures."

If the Durable Power of Attorney is to be useful, however, it must be accompanied by written instructions about specific problems that family and health care givers must face in making life and death decisions. Culver and Gert propose using "life-sustaining treatment" for what has been termed heroic, or extraordinary, measures. Instructions should cover such questions as whether life-sustaining treatment is to be continued when the patient is terminally ill and permanently incompetent to make that decision, and whether such treatment should be continued when the patient is not terminally ill but is permanently unconscious. Instructions must also address whether life-sustaining treatment is to be provided when there is very little chance of recovery, especially if the patient is likely to be brain-damaged even if recovery occurs. Whether nutrition and fluids are ever to be discontinued must also be spelled out. A Durable Power of Attorney is a stronger instrument than a living will if it gives specific instructions, because it creates an agent who can represent one's wishes and make fine-grained decisions impossible by means of a general document.

Psychological and Social Death

Although we know that there are times when body functions, even spontaneous heart rate and respiration, continue but the personality is dead, there are no standard measures for **psychological death.** One attempt at clarification is offered by Veatch (1979, 1981, 1989) as he elaborates on the notion that life includes the "capacity for integrating one's self, including one's body, with the social environment through consciousness, which permits interaction with other persons." He has argued that although it is immoral to end a life that might be resuscitated by mechanical means, it is also immoral to treat a body that is essentially without personhood as a person, that once personhood is lost, the body should not be endlessly maintained. Veatch's definition, of course, depends on the capacity for social interaction as well as consciousness, indicating how closely we identify psychological and social death. Robert Kastenbaum (1981b, 1985) raises an even more problematic issue when he suggests that we define psychological death in terms of whether the person is dead to herself or himself. In that sense, many people suffer partial deaths through loss of capacity or even through psychological disturbances such as depression or depersonalization.

Psychological death is usually defined, at least in part, in terms of social interaction, but it is also possible to look at the purely social aspects of death. Once a person appears to be psychologically dead, the behavior of others is changed. Social death begins. Eye contact, touching, and conversation with the deceased end, and the survivors begin to speak of someone who is psychologically dead as though biologically dead as well. Survivors begin to make decisions for someone who is psychologically dead without the pretense of consultation.

Complete biological and psychological death usually occur at the same moment, and social death follows. Through the funeral and bereavement, sometimes over a period of years, survivors cease looking at, talking to, and eventually thinking of, the deceased. But there is certainly no reason to believe that this order is sacred. We have talked about the problems of a biological death that follows a psychological one. Social death can precede psychological death, as occurs when a person is shunned for breaking a social taboo. There is even evidence that biological death can precede psychological death. Evidence of near-death experiences document the possibility.

Near-death experiences are not necessarily evidence of life after death, but they do make it clear that the biological and psychological aspects of death can occur independently. Common features of positive near-death experiences as described by Michael Simpson (1979) and Raymond Moody (1975, 1988) appear in Box 12.3. Negative near-death experiences also occur, although it is estimated that they represent less than 1 percent of all cases (Ring, 1984; Moody, 1988). Negative experiences seem to consist of two phases, one in which feelings of fear, anxiety, panic, and desperation predominate and a second that is characterized by the qualities of archetypal hell (Serdahely & Walker, 1990).

Carol Zaliski (1988) has suggested that we need to find an explanation for these experiences that bridges the gap between their being dismissed as nothing and their being embraced as proof of an afterlife. She reminds us that it is important to explore such phenomena because what we believe about death influences how we treat the dying—whether we try to sustain their life or not, how we respond to their needs, how we cope with their loss.

All of which brings us to the question of what dying is. Whereas death is a state or an event, dying is a process, the starting point of which is difficult to determine. In a sense, dying begins when the developments that will ultimately cause the moment of death begin. The process may take many years, and we may be unaware of it for most of them, but at some point, many of us will know. Then we say we are dying.

Dying, according to Kastenbaum (1981a, 1985) is a sequence of psychosocial events that begins with the recognition of the biomedical situation and the communication of those facts to the dying person. Other authors (Marshall

---

Box 12.3 Common aspects of the near-death experience

1. *Mystification:* The feeling that one understands everything; the experience of joy; feelings of unity, harmony, and peace.

2. *Depersonalization:* The experience of the self as strange or unreal, as set apart or detached from the body.

3. *Hyperalertness:* The feelings that one's thoughts are sharp, one's vision is keen, and the experience of an altered sense of time passing.

4. *Perceptual phenomena:* Awareness of a loud noise that is sensed rather than heard, the sensation of moving through a dark tunnel or funnel toward a bright light, the experience of "seeing" one's life pass by in a panoramic view.

5. *Cognitive interpretations:* The idea that one is being required to judge one's own life; awareness of a comforting being or presence; the notion that one is about to cross some barrier or frontier; the awareness that one's time has not yet come and one must return to complete the normal life span.

SOURCE: Based on Simpson (1979) and Moody (1975).

& Levy, 1990) have argued that we all participate in a **dying career,** in the sense that a career is a progression of statuses or functions that emerge in a more or less orderly fashion over time. Dying, as a final career, begins with the awareness that time is limited. As age peers and parents die, one becomes increasingly aware of those limits and may also experience increased self-reflection along with the exploration of the meaning of death (Levy, 1987). As a dying career progresses, the meaning of death changes. Part of the research in this area has addressed the impact of death at various points over the life cycle.

Death, Dying, and the Cycle of Life

Just as the meaning of death changes with age, so does the personal meaning of one's own dying. To an infant, it may have no meaning at all if the concept is learned. On the other hand, the evidence suggests that even very young children are often far more aware of their own dying than anyone close to them wants to admit. The meaning of a child's death or the impact of the death of someone close during childhood is quite different from the death that comes at the end of a long life. Generally, the loss of a young person is considered more tragic than the death of someone elderly, and the impact of a significant loss early in life is thought to be more traumatic than loss in adolescence or adulthood (Moss & Moss, 1983–84; Taylor, 1983–84).

The Loss of a Child

No one wants to think about the death of a child. The loss of a child may be the most painful experience one can have in adulthood. Perhaps because adults expect to care for children, to help them, even to save them, it is particularly devastating to be close to a child who cannot be saved. Often, people who must deal with a dying child prefer to keep the truth away from the child. But children know that something is dreadfully wrong even when they have not been specifically informed that they are dying. Most writers advocate honesty (Singher, 1974) but place the emphasis on addressing the child's fears about safety and loneliness or pain, rather than dwelling on death (Stillion & Wass, 1979).

Like adults, dying children become depressed and angry when they are not permitted to talk about their experiences. And, like adults, the fears they have are analogies from life and living. They fear separation, pain, and the loss of control over bodily functions, and one can deal with these, even if there is nothing to be done about the child's illness. Adults, especially parents, are often unable to meet these basic needs, however, because caring for a dying child is an anxiety-provoking, frustrating task. For many, anger and guilt follow on the heels of the frustration, and the parent feels more distant from the child than ever. Parents need honesty and emotional support, someone who understands and can outline the emotional reactions. The emotional responses of siblings, from anger and jealousy to guilt, must also be explained, and parents must be encouraged to continue setting limits for the child. Like any child, a dying child can be overindulged and begin behaving badly, creating havoc in an already difficult situation (Stillion & Wass, 1979).

The parents of a dying child experience powerful anger, which can be directed at each other or other family members, or even at those who are trying to help. Because they are helpless, the parents can be overwhelmed by anxiety or fear, and they usually withdraw from friends and family who have healthy children. Often, the best thing that can be done is to channel the caring and the energy into work. When parents take on the care of other children in the hospital, they are often better able to adjust because they feel less helpless and less isolated (Easson, 1970).

The death of an adult child may also be deeply disturbing for older people. In fact, it has been argued (DeSpelder & Strickland, 1992) that this is the most difficult of all griefs to resolve. Not only is the death usually untimely, but the parent suffers guilt at having survived the child. It seems unnatural. An elderly person may also lose a caregiver when a child dies or feel competition with the spouse of an adult child for the place of "most bereaved." If the child is a young adult, there may be grandchildren and grandparents may have to step in, an eventuality that can be both emotionally and economically disruptive for older people as well as the children.

Clearly, the death of a child is a highly disruptive experience. Perhaps of even greater concern, however, is the impact of parental death on children, an impact that can be seen even in adulthood. Grief hits children especially hard both because it takes away a parent and because the other parent is often lost to the child through bereavement. Intense anger toward the dead parent is common, and anniversary reactions or even anxiety about having children of one's own in adulthood are quite likely too (Kastenbaum, 1981a). Studies of adults who suffered early losses as well as studies of the key events in the lives of adults point to the long-term significance of early parental death. In one report on attitudes in a college-aged sample (Taylor, 1983–84), subjects who had suffered early loss used more death and suicide themes in describing pictures from the Thematic Apperception Test than subjects who had not experienced such losses. The Thematic Apperception Test consists of a group of pictures about which subjects are asked to tell stories. Well over one-half of all suicides and suicide attempts are reported to have experienced the loss of one parent in childhood, and disproportionate numbers of depressed patients have also experienced parental deaths as children. We have only begun to study the impact of death and dying on the way adult life is lived, but these tentative results suggest that early experience with death may be an extremely important predictor of adult behavior and personality.

Except for the literature on children, researchers have rarely focused on the age of a dying person specifically. Comparisons do exist in some areas, for example, in the study of how widowhood affects the surviving spouse, and there is some preliminary work on the effect of parental death on middle-aged children. Most of what we know about the death of a young adult comes from research on the responses of survivors to sudden or unexpected death, especially information about early widowhood.

Death in the Midst of the Life Cycle

One should ever be booted and spurred and ready to depart.

—Montaigne

As we saw in Chapter 10, by age fifty-six, over 50 percent of the female population in the United States and nearly 20 percent of all males are widowed. A number of these individuals were widowed very early, usually as the result of an accident; such early loss has a number of implications. When sudden, unexpected death is combined with youth, the impact is often disastrous. Young adults who are widowed are most likely to develop physical or emotional problems and to suffer from delayed or prolonged grief (Busse & Maddox, 1985). The younger a widowed person is, the more often she or he feels guilt about the circumstances surrounding the death, and the more angry and cheated the survivor feels. "If only I had done things differently . . ." is probably the dominating theme of the experience (Glick, Weiss, & Parkers, 1974).

The social and personal lives of younger people are more strongly affected by bereavement than the old. A young widow or widower is isolated. Few will ever share the experience, there is no one who can comfort the survivor with the confidence of experience. This society permits very limited expressions of grief, and young people especially are expected to rebound quickly. Young people who are bereaved are often pushed to take up their social lives, and even to date before they are finished mourning the spouse.

A sudden death is like a natural disaster, and the responses people make often include dullness, shock, feelings of worthlessness, somnolence, amnesia, suggestibility, increases in dependence, and even a loss of identity, as though one had survived a terrible earthquake or a fire. Anger, shame, and guilt are often present, and anger is especially likely when someone dies young. It seems so unfair (Shneidman, 1980). Searching and yearning are also most acute among mourners who have experienced an unexpected death, and therefore among the survivors of a young adult. People feel very sensitive to stimuli, especially events or objects associated with the loved one, and they often feel that they are "going crazy" because of episodes in which the mourner senses the return of the deceased. Sometimes, survivors may actually go out looking for the deceased; even though the behavior seems quite irrational, it seems to help (Davidson, 1979). Figure 12.1 shows the course of various responses that are especially strong after the death of a loved one. Note that disorientation is very intense, peaking during the first four to six months, the period considered the most important in terms of maintaining the health of a survivor.

Finally, young adults are likely to experience great personal and social disorganization because the spouse is unlikely to have left financial and personal accounts in order. A young widow may have several young children and suddenly have no means of support for herself. A young widower may find himself without household help or day care, and may have only a week or so of personal leave in which to straighten out all of the details. In the meantime, the children are suffering through the death of a parent, which is a most traumatic kind of loss, requiring some very special attention and caring (Lowenthal, Thurnher, & Chiriboga, 1975; Stillion & Wass, 1979).

Recent work (Thomas, DiGiulio, and Sheehan, 1988) does suggest, however, that most young widows find the strength to deal with bereavement, even reporting some positive experiences like growing independence and personal development.

Some note should be made here about the particularly devastating effects of murder and suicide on the survivors. These violent acts represent a special burden for the living, not only because they are almost always unexpected and sudden, but also because of the stigma associated with a violent or criminal death. Murder and suicide raise especially hard questions for the living, making those close to the victim feel terribly vulnerable as well as angry. Survivors typically become obsessed with who, what, why, and if. These thoughts can persist for years and can motivate accusations toward the self, family, and friends. Edwin Shneidman (1980, 1992) has reported that even as long as six years after the events, survivors still show low-grade sadness and seem unable to adapt completely.

Adding to the burden of the survivors of such deaths is the fact that the

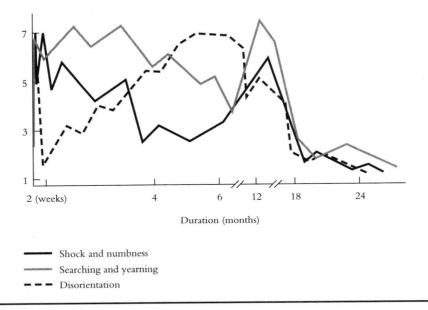

Duration (months)

——— Shock and numbness
▬▬▬ Searching and yearning
━ ━ ━ Disorientation

Figure 12.1 Intensity of responses after death of a loved one.

Characteristics of *shock and numbness* are resistance to stimuli, difficulty making judgments, impaired functioning, emotional outbursts, and stunned feelings.

Characteristics of *searching and yearning* are extreme sensitivity to stimuli, anger and guilt, restlessness and impatience, ambiguous feelings, and need to test reality.

Characteristics of *disorientation* are disorganization, depression, guilt, anorexia, and lack of awareness of reality.

SOURCE: After Wass, 1979, pp. 175, 177.

events and circumstances surrounding violence or suicide are often confusing. Only the perpetrator and the victim know exactly what happened, and so no one else ever knows. Survivors feel alternately depressed, guilty, angry, or confused, depending on the particular construction of the event they believe at a particular moment. Furthermore, the suddenness of the death along with the horror of the circumstances delays acceptance. One mother, coping with the death of her twenty-two-year-old son by what may have been accidental hanging (the result of a prank), reported that the most difficult time of day was morning. For weeks, as she woke up, she hoped it had all been a horrible nightmare. Slowly, she would have to convince herself that it was true; her son was dead (Hodges, 1987).

As people—especially women—get older, many will experience the death of a child, and most will be unprepared. The death of a child is always an "off-time" event, for we all expect our children to outlive us. Whether we are discussing the parental loss of a child or the loss of a spouse in young adulthood or early middle age, an important aspect of such events has to do with being "off-time." Parental death in childhood is relatively rare, as is early widowhood. Another kind of "off-time" loss that has been examined is the impact of the death of parents of young or early-middle-aged adults.

Interview data collected by Miriam and Sidney Moss (1983–84) showed that subjects aged thirty to fifty who had experienced the death of a parent rarely felt that the parent had lived long enough or had died well. They often expressed guilt about their own carelessness in the relationship with the parent, or about omissions and unanswered questions. Furthermore, subjects felt they had lost a buffer between themselves and death. They felt more vulnerable, closer to the end of life. The idea is nicely expressed by R. I. Fitzhenry: "When our parents are living we feel that they stand between us and death; when they go, we move to the edge of the unknown."

Even the elderly appear to see the death of a young person as more stressful than the death of someone older. Elderly people tend to avoid encounter with a young person who is dying, just as other adults do (Smith, Sherman, & Sherman, 1982–83). But they are not as likely to avoid another elderly person who is dying, in the way that younger people avoid a dying person of their own age. There are several possible explanations for these data, but one of the most likely is that the death of someone old is not viewed as tragic.

It has been suggested that the death of an older person is less tragic because older people are less valued. From another vantage point, however, death might be seen as a natural part of life, not a tragedy or a catastrophe. If the death of an older person is seen as less tragic, it may also reflect the perception that older people have had a chance for a full life, the opportunity to fulfill their own personal goals and to make whatever contribution they were capable of making. Yet the death of an elderly person causes some special problems, for many of that person's closest survivors are likely to be elderly themselves.

Kastenbaum (1981) has written of **bereavement overload.** Often an elderly survivor experiences the death of several close friends and relatives in a very short time. The survivor may not have recovered from the grief process after the death of a brother when a sister dies, or a spouse, or a friend. Bereavement overload can produce physical symptoms, depression, and even suicidal feelings. Many people who must cope with new stresses soon after the death of someone close are still disturbed and depressed two years or more after the death (Saunders, 1981).

To this point, we have treated death and dying as though it were a single, unitary phenomenon that affects people in a particular way depending on their age, social and personal circumstances, and, perhaps, emotional resources. But that is really a simplified notion, for no two deaths and no two dying people are alike. Although there are some common responses, people die much as they live, expressing all the individual differences that make each human being unique in some sense. To understand the meaning of a particular death one must also understand the dying. Therefore, we turn to a description of the literature on dying, the terminal stage of the life cycle.

Dying: The Terminal Stage of Life

The most widely publicized and influential account of the terminal stage of life is undoubtedly that first outlined by Elizabeth Kübler-Ross (1969). After interviewing hundreds of dying patients, Kübler-Ross concluded that the most likely sequence of reactions to awareness of one's own imminent death included five characteristic stages. The first of these, called *denial,* is dominated by shock and disbelief (There must be some mistake!).

After the shock wears off, a stage dominated by *anger* develops. Hostility may be directed at caregivers, friends, and family (Why me?). When the bitterness subsides, attempts to *bargain* often occur. Patients talk about making deals with God or fate, offering to be a better person, or husband, or wife, if allowed to live a little longer. The responses in this phase are not rational, of course, and if the patient outlives the bargain, a new one is struck.

Finally grief begins, and a stage Kübler-Ross calls *depression* emerges. As Edwin Shneidman (1992) observes: "People mourn themselves." They mourn not just for their own deaths but for lost abilities and well-being and for the loss of their experiences in the world. Shneidman has pointed out that self-mourning is a healthy sign of proper self-respect. Kübler-Ross believes that if patients successfully negotiate this stage, they will accept death and develop a sense of calm. *Acceptance* means that the patient achieves a kind of peace, not despair or remorse, but quiet expectation characterized by growing detachment from the outside world and the people that once were close.

Kübler-Ross's ideas were prime movers of the "death awareness movement" in the 1970s and 1980s. Most researchers now believe, however, that her five stages are too narrow to describe the complex patterns of knowing, denial, anger, depression, and acceptance that appear among dying patients. Simple acceptance and simple denial are unlikely adaptations. Although it is impossible to deny completely the notion that something is wrong, some denial may forestall the withdrawal of friends and family and make it possible to seek medical care and follow medical advice (Beilin, 1981–82).

Kübler-Ross's observations included many young adults and middle-aged people who were dying prematurely and more likely to experience anger and bargaining than older people (Marshall & Levy, 1990). The stages may also reflect the way dying is generally handled in this society; they may not be a universal experience at all. Furthermore, as Michael Simpson (1979) has argued:

> There is a great deal of seriously simplistic abuse of such terms as denial and knowledge throughout the sociological and psychological literature on death. The human mind is capable of so many levels of knowing, acknowledging, and ignoring, not only in rapid succession but even simultane-

ously, as to completely elude the naive classifications that are usually applied. In the hands of some writers on the subject, anything short of persistent direct statement of unequivocal certainty of one's imminent death is regarded as clear-cut denial. . . . Remember that however mortally ill one is, dying is not all one is doing, and failure to pay due attention to many other aspects of living would be truly inappropriate and would certainly represent a denial of reality. (p. 125)

Dying people are expected to settle unfinished business, manage strained relationships, and retain their composure. A "good death" is one in which friends and family are able to remain close, pain is controlled as are medications and technology, and one experiences personal growth (Levy & Gordon, 1987). All of this occurs in the context of a complex arrangement wherein there are varying levels of disclosure among the participants, from full knowledge to suspicion to complete ignorance (Marshall & Levy, 1990). A dying person is expected to handle all of this with grace and dignity. Little wonder it is difficult to describe how denial and acceptance may fluctuate, not only in the person who is dying, but also in the social network around that person. Such fluctuation must not only reflect but also create and reinforce a pattern that permits the dying person to do a great deal of social business in the terminal phase.

Instead of debating whether denial or acceptance dominates the terminal stage of life, Avery Weisman (1972) has offered the concept of an **appropriate death,** one that fulfills the patient's ideals and expectations. An appropriate death does not proceed by stages. Instead, three general phases have been suggested: an acute phase, coinciding with the patient's initial awareness that his or her condition is terminal; a chronic living-dying phase in which anticipatory grief usually occurs; and a terminal phase, which begins when the patient starts to withdraw from the outside world (Pattison, 1977). Figure 12.2 presents a graphic representation of the three phases.

Many varied emotions characterize each phase of an appropriate death, although certain reactions typify a particular phase. For example, shock and very acute anxiety, as well as anger and bargaining, characterize the acute phase, whereas fear of the unknown, fear of loneliness, and sorrow occur more often in the chronic living-dying stage. Denial and acceptance can occur in any phase, alternately or even simultaneously. Furthermore, patients display *hope* in every phase, even when it is clear that recovery or control of the disease is impossible. Looking forward to Christmas or Passover, another birthday, or another spring is hopeful. Hope motivates energetic attempts to control the disease or to establish continuity between oneself and one's survivors (Kastenbaum, 1981a).

In another version of the acceptance-denial controversy, Robert Kastenbaum warns that resistance may be mistaken for denial when the terminal stage is oversimplified. Resistance is sophisticated and resourceful. A resistant pa-

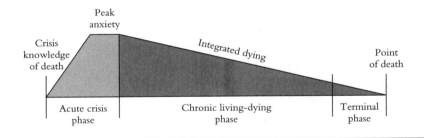

Figure 12.2 Phases in an appropriate death.

SOURCE: Pattison, 1977, p. 44.

tient sees the positive events, not dwelling on death, or finds that there is still much to accomplish. Just because one stresses living does not mean one has not accepted dying. An appropriate death is one in which personal identity and independence flourish alongside acceptance, denial, resistance, anger, or sorrow (Ryder & Ross, 1981).

Dealing with the Dying Patient: Family and Caregivers

For years, it seems, the main question researchers asked about terminal illness was whether or not one should inform the patient. The current answer is a resounding "yes," regardless of the circumstances of the patient, the desires of the family, or the predilections of the messenger. How much information to give and how to present it continue to raise conjecture, however. There are two principal objections to complete, detailed disclosure. First, it is argued, people cannot go on without some hope. Second, even the best of physicians and medical technicians can never be sure precisely how an illness will progress.

Despite the complexity of the issue, one set of guidelines that seem especially reasonable and fairly easy to implement includes the following nine points (Hogshead, 1978):

1. Keep it simple.
2. Try to see what the diagnosis means to the patient.
3. Try to keep on "cool" ground, where you have some idea of the possible response.
4. Don't deliver all the known information at once; patients will ask the questions of most interest to them when they are ready.

5. Wait for questions and answer them honestly.

6. Don't argue with an attempt to deny the news.

7. Ask the person to repeat what you have said.

8. Don't destroy all hope.

9. Don't say anything that is not true.

Box 12.4 presents some further thoughts about providing support to people in crisis, generally, and most especially when faced with a life-threatening illness.

Ordinarily, of course, the person delivering the bad news is a physician. In the twentieth century, medical caregivers have become core members of the **death system,** or the "sociophysical network by which the relationship to mortality is mediated and expressed" (Kastenbaum, 1981a, p. 67). People who are dying are generally institutionalized, and doctors and nurses become the purveyors of the system. Unfortunately, medical caregivers are poorly prepared for this aspect of their role. Trained to save lives, they often experience a patient's death as a personal and professional failure and have a difficult time establishing the correct distance from a dying patient. If they define helping as curing, they may experience much confusion, guilt, and defensiveness when it becomes clear that a cure is not possible (DeSpelder & Strickland, 1992). Doctors and nurses (along with fire fighters and police officers, who are also trained to save lives) express stronger fear of death than do other groups (Feifel, 1965; Martin, 1982–83; Lester, 1990).

Furthermore, because medical caregivers cannot grieve for each patient they lose, caregivers may end up at odds with the patient's family. Most writers agree that family members begin their **grief work** when they first learn of the patient's illness. Grief work includes shock and anger, depression and guilt, self-recrimination, and the need to handle unfinished business. According to Kübler-Ross (1969, 1974), the family usually lags behind the patient in the mourning process and must be encouraged to catch up. Medical caregivers, however, usually do not engage in grief work, although they do experience sorrow. As a consequence, many families accept a patient's death better than do staff. At times, when their grief work is done, the family withdraws from the patient, but then hostilities erupt because staff are still experiencing sorrow. Of course, such conflict increases the stress on everyone (Fulton, 1981).

Hospital staff need effective support and referral services in dealing with the stress of terminal care. They need to be able to discuss their feelings and to take time off to attend a funeral or to recuperate from difficult experiences.

The emotional responses of both patient and family may be controlled with drugs. The trade-off of such sophisticated care is less personal comfort and less attention to the emotional and social aspects of dying. All in all, a hospital may be an inappropriate place to die. Dedicated to life saving, it often relegates the family to a kind of hallway deathwatch. In a hospital, the operative response is denial. The job is to prevent death and treatment may become depersonalized

---

Box 12.4 Your caring presence: Ways of effectively providing support to others

---

1. Be honest about your own thoughts, concerns, and feelings.

2. When in doubt, ask questions:
   How is that for you?
   How do you feel right now?
   Can you tell me more about that?
   Am I intruding?
   What do you need?
   What are the ways you can take care of yourself?

3. When you are responding to a person facing a crisis situation, be sure to use statements such as:
   I feel _____
   I believe _____
   I would want _____
   Rather than:
   You should
   That's wrong
   Everything will be ok.
   which are statements that may not give the person the opportunity to express his/her own unique needs and feelings.

4. Stay in the present as much as possible: How do you feel RIGHT NOW? What do you need RIGHT NOW?

5. Listening is profoundly healing. You don't have to make it better. You don't have to have the answers. You don't have to take away the pain. It's his/her pain. He/She needs to experience it in his/her own time and in his/her own way.

6. People in crisis need to know they have decision-making power. It may be appropriate to point out alternatives.

7. Offer any practical assistance that you feel comfortable giving.

8. If the situation warrants it, feel free to refer individual to appropriate agency.

SOURCE: The Centre for Living with Dying.

---

and abstract in the effort to evade the recognition that a patient is dying (De-Spelder & Strickland, 1992).

Fortunately, the death system has expanded in the past few decades to include a facility especially designed for dying patients and their families. **Hospices** help people make the shift from delaying death to improving what remains of life.

Hospices

Time is not a question of length, it's a question of depth, isn't it?

—Cicely Saunders

The purpose of a hospice is to support the patient in achieving an appropriate death. The maintenance of life through the use of heroic measures is shunned and emphasis is placed instead on providing a comfortable, peaceful atmosphere, on maintaining the patient in a pain-free, independent lifestyle, and on permitting patients to live through the last months or days or moments exactly as they wish, insofar as it is possible.

Pain medication is provided every few hours, whether the patient requests it or not. The idea is to free the patient not only from pain itself but from the fear of it as well. The hospice staff is there to listen and just to be with the patient, rather than to do the objective, physical tasks medical personnel usually do. It is assumed that the patient knows best (Saunders, 1969). Some hospices are designed more like homes than hospitals. Bright furnishings and comfortable furniture is the order of the day, and the staff is dedicated to keeping emotional and social impoverishment at a minimum. Often this means providing strong support for family members and helping patients find ways to resolve old conflicts or fulfill realistic wishes (Saunders, 1976).

In the United States, however, hospice is not usually a place at all, but rather an organization within a hospital that provides support to families wishing to keep a dying person at home. Volunteers are trained to support the family in recognizing and fulfilling their own needs as well as the needs of the patient. Home care often alleviates guilt and eases the family's feeling of helplessness. It also provides a humane, caring environment for the patient and eases the guilt associated with extremely expensive, and often unwanted, hospital care (Ryder & Ross, 1981). In the case of home care, hospice workers usually visit the family once a week or more, often taking over care for a while to give the family a much needed vacation or a regular day off (Buckingham, 1982–83).

Many elderly people would prefer to die at home, but, as Richard Kalish (1985) has pointed out, it can be a great burden for families to take on the responsibility for a dying patient in this era of complex medical treatment. After the death occurs, caretakers often report feeling that the dying person should have been in a hospital. Home care is most appropriate when the patient is alert and able to relate to the caretaker and can benefit from familiar surroundings and family support, and when treatment can be carried out at home with reasonable ease. For these reasons, Kalish argues that hospice in the United States underserves the elderly population, as many older people are not cognitively intact and are not living with someone who could provide care.

Finally, hospice may consist of a set of special services integrated within the hospital setting. There may be a hospice ward in which it is possible to relax the usual rules and regulations, allowing children to visit, for instance, or permitting family members to stay beyond the usual hours. Special wards are problematic, however, because assignment to the ward itself is a cause for anxiety and the maintenance of special wards can be costly. As Lynne DeSpelder and Albert Strickland (1992) have emphasized, however, where hospice is integrated in the ordinary hospital setting, it requires a very strong, vocal advocate. The ordinary services and settings of hospitals simply do not support the concept that the patient knows best.

On the other hand, maintaining a dying patient at home to the very end requires a variety of services that are not only expensive but often cannot be purchased at any price. House calls by physicians and nurses, the provision of health aides, social workers, and even clergy might keep a family from rushing to the hospital with every new crisis (Magno, 1990). There are many challenges for hospice in the 1990s, but perhaps the biggest one is the involvement of physicians. Often, doctors are reluctant to refer a patient to hospice care until the very end. Physicians have not been trained in how best to utilize hospice. This situation may change, as younger doctors appear to show lower death anxiety and have more experience with hospice than older cohorts (Cochrane, Levy, Fryer, & Oglesby, 1990–91), especially doctors who self-select into specialities, such as oncology, where the probability of dealing with a terminal patient is high.

Whether in a hospital or a hospice or a home, however, dying eventually comes to an end, and the survivors must begin to cope with life bereft of someone close. Despite the amount of difficult grief work accomplished before the death, families are still bereaved. A natural part of bereavement, even when death was welcomed as an end to suffering, sorrow can be a very intense experience, both physically and emotionally.

Bereavement, Funerals, and Recovery

Physical distress is a common experience among people who are recently bereaved. In addition to feeling agitated or restless, and being unable to sleep or eat properly, bereaved people report sensations like choking or tightness that seem to come in waves. At least one researcher (Fredrick, 1976–77, 1983–84) has argued that bereaved people should be treated as though they were physically ill. His studies have demonstrated that the levels of a very powerful group of hormones known as the **corticosteroids** increase during bereavement and remain high for a very long time. The death rates of bereaved people are much higher than those of the general population, and rates for infection and malignancy have been reported at 2.5 to 5 times the national average.

Fredrick believes that the reason for increases in physical vulnerability lie in the adverse affect corticosteroids have on the function of the immune system.

High levels of these hormones appear to block normal immune function, leaving the victim more vulnerable to disease processes. If grief is unusually prolonged, high levels of corticosteroids are also found over longer periods. Fredrick feels that the expression of grief and the acceptance of death are essential if the survivor is to recover from the physical as well as the emotional aspects of grief.

Recently, however (Thomas, DiGiulio, & Sheehan, 1988), the medical or disease model of bereavement has met with some criticism. Attempts to document increased mortality among widows have produced mixed results (Osterwis, Solomon, & Green, 1984), and some studies have suggested that the idea that bereavement is an unremittingly negative event is inaccurate. L. Eugene Thomas, Robert DiGiulio, and Nancy Sheehan have shown, for example, that widows often perceive themselves as having experienced positive as well as negative changes with the death of a spouse. These researchers were unable to find any effect of widowhood on a widow's sense of identity, her self-esteem, or level of adaptation. Many of the women in this study were able to interpret their experience in such a way as to find meaning in the death of a spouse. In fact, "the widows in this study exhibited signs of psychological well-being that compare favorably to those who are not bereaved" (p. 235). The widows in this sample were relatively well educated and financially secure, though none of this means that they did not grieve. However, these results do raise the question of whether bereavement ought to be treated as a physical disorder. Like most psychosocial events, it is probably too complex to describe in any simple way.

For most people, bereavement is indeed complicated. Along with sorrow and despair, feelings occur that are not as well recognized. Few people are prepared for the anger, shame, guilt, and self-doubt that often accompany a death in the family. In part, the death awareness movement was mounted to familiarize people with such reactions, helping prevent the more serious mental and physical problems that can result when people deny or suppress their feelings. Concomitantly, **thanatologists** have devised **postvention** programs designed to intervene in the lives of survivors after a death has occurred. Postvention emphasizes the expression of feelings, especially feelings of anger, shame, and guilt. Survivors are offered empathy and are encouraged to feel that these responses are legitimate and normal (Shneidman, 1992). Above all, perhaps, postvention emphasizes patience. Society has no time to stop for death—the survivors are expected to hustle along with everyone else. Postvention reminds people that recovery takes time. Grief cannot be rushed.

Hospice Outreach is an organization that helps provide hospice care at home and postvention after the loss of someone close. Barbara Costa (1989) writes of her long experience with this program in the *Handbook for the Bereaved and Those Who Want to Help*. She describes the mix of denial, anger, guilt, depression, and isolation survivors often feel. Denial may even include momentary lapses of memory that the death occurred or fleeting hallucinations that the deceased is present in the room, or just coming in the door. These are perfectly normal, common events.

Costa reminds us that anger may be most prevalent when the relationship between survivors and the deceased was ambivalent. It's important to find a safe way to express such anger, which may be directed at family, friends, doctors and nurses, or the self. Costa suggests writing in a journal or composing letters (one may choose not to send them), physical exercise, playing music, even chopping wood, beating rugs, or finding an out-of-the-way place just to scream for a while.

Survivors often feel guilty, too, even though guilt is almost always unwarranted. They need to be reminded how much they loved the one that died, or if there is a real reason to feel guilty, bereaved people may need to learn to accept what happened, forgive themselves, and go on. Depression, feelings of isolation, and loneliness are mixed with guilt and anger, a combination that can be confusing for everyone.

In a series of letters designed to be sent to recently bereaved people, Costa paints a portrait of the most likely emotional responses month by month for the first year. In the first month or two, she talks about feelings of unreality and numbness and the need to maintain routine and take care of oneself physically. During this period, a bereaved person may actually be surprised at how well they are doing, believing that the worst is behind them. But often the most difficult phase occurs at three to six months, when the shock wears off and one has to deal with the pain. During this period, Costa encourages bereaved people to stick to a routine, get out of bed and get dressed everyday and plan something, no matter how trivial. She reminds us that grief is not a weakness; it is an adjustment to a significant loss that can last for a number of months, or even longer, but that will eventually ease.

At seven months, she discusses setbacks, feelings of disorganization, or anxiety. She suggests making lists of things to do, friends to call, places to go, books, music, projects, and letters. She advises posting these where they are handy for the difficult moments when one just can't think of anything worth doing. By ten months, she writes of feeling more secure, of a returning sense of humor and the ability to relax. She points out there is no need to feel disloyal or guilty about such improvements. She also warns that temporary setbacks can still occur. At a year, she talks about how common it is to feel some fresh pain, an anniversary reaction, but assures the reader it will pass. This is the time to write down new accomplishments, list problems overcome, new goals, skills, and activities. Box 12.5 presents Costa's advice for getting through the holidays in the first year of bereavement, often the most difficult period.

In the absence of any kind of formal postvention programs in this country, the people who most often end up dealing with the immediate problems of bereaved family and friends are the mortician and the funeral director. This role has fallen to them because funeral services have become the major channel

---

Box 12.5 Holidays in the first year of bereavement

Here are some of the questions it makes sense to ask if you are coping with the death of a loved one or trying to help someone who is:

- Do you want to stay home or run away to someplace entirely different? It's OK to want to go away if it helps.

- What kind of changes might make the holidays easier? If it is possible to let someone do some of the tasks you usually do yourself, don't be stuck in a holiday routine.

- What gifts will you need to purchase? Make a list well in advance so you can get the shopping done on your "good" days.

- Is there a memorial that might seem appropriate? Planting a garden, having a short ceremony, making a contribution can give you something to focus on and provide an opportunity for friends and family to participate and offer support.

- Do you want to be alone? Being alone is a legitimate choice.

SOURCE: Costa, 1989, pp. 19–20.

---

through which this society affords the bereaved an opportunity to express their misery, sorrow, and despair—a controversial solution at best.

Funerals

The American funeral is, for the most part, highly ritualized, and so expensive that many dying people hope their families will avoid all but the basic costs. In making funeral arrangements, bereaved people find themselves unable to make decisions that express their own needs, that respect the wishes of the deceased, and that are considered decent and right in the eyes of their friends and neighbors. An elaborate funeral is disparaged, but too little ceremony is equally unsatisfactory. On the one hand, social critics argue that American customs are needlessly expensive and distressing, especially if the body is to be displayed (Baird, 1976; Mitford, 1963). Embalming and cosmetics, as well as the purchase of an elaborate casket, have probably received the worst reviews. The traditional eulogy, flowers, music, funeral parlor, and nearly every other aspect of the average funeral have also been roundly criticized.

On the other hand, thanatologists have argued that American customs may be too simple, too informal, and too short-lived to provide emotional support and catharsis for the bereaved (Gorer, 1965). Kübler-Ross (1974) believes that encountering the body of the deceased is an important part of the process involved in accepting death and ought not to be considered morbid or unusual. If the body has been damaged in some way, if organs have been donated, or if it must be preserved for even a few days, the opportunity to touch or even talk to the deceased will depend on embalming and cosmetics, yet critics assert that these are the most barbaric and gruesome aspects of the ritual.

Survey research has demonstrated that people who consider themselves "very close" to the deceased feel that the presence of the body at the funeral service is an important aspect of the ceremony. Those who do not feel as close say the burial of the body prior to the service is a good idea. It seems that those who are most affected by the death are most likely to benefit from the presence of the body (Swanson & Bennett, 1982–83). Seeing is believing, and may help prevent long-term denial. Another line of evidence supporting this view suggests that the more "difficult" the death is for the family and those who feel close to the deceased, the more importance they are likely to attribute to the funeral (Swanson & Bennett, 1982–83). Finally, a recent study of alternative funeral practices indicates that arrangements offering more opportunity for individual participation are likely to be favorably perceived. Even among a group of less traditional survivors, however, a majority favored the presence of the body at the funeral service (Bergen & Williams, 1981–82).

Generally, one might well conclude that it is unwise for anyone, whether expert, critic, or friend of the family, to make pronouncements about what is or is not morbid or unnecessary. The survivors must decide for themselves, and they should not allow current fads or criticisms to dictate their decisions. Sometimes family traditions are best because they are familiar, and for no other more rational reason. Perhaps the one recommendation that can be made with some confidence is that a discussion of funeral matters should take place before the issues become critical. People who decide what to do before they are bereaved usually spend about one-third less than those who wait until they are distressed and overwhelmed (Stevens-Long, 1979).

Some of the basic decisions that must be made by family members and the financial implications of those decisions are presented in Boxes 12.6 and 12.7. Prices are based on data from Forest Lawn Memorial Park in Glendale, California. Forest Lawn has served as a model for the American middle-class funeral. It emphasizes traditional religious symbols while deemphasizing individual monuments. Flat brass plates are installed over each grave site, and even the notion of comparison shopping is advocated by the advertising program first developed for Forest Lawn.

Yet, as the people at Forest Lawn are quick to point out, things are changing even in the funeral business. More and more people are interested in the low-cost funeral and burial services offered by memorial associations (Consumers Union, 1981). Through contractual arrangements with local mortuaries and cemeteries, memorial societies are able to offer members substantially reduced prices on conventional funeral arrangements. Sometimes the members only have a verbal agreement that depends on a particular mortician; however, the advice and information offered by such groups is ordinarily quite useful.

"A man's death is more the survivors' affair than his own." Thomas Mann

There are those who argue that death is the ultimate commercial transaction, the last rite of the American consumer.

Box 12.6 Some important decisions about funerals, burials, and cremations

1. Which mortuary and cemetery are most appropriate?
   Considerations: Cost, distance, family mobility patterns, philosophy and training of the service personnel, range of services available.

2. What kind of funeral is most appropriate for the survivors?
   Considerations: Open or closed casket versus memorial services before or after interment, degree of formality, use of eulogy or personal statement.

3. Who should officiate?
   Considerations: Denomination of officiant, officiant's knowledge of deceased and family, designation of individual if officiant to be nonreligious.

4. Where should the funeral take place?
   Considerations: Choice of a specific church, within the mortuary-cemetery complex or in a traditional place of worship, any special nontraditional preferences such as services in the home or outdoors.

5. What kind of creative or artistic works might be used at the funeral or memorial service?
   Considerations: Choice of instruments and/or singers, type of musical composition, use of special poetry or prose selections, use of visual art.

6. What kind of interment seems appropriate and where shall it take place?
   Considerations: Cremation versus burial, scattering of ashes versus interment in the ground or in cremation urn, location of cemetery property, costs.

7. What arrangements should be made with regard to the body?
   Consideration: Type and cost of casket for burial or cremation, type and cost of sectional concrete box for grave, clothing and disposition of jewelry that is ordinarily worn, use of religious symbols (rosary, Bible), use of a slumber or viewing room prior to funeral.

8. What exchanges between family and friends seem most appropriate?
   Considerations: Use of flowers, suggestions for contributions to charity, special wishes with regard to cards or memorial notices.

Education is the main goal of all such associations. They hope to make the public more aware of the impact of funerals, their costs, and the importance of planning before the family is under the stress of bereavement.

In recent years, the funeral trade has come under regulation by the Federal Trade Practices Commission, which requires that funeral providers give detailed information to consumers. The FTC has mandated itemized pricing and requires that such prices be quoted over the phone as well as in writing. Funeral businesses are prohibited from misrepresenting how the remains will be handled and they are not allowed to embalm for a fee without prior permission. Practices that require customers to purchase caskets for cremation or that

---

Box 12.7 Minimum prices for various funeral purchases and mortuary services at Forest Lawn Cemetery, March 1991

Burial	*Cremation*

Property:
  Glendale: $595
  Hollywood Hills: $345
  Covina Hills: $275
	Niche:
	  Glendale: $150
	  Hollywood Hills: $90

Endowment care (includes maintenance of streets, art work, grounds and burial property):
  Glendale and Hollywood Hills: 10% of purchase price of property
	Endowment care:
	  Glendale: 10% of purchase price of niche

	Interment and Recording: $52
Sectional concrete box: $175	Cremation casket (cardboard): $29
Interment and recording (includes opening and closing grave, use of greens, setting up chairs, replacements of grass, record-keeping): $310	Cremation: $100
Casket: $300 and up, plus sales tax	Funeral casket: $300 and up (replaces cremation casket for casket-present funeral)
Memorial tablet: $300 and up	

Mortuary and Funeral Costs

Mortuary services only (includes the call to pick up the body, the disposition of the body, and record-keeping): $761

Mortuary services and funeral services (includes the first call, disposition of the body, record-keeping, embalming, the use of a slumber room, church attendants, and use of any Forest Lawn church, hearse rental, funeral direction and counselor services, an organist, valet services, transportation of the flowers, direction of the procession): $985

Total with funeral or memorial service (minimum):	under $2500 (burial) under $1000 (cremation)

make the purchase of any funeral good or service conditional on the purchase of another have been banned.

Strong regulation of the funeral industry is necessary partly because most Americans exhibit such a strong aversion to death. Most people don't want to touch or even be in the presence of a corpse and they certainly don't want to handle the disposition of the body or the burial. Regulation is probably appropriate in this sensitive industry; however, it seems equally appropriate that people learn to deal with death in a more direct, less stylized way. This is the purpose of **death education,** a movement that started in hospitals and universities and that has spread through public education even to the elementary school level.

Death Education

Death education focuses on the idea that dying is a human affair, not just a series of biological events. Death educators are concerned about the need to control technology as a response to dying and how to emphasize the moral, spiritual, and ethical dimensions of the process. They believe that the acceptance of personal mortality is necessary to keep human beings in touch with nature and with their own potential for creativity. They argue that death education should begin in childhood and be a lifelong affair (Feifel, 1990).

Exactly what form such an education might best take seems unclear, however. Research suggests that formal courses in death education are more effective at changing attitudes about death when they are experiential rather than didactic. That is, courses that include films, videos, field trips, and personal discussions, with an emphasis on working through feelings, appear to be more effective than those that rely on traditional lectures (Durlak & Riesenberg, 1991). Didactic courses may actually increase the anxiety level of students. Even experiential courses, however, are more effective at changing attitudes about death-related issues (like hospices or funerals) than feelings about one's own personal dying. Furthermore, many programs demonstrate few immediate effects but produce changes only weeks later (Lonetto & Templar, 1986), making it more difficult to evaluate such educational efforts.

The current literature contains few studies that are well designed. Experimental controls are seldom reported, there is little follow-up in most cases, and multiple outcome measures are rarely employed. Joseph Durlak and Lee Ann Riesenberg (1991) suggest that good research will have to assess many behaviors as well as attitude changes. The ability to express oneself and to discuss death and dying outside the class, contact with the terminally ill, and concrete actions like signing up to be an organ donor or preparing a will are just some of the measures that might be employed. They write that "Ultimately, in death education we need to know which participants change in which ways on which dimensions as a result of which instructional techniques. Providing answers to this question presents a great challenge for future investigators" (p. 54).

Beyond learning to handle death and dying better, however, one might also expect death education to teach people how to live more fully. In the last part of this chapter, we will address the question first raised. What is the point of studying death? What does a dying person have to offer the living?

Renewal and Revitalization

Death tugs at my ear and says "Live, I am coming."
    —Oliver Wendell Holmes, Sr.

Think about what life would be like without death. Time, work, love, all of the important human institutions would have different meaning in a deathless universe. The motivations people experience would be quite different if life were not finite and the time to live, limited. Certainly, an important part of death education is to understand better how to care for a dying person and for the survivors. But another, less easily described aspect involves the study of what death awareness means to the living. When people deny the notion that they will die and are afraid to encounter death, life may be less meaningful; certainly it is less urgent.

As Charles Corr (1979) pointed out, those who ignore death and avoid the dying suffer a loss of community in at least three different ways. First, they must shut themselves off from those who become associated with death. Not only from the dying, of course, but also from those who are bereaved, and from those who are intimately involved in the death system. They must also shut out certain kinds of places: hospitals (especially convalescent hospitals), cemeteries, mortuaries, and so on.

Second, those who cannot encounter death lose some sense of wholeness as a person when they cannot face a central human experience and when they must respond to people who are dealing with that experience in strained and unnatural ways. Corr argues that "in order to satisfy a particular model of conduct, we restrain our natural sensitivity and imagination, sometimes to the point of permitting a certain atrophy of our personhood" (p. 66).

Finally, the denial of death changes one's relationship to nature. Death is one of the things that we share with other forms of life. According to Corr: "Our problem is the tendency to withdraw from nature and construct an artificial living space populated by plastic flowers, glass figurines, and pet rocks—none of which ever die" (p. 67). Together, these losses diminish our humanity because they put us out of touch with ourselves as creatures of nature and as members of a larger social community, and out of touch with a primitive source of motivation in all great human endeavor, the struggle to leave something behind, something significant that contributes to the development of all human life. As one of the founders of the death education movement wrote: "Death education relates not only to death itself but to our feelings about ourselves and nature and the universe we live in. It has to do with our values and ideals, the way we relate to one another and the kind of world we are building. Thoughtfully pursued, it can deepen the quality of our lives and of our relationships" (Morgan, 1977, p. 3).

Coming face-to-face with one's own mortality can invigorate, providing a revitalized perspective for decision making about marriage, career, family, and morality. It snaps us out of the day-to-day irritations and boredoms and reminds us that we have only so much time after all. Over and over again, dying people have affirmed the impact of encountering one's own mortality by throwing themselves into life. When Senator Richard L. Neuberger discovered the cancer that would finally take his life, he remarked on his "new appreciation of things I once took for granted—eating lunch with a friend, scratching my cat Muffet's ears and listening for his purrs, the company of my wife, reading a book or magazine in the quiet of my bed lamp at night, raiding the refrigerator for a glass of orange juice or a slice of toast. For the first time, I think I actually am savoring life" (Peter, 1979, p. 137). Contact with the dying can serve as a source of personal courage for the survivor and as a wellspring for action, decisiveness, and motivation, propelling one toward a more meaningful, integrated existence (Kastenbaum, 1964).

As Herman Feifel (1990) concludes: "In emphasizing awareness of death, we sharpen and intensify our appreciation of the uniqueness and preciousness of life. In responding to our temporality, we shall find it easier to define values, priorities, and life goals" (p. 542).

Of course, thanatology and death education are also designed to protect people from undue suffering and anguish, to inform survivors about the process of grieving, and to help them maintain relationships with dying people that continue to make sense. The study of death helps people deal with the anger, shock, guilt, and self-recriminations, and offers activities and ways of relating that ease the pain, rather than adding to it. Avoiding death doesn't help us; it only limits our options (DeSpelder & Strickland, 1992).

Finally, the study of death offers a point of view about dying that makes a contribution to development in the terminal phase of life. It is in the terminal phase of life that one is given a final and perhaps most powerful opportunity to express integrity, courage, humor, and grace. The certainty of death creates anxiety of one sort, but reduces another. When we know we are about to die, we need no longer fear living. Shneidman has pointed out that dying people exhibit a strong need for closure, for achievement, for being remembered.

Erikson (1982) believes that one of the most important expressions of wisdom and integrity is the maintenance of order and meaning in the disintegration of body and mind. "The key . . ." Shneidman adds, is "to participate in one's own life, including one's pain and dying, with as much *grace* (elegance, poise, self-possession, pride, good manners, good cheer) as one can" (1980, p. 188). Dying frees one to risk everything, in a way, to be creative in a way not possible when limited by the fear of all the little risks in life. It can be seen as an adventure, even as beautiful.

> Dying is beautiful—even the first time around, at the ripe old age of 20. It's not easy most of the time, but there's a real beauty to be found in knowing that your end is going to catch up with you faster than you had expected, and that you have to get all your loving and laughing and crying done as soon as you can. . . . (Helton, 1972, p. 8)

There is no one best way to die. Shneidman's description is, as he is quick to note, only one possible pattern, and Helton's is another. Meaning and beauty can be communicated in acceptance and grace, or in resistance, even defiance. We are inspired by those who die with equanimity, but no less by those who "rage against the dying of the light." As Dylan Thomas wrote so eloquently: "Though wise men at their end know dark is right, / Because their words had

"The more complete one's life is, the more . . . one's creative capacities are fulfilled, the less one fears death. . . . People are not afraid of death per se, but of the incompleteness of their lives." Lisa Marburg Goodman

forked no lightning they / Do not go gentle into that good night." Perhaps there are as many good ways to die as there are good ways to live, and each of them can serve to instruct and motivate the living.

Summary

I. Death: Personal and Professional Meanings
    A. Recent social issues like abortion, AIDS, euthanasia, and violence are forcing us to reconsider death and dying.
        1. Existential psychologists have suggested that denial of death occurs because modern life robs us of meaning.
        2. Most Americans still appear to believe in some form of afterlife or social immortality.
        3. Death anxiety may be learned by association with isolation and inactivity.
    B. The concept of death develops over the life cycle, even through middle age.

C. Biologists, psychologists, and sociologists all have developed definitions of death from different perspectives.

   1. Biological death used to be defined in terms of reflexes, respiration, and heart function. Today more sophisticated criteria like the Harvard Criteria for Total Brain Death are necessary.

      a. There is still argument, however, that these criteria are unnecessarily rigid; however, the President's Commission of 1981 recommended their use in the Uniform Death Act.

      b. The ability to maintain life artificially leads to the question of how personality relates to biological death.

      c. The use of a Durable Power of Attorney and specific written instructions is the best way for a dying person to express their wishes about life-sustaining efforts.

   2. Psychological death is usually defined in terms of consciousness and social interaction, although the question of whether a person is alive to himself or herself has been raised.

   3. Social death refers to changes in the behavior of survivors, like touching, looking at, talking about, or even thinking of the deceased.

   4. There is evidence that biological, psychological, and social death may occur in several patterns or sequences.

D. Death, dying, and the cycle of life

   1. Death is not only a state, it is also a process, and as a process, its meaning varies over different stages of the life cycle.

   2. The death of a child is especially difficult for caretakers and is likely to evoke anger and helplessness, and the desire to keep the truth from the child.

      a. Dying children become more depressed and angry when they are not allowed to talk about death, for clearly they know something is terribly wrong, and they fear isolation, pain, and loss of control.

      b. The death of an adult child has also been shown to be very difficult.

      c. The most disruptive form of loss over the life cycle is generally thought to be parental death during childhood. Depressed and suicidal adults often report having experienced such parental loss.

   3. Coping with a death as a young adult is especially difficult because the loss is unexpected.

      a. Lacking anticipatory socialization, survivors often respond like victims of a natural disaster, with shock, amnesia, dependence, and a loss of identity.

      b. Personal, social, and economic disorganization are likely, especially if the survivor is a young widow or widower with children.

4. The loss of a parent in young adulthood or early middle age is likewise accompanied by strong feelings, because the death is experienced as unfair and because adult children feel more vulnerable when their own parents die.

5. The death of an older person is viewed as less tragic, perhaps because the old are not as highly valued as the young, but more likely because older people are seen as having had a chance to live a full life.

    a. The special problems of the elderly survivor include bereavement overload, when several significant deaths follow one another closely.

    b. Depression, physical symptoms, and suicidal feelings can accompany overload.

E. Dying as a terminal stage of life

1. Kübler-Ross's influential account of dying includes five stages: denial, anger, bargaining, depression, and acceptance.

2. Criticism of her point of view involves the notion that acceptance and denial cannot be seen as simple opposites, but may alternate or even occur simultaneously. It has also been pointed out that her work emphasizes the reactions of young and middle-aged adults.

3. The concept of an appropriate death as one that fulfills the ideas and expectations of the patient permits a variety of patterns, including hope, resistance, anger, and sorrow.

F. Dealing with the dying patient

1. Most writers now agree that dying people must be informed of their condition but that the information should be kept simple and the patient should lead the way by asking questions.

2. Medical caregivers are usually assigned the task of giving information, but they are rarely trained to deal with dying and may end up as surrogate mourners at odds with the patient's family.

3. Hospice has developed as a place or an approach specifically designed to encourage an appropriate death.

    a. Patients are maintained pain-free, independence is encouraged, and patients are supported in fulfilling realistic goals.

    b. Some hospices are designed to support the family members who are keeping a dying patient at home.

    c. Many American hospices require a vocal advocate to become and remain integrated in the regular, acute-care hospital setting.

II. Bereavement, Funerals, and Recovery

A. Bereaved people suffer both physical and psychological distress.

1. Some research shows those who have suffered a recent loss exhibit high levels of corticosteroids, which probably interfere with proper immune system function.

2. Other researchers have shown that bereaved people may exhibit

positive growth as well as negative responses, suggesting that a disease model of bereavement may be inadequate.

3. Programs of postvention are designed to help family members deal with the strong emotional reactions they often have, especially with anger, shame, and guilt.

   a. Hospice outreach emphasizes the range of emotional responses survivors may feel.

   b. The emotional experience of bereavement may last for months with several changes in the type and intensity of feelings.

B. Most people, however, must turn to the funeral industry as the main source of assistance as a channel of expression for their grief.

1. The assistance offered by the funeral industry is riddled with conflict and contradiction. Funerals are seen as too elaborate, expensive, and even gruesome on the one hand, and as too simple, informal, and short-lived on the other.

2. Survey research has shown that most people who are very affected by a death do experience benefit from the ritual of a funeral, even from the presence of the body.

3. Families must make decisions based on their own needs and the desires of the deceased, rather than on current fads or criticisms.

C. Death education emphasizes the experience of dying as a human affair.

1. Experiential courses appear to be more effective than didactic ones.

2. Much more research using various approaches and measures is needed to evaluate death education.

D. Renewal and revitalization

1. Encounter with death, especially through thanatology and death education, permits us a sense of community with the dying, adds to our wholeness as people, and strengthens our concept of ourselves as creatures of nature.

2. Thanatology and death education are designed to protect survivors from undue suffering and anguish, and to help them continue to relate to dying people in a meaningful way.

3. Death education also reminds us that dying is a final opportunity for development; for the emergence of integrity; and for the expression of audacity, determination, courage, humor, and grace.

4. An increased sense of one's own mortality can invigorate, revitalizing decision making and propelling one toward a more meaningful, integrated existence.

Glossary

Abstract operations Beginning formal operations that allow people to make generalizations and participate in bidirectional causal linking.

Action theory A theoretical framework for understanding how internal processes like beliefs, plans, and expectations influence subsequent behavior.

Active mastery A mode of dealing with the environment; thought to be characteristic of young and middle-aged men; the environment is viewed as malleable, and the self is seen as a source of energy and change; independence and energy are valued.

Activity theory The hypothesis that successful aging is associated with the maintenance of social, physical, and intellectual activity.

Acute brain syndrome A reversible, organic brain disorder characterized by fluctuating levels of awareness, emotional and intellectual dysfunction.

Adjustment model of marriage The clinical representation of a good marriage as one in which there is agreement between the partners and with the conventional standards for a successful marriage.

Affection Attachment or the kind of friendship associated with familiarity.

Aficionado Married person who chooses a child-free lifestyle for the freedom and the privacy.

Agape Altruistic love without passion or even intimacy.

Age density The proportion of residents of a particular age group living in a community.

Age equivalence An attribute of a measure, experimental task, or observation that implies that (1) the same set of abilities or traits is measured for all ages in the sample, and (2) the abilities or traits are equally important, in the experimental hypothesis, for all age groups.

Ageism The notion that chronological age is a primary determinant of human traits and capacities and, thus, that one age is superior to another.

Age-related change Change occurring over the life course and correlated with chronological age.

Age simulation A form of experimental research in which developmental researchers try to create in the laboratory the conditions thought to produce age-related change.

Agreeableness A personality trait that reflects sympathy, trust, cooperativeness, and altruism.

Alpha rhythm Brain-wave patterns with a frequency of from 9 to 12 cycles per second.

Alzheimer's disease An irreversible brain syndrome caused by the dissolution of brain cells and characterized by early onset when compared to senile dementia.

Androgyny The acceptance of both male and female characteristics in oneself.

Anima The primitive female force posited by Jung and thought to be part of the collective unconscious.

Animus The primitive male force posited by Jung and thought to be part of the collective unconscious.

Anomie Feelings of loneliness or loss of identity.

Anticipation interval A brief period during which a subject is asked to recall the second member of a pair of words or syllables when only one member has been presented.

Anticipatory socialization The process by which people are rehearsed and prepared for an event by the so-

cial delivery of information and training.

Antihero Male midlife personality type described by Farrell and Rosenberg as experiencing a strong sense of crisis and feeling alienated and dissatisfied.

Apportioned grandmother A type of grandmother defined by her concern about doing what is right for the grandchild and by her ability to derive significant emotional satisfaction from the role of grandmother.

Appropriate death A death that fulfills the ideals and expectations of the dying individual.

Arrangement An agreement between an unmarried male and female to share living quarters, expenses, and regular sexual intercourse.

Arteriosclerosis A disease of the blood vessels in which the walls of the smaller arteries thicken and harden.

Associative network A neural network thought to produce mutual stimulation during memory-related processes.

Associative strength The power of one word to call up or be associated with another

Assumption A fact or statement taken for granted or believed to be correct.

Asynchronous Not happening or taking place, not developing, at the same time or instant.

Atherosclerosis A disease of the blood vessels involving hardening of the arteries, as in arteriosclerosis, but affecting the larger arteries and usually including the formation of plaques.

Attachment A relationship characterized by feelings of intimacy and commitment but not necessarily by current positive feelings or by self-disclosure.

Appendix

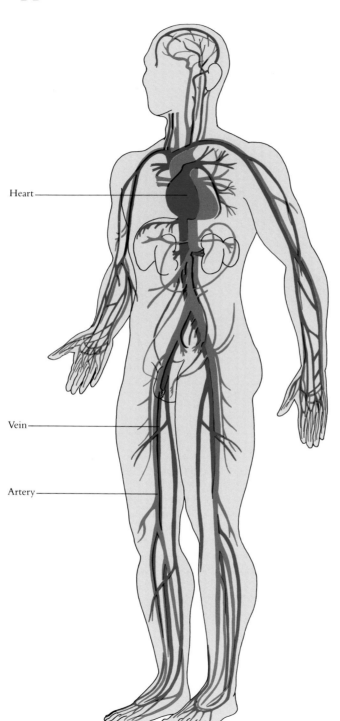

Heart

Vein

Artery

The Cardiovascular System
The heart and blood vessels (veins, arteries, and capillaries) make up the cardiovascular system. Veins carry blood to the heart, and arteries carry it away from the heart. The right side of the heart pumps blood to and from the lungs, where carbon dioxide gases are exchanged for fresh oxygen; this is called the pulmonary circulation. The right side of the heart then pumps the oxygen-rich blood to the rest of the body; this is called the systemic circulation.

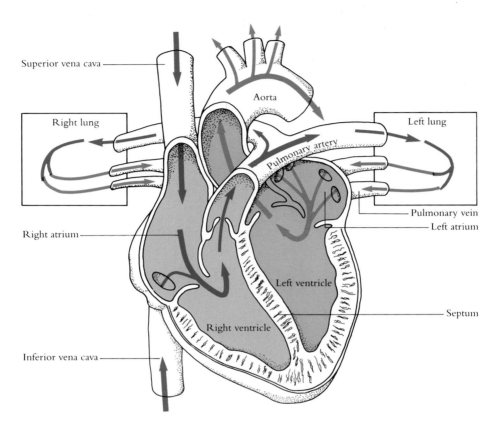

Circulation in the Heart

The heart is a four-chambered muscle, about the size of a fist. Each side of the heart contains two separate spaces separated by a valve. The thin-walled upper chamber is called the atrium, and the thick-walled lower chamber is called the ventricle.

Used blood returns to the heart via the vena cava, the body's largest vein, and enters the right atrium. It then flows down into the right ventricle. The ventricle contracts, forcing the blood through the pulmonary artery into the lungs, where carbon dioxide is removed and oxygen is added. The clean, oxygenated blood returns to the heart via the pulmonary veins into the left atrium and then down into the left ventricle. The powerful muscular wall of the left ventricle forces the blood up through the aorta, the body's largest artery, and into the systemic circulation. The familiar "lub-dub" sound of the heartbeat is caused by the alternating contraction (systole) and relaxation (diastole) of the chambers of the heart.

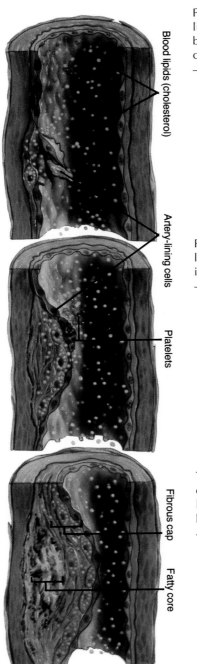

Blood lipids (cholesterol)

Artery-lining cells

Platelets

Fibrous cap

Fatty core

Plaque buildup begins when excess fat particles, called lipids, collect beneath cells lining the artery that have been damaged by smoking, high blood pressure, or other causes.

Platelets, one of the body's protective mechanisms, collect at the damaged area and cause a cap of cells to form, isolating the plaque within the artery wall.

The narrowed artery is now vulnerable to blockage by clots that can form if the cap breaks and the fatty core of lesion combines with the clot-producing factors in the blood.

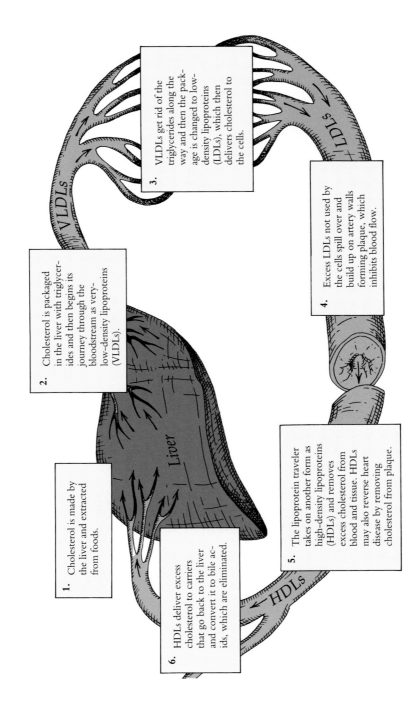

1. Cholesterol is made by the liver and extracted from foods.

2. Cholesterol is packaged in the liver with triglycerides and then begins its journey through the bloodstream as very-low-density lipoproteins (VLDLs).

3. VLDLs get rid of the triglycerides along the way and then the package is changed to low-density lipoproteins (LDLs), which then delivers cholesterol to the cells.

4. Excess LDLs not used by the cells spill over and build up on artery walls forming plaque, which inhibits blood flow.

5. The lipoprotein traveler takes on another form as high-density lipoproteins (HDLs) and removes excess cholesterol from blood and tissue. HDLs may also reverse heart disease by removing cholesterol from plaque.

6. HDLs deliver excess cholesterol to carriers that go back to the liver and convert it to bile acids, which are eliminated.

Liver

VLDLs

LDLs

HDLs

The Three Forms of Cholesterol

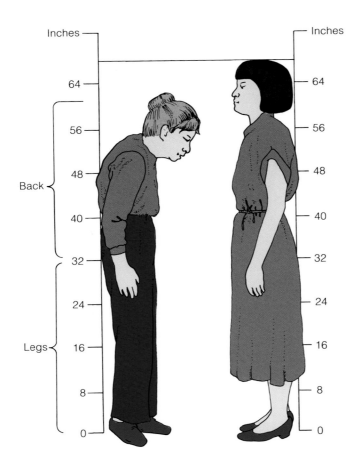

Osteoporosis: Reducing the Risk

After age 30, and especially after menopause in women, bone loss begins. Osteoporosis is an extreme form of the bone loss and mineralization that ordinarily occur with age. As bones become more brittle, fractures in the wrist, spine, and hip become more likely. Back pain, a bent spine, and loss of height also occur.

In fact, osteoporosis can first be detected by a loss of height. A decrease of more than one inch from the baseline height at age twenty is a sign that significant bone loss is taking place. The likelihood of osteoporosis can be minimized by starting as a young adult to maintain a good calcium intake, to engage in weight-bearing exercise, and to get a moderate amount of sun (in order to manufacture vitamin D), as well as by restricting alcohol intake and not smoking. After menopause, women should consult a doctor about estrogen replacement therapy and calcium supplements.

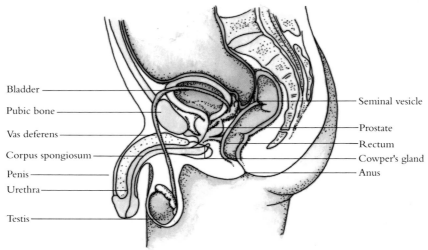

Male Sex Organs

Bladder

Pubic bone

Vas deferens

Corpus spongiosum

Penis

Urethra

Testis

Seminal vesicle

Prostate

Rectum

Cowper's gland

Anus

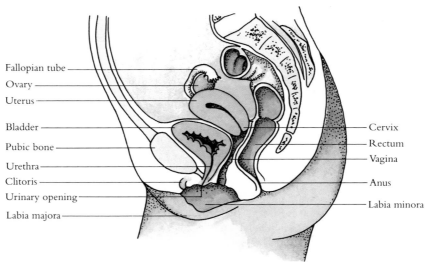

Female Sex Organs

Fallopian tube

Ovary

Uterus

Bladder

Pubic bone

Urethra

Clitoris

Urinary opening

Labia majora

Cervix

Rectum

Vagina

Anus

Labia minora

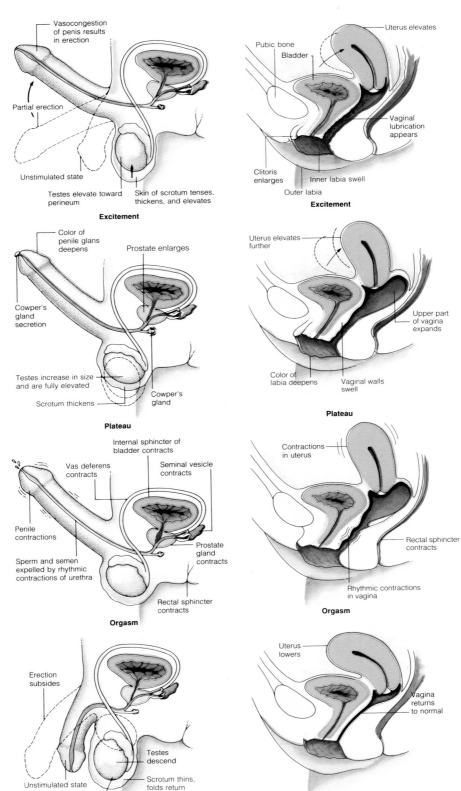

Vasocongestion of penis results in erection

Partial erection

Unstimulated state

Testes elevate toward perineum

Skin of scrotum tenses, thickens, and elevates

Excitement

Uterus elevates

Pubic bone

Bladder

Vaginal lubrication appears

Clitoris enlarges

Inner labia swell

Outer labia

Excitement

Color of penile glans deepens

Prostate enlarges

Cowper's gland secretion

Testes increase in size and are fully elevated

Cowper's gland

Scrotum thickens

Plateau

Uterus elevates further

Upper part of vagina expands

Color of labia deepens

Vaginal walls swell

Plateau

Internal sphincter of bladder contracts

Vas deferens contracts

Seminal vesicle contracts

Penile contractions

Sperm and semen expelled by rhythmic contractions of urethra

Prostate gland contracts

Rectal sphincter contracts

Orgasm

Contractions in uterus

Rectal sphincter contracts

Rhythmic contractions in vagina

Orgasm

Erection subsides

Testes descend

Unstimulated state

Scrotum thins, folds return

Loss of testicular congestion

Resolution

Uterus lowers

Vagina returns to normal

Resolution

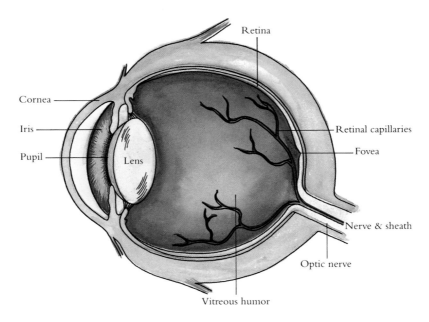

Major Structures of the Eye

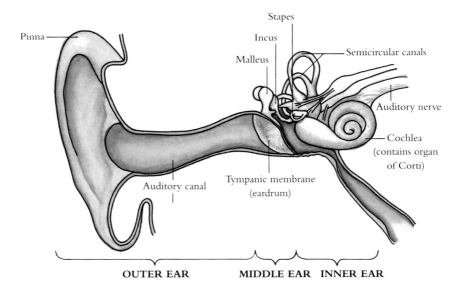

OUTER EAR   **MIDDLE EAR**   **INNER EAR**

Major Structures of the Ear

Autonomic nervous system The part of the nervous system that supplies smooth muscles in the internal organs, the cardiac muscle, and glandular tissues with nerves and governs involuntary action.

Autonomous mother Woman who views her children as individuals, and who is rewarded by the autonomy and independence of her children.

Autonomous thought The ability to see one's own role in the creation of truth and the construction of reality.

Autonomy One of Heath's five dimensions of maturity; with stability, allows an individual to think independently of the particulars of a situation and frees cognitive processes from emotional bias.

Axiom A statement regarded as a self-evident truth.

Basal metabolic rate The rate at which energy is used by an organism at rest.

Baseline data Information about the frequency or intensity of behavior prior to experimental intervention in a behavioral analysis design.

Bereavement The state of having lost a significant relationship, usually through death.

Bereavement overload The state of having lost a number of close friends or relatives during a short period.

Biological death The cessation of all physical signs of life, including heartbeat, respiration, and reflexes.

Biological renewal A type of meaning attributed to the role of grandparent; refers to perpetuation of the family.

Birren hypothesis The idea, advanced by James Birren, that all neural activity slows with age.

Brain death One of several definitions of biological death; involves the measurement of activity in the neocortex and brain stem.

Cardiac output The quantity of blood ejected each minute by one of the ventricles of the heart.

Career Any organized path taken by an individual across space and time; consistent involvement in any role over time.

Cataract Opacity in the lens of the eye.

Childhood creativity Creativity that exhibits precociousness and may be original or programmatic, but is not generative; that is, it does not represent a significant social contribution.

Chronic brain syndrome An irreversible organic brain syndrome from which full recovery is not possible, as in senile psychosis and the deterioration associated with cerebral arteriosclerosis; affects emotion and social and cognitive behavior.

Classical conditioning The pairing of a neutral stimulus and a stimulus known to evoke a reflexive response until the neutral stimulus evokes the response when presented alone; association through temporal contiguity.

Climacteric A period or point in human life during which some great change in health or constitution takes place, as at menopause.

Clinical threshold The point at which the symptoms of a disease appear or are diagnosable.

Cognition Internal mental activity, including knowledge, consciousness, thinking, imagining, and dreaming.

Cognitive generativity Development that occurs when an individual actively recombines experience with logic, memory, and imagination.

Cognitive investment The value an individual places on intellectual matters; breadth of interests, fluency, and introspection.

Cohabitation   Living together as husband and wife without being legally married; common-law marriage.

Cohort   A group of people all born during the same period of time.

Cohort difference   A difference between people of different age groups and attributable to the different social and cultural experiences or other environmental conditions associated with those particular age groups.

Collagen   A protein that makes up about one third of the protein in the human body.

Collagen theory   The hypothesis that biological aging is primarily attributable to the progressive cross-linking of large protein molecules, particularly collagen, that make up the tissues of the body.

Collective unconscious   Jung's term for a repository of memories from the entire human history of experience.

Comarital sex   Extramarital sexual activity under a consensual arrangement.

Companionate love   Intimacy plus commitment without strong physical attraction.

Companionship marriage   A marriage in which the relationship between husband and wife is of paramount concern to the partners and serves as a primary source of marital satisfaction.

Competence   The total range of biological, sensorimotor, and cognitive abilities one can bring to bear in adapting to the environment.

Complementarity hypothesis   The notion that individuals who choose each other as mates are similar in most physical, intellectual, and psychological traits.

Concept learning   Learning which demonstrates that ability to define an instance of a class of objects and rules for the discrimination of members of that class.

Conditioning   A process by which response frequency is altered by association with external environmental events, as in classical or operant conditioning.

Conflict-habituated marriage   A subtype of institutional marriage; characterized by constant arguments, bickering, and nagging; discord is seen not as a basis for ending the relationship, but as normal communication.

Congregation   The requirement that people in institutions do things at the same time and place.

Conscientiousness   A personality trait that reflects organization, scrupulousness, persistence, and achievement motivation.

Consolidation   The strengthening or securing of useful knowledge gained in childhood; takes place during the development of formal operations in adolescence or young adulthood.

Constraint   Degree to which activity must be done in a particular way, at a particular time with regard to speed, time, etc.

Constraint seeking   A problem-solving strategy in which each question is designed to eliminate the greatest number of alternative solutions.

Consummate love   Love in which passion, intimacy, and commitment are all present.

Content-free ability   An intellectual capacity or cognitive operation that can be applied to various subjects.

Contrasexual transition   The leveling of sex-role distinctions that is believed to occur during midlife and later, as men exhibit a tendency toward passive mastery and women show more active, aggressive forms of mastery.

Control   The degree of autonomy permitted in institutional settings. Also refers to the number of attempts partners in a relationship make at influencing each other.

Control beliefs   Beliefs concerning the degree to which one has control over or is able to make successful decisions concerning the important events of the life cycle.

Control center   An environmental arrangement that permits an individual with limited mobility to make maximum use of a constricted space for information gathering, stimulus variety, and social integration.

Convoy   The network of social support an individual has over the life span.

Corticosteroids   A powerful group of hormones produced by the adrenals. Levels of corticosteroids appear to increase in bereavement.

Coupled mother   Woman who experiences feeling special and irreplaceable as the main reward of motherhood.

Cross-linking theory   The hypothesis that biological aging is primarily a product of the loss of elasticity and flexibility in tissues; this loss results from the linking of large molecules, such as collagen, or from mutations that occur when DNA or RNA become cross-linked.

Cross-sectional design   A research format that includes the observation of subjects from two or more cohorts as representatives of as many different age groups; observations are made at one and only one time of measurement.

Culture   A set of assumptions, beliefs, attitudes, and ways of doing things that are unique to a group, as in organizational culture.

Crystallization   One of five proposed stages of vocational development postulated by Super; characterized by the firm establishment of one's ideas about the type of work one desires to do.

Crystallized intelligence   Mechanical and social knowledge, spatial reasoning and visualization, accuracy of perceptual and motor performance, vocabulary, and information skills; thought to increase with age.

Dark adaptation   The gradual increase in visual sensitivity that occurs under conditions of low illumination.

Deathbed scene   The scenario one imagines will accompany one's own death.

Death clock   A hypothetical genetic mechanism or program that controls the number of divisions of the labile cells and thus ensures that tissues will eventually die.

Death education   A movement in hospitals, universities, and the public schools to teach people how to deal with death in a more direct, less stylized way.

Death system   The social and physical network by which the relationship between a society and death or mortality is mediated and expressed.

Defensive adapters   Those elderly persons who tend to cope with the problems of later life by rationalizing and appear to be haunted by doubt.

Demand quality   The potential of the physical setting for evoking behavior.

Density of ties   The number of social ties a person maintains and their potential for interconnectedness.

Despair   The inability to accept one's own life, fate, and death, accompanied, according to Erikson, by regret, frustration, and discouragement.

Desynchronization   Change from synchronous or harmonious relationship between parts or processes to relationships not in harmony; unaligned.

Development   Change in the organization of behavior from simple to more complex forms, from small to large repertoires of behavior, from fixed ways of responding to demands and needs to strategic choice from a large repertoire of behavior. Orderly changes presumed to be evidenced by individuals as they progress in time toward maturity and through adult phases toward old age.

Developmentalists   A group of theorists who suggest that vocational choices are determined by one's early experiences.

Developmental task   A prescription, obligation, or responsibility thought to contribute to healthy, satisfactory growth in a particular society.

Devitalized marriage   A subtype of institutional marriage in which the partners are congenial but are bored or disenchanted with their relationship.

Dialectical paradigm   A general set of assumptions about human nature and developmental change; represents the organism and the world around it as existing in a state of continuous change.

Dialectical thinking   A final stage of adult cognition that builds on formal operations and allows one to analyze competing systems.

Dichotic listening   A memory task involving the recall of a short series of digits presented to one ear when a different series of digits is presented simultaneously to the other ear.

Differential approach   A mode of developmental study devoted to

discovery of predictable relationships through research that proceeds from a framework consisting of assumptions common to several theories.

Disdain   The opposite of wisdom; a reaction to feeling increasingly finished, confused, helpless.

Disenchantment   Third of Atchley's six-stage model of retirement. In this stage one learns to restructure one's time in a constructive manner.

Disengagement theory   A theory positing a process of mutual withdrawal between older people and society. Thought to begin in middle age, disengagement has been described as successful adjustment to growing old.

Disjunctive response time   Time required to respond to a complex stimulus defined by the presence of one element and the absence of another.

Disorganized personalities   Those elderly persons who exhibit tangential thinking and often appear immobilized by the problems of later life.

Distal behaviors   Attachment behaviors that do not require contact, such as eye contact or verbal behavior.

Distress   Stress caused by events ordinarily evaluated as negative such as the loss of a job or a divorce.

Distribution   An objective property of an event, referring to whether the event is experienced by many people, whether it is age-related, and whether it is likely to occur in the life of a particular person.

Divergent thinking   The intellectual process that allows an individual to generate alternative correct or possible solutions to a problem.

Dogmatism   Resistance to change, particularly in one's ideas or opinions.

Double jeopardy   The hypothesis that the gap between elderly members of minority groups and whites should increase with age as racial discrimination is compounded by age discrimination.

Dual-process model   The hypothesis that different classes of abilities show different courses of development over the life span. The pragmatic processes of intelligence are said to improve while the mechanics of intelligence decline.

Dual-track women   Women equally committed to work and family in a study by Janet Stroud.

Durable Power of Attorney   An instrument that gives another person the power to make decisions for oneself should one be unable to do so.

Dying career   The progression of statuses that emerge in a more or less orderly fashion in the course of acknowledging and coping with one's own personal death.

Early articulators   Women who consider child-freeness as a characteristic of the self rather than a product of a particular relationship or life style.

Ecological validity   Validity that is determined by examining experimenter effects, subject effects, situational effects, and the more general effect of the social and cultural environment on a piece of research.

Ecology   The science of plants and animals as they are related to their environment.

Elastin   Large protein molecules that make up the elastic fibers of the body; similar to collagen but more flexible.

Elderspeak   A pattern of speech that places stress at locations optimal for linguistic processing.

Electroencephalograph   An instrument designed to measure the wavelike activity of the brain.

Elementarism   The philosophical position that human behavior can be productively analyzed and understood in terms of its basic elements.

Embeddedness   Lack of awareness of the context of one's own thoughts, beliefs, values, or feelings.

Empty love   A relationship in which mutual emotional involvement and physical attraction have been lost.

Empty-nest syndrome   A group of symptoms thought to be associated with launching children from the home; most often described in terms of depression or anxiety.

Encoding   Conversion of information from the environment to the memory systems or to the kind of symbolization useful in the memory process.

Engagement   Maintenance or increase of activity level and involvement in social roles during later adulthood.

Environmental press   The degree of demand for competent behavior produced by various environmental conditions.

Epigenetic principle   Erikson's statement that anything that grows has an internal ground plan that determines the special times or critical periods during which specific developments can occur.

Equal-partner relationship   Couples who hold less conventional ideologies and share in decision making.

Equitable relationship   A relationship characterized by equal autonomy for both persons and by fairness.

Equity theory   A theory which proposes that successful intimate relationships are based on equality of the outcome for both partners, where outcome is equal to the sum of a person's assets minus the sum of his or her liabilities.

Eros   Romantic love based around the component of sexual desire.

Error catastrophe   A critical accumulation of cellular errors; the result of mutation that is thought to curtail functioning enough to cause the death of the organism.

Ethnic endogamy   Marriage within one's own racial and ethnic group.

Ethnocentrism   The tendency to see the behaviors that are valued in one's own culture as universally optimal or mature.

Eustress   Stress caused by events ordinarily evaluated as positive such as childbirth or marriage.

Event-related potential   Specific brain activity correlated with the onset of a stimulus.

Excitation   First stage of the human sexual response as defined by Masters and Johnson. This stage is characterized by vasocongestion and increased myotonia.

Executive processes   Subjective aspects of experience, such as self-awareness, perception of environmental quality, perception of time, and mode of dealing with the environment.

Existentialists   Psychologists who argue that life in modern times is experienced by people as meaningless and insignificant leading them to deny large parts of their experience, including the inevitability of personal death.

Experiential change   Personality change characterized by an increase or decrease in the strength of a particular trait from one time of measurement to another, and by changes in the rank ordering of individuals tested on that trait.

Experimental mortality   The phenomenon of dropout, or refusal of subjects to continue to participate in a longitudinal development research study.

Expiratory reserve   The amount of air one can still exhale after a normal breath.

Explicit memory   Intentional memory—memory that occurs when one attempts to remember material as it is presented.

Exploration   First stage of career development during which one learns about the fit between one's abilities and preferences and the available career opportunities.

Expressive activity   Behavior that offers immediate gratification or satisfaction; leisure.

External career path   The stages encountered in the pursuit of a particular occupation, such as apprentice, journeyman, master.

External validity   The degree to which conclusions drawn from data about one sample can be generalized to other samples with similar characteristics.

Extroversion   A personality trait reflected in high scores on tests measuring warmth of personality, assertiveness, gregariousness, excitement-seeking, activity, and positive emotions.

Family life cycle   A proposed division of married life into eight stages; includes beginning families, childbearing families, families with preschool children, families with school-age children, families with teenagers, families as launching centers, families in the middle years, and aging families.

Fatuous love   Passion and commitment without intimacy.

Filial maturity   The ability to view one's parent as a real and separate person—acknowledging that the parent was formed by a social history that took place before as well as after one's own birth, relinquishing adolescent rebellion, and allowing the parent to develop some dependence on oneself.

Fluid intelligence   Innate general cognitive capacity reflected in performance on tests that require relational thinking (such as memory span and block design); believed to peak in late adolescence or early adulthood.

Formal operations   The final stage of cognitive development, as described by Piaget, in which the individual is able to think abstractly and systematically about complex propositions and problems.

Free radicals   Molecules produced during normal metabolism that exhibit fewer or greater than the usual number of electrons.

Functional mental disorder   A psychiatric disorder or set of symptoms that have no apparent physiological basis.

Galvanic skin response   A physiological measure of palmar sweat associated with arousal.

Gender identity   Psychological identification of the self-concept as either masculine or feminine.

General adaptation syndrome   The totality of the physiological changes that accompany stress.

Generational stake   The tendency of the younger generation to establish a unique identity vs. the desire of the older generation to maintain generational continuity.

Generativity   The positive pole of the crisis of middle age as proposed by Erikson; a deep concern for the establishment and nurturance of the next generation; direction of one's creativity and energy in a way that will produce a lasting accomplishment.

Genetic imperative   A theoretical construct suggesting that parenthood constitutes a social emergency and sharpens the sex-role distinctions of the parents.

Genotypic continuity   Changes in the personality that are predictable but are not necessarily characterized by the persistence of particular traits.

Gerontology   The study of aging and the problems of the aged.

Global personality trait   A general characteristic, such as agreeableness, that may be defined but not broken into subfactors by personality tests.

Grief   Emotional suffering caused by bereavement or deprivation; characterized by sadness, anger, depression, and often by physical symptoms such as nausea.

Grief work   The anger and self-recrimination that accompany bereavement.

Ground substance   The biological matter that surrounds the cells of the skin.

Habituation   Development that is largely dependent on external environmental conditions, such as the acquisition of social mores.

Hawthorne effect   The effect of observation or inclusion alone on the behavior of participants in a research study. *See also* Placebo effect.

Hierarchical stage   A stage, as in Piaget's theory, that is built on and includes the elements of previous stages.

History-graded influences   The general social and historical background of a particular group of people born into a culture at the same time.

Holism   The philosophical position that the organism can be understood only as an entity that is greater than the sum of its parts and cannot be analyzed as a series of simple events.

Homogamy   The tendency of individuals to marry those of similar social and educational backgrounds, intellectual and personality characteristics, physical attributes, and value structures.

Honeymoon   Second of six stages of retirement proposed by Atchley. In this stage, one plays out the fantasies of the preretirement period.

Hospice   A facility for the dying patient; offers medical services necessary to allay pain or restore function, but focuses on emotional care of the patient and his or her family.

Hypertrophy   Growth beyond normal size.

Immune theory   The hypothesis that biological aging is primarily attributable to detrimental changes in the autoimmune system that diminish its ability to identify foreign material.

Implementation   One proposed stage of vocational development; usually occurs between the ages of eighteen and twenty-one; includes training for and entry into one's first job.

Implicit memory   Memory that occurs without any conscious attempt to remember.

Independents   Women equally committed to work and family in a study by Florine Livson. Also used by Fitzpatrick to refer to married women and men who believe in sharing both household and decision-making responsibilities.

Individualized grandmother   A grandmother who is concerned primarily about deriving emotional satisfaction from her grandchildren, rather than about seeing that they are properly reared.

Infatuation   Love at first sight. May become an obsession with an unrealistic ideal of the partner.

Infidelity   Clandestine adultery as opposed to consensual extramartial sex.

Information processing   The manner in which people store and retrieve ideas.

Inspection interval   In paired associate learning, the period during which both members of a pair are presented together for study.

Inspiratory reserve   The difference between the amount of air one takes in in a normal breath and maximum capacity.

Institutional discrimination   Factors in the nature of work and its relationship to family or society that prevent disadvantaged groups from gaining employment and advancement.

Institutional marriage   A marriage in which the partners derive their major satisfactions from relationships and activities outside of the husband-wife relationship (for example, from parenting or from community activities).

Institutional racism   Indirect discrimination on the basis of race, such as inadequate education and training rather than denial of employment.

Instrumental activity   Behavior that is rewarded by future gratification, such as work for pay, rather than by immediate gratification intrinsic to the activity.

Instrumental marriage   A marriage relationship based on generally accepted role distinctions and cultural standards for men and women.

Integration   One of Heath's five dimensions of maturity; an integrated person has a coherent system of values, motives, personality traits, and beliefs that permit the organization of life events in a meaningful way.

Integrity   The central achievement of Erikson's final stage; the accrued sense of order and meaning that allows one to see one's own life as meaningful and as a contribution to the human world.

Intelligence   The ability to learn or to reason and solve problems; the potential or innate ability of the individual to adapt.

Intelligence quotient   The score one receives on a traditional test of intelligence (such as the Stanford-Binet or the Wechsler Adult Intelligence Scale); used as a measure of general ability to learn.

Intentional behavior   Self-planned behavior under personal control that can be explained in terms of beliefs, goals, and opportunities.

Interactional factors   Human relationships and social processes that characterize a job.

Interiority   Decreasing attachment to persons and objects in the external world.

Internal career path   A set of individual expectations and perceptions about one's career; may include transitions through several external career paths.

Internal validity   The degree to which a particular piece of research or a general research format allows one to draw unambiguous conclusions about the relationships observed in the data obtained.

Interpretive science   Research methods such as interview, analysis of literary texts, and participant observation, aimed at understanding human experience rather than predicting behavior.

Intersystemic thought   The ability to understand several systems of relationships and how each generates its own version of the truth.

Intervention   Intrusion of the experimenter into the research design in order to manipulate or control some aspect of the environment and so produce an observable change in a developmental process.

Intervention research   Any research format based on the observation of phenomena resulting from manipulation of the experimental environment by the researcher.

Intimacy   The quality of closeness and rapport found in relationships characterized by self-disclosure, mutuality, similarity, and compatibility.

Intrasystemic thought   The ability to understand the relationships within a closed, finite system.

Involution   The reversal of some aspects of biological development as when the uterus and other sex organs return to normal size and condition after pregnancy or when changes occur in the genital tract and reproductive organs during climacteric.

Irreversible decrement   A general decline or degeneration of biological, emotional, and social capacities; characteristic of development in later life as pictured by the cultural stereotype.

Junior-partner relationship   Couples in which one of the partners has some decision-making power, but less than a fully equal share.

Kin keepers   Family members, usually women, responsible for maintaining family contact, monitoring family needs and offering help when necessary.

Learning   The acquisition of new information, skills, or rules.

Leisure ethic   A set of attitudes and beliefs about the value of leisure as a role in adult life.

Life course   The years assigned important social and personal meaning by the society.

Life cycle   The series of events that are associated with human development over generations as well as within individual lives.

Life review   The tendency to review one's life course in old age; reminiscence in later life.

Life span   The actual chronological length of human life as in average life span.

Lifestyle   The environmental characteristics, social choice of personal and group relationships, degree of involvement in leisure and work, and investment in various roles that typify an individual's life.

Lifetime family   The nuclear family, including two generations only.

Lightening   An event in the final month of pregnancy, when the fetus drops, or settles, down into the pelvic area.

Limerance   The very intense phase of romantic love usually called "falling in love."

Lineage family   The extended family, including the older, middle, and younger generations (married or unmarried); may be more than three generations.

Longitudinal design   A research format that involves the observation of one cohort over two or more times of measurement (the same individuals are observed repeatedly).

Long-term memory   The process by which, or the stores into which, information is transferred as it exceeds one's immediate capacity for retention; believed to be of infinite capacity and of infinite duration.

Ludis   Game-playing love.

Maintenance   Career stage at midlife in which one is expected to achieve maximum productivity and to be privy to organizational secrets; also called plateau.

Mania   Possessive love.

Matrix   An array of elements arranged in rows and columns.

Measurement   Appraisal of a phenomenon through the application of tests, observation of performance, description of natural behavior, or any other objective means.

Mechanical model   A set of assumptions about human nature and developmental change; represents the organism as if it were a machine; suggests that behavior can be analyzed and understood as a series of simple events or elements.

Mechanical presbycusis   The loss of high frequency hearing due to the decreased flexibility of the basal membrane.

Mechanics of intelligence   The basic tasks required for logical thought, including logical reasoning and classification.

Mediator   An unobservable, internal process or response that influences external behavior by evoking related prior experience or stimulation.

Memory   The several processes by which, or the stores in which, information from current experience is filed and retrieved later; each process has different characteristics, capacities, and functions.

Metabolic presbycusis   The loss of pure tone hearing due to atrophy of the stria vasculis.

Metamemory   The knowledge a person possesses about memory processes or a person's perception of his or her own memory function.

Metamorphosis   Change in vocational status, from novice to probationary member; sometimes acknowledged by the ritual of a new title or position.

Meta-needs   According to Maslow, those needs associated with self-actualization including the need for self-sufficiency, the need to be creative, to know the truth, to discover beauty, etc.

Methodology   The principles and strategies involved in the pursuit of knowledge about any scientific question or problem.

Midlife transition   A period of turmoil and reassessment identified by the clinical literature and thought to occur between ages thirty-nine and forty-three.

Mnemonics   A technique for improving the memory through the use of codes to help one store and recall information.

Model   A general set of assumptions about, and definitions of, the nature of a phenomenon—specifically, human nature and human development—from which theories and hypotheses proceed.

Motor unit   A single motor neuron and all the fibers it innervates.

Multiple orgasm   Two or more orgasms during a single episode of sexual activity, as defined by contractions of the vaginal musculature.

Mutuality   A proposed final stage in the development of friendships; includes shared knowledge of each other, a sense of commitment, and behavior regulated by private rather than general social norms.

Myotonia   Involuntary muscular contraction that builds throughout sexual arousal to the point of orgasm.

Nature/nurture controversy   Debate among developmentalists over how much of human behavior is determined by external, environmental forces and how much by internal, maturational forces.

Near point of vision   The nearest point at which an object can be seen clearly without a blur.

Nephron unit   One of many tiny filters in the kidney that constitute the central mechanisms by which waste is removed from the bloodstream.

Neural noise   Random activity of neurons in the cortex; assumed to increase in frequency with age and believed to make it more difficult to detect sensory signals from the external environment.

Neural presbycusis   The hearing loss that affects speech discrimination and is thought to be caused by neural losses.

Neuroticism   A personality trait that is reflected in high scores on tests of anxiety, depression, self-consciousness, vulnerability, impulsiveness, and hostility.

Nonnormative influences   Environmental and biological events that do not occur to everyone or cannot be specified as most likely to occur at a particular phase of life.

Normative age-graded influences   The biological and environmental events that are strongly associated with chronological age.

Normative history-graded influences   Social and historical events affecting particular groups of people born into a culture at the same time.

Object relations   A theory of psychic development based on the work of Melanie Klein and Freud that focuses on how people relate to the significant people, objects, and ideas they encounter over the life course.

Occupation   The principal business of one's life; vocation.

Off-time   Experiencing the normal events of the life course at an atypical time, as by a late marriage or early retirement.

Open-mindedness   A personality trait associated with high scores on tests that tap attitudes such as openness to new ideas and feelings, interest in the aesthetic features of experience, and willingness to explore alternative values and behavior.

Organic brain syndrome   Dementia caused by the physical damage of the brain tissue.

Organismic model   A set of assumptions about human nature; presents the organism as active, organic, and holistic, and presents human development as structural and emergent.

Organizational culture   A set of important assumptions (often unstated) members of a community share.

Organizational policy   Company benefits such as flextime, fringe benefits, job security, etc.

Orgasm   Rhythmic contractions of the pelvic musculature that produce intense physical sensations.

Osteoarthritis   Inflammation of the joints, due to changes in bone and cartilage.

Osteoporosis   A disease in which material is lost from the bones, leaving them brittle and vulnerable to fracture.

Overarousal hypothesis   The proposal that older people perform poorly on tests of learning because they experience greater excitement of the autonomic nervous system under conditions of fast pacing than do the young.

Paired associates   Two nonsense syllables used in a verbal learning experiment. Subjects must learn to call out one in response to hearing or seeing the other.

Paradigm   An untestable set of assumptions about the nature of a phenomenon, such as the nature of human development.

Paraphrenia   Functional syndrome of the elderly characterized by paranoid ideation and hallucinations.

Parental imperative   The genetic emergency believed to occur at the birth of the first child and to sharpen sex-role distinctions between father and mother.

Passive-congenial marriage   A type of institutional marriage; described as amicable but characterized by a lack of emotional involvement between the partners.

Passive mastery   The tendency to cope with environmental change, or with dissatisfaction with the environment, by accommodating to circumstances rather than by attempting to alter external events.

Path analysis   A statistical technique that allows researchers to determine which factors analyzed in a multiple regression act through other factors included in that regression.

Perception   Interpretation of sensory stimulation in terms of prior experience, environmental demands, or other personal and situational factors.

Perceptual masking   The presentation of a visual figure followed, after a short interval, by another stimulus known to erase the perception of the first figure.

Perceptual regression hypothesis   The notion that elderly people perform more like adolescents than do young or middle-aged adults in response to visual illusions, embedded figures, and other such complex stimuli.

Personal fable   The adolescent belief that one is special and what happens to others will not happen to the self.

Personal unconscious   Jung's term of primitive thoughts, feelings, and ideas from one's own personal history.

Person-environment congruence
The match between the therapeutic and prosthetic needs of the person and what is offered by the environment; the match between demand quality and competence.

Phenotypic persistence   Stability of personality traits or dispositions over the life course.

Physical ontogeny   Development that is largely dependent on biological regulation, such as physical growth.

Placebo effect   The improvement of subject performance or health or function during participation in an experiment when the subject does not, in fact, receive the experimental treatment.

Plaque   Abnormal formation on the wall of a blood vessel where fat, cholesterol, and other wastes build up, eventually forming an obstruction to normal circulation of the blood.

Plastic   Capable of being modeled or changed; mutable.

Plateau   State of extremely high sexual arousal in both men and women. Also refers to the stage of maximum productivity entered during middle age (*see* Maintenance).

Portent of embarrassment   The fear of appearing foolish due to poor performance at a new activity.

Postponers   Those who put off the decision to have children again and again, finally realizing that a decision has been made.

Postvention   A program of therapeutic intervention for the bereaved, begun as soon as an individual experiences a loss or offered to those who experience very intense or prolonged grief.

Practice effect   Changes in subject behavior produced by repeated exposure to a test or an experimental task.

Pragma   A type of love in which the lover chooses a mate based on practical compatibility, thereby making the "correct" match.

Pragmatics of intelligence   The application of knowledge or social wisdom.

Preretirement   First of six stages of retirement proposed by Atchley. In this stage, short timers in the work force entertain fantasies about retirement.

Presbycusis   Progressive loss of hearing for high frequency tones; associated with degenerative changes in the auditory system.

Primary memory   *See* Long-term memory.

Principle of justice   The idea that what is morally best is respect for individual rights and dignity.

Pronatalist attitude   The beliefs and emotional responses underlying the position that childbearing and child rearing are natural, basic, and necessary activities for all human adults.

Propinquity   Physical proximity.

Prosthetic environment   An environment that provides some form of permanent support for functioning; allows the individual to function more fully as long as the supports are present, but produces no permanent therapeutic effect.

Proximal behaviors   Attachment behaviors that involve contact.

Pseudodementia   A condition in which all the symptoms of senile dementia appear without any apparent brain damage.

Pseudo-developed   Male midlife personality type identified by Farrell and Rosenberg as denying the stress of the midlife transition and experiencing dissatisfaction and hopelessness.

Psychological death   The cessation of thought, feelings, and needs and the disappearance of the personality characteristics and abilities associated with a particular individual.

Psychomotor skill   An ability that requires dexterity and agility and is believed to improve with practice.

Punitive-disenchanted   Male midlife personality type identified by Farrell and Rosenberg as denying crisis and functioning in a bigoted, authoritarian way.

Pure job   Degree to which an activity is characterized by constraint and motivated by external rewards.

Pure leisure   Degree to which an activity provides freedom and intrinsic motivation.

Pure work   Activity that is constrained—that is, it must be done in a particular way, at a particular time or speed—but that also offers intrinsic value, thereby affording enjoyment and/or satisfaction to the worker.

Qualitative approach   The study of intelligence or other aspects of human development that assumes the emergence of stages, as in the work of Piaget, Commons, or Labouvie-Vief.

Quantitative approach   The study of intelligence or other aspects of human development that assumes that the existence of a variety of factors, abilities, or traits accounts for people's performances on standardized tests.

Quasi-experimental   Research designs in which the assignment of subjects to conditions cannot be controlled, such as the assignment of subjects to age groups.

Racial mortality crossover   Data suggesting that older blacks live longer than older whites.

Reaction time   The amount of time an individual requires to respond to a stimulus that signals a response.

Reality shock   The experience of disparity between the conception of an occupation created by education or by anticipatory socialization and the reality of that occupation.

Reciprocity   The Kantian Principle; the definition of optimal behavior as behavior that never involves the use of another person to gain one's own ends.

Refractory period   The period after a response when an individual cannot be rearoused (for example, the period following ejaculation in the male sexual response).

Rehearsal   A form of processing that transfers information from short-term memory to long-term memory; involves repetition of information in short-term stores.

Rejectors   Women who articulate early that they do not want children because they dislike them and are committed to a childless lifestyle.

Reliability   The extent to which a subject's response to an item on a test, or performance on an experimental task, is stable from one time of measurement to another.

Reminiscence   Review of one's past life during old age; a part of the life review process.

Reorientation   Fourth of six stages of retirement proposed by Atchley. In this stage, one becomes realistically involved with the world.

Residential propinquity   Physical closeness of one's dwelling to that of another individual.

Retirement   A period late in life when an individual does not hold a full-time, year-round job and receives at least part of his or her income from Social Security or a pension program.

Rheumatoid arthritis   Inflammation of the joints caused by immunological dysfunction; develops early in life and becomes progressively worse.

Role compatibility   The final phase in mating, according to Murstein, when a couple learns if their perceptions of the wife and husband roles are compatible.

Role cycling   The timing of movement through various roles such as spouse, parent, and worker that is experienced by people in families.

Role involution   The leveling of sex-role distinctions that is believed to occur during middle and later life, as men exhibit a tendency toward passive mastery and women display more aggressive, active forms of mastery.

Role overload   Conflict between the demands and expectations of two or more roles; characteristic of particular life styles (for example, the conflict between the mother/wife role and the career expectations of a woman in a dual-career marriage).

Role reversal   The taking on of some of the obligations and responsibilities of a parent by adult children as their parents become very elderly.

Romantic love   A relationship characterized by emotional and physical attraction but not necessarily commitment.

Secondary memory   *See* Long-term memory.

Segregation   The degree to which people in institutions are isolated from the outside world.

Selective attention   The ability to filter out irrelevant information and focus on relevant information from the environment.

Self   A unifying force in personality, according to Jung, responsible for integration of conflicting aspects.

Self-actualization   According to Maslow, the degree to which the meta-needs are fulfilled. According to Jung, the degree to which one is able to tolerate and/or transcend conflict even within the self.

Self-disclosure   Revelation of personal information; considered essential to the development of an intimate relationship.

Self-efficacy   The feeling that one can successfully make decisions about important life choices.

Self-initiating widows   Widows who are able to maintain aspects of old roles that are appropriate to their new status, who take over, reassign, or give up the function of their husbands.

Self-produced feedback   Any sensory, cognitive, or emotional stimulation following self-initiated behavior.

Senescence   Changes that accompany the aging process.

Senile dementia   A chronic, irreversible brain syndrome associated with the dissolution of the brain cells.

Senile osteoporosis   Pathological or extreme porousness of the bones of an elderly individual.

Senility   The characteristics associated with old age, especially mental and physical infirmities.

Sensation   Awareness of simple stimuli in the environment.

Sensory memory   The first stage in a three-process model of memory, in which information is registered autonomatically as an exact copy of the environment.

Sensory presbycusis   The loss of hearing for high pitched tones caused by atrophy of hair cells in the inner ear.

Sensual transcendence   Cognitive, emotional, or physical activity of great intensity; provides high levels of involvement and gratification of the senses; peak experience.

Separates   Couples who hold conventional sex role ideologies but report little conflict because they experience low levels of interdependence.

Sequential design   A format for developmental research; uses two or more simple cross-sections or longitudinal studies in one research project.

Shadow   Embodiment of animal instincts posited by Jung and thought to be a part of the collective unconscious.

Short-term memory   The second stage in a three-process model of memory; in this stage information exists as bits or single items, and memory is characterized by limited capacity and the rapid displacement of old information by new data from the sensory register.

Similarity hypothesis   The proposal that mate selection proceeds on the basis of similarity of values and attributes, including physical attractiveness, intelligence, and beliefs about role behaviors and lifestyle.

Simple response time   The time it takes to respond to the onset or offset of a simple stimulus used to signal the beginning of a response.

Social clock   The culturally accepted ordering and scheduling of social and environmental events; provides information about whether an individual's life is meeting the expectations of society.

Social death   Cessation of institutional and cultural processes surrounding the life and death of an individual (for example, mourning and bereavement).

Social exchange theory   Interpretation of close relationships by social-learning theorists positing that intimacy is the product of a reward-cost history in the interaction between two people.

Social gerontology   The study of the influence of social and environmental

events and processes on the life course in adulthood.

Social intelligence   The abilities and skills that are predictive of success and adaptation.

Socialization   The process of learning skills, attitudes, and values, as well as the cognitive and emotional patterns that relate people to their sociocultural settings.

Social-learning theory   The notion that human development proceeds through the association of environmental events or learning.

Social maturity   The ability to live comfortably with others, respond appropriately to stress, and depart from conventional norms when necessary or desirable.

Somatization   The expression of anxiety in terms of physical symptoms like headaches or indigestion.

Specification   A proposed stage of vocational choice; believed to occur between the ages of eighteen and twenty-one; characterized by development of an explicit vocational choice.

Speech discrimination   The ability to differentiate between different sounds in the language one hears.

Split dream   A term used to describe the phenomenon that women believe they can be successful in both family and occupational roles.

Stability   Fifth of six stages of retirement proposed by Atchley. In this stage, activities established during reorientation are carried on.

Stagnation   The negative pole of the developmental crisis of middle age as proposed by Erikson; characterized by impoverishment and self-indulgence.

Stenosis   The narrowing of the coronary artery.

Stepparent adoption   Legal adoption of a child by a stepparent.

Storge   The love of friends.

Striped muscle   A muscle that produces discrete, voluntary movements (such as lifting the leg or flexing the arm).

Structural analytic stage   A proposed final stage of cognitive development; believed to occur in adulthood and to follow from and build upon formal operations, enabling the individual to analyze relationships between whole systems and paradigms of thought.

Sublimation   The defensive redirection of anxiety into productive activities.

Substitution theory   The proposal that successful adaptation to retirement is based on the replacement of the work role with activities that provide similar kinds of gratification.

Symbolic grandmother   A grandmother who reports that the most important aspects of grandparenting involve doing what is morally right for the child and setting a good example.

Syndrome   A group of signs and symptoms that occur together and characterize a particular abnormality or disorder.

System   Any coherent set of relationships.

Systematic operations   The ability to understand systems of relations and to describe how these systems are alike or different from each other.

Termination   Last of six stages of retirement proposed by Atchley. In this stage, the role of retiree is lost, usually through disability.

Test-retest effect   Any change in subject behavior or performance produced by repeated exposure to an experimental test or measure; practice effect.

Thanatology   The study of death and dying.

Theme   The basic motivation for pursuit of an occupation at a particular point in one's career.

Theorem   An idea that is proposed as a demonstrable truth; often occurs as part of a general theory.

Theory   A principle or set of principles offered as an explanation for some phenomenon.

Therapeutic environment   Living arrangements that provide rich and varied opportunities for growth and development.

Threshold   The point at which sensory stimulation is intense enough to produce an effect that is psychologically noticeable.

Time compression   The speeding of natural processes that often is produced in the laboratory to facilitate experimental observation of some long-term developmental change.

Time-lag design   Observation of one age group over at least two different times of measurement.

Time of measurement   The moment in history when a set of observations is made in the course of a developmental research project.

Time perspective   The way an individual experiences the passage of time; the way an individual regards the past, present, and future.

Time-related change   Developmental change that occurs over the life course as a result of an individual's personal history and social, economic, and historical circumstances.

Timetable   A subjective deadline for evaluation of progress in one's occupational career, especially progress related to the theme one has developed for a particular stage of that career.

Total brain death   Cessation of function in the brain and the brain stem as defined by such criteria as the cessation of spontaneous breathing and movement and the presence of a flat electroencephalogram record.

Total marriage A subtype of companionship marriage, in which the marital couple share every area of their lives, including feelings, responsibilities, hobbies, thoughts, and dreams.

Traditionals Persons holding a more conventional set of beliefs or values, especially with regard to marriage and/or sex roles.

Transcendence The ability, according to Lowenthal and her associates, to expand one's behavioral repertoire when loss is encountered.

Transcendent generative Male personality type identified by Farrell and Rosenberg as experiencing no crisis of midlife yet exhibiting growth, self-confidence, and satisfaction.

Transformation A major change in the form, nature, or function of a thing so that it can be put to a use not originally intended.

Transudation Process whereby lubrication of the vaginal walls occurs, during the first stages of sexual arousal.

Triangular theory of love The hypothesis that love can be defined in terms of three basic forces: intimacy, passion, and decision/commitment.

Two-path career model The hypothesis that some workers prefer lower involvement in work, more extrinsic rewards, and a less stressful workload, whereas others enjoy high involvement, are internally motivated, and desire to participate in the decisions that affect the organization.

Unstable workers Women, in a study by Janet Stroud, who worked on and off during their married lives, but enjoy neither work nor marriage.

Utilitarian principle The idea that what is morally best is what maximizes human happiness.

Validity In experimentation, a term referring to how accurately research procedures measure what they are supposed to measure.

Value matching A phase in mate selection, according to Murstein, when a couple focuses on similarity of values.

Vasocongestion The flooding or congestion of an area with blood from the capillaries; occurs in many areas of the body during sexual arousal.

Verbal mediation An internal use of language that affects one's response to a particular stimulus (for example, the use of a rhyme or a system of key words to aid memory).

Vicarious achievement A perception of the grandparent role as one who values the possibility that grandchildren may be able to achieve goals preceding generations have not achieved.

Visual acuity The ability to see accurately small details in the visual field.

Visual mediation Use of imagery in a way that affects one's response to an external stimulus (for example, the generation or adoption of an image as a device to aid memory).

Vital capacity The sum of the excess capacity of the lungs, both for inspiration and for expiration, after a normal breath has been taken and expelled.

Vital marriage A subtype of companionship marriage; the marital couple participate in and share many common activities and areas of concern, such as social and family activities and financial management.

Wisdom Informed and detached concern with life itself in the face of death itself.

Working memory The ability to store recently presented material while continuing to process additional information.

References

Abbott, W. (1977). Work in the year 2001. *The Futurist,* February, 25–29.

Abramson, J., & Franklin, B. (1986). *Where they are now.* Garden City, NY: Doubleday.

Achenbach, T. (1978). *Research in developmental psychology: Concepts, strategies, methods.* New York: Free Press.

Achenbaum, W. A. (1985). Societal perceptions of the aging and the aged. In R. H. Binstock & E. Shanas (Eds.), *Handbook of aging and the social sciences* (2nd ed.). New York: Van Nostrand Reinhold.

Adams, M. (1971). The single woman in today's society: A reappraisal. *American Journal of Orthopsychiatry, 41,* 776–786.

A definition of irreversible coma: Report of the ad hoc committee of the Harvard School to Examine the Definition of Brain Death. (1968). *Journal of the American Medical Association, 205,* 337–340.

Adelson, J., Doehrman, M. J. (1980). The psychodynamic approach to adolescence. In J. Adelson (Ed.), *Handbook of the psychology of adolescence.* New York: Wiley.

Adler, W. (1974). An autoimmune theory of aging. In M. Rockstein (Ed.), *Proceedings of a symposium on the theoretical aspects of aging.* New York: Academic Press.

Ainsworth, L. & Vaune, A. (1982). Imaging and creativity: An integrating perspective. *Journal of Creative Behavior, 16,* 5–28.

Aizenberg, R., & Treas, J. (1985). The family in late life: Psychosocial and demographic considerations. In J. E. Birren & K. W. Schaie (Eds.), *Handbook of the psychology of aging* (2nd ed.). New York: Van Nostrand Reinhold.

Aldous, J. (1990). Family development and the life course: Two perspectives on family change. *Journal of Marriage and the Family, 51,* 571–581.

Alexander, C. N., & Langer, E. J. (Eds.). (1990). *Higher stages of human development: Perspectives on adult growth.* New York: Oxford University Press.

Alpert, J. L., & Richardson, M. S. (1980). Parenting. In L. W. Poon (Ed.), *Aging in the 1980s.* Washington, DC: American Psychological Association.

Anderson, B., Jr., & Palmore, E. (1974). Longitudinal evaluation of ocular functions. In E. Palmore (Ed.), *Normal aging II.* Durham, NC: Duke University Press.

Anderson, S., Russell C., & Schumm, W. (1983). Perceived marital quality and family life cycle categories: A further analysis. *Journal of Marriage and the Family,* 45, 127–138.

Antonucci, T. C. (1985). Personal characteristics, social support, and social behavior. In R. H. Binstock & E. Shanas (Eds.), *Handbook of aging and the social sciences* (2nd ed.). New York: Van Nostrand Reinhold.

Antonucci, T. C. (1990). Social supports and social relationships. In R. H. Binstock & K. K. George (Eds.), *Handbook of aging and the social sciences* (3rd ed.). New York: Academic Press.

Antonucci, T. C., & Akiyama, H. (1987). Social networks in adult life and a preliminary examination of the convoy model. *Journal of Gerontology, 42,* 519–527.

Arenberg, D. (1968). Concept problem-solving in young and old adults. *Journal of Gerontology, 23,* 279–282.

Arenberg, D. (1973). Cognition and aging: Verbal learning, memory, and problem-solving. In C. Eisdorfer & M. P. Lawton (Eds.), *The psychology of adult development and aging.* Washington, DC: American Psychological Association.

Arenberg, D. (1983). Memory and learning do decline late in life. In J. E. Birren et al. (Eds.), *Aging: A challenge to science and society* (Vol. 3). New York: Oxford.

Arenberg, D., & Robertson-Tchabo, E. A. (1977). Learning and aging. In J. E. Birren & K. W. Schaie (Eds.), *Handbook of the psychology of aging.* New York: Van Nostrand Reinhold.

Ariés, P. (1985). Thoughts on the history of homosexuality. In P. Ariés & A. Bejin (Eds.), *Western sexuality.* New York: Basil Blackwell.

Arlin, P. (1983). Adolescent and adult thought: A structural interpretation. In M. Commons & S. Benack (Eds.), *Post-formal operations.* New York: Praeger.

Armon, C. (1984a). Ideals of the good life and moral judgment: Ethical reasoning across the life span. In M. L. Commons, F. A. Richards, & C. Armon (Eds.), *Beyond formal operations, Vol. 1: Late adolescent and adult cognitive development.* New York: Praeger.

Armon, C. (1984b). *Ideals of the good life: A cross-sectional/longitudinal study of evaluative reasoning in children and adults.* Unpublished doctoral dissertation, Harvard Graduate School of Education, Cambridge, MA.

Armon, C. (1984c). Ideals of the good life and moral judgement: Evaluative reasoning in children and adults. *Moral Education Forum,* 9, 357–380.

Armon, C. (1988). The place of the good in a justice reasoning approach to moral education. *Journal of Moral Education,* 17, 220–229.

Armon, C. (1989). Individuality and autonomy in adult ethical reasoning. In M. L. Commons, J. D. Sinnott, F. A.

Richards, & C. Armon (Eds.), *Adult development, Vol. 1: Comparisons and applications of adolescent and adult developmental models*. New York: Praeger.

Armon, C. (1991, July 12–14). The development of reasoning about the good life. Paper presented at the Sixth Adult Development Symposium of the Society for Research in Adult Development, Boston, MA.

Ashton, P. T. (1975). Cross-cultural Piagetian research: An experimental perspective. *Harvard Educational Review, 45*, 475–506.

Astrachan, A. (1986). *How men feel*. New York: Doubleday.

Atchley, R. C. (1969). Respondents and refusers in an interview study of retired women. *Journal of Gerontology, 24*, 42–47.

Atchley, R. C. (1974). The meaning of retirement. *Journal of Communications, 24*, 97–101.

Atchley, R. C. (1976). *The sociology of retirement*. Cambridge, MA: Schenkman.

Atchley, R. C. (1980). *The social forces in later life* (3rd ed.). Belmont, CA: Wadsworth.

Atchley, R. C., & Miller, S. (1980). Older people and their families. In C. Eisdorfer (Ed.), *Annual review of gerontology and geriatrics* (Vol. 1). New York: Springer.

Atchley, R. C. (1988). A continuity theory of normal aging. *The Gerontologist, 29*, 183–190.

Babbie, E. (1977). *Society by agreement: An introduction to sociology*. Belmont, CA: Wadsworth.

Babins, L. H. (1987–88). Cognitive processes in the elderly: General factors to consider. *Gerontology and Geriatrics Education, 8*, 9–22.

Bachman, J. G., O'Malley, P. M., & Johnston, J. (1978). *Youth in transition*

(Vol. 6). Ann Arbor, MI: Institute for Social Research.

Bachrach, C. A. (1983). Children in families: Characteristics of biological, step- and adopted children. *Journal of Marriage and the Family, 45*, 171–179.

Bahr, S. J. (1989). The economic well-being of aging families. In S. Bahr & E. Peterson (Eds.), *Aging and the family*. Lexington, MA: D. C. Heath.

Baillargeon, R., Spelke, E., & Wasserman, S. (1985). Object permanence in five-month-old infants. *Cognition, 20*, 191–208.

Bailyn, L. (1970). Career and family orientations of husbands and wives in relation to marital satisfaction. *Human Relations, 23*, 97–113.

Bailyn, L. (1977). Involvement and accommodation in technical careers: An inquiry into the relation to work at midcareer. In J. Van Maanen (Ed.), *Organization careers: Some new perspectives*. New York: Wiley.

Baird, J. (1976). The funeral industry in Boston. In E. Shneidman (Ed.), *Death: Current perspectives*. Palo Alto, CA: Mayfield.

Bakerman, S. (Ed.). (1969). *Aging life processes*. Springfield, IL: Charles C. Thomas.

Baldwin, A. L. (1980). *Theories of child development*. New York: Wiley.

Ball, L. J., and Pollack, R. H. (1989). Simulated aged performance on the Embedded Figures Test. *Experimental Aging Research, 15*, 27–32.

Baltes, M. M., & Wahl, W. W. (1987). Dependency in aging. In L. L. Carstensen & B. A. Edelstein (Eds.), *Handbook of clinical gerontology*. New York: Pergamon.

Baltes, P. B. (1978). Life-span developmental psychology: Observations on history and theory revisited. In R. J. Lerner (Ed.), *Developmental psychol-*

ogy: Historical and philosophical perspectives. Hillsdale, NJ: Lawrence Erlbaum.

Baltes, P. B. (1979). Life-span developmental psychology: Some converging observations on history and theory. In P. B. Baltes & O. G. Brim, Jr. (Eds.), *Life-span development and behavior* (Vol. 2). New York: Academic Press.

Baltes, P. B. (1984). Discussion: Some constructive caveats on action psychology and the study of intention. *Human Development, 27,* 135–139.

Baltes, P. B., & Baltes, M. M. (1988). Psychological perspectives on successful aging: A model of selective optimization with compensation. In P. B. Baltes & M. M. Baltes (Eds.), *Successful aging: Research and theory.* New York: Academic Press.

Baltes, P. B., Dittmann-Kohli, F., & Dixon, R. A. (1984). New perspectives on the development of intelligence in adulthood: Toward a dual process conception and a model of selective optimization with compensation. In P. B. Baltes & O. G. Brim, Jr. (Eds.), *Life-span development and behavior* (Vol. 6). New York: Academic Press.

Baltes, P. B., Reese, H. W., & Nesselroade, J. R. (1977). *Life-span developmental psychology: Research and theory.* New York: Academic Press.

Baltes, P. B., & Schaie, K. W. (1976). On the plasticity of adult and gerontological intelligence: Where Horn and Donaldson fail. *American Psychologist, 31,* 720–725.

Baltes, P. B., & Willis, S. L. (1977). Toward psychological theories of aging and development. In J. E. Birren & K. W. Schaie (Eds.), *Handbook of the psychology of aging.* New York: Van Nostrand Reinhold.

Bammer, L. M. (1990). Self-actualization. In R. M. Thomas (Ed.), *The encyclopedia of human development and education theory, research and studies.* New York: Pergamon.

Bandura, A. (1981). Self-referent thought: A developmental analysis of self-efficacy. In I. H. Flavell & L. Ross (Eds.), *Social cognitive development: Frontiers and possible futures.* London and New York: Cambridge Press.

Barber, C. E. (1989). Transition to the empty nest. In S. J. Bahr & E. T. Peterson (Eds.), *Aging and the family.* Lexington, MA: D. C. Heath.

Bardwick, J. M. (1990). Where we are and what we want: A psychological model. In R. A. Nemiroff & C. A. Colarusso (Eds.), *New dimensions in adult development.* New York: Basic Books.

Barnett, M. (1985). *The psychological processes behind decision-making in a university setting.* Honors thesis in psychology and social relations, Harvard University, Cambridge, MA.

Baruch, G., & Barnett, R. (1983). Adult daughters' relationships with their mothers. *Journal of Marriage and the Family, 45,* 601–612.

Baruch, G., Barnett, R., & Rivers, C. (1983). *Life prints: New patterns of love and work for today's women.* New York: McGraw-Hill.

Baruch, R. (1967). The achievement motive in women: Implications for career development. *Journal of Personality and Social Psychology 5,* 260–267.

Barzel, U. (1989). Osteoporosis. In G. L. Maddox (Ed.), *The encyclopedia of aging.* New York: Springer.

Barzel, U. S., & Wasserman, S. H. (October 1987). Osteoporosis—The state of the art 1987: A review. *Seminar on Nuclear Medicine, 17,* 283–292.

Basse, R., & Ekerdt, D. (1981). Change in self-perception of leisure activities with retirement. *The Gerontologist, 21,* 650–654.

Basseches, M. (1984). *Dialectical thinking and adult development.* Norwood, NJ: Ablex.

Bear, M. (1990). Social network characteristics and the duration of primary relationships after entry into long-term care. *Journal of Gerontology: Social Sciences, 45,* 156–162.

Beaubier, J. (1980). Biological factors in aging. In C. L. Fry (Ed.), *Aging in culture and society.* Brooklyn, NY: J. F. Bergin.

Beck, P. (1982). Two successful interventions in nursing homes: The therapeutic effects of cognitive activity. *The Gerontologist, 22,* 378–383.

Becker, E. (1973). *The denial of death.* New York: Free Press.

Beckhard, R. (1977). Managerial careers in transition: Dilemmas and directions. In J. Van Maanen (Ed.), *Organizational careers: Some new perspectives.* New York: Wiley.

Beilin, R. (1981–82). Social functions of the denial of death. *Omega, 12,* 25–35.

Belkin, G. S., & Goodman, N. (1980). *Marriage, family and intimate relationships.* Chicago: Rand McNally.

Bell, A. P., & Weinberg, M. S. (1978). *Homosexualities: A study of diversity among men and women.* New York: Simon and Schuster.

Bell, R. Q. (1968). A reinterpretation of the direction of effects in studies of socialization. *Psychological Review, 75,* 81–95.

Bell, R., Turner, S., & Rosen, L. (1975). Multivariate analysis of female extramarital coitus. *Journal of Marriage and the Family, 37,* 375–385.

Belsky, J., & Pensky, E. (1988). Marital change across the transition to parenthood. *Marriage and Family Review, 12,* 133–156.

Belsky, J., & Rovine, M. (1900). Patterns of marital change across the transition to parenthood: Pregnancy to three years postpartum. *Journal of Marriage and the Family, 51,* 6–19.

Benack, S. (1984). Postformal epistemologies and the growth of empathy. M. L. Commons, F. A. Richards, and C. R. Armon (Eds.), *Beyond formal operations: Late adolescent and adult development.* New York: Praeger.

Bengston, V. L., Cutler, N. E., Mangen, D. J., & Marshall, V. W. (1985). Generations, cohorts, and relations between age groups. In R. H. Binstock & E. Shanas (Eds.), *Handbook of aging and the social sciences* (2nd ed.). New York: Van Nostrand Reinhold.

Bengston, V. L., Mangen, D. J., & Landry, P. H., Jr. (1984). The multigenerational family: Concepts and findings. In V. Garms-Holova, E. M. Hoerning, D. Schaeffer (Eds.), *Intergenerational relationships.* Lewiston, NY: C. J. Hogrefe.

Bengston, V. L., Reedy, M., & Gordon, C. (1985). Aging self conceptions: Personality processes and social context. In J. E. Birren & K. W. Schaie (Eds.), *Handbook of the psychology of aging* (2nd ed.). New York: Van Nostrand Reinhold.

Bengston, V., Rosenthal, C., & Burton, L. (1990). Families and aging: Diversity and heterogeneity. In R. H. Binstock & L. K. George (Eds.), *Handbook of aging and the social sciences* (3rd ed.). New York: Academic Press.

Bergen, M., & Williams, R. R. (1981–82). Alternative funerals: An exploratory study. *Omega, 12,* 71–78.

Bergmann, M. S. (1980). On the intrapsychic function of falling in love. *Psychoanalytic Quarterly, 69,* 56–78.

Bergmann, M. S. (1987). *The anatomy of love*. New York: Columbia University Press.

Berkowitz, L. (1990). On the formation and regulation of anger and aggression. *American Psychologist, 45,* 494–503.

Berkowitz, M. W. (1985). The role of discussion in moral education. In M. W. Berkowitz & F. Oser (Eds.), *Moral education theory and application*. Hillsdale, NJ: Lawrence Erlbaum.

Berman, W. H., & Turk, D. C. (1981). Adaption to divorce: Problems and strategies. *Journal of Marriage and the Family, 43,* 179–189.

Bernard, J. (1975). Notes on changing life styles: 1970–1974. *Journal of Marriage and the Family, 37,* 582–593.

Bernard, J. (1981). *The female world*. New York: Free Press.

Bernard, J. (1984). The good provider role: The rise and fall. In P. Voydanoff (Ed.), *Work and family: Changing roles of men and women*. Palo Alto, CA: Mayfield.

Bernardo, F. M. (1968). Widowhood status in the United States: Perspectives on a neglected aspect of the family life cycle. *Family Coordinator, 17,* 191–203.

Bernardo, F. M. (1970). Survivorship and social isolation. *Family Coordinator, 19,* 11–15.

Berscheid, E. (1982). Attraction and emotion in interpersonal relations. In M. S. Clark & S. T. Fiske (Eds.), *Affect and cognition*. Hillsdale, NJ: Lawrence Erlbaum.

Berscheid, E. (1988). Some comments on love's anatomy. In R. J. Sternberg & M. L. Barnes (Eds.), *The psychology of love*. New Haven, CT: Yale University Press.

Berscheid, E., & Walster, E. (1974). Physical attractiveness. In L. Berkowitz (Ed.), *Advances in experimental and social psychology* (Vol. 7). New York: Academic Press.

Berscheid, E., Walster, E., & Bohrstedt, G. (1973). The body image report. *Psychology Today, 7,* 119–131.

Best, F. (1980). *Flexible life scheduling*. New York: Praeger.

Beswick, H. T., & Harding, J. J. (1987). Conformational changes induced in lens alpha and gamma crystalline by modification with glucose-6 phosphate. *Biochemistry Journal, 246,* 761–764.

Betz, E. (1984). A study of career patterns of college graduates. *Journal of Vocational Behavior, 24,* 249–264.

Betz, N. E. (1984). A study of career patterns of college graduates. *Journal of Vocational Behavior, 24,* 249–264.

Betz, N. E., & Hackett, G. (1987). Concept of agency in educational and career development. *Journal of Counseling Psychology, 34,* 299–308.

Biller, H. B. (1982). Implications for child and adult development. In B. B. Wolman (Ed.), *Handbook of developmental psychology*. Englewood Cliffs, NJ: Prentice-Hall.

Birns, B., & Hay, D. (1988). *The differing faces of motherhood*. New York: Plenum.

Birren, J. E. (1964). *The psychology of aging*. Englewood Cliffs, NJ: Prentice-Hall.

Birren, J. E. (1970, March). The abuse of the urban aged. *Psychology Today,* 36–38.

Birren, J. E. (1980). Progress in research on aging in the behavioral and social sciences. *Human Development, 23,* 33–45.

Birren, J. E., & Birren, B. B. (1990). The concepts, models, and history of the psychology of aging. In J. E. Birren & K. W. Schaie (Eds.), *Handbook of* the psychology of aging (3rd ed.). New York: Academic Press.

Birren, J. E., & Botwinick, J. (1951). The relation of writing speed to age and to the senile psychoses. *Journal of Consulting Psychology, 15,* 243–249.

Birren, J. E., Butler, R. N., Greenhouse, S. W., Sokoloff, L., & Yarrow, M. R. (Eds.). (1963). *Human aging.* Washington, DC: The Government Printing Office.

Birren, J. E., & Cunningham, W. (1985). Research on the psychology of aging: Principles, concepts, and theories. In J. E. Birren & K. W. Schaie (Eds.), *Handbook of the psychology of aging* (2nd ed.). New York: Van Nostrand Reinhold.

Birren, J. E., & Renner, J. V. (1977). Research on the psychology of aging: Principles and experimentation. In J. E. Birren & K. W. Schaie (Eds.), *Handbook of the psychology of aging.* New York: Van Nostrand Reinhold.

Birren, J. E., & Stacey, C. A. (1988). Paradigms of aging: Growth vs. decline. In J. E. Thornton & E. R. Winkler (Eds.), *Ethics and aging.* Vancouver, British Columbia, Canada: University of British Columbia Press.

Birren, J. E., Woods, A. M., & Williams, M. V. (1980). Behavioral slowing with age: Causes, organization, and consequences. In L. Poon (Ed.), *Aging in the 1980s.* Washington, DC: American Psychological Association.

Blackburn, R. T., Lawrence, J. H. (1986). Aging and the quality of faculty job performance. *Review of Educational Research, 56,* 265–290.

Blasi, A. (1980). Bridging moral cognition and moral action: A critical review of the literature. *Psychological Bulletin, 88,* 1–45.

Blau, F. D. (1975). Women in the labor force: An overview. In J. Freeman (Ed.), *Women: A feminist perspective.* Palo Alto, CA: Mayfield.

Blumstein, P., & Schwartz, P. (1983). *American couples.* New York: Pocket Books.

Bortner, R. W., & Hultsch, D. F. (1972). Personal time perspective in adulthood. *Developmental Psychology, 7,* 98–103.

Botwinick, J. (1959). Drives, expectations & emotions. In J. E. Birren (Ed.), *Handbook of aging and the individual.* Chicago: University of Chicago Press.

Botwinick, J. (1981). *We are aging.* New York: Springer.

Bowmer, L. F., & Bahr, S. J. (1989). Remarriage among the elderly. In S. J. Bahr & E. T. Peterson (Eds.), *Aging and the family.* Lexington, MA: D. C. Heath.

Bowlby, J. (1958). The nature of a child's tie to his mother. *International Journal of Psychoanalysis, 39,* 350–373.

Bowlby, J. (1969). Attachment and love. In *Attachment* (Vol. 1). New York: Basic Books.

Bowles, N. L. (1989). Age and semantic inhibition in word retrieval. *Journal of Gerontology, 44,* P88–P90.

Bowmer, L. F. (1980). America's baby boom generation: The fateful bulge. *Population Bulletin, 35,* 29–33.

Brabeck, M. M., & Wood, P. K. (1990). Cross-sectional and longitudinal evidence for differences between well-structured and ill-structured problem solving abilities. In M. L. Commons, C. Armon, L. Kohlberg, F. A. Richards, T. A. Grotzer, & J. D. Sinnott (Eds.), *Adult development, Vol. 2: Models and methods in the study of adolescent and adult thought.* New York: Praeger.

Bradbury, W. (Ed.). (1975). *The adult years.* New York: Time-Life Books.

Brandtstädter, J. (1984a). Personal and social control over development: Some implications of an action perspective in life-span developmental psychology. In P. B. Baltes & O. G. Brim, Jr. (Eds.), *Life-span development and behavior* (Vol. 6). New York: Academic Press.

Brandtstädter, J. (1984b). Action development and development through action. *Human Development, 27,* 11–19.

Brandtstädter, J. (1990). Commentary. *Human Development, 33,* 160–164.

Brash, D. E., & Hart, R. W. (1978). Molecular biology of aging. In A. Behnke, C. Finch, & G. Moment (Eds.), *The biology of aging.* New York: Plenum.

Bray, D. W., & Howard, A. (1988). Management career motivation: Life change in social vicissitudes. In M. London & E. Mone (Eds.), *Career management and human resource strategies.* New York: Quorum.

Brenton, M. (1976). The breadwinner. In D. S. David & R. Brannon (Eds.), *The forty-nine percent majority.* Reading, MA: Addison-Wesley.

Bridgewater, C. A. (1982). Throbbing makes the heart grow fonder. *Psychology Today, 19,* 12, 13.

Brim, O. G., & Ryff, C. (1980). On the properties of life events. In P. B. Baltes and O. G. Brim, Jr. (Eds.), *Life-span development and behavior* (Vol. 3). New York: Academic Press.

Broderick, C. (1982). Adult sexual development. In B. B. Wolman (Ed.), *Handbook of developmental psychology.* Englewood Cliffs, NJ: Prentice-Hall.

Brody, H., & Vijayashankar, N. (1977). Anatomical changes in the nervous system. In C. E. Finch & L. Hayflick (Eds.), *Handbook of the biology of aging.* New York: Van Nostrand Reinhold.

Broman, C. L., Neighbors, H. W., & Jackson, J. S. (1988). Racial group identification among black adults. *Social Forces, 67,* 146–158.

Bromley, D. B. (1974). *The psychology of human aging* (2nd ed.). Baltimore: Penguin.

Brooks, B., & Impleman, D. (1981). Special senses. In E. J. Masoro (Ed.), *CRC handbook of physiology in aging.* Boca Raton, FL: CRC Press.

Brooks, J. B. (1981). Social maturity in middle-age and its developmental antecedents. In D. Eichorn, N. Haan, J. Calusen, M. Honzik, & P. Mussen (Eds.), *Present and past in middle life.* New York: Academic Press.

Brown, F. H. (1989). The post-divorce family. In B. Carter & M. McGoldrick (Eds.), *The changing family life cycle.* Boston: Allyn and Bacon.

Bruce, R., & Stevenson, J. C. (1990). Current understanding of osteoporosis. *Comprehensive Therapy, 16,* 9–16.

Buckingham, R. W. (1982–83). Hospice care in the United States: The process begins. *Omega, 13,* 159–171.

Buck-Morss, S. (1979). Socioeconomic bias in Piaget's theory: Implication for cross-cultural studies. In A. Buss (Ed.), *Psychology in social context.* New York: Irvington.

Buhler, C. (1972). The course of human life as a psychological problem. In W. R. Looft (Ed.), *Developmental psychology: A book of readings.* New York: Holt, Rinehart and Winston.

Burgess, J. K. (1970). The single-parent family: A social and sociological problem. *Family Coordinator, 19,* 141.

Burgess, R. L., & Huston, T. L. (1979). *Social exchange in developing relationships.* New York: Academic Press.

Burrus-Bammel, L. L., & Bammel, G. (1985). Leisure and recreation. In

J. E. Birren & K. W. Schaie (Eds.), *Handbook of the psychology of aging* (2nd ed.). New York: Van Nostrand Reinhold.

Buskirk, E. R. (1985). Health maintenance and longevity: Exercise. In C. E. Finch & E. L. Schneider (Eds.), *Handbook of the biology of aging* (2nd ed.). New York: Van Nostrand Reinhold.

Buss, A. (1979). Dialectics, history and development: The historical roots of the individual-society dialectic. In P. B. Baltes & O. G. Brim (Eds.), *Life-span development and behavior* (Vol. 2). New York: Academic Press.

Busse, E. W., & Maddox, G. L. (1985). *The Duke longitudinal studies of normal aging: 1955–1980.* New York: Springer.

Butler, R. N. (1970, June). The burnt out and the bored. *The Futurist*, p. 82.

Cahn, A. F. (1979). Summary. In A. F. Cahn (Ed.), *Women in the U.S. labor force*. New York: Praeger.

Cairo, P. C. (1982). Measured interest versus expressed interests as predictors of long-term occupational membership. *Journal of Vocational Behavior, 20*, 343–353.

Cameron, P. (1972). Stereotypes about generational fun and happiness versus self-appraised fun and happiness. *The Gerontologist, 12*, 120–123.

Cameron, P. (1975). Mood as an indicant of happiness: Age, sex, social class, and situational differences. *Journal of Gerontology, 30*, 216–224.

Campbell, A. (1975, May). The American way of mating: Marriage si, children, only maybe. *Psychology Today*, pp. 39–42.

Campbell, D. T., & Stanley, J. C. (1963). *Experimental and quasi-experimental designs for research*. Chicago: Rand McNally.

Campbell, R. L., & Richie, D. M. (1983). Problems in the theory of developmental sequences. *Human Development, 26*, 156–172.

Capra, F. (1982). *The turning point*. New York: Simon and Schuster.

Carey, R. G. (1979). Weathering widowhood: Problems and adjustment of the widowed during the first year. *Omega, 10*, 163–174.

Cargan, L., & Melko, M. (1982). *Singles: Myths and realities*. Beverly Hills, CA: Sage.

Carp, F. M. (1966). *A future for the aged*. Austin: University of Texas Press.

Carp, F. M. (1975). Long-range satisfaction with housing. *The Gerontologist, 15*, 27–34.

Carp, F. M. (1977). Housing and living environments of older people. In R. H. Binstock & E. Shanas (Eds.), *Handbook of aging and the social sciences*. New York: Van Nostrand Reinhold.

Carp, F. M. (1987). Environment and aging. In D. Stokols & I. Altman (Eds.), *Handbook of environmental psychology*. New York: Wiley.

Carter, R. T., & Swanson, J. L. (1990). The validity of the strong inventory with Black Americans. *Journal of Vocational Behavior, 36*, 195–209.

Center for the Study of Social Policy (1983). *A dream deferred: The economic status of Black Americans*. Washington, DC: Center for the Study of Social Policy.

Centers for Disease Control (1989). Cigarette smoking trends—Wisconsin, 1950–1988. *Journal of the American Medical Association, 262*, 252–260.

Cerella, J. (1990). Aging and information-processing rate. In J. E. Birren & K. W. Schaie (Eds.), *Handbook of the psychology of aging* (3rd ed.). New York: Academic Press.

Chao, G. T. (1988). The socialization process: Building newcomer commitment. In M. London & E. Mone (Eds.), *Career growth and human resource strategy*. New York: Quorum.

Charness, N. (1981). Aging and skilled problem solving. *Journal of Experimental Psychology: General, 110*, 21–38.

Charness, N. (1989). Age and expertise: Responding to Talland's challenge. In L. W. Poon, D. C. Rubin, & B. A. Wilson (Eds.), *Everyday cognition in adulthood and old age*. New York: Cambridge University Press.

Charness, N., & Bosman, E. (1990). Human factors design for older adults. In J. E. Birren & K. W. Schaie (Eds.), *Handbook of the psychology of aging* (3rd ed.). New York: Academic Press.

Chen, Y. (1985). Economic status of the aged. In R. H. Binstock & E. Shanas (Eds.), *Handbook of aging and the social sciences* (2nd ed.). New York: Van Nostrand Reinhold.

Chen, Y. (1989). Low confidence in social security is unwarranted. In S. Bahr & E. Peterson (Eds.), *Aging and the family*. Lexington, MA: D. C. Heath.

Cherlin, A. (1981). *Marriage, divorce, remarriage*. Cambridge, MA: Harvard University Press.

Chinen, A. B. (1984). Modal logic: A new paradigm of development and late life potential. *Human Development, 27*, 52–56.

Chiriboga, D. (1989). Mental health at the midpoint: Crisis, challenge or relief? In S. Hunter & M. Sundel (Eds.), *Midlife myths*. Newbury Park, CA: Sage.

Chiriboga, D., & Cutler, L. (1980). Stress and adaptation: A life-span perspective. In L. W. Poon (Ed.), *Aging in the 1980s*. Washington, DC: American Psychological Association.

Chown, S. M. (1977). Morale, careers, and personal potentials. In J. E. Birren & K. W. Schaie (Eds.), *Handbook of the psychology of aging*. New York: Van Nostrand Reinhold.

Cicirelli, V. (1980). Sibling relationships in adulthood: A life-span perspective. In L. W. Poon (Ed.), *Aging in the 1980s*. Washington, DC: American Psychological Association.

Clarkson-Smith, L., Hartley, A. A. (1989). Relationships between physical exercise and cognitive abilities in older adults. *Psychology and Aging, 4*, 183–189.

Clausen, J. A. (1976). Glimpses into the social world of middle age. *International Journal of Aging and Human Development, 7*, 99–106.

Clausen, J. A. (1981). Men's occupational careers in the middle years. In D. H. Eichorn, N. Haan, J. Clausen, M. Honzik, & P. Mussen (Eds.), *Present and past in middle life*. New York: Academic Press.

Clausen, J. A., Mussen, P., & Kuypers, J. (1981). Involvement, warmth, and parent-child resemblances in three generations. In D. Eichorn, N. Haan, J. Clausen, M. Honzik, & P. Mussen (Eds.), *Present and past in middle life*. New York: Academic Press.

Cochrane, J. B., Levy, M. T., Fryer, J. E., & Oglesby, C. A. (1990–91). Death anxiety, disclosure behaviors, and attitudes of oncologists toward terminal care. *Omega, 22*, 1–12.

Coen, S. J. (1981). Sexualization as a predominant mode of defense. *Journal of the American Psychoanalytic Association, 29*, 893–921.

Coffman, T. L. (1981). Relocation and survival of institutionalized aged: A reexamination of the evidence. *The Gerontologist, 21*, 483–500.

Cohen, G. (1979). Language and comprehension in old age. *Cognitive Psychology, 11*, 412–429.

Cohen, G., & Faulkner, D. (1986). Age differences in source forgetting: Effects on reality monitoring and on eyewitness testimony. *Psychology and aging, 4*, 10–17.

Cohen, G., & Faulkner, D. (1986). Memory for proper names: Age differences in retrieval. *British Journal of Developmental Psychology, 4*, 187–197.

Cohen, J. (1969). *Sensation and perception II: Audition and the minor senses.* Chicago: Rand McNally.

Cohler, B. J., & Galatzer-Levy, R. M. (1990). Self, meaning, and morale across the second half of life. In R. Nemiroff & C. Colarusso (Eds.), *New dimensions in adult development.* New York: Basic Books.

Colarusso, C. A., & Nemiroff, R. A. (1981). *Adult development.* New York: Plenum.

Colby, A., & Kohlberg, L. (Eds.), (1987a). *The measurement of moral judgment, Vol. 1: Theoretical foundations and research validation.* New York: Cambridge University Press.

Colby, A., & Kohlberg, L. (Eds.), (1987b). *The measurement of moral judgment, Vol. 2: Standard form scoring manuals.* New York: Cambridge University Press.

Cole, S. (1979). Age and scientific performance. *American Journal of Sociology, 84*, 958–977.

Coleman, J. (1988). *Intimate relationships, marriage, and families.* New York: Macmillan.

Coleman, L., & Antonucci, T. (1983). Impact of work on women at midlife. *Developmental Psychology, 19*, 290–294.

Collins, R. (1985). *Sociology of marriage and the family: Gender, love, property.* Chicago: Nelson-Hall.

Colwill, N. (1982). *The new partnership: Men and women in organizations.* Palo Alto, CA: Mayfield.

Colwill, N., & Lips, H. (1988). Issues in the workplace. In H. Lips (Ed.), *Sex and gender.* Palo Alto, CA: Mayfield.

Comalli, P. E., Jr. (1962). *Differential effects of context on perception in young and aged groups.* Paper presented at the meeting of the Gerontological Society, Miami Beach, FL.

Comalli, P. E., Jr. (1965). Cognitive functioning in a group of eighty to ninety year old men. *Journal of Gerontology, 20*, 14–17.

Comalli, P. E., Jr. (1970). Life-span changes in visual perception. In L. R. Goulet & P. B. Baltes (Eds.), *Life-span developmental psychology: Research and theory.* New York: Academic Press.

Comalli, P. E., Jr., Wapner, S., & Werner, H. (1959). Perception of verticality in middle and old age. *Journal of Psychology, 47*, 259–266.

Comfort, A. (1976). *A good age.* New York: Crown.

Commons, M. L. (1991). A comparison and synthesis of Kohlberg's and Gewirtz's theories of attachment. In J. L. Gewirtz & W. M. Kurtines (Eds.), *Intersections with attachment.* Hillsdale, NJ: Lawrence Erlbaum.

Commons, M. L. (in preparation). On being creative.

Commons, M. L., Armon, C., Richards, F. A., & Schrader, D. E., with Farrell, E. W., Tappan, M. B., & Bauer, N. F. (1989). A multidomain study of adult development. *Adult development, Vol. 1: Comparisons and applications of adolescent and adult developmental models.* New York: Praeger.

Commons, M. L., & Barnett, M. A. (1984). Action as a function of stage, bonding, and affiliative experience. *The Genetic Epistemologist, 14,* 17–23.

Commons, M. L., Broderick, M. A., Gewirtz, J. L., & Kohlberg, L. (in preparation). *From moral action to judgment and back.* Cambridge, MA: Harvard University Press.

Commons, M. L., Grossberg, S., & Staddon, S. E. G. (Eds.). (1991). *Neural network models of conditioning and action, Vol. 10: Quantitative analysis of behavior.* Hillsdale, NJ: Lawrence Erlbaum.

Commons, M. L., & Grotzer, T. A. (1990). The relationship between Piagetian and Kohlbergian stage: An examination of the "necessary but not sufficient relationship." In M. L. Commons, C. Armon, L. Kohlberg, F. A. Richards, T. A. Grotzer, & J. D. Sinnott (Eds.), *Adult development, Vol. 2: Models and methods in the study of adolescent and adult thought.* New York: Praeger.

Commons, M. L., & Hallinan, P. W., with Fong, W., & McCarthy, K. (1989). Intelligent pattern recognition: Hierarchical organization of concepts and hierarchies. In M. L. Commons, R. J. Herrnstein, S. M. Kosslyn, & D. B. Mumford (Eds.), *Quantitative analyses of behavior, Vol. 9: Computational and clinical approaches to pattern recognition and concept formation.* Hillsdale, NJ: Lawrence Erlbaum.

Commons, M. L., Mazur, J. E., Nevin, J. A., & Rachlin, H. (1987). *Quantitative analyses of behavior, Vol. 5: Effect of delay and intervening events on value.* Hillsdale, NJ: Lawrence Erlbaum.

Commons, M. L., & Richards, F. A. (1978, April). *The structural analytic stage of development: A Piagetian postformal operational stage.* Paper presented at the meeting of the Western Psychological Association, San Francisco, CA.

Commons, M. L., & Richards, F. A. (1982). A general model of stage theory. In M. L. Commons, F. A. Richards, & C. Armon (Eds.), *Beyond formal operations: Late adolescent and adult cognitive development.* New York: Praeger.

Commons, M. L., & Richards, F. A. (1984a). A general model of stage theory. In M. L. Commons, F. A. Richards, & C. Armon (Eds.), *Beyond formal operations, Vol. 1: Late adolescent and adult cognitive development* (pp. 120–140). New York: Praeger.

Commons, M. L., & Richards, F. A. (1984b). Applying the general stage model. In M. L. Commons, F. A. Richards, & C. Armon (Eds.), *Beyond formal operations, Vol. 1: Late adolescent and adult cognitive development.* New York: Praeger.

Commons, M. L., & Rodriguez, J. A. (1990). "Equal access" without "establishing" religion: The necessity for assessing social perspective-taking skills and institutional atmosphere. *Developmental Review, 10,* 323–340.

Commons, M. L., Stein, S. A., Richards, F. A., Trudeau, E. J., & Galez-Fontes, J. F. (in preparation). *Implicity and explicit rule-governed behavior and hierarchical task complexity.* Cambridge, MA: Harvard University Press.

Commons, M. L., Woodford, M., & Trudeau, E. J. (1991). How each reinforcer contributes to value: "Noise" must reduce reinforcer value hyperbolically. In M. L. Commons, M. C. Davison, J. A. Nevin (Eds.), *Quantitative analyses of behavior, Vol. 11: Signal detection.* Hillsdale, NJ: Lawrence Erlbaum.

Condie, S. J. (1989). Older married couples. In S. J. Bahr & E. T. Peterson (Eds.), *Aging and the family*. Lexington, MA: D. C. Heath.

Conger, J. J., & Peterson, A. C. (1984). *Adolescence and youth* (3rd ed.). New York: Harper and Row.

Conley, J. J. (1985). Longitudinal stability of personality traits. *Journal of Personality and Social Psychology, 54,* 1266–1282.

Connidis, I. G., & Davies, L. (1990). Confidants and companions in later life: The place of family and friends. *Journal of Gerontology: Social Sciences, 45,* S141–149.

Consumers Union (1981). Funerals: The memorial society alternative. In R. Fulton, E. Markusen, G. Owne, & J. L. Scheiber (Eds.), *Death and dying: Challenge and change*. San Francisco: Boyd & Fraser.

Cooney, T. M., & Uhlenberg, P. (1990). The role of divorce in men's relations with their adult children after midlife. *Journal of Marriage and the Family, 52,* 677–688.

Cornelius, S. W., Caspi, A. (1987). Everyday problem solving in adulthood and old age. *Psychology and Aging, 2,* 144–153.

Corr, C. (1979). Reconstructing the changing face of death. In H. Wass (Ed.), *Dying: Facing the facts*. New York: McGraw-Hill.

Corso, J. F. (1957). Confirmation of normal discrimination loss for speech on CID auditory test W-22. *Laryngoscope, 67,* 365–370.

Corso, J. F. (1977). Auditory perception and communication. In J. E. Birren & K. W. Schaie (Eds.), *Handbook of the psychology of aging*. New York: Van Nostrand Reinhold.

Corso, J. F. (1981). *Aging sensory systems and perception*. New York: Praeger.

Cosby, A. (1974). Occupational expectations and the hypothesis of increasing realism of choice. *Journal of Vocational Behavior, 5,* 53–65.

Costa, B. J. (1989). *Handbook for the bereaved and those who want to help*. Fall River, MA: Hospice Outreach.

Costa, P. T., & McCrae, R. R. (1981). Age differences in personality structure revisited: Studies in validity, stability, and change. In J. Hendricks (Ed.), *Being and becoming old*. Farmingdale, NY: Baywood.

Costa, P. T., Jr., & McCrae, R. R. (1988). Personality in adulthood: A six-year longitudinal study of self-reports and spouse ratings on the NEO Personality Inventory. *Journal of Personality and Social Psychology, 54,* 853–863.

Craik, F. I. M. (1977). Age differences in human memory. In J. E. Birren & K. W. Schaie (Eds.), *Handbook of the psychology of aging*. New York: Van Nostrand Reinhold.

Craik, F. I. M., Byrd, M., & Swanson, J. M. (1987). Patterns of memory loss in three elderly samples. *Psychology and Aging, 2,* 79–86.

Craik, F. I. M., & Lockhart, R. S. (1972). Level of processing: A framework for memory research. *Journal of Verbal Learning and Verbal Behavior, 11,* 671–684.

Craik, F. I. M., Morris, R. G., & Gick, M. L. (1989). Adult age differences in working memory. In G. Vallar & T. Shallice (Eds.), *Neuropsychological impairments of short-term memory*. New York: Cambridge University Press.

Crain, W. C. (1980). *Theories of personality*. Englewood Cliffs, NJ: Prentice-Hall.

Crane, D. (1965). Scientists at major and minor universities: A study of productivity and recognition. *American Sociological Review, 30,* 699–713.

Crohan, S., & Veroff, J. (1989). Dimensions of marital well-being among white and black newlyweds. *Journal of Marriage and the Family, 51,* 373–383.

Crohan, S. E., & Antonucci, T. C. (1989). Friends as a source of social support in old age. In R. Adams & R. Blieszner (Eds.), *Older adult friendship: Structure & process.* Beverly Hills, CA: Sage.

Cuber, J. F., & Harroff, P. B. (1965). *Sex and the significant Americans.* Baltimore: Penguin.

Culver, C. M., & Girt, B. (1990). Beyond the living will: Making advance directives more useful. *Omega, 21,* 253–258.

Cumming, E., & Henry, W. (1961). *Growing old.* New York: Basic Books.

Curtis, H. J. (1965). The somatic mutation theory. In R. Kastenbaum (Ed.), *Contributions to the psychobiology of aging.* New York: Springer.

Cutler, S. J. (1975). Evolution of human longevity and the genetic complexity governing aging rate. *Proceedings of the National Academy of Sciences, 72,* 4664–4668.

Cutler, S. J., & Hendricks, J. (1990). Leisure and time use across the life course. In R. H. Binstock & L. K. George (Eds.), *Handbook of aging and the social sciences* (3rd ed.). New York: Academic Press.

Cytrynbaum, S., Blum, L., Patrick, R., Stein, J., Wadner, D., & Wilk, C. (1980). Midlife development: A personality and social systems perspective. In L. W. Poon (Ed.), *Aging in the 1980s.* Washington, DC: American Psychological Association.

Dahl, A. S., Cowgill, K. M., & Asmundsson, R. (1987). Life in remarriage families. *Social Work, 32,* 40–44.

Daniels, P., & Weingarten, K. (1980). *Sooner or later: The timing of parenthood in adult lives.* New York: Norton.

Dannefer, D., & Perlmutter, M. (1990). Development as a multidimensional process: Individual and social constituents. *Human Development, 33,* 108–137.

Dasen, P., & Heron, A. (1981). Cross-cultural tests of Piaget's theory. In H. Trindis & A. Heron (Eds.), *Handbook of cross-cultural psychology: Developmental psychology* (Vol. 4). Boston: Allyn and Bacon.

Dattell, A. R., Neimeyer, R. A. (1990). Sex differences in death anxiety: Testing the emotional expressiveness hypothesis. *Death Studies, 14,* 1–11.

David, D. S., & Brannon, R. (Eds.). (1976). *The forty-nine percent majority: The male sex role.* Reading, MA: Addison-Wesley.

Davidson, G. W. (1979). Hospice care for the dying. In H. W. Wass (Ed.), *Death: Facing the facts.* New York: McGraw-Hill.

Dawis, R. V., & Lofquist, L. H. (1984). *A world of work adjustment.* Minneapolis: University of Minnesota Press.

Decker, D. L. (1980). *Social gerontology.* Boston: Little, Brown.

Demetriou, A. (1990). Structural and developmental relations between formal and postformal capacities: Towards a comprehensive theory of adolescent and adult cognitive development. In M. L. Commons, C. Armon, L. Kohlberg, F. A. Richards, T. A. Grotzer, & J. D. Sinnott (Eds.), *Adult development, Vol. 2: Models and methods in the study of adolescent and adult thought.* New York: Praeger.

Demetriou, A., & Efklides, A. (1985). Structure and sequence of formal and postformal thought: General patterns and individual differences. *Child Development, 56,* 1062–1091.

Demon, V. (1990). Black family studies in the *Journal of Marriage and the*

Family and the issue of distortion: A trend analysis. *Journal of Marriage and the Family, 51,* 603–612.

Denney, N. W. (1982). Aging and cognitive abilities. In B. B. Wolman (Ed.), *Handbook of developmental psychology.* Englewood Cliffs, NJ: Prentice-Hall.

Denney, N. W., & Palmer, A. M. (1982). *Adult age differences on traditional and practical problem-solving measures.* Unpublished manuscript, University of Kansas.

Denney, N. W., & Pearce, K. A. (1982). *A developmental study of adult performance on traditional and practical problem-solving tasks.* Unpublished manuscript, University of Kansas.

Dennis, W. (1966). Creative productivity between the ages of twenty and eighty years. *Journal of Gerontology, 21,* 1–8.

Derbyshire, R. L. (1968). Adolescent identity crisis in urban Mexican-Americans in East Los Angeles. In E. B. Brody (Ed.), *Minority-group adolescents in the United States.* Baltimore: Williams and Wilkins.

DeSpelder, L. A., & Strickland, A. L. (1992). *The last dance* (2nd ed.). Palo Alto, CA: Mayfield.

Deutsch, C. H. (1990, April 29). Challenging the career vs. family myth. *Seattle Post-Intelligence,* p. B5.

Diamond, N. (1982). Cognitive theory. In B. B. Wolman (Ed.), *Handbook of developmental psychology.* Englewood Cliffs, NJ: Prentice-Hall.

Dixon, R. A. (1990). History of research in human development. In R. M. Thomas (Ed.), *The encyclopedia of human development and education: Theory, research and studies.* New York: Pergamon.

Dixon, R. A., & Hultsch, D. F. (1983). Structure and development of metamemory in adulthood. *Journal of Gerontology, 38,* 682–688.

Dobbs, A. R., & Rule, B. G. (1987). Prospective memory and self-reports of memory abilities in older adults. Special Issue: Aging and cognition. *Canadian Journal of Psychology, 41,* 209–222.

Dodson, F. D. (1974). *How to father.* New York: New American Library.

Doherty, W., & Jacobson, N. (1982). Marriage and the family. In B. B. Wolman (Ed.), *Handbook of developmental psychology.* Englewood Cliffs, NJ: Prentice-Hall.

Douvan, E. (1977). Interpersonal relationships: Some questions and observations. In G. Levinger & H. L. Raush (Eds.), *Close relationships and the meaning of intimacy.* Amherst: University of Massachusetts Press.

Douvan, E. (1983). Learning to listen to a different drummer. *Contemporary Psychology, 28,* 261–262.

Dunn, J. (1984). Sibling studies and the developmental impact of critical incidents. In P. B. Baltes & O. G. Brim, Jr. (Eds.), *Life-span development and behavior* (Vol. 6). New York: Academic Press.

Durlak, J. A., & Riesenberg, L. A. (1991). The impact of death education. *Death Studies, 15,* 39–58.

Dustman, R. E., Emmerson, R. Y., Ruhling, R. O., Shearer, D. E., Steinhaus, L. A., Johnson, S. C., Bonekat, H. W., & Shigeoka, J. W. (1990). Age and fitness effects on EEG, ERPs, visual sensitivity, and cognition. *Neurobiology of Aging, 11,* 193–200.

Dutton, D., & Aron, A. P. (1974). Some evidence of heightened sexual attraction under conditions of high anxiety. *Journal of Personality and Social Psychology, 30,* 510–517.

Dyer, E. D. (1963). Parenthood as crisis: A restudy. *Marriage and Family Living, 25,* 196–201.

Easson, W. M. (1970). *The dying child.* Springfield, IL: Charles Thomas.

Eckensburger, L. H. (1973). Methodological issues of cross-cultural research in developmental psychology. In J. R. Nesselroade & H. W. Reese (Eds.), *Life-span developmental psychology: Methodological issues.* New York: Academic Press.

Eckensburger, L. H., & Meacham, J. A. (1984). The essentials of action theory: A framework for discussion. *Human Development, 27,* 166–173.

Edelstein, W., & Noam, G. (1982). Regulatory structures of self and "post-formal" stages in adulthood. *Human Development, 25,* 407–422.

Edwards, C. P. (1980). The comparative study of the development of moral judgment and reasoning. In R. H. Munroe, R. L. Munroe, & B. B. Whiting (Eds.), *Handbook of cross-cultural human development.* New York: Garland STM Press.

Eichorn, D. H., Hunt, J. B., & Honzik, M. P. (1981). Experience, personality and I.Q.: Adolescence to middle age. In D. H. Eichorn, N. Haan, J. Clausen, M. Honzik, & P. Mussen (Eds.), *Present and past in middle life.* New York: Academic Press.

Einstein, A. (1950). *The meaning of relativity.* Princeton, NJ: Princeton University Press.

Eisenhandler, S. (1989). More than counting: Social aspects of time and the identity of elders. In L. Thomas (Ed.), *Research on adulthood and aging.* Albany, NY: State University of New York Press.

Elder, G. H. (1985). Perspectives on the life course. In G. H. Elder (Ed.), *Life course dynamics: Trajectories and transition, 1968–1980.* Ithaca, NY: Cornell University Press.

Elias, M. F., Elias, P. K., & Elias, J. W. (1977) *Basic processes in adult developmental psychology.* St. Louis, MO: C. V. Mosby.

Elkind, D. (1978). Understanding the young adolescent. *Adolescence 13,* 127–134.

Erikson, E. H. (1963). *Childhood and society* (2nd ed.). New York: Norton.

Erikson, E. H. (1968a). Generativity and ego integrity. In B. L. Neugarten (Ed.), *Middle age and aging.* Chicago: University of Chicago Press.

Erikson, E. H. (1968b). *Identity, youth, and crisis.* New York: Norton.

Erikson, E. H. (1982). *The life cycle completed: Review.* New York: Norton.

Eustis, N. (1981). Symposium: Relocation-interpretation and application. *The Geronotologist, 21,* 481–483.

Farrell, M. P., & Rosenberg, S. D. (1981). *Men at midlife.* Boston: Auburn House.

Farrell, W. (1986). *Why men are the way they are.* New York: McGraw-Hill.

Featherman, D. L., & Marks, N. F. (1990). Commentary. *Human Development, 33,* 171–178.

Feifel, H. (1959). The meaning of death. New York: McGraw-Hill.

Feifel, H. (1965). The function of attitudes toward death. In Group for the Advancement of Psychiatry (Eds.), *Death and dying: Attitudes of patient and doctor.* New York: Mental Health Materials Center.

Feifel, H. (1990). Psychology and death. *American Psychologist, 45,* 537–543.

Feifel, H., & Branscomb, A. B. (1973). Who's afraid of death? *Journal of Abnormal Psychology, 81,* 282–288.

Feldman, D. C., & Arnold, H. J. (1983). *Managing individual and group behavior in organizations.* New York: McGraw-Hill.

Feldman, D. H., with Goldsmith L. T. (1986). *Nature's gambit: Child prodigies*

and the development of human potential.
New York: Basic Books.

Ferraro, K. F. (1990). Cohort analysis of
retirement preparation, 1974–1981.
Journal of Gerontology: Social Sciences,
45, S21–31.

Field, T. M., & Widmayer, S. M. (1982).
Motherhood. In B. B. Wolman (Ed.),
Handbook of developmental psychology.
Englewood Cliffs, NJ: Prentice-Hall.

Finch, C. (1978). The brain and aging. In
J. Behnke, C. Finch, & G. Moment
(Eds.), *Biology of aging.* New York:
Plenum.

Fine, M. (1986). Perceptions of stepparents: Variation in stereotypes as a
function of current family structure.
Journal of Marriage and the Family, 48,
537–543.

Fiske, M. L. (1980). Changing hier-
archies of commitment in adulthood.
In N. J. Smelser & E. Erikson (Eds.),
Themes of love and work in adulthood.
Cambridge, MA: Harvard University
Press.

Fiske, S. T. (1982). Schema-triggered
affect: Applications to social perception. In M. S. Clark & S. T. Fiske
(Eds.), *Affect and cognition.* Hillsdale,
NJ: Lawrence Erlbaum.

Fitzpatrick, M. A. (1988). *Between hus-*
bands and wives: Communication in mar-
riage. Newbury Park, CA: Sage.

Flandrin, J. (1985). Sex in married life in
the early Middle Ages: The church's
teaching and behavioral reality. In P.
Ariés & A. Bejin (Eds.), *Western sexu-*
ality. New York: Basil Blackwell.

Flavell, J. H. (1963). *The developmental*
psychology of Jean Piaget. New York:
Van Nostrand Reinhold.

Flavell, J. H. (1970). Cognitive changes
in adulthood. In L. R. Goulet & P. B.
Baltes (Eds.), *Life-span developmental*
psychology: Research and theory. New
York: Academic Press.

Flavell, J. H. (1977). *Cognitive develop-*
ment. Englewood Cliffs, NJ: Prentice-
Hall.

Flavell, J. H., & Ross, L. (1981). *Social*
cognitive development: Frontiers and pos-
sible futures. London and New York:
Cambridge Press.

Ford, A. B., Haug, M. R., Jones, P. K.,
Roy, A. W., & Folman, S. J. (1990).
Race-related differences among
elderly urban residents: A cohort
study 1975–1984. *Journal of Geron-*
tology, 45, 163–171.

Ford, J. M., & Pfefferbaum, A. (1980).
The utility of brain potentials in determining age-related changes in central nervous system and cognitive
functioning. In L. W. Poon (Ed.),
Aging in the 1980s. Washington, DC:
American Psychological Association.

Fozard, J. L. (1980). The time for re-
membering. In L. W. Poon (Ed.),
Aging in the 1980s. Washington, DC:
American Psychological Association.

Fozard, J. L., & Thomas, J. C. (1975).
Psychology of aging: Basic findings
and their psychiatric application. In
J. G. Howells (Ed.), *Modern perspec-*
tives in the psychiatry of old age. New
York: Brunner-Mazel.

Fozard, J. L., Wolf, E., Bell, B.,
McFarland, R., & Podolsky, S.
(1977). Visual perception and communication. In J. E. Birren & K. W.
Schaie (Eds.), *Handbook of the psychol-*
ogy of aging. New York: Van Nostrand
Reinhold.

Franke, K. J., & Durlak, J. A. (1990). Impact of life factors on attitudes toward
death. *Omega, 21,* 41–49.

Fredrick, J. F. (1976–77). Grief as a disease process. *Omega, 7,* 197–305.

Fredrick, J. F. (1983–84). The biochemistry of bereavement: Possible bias for
chemotherapy. *Omega, 13,* 295–303.

Freedman, J. L., Sears, D. O., & Carl-
smith, J. M. (1981). *Social psychology*

(2nd ed.). Englewood Cliffs, NJ: Prentice-Hall.

Frengley, J. D. (1985). The special knowledge of geriatric medicine. *Rehabilitation Literature, 46,* 133–137.

Friedman, E. A., & Havighurst, R. J. (1954). *The meaning of work and retirement.* Chicago: University of Chicago Press.

Friedman, M., & Rosenman, R. H. (1974). *Type A behavior and your heart.* New York: Knopf.

Fries, J. E., & Crapo, L. M. (1981). *Vitality and aging.* San Francisco: Freeman.

Fries, J. G., & Vickery, D. M. (1989). *Take care of yourself.* New York: Addison-Wesley.

Fulton, R. (1981). Anticipatory grief, stress, and the surrogate griever. In R. Fulton, E. Markusen, G. Owen, J. L. Scheiber (Eds.), *Death and dying: Challenge and change.* San Francisco: Boyd and Fraser.

Funk, J. D. (1989). Postformal cognitive theory and developmental stages of musical composition. In M. L. Commons, F. A. Richards, & C. Armon (Eds.), *Beyond formal operations, Vol. 1: Late adolescent and adult cognitive development.* New York: Praeger.

Furstenberg, F. F. (1987). The new extended family: The experience of parents and children after remarriage. In K. Pasley & M. Ihinger-Tallman (Eds.), *Remarriage and stepparenting.* New York: Guilford Press.

Gagnon, J. H., & Greenblatt, C. S. (1978). *Life designs: Individual marriages and families.* Glenville, IL: Scott, Foresman.

Galaz-Fontes, J. F., Ceron-Esquivel, F., Commons, M. L., Richard, D. C., Hauser, M. J., & Gutheil, T. G. (1988). *Life-based demands and development of moral reasoning among Mexi-*

cans. Paper presented at the 18th Symposium of the Jean Piaget Society. Philadelphia, PA, June 2.

Galaz-Fontes, J. F., & Commons, M. L. (1989). Desarrollo moral y educasión. *Revista travesia, 15,* 21–25.

Galaz-Fontes, J. F., & Commons, M. L. (1990). La experinecia universitaria y el desarrollo moral. *Revista travesia, 18,* 5–8.

Galaz-Fontes, J. F., Pacheco-Sanchez, M. E., Sierra-Morales, I., Commons, M. L., Gutheil, T. G., & Hauser, M. J. (1989, July 29). *Medical school training and moral reasoning in Mexico.* Paper presented at the Fourth Adult Development Symposium. Cambridge, MA.

Gardner, H. (1982). *Art, mind and brain: A cognitive approach to creativity.* New York: Basic Books.

Garn, S. M. (1975). Bone loss and aging. In R. Goldman & M. Rockstein (Eds.), *The physiology and pathology of human aging.* New York: Academic Press.

Gatz, M., Bengtson, V. L., & Blum, M. (1990). Caregiving families. In J. E. Birren & K. W. Schaie (Eds.), *Handbook of the psychology of aging* (3rd ed.). New York: Academic Press.

Genevie, L., & Margolis, E. (1987). *The motherhood report.* New York: Macmillan.

Gennari, C., Agnusdel, D. (1990). Calcitonin, estrogens and the bone. *Journal of Steroid Biochemistry and Molecular Biology, 37,* 451–455.

George, L. (1981). Subjective well-being: Conceptual and methodological issues. In C. Eisdorfer (Ed.), *Annual review of gerontology and geriatrics* (Vol. 2). New York: Springer.

George, L. K. (1988). Social participation in later life: Black-white differences. In J. S. Jackson (Ed.), *The black American elderly.* New York: Springer.

Gergen, K. J. (1977). Stability, change, and chance in understanding human development. In N. Datan & H. W. Reese (Eds.), *Life-span developmental psychology: Dialectical perspectives on experimental research*. New York: Academic Press.

Gergen, K. J. (1980). The challenge of phenomenal change for research methodology. *Human Development, 23*, 254–265.

Gergen, K. J. (1985). The social constructivist movement in modern psychology. *American Psychologist, 40*, 266–273.

Gewirtz, J. L. (1991). Identification, attachment, and their developmental sequencing in a conditioning frame. In J. L. Gewirtz & W. M. Kurtines (Eds.), *Intersections with attachment*. Hillsdale, NJ: Lawrence Erlbaum.

Gewirtz, J. L., & Kurtines, W. M. (Eds.), (1991). *Intersections with attachment*. Hillsdale, NJ: Lawrence Erlbaum.

Giambra, L. M., & Arenberg, D. (1980). Problem-solving, concept learning and aging. In L. W. Poon (Ed.), *Aging in the 1980s*. Washington, DC: American Psychological Association.

Gibson, R. C. (1989). Guest editorial: Minority aging research: Opportunity and challenge. *Journal of Gerontology: Social Sciences, 44*, S2–3.

Giles-Sims, J. (1984). The stepparent role. *Journal of Family Issues, 5*, 116–130.

Gilbert, L. A., & Davidson, S. (1989). Dual career families at midlife. In S. Hunter & M. Sundel (Eds.), *Midlife myths*. Newbury Park, CA: Sage.

Gilligan, C. (1982). *In a different voice: Psychological theory and women's development*. Cambridge, MA: Harvard University Press.

Ginsberg, E. (1972). Toward a theory of occupational choice: A restatement.

Vocational Guidance Quarterly, 20, 169–176.

Glass, J. C., Jr. (1990). Changing death anxiety through education in the public schools. *Death Studies, 14*, 31–52.

Glenn, N. D. (1975). Psychological well-being in the postparental stage: Some evidence from national surveys. *Journal of Marriage and the Family, 37*, 105–109.

Glenwick, D. S., & Whitbourne, S. K. (1978). Beyond despair and disengagement: A transactional model of personality development in later life. *International Journal of Aging and Human Development, 8*, 261–267.

Glick, I. O., Weiss, R. S., & Parkes, C. M. (1974). *The first year of bereavement*. New York: Wiley.

Glick, P. C. (1977). Updating the life cycle of the family. *Journal of Marriage and the Family, 39*, 5–15.

Glick, P. C. (1980). Remarriage: Some recent changes and variations. *Journal of Family Issues, 1*, 455–478.

Glick, P. C., & Carter, H. (1976). *Marriage and divorce: A social and economic study* (2nd ed.). Cambridge, MA: Harvard University Press.

Gloger-Tippelt, G. (1983). A process model of the pregnancy course. *Human Development, 26*, 134–148.

Gödel, K. (1977). Some meta-mathematical results on completeness and consistency; On formal undecidable propositions of *Principia Mathematica* and related systems I; On completeness and consistency. In J. Heijehoort (Ed.), *From from Frege to Gödel: A source book in mathematical logic 1879–1931*. Cambridge, MA: Harvard University Press. (Originally published 1930, 1931, 1931, respectively.)

Godwin, D., & Scanzoni, J. (1990). Couple consensus during joint decision-making: A context, process, outcome model. *Journal of Marriage and the Family, 51,* 943–955.

Gohmann, S. F. (1990). Retirement differences among the respondents to the retirement history survey. *Journal of Gerontology: Social Sciences, 45,* S120–127.

Gold, D. T., Woodbury, M. A., & George, L. K. (1990). Relationship classification using grade of membership analysis: A typology of sibling relationships in later life. *Journal of Gerontology: Social Sciences, 45,* S43–51.

Goldstein, M. S. (1951). Physical status of men rejected through selective service in World War II. *Public Health Reports, 66,* 587–609.

Gorden, J. (1984). *The relationship between the ability to make transformations and intelligence, creativity, and field-dependence/field-independence.* Unpublished dissertation. Hofstra University, Hempstead, NY.

Gordon, C., & Gaitz, C. M. (1983). Leisure activities late in the life span. In J. E. Birren, J. M. A. Munnichs, H. Thomae, & M. Marois (Eds.), *Aging: A challenge to science and society* (Vol. 3). New York: Oxford University Press.

Gordon, C., Gaitz, C. M., & Scott, J. (1977). Leisure and lives: Personal expressivity across the life span. In R. H. Binstock & E. Shanas (Eds.), *Handbook of aging and the social sciences.* New York: Van Nostrand Reinhold.

Gorer, G. (1965). *Death, grief, and mourning.* Garden City, NY: Doubleday.

Gould, R. L. (1972). The phases of adult life: A study in developmental psychology. *American Journal of Psychiatry, 129,* 521–531.

Gould, R. L. (1980). Transformations during early and middle adult years. In N. J. Smelser & E. H. Erikson (Eds.), *Themes of work and love in*

adulthood. Cambridge, MA: Harvard University Press.

Green, M., & Tyron, H. (1969). *Preretirement counseling: Retirement, adjustment, and the older employee.* Eugene, OR: University of Oregon Graduate School of Management.

Greenfield, P. M. (1976). Cross-cultural research and Piagetian theory: Paradox and progress. In K. F. Riegel & J. A. Meacham (Eds.), *The developing individual in a changing world.* Chicago: Aldine.

Greenfield, P. M., & Childs, C. (in press). Weaving, color terms and pattern representation: Cultural influences and cognitive development among the Zinacanecos. *International Journal of Psychology.*

Greenhaus, J. H. (1988). Career exploration. In M. London & E. Mone (Eds.), *Career growth and human resource strategy.* New York: Quorum.

Greenstein, T. N. (1990). Marital disruption and the employment of married women. *Journal of Marriage and the Family, 51,* 657–675.

Greer, J. H. (1965). The development of a scale to measure fear. *Behavior Research and Therapy, 3,* 45–53.

Gribben, K., & Schaie, K. W. (1976). Monetary incentive, age, and cognition. *Experimental Aging Research, 2,* 461–468.

Gubrium, J. F. (1974). On multiple realities in a nursing home. In J. F. Gubrium (Ed.), *Late life communities and environmental policies.* Springfield, IL: Charles C. Thomas.

Gruber, H. E. (1985). From epistemic subject to unique creative person at work. *Archives de Psychologie, 53,* 167–185.

Guidano, V. F. (1987). *Complexity of self.* New York: Guilford Press.

Grzegoczyk, P. B., Jones, S. W., & Mistretta, C. M. (1979). Age-related differences in salt taste acuity. *Journal of Gerontology, 34,* 836–839.

Guilford, J. P. (1950). Creativity. *American Psychologist, 5,* 444–445.

Guilford, J. P. (1959). Traits of creativity. In H. H. Anderson (Ed.), *Creativity and its cultivation.* New York: Harper.

Gurin, P., & Brim, O. G., Jr. (1984). Change in the self in adulthood: The example of sense of control. In P. B. Baltes & O. G. Brim, Jr. (Eds.), *Life-span development and behavior* (Vol. 6). New York: Academic Press.

Gurland, B. J., & Toner, J. A. (1982). Depression in the elderly: A review of recently published studies. In C. Eisdorfer (Ed.), *Annual review of gerontology and geriatrics* (Vol. 3). New York: Springer.

Gutmann, D. L. (1964). An exploration of ego configurations in middle and later life. In B. G. Neugarten & Associates (Eds.), *Personality in middle and later life.* New York: Atherton Press.

Gutmann, D. L. (1969). *The country of old men: Cross-cultural studies in the psychology of later life.* Occasional Papers in Gerontology (No. 5). Ann Arbor, MI: Institute of Gerontology, University of Michigan-Wayne State.

Gutmann, D. L. (1975). Parenthood, key to comparative study of the life cycle. In N. Datan & L. Ginsberg (Eds.), *Life span developmental psychology: Normative life crises.* New York: Academic Press.

Gutmann, D. L. (1977). The cross-cultural perspective: Notes toward a comparative psychology of aging. In J. E. Birren & K. W. Schaie (Eds.), *Handbook of the psychology of aging.* New York: Van Nostrand Reinhold.

Gutmann, D. L. (1978). *Personal transformation in the post-parental period: A cross-cultural view.* Washington,

DC: American Association for the Advancement of Science.

Gutmann, D. L. (1990). Psychological development and pathology in later adulthood. In R. A. Nemiroff & C. A. Colarusso (Eds.), *New dimensions in adult development.* New York: Basic Books.

Haan, N. (1976). Personality organization of well-functioning younger people and older adults. *International Journal of Aging and Human Development, 7,* 117–127.

Haan, N. (1981). Common dimensions of personality: Early adolescence to middle life. In D. H. Eichorn, N. Haan, J. Clausen, M. Honzik, & P. Mussen (Eds.), *Present and past in middle life.* New York: Academic Press.

Haan, N. (1985). Common personality dimensions or common organizations across the life-span? In J. M. A. Munnichs, P. Mussen, E. Olbrich, & P. G. Coleman (Eds.), *Life-span and change in a gerontological perspective.* New York: Academic Press.

Haan, N. (1989). Personality at midlife. In S. Hunter & M. Sundal (Eds.), *Midlife myths.* Newbury Park, CA: Sage.

Haan, N., Smith, M. B., & Block, J. (1968). Political, family and personality correlates of adolescent moral judgment. *Journal of Personality and Social Psychology, 10,* 183–201.

Habib, J. (1985). The economy and the aged. In R. A. Binstock & E. Shanas (Eds.), *Handbook of aging and the social sciences* (2nd ed.). New York: Van Nostrand Reinhold.

Habib, J. (1990). Population aging and the economy. In R. Binstock & L. George (Eds.), *Handbook of aging and the social sciences* (3rd ed.). New York: Academic Press.

Hagestad, G. O. (1984). Multi-generational families, socialization, support, and strain. In V. Garms-Homolova, E. M. Hoerning, & D. Schaeffer (Eds.), *Intergenerational relationships*. Lewiston, NY: C. J. Hogrefe.

Hagestad, G. O. (1988). Demographic change and the life course: Some emerging trends in the family realm. *Family Relations, 37*, 405–410.

Hagestad, G. O. (1990). Social perspectives on the life course. In B. H. Binstock & L. K. George (Eds.), *Handbook of aging and the social sciences*. New York: Academic Press.

Hagestad, G., & Neugarten, B. L. (1985). Age and the life course. In B. H. Binstock & E. Shanas (Eds.), *Handbook of aging and the social sciences* (2nd ed.). New York: Van Nostrand Reinhold.

Hagestad, G. O., Smyer, M. A., & Stierman, K. L. (1983). Parent-child relations in adulthood: The impact of divorce in middle age. In R. Cohen, S. Weissman, & B. Cohler (Eds.), *Parenthood: Psychodynamic perspectives*. New York: Guilford Press.

Hall, D. T., & Rabinowitz, S. (1988). Maintaining employee involvement in a plateaued career. In M. London & E. Mone (Eds.), *Career management and human resource strategies*. New York: Quorum.

Hamon, R. R., & Blieszner, R. (1990). Filial responsibility expectations among adult child-older parent pairs. *Journal of Gerontology: Psychological Sciences, 45*, P110–P112.

Hancock, E. (1985). Age or experience? In B. J. Reinke, A. M. Ellicott, R. L. Harris, & E. Hancock (Eds.), Timing of psychosocial change in women's lives, *Human Development, 28*, 259–280.

Harkins, S. W. (1980). Psychophysiological issues: Brain evoked potentials. In L. W. Poon (Ed.), *Aging in the 1980s*. Washington, D.C.: American Psychological Association.

Harrington, D. M., Block, J., Block, J. H. (1983). Predicting creativity in preadolescence from divergent thinking in early childhood. *Journal of Personality and Social Psychology, 45*, 609–623.

Harris, A. (1984). Action theory, language, and unconscious. *Human Development, 27*, 196–204.

Harris, L., and associates (1975). *The myth and reality of aging in America*. Washington, DC: The National Council on Aging, Inc.

Harris, R. (1975). Cardiac changes with age. In R. Goldman & M. Rockstein (Eds.), *The physiology and pathology of human aging*. New York: Academic Press.

Harry, J. (1976). Evolving sources of happiness for men over the life cycle: A structural analysis. *Journal of Marriage and the Family, 38*, 289–296.

Hartley, J. T., Harker, J. O., & Walsh, D. A. (1980). Contemporary issues and new directions in adult development of learning and memory. In L. W. Poon (Ed.), *Aging in the 1980s*. Washington, DC: American Psychological Association.

Hass, H., Fink, H., & Hartfelder, G. (1963). The placebo problem. *Psychopharmacology Service Center Bulletin, 2*, 1–65.

Hatchett, S., Veroff, J., & Douvan, E. (1990). *Marital instability among black and white couples in early marriage*. Unpublished manuscript, Ann Arbor, University of Michigan.

Hatfield, E. (1988). Passionate and companionate love. In R. J. Sternberg & M. L. Brown (Eds.), *The psychology of love*. New Haven, CT: Yale University Press.

Hatfield, E., Utne, M. K., & Traupmann, J. (1979). Equity theory and intimate relationships. In R. L. Burgess & T. L. Huston (Eds.), *Social exchange in developing relationships*. New York: Academic Press.

Hausman, P. B., & Wekster, M. E. (1985). Changes in the immune response with age. In C. E. Finch & E. L. Schneider (Eds.), *Handbook of the biology of aging* (2nd ed.). New York: Van Nostrand Reinhold.

Havighurst, R. J. (1969). Research and development in social gerontology: A report of a special committee of the Gerontological Society. *The Gerontologist, 9,* 1–90.

Havighurst, R. J. (1972). *Development tasks and education*. New York: McKay.

Havighurst, R. J. (1982). The world of work. In B. B. Wolman (Ed.), *Handbook of developmental psychology*. Englewood Cliffs, NJ: Prentice-Hall.

Havighurst, R. J., Neugarten, B. L., & Tobin, S. C. (1968). Disengagement and patterns of aging. In B. L. Neugarten (Ed.), *Middle age and aging*. Chicago: University of Chicago Press.

Hayflick, L. (1974). Cytogerontology. In M. Rockstein (Ed.), *Theoretical aspects of aging*. New York: Academic Press.

Hayflick, L. (1979). Cell aging. In A. Cherkin & C. Finch et al. (Eds.), *Physiology and cell biology of aging* (Aging Series, Vol. 8). New York: Raven Press.

Hayflick, L. (1981). Prospects for increasing longevity. In P. Johnston (Ed.), *Perspectives on aging*. Cambridge, MA: Ballinger.

Heaney, R. P. (1982). Age-related bone loss. In M. E. Riff & E. L. Schneider (Eds.), *Biological markers of aging*. National Institute of Health Publication No. 82-2221.

Heath, D. (1965). *Explorations of maturity*. New York: Appleton-Century-Crofts.

Heath, D. (1977). *Maturity and competence*. New York: Gardner Press.

Helson, R., & Moane, G. (1987). Personality change in women from college to midlife. *Journal of Personality and Social Psychology, 53,* 531–541.

Hernandez-Morrelos, I. G. (1990). *Razonamiento moral in adultos noescolarizados* [*Moral reasoning in nonliterate adults*]. Unpublished bachelor thesis, Carreras de Psicología, Escuela de Ciencias de la Educacíon, Universidad Autónoma en Baja California, P.O. 3280, Calexico, CA 92231.

Hendricks, J., & Hendricks, C. D. (1981). *Aging in mass society* (2nd ed.). Cambridge, MA: Winthrop.

Hennig, M. M. (1970). *Career development for women executives*. Doctoral dissertation, Harvard University.

Hershey, D. (1974). *Life-span and factors affecting it*. Springfield, IL: Charles C. Thomas.

Hess, B. B., & Waring, J. M. (1978). Parent and child in later life: Rethinking the relationship. In R. Lerner & G. Spanier (Eds.), *Child influences on marital and family interaction*. New York: Academic Press.

Hetherington, E. (1987). Family relations six years after divorce. In K. Pasley & M. Ihinger-Fallman (Eds.), *Remarriage and stepparenting*. New York: Guilford Press.

Hicks, M. W., & Platt, M. (1970). Marital happiness and stability. *Journal of Marriage and the Family, 32,* 553–574.

Hiller, D., & Philliber, W. (1986). The division of labor in contemporary marriage: Expectations, perceptions, and performance. *Social Problems, 35,* 191–201.

Hines, T., & Fozard, J. (1980). Memory and aging: Relevance of recent developments for research and application. In C. Eisdorfer (Ed.), *Annual review of gerontology and geriatrics* (Vol. 1). New York: Springer.

Hite, S. (1981). *The Hite report: A nationwide study of female sexuality.* New York: Dell.

Hobbs, D. F., Jr. (1965). Parenthood as crisis: A third study. *Journal of Marriage and the Family, 27,* 367–372.

Hobbs, D. F., Jr., & Cole, S. P. (1976). Transition to parenthood: A decade of replication. *Journal of Marriage and the Family, 38,* 723–731.

Hochschild, A. R. (1983). *The managed heart.* Berkeley: University of California Press.

Hodges, P. (1987). Personal communication. California State University, Los Angeles.

Hoffman, L. W., & Manis, J. D. (1978). Influences of children on marital interaction and parental satisfactions and dissatisfactions. In R. M. Lerner & G. B. Spanier (Eds.), *Child influences on marital and family interaction.* New York: Academic Press.

Hoffman, M. L. (1980). Moral development in adolescence. In J. Adelson (Ed.), *Handbook of adolescent psychology.* New York: Wiley.

Hoffman, M. L. (1984). Empathy, its limitations, and its role in a comprehensive moral theory. In W. M. Kurtines & J. L. Gewirtz, *Mortality, moral behavior, and moral development.* New York: Wiley.

Hogshead, H. P. (1978). The art of delivering bad news. In C. Garfield (Ed.), *Psychological care of the dying person.* New York: McGraw-Hill.

Holder, D. P., & Anderson, C. M. (1989). Women, work and the family. In M. McGoldrick, C. M. Anderson, & F. Walsh (Eds.), *Women in families: A framework for family therapy.* New York: Norton.

Holland, J. L. (1966). *The psychology of vocational choice: A theory of personality types and model environments.* Waltham, MA: Blaisdell.

Holland, J. L., Sorensen, A. B., Clark, S. P., Najziger, D. H., & Blum, Z. D. (1973). Applying an occupational classification to a representative sample of work histories. *Journal of Applied Psychology, 58,* 34–41.

Holmes, T. H., & Rahe, R. H. (1967). The social readjustment rating scale. *Journal of Psychosomatic Research, 11,* 213–218.

Hooper, J. O., Hooper, F. H., Colbert, K., & McMahan, R. (1986). Cognition, memory, and personality in elderly students. *Education Gerontology, 12,* 219–229.

Horn, J. L. (1970). Organization of data on life-span development of human abilities. In L. R. Goulet & P. B. Baltes (Eds.), *Life-span developmental psychology: Research and theory.* New York: Academic Press.

Horn, J. L. (1978). Human ability systems. In P. B. Baltes (Ed.), *Life-span development and behavior* (Vol. 1). New York: Academic Press.

Horn, J. L. (1982). The theory of fluid and crystallized intelligence in relation to concepts of cognitive psychology and aging in adulthood. In F. I. M. Craik & S. E. Trehub (Eds.), *The 1980 Erindale symposium.* Beverly Hills, CA: Sage.

Horn, J. L., & Cattell, R. B. (1982). Some comments on whimsy and misunderstandings of Gf-Gc theory. *Psychological Bulletin, 90,* 623–633.

Horn, J. L., Donaldson, G., & Engstrom, R. (1981). Apprehension, memory and fluid intelligence decline in adulthood. *Research on Aging, 3,* 33–84.

Horner, K. L., Rushton, J. P., & Vernon, P. A. (1986). Relation between aging and research productivity. *Psychology and Aging, 1,* 319–324.

Houseknecht, S. K. (1977). Reference group support for voluntary childlessness: Evidence for conformity. *Journal of Marriage and the Family, 39,* 285–291.

Howard, A., & Bray, D. W. (1988). *Managerial lives in transition: Advancing age and changing times.* New York: Guilford Press.

Howard, A., & Scott, R. A. (1965). Cultural values and attitudes toward dying. *Journal of Existentialism, 6,* 161–174.

Howell, S. C. (1978). *Shared spaces in housing for the elderly.* Cambridge: Laboratory of Architecture and Planning, Massachusetts Institute of Technology.

Howell, S. C. (1980a). Environment as hypothesis in human aging research. In L. Poon (Ed.), *Aging in the 1980s.* Washington, DC: American Psychological Association.

Howell, S. C. (1980b). Environments and aging. In C. Eisdorfer (Ed.), *Annual review of geriatrics and gerontology* (Vol. 1). New York: Springer.

Hoyer, W. J., & Plude, D. J. (1980). Attentional and perceptual processes in the study of cognitive aging. In L. W. Poon (Ed.), *Aging in the 1980s.* Washington, DC: American Psychological Association.

Hulicka, I. M. (1967). Age differences in retention as a function of interference. *Journal of Gerontology, 22,* 180–184.

Hulicka, I. M., & Grossman, J. L. (1967). Age-group comparisons of paired-associate learning as a function of paced and self-paced association and response time. *Journal of Gerontology, 22,* 274–280.

Hultsch, D. F., & Dixon, R. A. (1983). The role of pre-experimental knowledge in text processing in adulthood. *Experimental Aging Research, 9,* 17–22.

Hultsch, D. F., & Dixon, R. A. (1984). Memory for text materials in adulthood. In P. B. Baltes & O. G. Brim, Jr. (Eds.), *Life-span development and behavior* (Vol. 6). New York: Academic Press.

Hultsch, D. F., & Dixon, R. A. (1990). Learning and memory in aging. In J. E. Birren & K. W. Schaie (Eds.), *Handbook of the psychology of aging* (3rd ed.). New York: Academic Press.

Hultsch, D. F., Hertzog, C., Dixon, R. A. (1987). Age differences in metamemory: Resolving the inconsistencies. Special Issue: Aging and cognition. *Canadian Journal of Psychology, 41,* 193–208.

Hultsch, D. F., & Pentz, C. A. (1980). Encoding, storage and retrieval in adult memory: The role of assumptions. In L. W. Poon, J. L. Fozard, L. S. Cremak, D. Arenberg, & L. W. Thompson (Eds.), *New directions in memory and aging: Proceedings of the George Talland Memorial Conference.* Hillsdale, NJ: Lawrence Erlbaum.

Hunt, M. (1974). *Sexual behavior in the 1970s.* Chicago: Playboy Press.

Hunter College Women's Studies Collective (1983). *Women's realities, women's choices.* New York: Oxford University Press.

Hurlock, E. (1975). *Developmental psychology* (4th ed.). New York: McGraw-Hill.

Huston, T. L., & Burgess, R. L. (1979). Social exchange in developing relationships: An overview. In T. L. Huston & R. L. Burgess (Eds.), *Social exchange in developing relationships*. New York: Academic Press.

Hutson, P. W. (1962). Vocational choices, 1930 and 1961. *Vocational Guidance Quarterly, 10,* 218–222.

Huyck, M. J. (1990). Gender differences in aging. In J. E. Birren & K. W. Schaie (Eds.), *Handbook of the psychology of aging* (3rd ed.). New York: Academic Press.

Insel, P., & Roth, W. T. (1988). *Core concepts in health* (4th ed.). Palo Alto, CA: Mayfield.

Insel, P., & Roth, W. T. (1991). *Core concepts in health* (5th ed.). Palo Alto, CA: Mayfield.

Izard, C. E. (1982). Comments on emotion and cognition: Can there be a working relationship? In M. S. Clark & S. T. Fiske (Eds.), *Affect and cognition*. Hillsdale, NJ: Lawrence Erlbaum.

Jacobs, S. S., & Ho, S. S. (1975). Interrelationships among intelligence, product dimension of Guilford's model and multi-level measure of cognitive functioning. *Psychological Reports, 37,* 903–910.

Jackson, J. S., Antonucci, T. C., & Gibson, R. C. (1990). Cultural, racial, and ethnic influences in aging. In J. E. Birren & K. W. Schaie (Eds.), *Handbook of the psychology of aging* (3rd ed.). New York: Academic Press.

Jacoby, S. (1982, June). The truth about two-job marriages. *McCall's,* pp. 127–128.

Janson, H. W. (1962). *History of art.* Englewood Cliffs, NJ: Prentice-Hall.

Jensen, R. (1989). *The life course of independent women: Career and relationship development of mid-life single women in male dominated professions.* Doctoral dissertation, The Fielding Institute, 1989. (University Microfilms, Int. No. 8917277)

Johnson, C. L. (1989). Divorce related changes in relationships: Parents, their adult children, and children-in-law. In J. A. Mancini (Ed.), *Aging parents and adult children.* Lexington, MA: D. C. Heath.

Johnson, C. L., & Barer, B. (1987). American kinship relationships with divorce and remarriage. *The Gerontologist, 23,* 612–618.

Johnson, E., & Williamson, J. B. (1987). Retirement in the United States. In K. Markides & C. L. Cooper (Eds.), *Retirement in industrialized countries.* New York: Wiley.

Johnson, E. S., & Bursk, B. J. (1977). Relationships between the elderly and their adult children. *The Gerontologist, 17,* 90–96.

Jung, C. G. (1933). *Modern man in search of a soul.* New York: Harcourt, Brace, & World.

Jung, C. G. (1960). *Collected works* (H. Read, M. Fordham, & G. Adler, (Eds.). Princeton, NJ: Princeton University Press.

Jung, C. G. (1971). The stages of life. In Joseph Campbell (Ed.), *The portable Jung.* New York: Viking.

Jung, J. (1971). *The experimenter's dilemma.* New York: Harper and Row.

Kagan, J. (1983). Developmental categories and the premise of connectivity. In R. M. Lerner (Ed.), *Developmental psychology: Historical and philosophical perspectives.* Hillsdale, NJ: Lawrence Erlbaum.

Kahana, B. (1982). Social behavior and aging. In B. B. Wolman (Ed.). *Handbook of developmental psychology.* Englewood Cliffs, NJ: Prentice-Hall.

Kahana, E. (1973). The humane treatment of old people in institutions. *The Gerontologist, 13,* 282–289.

Kahana, E. (1975). A congruence model of person-environment interaction. In P. G. Windley & G. Ernst (Eds.), *Theory development in environment and aging.* Washington, D.C.: Gerontological Society.

Kahana, E., Kahana, B., & McLenigan, P. (1980). *The adventurous aged: Voluntary relocation in the later years.* Thirty-third Annual Scientific Meeting of the Gerontological Society, San Diego, CA.

Kalish, R. A. (1982). *Late adulthood: Perspectives on human development* (2nd ed.). Monterey, CA: Brooks-Cole.

Kalish, R. A. (1985). The social context of death and dying. In R. H. Binstock & E. Shanas (Eds.), *Handbook of aging and the social sciences* (2nd ed.). New York: Van Nostrand Reinhold.

Kalish, R. A., & Knudtson, F. W. (1976). Attachment versus disengagement: A life-span conceptualization. *Human Development, 19,* 135–182.

Kalish, R. A., & Reynolds, D. K. (1976). *Death and ethnicity: A psychocultural study.* Los Angeles: University of Southern California Press.

Kangas, J., & Bradway, K. (1971). Intelligence at middle age: A thirty-eight-year follow-up. *Developmental Psychology, 5,* 333–337.

Kanter, R. (1989). *When giants learn to dance.* New York: Simon and Schuster.

Kaplan, H. S. (1980). *The new sex therapy* (2nd ed.). New York: Brunner/Mazel.

Kaplan, M. (1979). *Leisure: Lifestyle and lifespan.* Philadelphia: W. B. Saunders.

Karp, D. A. (1988). A decade of reminders: Changing age consciousness between fifty and sixty years old. *The Gerontologist, 6,* 727–738.

Kastenbaum, R. (1964). Young people view old age. In R. Kastenbaum (Ed.), *New thoughts on old age.* New York: Springer.

Kastenbaum, R. (1981a). *Death, society, and human experience* (2nd ed.). St. Louis, MO: Mosby.

Kastenbaum, R. (1981b). Exit and existence: Alternative scenarios. In S. Wilcox & M. Sutton (Eds.), *Understanding death and dying* (2nd ed.). Palo Alto, CA: Mayfield.

Kastenbaum, R. (1985). Dying and death: A life-span approach. In J. E, Birren & K. W. Schaie (Eds.), *Handbook of the psychology of aging* (2nd ed.). New York: Van Nostrand Reinhold.

Kastenbaum, R. (1987–88). Theory, research, and application: Some critical issues for thanatology. *Omega, 18,* 397–410.

Kastenbaum, R., & Norman, C. (1990). Deathbed scenes imagined by the young and experienced by the old. *Death Studies, 14,* 201–217.

Katz, R., & Van Maanen, J. (1974). *The loci of satisfaction: Job interaction and policy.* (Sloan School of Management Working Paper 741–774.) Cambridge: Massachusetts Institute of Technology.

Kay, E. (1974). *The crisis in middle management.* New York: AMACOM.

Keating, D. P., & MacLean, D. J. (1988). Reconstruction in cognitive development: A post-structuralist agenda. In P. B. Baltes, D. L. Featherman, & R. M. Lerner (Eds.), *Life-span development and behavior* (Vol. 8). Hillsdale, NJ: Lawrence Erlbaum.

Keating, N. C., & Cole, P. (1980). What do I do with him 24 hours a day? Changes in the housewife role after retirement. *The Gerontologist, 20,* 84–89.

Kegan, R. (1982). *The evolving self.* Cambridge, MA: Harvard University Press.

Kelley, J. R. (1987a). *Freedom to be: A new sociology of leisure.* New York: Macmillan.

Kelley, J. R. (1987b). *Peoria winter: Styles and resources in later life.* Lexington, MA: D. C. Heath.

Kelly, H. H., Berscheid, E., Christensen, A., Harvey, J. H., Huston, T. L., Levinger, G., McClintock, E., Peplau, L. A., & Peterson, D. R. (Eds.). (1983). *Close relationships.* San Francisco: Freeman.

Kelly, J. B. (1982). Divorce: The adult perspective. In B. B. Wolman (Ed.), *Handbook of developmental psychology.* New York: Van Nostrand Reinhold.

Kendig, H. L. (1990). Comparative perspectives on housing, aging, and social structure. In R. H. Binstock and L. K. George (Eds.), *Handbook of aging and the social sciences* (3rd ed.). New York: Academic Press.

Kernberg, O. (1976). Mature love: Prerequisites and characteristics. In O. Kernberg (Ed.), *Object relations theory and clinical psychoanalysis.* New York: Jason Aronson.

Kernberg, O. (1980). Love, the couple, and the group: A psychoanalytic frame. *The Psychoanalytic Quarterly, 69,* 78–108.

Keshna, R. (1980). Relevancy of tribal interests and tribal diversity in determining the educational needs of American Indians. In *Conference on the Education and Occupational Needs of American Indian Work.* Washington, D.C.: U.S. Department of Education, National Institute of Education.

Kessen, W. (1965). *The child.* New York: Wiley.

Keyserling, M. D. (1979). Women's stake in full employment: Their disadvantaged role in the economy—challenge to action. In A. F. Cahn (Ed.), *Women in the U.S. labor force.* New York: Praeger.

Khatena, J. (1983). Analogy imagery and the creative imagination. *Journal of Mental Imagery, 7,* 127–134.

Kimmel, D. C. (1982). Gay people grow old too: Life history interviews of aging gay men. *International Journal of Aging and Human Development, 10,* 239–248.

Kimmel, D. C. (1988). Agism, psychology, and public policy. *American Psychologist, 43,* 175–178.

Kinsey, A. C., Pomeroy, W. B., & Martin, C. (1948). *Sexual behavior in the human male.* Philadelphia, PA: Saunders.

Kitchener, R. F. (1978). Epigenesis: The role of biological models in developmental psychology. *Human Development, 21,* 141–160.

Kitson, G. C., & Sussman, M. B. (1982). Marital complaints, demographic characteristics, and symptoms of mental distress in divorce. *Journal of Marriage and the Family, 44,* 87–102.

Kivnick, H. Q. (1982). Grandparenthood: An overview of meaning and mental health. *The Gerontologist, 22,* 59–66.

Kivnick, H. Q. (1985). Grandparenthood and mental health. In V. L. Bengston & J. F. Robertson (Eds.), *Grandparenthood.* Beverly Hills, CA: Sage.

Klassen, A. D., Williams, C. J., & Levitt, E. E. (1989). *Sex and morality in the United States: An empirical inquiry under the auspices of the Kinsey Institute.* Middleton, CT: Wesleyan Press.

Kleemier, R. W. (1959). Behavior and organization and external environment. In J. E. Birren (Ed.), *Handbook of aging and the individual.* Chicago: University of Chicago Press.

Klein, S. P., & Evans, F. R. (1969). Early predictors of later creative achievements. *Proceedings of the 77th Annual Convention of the American Psychological Association, 4,* 153–154.

Kline, D. W., & Schieber, F. (1985). Vision and aging. In K. W. Schaie & J. E. Birren (Eds.), *Handbook of the psychology of aging* (2nd ed.). New York: Van Nostrand Reinhold.

Knekt, P., Albanes, D., Seppanen, R., Aromaa, A., Jarvinen, R., Hyvonen, L., Teppo, L., & Pukkala, E. (1990). Dietary fat and risk of breast cancer. *American Journal of Clinical Nutrition, 52,* 808–812.

Knipscheir, K. (1985). The quality of relationships between elderly people and their adult children. In V. Garms-Homolova, E. M. Hoerning, & D. Schaeffer (Eds.), *Intergenerational relationships.* Lewiston, NY: C. J. Hogrefe.

Kogan, N. (1990). Personality and aging. In J. E. Birren & K. W. Schaie (Eds.), *Handbook of the psychology of aging* (3rd ed.). New York: Academic Press.

Kohlberg, L. (1968). The child as a moral philosopher. *Psychology Today, 2,* 25–30.

Kohlberg, L. (1969). Stage and sequence: The cognitive-developmental approach to socialization. In D. A. Goslin (Ed.), *Handbook of socialization theory and research.* Chicago: Rand McNally.

Kohlberg, L. (1973). The claim to moral adequacy of a highest stage of moral development. *Journal of Philosophy, 70,* 630–646.

Kohlberg, L. (1986). A current statement on some theoretical issues. In S. Modgil & C. Modgil (Eds.), *Lawrence Kohlberg: Consensus and controversy.* Philadelphia: PA: Falmer Press.

Kohlberg, L. (1990). Which postformal levels are stages? In M. L. Commons, C. Armon, L. Kohlberg, F. A. Richards, T. A. Grotzer, & J. D. Sinnott (Eds.), *Adult development, Vol. 2: Models and methods in the study of adolescent and adult thought.* New York: Praeger.

Kohlberg, L. (1991). In J. L. Gewirtz & W. M. Kurtines (Eds.), *Intersections with attachment.* Hillsdale, NJ: Lawrence Erlbaum.

Kohlberg, L., Boyd, D. R., & Levine, C. (1990). The return of stage 6: Its principle and moral point of view. In T. E. Wren (Ed.), *The moral domain.* Cambridge: MA: MIT Press.

Kohlberg, L., with Ryncarz, R. A. (1990). Beyond justice reasoning: Moral development and considerations of a seventh stage. In C. N. Alexander & E. J. Langer (Eds.), *Higher stages of human development: Perspectives on adult growth.* New York: Oxford University Press.

Kohlberg, L., & Candee, D. (1984). The relationship of moral judgment to moral action. In W. M. Kurtines & J. L. Gewirtz (Eds.), *Morality, moral behavior, and moral development.* New York: Wiley.

Kohlberg, L., Levine, C., & Hewer, A. (1983). Moral stages: A current formulation and a response to critics. *Contributions to Human Development, 10.* Basel, Switzerland: S. Karger.

Kohn, M. (1980). Job complexity and adult personality. In N. J. Smelser & E. H. Erikson (Eds.), *Themes of work and love in adulthood.* Cambridge, MA: Harvard University Press.

Kohn, R. R. (1977). Heart and cardiovascular system. In C. E. Finch & L. Hayflick (Eds.), *Handbook of the biology of aging.* New York: Van Nostrand Reinhold.

Komarovsky, M. (1973). Cultural contradictions and sex roles: The masculine case. *American Journal of Sociology, 78,* 873–884.

Korman, A. K. (1989). Career success and personal failure: Mid to late career feelings and events. In M. London & E. Mone (Eds.), *Career management and human resource strategies.* New York: Quorum.

Kotre, J. (1984). *Outliving the self: Generativity and the interpretation of lives.* Baltimore, MD: Johns Hopkins Press.

Krause, E. A. (1971). *The sociology of occupations.* Boston: Little, Brown.

Kruse, A. (1984). The five generation family: A pilot study. In V. Garms-Homolova, E. M. Hoerning, & D. Schaeffer (Eds.) *Intergenerational relationships.* Lewiston, NY: C. J. Hogrefe.

Kübler-Ross, E. (1969). *On death and dying.* New York: Macmillan.

Kübler-Ross, E. (1974). *Questions and answers on death and dying.* New York: Macmillan.

Kuhn, D. (1989). Children and adults as intuitive scientists. *Psychological Review, 96,* 674–689.

Kuhn, D., Amsel, E., & O'Loughlin, M. (1988). *The development of scientific thinking skills.* Orlando, FL: Academic Press.

Kuhn, D., Langer, J., Kohlberg, L., & Haan, N. (1977). The development of formal operation in logical and moral judgment. *Genetic Psychology Monographs, 95,* 97–188.

Kuhn, T. S. (1962, 1972). *The structure of scientific revolutions* (2nd ed.). Chicago: University of Chicago Press.

Kurtines, W. M. (1984). Moral behavior as rule-governed behavior: A psychosocial role-theoretical approach to moral behavior and development. In W. M. Kurtines & J. L. Gewirtz (Eds.), *Morality, moral behavior, and moral development.* New York: Wiley.

Kurtines, W. M., & Gewirtz, J. L. (Eds.). (1984). *Morality, moral behavior, and moral development.* New York: Wiley.

Kuypers, J. A. (1981). Ego functioning in old age: Early adult life antecedents. In J. Hendricks (Ed.), *Being and becoming old.* Farmingdale, NY: Baywood.

Labouvie, E. W. (1982). Issues in life span development. In B. B. Wolman (Ed.), *Handbook of developmental psychology.* Englewood Cliffs, NJ: Prentice-Hall.

Labouvie-Vief, G. (1982a). Dynamic development and mature autonomy. *Human Development, 25,* 161–191.

Labouvie-Vief, G. (1982b). Growth and aging in life-span perspective. *Human Development, 25,* 65–78.

Labouvie-Vief, G. (1984). Logic and self-regulation from youth to maturity: A model. In M. L. Commons, F. A. Richards, & C. Armon (Eds.), *Beyond formal operations, Vol. 1: Late adolescent and adult cognitive development.* New York: Praeger.

Labouvie-Vief, G. (1985). Intelligence and cognition. In J. E. Birren & K. W. Schaie (Eds.), *Handbook of the psychology of aging* (2nd ed.). New York: Van Nostrand Reinhold.

Labouvie-Vief, G. (1990). Modes of knowledge and the organization of development. In M. L. Commons, C. Armon, L. Kohlberg, F. A. Richards, T. A. Grotzer, & J. D. Sinnott (Eds.), *Adult development, Vol. 2: Models and methods in the study of adolescent and adult thought.* New York: Praeger.

Labouvie-Vief, G., Adams, C., Hakim-Larson, J., & Hayden, M. (1983). *Contexts of logic: The growth of interpretation from pre-adolescence to mature adulthood.* Paper presented at the meeting of the Society for Research in Child Development, Detroit, MI.

Labouvie-Vief, G., & Blanchard-Fields, F. (1982). Cognitive aging and psychological growth. *Ageing and Society, 2,* 183–209.

Labouvie-Vief, G., & Schell, D. A. (1982). Learning and memory in later life. In B. B. Wolman (Ed.), *Handbook of developmental psychology.* Englewood Cliffs, NJ: Prentice-Hall.

Lamb, M. E. (1978). Fathers and child development: An integrative overview. In M. E. Lamb (Ed.), *Child influences on marital and family interaction.* New York: Academic Press.

Lamb, M. E. (1981). Fathers and child development: An integrative overview. In M. E. Lamb (Ed.), *The role of the father in child development.* New York: Wiley.

Lamb, M. E., & Goldberg, W. A. (1982). The father-child relationship: A synthesis of biological, evolutionary, and social perspective. In L. W. Hoffman, R. Gandelman, & H. R. Schiffman (Eds.), *Parenting: Its causes and consequences.* Hillsdale, NJ: Lawrence Erlbaum.

Lamb, M. E., Thompson, R. A., Gardner, W., & Charnov, R. L. (1985). *Infant-mother attachment: The origins and developmental significance of individual differences in stranger situation behavior.* Hillsdale, NJ: Lawrence Erlbaum.

La Rossa, R., & La Rossa, M. M. (1981). *Transition to parenthood: How infants change families.* Beverly Hills, CA: Sage.

LaRue, A., Dessonville, C., & Jarvik, J. (1985). Aging and mental disorders. In J. E. Birren & K. W. Schaie (Eds.), *Handbook of the psychology of aging.* (2nd ed.). New York: Van Nostrand Reinhold.

LaRue, A., & Jarvik, L. (1982). Old age and biobehavioral changes. In B. B. Wolman (Ed.), *Handbook of developmental psychology.* Englewood Cliffs, NJ: Prentice-Hall.

Laslett, P. (1985). Societal development and aging. In R. A. Binstock & E. Shanas (Eds.), *Handbook of aging and the social sciences.* (2nd ed.). New York: Van Nostrand Reinhold.

Lasswell, M., & Lobsenz, N. (1980). *Styles of loving.* Garden City, NY: Doubleday.

Lavery, M. A., Loewy, J. W., Kapadia, A. S., Nichaman, M. S., Foreyt, J. B., & Gee, M. (1990). Long-term follow-up of weight status off subject in a behavioral weight control program. *Journal of the American Dietary Association, 90,* 512–517.

Lawton, M. P. (1970). Ecology and aging. In L. A. Pastalan & D. H. Carson (Eds.), *The spatial behavior of older people.* Ann Arbor: Michigan Institute of Gerontology.

Lawton, M. P. (1975). *Planning and managing housing for the elderly.* New York: Wiley.

Lawton, M. P. (1977). The impact of environment on aging and behavior. In J. E. Birren & K. W. Schaie (Eds.), *Handbook of the psychology of aging.* New York: Van Nostrand Reinhold.

Lawton, M. P. (1980). *Environment and aging.* Monterey, CA: Brooks-Cole.

Lawton, M. P. (1985). Housing and living arrangements of older people. In R. A. Binstock & E. Shanas (Eds.), *Handbook of aging and the social sciences* (2nd ed.). New York: Van Nostrand Reinhold.

Lawton, M. P. (1990). Residential environment and self-directedness among older people. *American Psychologist, 45,* 638–640.

Lawton, M. P., & Cohen, J. (1974). Housing impact on older people. *Journal of Gerontology, 29,* 194–204.

Lawton, M. P., & Nahemow, L. (1973).

Ecology and the aging process. In C. Eisdorfer & M. P. Lawton (Eds.), *The psychology of adult development and aging*. Washington, DC: American Psychological Association.

Lazarus, R. S. (1981). The stress and coping paradigm. In C. Eisdorfer, D. Cohen, A. Kleinman, & P. Maxim (Eds.), *Theoretical bases in psychopathology*. New York: Spectrum.

Lee, D. J., & Markides, K. S. (1990). Activity and mortality among aged persons over an eight year period. *Journal of Gerontology: Social Sciences, 45,* S38–S42.

Lee, G. R., & Shehan (1989). Elderly parents and their children: Normative influences. In J. A. Mancini (Ed.), *Aging parents and adult children*. Lexington, MA: D. C. Heath.

Lee, J. (1988). Styles of loving. In R. J. Sternberg & M. L. Brown (Eds.), *The psychology of love*. New Haven, CT: Yale University Press.

Lee, J. A. (1974). Styles of loving, *Psychology Today, 8,* 43–51.

Lee, J. A. (1977). A typology of styles of loving. *Personality and Social Behavior, 3,* 173–182.

Lehman, H. C. (1953). The age decrement in outstanding scientific creativity. *American Psychologist, 15,* 128–134.

Lehr, U. (1984). The role of women in the family generational context. In V. Garms-Holova, E. M. Hoerning, & D. Schaeffer (Eds.), *Integenerational relationships*. Lewiston, NY: C. J. Hogrefe.

Leifer, M. (1977). Psychological changes accompanying pregnancy and motherhood. *Genetic Psychology Monographs, 95,* 55–96.

Le Masters, E. E. (1957). Parenthood as crisis. *Marriage and Family Loving, 19,* 352–355.

Lerner, R. M. (1976). *Concepts and theories of human development*. Reading, MA: Addison-Wesley.

Lerner, R. M. (1983). *Developmental psychology*. Hillsdale, NJ: Lawrence Erlbaum.

Lerner, R. M., & Mulkeen, P. (1990). Commentary. *Human Development, 33,* 179–184.

Lerner, R. M., & Ryff, C. D. (1978). Implementation of the life-span view of human development: The sample case of attachment. In P. B. Baltes & O. G. Brim, Jr. (Eds.), *Life-span development and behavior* (Vol. 1). New York: Academic Press.

Lester, D. (1990). The Collett-Lester fear of death scale: The original version and a revision. *Death Studies, 14,* 451–468.

Leventhal, H. (1982). The integration of emotion and cognition: A view from the perceptual-motor theory of emotion. In M. S. Clark & S. T. Fiske (Eds.), *Affect and cognition*. Hillsdale: NJ: Lawrence Erlbaum.

Levin, R. J. (1975, October). The Redbook report on premarital and extramarital sex. *Redbook*, pp. 51–58.

Levine, C., Kohlberg, L., & Hewer, A. (1985). The current formulation of Kohlberg's theory and a response to critics. *Human Development, 28,* 94–100.

Levinson, D. J. (1986). A conception of adult development. *American Psychologist, 41,* 3–14.

Levinson, D. J. (in press). *Seasons of a woman's life*. New York: Knopf.

Levinson, D. J., Darrow, C. N., Klein, E. B., Levinson, M. H., & McKee, B. (1974). The psychosocial development of men in early adulthood and the midlife transition. In D. F. Ricks, A. Thomas, & M. Roff (Eds.), *Life history research in psychopathology*

(Vol. 3). Minneapolis: University of Minnesota Press.

Levinson, D. J., Darrow, C. N., Klein, E. B., Levinson, M. H., & McKee, B. (1978). *Seasons of a man's life*. New York: Knopf.

Levy, J. A., (1987). A life course perspective on hospice and the family. *Marriage and Family Review, 11*, 39–64.

Levy, J. A., & Gordon, A. (1987). Stress and burnout in the social world of hospice. *Hospice Journal, 3*, 29–51.

Levy, S. M., Derogatis, L. R., Gallagher, D., & Gatz, M. (1980). Intervention with older adults and the evaluation of outcome. In L. W. Poon (Ed.), *Aging in the 1980s*. Washington, DC: American Psychological Association.

Li, T., & Liu, S. (1991, July 12–14). *Moving from moral moratorium in Chinese youth: Equilibrium effect of experiencing estranging events*. Paper presented at the Sixth Adult Development Symposium of the Society for Research in Adult Development, Boston, MA.

Libby, R. W. (1977). Extramarital and comarital sex: A critique of the literature. In R. W. Libby & R. N. Whitehurst (Eds.), *Marriage and alternative: Exploring intimate relationships*. Glenview, IL: Scott Foresman.

Lieberman, L. R. (1970). Life satisfaction in the young and the old. *Psychological Reports, 27*, 75–79.

Lieberman, M. A. (1981). Social and psychological determinants of adaptation. In J. Hendricks (Ed.), *Being and becoming old*. Farmington, NY: Baywood.

Liebert, R. M. (1984). What develops in moral development? In W. M. Kurtines & J. L. Gewirtz, (Eds.), *Morality, moral behavior, and moral development*. New York: Wiley.

Lieblich, A. (1986). Successful career women at midlife: Crises and transitions. *International Journal of Aging and Human Development, 23*, 301–312.

Lifton, R. J. (1981). Witnessing survival. In R. Fulton, E. Markusen, G. Owne, & J. L. Scheiber (Eds.), *Death and dying: Challenge and change*. San Francisco: Boyd and Fraser.

Lifton, R. J., & Olson, E. (1974). *Living and dying*. New York: Praeger.

Light, L. L. (1988). Preserved implicit memory in old age. In M. M. Gruneberg, P. E. Morris, & R. N. Sykes (Eds.), *Practical aspects of memory: Current research issues* (Vol. 2). New York: Wiley.

Light, L. L. (1990). Interactions between memory and language in old age. In J. E. Birren & K. W. Schaie (Eds.), *Handbook of the psychology of aging* (3rd ed.). New York: Academic Press.

Lindeman, R. D. (1975). Changes in renal function. In R. Goldman & M. Rockstein (Eds.), *The physiology and pathology of human aging*. New York: Academic Press.

Linville, P. W. (1982). Affective consequences of complexity regarding the self and others. In M. S. Clark & S. T. Fiske (Eds.), *Affect and cognition*. Hillsdale, NJ: Lawrence Erlbaum.

Lips, H. M. (1988). *Sex and gender*. Palo Alto, CA: Mayfield.

Litewka, J. (1977). The socialized penis. In J. Snodgrass (Ed.), *A book of readings for men against sexism*. Albion, CA: Times Change Press.

Livingston, K. R. (1980). Love as a process of reducing uncertainty—cognitive theory. In K. S. Pope (Ed.), *On loving and being loved*. San Francisco: Jossey-Bass.

Livson, F. B. (1981a). Paths to psychological health in the middle years: Sex differences. In D. H. Eichorn, N. Haan, J. Clausen, M. Honzik, & P. Mussen (Eds.), *Present and past in middle life*. New York: Academic Press.

Livson, F. B. (1981b). Patterns of personality development in middle-aged women: A longitudinal study. In J. Hendricks (Ed.), *Being and becoming old*. Farmingdale, NY: Baywood.

Livson, N. (1973). Developmental dimensions of personality: A life-span formulation. In P. B. Baltes & K. W. Schaie (Eds.), *Life-span developmental psychology: Personality and socialization*. New York: Academic Press.

Livson, N., & Peskin, H. (1981). Psychological health at 40: Prediction from adolescent personality. In D. H. Eichorn, N. Haan, J. Clausen, M. Honzik, & P. Mussen (Eds.), *Present and past in middle life*. New York: Academic Press.

Locke, D. (1983). Doing what comes morally: The relation between behavior and stages of moral reasoning. *Human Development, 26,* 11–25.

Lonetto, R., & Templer, D. (1986). *Death anxiety*. Washington, DC: Hemisphere Publishing.

Long, J. K., & Mancini, J. A. (1989). The parental role and parent-child relationship provisions. In J. A. Mancini (Ed.), *Aging parents and adult children*. Lexington, MA: D. C. Heath.

Lopata, H. Z. (1971). *Occupation: Housewife*. New York: Oxford University Press.

Lopata, H. Z. (1973). *Widowhood in an American city*. New York: Schenkman.

Lopata, H. Z. (1975). Widowhood: Societal factors in life-span disruptions and alternatives. In N. Datan & L. Ginsberg (Eds.), *Life-span developmental psychology: Normative life crises*. New York: Academic Press.

Los Angeles Times (1983). Life Expectancy Increase Announced. Part IV, Wednesday, June 8, pp. 1, 8.

Lovibond, S. H., Birrell, P. C., & Langeluddecke, P. (1986). Changing coronary heart disease risk-factor status: The effects of three behavioral programs. *Journal of Behavioral Medicine, 9,* 415–437.

Lowenthal, M., Thurnher, M., & Chiriboga, D. (1975). *Four stages of life*. San Francisco: Jossey-Bass.

Lowenthal, M., & Weiss, L. (1976). Intimacy and crisis in adulthood. *Counseling Psychologist, 6,* 10–15.

Lowenthal, M. F., & Robinson, B. (1977). Social networks and isolation. In R. H. Binstock & E. Shanas (Eds.), *Handbook of aging and the social sciences*. New York: Van Nostrand Reinhold.

Lunneborg, C. E., & Lunneborg, P. W. (1975). Factor structure of the vocational interest models of Roe and Holland. *Journal of Vocational Behavior, 7,* 313–326.

Lutsky, N. (1980). Attitudes toward old age and elderly persons. In C. Eisdorfer (Ed.), *Annual review of gerontology and geriatrics* (Vol. 1). New York: Springer.

Maas, H. S. (1985). The development of adult development: Recollections and reflections. In J. M. A. Munnichs, P. Mussen, E. Olbrich, & P. G. Coleman (Eds.), *Life-span and change in a gerontological perspective*. New York: Academic Press.

Maas, H. S. (1989). Social responsibility in middle age: Prospects and preconditions. In S. Hunter & M. Sundel (Eds.), *Midlife myths*. Newbury Park, CA: Sage.

Maas, H. S., & Kuypers, J. A. (1974). *From thirty to seventy*. San Francisco: Jossey-Bass.

Maccoby, E. (1990). Gender and relationships. *American Psychologist, 45,* 513–520.

Maccoby, E., Depner, C., & Mnooken,

R. (1989). Coparenting in the second year after divorce. *Journal of Marriage and the Family, 50,* 141–155.

MacDermid, S. M., Huston, T. L., & McHale, S. (1990). Changes in marriage associated with the transition to parenthood: Individual differences as a function of sex-role attitudes and changes in the division of household labor. *Journal of Marriage and the Family, 51,* 475–486.

Maddi, S. (1980). *Personality theories: A comparative analysis* (4th ed.). Homewood, IL: Dorsey Press.

Maddox, B. (1976). Neither witch nor good fairy. *New York Times Magazine,* August 8, p. 16.

Maddox, G. L. (1962). A longitudinal multidisciplinary study of human aging: Selected methodological issues. *Proceedings of the Social Statistics Section of the American Statistical Association.* Washington, DC: American Statistical Association.

Magno, J. B. (1990). The hospice concept of care: Facing the 1990s. *Death Studies, 14,* 109–119.

Magnusson, David. (1988). *Individual development from an interactional perspective.* Hillsdale, NJ: Lawrence Erlbaum.

Mahrer, A. R., & Gervaize, P. A. (1990). Humanistic theory of development. In R. Murray Thomas (Ed.), *The encyclopedia of human development and education theory, research, and studies.* New York: Pergamon.

Maltzman, I. (1960). On the training off originality. *Psychological Review, 67,* 229–242.

Mandler, G. (1982). The structure of value: Accounting for taste. In M. S. Clarke & S. T. Fiske (Eds.), *Affect and cognition.* Hillsdale, NJ: Lawrence Erlbaum.

Markides, K. S., & Lee, D. J. (1990).

Predictors of well-being and functioning in older Mexican-Americans and Anglos: An eight-year follow-up. *Journal of Gerontology: Social Sciences, 45,* S69–S73.

Markides, K., Liang, J., & Jackson, J. S. (1990). Race, ethnicity, and aging: Conceptual and methodological issues. In R. Binstock & L. George (Eds.), *Handbook of aging and the social sciences* (3rd ed.). New York: Academic Press.

Marsh, G. R., & Thompson, L. W. (1977). Psychophysiology of aging. In J. E. Birren & K. W. Schaie (Eds.), *Handbook of the psychology of aging.* New York: Van Nostrand Reinhold.

Marshall, V., & Levy, J. A. (1990). Aging and dying. In R. H. Binstock & L. K. George (Eds.), *Handbook of aging and the social sciences* (3rd ed.). New York: Academic Press.

Martin, T. O. (1982–83). Death anxiety and social desirability among nurses. *Omega, 13,* 51–58.

Maslow, A. H. (1968). *Toward a psychology of being.* New York: Van Nostrand Reinhold.

Maslow, A. H. (1970). *Motivation and personality* (2nd ed.). New York: Harper and Row.

Masters, W. H., & Johnson, V. E. (1966). *Human sexual response.* Boston: Little, Brown.

Masters, W. H., & Johnson, V. E. (1970). *Human sexual inadequacy.* Boston: Little, Brown.

Masters, W. H., Johnson, V. E., & Kolodny, R. C. (1982). *Human sexuality.* Boston: Little, Brown.

Masters, W. H., Johnson, V. E., & Kolodny, R. C. (1985). *Human sexuality* (2nd ed.). Boston: Little, Brown.

Masters, W. H, Johnson, V. E., & Kolodny, R. C. (1991). *Human sexuality* (3rd ed.). Boston: Little, Brown.

Matthews, K. A., & Rodin, J. (1989). Women's changing work roles: Impact on health, family and public policy. *American Psychologist, 44,* 1389–1393.

Matthews, K. A., Wing, R. R., Kuller, L. H., Meilahn, E. N., Kelsey, S. F., Costello, E. J., & Caggiula, A. W. (1990). Influence of natural menopause on psychological characteristics and symptoms of middle-aged women. *Journal of Consulting and Clinical Psychology, 58,* 345–351.

McAdams, D. P., Ruetzel, K., & Foley, J. M. (1986). Complexity and generativity at mid-life: Relations among social motives, ego development, and adults' plans for the future. *Journal of Personality and Social Psychology, 50,* 800–807.

McBride, A. (1990). Mental health effects of women's multiple roles. *American Psychologist, 45,* 381–384.

McCarthy, D. C. (1991). Behavioral detection theory: Some implications for applied human research. In M. L. Commons, M. C. Davison, J. A. Nevin (Eds.), *Quantitative analyses of behavior, Vol. 11: Signal detection.* Hillsdale, NJ: Lawrence Erlbaum.

McCary, J. L., & McCary, S. P. (1982). *McCary's human sexuality* (4th ed.). Belmont, CA: Wadsworth.

McCrae, R., & Costa, P. T., Jr. (1982). Aging, the life course, and models of personality. In T. M. Field, A. Huston, H. C. Quay, L. Troll, & G. E. Finley (Eds.), *Review of human development.* New York: Wiley-Interscience.

McCrae, R., & Costa, P. T., Jr. (1984). *Emerging lives, enduring dispositions: Personality in adulthood.* Boston: Little Brown.

McCrae, R. R., & Costa, P., Jr. (1987). Validation of the five factor model of personality across instruments and observers. *Journal of Personality and Social Psychology, 52,* 81–90.

McCrae, R. R., & Costa, P. T., Jr. (1989). Reinterpreting the MBTI from the perspective of the five factor model. *Journal of Personality, 59,* 17–40.

McDowd, J. M., & Birren, J. E. (1990). Aging and attentional processes. In J. E. Birren and K. W. Schaie (Eds.), *Handbook of the psychology of aging* (3rd ed.). New York: Academic Press.

McDowd, J. M., & Craik, F. I. M. (1988). Effects of aging and task difficulty on divided attention performance. *Journal of Experimental Psychology: Human Perception and Performance, 14,* 267–280.

McGee, J., & Wells, K. (1982). Gender typing and androgyny in later life: New direction for theory and research. *Human Development, 25,* 116–139.

McGoldrick, M. (1989). Ethnicity and the family life cycle. In B. Carter & M. McGoldrick (Eds.), *The changing family life cycle.* Boston: Allyn and Bacon.

McGoldrick, M. (1989). Women and the family life cycle. In B. Carter & M. McGoldrick (Eds.), *The changing family life cycle.* Boston: Allyn and Bacon.

McGoldrick, M., & Carter, B. (1989). Forming a remarried family. In B. Carter & M. McGoldrick (Eds.), *The changing family life cycle.* Boston: Allyn and Bacon.

McHale, S. M., & Lerner, R. M. (1990). Definitions of stage and rate. In R. M. Thomas (Ed.), *The encyclopedia of human development and education: Theory, research and studies.* New York: Pergamon.

McIntyre, J., & Craik, F. (1987) Age differences in memory for item and source information. Special Issue: Aging and cognition. *Canadian Journal of Psychology, 41,* 175–192.

McKeown, F. (1965). *Pathology of the aged.* London: Butterworth.

McLanahan, S. S., & Sorensen, A. G. (1985). Life events and psychological well-being over the life course. In G. H. Elder, Jr. (Ed.), *Life course dynamics.* Ithaca, NY: Cornell University Press.

McLeish, J. A. B. (1981). The continuity of creativity. In P. Johnston (Ed.), *Perspectives on aging.* Cambridge, MA: Ballinger.

Meacham, J. A. (1977). A transactional model for remembering. In N. Datan & H. W. Reese (Eds.), *Life-span developmental psychology: Dialectical perspectives on research.* New York: Academic Press.

Meacham, J. A. (1980). Research on remembering: Interrogation or conversation, monologue or dialogue? In D. F. Hultsch (Ed.), Implications of a dialectical perspective for research methodology. *Human Development, 23,* 236–245.

Meir, E. K., & Ben-Yehuda, A. (1976). Inventories based on Roe and Holland yield similar results. *Journal of Vocational Behavior, 8,* 269–274.

Melville, K. (1988). *Marriage and family today* (4th ed.). New York: Random House.

Meyer, B. J. F., & Rick, G. E. (1989). Prose processing in adulthood: The text, the learner, and the task. In L. W. Poon, D. C. Rubin, & B. A. Wilson (Eds.), *Everyday cognition in adulthood and old age.* New York: Cambridge University Press.

Miernyk, W. H. (1975). The changing life cycle of work. In N. Datan & L. Ginsberg (Eds.), *Life-span developmental psychology: Normative life crises.* New York: Academic Press.

Mileski, M., & Black, D. J. (1972). The social organization of homosexuality. *Urban Life and Culture, 1,* 187–199.

Miller, B. C. (1976). A multivariate developmental model of marital satisfaction. *Journal of Marriage and the Family, 36,* 643–657.

Miller, P. H. (1983). *Theories of developmental psychology.* San Francisco: Freeman.

Miller, S. S., & Cavanaugh, J. C. (1990). The meaning of grandparenthood and its relationship to demographic, relationship and social participation variables. *Journal of Gerontology, 45,* P244–P246.

Minhas, L. S., & Kaur, F. (1983). A study of field-dependent-independent cognitive styles in relation to novelty and meaning contexts of creativity. *Personality Study and Group Behavior, 3,* 20–34.

Mischel, W. (1969). Continuity and change in personality. *American Psychologist, 24,* 1012–1018.

Mitford, J. (1963). *The American way of death.* New York: Simon and Schuster.

Montgomery, R. (1982). Impact of institutional care policies on family integration. *The Gerontologist, 22,* 54–58.

Moody, R. A. (1975). *Life after life.* New York: Bantam.

Moody, R. A., Jr. (1988). *The light beyond.* New York: Bantam Books.

Moore, L. M., Nielsen, C. R., & Mistretta, C. M. (1982). Sucrose-taste thresholds: Age-related difference. *Journal of Gerontology, 37,* 64–69.

Moos, R., & Lemke, S. (1985). Specialized living environments of older people. In J. E. Birren & K. W. Schaie (Eds.), *Handbook of the psychology of aging* (2nd ed.). New York: Van Nostrand Reinhold.

Morbidity and mortality weekly report (1989, July 21). HIV infection reporting—United States (Vol. 38, pp. 496–499). Department of Health and Human Services, Public Health Service, Centers for Disease Control, Atlanta, GA.

Morgan, E. (1977). *A manual of death education and simple burial* (8th ed.). Burnsville, NC: Celo Press.

Morgan, L. A. (1982). Social roles in later life. *Annual review of gerontology and geriatrics* (Vol. 3). New York: Springer.

Morrison, J. D., & McGrath, C. (1985). Assessment of the optical contributions to the age-related deterioration in vision. *Quarterly Journal of Experimental Physiology, 70,* 249–269.

Mortimer, J. T., & London, J. (1984). The varying linkages of work and family. In P. Voydanoff (Ed.), *Work and family: Changing roles of men and women.* Palo Alto, CA: Mayfield.

Moss, M., & Moss, S. (1983–84). The impact of parental death on middle-aged children. *Omega 14,* pp. 74–80.

Mulvey, A., & Dohrenwend, B. S. (1984). The relation of stressful life events to gender. In A. Rickel, M. Gerrard, & I. Iscoe (Eds.), *Social and psychological problems of women.* New York: Hemisphere.

Munnichs, J. M. A., Mussen, P., Olbrich, E., & Coleman, P. G. (Eds.) (1985). *Life-span and change in gerontological perspective.* New York: Academic Press.

Murstein, B. (1973). Self-ideal-self discrepancy and choice of marital partner. In M. E. Lasswell & T. E. Lasswell (Eds.), *Love, marriage and family: A developmental approach.* Glenview, IL: Scott, Foresman.

Murstein, B. (1988). A toxonomy of love. In R. J. Sternberg & M. L. Brown (Eds.), *The psychology of love.* New Haven, CT: Yale University Press.

Murstein, B. I. (1982). Marital choice. In B. B. Wolman (Ed.), *Handbook of developmental psychology.* Englewood Cliffs, NJ: Prentice-Hall.

Mussen, P. (1985). Early adult antecedents of life satisfaction at age 70. In J. M. A. Munnichs, P. Mussen, E. Olbrich, & P. G. Coleman (Eds.), *Life-span and change in gerontological perspective.* New York: Academic Press.

Myers, G. C. (1985). Aging and worldwide population change. In J. E. Birren & K. W. Schaie (Eds.), *Handbook of the psychology of aging* (2nd ed.). New York: Van Nostrand Reinhold.

Myers, G. C. (1990). Demography of aging. In B. H. Binstock & L. K. George (Eds.), *Handbook of aging and the social sciences* (3rd ed.). New York: Academic Press.

Nagy, M. (1948). The child's theories concerning death. *Journal of Genetic Psychology, 73,* 3–27.

Nahemow, L., & Kogan, L. S. (1971). *Reduced fare for the elderly.* New York: Mayor's Office for the Aging.

Nahemow, L., McCluskey-Fawcett, K., & McGhee, P. E. (1986). *Humor and aging.* New York: Academic Press.

Neff, W. S. (1985). *Work and human behavior* (3rd ed.). New York: Aldine.

Neisser, U. (1976). *Cognition and reality: Principles and implications of cognitive psychology.* San Francisco: Freeman.

Nemeth, C. J., & Kwan, J. L. (1985). Originality of word association as a function of majority versus minority influence. *Social Psychology Quarterly, 48,* 277–282.

Nesselroade, J. R. (1977). Issues in studying developmental change in adults from a multivariate perspective. In J. E. Birren & K. W. Schaie (Eds.), *Handbook of the psychology of aging.* New York: Van Nostrand Reinhold.

Nesselroade, J. R. (1988). Some implications of the trait-state distinction for the study of development over the life-span: The case of personality. In P. B. Baltes, D. L. Featherman, & R. M. Lerner (Eds.), *Life-span development and behavior.* (Vol. 8). Hillsdale, NJ: Lawrence Erlbaum.

Nesselroade, J. R. (1990). Sampling and generalizability: Adult development and aging research issues examined within the general methodological framework of selection. In K. W. Schaie, R. T. Campbell, W. Meredith, & S. E. Rawlings (Eds.), *Methodological issues in aging research.* New York: Springer.

Nesselroade, J. R., & Labouvie, E. W. (1985). Experimental design in research on aging. In J. E. Birren & K. W. Schaie (Eds.), *Handbook of the psychology of aging* (2nd ed.). New York: Van Nostrand Reinhold.

Neugarten, B. L. (1967, December). A new look at menopause. *Psychology Today,* pp. 42–45.

Neugarten, B. L. (1968a). Adult personality: Toward a psychology of the life cycle. In B. L. Neugarten (Ed.), *Middle age and aging.* Chicago: University of Chicago Press.

Neugarten, B. L. (1968b). The awareness of middle age. In B. L. Neugarten (Ed.), *Middle age and aging.* Chicago: University of Chicago Press.

Neugarten, B. L. (1973). Personality change in later life: A developmental perspective. In C. Eisdorfer & M. P. Lawton (Eds.), *The psychology of adult development and aging.* Washington, DC: American Psychological Association.

Neugarten, B. L. (1974). Age groups in American society and the rise of the young old. *Annals of American Academy of Science,* pp. 187–198.

Neugarten, B. L. (1977). Personality and aging. In J. E. Birren & K. W. Schaie (Eds.), *Handbook of the psychology of aging.* New York: Van Nostrand Reinhold.

Neugarten, B. L., & Associates (1964). *Personality in middle and later life.* New York: Atherton Press.

Neugarten, B. L., & Datan, N. (1974). The middle years. In S. Arieti (Ed.), *American handbook of psychiatry* (Vol. 1, 2nd ed.). New York: Basic Books.

Neugarten, B. L., & Hagestad, G. O. (1977). Age and the life course. In R. H. Binstock & E. Shanas (Eds.), *Handbook of aging and the social sciences.* New York: Van Nostrand Reinhold.

Neugarten, B. L., Kraines, R. J., & Wood, V. (1965). *Women in the middle years.* Unpublished manuscript of the Committee on Human Development, University of Chicago.

Neugarten, B. L., & Weinstein, K. K. (1964). The changing American grandparent. *Journal of Marriage and the Family, 26,* 199–206.

Neugarten, B. L., Wood, V., Kraines, R. J., & Loomis, B. (1963). Women's attitudes toward the menopause. *Vita Humana, 6,* 140–151.

Neulinger, J. (1980). *To leisure: An introduction.* Boston: Allyn and Bacon.

Newman, B. M. (1982). Midlife development. In B. B. Wolman (Ed.), *Handbook of developmental psychology.* Englewood Cliffs, NJ: Prentice-Hall.

Nickols, S. Y., & Fox, K. D. (1983). Buying time and saving time: Strategies for managing household production. *Journal of Consumer Research, 10,* 197–208.

Northwest Indian Child Welfare Association, Inc. (1990). *Watchful eyes*. Portland, OR: Northwest Indian Child Welfare Association.

Nowak, C. (1977). Does youthfulness equal attractiveness. In L. Troll, J. Israel, & K. Israel (Eds.), *Looking ahead: A woman's guide to the problems and joys of growing old*. Englewood Cliffs, NJ: Prentice-Hall.

Nucci, L. P., & Turiel, E. (1978). Social interactions and the development of social concepts in preschool children. *Child Development, 49*, 400–407.

Nuessel, F. H. (1982). The language of ageism. *The Gerontologist, 22*, 273–275.

Nunnally, J. C. (1982). The study of human change: Measurement, research strategies, and methods of analysis. In B. B. Wolman (Ed.), *Handbook of developmental psychology*. Englewood Cliffs, NJ: Prentice-Hall.

Oerter, R. (1988). Developmental tasks through the life span: A new approach to an old concept. In P. B. Baltes, D. L. Featherman, & R. M. Lerner (Eds.), *Life-span development and behavior* (Vol. 8). Hillsdale, NJ: Lawrence Erlbaum.

Offenbach, S. I. (1990). Relationship between physiological status, cognition, and age in adult men. *Bulletin of the Psychonomic Society, 28*, 112–114.

Offer, D., & Sabshin, M. (1984). *Normality and the life cycle*. New York: Basic Books.

Ohnmacht, F. W., & McMorris, R. F. (1971). Creativity as a function of field independence and dogmatism. *Journal of Psychology, 79*, 165–168.

Olsho, L. W., Harkins, S. W., & Lenhardt, M. L. (1985). Aging and the auditory system. In J. E. Birren & K. W. Schaie (Eds.), *Handbook of the psychology of aging* (2nd ed.). New York: Van Nostrand Reinhold.

O'Rand, A. M., & Krecker, M. L. (1990). Concepts of the life cycle: Their history, meanings, and uses in the social sciences. *Annual Review of Sociology, 16*, 241–262.

Ordy, J. M. (1975). The nervous system, behavior, and aging. In J. M. Ordy & K. R. Brizzie (Eds.), *Neurobiology of aging: An interdisciplinary life-span approach*. New York: Plenum.

Orgel, L. E. (1963). The maintenance of the accuracy of protein synthesis and its relevance to aging. *Proceedings of the National Academy of Sciences, 49*, 517–521.

Orlofsky, J. L. (1976). Intimacy status: Relationship to interpersonal perception. *Journal of Youth and Adolescence, 5*, 73–88.

Orlofsky, J. L., Marcia, J. E., & Lesser, J. J. (1973). Ego identity status and the intimacy vs. isolation crisis of young adulthood. *Journal of Personality and Social Psychology, 27*, 211–219.

Orne, M. T. (1962). On the social psychology of the psychological experiment: With particular reference to demand characteristics and their implications. *American Psychologist, 17*, 776–783.

Ornstein, S., Cron, W. L., & Slocum, J. A., Jr. (1989). Life stage versus career stage: A comparative test of the theories of Levinson and Super. *Journal of Organizational Development, 10*, 117–133.

Ornstein, S., & Isabella, L. (1990). Age vs. stage models of career attitudes of women: A partial replication and extension. *Journal of Vocational Behavior, 36*, 1–9.

Orwell, G. (1963). The art of Donald McGill. In *A collection of essays*. New York: Harcourt, Brace, World. (Original essay published 1946)

Osborn, D. P. (1990). A reexamination of organizational choice process. *Journal of Vocational Behavior, 36,* 45–60.

Osborne, L. (1986). *The effects of age, modality and complexity of response, and practice on reaction time.* Unpublished master's thesis, University of Texas, Austin.

Osipow, S. (1990). Convergence in theories of career choice and development: Review and prospect. *Journal of Vocational Behavior, 39,* 122–131.

Osterwis, M., Solomon, F., & Green, M. (1984). (Eds.). Bereavement: Reactions, consequences, and care. Washington, DC: National Academy Press.

Oswalt, W. H. (1986). *Life cycles and lifeways.* Palo Alto, CA: Mayfield.

Overton, W. F., & Reese, H. W. (1973). Models of development: Methodological implication. In J. R. Nesselroade & H. W. Reese (Eds.), *Life-span developmental psychology: Methodological issues.* New York: Academic Press.

Pacaud, S. (1989). Performance in relation to age and educational level: A monumental research. *Experimental Aging Research, 15,* 123–136.

Palmore, E. (1968). The effects of aging on activities and attitudes. *The Gerontologist, 8,* 259–263.

Palmore, E. (1977). Facts on aging: A short quiz. *The Gerontologist, 17,* 315–320.

Palmore, E. (1979). Predictors of successful aging. *The Gerontologist, 19,* 427–431.

Palmore, E., & Luikart, C. (1974). Health and social factors related to life satisfaction. In E. Palmore (Ed.), *Normal aging II.* Durham, NC: Duke University Press.

Palmore, E. B., Rowlin, J. B., & Wang, H. S. (1985). Predictors of function among the old-old: A ten year follow-up. *Journal of Aging and Health, 1,* 50–66.

Parker, S. P. (1982) *Work and retirement.* Boston: George Allen and Unwin.

Parkes, C. M. (1972). *Bereavement: Studies of grief in adult life.* New York: International Universities Press.

Parks, R. D., & Swain, D. B. (1976). The father's role in infancy: A reevaluation. *Family Coordinator, 25,* 365–371.

Parmelee, P., & Lawton, M. P. (1990). The design of special environments for the aged. In J. E. Birren & K. W. Schaie (Eds.), *Handbook of the psychology of aging* (3rd ed.). New York: Academic Press.

Parr, J. (1980). The interaction of person and living environments. In L. W. Poon (Ed.), *Aging in the 1980s.* Washington, DC: American Psychological Association.

Pascual-Leone, J. (1984). Attention, dialectic, and mental effort: Toward an organismic theory of life stages. In M. L. Commons, F. A. Richards, and C. Armon (Eds.), *Beyond formal operations, Vol. 1: Late adolescent and adult cognitive development.* New York: Praeger.

Pascual-Leone, J. (1990). Reflections on life-span intelligence, consciousness, and ego development. In C. N. Alexander & E. J. Langer (Eds.), *Higher stages of human development: Perspectives on adult growth.* New York: Oxford University Press.

Peacock, J. C., Rush, A. C., & Milkovich, G. T. (1980). Career stages: A partial test of Levinson's model of life/career stages. *Journal of Vocational Behavior, 16,* 347–359.

Peck, R. (1968). Psychological developments in the second half of life. In B. L. Neugarten (Ed.), *Middle age and aging.* Chicago: University of Chicago Press.

Perkins, D. N. (1981). *The mind's best work*. Cambridge, MA: Harvard University Press.

Perlmutter, M. (1983). Learning and memory through adulthood. In M. W. Riley, B. B. Hess, & K. Bond (Eds.), *Aging in society: Selected reviews of recent research*. Hillsdale, NJ: Lawrence Erlbaum.

Peskin, H., & Livson, N. (1981). Uses of the past in adult psychological health. In D. H. Eichorn, N. Haan, J. Clausen, M. Honzik, & P. Mussen (Eds.), *Present and past in middle life*. New York: Academic Press.

Peter, L. J. (1979). *Peter's quotations*. New York: Bantam Books.

Peters, T. (1987). *Thriving on chaos*. New York: Harper and Row.

Peterson, E. T. (1989). Grandparenting. In S. J. Bahr & E. T. Peterson (Eds.), *Aging and the family*. Lexington, MA: D. C. Heath.

Pfeiffer, E., & Davis, G. C. (1974). The use of leisure time in middle life. In E. Palmore (Ed.), *Normal aging II*. Durham, NC: Duke University Press.

Phillips, S. (1982a). Career exploration in adulthood. *Journal of Vocational Behavior, 20,* 129–140.

Phillips, S. (1982b). The development of career choices: The relationship between patterns of commitment and career outcomes in adulthood. *Journal of Vocational Behavior, 20,* 141–152.

Pitcher, B. L., & Larson, D. C. (1989). Elderly widowhood. In S. J. Bahr & E. T. Peterson (Eds.), *Aging and the family*. Lexington, MA: D. C. Heath.

Pitts, D. G. (1982). The effects of aging on selected visual functions: Dark adaptation, visual acuity, steropsis and brightness contrast. In R. Sekuler, D. W. Kline, & K. Dismukes (Eds.), *Aging and human visual function*. New York: Alan R. Liss.

Plomin, R., Pederson, N. L., McClean, G. E., Nesselroade, J. R., & Bergeman, C. S. (1988). EAS temperament during the last half of the life span: Twins reared apart and together. *Psychology and Aging, 3,* 43–50.

Plomin, R., & Thompson, L. (1988). Life-span developmental behavioral genetics. In P. B. Baltes, D. L. Featherman, & R. M. Lerner (Eds.), *Life-span development and behavior* (Vol. 8). Hillsdale, NJ: Lawrence Erlbaum.

Plude, D. J., Milberg, W. P., & Cerella, J. (1986). Age differences in depicting and perceiving tridimensionality in simple line drawings. *Experimental Aging Research, 12,* 221–225.

Pollack, R. H., & Atkeson, B. M. (1978). A life-span approach to perceptual development. In P. B. Baltes (Ed.), *Life-span development and behavior* (Vol. 1). New York: Academic Press.

Poon, L. W. (1985). Differences in human memory with aging: Nature, causes, & clinical impressions. In J. E. Birren & K. W. Schaie (Eds.), *Handbook of the psychology of aging* (2nd. ed.). New York: Van Nostrand Reinhold.

Poon, L. W., Rubin, D. C., & Wilson, B. A. (Eds.). (1989). *Everyday cognition in adult and later life*. New York: Cambridge University Press.

Power, F. C., Higgins, A., & Kohlberg, L. (1989). *Lawrence Kohlberg's approach to moral education: A study of three democratic high schools*. New York: Columbia University Press.

Prado, C. G. (1988). Narrative perspective and aging. In J. E. Thornton & E. R. Winkler (Eds.), *Ethics and aging*. Vancouver, British Columbia, Canada: University of British Columbia Press.

Price-Williams, D. (1981). Concrete and formal operations. In R. H. Munroe, R. L. Munroe, & B. B. Whiting (Eds.), *Handbook of cross-cultural hu-*

man development. New York: Garland STM Press.

Quinn, J. F., & Burkhauser, R. V. (1990). Work and retirement. In R. H. Binstock & L. K. George (Eds.), *Handbook of aging and the social sciences* (3rd ed.). New York: Academic Press.

Quinn, J. F., Burkhauser, R. V., & Myers, D. C. (1990). Passing the torch: The influence of economic incentives on work and retirement. Kalamazoo, MI: Upjohn Institute for Employment Research.

Rabbit, P. (1977). Changes in problem-solving ability in old age. In J. E. Birren & K. W. Schaie (Eds.), *Handbook of the psychology of aging*. New York: Van Nostrand Reinhold.

Rapoport, R., & Rapoport, R. (1971). *Dual career families*. Baltimore: Penguin.

Rathus, S. (1981). *Psychology*. New York: Holt, Rinehart and Winston.

Ravussin, E., & Pogardus, C. (1989). Relationship of genetics, age, and physical fitness to daily energy expenditure and fuel utilization. *American Journal of Clinical Nutrition, 49,* 968–975.

Ray, W. J., & Ravizza, R. (1985). *Methods toward a science of behavior and experience* (2nd ed.). Belmont, CA: Wadsworth.

Reedy, M. N., Birren, J. E., & Schaie, K. W. (1982). Age and sex differences in satisfying love relationships across the life-span. *Human Development, 24,* 52–66.

Reese, H. W., & Overton, W. F. (1970). Models of development and theories of development. In L. R. Goulet & P. B. Baltes (Eds.), *Life-span development psychology: Research and theory*. New York: Academic Press.

Reese, H. W., & Rodeheaver, D. (1985). Problem solving and complex decision making. In J. E. Birren & K. W. Schaie (Eds.), *Handbook of the psychol-*

ogy of aging (2nd ed.). New York: Van Nostrand Reinhold.

Reese, H. W., & Smyer, M. (1983). The dimensionalization of life events. In E. Callahan & K. McClusky (Eds.), *Life-span developmental psychology: Nonnormative life events*. New York: Academic Press.

Reid, B. V. (1984). An anthropological reinterpretation of Kohlberg's stages of moral development. *Human Development, 27,* 57–64.

Reinke, B. J., Ellicott, A. M., Harris, R. L., & Hancock, E. (1985). Timing of psychosocial change in women's lives. *Human Development, 28,* 259–280.

Reiss, I. (1980). *Family systems in America* (3rd ed.). New York: Holt, Rinehart and Winston.

Relethford, J. H. (1990). The human species: An introduction to biological anthropology. Mountain View, CA: Mayfield.

Rice, D. G. (1979). *Dual-career marriage*. New York: Free Press.

Rice, P. R. (1990). *Intimate relationships, marriages and families*. Mountain View, CA: Mayfield.

Richards, F. A. (1990). Equilibrational models and the framework of postformal cognition. *Adult development, Vol. 2: Models and methods in the study of adolescent and adult thought*. New York: Praeger.

Richards, F. A., & Commons, M. L. (1982). Systematic, metasystematic, and cross-paradigmatic reasoning: A case for stages of reasoning beyond formal operations. In M. L. Commons, F. A. Richards, & C. Armon (Eds.), *Beyond formal operations: Late adolescent and adult cognitive development*. New York: Praeger.

Richards, F. A., & Commons, M. L. (1984). Systematic, metasystematic, and cross-paradigmatic reasoning: A case for stages of reasoning beyond formal operations. In M. L. Commons, F. A. Richards, and C. Armon (Eds.), *Beyond formal operations, Vol. 1: Late adolescent and adult cognitive development* (pp. 92–119). New York: Praeger.

Richards, F. A., & Commons, M. L. (1990a). Applying signal detection theory to measure subject sensitivity to metasystematic, systematic and lower developmental stage signals. In M. L. Commons, C. Armon, L. Kohlberg, F. A. Richards, T. A. Grotzer, & J. D. Sinnott (Eds.), *Adult development, Vol. 2: Models and methods in the study of adolescent and adult thought*. New York: Praeger.

Richards, F. A., & Commons, M. L. (1990b). Postformal cognitive-developmental theory and research: A review of its current status. In C. N. Alexander & E. J. Langer (Eds.), *Higher stages of human development: Perspectives on adult growth*. New York: Oxford University Press.

Ridley, C. A. (1973). Exploring the impact of work satisfaction and involvement on marital interaction when both partners are employed. *Journal of Marriage and the Family, 35,* 229–237.

Riegel, K. F. (1975a). Adult life crises: A dialectic interpretation of development. In N. Datan & L. H. Ginsberg (Eds.), *Life-span developmental psychology: Normative life crises*. New York: Academic Press.

Riegel, K. F. (1975b). From traits and equilibrium toward developmental dialectics. In W. J. Arnold & J. K. Cole (Eds.), *1974–75 Nebraska symposium on motivation*. Lincoln: University of Nebraska Press.

Riegel, K. F. (1977). History of psychological gerontology. In J. E. Birren & K. W. Schaie (Eds.), *Handbook of the psychology of aging*. New York: Van Nostrand Reinhold.

Riegel, K. F., Riegel, R. M., & Meyer, G. (1967). A study of the dropout rates of longitudinal research on aging and the prediction of death. *Journal of Personality and Social Psychology, 5,* 342–348.

Ring, K. (1984). *Heading toward omega*. New York: William Morrow.

Risman, B., Hill, C., Rubin, Z., & Peplau, A. (1981). Living together in college: Implications for courtship. *Journal of Marriage and the Family, 42,* 77–117.

Ritzer, G. (1977). *Working: Conflict and change* (2nd ed.). Englewood Cliffs, NJ: Prentice-Hall.

Robbins, S. L. (1967). *Pathology* (3rd ed.). Philadelphia: Saunders.

Roberts, P., & Newton, P. M. (1987). Levinsonian studies of women's development. *Psychology and Aging, 2,* 154–163.

Roberts, R. E. L., & Bengston, V. L. (1990). Is intergenerational solidarity a unidimensional construct? A second test of a formal model. *Journal of Gerontology: Social Sciences, 45,* S12–S20.

Robertson, J. F. (1977). Grandmother: A study of role conceptions. *Journal of Marriage and the Family, 39,* 165–174.

Robinson, P. B., Jr., & Peterson, E. T. (1989). Leisure among the elderly. In S. Bahr & E. Peterson (Eds.), *Aging and the family*. Lexington, MA: D. C. Heath.

Robinson, P. K., Coberly, S., & Paul, C. E. (1985). Work and retirement. In R. H. Binstock & E. Shanas (Eds.), *Handbook of aging and the social sciences* (2nd ed.). New York: Van Nostrand Reinhold.

Rockstein, M. (1975). The biology of aging in humans: An overview. In R. Goldman & M. Rockstein (Eds.), *The physiology and pathology of human aging*. New York: Academic Press.

Rodeheaver, D. (1987). Problem solving. In G. L. Maddox (Ed.), *The encyclopedia of aging*. New York: Springer.

Rodeheaver, D., & Datan, N. (1988). The challenge of double jeopardy: Toward a mental health agenda for aging women. *American Psychologist, 43,* 648–654.

Rodin, J. (1980). Managing the stress of aging. The role of control and coping. In S. Levine & H. Ursin (Eds.), *Coping and health.* New York: Plenum.

Rodriguez, J. A. (1989). *Exploring the notion of higher stages of social perspective taking.* Unpublished qualifying paper, Harvard Graduate School of Education, Cambridge, MA.

Rodriguez, J. A. (1991). *Adult social-perspective-taking stages and the doctor-patient relationship.* Unpublished dissertation, Harvard Graduate School of Education, Cambridge, MA.

Rogosa, D. (1988). Myths about longitudinal research. In K. W. Schaie, R. T. Campbell, W. Meredith, & S. E. Rawlings (Eds.), *Methodological issues in aging research.* New York: Springer.

Roiphe, A. (1975). *Can you have everything and still want babies?* New York: Brandt and Brandt Literary Agency.

Rollins, B. C. (1989). Marital quality at midlife. In S. Hunter & M. Sundel (Eds.), *Midlife myths.* Newbury Park, CA: Sage.

Rollins, B. C., & Feldman, H. (1970). Marital satisfaction over the life cycle. *Journal of Marriage and the Family, 32,* 20–28.

Rook, K. S., & Pietromonaco, P. (1987). Close relationships: Ties that heal or ties that bind? In W. H. Jones & D. Perlman (Eds.), *Advances in personal relationships* (Vol. 1). Greenwich, CT: JAI Press.

The Roper Organization (1985). *The Virginia Slims American women's opinion poll.* New York: Roper.

Rosenberg, S. D., & Farrell, M. P. (1976). Identity and crisis in middle-aged men. *International Journal of Aging and Human Development, 7,* 153–170.

Rosenfield, S. (1980). Sex differences in depression: Do women always have higher rates? *Journal of Health and Social Behavior, 21,* 33–42.

Rosenman, I., Friedman, M., Straus, R., Jenkins, C. D., Zyzanski, S., Jr., Wurm, M., & Kositcheck, R. (1970). Coronary heart disease in the western collaborative group study: A follow-up experience of four and one-half years. *Journal of Chronic Diseases, 23,* 173–190.

Rosenmayr, L. (1985). Changing values and the position of the aged in Western cultures. In J. E. Birren & K. W. Schaie (Eds.), *Handbook of the psychology of aging* (2nd ed.). New York: Van Nostrand Reinhold.

Rosenthal, R. (1966). *Experimenter effects in behavioral research.* New York: Appleton-Century-Crofts.

Rosenthal, R. (1969). Interpersonal expectations: Effects of the experimenter's hypothesis. In R. Rosenthal & R. Rosnow (Eds.), *Artifact in behavioral research.* New York: Academic Press.

Rosenthal, R. (1979). How often are numbers wrong? *American Psychologist, 33,* 1005–1008.

Rosow, I. (1967). *Social integration of the aged.* New York: Free Press.

Ross, B. L. (1977). *Interrelationships of five cognitive constructs: Moral development, locus of control, creativity, field dependence–field independence, and intelligence in a sample of 167 community college students.* Los Angeles: University of Southern California.

Rossi, A. S. (1980). Aging and parenthood in the middle years. In P. B. Baltes & O. G. Brim, Jr. (Eds.), *Life-span development and behavior* (Vol. 3). New York: Academic Press.

Rossman, I. (1977). Anatomic and body composition changes with aging. In C. E. Finch & L. Hayflick (Eds.), *Handbook of the biology of aging*. New York: Van Nostrand Reinhold.

Rubenstein, R. L. (1989). The home environments of older people: A description of psychosocial processes linking person to place. *Journal of Gerontology, 44,* S45–S53.

Rubin, A., Peplau, L. A., & Hill, C. T. (1976). *Becoming intimate: The development of male-female relationships*. Working manuscript.

Rubin, Z. (1973). *Liking and loving: An invitation to social psychology*. New York: Holt, Rinehart and Winston.

Rubin, Z. (1981, May). Does personality really change after 20? *Psychology Today, 15,* 18–27.

Rupp, R. R. (1970). Understanding the problems of presbycusis: An overview. *Geriatrics, 25,* 100.

Rusin, M. J., & Siegler, I. C. (1975, October). *Personality differences between participants and dropouts in a longitudinal aging study*. Paper presented at the 28th Annual Meeting of the Gerontological Society, Louisville, KY.

Russell, C. S. (1974). Transition to parenthood: Problems and gratifications. *Journal of Marriage and the Family, 36,* 294–301.

Russell, J. A. (1980). A circumplex model of emotion. *Journal of Personality and Social Psychology, 39,* 1161–1178.

Rybash, J. M., Hoyer, W., & Roodin, P. (1986). *Adult cognition and aging*. New York: Pergamon Press.

Rybash, J. M., Roodin, P., & Santrock (1991). J. W. *Adult development*. Dubuque, IA: W. C. Brown.

Ryder, C. F., & Ross, D. M. (1981). Terminal care: Issues and alternatives. In R. Fulton, E. Markusen, G. Owen, J. L. Scheiber (Eds.), *Death and dying: Challenge and change*. San Francisco: Boyd and Fraser.

Ryff, C. (1984). Personality development from the inside: The subjective experience of change in adulthood and aging. In P. B. Baltes & O. G. Brim (Eds.), *Life-span development and behavior* (Vol. 6). New York: Academic Press.

Ryon, R. (1978). Seniors want some surprising things. *Los Angeles Times,* January 22, Part VIII, pp. 1, 24.

Safilios-Rothschild, C. (1977). *Love, sex, and sex roles*. Englewood Cliffs, NJ: Prentice-Hall.

Sales, A., & Mirvis, P. H. (1984). When cultures collide: Issues in acquisition. In J. R. Kimberly & R. E. Quinn (Eds.), *New futures: The challenge of managing corporate transitions*. Homewood, IL: Dow Jones-Irwin.

Salthouse, T. (1985a). *A theory of cognitive aging*. New York: North-Holland.

Salthouse, T. (1985b). Speed of behavior and its implications for cognition. In K. W. Schaie & J. E. Birren (Eds.), *Handbook of the psychology of aging* (2nd ed.). New York: Van Nostrand Reinhold.

Salthouse, T. A. (1987). Age, experience and compensation. In C. Schooler & K. W. Schaie (Eds.), *Cognitive function and social structure over the life course*. New York: Ablex.

Salthouse, T. A. (1988). Initiating the formalization of theories of cognitive aging. *Psychology and Aging, 3,* 3–16.

Salthouse, T. A. (1990). Cognitive competence and expertise. In J. E. Birren & K. W. Schaie (Eds.), *Handbook of the psychology of aging* (3rd ed.). New York: Academic Press.

Salthouse, T. A., Kausler, D. H., &

Saults, J. S. (1990). Age, self-assessed health status, and cognition. *Journal of Gerontology, 45,* 156–60.

Sanders, J. L., Sterns, H. L., Smith, M., & Sanders, R. E. (1975). Modification of concept identification performance in older adults. *Developmental Psychology, 11,* 824–829.

Sanders, R. E., Wise, J. L., Liddle, C. L., Murphy, M. D. (1990). Adult age comparisons in the processing of event frequency information. *Psychology and Aging, 5,* 172–177.

Santrock, J. W., & Sitterle, K. A. (1987). Parent-child relationships in stepmother families. In K. Pasley & M. Ihinger-Tallman (Eds.), *Remarriage and stepparenting.* New York: Guilford Press.

Sapiro, V. (1990). *Women in American society* (2nd ed.). Palo Alto, CA: Mayfield.

Sarason, I. G., Sarason, B. R., Pierce, G. R. (1989). *Social support: An interactional view.* New York: Wiley.

Sarton, M. (1981). A literary perspective. In P. Johnson (Ed.), *Perspectives on aging.* Cambridge, MA: Ballinger.

Sathe, V. (1985). *Culture and related corporate realities.* Homewood, IL: Richard D. Irwin.

Saunders, C. (1969). *The moment of truth: Care of the dying person.* Cleveland: Case Western University.

Saunders, C. (1976). St. Christopher's hospice. In E. Shneidman (Ed.), *Death: Contemporary perspectives.* Palo Alto, CA: Mayfield.

Saunders, C. (1981). Should a patient know? In R. Fulton, E. Markusen, G. Owen, & J. L. Scheiber (Eds.), *Death and dying: Challenge and change.* San Francisco: Boyd and Fraser.

Scanzoni, J., Polonko, K., Teachman, J., & Thompson, L. (1989). *The sexual bond: Rethinking families and close relationships.* Newbury Park, CA: Sage.

Scarr, S., Phillips, D., & McCartney, K. (1989). Working mothers and their families. *American Psychologist, 44,* 1402–1409.

Schacter, D. L. (1987). Implicit memory: History and current status. *Journal of Experimental Psychology: Learning, Memory, and Cognition, 13,* 501–518.

Schacter, D., & Singer, J. F. (1962). Cognitive, social, and physiological determinants of emotional state. *Psychological Review, 69,* 379–399.

Schaie, K. W. (1967). Age changes and age differences. *The Gerontologist, 7,* 128–132.

Schaie, K. W. (1973). Developmental processes and aging. In C. Eisdorfer & M. P. Lawton (Eds.), *The psychology of adult development and aging.* Washington, DC: American Psychological Association.

Schaie, K. W. (1977). Quasi-experimental research designs in the psychology of aging. In J. E. Birren & K. W. Schaie (Eds.), *Handbook of the psychology of aging.* New York: Van Nostrand Reinhold.

Schaie, K. W. (1979). The primary mental abilities in adulthood: An exploration in the development of psychometric intelligence. In P. B. Baltes & O. G. Brim, Jr. (Eds.), *Life-span development and behavior* (Vol. 2). New York: Academic Press.

Schaie, K. W. (1988). Ageism in psychological research. *American Psychologist, 43,* 179–183.

Schaie, K. W. (1988). Methodological issues in aging research: An introduction. In K. W. Schaie, R. T. Campbell, W. Meredith, & S. E. Rawlings (Eds.), *Methodological issues in aging research.* New York: Springer.

Schaie, K. W., & Geiwitz, J. (1982), *Adult development and aging.* Boston: Little, Brown.

Schaie, K. W., & Hertzog, C. (1982).

Longitudinal methods. In B. B. Wolman (Ed.), *Handbook of developmental psychology.* New York: Van Nostrand Reinhold.

Schaie, K. W., & Hertzog, C. (1983). Fourteen-year cohort-sequential studies of adult intellectual development. *Developmental Psychology, 19,* 531–543.

Schaie, K. W., & Hertzog, C. (1985). Measurement in the psychology of adulthood and aging. In J. E. Birren & K. W. Schaie (Eds.), *Handbook of the psychology of aging* (2nd ed.). New York: Van Nostrand Reinhold.

Schaie, K. W., & Labouvie-Vief, G. (1974). Generational versus ontogenetic components of change in adult cognitive behavior. *Developmental Psychology, 10,* 305–320.

Schaie, K. W., & Willis, S. L. (1991). *Adult development and aging.* New York: Harper Collins.

Scheidt, R. J., & Windley, P. G. (1985). The ecology of aging. In J. E. Birren & K. W. Schaie (Eds.), *Handbook of the psychology of aging* (2nd ed.). New York: Van Nostrand Reinhold.

Schein, E. (1987). *Organizational culture and leadership.* San Francisco: Jossey-Bass.

Schlesinger, B. (1977). One-parent families in Britain. *Family Coordinator, 26,* 139–141.

Schludermann, E. H., Schludermann, P. W., & Brown, B. W. (1983). Halstead's studies in the neurophysiology of aging. *Archives of Gerontology and Geriatrics, 2,* 49–172.

Schmid-Kitsikis, E. (1990). Development of mental functioning. *Human Development, 33,* 189–209.

Schmidt, M. G. (1981–82). Exchange and power in special settings for the aged. *International Journal of Aging and Human Development, 14,* 157–166.

Schmitt, R. L. (1982–83). Symbolic mortality in ordinary contexts: Impediments to the nuclear era. *Omega, 13,* 95–116.

Schneider, E. L., & Reed, J. D. (1985). Modulations of the aging process. In C. E. Finch & E. L. Schneider (Eds.), *Handbook of the biology of aging* (2nd ed.). New York: Van Nostrand Reinhold.

Schneidman, E. (1992). *Death: Current perspectives* (3rd ed.). Mountain View, CA: Mayfield.

Schnurr, P., Vaillant, C., & Vaillant, G. (in press). Predicting exercise in late middle life from young adult personality. *International Journal of Aging and Human Development.*

Schonfield, D. (1982). Who is stereotyping whom? *The Gerontologist, 22,* 269–271.

Schroots, J. J. F., & Birren, J. E. (1990). Concepts of time and aging in science. In J. E. Birren & K. W. Schaie (Eds.), *Handbook of the psychology of aging* (3rd ed.). New York: Academic Press.

Schuknecht, H. F., & Igarashi, M. (1964). Pathology of slowly progressive sensorineural deafness. *Transactions: American Academy of Ophthalmology and Otolaryngology, 68,* 222–242.

Schulz, R. (1985). Emotion and affect. In J. E. Birren & K. W. Schaie (Eds.), *Handbook of the psychology of aging* (2nd ed.). New York: Van Nostrand Reinhold.

Schulz, R. (1988, August). *Psychological perspectives on caregiving.* Invited address presented at the annual convention of the American Psychological Association, Atlanta, GA.

Schulz, R., & Curnow, C. (1988). Peak performance and age among super athletes, track and field, swimming, baseball, and golf. *Journal of Gerontology, 43,* P113–P120.

Schulz, R., Visintainer, P., & Williamson, G. M. (1990). Psychiatric and physical morbidity of caregiving. *Journal of Gerontology, 45,* P181–P191.

Schwartzman, A., Gold, D., Andres, D., Arbuckle, T., et al. (1987). Stability of intelligence: A 40-year follow-up. Special Issue: Aging and cognition. *Canadian Journal of Psychology, 41,* 244–256.

Scott, A. (1981). Old wives' tales. In P. Johnston (Ed.), *Perspectives on aging.* Cambridge, MA: Ballinger.

Self, P. (1975). The further evolution of the parental imperative. In N. Datan & L. Ginsberg (Eds.), *Life-span developmental psychology: Normative life crises.* New York: Academic Press.

Selmanowitz, O. J., Rizer, R. L., & Orentreich, N. (1977). Aging of the skin and its appendages. In C. E. Finch & L. Hayflick (Eds.), *Handbook of the biology of aging.* New York: Van Nostrand Reinhold.

Selye, H. (1976). *The stress of life.* New York: McGraw-Hill.

Selzer, S. C., & Denney, N. W. (1980). Conservation abilities among middle-aged and elderly adults. *Aging and Human Development, 11,* 135–146.

Serdahely, W., & Walker, B. (1990). A near death experience at birth. *Death Studies, 14,* 177–183.

Shanan, J., & Jacobowitz, J. (1982). Personality and aging. In C. Eisdorfer (Ed.), *Annual review of gerontology and geriatrics* (Vol. 3). New York: Springer.

Shanas, E. (1972). Adjustment to retirement. In F. M. Carp (Ed.), *Retirement.* New York: Behavioral Publications.

Shantz, C. U. (1983). Social cognition.

In P. Mussen (Ed.), *Handbook of child psychology* (4th ed.), *Vol. 3: Cognitive development.* New York: Wiley.

Sheehy, G. (1976). *Passages: The predictable crises of adult life.* New York: Dutton.

Sheehy, G. (1977). The mentor connection. In D. Elkind & D. C. Hertzel (Eds.), *Readings in human development: Contemporary perspective.* New York: Harper and Row.

Sheehy, G. (1981). *Pathfinders.* New York: Dutton.

Shehan, C., & Dwyer, J. W. (1989). Parent child exchanges in the middle years: Attachment and autonomy in the transition to adulthood. In J. A. Mancini (Ed.), *Aging parents and adult children.* Lexington, MA: D. C. Heath.

Sherman, S. R. (1974). Leisure activities in retirement housing. *Journal of Gerontology, 29,* 325–335.

Sherwood, S., Greer, D. S., Morris, J. N., & Sherwood, C. C. (1972). *The Highland Heights experiment.* Washington, DC: U.S. Department of Housing and Urban Development.

Shneidman, E. (1984). *Death: Current perspectives* (3rd ed.). Palo Alto, CA: Mayfield.

Shumaker, S. A., & Czajokowski, S. M. (1989). Social support and quality of life. In S. A. Shumaker & S. M. Czajokowski (Eds.), *Social support and cardiovascular disease.* New York: Plenum.

Siegler, I. C. (1975). The terminal drop hypothesis: Fact or artifact? *Experimental Aging Research, 1,* 169.

Siegler, I. C., & Costa, P. T., Jr. (1985). Health behavior and relationships. In J. E. Birren & K. W. Schaie (Eds.), *Handbook of the psychology of aging* (2nd ed.). New York: Van Nostrand Reinhold.

Siegler, I. C., Nowlin, J. B., & Blumenthal, J. A. (1980). Health and behavior: Methodological considerations for adult development and aging. In L. Poon (Ed.), *Aging in the 1980s.* Washington, DC: American Psychological Association.

Sih, P. K. T., & Allen, L. B. (1976). *The Chinese in America.* New York: St. John's University.

Silverman, P. R. (1977). Widowhood and preventive intervention. In S. H. Zarit (Ed.), *Reading in aging and death: Contemporary perspectives.* New York: Harper and Row.

Simenauer, J., & Carroll, D. (1982). *Singles: The new Americans.* New York: Simon and Schuster.

Simon, E. W., Dixon, R. A., Nowak, C. A., & Hultsch, D. F. (1982). Orienting task effects on text recall in adulthood. *Journal of Gerontology, 31,* 575–580.

Simonton, D. K. (1980). Thematic fame, melodic originality, and musical zeitgeist: A biographical and transhistorical content analysis. *Journal of Personality and Social Psychology, 39,* 972–983.

Simonton, D. K. (1985). Quality, quantity, and age: The careers of 10 distinguished psychologists. *International Journal of Aging and Human Development, 21,* 241–254.

Simonton, D. K. (1986). Popularity, content, and context in 37 Shakespeare plays. *Poetics, 15,* 493–510.

Simonton, D. K. (1988a). Age and outstanding achievement: What do we know after over a century of research? *Psychological Bulletin, 104,* 251–267.

Simonton, D. K. (1988b). Creativity, leadership and chance. In R. J. Sternberg (Ed.), *The nature of creativity.* Cambridge, MA: Harvard University Press.

Simonton, D. K. (1988c). *Scientific genius: A psychology of science.* Cambridge, MA: Harvard University Press.

Simonton, D. K. (1990). Creativity and wisdom in aging. In J. E. Birren and K. W. Schaie, (Eds.), *Handbook of the psychology of aging* (3rd ed.). New York: Academic Press.

Simpson, M. (1979). Social and psychological aspects of dying. In H. W. Wass (Ed.), *Death: Facing the facts.* New York: McGraw-Hill.

Sinclair, D. (1969). *Human growth after birth.* London: Oxford University Press.

Singher, L. J. (1974). The slowly dying child. *Clinical Pediatrics, 13,* 861–867.

Singleton, J. F. (1985). Retirement: Its effect on the individual. *Activities, Adaptation, & Aging, 6,* 1–7.

Sinnot, J. D. (1982). Correlates of sex roles of older adults. *Journal of Gerontology, 37,* 587–594.

Sinnott, J. D. (Ed.). (1989). *Everyday problem solving: Theory and applications.* New York: Praeger.

Sistrunk, F., & McDavid, J. W. (1971). Sex variable in conforming behavior. *Journal of Personality and Social Psychology, 17,* 200–207.

Skinner, B. F. (1953). *Science and human behavior.* New York: Macmillan.

Skinner, B. F. (1971). *Beyond freedom and dignity.* New York: Knopf.

Skinner, D. A. (1984). Dual-career family and stress. In P. Voydanoff (Ed.), *Work and family.* Palo Alto, CA: Mayfield.

Skolnick, A. (1978). *The intimate environment: Exploring marriage and family* (2nd ed.). Boston: Little, Brown.

Skolnick, A. (1981). Married lives: Longitudinal perspectives on marriage. In D. Eichorn, N. Haan, J. Clausen,

M. Honzik, & P. Mussen (Eds.), *Present and past in middle life*. New York: Academic Press.

Skolnick, A. (1986a). *The intimate environment: Exploring marriage and family* (4th ed.). Boston: Little, Brown.

Skolnick, A. (1986b). *The psychology of human development*. Orlando, FL: Harcourt, Brace, Jovanovich.

Skolnick, A. (1986c). Early attachment and personal relationships across the life-span. In P. B. Baltes, D. L. Featherman, & R. M. Lerner (Eds.), *Life-span development and behavior* (Vol. 7). Hillsdale, NJ: Lawrence Earlbaum.

Smith, C. (1979). Use of drugs in the aged. *Johns Hopkins Medical Journal, 145*, 61–64.

Smith, G. J., Carlsson, I., Sandstrom, S. (1985). Artists and artistic creativity—elucidated by psychological experiments. *Psychological Research Bulletin, 25*, 9–10.

Smith, J., Dixon, R. A., & Baltes, P. B. (1987). Age differences in responses to life planning problems: A research analog for the study of wisdom-related knowledge. In M. L. Commons, J. O. Sinnott, F. A. Richards, & C. Armon (Eds.), *Adult development, Vol. 1: Comparisons and applications of developmental models*. New York: Praeger.

Smith, J., Dixon, R. A., & Baltes, P. B. (1989). Expertise in life planning: A new research approach to investigating aspects of wisdom. In M. L. Commons, J. D. Sinnott, F. A. Richards, & C. Armon (Eds.), *Adult development, Vol. 1: Comparisons and applications of developmental models*. New York: Praeger.

Smith, K. F., & Bengston, F. L. (1979). Positive consequences of institutionalization: Solidarity between elderly parents and their middle-aged children. *The Gerontologist, 19*, 609–615.

Smith, R. J., Sherman, M. F., & Sherman, N. C. (1982–83). The elderly's reactions toward the dying: The effects of perceived age similarity. *Omega, 13*, 319–331.

Snarey, J. R. (1985). Cross-cultural universality of social-moral development: A critical review of Kohlbergian research. *Psychological Bulletin, 97*, 202–232.

Snarey, J., Son, L., Kuehne, V. S., Hauser, S., & Vaillant, G. (1987). The role of parenting in men's psycho-social development: A longitudinal study of early adulthood infertility and midlife generativity. *Developmental Psychology, 23*, 593–603.

Snodgrass, J. (1986). *Observing organizations: How to uncover the informal power structure*. Working paper, California State University, Los Angeles.

Snyder, M., & Swann, W. B., Jr. (1978a). Behavioral confirmation in social interaction. *Journal of Experimental Social Psychology, 14*, 148–162.

Snyder, M., & Swann, W. B., Jr. (1978b). Hypothesis testing in social interaction. *Journal of Personality and Social Psychology, 36*, 1202–1212.

Sonnenborn, T. (1978). The origin, evolution, nature and causes of aging. In J. Behnke, C. Finch, & G. Moment (Eds.), *The biology of aging*. New York: Harper and Row.

Sonnert, J. G., & Commons, M. L. (in preparation). *A definition of moral stage 6*. Cambridge, MA: Harvard University Press.

Sonnert, J. G., & Commons, M. L. (1991, July 12–14). *Society and the highest stages of moral development*. Paper presented at the Fourteenth Annual Meeting of the International

Society of Political Psychology, Helsinki, Finland. July 1–6.

Sonstroem, R. J. (1984). Exercise and self-esteem. *Exercise and Sports Sciences Review, 12,* 123–155.

Spector, A. (1982). Aging of the lens and cataract formation. In R. Sekuler, D. W. Kline, & K. Dismukes (Eds.), *Aging and human visual function.* New York: Alan Liss.

Spence, J. (1985). *Achievement American style: The rewards and costs of individualism.* Presidential Address, American Psychological Association Convention, Los Angeles, CA.

Spock, B. (1974). *Baby and child care.* New York: Pocket Books.

Srole, L., Langner, T. S., Michael, S. T., Opler, M. K., & Rennie, T. A. (1962). Mental health in the metropolis: The Midtown Manhattan Study. New York: McGraw-Hill.

Sroufe, L. A. (1979). The coherence of individual development. *American Psychologist, 34,* 834–841.

Sroufe, L. A. (1985). Attachment classification from the perspective of infant-caregiver relationships and infant temperament. *Child Development, 56,* 1–14.

Stafford, R., Blackman, E., & Debona, P. (1977). The division of labor among cohabiting and married couples. *Journal of Marriage and the Family, 39,* 43–58.

Stagner, R. (1985). Aging in industry. In J. E. Birren & K. W. Schaie (Eds.), *Handbook of the psychology of aging* (2nd ed.). New York: Van Nostrand Reinhold.

Stankov, L. (1988). Aging, attention and intelligence. *Psychology and Aging, 3,* 59–74.

Sternberg, R. J. (1984). Postformal operational thought. In M. L. Commons & F. A. Richards (Eds.), *Beyond formal operations, Vol. 1: Late adolescent and adult cognitive development.* New York: Praeger.

Sternberg, R. J. (1985). *Beyond IQ: A triarchic theory of human intelligence.* Cambridge, England: Cambridge University Press.

Sternberg, R. J. (1988). Triangulating love. In R. J. Sternberg & M. L. Brown (Eds.), *The psychology of love.* New Haven: CT: Yale University Press.

Stevens-Long, J. (1979). *Adult life.* Palo Alto, CA: Mayfield.

Stevens-Long, J. (1979). *Planning a funeral.* Working manuscript. Los Angeles: California State University.

Stevens-Long, J., & Cobb, N. (1983). *Adolescence and young adulthood.* Palo Alto, CA: Mayfield.

Stevens-Long, J., & Macdonald, S. (1991). *The relationship of empathy to ego development and cognitive generativity.* Paper presented at the conference of the Society for Research in Adult Development. Boston: Suffolk University, July 12–14.

Stevenson, J. S., & Topp, R. (1990). Effects of moderate and low intensity long-term exercise by older adults. *Research in Nursing and Health, 13,* 209–218.

Stillion, J., & Wass, H. (1979). Children and death. In H. Wass (Ed.), *Dying: Facing the facts.* New York: McGraw-Hill.

Stinnett, N., & Walters, J. (1977). *Relationships in marriage and family.* New York: Macmillan.

Storr, C. (1972). Freud and the concept of parental guilt. In J. Miller (Ed.), *Freud: The man, his world, his influence.* Boston: Little, Brown.

Strehler, B. L. (1979). The future and aging research. In A. Cherkin & C. Finch et al. (Eds.), *Physiology and cell biology of aging.* New York: Raven Press.

Streib, G. (1983). The social psychology of retirement: Theoretical perspectives and research priorities. In J. E. Birren, J. M. A. Munnichs, H. Thomae, & M. Marois (Eds.), *Aging: A challenge to science and society* (Vol. 3). New York: Oxford University Press.

Streib, G., & Schneider, C. J. (1971). *Retirement in American society: Impact and progress.* Ithaca, NY: Cornell University Press.

Stromberg, A., & Harkess, S. (1988). *Women working: Theories and facts in perspective.* Mountain View, CA: Mayfield.

Stroud, J. G. (1981). Women's careers: Work, family, and personality. In D. Eichorn, N. Haan, J. Clausen, M. Honzik, & P. Mussen (Eds.), *Present and past in middle life.* New York: Academic Press.

Struyk, R. (1981). The changing housing and neighborhood environment of the elderly: A look at the year 2000. In J. G. Marsh (Ed.), *Aging: Social change.* New York: Academic Press.

Suchet, M., & Barling, J. (1986). Employed mothers' interrole conflict, spouse support and marital functioning. *Journal of Occupational Behavior, 7,* 167–178.

Sunderland, T., Tariot, P. N., Newhouse, P. A. (1988). Differential responsivity of mood, behavior, and cognition to cholinergic agents in elderly neuropsychiatric populations. *Brain Research Reviews, 13,* 371–389.

Super, D. E. (1957). *The psychology of careers.* New York: Harper.

Super, D. E. (1984). Career and life development. In D. Brown & L. Brooks (Eds.), *Career choice and development.* San Francisco: Jossey-Bass.

Super, D. E., Starishevsky, R., Matlin, N., & Jordaan, J. P. (1963). *Career development: Self concept theory.* New York: College Entrance Examination Board.

Super, D. E., Thompson, A. S., & Lindeman, R. H. (1988). *Adult career concerns inventory: Manual for research and exploratory use in counseling.* Palo Alto, CA: Consulting Psychologists Press.

Sussman, M. (1977). Family life of old people. In R. H. Binstock & E. Shanas (Eds.), *Handbook of aging and the social sciences.* New York: Van Nostrand Reinhold.

Sussman, M. (1985). Family life of old people. In R. H. Binstock & E. Shanas (Eds.), *Handbook of aging and the social sciences* (2nd ed.). New York: Van Nostrand Reinhold.

Sussman, M. B. (1972). An analytic model for the sociological study of retirement. In F. M. Carp (Ed.), *Retirement.* New York: Behavioral Publications.

Swanson, E. A., & Bennett, T. F. (1982–83). Degree of closeness: Does if affect the bereaved's attitudes toward selected funeral practices? *Omega, 13,* 43–50.

Szinovacz, M. (1989). Retirement, couples, and household work. In S. Bahr & E. Peterson (Eds.), *Aging and the family.* Lexington, MA: D. C. Heath.

Talbert, G. (1977). Aging of the reproductive system. In C. E. Finch & L. Hayflick (Eds.), *Handbook of the biology of aging.* New York: Van Nostrand Reinhold.

Tamir, L. (1982). *Men in their forties.* New York: Springer.

Tamir, L. M. (1989). Modern myths about men at midlife: An assessment. In S. Hunter & M. Sundel (Eds.), *Midlife myths.* Newbury Park, CA: Sage.

Tanfer, K. (1987). Patterns of premarital cohabitation among never married women in the United States. *Journal of Marriage and the Family, 49,* 483–497.

Taylor, D. (1983–84). Views of death from sufferers of early loss. *Omega, 14,* 77–83.

Taylor, D. A. (1968). Some aspects of the development of interpersonal relations: Social penetration process. *Journal of Social Psychology, 75,* 79–90.

Taylor, K. M., & Popma, J. (1990). An examination of the relationships among career decision-making, self-efficacy, career salience, locus of control, and vocational interests. *Journal of Vocational Behavior, 37,* 17–31.

Taylor, P. (1984, May 28). Hispanic Americans haven't found their pot of gold. *Washington Post National Weekly Edition,* pp. 9–10.

Teague, M. L. (1980). Aging and leisure: A social psychological perspective. In S. E. Iso-Ahola (Ed.), *Social psychological perspectives on leisure and recreation.* Springfield, IL: Charles C. Thomas.

Tennov, D. (1980). *Love and limerance.* New York: Stein and Day.

Terkel, S. (1974). *Working.* New York: Pantheon Books.

Tesch, S., & Whitbourne, S. (1981). Friendship, social interaction and subjective well-being of older men in an institutional setting. *International Journal of Aging and Human Development, 13,* 317–327.

Thomae, H. (1970). Theory of aging and cognitive theory of personality. *Human Development, 13,* 1–16.

Thomae, H. (1979). The concept of development and life-span developmental psychology. In P. B. Baltes & O. G. Brim, Jr. (Eds.), *Life-span development and behavior* (Vol. 2). New York: Academic Press.

Thomas, L. E. (1982). Sexuality and aging: Essential vitamin or popcorn? *The Gerontologist, 22,* 240–243.

Thomas, L. E. (1989). The human science approach to understanding adulthood and aging. In L. E. Thomas (Ed.), *Research on adulthood and aging.* New York: State University of New York Press.

Thomas, L. E., DiGiulio, R. C., & Sheehan, N. W (1988). Identity loss and psychological crisis in widowhood: A reevaluation. *Internation Journal of Aging and Human Development, 26,* 225–239.

Thompson, A. P. (1984). Emotional and sexual components of extramarital relations. *Journal of Marriage and the Family, 42,* 133–139.

Thompson, L., & Walker, A. (1990). Gender in families: Women and men in marriage, work, and parenthood. *Journal of Marriage and the Family, 51,* 845–869.

Thorson, J. A., & Powell, F. C. (1988). Elements of death anxiety and meanings of death. *Journal of Clinical Psychology, 44,* 691–701.

Time Magazine (1986, May 19). The baby boom reaches forty, pp. 25–34.

Time Magazine (1987, February 16). McDonald's McMasters, pp. 44–48.

Time Magazine (1990, Fall). *Women: The road ahead.* Special Issue.

Timiras, P. S. (Ed.) (1972). *Developmental physiology and aging.* New York: Macmillan.

Timiras, P. S., & Vernadakis, A. (1972). Structural, biochemical, and functional aging of the nervous system. In P. S. Timiras (Ed.), *Developmental physiology and aging.* New York: Macmillan.

Timko, C., Moos, R. (1990). Determinants of interpersonal support and self-direction in group residential facilities. *Journal of Gerontology: Social Sciences, 45,* S184–S192.

Toffler, A. (1970). *Future shock.* New York: Random House.

Toffler, A. (1980). *The third wave.* New York: Morrow.

Tolman, C. (1983). Further comments on the meaning of dialectic. *Human Development, 26,* 320–324.

Tonna, E. A. (1977). Aging of skeletal-dental systems and supporting tissues. In C. E. Finch & L. Hayflick (Eds.), *Handbook of the biology of aging.* New York: Van Nostrand Reinhold.

Traupmann, J., & Hatfield, E. (1983). How important is marital fairness over the lifespan. *International Journal of Aging and Human Development, 17,* 89–102.

TRB (1985, October 14). Dohrn again. *New Republic,* pp. 4, 41.

Treas, J., & Bengston, V. L. (1987). Family in later years. In M. Sussman & S. Steinmitz (Eds.), *Handbook on marriage and the family.* New York: Plenum.

Troll, L. E. (1971). The family in later life: A decade review. *Journal of Marriage and the Family, 33,* 263–290.

Troll, L. E. (1977). Poor, dumb, and ugly. In L. E. Troll, J. Israel, & K. Israel (Eds.), *Looking ahead: A woman's guide to growing old.* Englewood Cliffs, NJ: Prentice-Hall.

Troll, L. E. (1980). Grandparenting. In L. W. Poon (Ed.), *Aging in the 1980s.* Washington, DC: American Psychological Association.

Troll, L. (1989). Myths of midlife intergenerational relationships. In S. Hunter & M. Sundel (Eds.), *Midlife myths.* Newbury Park, CA: Sage.

Troll, L. E., & Bengston, V. (1982). Intergenerational relations throughout the life-span. In B. B. Wolman (Ed.), *Handbook of developmental psychology.* Englewood Cliffs, NJ: Prentice-Hall.

Troll, L. E., Miller, S., & Atchley, R. (1979). *Families of later life.* Belmont, CA: Wadsworth.

Troll, L. E., & Smith, J. (1976). Attachment through the life span: Some questions about dyadic bonds among adults. *Human Development, 19,* 135–182.

Trudeau, E. J., & Commons, M. L. (1991, July 12–14). *Evolution and learning of assortiveness in adults.* Paper presented at the Sixth Adult Development Symposium of the Society for Research in Adult Development. Boston, MA.

Tucker, D. M., Penland, J. G., Sandstead, H. H., Milne, D. B., Heck, D. G., & Klevay, L. M. (1990). Nutrition status and brain function in aging. *American Journal of Clinical Nutrition, 52,* 93–102.

Turiel, E. T., & Smetana, J. G. (1984). Social knowledge and action: The coordination of domains. In W. M. Kurtines & J. L. Gewirtz (Eds.), *Morality, moral behavior, and moral development.* New York: Wiley.

Turner, B. F. (1982). Sex related differences in aging. In B. B. Wolman (Ed.), *Handbook of developmental psychology.* New York: Van Nostrand Reinhold.

Uhlenberg, P., Cooney, T., & Boyd, R. (1990). Divorce for women after midlife. *Journal of Gerontology: Social Sciences, 45,* S3–S11.

Updike, J. (1975). *A month of Sundays.* New York: Knopf.

Ure, M. C. D., & Colinvaux, D. (1985). New results on the reasoning of unschooled adults. *The Quarterly Newsletter of the Laboratory of Comparative Human Cognition, 7,* 27–29.

U.S. Bureau of the Census (1987). *Household, families, marital status, and living arrangements.* (Current Population Reports, Series. P-20, No. 417.)

Washington, DC: U.S. Government Printing Office.

U.S. Bureau of the Census (1989). *Population profile of the United States.* (Current Population Reports, Series P-23, No. 159.) Washington, DC: U.S. Government Printing Office.

U.S. Department of Commerce (1979). *Social indicators.* Washington, DC: U.S. Government Printing Office.

U.S. Department of Commerce, Bureau of the Census (1980). *Population estimates and projection series.* (Current Population Reports, Series P-25, No. 889.) Washington, DC: U.S. Government Printing Office.

U.S. Department of Commerce, Bureau of the Census (1981). *Population profile of the United States: 1980.* (Current Population Reports, Series P-20, No. 350.) Washington, DC: U.S. Government Printing Office.

U.S. Department of Commerce, Bureau of the Census (1982). *Statistical abstract of the United States, 1982–83* (103rd edition). Washington, DC: U.S. Government Printing Office.

U.S. Department of Commerce (1984). *Families at work: The jobs and the pay.* Washington, DC: U.S. Government Printing Office.

U.S. Public Health Service (1979). *Alzheimer's disease: Q & A.* (NIH Pub. No. 80-1646.) Washington, DC: U.S. Government Printing Office.

Valdez, R. L., & Gutik, B. A. (1987). Family roles: A help or a hindrance for working women? In B. A. Gutek & L. Larwood (Eds.), *Women's career development.* Newbury Park, CA: Sage.

Vaillant, G. E. (1977). *Adaptation to life.* Boston: Little, Brown.

Vaillant, G. E., & McArthur, C. C. (1972). Natural history of male psychological health: The adult life cycle

from eighteen to fifty. *Seminars in Psychiatry, 4,* 415–427.

Van-Bezooijen, C. F. (1987). Biomedical gerontology in the Netherlands. Special Issue: Forty years of gerontology research in the Netherlands. *Tijdschrift-voor-Gerontolgie-en-geriatrie, 18,* 139–146.

Van-Gaal, L. (1989). Body fat mass distribution. Influence on metabolic and atherosclerotic parameters in non-insulin dependent diabetics and obese subjects with and without impaired glucose tolerance, influence of weight reduction. *Verh-K-Acad-Geneeskd-Belg, 51,* 47–80.

Van Geert, P. (1987). The structure of Erikson's model of the eight ages: A generative approach. *Human Development, 30,* 236–254.

Van Hoose, W. H., & Worth, M. R. (1988). *Adulthood in the life cycle.* Dubuque, IA: W. C. Brown.

Van Maanen, J. (1977). Summary: Toward a theory of the career. In J. Van Maanen (Ed.), *Organizational careers.* New York: Wiley.

Van Maanen, J., & Schein, E. H. (1977). Career development. In J. R. Hackman & J. L. Suttle (Eds.), *Improving life at work.* Santa Monica, CA: Goodyear.

Vasudev, J. (1987, June). *Maturity in adulthood: A cross-cultural perspective.* Paper presented at the Third Beyond Formal Operations Symposium held at Harvard: Positive Development During Adolescence and Adulthood, Cambridge, MA.

Vasudev, J., and Hummel, R. C. (1987). Moral stage sequence and principled reasoning in an Indian sample. *Human Development, 30,* 105–118.

Veatch, R. M. (1976). *Death, dying and the biological revolution: Our last quest for responsibility.* New Haven, CT: Yale University Press.

Veatch, R. M. (1979). Defining death anew. In H. Wass (Ed.), *Dying: Facing the facts*. New York: McGraw-Hill.

Veatch, R. M. (1981). *A theory of medical ethics*. New York: Basic Books.

Veatch, R. M. (1984). Brain death. In Shneidman (Ed.), *Death: Current perspectives* (3rd ed.). Palo Alto, CA: Mayfield.

Veatch, R. M. (1989). *Death, dying, and the biological revolution: Our last quest for responsibility* (2nd ed.). New Haven, CT: Yale University Press.

Veevers, J. E. (1980). *Childless by choice*. Toronto: Butterworth.

Veroff, J. E., & Feld, S. (1970). *Marriage and work in America: A study of motives and roles*. New York: Van Nostrand Reinhold.

Veroff, J., Douvan, E., & Hatchett, S. (1990). *Marital interaction and marital quality in the first year of marriage*. Unpublished manuscript, University of Michigan, Ann Arbor.

Veroff, J., & Oggins, J. (1988, November). *Processes of marital interaction among black and white newlyweds*. Paper presented at NCFR meetings, Philadelphia.

Veroff, J., Reuman, D., & Feld, S. (1984). Stability and changes in adult personality over 12 and 24 years. *Developmental Psychology, 21*, 568–584.

Videk, A. (1982). Biological aging: Searching for the mechanisms of aging. In H. Thomae & G. I. Maddox (Eds.), *New perspectives on old age*. New York: Springer.

Vigod, Z. (1972). The relationship between occupational choice and parental occupation. *Alberta Journal of Educational Research, 18*, 287–294.

Viney, L. (1987). A socio-phenomenological approach to life-span development complementing Erikson's sociodynamic approach. *Human Development, 30*, 125–136.

Vondracek, F. W., & Lerner, R. M. (1982). Vocational role development in adolescence. In B. B. Wolman (Ed.), *Handbook of developmental psychology*. Englewood Cliffs, NJ: Prentice-Hall.

Voneche, J. (1985). Preliminary remarks on constructivism. *Archives de Psychologie, 533*, 19–20.

Von Kondratowitz, H. J. (1984). Long-term changes in attitudes toward "old age." In V. Garms-Homolova, E. M. Herning, & D. Schaeffer (Eds.), *Intergenerational relations*. Lewiston, NY: C. J. Hogrefe.

Walker, L. J. (1984). Sex differences in the development of moral reasoning: A critical review. *Child Development, 55*, 677–691.

Walker, L. J. (1986). Experiential and cognitive sources of moral development in adulthood. *Human Development, 29*, 113–124.

Wallace, P. M., & Gotlib, I. H. (1990). Marital adjustment during the transition to parenthood: Stability and predictors of change. *Journal of Marriage and the Family, 51*, 21–29.

Wallerstein, J. S., & Kelly, J. B. (1972). The effects of parental divorce: The adolescent experience. In E. J. Anthony & C. Koupernik (Eds.), *The child in his family: Children at psychiatric risk* (Vol. 3). New York: Wiley.

Wallerstein, J. S., & Kelly, J. B. (1980). *Surviving the breakup: How children actually cope with divorce*. New York: Basic Books.

Walsh, D. (1975). Age differences in learning and memory. In D. S. Woodruff & J. E. Birren (Eds.), *Aging: Scientific perspectives and social issues*. New York: Van Nostrand Reinhold.

Walsh, F. (1989). Reconsidering gender in the marital quid pro quo. In M. McGoldrick, C. M. Anderson, & F. Walsh (Eds.) *Women in families: A framework for family therapy.* New York: Norton.

Walster, E., Walster, G. W., & Traupmann, J. (1978). Equity and premarital sex. *Journal of Personality and Social Psychology, 36,* 82–92.

Walters, J., & Stinnet, N. (1971). Parent-child relationships: A decade of research. *Journal of Marriage and the Family, 33,* 70–118.

Wanous, J. (1980). *Organizational entry.* Reading, MA: Addison-Wesley.

Washington, V. (1988). The black mother in the United States. In B. Birns & D. Hay (Eds.), *The different faces of motherhood.* New York: Plenum.

Wass, H. (1979). *Death: Facing the facts.* New York: McGraw-Hill.

Weintraub, W., & Aronson, H. (1968). A survey of patients in classical psychoanalysis: Some vital statistics. *Journal of Nervous and Mental Disorders, 146,* 98–102.

Weisman, A. T. (1972). *On dying and denying: A psychiatric study of terminality.* New York: Behavioral Publications.

Welford, A. T. (1977). Motor performance. In J. E. Birren & K. W. Schaie (Eds.), *Handbook of the psychology of aging.* New York: Van Nostrand Reinhold.

Wells, L. E., & Stryker, S. (1988). Stability and change in self over the life course. In P. B. Baltes, D. L. Featherman, & R. M. Lerner (Eds.), *Life-span development and behavior* (Vol. 8). Hillsdale, NJ: Lawrence Erlbaum.

Werts, C. E. (1968). Paternal influence on career choice. *Journal of Counseling Psychology, 15,* 48–52.

Whitbourne, S. (1985a). The psychological construction of the life-span. In J. E. Birren & K. W. Schaie (Eds.), *Handbook of the psychology of aging*

(2nd ed.). New York: Academic Press.

Whitbourne, S. (1985b). *The aging body.* New York: Springer-Verlag.

White, R. (1975). *Lives in progress: A study of the natural growth of personality* (3rd ed.). New York: Holt, Rinehart and Winston.

Willett, W. C., Stamper, M. J., Colditz, G. A., Rosner, B. A., & Speizer, F. E. (1990). Relation of meat, fat and fiber intake to the risk of colon cancer in a prospective study among women. *New England Journal of Medicine, 323,* 1664–1672.

Willis, S. L. (1985). Towards an educational psychology of the older adult learner: Intellectual and cognitive bases. In J. E. Birren & K. W. Schaie (Eds.), *Handbook of the psychology of aging* (2nd ed.). New York: Van Nostrand Reinhold.

Willis, S. L., & Baltes, P. B. (1980). Intelligence in adulthood and aging: Contemporary issues. In L. W. Poon (Ed.), *Aging in the 1980s.* Washington, DC: American Psychological Association.

Williams, C. P., & Savickas, M. L. (1990). Developmental tasks of career maintenance. *Journal of Vocational Behavior, 36,* 166–175.

Winch, R. F. (1974). Complementary needs and related notions about voluntary mate selection. In R. F. Winch & G. B. Spanier (Eds.), *Selected studies in marriage and the family.* New York: Holt, Rinehart and Winston.

Windley, P. G., & Scheidt, R. J. (1980). Person-environment dialectics: Implications for competent functioning in old age. In L. W. Poon (Ed.), *Aging in the 1980s.* Washington, DC: American Psychological Association.

Winocur, G., Moscovitch, M., Freedman, J. (1987). An investigation of cognitive function in relation to psychosocial variables in institutionalized old people. Special Issue: Aging and cognition. *Canadian Journal of Psychology, 41,* 257–269.

Witkin, H. A. (1949). Perception of body position and of the position of visual field. *Psychological Monographs, 63,* 1–50.

Witkin, H. A., Lewis, H. B., Hertzman, M., Machover, K., Meissner, P. B., Wapner, S. (1954). *Personality through perception.* New York: Harper.

Wolkind, S., & Zajicek, E. (1981). *Pregnancy: A psychological and social study.* New York: Academic Press.

Woodruff, D. (1972). *Biofeedback control of the EEG alpha rhythm and its effect on reaction time in the young and old.* Doctoral dissertation, University of Southern California.

Worthington-Roberts, B., & Hazzard, W. (1982). Nutrition and aging. In C. Eisdorfer (Ed.), *Annual review of gerontology and geriatrics* (Vol. 3). New York: Springer.

Wright, L. S. (1988). *Personality development in adulthood.* Newbury Park, CA: Sage.

Young, N. F. (1972). Socialization of patterns among the Chinese in Hawaii. *Amerasian Journal, 1,* 31–51.

Zaliski, C. (1988). *Otherworld journeys: Accounts of the near death experiences in medieval and modern times.* New York: Oxford University Press.

Zarit, S. (1977). Don't cry in front of your friends. In S. Zarit (Ed.), *Readings in aging and death: Contemporary perspectives.* New York: Harper and Row.

Zarit, S. H. (1989). Issues and directions in family intervention research. In E. Light & B. D. Lebowitz (Eds.), *Alzheimer's disease treatment and family stress: Directions for research.* Washington, DC: National Institutes of Mental Health. (DHHS Publication No. ADM 89-1569)

Zedeck, S., & Mosier, K. (1990). Work in the family and employing organizations. *American Psychologist, 45,* 240–251.

Zeits, C., & Prince, R. (1982). Child effects on parents. In B. B. Wolman (Ed.), *Handbook of developmental psychology.* Englewood Cliffs, NJ: Prentice-Hall.

Ziajka, A. (1972). The black youth's self-concept. In W. Looft (Ed.), *Developmental psychology: A book of readings.* Hillsdale, IL: Dryden Press.

Zuckerman, S. (1981). Female midlife issues in prose and poetry. In C. Colarusso & R. Nemiroff (Eds.), *Adult development: A new dimension in psychodynamic theory and practice.* New York: Plenum.

Name Index

Subject Index

Page numbers in bold type indicate glossary entries.